Making School Reform Happen

Making School Reform Happen

PAMELA BULLARD

BARBARA O. TAYLOR
University of Wisconsin, Madison

ALLYN AND BACON
Boston London Toronto Sydney Tokyo Singapore

A Division of Simon & Schuster, Inc.
160 Gould Street
Needham Heights, Massachusetts 02194

Library of Congress Cataloging-in-Publication Data

Bullard, Pamela.
Making school reform happen / Pamela Bullard and Barbara O. Taylor.
p. cm.
Includes bibliographical references (p.) and index.
ISBN 0-205-14115-3
1. Public schools—United States. 2. Educational change—United States. I. Taylor, Barbara O. II. Title.
LA217.2.B85 1992 92-13428
371'.01'0973—dc20 CIP

Printed in the United States of America
10 9 8 7 6 5 4 3 2 1 96 95 94 93 92

For Ashley Elizabeth, Kyle, Francis, Whitney,
David, Franklin, and Jayne Morgan

And for all *children and their dreams.*

Contents

Preface

This book is about Effective Schools—how they work, the people who make them work, and why. It is not an examination so much of specific programs but of the people who make those programs vital and the process in which those programs flourish. It looks at educational reform through two very distinct lenses. First is that of Effective Schools as an ongoing, vibrant change process, a process that is its own structure. Second is that it is the people, the practitioners—their willingness to learn and change, their enhanced teaching and leadership skills, their intense accountability, and their uncomprising commitment to the moral imperative of teaching for learning for *all*—that make Effective Schools happen.

Making School Reform Happen is a book of hope. Since the early sixties, America's public schools and the people working within them have been under a suffocating avalanche of criticism from parents, politicians, academia, and, in particular, the media. Much of that criticism is warranted. But in the last decade there has been a growth of Effective teaching and leadership that is dramatically transforming schools—not just urban schools, but *all* schools, for *all* children. This book is a thorough examination—told honestly and passionately—of the people who are creating that transformation and the manner in which they are restoring pride in U.S. public education.

This book is the result of over 450 interviews with teachers, principals, superintendents, secretaries, custodians, students, parents, board members, police, politicians, zoning specialists, sociologists, psychologists, professors of education, officials of City Halls and State Houses, Washington politicians and their staffs, lobbyists, union leaders, and consultants. The stack of interviews is equaled only by the stack of accompanying research, background literature, and individual school and district status reports and test scores. This look at Effective Schools goes from the migrant communities in northern Washington, to the barrios and cattle baron estates of Texas, the farms and military bases of Kansas, the Washington beltway, Spanish Harlem, and the working and middle-class districts of upstate New York.

There have been books published recently that discuss successful programs as well as neglect in the public schools and the failure of school change.

These books, rather than detracting from *Making School Reform Happen,* pave the way for it. Not one of these books examines an entire, comprehensive process that is making schools work. They do not look at the why or the how behind programs of promise. This book does. In that sense, it is unique; it is a book of *hope.* It tells you not only what an Effective School is and why it works but how the process is begun and carried out, and how the people and schools transform and are transformed.

You will learn a great deal about the philosophy of Ron Edmonds and the Effective Schools Improvement Process in this book. You will learn the reasons behind the seven correlates, initial applications of the correlates, and what the latest, ongoing research of those correlates shows, and how they have grown into what is being referred to as the *second generation.* You will also realize the complex, far-reaching impact that business strategies of the eighties and nineties are having on the push for outcome-based accountability.

But most important, you will see beyond the rhetoric of school reform. You will see how people apply the correlates in their daily tasks, and how that application is turning schools around and bringing new life to demoralized faculties and staffs. The seven correlates—safe and orderly environment, instructional leadership, climate of high expectations, frequent monitoring, clear and focused mission, opportunity to learn, and positive home-school relations—provide the means to carry out the moral imperative of teaching for learning for *all.*

That is what this book focuses on: the power of that moral imperative that is the driving belief system for people working at Effective Schools. That is what sets the Effective Schools Process apart from other reform and restructuring attempts. And that is why it is the *people* of those schools who are most important. If they do not have that will to change, to buck the past, to embrace new teaching and learning skills, our schools will never improve. This book is about those people who live the moral commitment of the Effective Schools Process and prove that accountability is not a threat, but a motivator and its own reward.

In their own words, superintendents, principals, teachers, and board members discuss what they believed were their shortcomings prior to being awakened professionally by the Effective Schools Process. They talk about the change in their personal beliefs, and the ramifications in their professional lives. They examine their own struggle, their successes as well as their failures. They talk of a system so obsessed with protecting the status quo that it still discriminates not only against the children of the lower socioeconomic classes but those within the schools who struggle to change that system of discrimination. They talk honestly about what they see as the only hope for public school reform. Their opinions are sometimes gruff, often laced with anger and frustration at politicians who play to false fears, petty biases, personal aspirations, and at academicians who equivocate and cajole, and fail to understand the day-to-day operations, machinations, and polemics of the schoolroom, the schoolhouse, and the school district.

The format for this book is journalistic. The schools, the people, and the programs are presented for the most part in the exact words of those who are most closely involved. No one can better explain what is happening in the schools than the practitioners themselves. The book follows the adage: Let the people tell their story; let the public decide its validity. Finally given the chance to speak, and knowing there would be an objective presentation of the facts—leaving the judgments up to the individual readers—the practitioners spoke their minds and hearts. These are people whose expertise, courage, and devotion are restoring the American dream for thousands of public school children.

But this book does not show just the polished parts of the Effective Schools Process trophy. On the contrary, it shows where the process is still weak and needs work, and interviews many who have been hesitant in their praise of the process. It tells the story of struggling schools and districts, and even how some districts allege Effectiveness and don't even know how to spell the word.

Because there is a great deal of truth in the phrase "the road to hell is paved with good intentions," this book goes behind the stories of inspiration to what *exactly* are the building blocks of Effective Schools and how they are constructed. In precise detail, superintendents discuss and analyze their implementation process. Principals discuss the first steps they took in transforming their schools. Teachers talk about the changes in their classrooms, as well as the changes in the faculty lounge and the faculty meetings. You will see not only why the rules, roles, and relationships changed but *how* they changed and continue to change. It is not the examination of one process set out by a group of experts, but it is a study of *this* school in Texas, *that* school in New York, *this* district in Kansas. You will see how every school personalizes the process with its own distinctive culture—how the brightly colored fabric that creates the design of an Effective School is woven from the same tough, durable thread of the distinctive change process of Effective Schools. That process evolves around professional accountability, the application of evolving business strategies, staff development, and school-based improvement.

There are already critics of school reform who say that in this time of recession in the United States it is enough just to keep schools open and teachers in the classroom, that there is no money for reform. That argument is a red herring—another excuse to do nothing, to continue the status quo and its inbred mediocrity.

The Effective Schools Improvement Process has been launched successfully in districts of 30,000 pupils for as little as $20,000. That is the cost of bringing in appropriate experts and facilitators to begin the assessment and training process. Future expenses primarily evolve around staff development, which consumes an average of less than 1 percent of a district's operating budget.

To the contrary of what we may think, this time of economic trauma just may be the right time for school reform. In times of crisis, the infrastructure is reexamined and priorities are realigned. Now is the best time for school districts to examine carefully what is essential, what is working, and what is not. Just as in business, the time of crisis, the time of financial trouble, can be the catalyst for long-lasting change that will result in alignment of policies and programs, therefore creating effective and efficient school districts.

In the Introduction of this book, you will be given the history of America's attitude toward public education, and the impact of that attitude on not just the lower socioeconomic classes but on all Americans. Has recent reform made any difference and why is the Effective Schools Improvement Process the most promising answer to the problems of public schools? And why should it matter to *all* of us?

In Chapter 1, we examine the philosophy of the Effective Schools Process, how the schools work and why we need them now. The correlates are explained along with a look at the growth of such schools since Ron Edmonds began in 1966. There is also a "rap sheet" on U.S. education—an explanation of where we stand and what we are doing, or failing to do, to so many of our 24 million public school children.

Chapter 2 is a profile of the Hollibrook Elementary School in Spring Branch, Texas. This is a school that George Bush could jog to from his condominium on the other side of the tracks (literally). Abandoned by a school district that was once one of the nation's finest, Hollibrook has gone through a transformation that has made it one of the most progressive and exciting schools in the United States.

Chapter 3 examines the changing business paradigm that is impacting how administrators run their schools and districts. We discuss contemporary business and leadership literature that is being adopted by school administrators striving for quality teaching for learning for all. We focus on how those principles are being applied, and how, at the heart of all this change, we must break free from the shackles of a psychic prison that has held U.S. education hostage since long before Horace Mann tried to implement his changes.

Chapters 4 and 5 take a personal and professional look at leadership as a moral act in the public schools. Chapter 4 concentrates on the thinking, and changes in the thinking, of Dr. Hal Guthrie, superintendent of the Spring Branch (Texas) Independent School District. We examine how he has used strategic planning and the power of his own will and commitment to the Effective Schools Process to transform that Texas school district. Chapter 5 looks at other superintendents who have dared to change. This is an honest look at some tough, controversial leaders who, like Guthrie, are not afraid to go up against their boards, their communities, and their peers to bring equity and quality to their school districts. The theme here is accountability *all the way down the line*. It is the driving force for these individuals who admit to having to change their own professional philosophy in order to become Effective, successful superintendents.

These educators speak honestly, sometimes even combatively, as they stand up for their beliefs, their schools, and their people. This style continues in Chapters 6 and 7 where new as well as seasoned principals discuss the changes that have been brought to their arenas. What is true instructional leadership in the schools? Principals from Spanish Harlem to Seattle to Kansas speak openly of their growth and change and how they fostered Effectiveness in their schools. In Chapter 7, principals, some who are veterans of 25 years' experience, discuss the often sudden change from a hierarchical, authoritarian style of management to collaborative decision making in a district with school-based management. How do they do it, how difficult was it, and are they pleased with the changes in them and their schools?

In Chapters 8 and 9, teachers have their say! In Chapter 8, the teachers discuss the instructional changes that come with the Effective Schools Process. There is a personal perspective on teaching in the fifties and how Effective School changes bring back the accountability, collegiality, and decision-making power of that time. Then teachers in the nineties talk frankly of their early biases, the failings of their formal training, the need for additional training, and the often extraordinary impact that new training has had in the classrooms.

In Chapter 9, teachers continue to talk about the new decision-making powers that have come with the Effective Schools Process and school-based management. The significant changes for teachers—their autonomy in the classroom and their involvement in school decisions—have led to ownership, accountability, and enthusiasm for their work heretofore unknown by most. Teachers praise their schools, the new leadership, and their new ownership. But they also speak of what happens when that ownership is just rhetoric.

By now you may be thinking, this all sounds great but how do I do it? Chapter 10 takes implementation of the Effective Schools Process from that first meeting between the board and the superintendent right down to the needs assessments, the faculty meetings, the teams drawing up objectives and strategies, the meetings with parents, and the constant monitoring and adjusting. Using the actual time lines of Effective districts, their own charts, graphs, and communications, you are taken step by step through the process—not just the acts themselves, but the reasoning for one strategy over another. The practitioners discuss the maneuverings, the mistakes, the shortcomings, and the promises that fell short. Teachers can see what superintendents were thinking when they took a particular step, principals can see what teachers were thinking, parents can see what everyone was thinking, and board members can try to figure out what really happened after that first vote.

Chapter 11 examines what these changes mean for parents and students in this process. Parents talk about the changes they have seen in the schools, and the impact their increased involvement has had with relationships with teachers. Teachers give their own feelings and observations, detailing the tangible improvements. And students, from the honors classes to the skinheads, offer their perspective on what the changes mean.

No one gets off the hook in Effective Schools, least of all those power brokers with the ultimate say. The Effective Schools Process requires dramatic change in rules, roles, and responsibilities, not the least of which are in the central office administration, the state departments of education, and the district boards or committees. Chapter 12 discusses those changes—how different boards and superintendents deal with and adjust to their changing roles and new accountability. It is a lesson in not just the changing of the way things are but the changing of the way things have been for 200 years.

But even the best laid plans go awry. Chapter 13 looks at those districts that have tried but failed to bring about true effectiveness. Three areas are examined. The first is South Carolina, where a state sales tax was approved for educational improvement via the Effective Schools Process. There has been significant progress, but it is coming kicking and screaming and in some places it isn't happening at all. Second is St. Louis, Missouri. This is the story of how one man, Rufus Young, bucked the system to bring in the Effective Schools Process, and, after achieving unprecedented increases in scores in several schools, and lighting a fire under a whole district, he was told basically to cease and desist. How great were those schools and that time of Effectiveness, and what is happening now? Third is the *illusion* of Effectiveness. There are numerous districts that call themselves effective, but do it by manipulating teachers and scores, and giving only lip service to the correlates and philosophy of the Effective Schools Process. We present a profile of a district, drawn from a compilation of several districts, that deceives the public into thinking teaching for learning for all is really happening. It is not. It is still an oppressive, dual school system, extremely authoritarian, with no true school-based management, but with a highly effective public relations team that is, for the moment, fooling almost everyone. We meet the players, see the schools, and study the tests and how they are given. We meet principals and teachers who have no intention of changing from the old ways. The lesson is sad but worth noting as more and more districts strive for effectiveness.

And Chapter 14 presents the conclusions of this book and the work of the Effective Schools Process. We look at Effective Schools as they grow into their next generation. The research continues to expand, as do the insights and the numbers of brave, dedicated individuals who daily work the mortar of learning in America's public schools. This book is about them—the keepers of the dream.

Acknowledgments

The seed for this book was planted some 29 years ago in the spirit of Barbara Taylor. Over the years, she has nurtured its growth with selfless passion, gutsy determination, and unflinching devotion. Her belief in Effective Schools and the people behind them, and her desire to enhance the future of America's schoolchildren, have been her gardener's tools. Those who gain insight and inspiration from this book owe their initial thanks to the vision and commitment of Barbara Taylor.

Thanks are also due to literally hundreds of people involved in the school districts examined in this book who gave their time, their experiences, and their thoughtful concerns. There are some who deserve special mention: Larry Lezotte, Gary Mathews, Jerry Bamberg, Edie Holcomb, Bob Sudlow, Kevin Castner, Pat Anderson, Jean Norman, Suzanne Still, Bonnie Seaburn, and, for their conscientious and expert analysis of the manuscript, Dr. Dan Levine (University of Missouri) and Dr. Richard E. Maurer (Middle School Principal, Ossining, NY).

It should also be noted that many districts and schools would not have become Effective without the commitment and competence of the many educators who train, consult, and facilitate in the name of the Effective Schools Process. These experts have been a lifeline of support and encouragement nationwide.

Finally, a personal thank you to Judith Stoia and Robert Ginn, who speculated on the chemistry between Dr. Taylor and myself. Somehow, we didn't blow up the lab. Indeed, once I realized Barbara Taylor's vision of Effective Schools, I knew the stories of dedication, of hope, and of intense, life-consuming hard work must be told. The people in this book are some of the true pioneers of education for the twenty-first century. I have been humbled by the brave eagerness of the students, the dogged courage of the teachers and their leaders, and how essential their Effectiveness is to *all of us*.

Pamela Bullard

We can, whenever and wherever we choose,
successfully teach all children
whose schooling is of interest to us.
We already know more than we need to do that.
Whether or not we do it must finally depend on
how we feel about the fact we haven't so far.

Ronald Edmonds, 1935–1983

INTRODUCTION

Why You Should Read This Book

Citizen, politician, parent, teacher, school administrator, all persons who care about the teaching and learning of all children: Do not put this book down until you have finished it. Whether or not we teach all children depends on your will, your strength of conviction, and your commitment to your local schools, the schools in your state, and the children who count on us for help.

We *do* know how to teach all children. We *do* know how to build good schools where teachers, administrators, parents, and support staff can decide together how to teach all of their children the course of study designed by the school community.

Today we have only to make up our minds that all children can learn, and that all children can be taught the intended curriculum. Then we set up our schools to support classroom teachers so that they are able to reach and teach all of their students.

This is precisely what the Effective Schools Process can do. This is precisely what practitioners all over the country are doing when they use the Effective Schools Process for school improvement—an implementation strategy that practitioners have worked out and championed over the past decade. True, the standards of achievement, the curricular content, and the policy and rules of the school will be set by the district, with consent from each school. But in school reform based on the Effective Schools Process, the teachers and administrators at the school site will decide how to reach and teach all of their children, and will be held accountable for that task by the board of education and the community, especially parents.

Indeed, practitioners have set about developing the Effective Schools Process because of their desire to make their vocational callings—teaching and educational administration—truly professional. They have embraced accountability to teach all children in order to begin to set their own high standards of competency and performance for all practitioners. In the last decade, our knowledge concerning instructional design and strategies for teaching low-achieving students has grown sufficiently to embrace professional status in the field of education. Practitioners worth their salt now want that knowledge diffused so that their colleagues become allies in the march to professionalism, and want the individual discretion that is the hallmark of that status.

The myth continues to be perpetrated by some interest groups that educators do not have a body of knowledge comprehensive enough to enable the teaching of all children; therefore, they should not be a profession, that is, be held responsible for the teaching and learning of all children. This myth must be dispelled. If we held doctors responsible only for the treatment of those patients they knew they could treat successfully, we would have questionable medical and surgical services. We are able to hold doctors responsible for their practices because so much is known about how the normal body functions, and how abnormal tissue or defective organs respond to tests or appear to the senses. The same is true for the field of education.

Some children are harder to teach than others, but we *can* teach them, given proper teaching practices, time, and understanding of their variety of learning styles. It is time to regard educators as professionals, and require of them the specialized knowledge, skills, and methods necessary to serve all children in our schools. We need to expect of our colleges and universities that they will teach would-be teachers the skills, methods, and scholarly and philosophical principles necessary to teach all children. Curricula in teachers' colleges must demonstrate what we know today, not what was acceptable in schools of education 30 years ago.

University and college faculties of education have, for the most part, not kept up with new developments in the field because there is no real accountability in the system of education as there is in the medical and legal systems of the United States. Medical and law schools that fall behind will fast lose their accreditation and standing in their professions. The word gets around long before the accreditation team writes its report. Schools of education, on the other hand, are responsible to no higher authority than the vaguely written state codes of law and their college or university board of trustees, who feel slightly embarrassed about their schools of education but do not know how to ask the tough questions to set them right.

Today there are few schools of education that have in their curricula courses of study that prepare our teachers and administrators for the urban and rural realities they will encounter. We still prepare our teachers for suburban or small-town schools, homogeneous student populations, and narrow pedagogical procedures. Few teachers emerge from undergraduate or even graduate training exposed to practices that anticipate the variety of learning styles they will find in the typical classroom of today.

Meanwhile, children flow through our schools, and many of them are refused the chance to learn—beginning with the school system's discriminant rationing of "equal opportunity" to learn, and ending with the local school board of education's dilution of high school graduation standards. The primary responsibility for learning is now mistakenly placed with the student—not with the teacher, where it should be placed and where it is placed in Effective Schools. Effective Schools regard teachers as professionals who know their stuff and are held accountable for what they do by parents, the board of education, and the community. Most schools today have no real systems of accountability.

The evaluation of teaching is almost nonexistent. With the responsibility for learning placed on the student, teachers are not held to high teaching standards or high levels of achievement for their students. And yet, good teachers have always set *their own* high standards and attempted to meet them. However, today many communities set educational standards *below* which no one falls, a sort of "safety net for the uneducable." Because setting the standards of academic achievement for students is a very political process, as it should be, many boards of education back away from this obligation and instead let the standardized norm-referenced tests and popular texts set the level. Over the years since the early sixties, this is how the individual teaching objectives of the curriculum, or what is expected to be learned each year by students, has been "dumbed down."

What does this mean for you? It means that your own children could be shortchanged if they happen to be more difficult to teach, from a different culture, or live on the wrong side of the railroad tracks. You do not have to be a person from a minority group, a person of color, or a person in poverty. Your child may not be taught if he or she is outside the narrow range of learning styles most teachers teach to—those that fit into the time and materials allocation of our present school system.

The unpleasant truth of the history of public education in this country is simply that it is a history filled with discrimination bordering on oppression. How can there be justice in an educational system that is set up so that certain children will fall behind in their studies? There is an unwritten rule that the new teacher learns during his or her period of socialization at the schoolhouse: Some children cannot learn; don't waste your scarce resources of time, energy, materials, and attention on them. Concentrate on those students who can learn. To quote Diane Ravitch, "American educators, despite their professed ideals, had never made sustained effort to break the correlation between social class and achievement" (1983, p. 153).

The bureaucracy of education is designed to sort out who is destined to learn and who will not be given an equal opportunity to learn. Decisions are made in ways that screen out poor children, migrant workers' children, children of recent immigrants to this country, children who for whatever reason just don't fit the mold of the "educable" student. Decisions are made so that schools in the wrong neighborhoods are not given attention when they need teaching materials, building maintenance, and the assignment of better teachers. The common knowledge from the board of education through superintendent, principal, and on to the teacher speaks to political and public relations, not to the educational issues involved. This common knowledge reinforces the unequal distribution of the scarce resources in school systems.

For instance, many principals are still appointed because of political patronage, not because they are competent. Members of some boards of education still believe they must make decisions to buttress the local political party in power, rather than having as their goal the teaching and learning of all children.

Statistics demonstrate conclusively how well the educational system has sorted and selected students throughout the twentieth century. In the twenties, less than 23 percent of students finished high school. In the forties, about 50 percent, and by 1964, 69 percent. College graduates numbered less than 5 percent of the cohort in the twenties, and nearly 13 percent in 1964 (Keppel, 1966, pp. 18–19). By 1985, over 70 percent of students finished high school, and about half of these went on to postsecondary education (colleges, universities, community colleges, technical training, two-year junior colleges, and the like).

Although this progress seems like an admirable achievement, and it is, if we break down these percentages according to socioeconomic class, we find that relatively little progress has been made to bring bright children from the working class and from poor families into four-year colleges and universities. We may criticize other nations for tracking their children into vocational and academic streams early on (usually by the sixth grade), but the United States accomplishes the same thing in a much more subtle way: by perpetrating a system of education that does not assist and support teachers in reaching and teaching individual children.

It is not fair to blame the teachers and administrators for this sad state of affairs. The genesis of tracking in the schools is in the societal fabric of the United States, starting high up, especially within the "power elite." In a land of unparalleled opportunity, those who were successful labeled those who were not as lazy, ignorant, and unAmerican. Individualism in the United States reinforced the "can do" philosophy across class lines. If your child was not learning, it was his or her own fault.

In the late nineteenth century, industrialists, politicians, and entrepreneurs wanted workers, especially immigrants and poor people, socialized to the work ethic, to follow orders and not question authority. It was part and parcel of the "scientific management" movement: The worker was treated like a cog in a machine, and the best worker came with no mind. In spite of the work of people like Horace Mann, Henry Barnard, John Dewey, and Jane Addams to educate people universally and encourage education for goals set by the individual student, the power elite demanded that students be taught according to their social class—that is, a course of college preparation for the upper and professional classes, and a more practical or vocational curriculum for all others. Oral and written grammar of students from low-income families often went uncorrected in the classrooms, because these students were not expected to need skills of rhetoric or logic. They needed only to do what they were told.

As time went on, more people gained a common education in the United States. When they became parents, they wanted a better education for their own children. High schools, which in the nineteenth century were found in urban settings for the most part, became commonplace in the twentieth century in rural and small-town settings. World Wars I and II served to put people in places they would not have known had there been no wars. Country boys went to Europe, others were trained all over the United States. Women held jobs they were "not able" or were not allowed to "qualify" for in peacetime, and for the first time they began to know what a modicum of independence was all about. For the first time, female workers were able to earn more than a bare subsistence wage as they manned the assembly lines in World War II. The voices of these citizens raised the level of educational expectations for working and middle-class families in their own communities, and they were heard in policy circles at the federal level.

The advent of the G.I. Bill of Rights gave veterans of World War II and the Korean War the chance to go back to school and to matriculate at postsecondary institutions. From this opportunity came educational demand that the country had never experienced. Men and women who had been trained in the armed forces, having become mature and disciplined, returned to school in great numbers. At the same time, the knowledge explosion—a result of many new thrusts in industry, built on knowledge generated in the field of war and encouraged by a growing global economy—was evolving. The confluence of these two events sent the educational planners around the country into a burst of activity that has not slowed until the present day.

But the emphasis was on higher education, not the public elementary and secondary schools. Until the last two decades, very little was known about teaching hard-to-reach children: those who are learning disabled, who are children of poverty, who are from families where English is a second language (if it is spoken at all). Worst of all, the district school systems did not change to meet the demands of universal education and the knowledge explosion. Because central offices became more and more entrenched in bureaucratic school codes and procedures, and because little research in education was done in actual central office and school sites, practitioners continued to be constrained within procedures not very different from those they knew when they were students in the public schools—procedures and systems not designed to address the learning of all children.

The present dilemma is this: the universal demand for good educational services and attention to the national interest in a global economy versus continuation of various forms of discrimination in our public schools.

The history of national interest and education is an intriguing one. Beginning in higher education with the National Defense Education Act of 1958, the federal government began to define national interests in education, granting scholarships to needy students, giving them the opportunity for higher education. Sputnik had just been launched by the USSR, and the Congress saw the need to encourage more scientists and mathematicians from all walks of life. Because the G.I. Bill of Rights program had been so successful in sending veterans from various backgrounds to postsecondary study, the 1958 legislation was patterned on this earlier experience.

This infusion of federal money in the early sixties coincided with the Civil Rights Act of 1964. The convergence of federal interest in education and growing civil rights pressure for equal opportunity in education made it impossible for politicians to sweep segregated schools under the rug.

The first efforts on a national scale to help children of poverty were the programs, especially Title 1 and Title 2, of the Elementary and Secondary Education Act of 1965. This legislation grew out of the National Education Improvement Act of 1963, which addressed the press of higher education issues confronting the nation. However, the 1963 act merely extended some federal programs in vocational and elementary and secondary education, and continued programs already started under the National Defense Education Act (1958).

The Elementary and Secondary Education Act of 1965 was the first federal program that recognized educational needs of children in low-income school districts. The act grew out of the War on Poverty and the Office of Economic Opportunity programs, which identified schooling as an economic good for the first time in U.S. history. Although "educators had often made this point to anyone who would listen" (Keppel, 1966, p. 50), the plea, usually made at the local level, was not heard until Sputnik (1958) and domestic crises brought the issue into national focus. Education had been seen as an "individual good, rather than the basis for an expanding economy" (Keppel, 1966, p. 50). The relationship between economics and education began to be discovered and redefined.

How education became known as an "individual good" is a mystery.* From the time of Thomas Jefferson, education was considered an essential part of freedom; "liberty for all" meant universal knowledge. Although Jefferson would educate classes and vocations differently (there was no vision here for a core education for all citizens), nevertheless he and others of his era considered a broadly educated citizenry essential to democracy. Jefferson believed all citizens had a right to choose to be a leader, to be educated for the "learned" class if they so chose. Or citizens could choose to be educated for the

*In economic terms, an individual or private good is one that is able to be consumed by just one person, the supply of which is dictated by market forces. A public good, on the other hand, is one that is generated by the government, and its supply is determined by central planning processes and revenues. A public good is consumed by all relevant groups as a corporate body, depending on the groups' "perceived utility function" of that good.

basic duties of their way of life. This sentiment would imply that education is a public good, to be valued by the society and its people.

It was not until economists developed better ways to measure growth of national product (GNP) that they realized they could not account for growth only by looking at investment in machinery and in production, including labor.

> *The missing factors were investment in research and development and education of the working force. Education, one of the primary ways to achieve both quality performance and equality of opportunity, is now understood also as a necessary national investment for an expanding society. It is not only a commodity to be consumed by the individual but an investment whose use brings returns both to the individual and to the society. (Keppel, 1966, pp. 26–27)*

The Educational Policies Commission (1965) of the National Education Association and the American Association of School Administrators "pointed out that the important question in the future is not, Who deserves to be educated? but rather Whom can society, in conscience and self-interest, exclude?" (Keppel, 1966, p. 25).

Education was finally recognized as a national interest and a public good. The stage was now set for federal intervention in educational matters, forcing the states to comply with certain "equal opportunity" imperatives.

The Real Costs of Discrimination: Wasted Lives, Lost Productivity, and the Taxpayers' Burden

The declaration of education as a national interest and public good allowed the federal government to pass legislation that would serve individual citizens across the land. The United States Constitution does not mention education, and so jurisdiction for education is left to the states. States set up educational standards, draw up School Codes of Law, and establish core high school graduation requirements and minimum standards in curricula from which the local boards of education can build. States continue to wrestle with formulas for property tax equalization, which will help those towns that suffer from a low tax base to finance their schools. But it is the local school boards that decide the ultimate standards to which students will be held—the curricular objectives, the school budget, and the job descriptions of those who teach and those who administer.

In order to keep control of the schools out of the hands of federal and state governments, the tradition in this country is to place curricular and employment questions (other than those negotiated at state levels by associations of teachers and of administrators) in the hands of local boards of education and professional or trade associations (unions). So, the declaration of education as a national interest had to be articulated as a relationship between federal government and individual citizens, or federal government and local state, rather than federal government and local school board. Title 1 and Title 2 programs of the Elementary and Secondary Education Act of 1965 were the first legislation to test the legaility of this relationship.

In order to promote equal opportunity, the federal government felt it was necessary to hold states responsible for seeing to it that no individual student was shortchanged when it came to those special emphases and privileges that made up the teaching practices that research found were necessary for efficacious teaching and learning of each child. Thus the "compensatory education" (later changed to "supplemental education") components presented for the "disadvantaged" students were named. Title 1 of the 1965 Act described these additions and declared this remedial education necessary to promote equal opportunity in the public schools.

In fact, most of the Title 1 classes were merely smaller groups of students doing more of the same practices at a slower rate than was carried out in the classroom. There was not much effort directed at meeting the needs of children from different cultures or children who learned differently from most. "Equal opportunity" at this early stage of federal intervention was focused on desegregation of schools, rather than differentiation of students' needs that fostered a variety of teaching practices and styles to meet the variety of learning styles of the students.

The policy dilemma was obvious: In order to keep strict legal and governance questions of desegregation honest, the federal government had to trade off strict compliance to (i.e., less discrimination in) the targeting of students for intervention, for categorical implementation of the program. What transpired was that needy students were served, but they were the best of the needy students. A creaming selection process took place as Title 1 students were selected across the land by their teachers. Then these students were ushered out of the classroom and given more of the same practices, but in a smaller group. Especially in the first decade of Title 1, students were selected with the purpose of keeping Title 1 funds coming into the districts: The students just under the norm would be brought up to speed, making the report of the program look good. Unfortunately, not only were those students most in need generally not served but this kind of remedial teaching (more of the same) did not address the special needs of individual students.

When the first reports of Title 1 programs came in, many citizens read into these evaluations proof that the poor, especially minorities, simply could not learn adequately. A spurious report that evaluated Head Start was also interpreted to mean that poor children reverted quickly to below-average achievement soon after leaving Head Start, and had to have benefits of Title 1 programs and other forms of remedial teaching to keep up. Both of these federal evaluations (under the Nixon Administration) depicted the entrenched national education policy of holding only certain students to a higher level of achievement. Discrimination in education programs was reiterated in federal evaluation procedures, which echoed the refrain, "What do you expect of poor black, brown, or even white kids?"

Fortunately these evaluations were not accepted by the education community or by university evaluators who replicated the evaluations and came to different conclusions. Citizen groups also lobbied for these remedial programs, because they sensed they were helping bring certain students into the mainstream. Both Title 1 and Title 2 programs were retained, as well as Head Start.

However, even as the politicians and academicians tinkered with evaluations, the cities were being deserted by those who could afford to move out from deteriorating neighborhoods. Stable working class, ethnic neighborhoods with middle-class values were being replaced by crime, drugs, and the sense of futility that belongs to many in low-income and poverty situations. "White flight" quickly lighted the tinderboxes of poor ethnic and racial groups who were left in the great urban cities to fight on both sides of the desegregation issue.

Children from lower classes were usually not welcomed anywhere, no matter what the tradition of the school before desegregation. Resegregation became a function of class as well as race and ethnicity.

All through these sad years, which saw good working-class neighborhoods disintegrate and become centers of racial hatred where ghetto residents were buried deep in despair, few people mentioned the obvious fact that schools that served these neighborhoods were left to fend on their own. Teachers, students, and administrators involved were not encouraged or trained to regard all students as educable; they were made to worry about simple survival.

What was really happening here was that *all* U.S. citizens were paying for unequal educational opportunity. Many children were not being taught, not just the children of the poor. Anticipating that poor students brought duller minds and broken families into the schools, achievement standards were lowered for everyone, so that teachers would not be expected to cover as much material. The curriculum in most school systems was "dumbed down." Grade inflation took the pressure off teachers as well as students. Tracking of students became more common and pervasive.

In some high schools, the unspoken contract between teacher and students included their knowing what questions would be asked on an exam beforehand. This way, the students looked good, the teachers looked good, and no one was the wiser. Because the grades were higher, the community these schools served often felt their children were getting a good education.

This is what happens when some students are prohibited from being included in the full, intended curriculum. Whether subject matter is not taught, or the process allows students to fall behind, or the system itself encourages administrators and teachers to play games with the birthright of all children—a good education with rigorous standards—no matter what the cause, *children of all backgrounds suffer.*

The best kept secret of our educational system today is this: Many children in some social classes, and some children in all social classes, are being robbed of their educational rights. A student doesn't have to be at risk to be ignored in the classroom.

A school where all children learn is the best school for all children. In an equitable school, where teaching for learning for all occurs, there are far less disciplined problems. More students are highly motivated to study and learn, because they know they will get a fair shot at the target. Higher student achievement of all students reflects the other ingredients of a good school: a climate of learning, school pride and individual rewards for students and practitioners alike, very low tardiness and absenteeism, and a sense of "can do." "All students winners" is the motto of one outstanding Effective School. Effective Schools are win-win schools.

But all children will not be taught unless the community—whether school, district, town, city, or county—demands that all our children be taught. Unless the grassroots produce this political will, putting pressure on public officials as well as on the education system, lives will continue to be wasted, and the cost of these wasted lives will be borne by taxpayers and the society in which we live. How much cost? A person out of work for a year who is an average "head of household" (earning $15,000 a year) will cost the society over $90,000 in lost productivity, opportunity costs, welfare payments, or unemployment compensation combined. If that person starts dealing drugs or abusing them, becomes a criminal, or abuses family, neighbors, or the community, the cost is doubled. And ultimately, the taxpayer pays for it all.

Discrimination in education is a costly policy, just as it is in employment and social relations. That's the bottom line. The argument has come full circle.

Education is no longer thought of as an individual good, but is seen as a national interest, a public good. As a public good, investments are made by federal, state, and local levels of government for educational services for all children for the sake of the country's well-being, as well as for the sake of all citizens' and children's well-being. The national interest is served by having educated citizens who can compete, add workplace competency, and participate in a free society by sharing informed decisions in political, social, and economic debates.

When the national investment in education is hedged by discrimination and the withholding of teaching to certain targeted groups, then all of society pays the costs in welfare burdens, crime, disease, and unproductive lives when these groups fail to respond to society's common demands.

When the investment in education is hedged by discrimination and the withholding of teaching from certain targeted groups, there is no group that is safe from classroom discrimination. All of society's parents take the chance that their children will be discriminated against, if only because there are not enough educational resources—good teachers, curriculums, schools, systems of public education—to go around. And this lack of adequate funding for educational programs at the federal, state, and local levels ultimately increases our society's costs.

Only by adopting a policy that states that all children are educable, therefore the schools will be held accountable for the teaching of all children to an agreed upon standard, do we make that public good that is education eminently available to all families, no matter what their resources.

Excellence in education without equity will not solve our problems. Excellence *with equity*—that is, a superior educational program available and taught to *all* children—is the goal we seek. This means that working-class parents, parents with low incomes, minority parents, and even parents who have daughters as well as sons can expect a solid education program for all their children. Especially those parents who are middle class will be served by such a policy. They can count on better schools where discipline is no longer a problem, where programs address the problems of the twenty-first century, and where teaching is focused on individual needs by teachers who hold themselves responsible for their students' success.

When this system is implemented through a change process like the Effective Schools Process, we will then be able to have educational choice that is as equitable as it is excellent. Only then can the American dream be realized by all children and their families.

CHAPTER ONE

All Children Can Learn

How many effective schools would you have to see to be persuaded of the educability of poor children? If your answer is more than one, then I submit that you have reasons of your own for preferring to believe that basic pupil performance derives from family background instead of school response to family background. —RON EDMONDS

Treat a man as he is, and he will remain as he is. Treat a man as he can and should be and he will become as he can and should be. —GOETHE

It's as American as apple pie.

Two first-graders walk into a classroom. One is wearing stiff, new corduroy slacks, a knit sweater, and fashionable top-siders. The other is in patched jeans, a worn sweatshirt, and scarred sneakers with frayed and knotted laces. Without hesitation, our mind classifies the child in the finer clothes as the one who will succeed. The other child is written off as a failure. Our reaction is as American as apple pie. We have been trained and conditioned to think this way. Although these two first-graders were different only in their clothing, that clothing, to the average observer, identified their class. And in the United States, lower socioeconomic class means "not so bright."

In this particular analogy, the child we placed in the lower socioeconomic class had on clean, just-pressed clothing. His mother had made sure his socks had no holes, his hair was combed, and his ears were clean. But all that didn't matter. All we saw was that he was poor. And that was enough. But what if, along with being poor, this child was black or Hispanic? What if his pants were not just worn but dirty? And what if he was sullen or angry and acted out?

We would shake our heads and say that the child had no future. He was obviously destined for the remedial classes, perhaps the educationally retarded classes. We would like to give him a good education, but the deck is stacked against him. He's from a disadvantaged family, his environment is harmful, he won't get the necessary support or resources, and he doesn't have the desire, anyway.

Excuses, excuses, excuses. Excuses for us. Excuses for the teachers and the school. Excuses for the child. Excuses that are as American as apple pie.

But, wait. Let's replay this scenario without the preordained judgments and without accepting any excuses for us, the teachers, the school, or the child. This time, let's have a teacher and a principal say to this poorly clad, minority child with the angry expression: "You're just as smart as anyone in this class. You can do everything they can do. Matter of fact, you can do just about anything you want. Want to be a doctor? Fine. A president of a multinational company? Fine. Want to be a judge, an artist, a movie director? Fine. And you know what? That goes for your sister, too."

The school then teaches the child accordingly. There are no limits set on the child's potential. Everyone, including the child, believes he can accomplish whatever he desires. The teacher and principal are accountable, and pleased to be accountable, for the child's learning. The child learns at grade level and then excels beyond it. He is happy, confident, and directed. He still wears a worn sweatshirt, but he's now a friend and equal of the boy in the slim, slick corduroys. They learn and share together. They *both* are on their way to productive lives.

In some schools, this scenario is in fact the way it is. In some schools, this equity and quality is as American as apple pie, and this is what Effective Schools are all about. Effective Schools are places where *all* children learn—not just kids with blue eyes and blond hair and Izod shirts, not just kids whose parents set up trust funds, not just kids who shout and demand, not just kids with brown skin and hand-me-downs, not just kids who never get a break and who we feel sorry for—but *all* kids.

The people in Effective Schools teach all children because they believe they have a moral responsibility to teach all children—a responsibility not just to the child but to the parent, the taxpayer, their bosses, their community, and society as a whole. They are accountable, and want to be accountable, insisting on regular testing and monitoring of their classrooms.

The superintendent, visible and demanding, runs the district, and the principals, informed and inspiring, run the schools, like a business. There are specific goals and objectives, and means of accomplishing those. Change is ongoing, maintenance of the status quo is unacceptable. The schools, dependent on their own internal leadership and responsibility, are in an ongoing improvement process that is judged by the viability and vitality of its outcomes.

At the heart of this Effective School is the belief that all children can learn. That belief drives and inspires people to prove that all children can learn and to be accountable for that learning. Accountability is not feared—it is welcomed and it becomes its own motivator.

By teaching all children, the school implements a process that begins to improve the school. Achievement scores rise. Teacher and student morale improve. The school becomes a more productive, accountable learning center because it is following a precise process of change based on every child learning. And that process of change emanates from 25 years of extensive research.

But isn't this what schools are supposed to be about anyway? Isn't this equity and quality what Horace Mann talked about 150 years ago? Certainly, but along the way. U.S. education, reflecting the values of society at large, as it is prone to do, decided that disadvantaged, minority children just didn't have what it takes to succeed in school. This belief was reinforced in 1966 when James Coleman and colleagues released their survey of Equal Educational Opportunity. The results stated that the reason black student performance was below that of white student performance was because of family background, and there wasn't a whole lot schools could do about it:

> *Schools bring little influence to bear on a child's achievement that is independent of his background and general social context . . . this very lack of an independent effect means that the inequalities imposed on children by their home, neighborhood, and peer environment are carried along to become the inequalities with which they confront life at the end of school. For equality of educational opportunity through the schools must imply a strong effect of schools that is independent of the child's immediate social environment, and that strong independent effect is not present in American schools.*

These conclusions were supported in 1972 by Christopher Jencks and other Harvard researchers in a study that essentially relieved the schools of any responsibility in the failure to educate disadvantaged children. The study concluded that the schools could make no impact on the economic and social inequalities brought into the classroom: "We cannot blame economic inequality on differences between schools, since differences between schools seem to have very little effect on any measurable attribute of those who attend them."

The implication of these findings—which were simply and flatly "schools don't make a difference"—was the subtle confirmation for parents, teachers, and administrators that disadvantaged students, because of their family background, just couldn't pull together the thinking skills like their more affluent classmates.

In later years, Coleman's methodological approach would be seriously challenged and Coleman himself would back off from his conclusions. We know now that Coleman and Jencks never looked at the schools that were teaching all children, and teaching all children very successfully. Of if they did look at them, they failed to mention them. Such schools did exist, and as early as 1971, researchers like George Weber were identifying these schools in Manhattan, Kansas City, and Los Angeles.

The research continued, and in the mid-seventies, Wilbur Brookover, Larry Lezotte, and Ron Edmonds began conducting detailed analyses of the differences between successful and unsuccessful schools for low-income children.

They published their results, citing specific characteristics that, according to their research, made these schools so successful in teaching all children.

In 1979, Ron Edmonds, then a project director at Harvard's Center for Urban Studies in the Graduate School of Education, published an article in *Educational Leadership* that brought together some of the most powerful and all-conclusive data on successful schools serving lower socioeconomic populations. This article, still cited today, became the clarion call for teaching for learning for all children. In the article, entitled "Effective Schools for the Urban Poor," Edmonds refuted Coleman and Jencks, citing schools where family background put *no limits* on the aspirations and abilities of disadvantaged children. He wrote plainly of the differences between the high-achieving and improving schools and the declining and low-achieving schools:

- Teachers believed all their students could learn.
- Teachers had specific goals.
- Teachers were more task oriented.
- Teachers were not satisfied with the status quo.
- Teachers had more supportive principals.
- The principal was a strong leader, visible and supportive.
- There was more student monitoring.
- Teachers had higher expectations for their students.
- Students were happier and worked harder.
- There was trust between students, faculty, and staff.

There was one predominant factor that Edmonds kept going back to when talking about the improving, high-achieving schools: The faculties and staffs were accountable and sought out that accountability. In fact, it seemed that the accountability motivated them.

At the conclusion of the article, Edmonds set forth what he believed the research concluded were six correlates of an Effective School. It is these same correlates, based on the philosophy that *all children can learn,* that have become the guiding principles of Effective Schools over the last 25 years. These correlates are in place in hundreds of school districts and thousands of schools throughout the United States. It is these correlates that practitioners claim, lay the foundation for healthy, exciting learning environments for the teaching for learning for all children.

Clear and Focused School Mission

There is a clearly articulated mission for the school through which the staff shares an understanding of and a commitment to instructional goals, priorities, assessment procedures, and accountability.

Safe and Orderly Environment

There is an orderly, purposeful atmosphere that is free from the threat of physical harm for both students and staff. However, the atmosphere is not oppressive and is conducive to teaching and learning.

High Expectations

The school displays a climate of expectation in which the staff believes and demonstrates that students can attain mastery of basic skills and that they (the staff) have the capability to help students achieve such mastery.

Opportunity to Learn and Time on Task

Teachers allocate a significant amount of classroom time to instruction in basic skills areas. For a high percentage of that allocated time, students are engaged in planned learning activities directly related to identified objectives.

Instructional Leadership

The principal acts as the instructional leader who effectively communicates the mission of the school to the staff, parents, and students, and who understands and applies the characteristics of instructional effectiveness in the management of the instructional program of the school.

Frequent Monitoring of Student Progress

Feedback on student academic progress is frequently obtained. Multiple assessment methods such as teacher-made tests, samples of students' work, mastery skills checklists, criterion-referenced tests, and norm-referenced tests are used. The results of testing are used to improve individual student performance and also to improve the instructional program.

A seventh correlate was later added by Edmonds.

Positive Home-School Relations

Parents understand and support the school's basic mission and are given opportunity to play an important role in helping the school achieve its mission.

This last correlate was not included initially because the Effective Schools Process holds as its base only those variables that the school has absolute control over. Edmonds realized that schools could not always depend on parental involvement and was fearful that schools would use the lack of parental involvement as an excuse for failure.

Positive home-school relations are, however, something that is encouraged and determinedly worked for by teachers and staff at Effective Schools. It is considered essential to all sound planning. Under the Effective Schools Process, the relationship with parents is far more open, inclusive, and has greater power than in ineffective schools. It is now listed as a vital correlate and considered one of the major inducements to community support. However, the original thinking still holds: Parents are a plus when they are involved, but if they are not, the schools cannot use their absence as an excuse for failure.

These seven correlates, as they were first set out in concrete terms by Edmonds in his 1979 article, and as they are applied today in Effective Schools, are not an end in themselves, but a means to an end. The correlates have expanded and intensified over the years, with more research and data added daily. Just as these correlates were initially based on years of research findings, so has all the subsequent Effective Schools literature been reinforced by years of extensive research and data collection.

Practitioners today still remember Edmonds's 1979 article. For many, it was their first contact with the Effective Schools Process, to be followed by additional study. The deeper into the research they traveled, the more reinforcement they discovered for Edmonds's philosophy and assertions, and the efficacy of the correlates. Most had strong instincts about the educability of all children; they were now ready to make the transition to rejecting flatly the contentions of Coleman and Jencks. For these practitioners, the Effective Schools research and literature began a process of their own professional renewal.

These were educators who like the call to accountability. They like the call to equity in excellence, to teaching all children to *the teacher's* fullest potential, to teaching for learning, to setting goals and working for *specific outcomes,* to making schools professional workplaces for teachers and administrators. It is a summons that good educators have been waiting for. Noel Farmer, Ed.D., superintendent of Frederick County (Maryland) Public Schools, echoes the sentiment of many superintendents, principals, and teachers: "I knew something was missing. I knew something out there in terms of how we were doing it, was just wrong. And I knew I was failing at some very important level."

Farmer adopted and implemented the Effective Schools Improvement Process and turned around his declining school system. In the 1990s, Frederick County has moved to the top tiers of the Maryland state performance tests. The scores are all above average, almost all students achieving at or above grade level. While many other Maryland counties are slipping down or barely holding steady, Frederick County is rising in all major categories. Plus, dropouts are down; graduates, attendance, and morale are up. Frederick County spends $4,853 per pupil. It is ranked 13th in per pupil expenditure for the state (out of 23 districts). The two districts it is tied with spend over $6,000 and $7,000 per student.

Frederick County is just one of the success stories—just one of many stories in this book of the genuine good work by teachers and students in U.S. public schools. Noel Farmer is just 1 of over 450 people interviewed whose life has been changed for the better by the Effective Schools Process.

What is the most important thing Farmer has going for him in making Effective Schools so successful? What is the one thing that every superintendent, every principal, and every teacher tells you is essential for school change? WILL. You have to have the will to change: the will to enhance your own knowledge, buck the past, and embrace new teaching and leadership skills; the will to live the moral imperative that is the driving force of Effective Schools. And if you have that will, the rest is simple—not easy, but simple.

The Call for Equity Must Begin at Tracking

In many of this country's over 16,000 school districts, there is not a significant will to change. The maintenance of the status quo, no matter how mediocre or debilitating, is the law of the land, comfortable and easy. That status quo is America's apple pie. It is that status quo that has kept children in carefully determined tracks of learning that existed long before the Coleman and Jencks reports. In fact, those reports just reinforced that status quo, the way people think about children and learning. And it is breaking that system of tracking, physical as well as psychological, that is the mission of the Effective Schools Process.

We have all been the victims of it, for good and ill. In school, someone decided, because of the color of our skin, our ethnic background, our religion, our gender, our style of dress, who our parents were, and where we lived, which track we would go into. In elementary school, it may have been decided in our homeroom whether we were with the bright kids or slow kids. In secondary school, we were tracked into college courses, business courses, or vocational courses—not because we chose but because someone else decided years ago that that was the track we were destined to be in.

Tracking decides which children can learn and how well they can learn. In a tracking school system, only certain children are allowed open access to knowledge. Only certain children are allowed high expectations. Only certain children are deemed "educable."

"You have to understand that teaching all children is not a natural act," says Larry Lezotte, now one of the premier experts on the Effective Schools Process. "Thinking that all children can learn is just not part of the American psyche. You don't have to scrape the surface very hard to find the real demon here. There are an awful lot of people who do not want all children to learn because of the social, economic implications of that. If they all learn, they ask, what is it that I'm going to use to say that I'm better than somebody else?"

It is not just a race struggle, it is a class struggle. This class struggle is part of our nation's heritage. It rode on the Mayflower and helped fire the shot heard 'round the world. As our country grew, inequities grew. People began to "know their place." And later, if they didn't know their place, someone directed them to that place. And hence we have tracking. Tracking was and is no accident.

The justification for tracking came about in the late nineteenth and early twentieth centuries when this country was hit with the onslaught of immigrants from eastern and southern Europe. As the cities bulged and politicians wondered what to do with the increase in immigrants, it fell to the schools to devise a solution. Public education was to be for every citizen, but not everyone can have the best education and enter white-collar professions. After all, someone has to work in the fields and factories, sweep the streets, collect the garbage, and so on.

The answer was tracking—ability grouping. One large group was tracked into programs that would feed the fields and factories. The other, "higher status," group was aimed toward management careers and colleges.

But how does a society decide who goes where? The United States got caught up in a debate that continues today. And although the debate is somewhat quieter today and has different nuances, its characteristics are still frighteningly similar. It was assumed then that the lighter-complexioned northern Europeans (the WASPs, for the most part) were a step above everyone on the evolutionary ladder. The darker-skinned southern and eastern Europeans (in particular Catholic and Jewish immigrants) were relegated to a lower evolutionary rung. Subtle, but very effective, it was the way things became, and stayed, in the public schools. Some children, the experts said, just cannot learn.

These subtleties were later reinforced when the founders of intelligence tests offered their interpretation of the results. Lewis Terman, an intelligence test pioneer, wrote in 1923, in *Intelligence Tests and School Reorganization,* referring to the immigrants from eastern and southern Europe: "Their dullness seems to be racial. . . . Children of this group should be segregated in special classes. . . . They cannot master abstractions, but they can often be made efficient workers."

And with statements like that came the official justification for the tracking of students. When minorities entered the system, they were directed into the already worn paths of tracking formerly trod by eastern and southern Europeans. Over time, the vicious cycle of tracking kept spinning, the low-level students walking out to the low-level jobs and raising families in low-income neighborhoods with schools that moved their children along the low-level tracks.

The reasoning behind tracking is that by putting students into groups according to what someone perceives as their ability, schools are able to cater to specific achievement levels, thus making teaching more efficient. It is also argued that tracking prevents psychological damage to lower-level students who would be competing with the higher achievers. Also, tracking is supposed to make the teaching task simpler; teachers can manage students more easily.

Jeannie Oakes, considered one of the foremost authorities on tracking, has conducted numerous studies of tracking and has concluded that there is little evidence to support any of the assumptions about tracking. Not only are students in the lower tracks adversely affected, she says, but also research shows that students in the top tracks do not have their learning significantly enhanced by tracking.

The students are isolated in a very controlled atmosphere, very often with preordained notions (though not as preordained as teachers for the lower-track students) as to what they should learn and how quickly. The atmosphere is extremely competitive, which at first blush seems right, but in fact the socialization of students is seriously impaired. In a society that increasingly values cooperation and teamwork, tracking encourages ego-driven individuality and self-improvement at the expense of others.

The students in the lower tracks have, for the most part, the less experienced, less enthusiastic, more punitive teachers. These students' access to knowledge is severely limited. There is little independent, critical thinking; the environment is not nurturing or positive; and there are fewer opportunities to learn, with much of the class emphasis dealing with student behavior. Researchers point out that limited access to knowledge is a damaging problem. Most low-track students never get a chance to encounter the knowledge and learning skills that our society values most. There is also the problem of interaction. By dividing students and keeping them separated, they are denied the chance to learn about others—not just other personalities, but often other races, religions, and customs. There is no sharing of ambitions or tasks. The value of knowing how to work with someone is rarely investigated or experienced.

By tracking the students into the lower achievement tracks, the school accomplishes the feat of keeping the children at lower achievement levels. Tracking becomes a self-fulfilling prophecy and a vicious circle. The reason why students fail is because they are placed in these low tracks with no expectations. The reason they are placed is because they have a history of failing. Tracking becomes its own reason for inequity. And it becomes an excuse for teachers and school systems.

"America buys into the tracking. It's something we expect, something we desire," says Noel Farmer of Frederick County, Maryland. "We're comfortable with grouping, with putting the poor, the African-American at the bottom. We like the idea of a caste system, of keeping certain people in place according to their race or gender. As long as our kids are at the top, of course."

Farmer says that it is part of our country's heritage to pay homage to students' ability to learn, or assessing the capacity to learn. The problem is, says Farmer, that the tests we use to assess that capacity (IQ tests) do not test capacity. They test rates of learning. And for immigrants unfamiliar with American ways, nuances, and vocabulary, that judgment—how quickly they did test problems—seems unreasonable and unfair.

"We are paying merit to someone learning something in a given period of time. And that's wrong. We cannot afford to let that happen anymore. We have been about an amoral business. To judge students by their rate of learning is evil," insists Farmer. "If we give students time and assistance, there is no cap to their capacity to learn."

This is Effective Schools: There is no limit to the learning ability of all students. All children can learn, given the chance and the time. And if schools operate on this premise, they will produce higher achievement scores and higher levels of satisfaction for the entire school community than those schools that track. Deciding whether or not a child can learn, and then deciding what that child is entitled to learn, and operating a school that reinforces that in procedure and policy, produces *ineffective* schools. Our policy of tracking, of selecting and sorting, is the major contributing factor to the failure of this country's public schools.

"Tracking just makes it so a small group of kids get the good stuff," insists Farmer. "And how do you run a successful school if you're only providing teaching for learning for one small, select group? Is it any wonder why we're in trouble?"

That trouble is exhibited in disgruntled teachers who no longer care, principals and superintendents who are only interested in political paybacks, parents who search for alternative education sites, and students who drop out and get their equal learning opportunity on the streets.

But the real villain is often overlooked. Since the early nineteenth century, public education has been based on the centralized factory model that sends students into designated tracks and places all learning on the notorious Bell curve. Effective Schools insist that our country must now move to a decentralized, information age model operating on shared decision making. This model is based on the J curve, with all students learning.

Unfortunately, dissolving the factory model and the tracking system does not sit well with everyone, in particular those affluent parents whose children are benefiting from it. Some parents view their schools as elite, private white schools, and they don't want that changed. Some districts, which you will read about later in this book, are still doing battle over tracking. But what is diminishing the viciousness of the argument is the results that the Effective Schools Process is pulling in. The achievement scores for children at all levels are rising.

"We have to be very careful here. We cannot have one group of students excel and another group falter. You just cannot bring up the lower socioeconomic students and have the middle and upper class kids slip, even slightly," explains Hal Guthrie, Ed.D., superintendent of Spring Branch (Texas) Independent School District. "The ideal is that everyone goes up, and thank God, so far that's what we're doing."

Spring Branch has a very wealthy and very conservative population. It also has a growing Hispanic and black population. Prior to Guthrie coming in, the entire district was starting to fail. He began the Effective Schools Improvement Process.

"Parents wanted it because they knew we needed major change because we were in trouble and heading for tough times," explains Guthrie. "But there's now been *a lot* of change, and although they may tell me they're not completely happy with it, they say they can't argue with the results."

Many parents feared that dissolving the tracking system would eliminate all programs for the gifted and talented students, that the school system would no longer recognize the exceptional talent of *some* students. That is an unnecessary fear. There will always be some students, especially at the high school level, who exhibit exceptional learning skills. But with the Effective Schools Process, these children are not chosen by superficial criteria of race, class, religion, or gender, but by a careful, extensive examination of their academic and leadership skills.

One of the essential components of Effective Schools is the disaggregation of test scores, the breakdown of test results according to specific criteria. Students are tested frequently, and the scores are disaggregated according to high, middle, and low socioeconomic status. If the district has no perceived low-income students, the scores are disaggregated according to the level of a mother's education. The scores are also disaggregated according to gender, and any additional criteria the school seeks.

Disaggregation of test scores is not common in the public schools. Only 42 percent of this country's 16,000 school districts have a program of school improvement, and of that 42 percent, *only 11 percent* (or 740) disaggregate their scores. The reason is that once a district or school disaggregates its scores, some ugly truths may come to the fore, and some myths may be blown apart.

A common example is the school that celebrates the fact that 70 percent of its students are reading at grade level. The school disaggregates its scores and discovers that maybe 95 percent of its white students are reading at grade level, but only 40 percent of its minority students are doing likewise. A further look shows that while 80 percent of the girls are reading well, only 50 percent of the boys are. The scores reveal that a big chunk of this school's population is in fact failing.

With an Effective School disaggregating its scores, this type of illusion would not be possible. The whole purpose of disaggregation is to see which students and which classes are failing, and to get help to those students. It is not a mark against teachers. It is the way teachers can make a call for help. The classes can now be split up, if necessary; the teacher can receive additional training to help her or him reach the students; and the school can allocate its time and resources accordingly. The frequent monitoring and the disaggregation are means for teachers to see where the trouble is. They force accountability on the teachers, but they also give teachers the tools to address and handle that accountability.

It is not fair, nor does it make sense, to ask teachers to accomplish a task they are not prepared to do. A common refrain from teachers today is that they were never properly trained to handle the learning needs of today's heterogeneous population. Effective schools recognize that, and did so right from the beginning, stating that teachers would never be asked to do something they were not properly trained to do. For that reason, staff development—renewal—is a key component of the Effective Schools Improvement Process.

As soon as a district begins implementation, it starts the process of enhancing teacher training. Experts and practitioners in the Effective Schools Process are brought in not only to run seminars on the philosophy and change process but to give instruction on how teachers can teach for learning for all.

"Good teachers instinctually know that all their children can learn. They just don't always know how to get the kids to that point where they can learn," explains Bonnie Seaburn, principal of the Munn Elementary School in Spencerport, New York, a predominantly middle-class suburb of Rochester. "What we did through our training was to reinforce the teachers' skills and to give them the training to reach all their kids. Some teachers, sure, you have to show them all these kids can learn. And we did that, too."

Through instructional changes like Teacher Expectation and Student Achievement (TESA), Mastery Learning, Cooperative Learning, and Outcomes Based Education, teachers saw how students, who would have previously been classified as low-level achievers, ended up competing with some of the best students in the class. It happens in Effective School districts across the country. Teachers proudly say they are in the business of killing off the stereotypes.

But this has not come easy to many teachers or principals. A whole culture, in and out of school, has been built up around the nineteenth-century factory model and Bell curve. Dismantling that means changing the way people think.

"The Effective Schools (Process) is a change in our culture and belief system," says Edie Holbrook, Ed.D., a former teacher, principal, and now head of training and technical assistance for the National Center for Effective Schools housed at the University of Wisconsin–Madison. "It is a threat to the values we hold dear, to the values we have defined ourselves with. We are being challenged, not just on how we teach, but on how we think, how we view the world."

This change is made even more difficult by what Holcomb calls the "norm of inertia" present in the public schools. "We want to continue to do things the way we always have, the way things have been worked in the past. And we're not interested in hearing how it didn't work. The need here is to change the norm of inertia without implying that anyone has done anything wrong."

Because of this norm of inertia, the Effective Schools Process is very precise in not only *how* it goes about change but *what* that change is demonstrating.

Sophisticated rhetoric is not enough. The schools have heard that song before. The teachers, principals and parents want facts and proof.

An Outcome-Based Business

"What gets measured gets done" is a familiar slogan around Effective Schools. How are the lower-income kids doing in history? Measure it, and if it's bad, change it. How many girls are involved in the science fair? Measure it, and if it's below the number for boys, find out why and change it. How many minorities are in the future business leaders club? Find out, and if there's a problem, figure out how to turn it around.

It is a matter of outcomes, and it is no secret that it is this push for results that is the appeal for many superintendents and community and business leaders. Hal Guthrie has never understood why schools are not more outcome based.

"Doesn't it make common sense? You aim for results?" he asks. "You set up a plan, with objectives, and you go about doing it. You reach for outcomes. If it's good enough for business, why isn't it good enough for us?"

Many still ask that. Why are some students not getting into colleges or not getting good jobs? Why in some districts are dropout rates between 35 and 50 percent accepted? Why are some school districts, like Boston, allowed to come in $50 million dollars over budget?

"Because we've never been forced to be accountable. We've never had to produce outcomes that justified policies and expenditures," says Noel Farmer. "We had excuses. We blamed it on the kids' background, the family, then we blamed the teachers, the principals. Somehow we never blamed the superintendents or the boards of education."

Effective Schools don't allow excuses. They operate like businesses. The superintendent is accountable, just as the board is. It is an outcome-based operation, with specific missions and goals. Effective Schools are adopting many of the practices of businesses of the eighties and nineties. The schools insist on instructional leadership that models behavior and performance: leadership that gets involved with the employees and the students; leadership that doesn't politic in the corner office all day, but spends time in the classrooms, watching and assessing teachers, principals, and students; leadership that understands organization and management skills, and is not afraid to take a stand or, if necessary, a risk.

It is an entirely new atmosphere in an Effective School district. The schools do not exist at the whim of the superintendent and the staff. The principals are instructional leaders, the teachers monitor and are monitored, and even the central office staff exists to serve the schools, not to appease the superintendent and the board.

Effective Schools believe in decentralized school-based management, shared decision making, putting the power to run the schools in the hands of those who must actually do it. Teachers are free to design their own school mission statement, the school's objectives, and how the school is going to accomplish those objectives. The teachers work on the school's curriculum, and choose the development and renewal courses they want. Teachers even take courses in group process skills and decision making in order to enhance their own leadership capabilities.

The school sets up its own improvement team, a team that is usually elected, not hand-picked by the political operatives in the principal's office. Parents and business and community leaders are on the team. The team meets regularly, often off campus during a specially set aside time. The needs of the students are seriously discussed. The means of addressing those needs are hammered out in preparation for presentation to the entire school community.

And the principal? There's a new breed of principal out there—a principal who supports the teachers, who understands instructional techniques, and who is a team player, but gives the teachers autonomy and trust. This principal knows about adult learning, management of professionals, and student behavior, and becomes a model for the school. This principal is a buffer, a cheerleader, an inspiration, and a driving force for the school. And in the Effective Schools district, if the principal cannot measure up to the new breed—even after special leadership training—the principal is moved out.

What Effective Schools are all about is getting rid of the status quo that failed to serve many students and that exasperated many teachers and parents. Under the Effective Schools Process, boards of education know what is truly happening in the schools and realize their job is not one of forwarding their political career and ensuring patronage jobs. Superintendents are accountable and have to produce specific outcomes. Principals must be instructional leaders that assist, support, and inspire their school communities. Teachers must now teach all children and are given the tools, autonomy, and power to do that.

The accountability moves from the board and superintendent right down to the students. In an Effective School, they are called to be involved in their education. They are empowered, just as their teachers. They know what is expected of them—everything—and they are given the time and assistance to deliver it.

"It's not just a big change from what schools have been; it's a big improvement," maintains Hal Guthrie. "We're finally empowering the right people. I'm setting up the framework, the schools are completing the process. I say to them, 'I don't care how the hell you teach *all* of those kids and deliver the outcomes this district demands, just *do it!*'"

There are those who see the Effective Schools Process and the correlates as nothing more than common sense, or the way schools should be. "I believe that basically Effective Schools put a working plan to good common sense," says Sue Rovin, president of the Frederick County (Maryland) School Board. "Here, finally, were the all encompassing guidelines on how to produce the outcomes that guaranteed we were educating all of our children."

Frederick County has changed many of its policies, including tracking. It had to in order to address the teaching for learning for all children. Rovin says that, as expected, complaints come from those parents in the upper classes. But so far, the results prove that the Effective Schools Process is in fact helping *all* children. And although that is the mission of Effective Schools, Rovin says that there is more to it; the shackles have been lifted from the entire school community and there is revitalization happening.

"Over the years, I saw the frustration of so many of our employees. They wanted to do better, but didn't know how. Now I see exuberant, dedicated teachers, and it's not just the newer teachers who picked this up quickly. I talk to veteran teachers and administrators who say the Effective Schools Process has afforded them the opportunity for growth. They are now aware, excited. And we include everyone in that growth. Secretaries, maintenance people, the community. It is a movement towards self-esteem, improvement, for all of us."

The Schools' Failing Report Card

For some school districts, the Effective Schools Process has come just in time. Unfortunately, for many, it is already too late. This year, 1 million students will drop out of school. Some 15 million of America's 40 million school children are at failure of academic risk. In this country 45 million people are functionally illiterate; 25 million are totally illiterate. Of those, 40 percent are English-speaking, white Americans; 22 percent are black, and 37 percent do not have English as their first language.

We know what all this means for our society: increased poverty, neglect, abuse, violence, and crime—not just in the inner city, but in our small towns and suburbs. Drug abuse continues to climb. Teen pregnancy continues to feed the welfare cycle. Each day, another 40 teenage girls give birth to their third child.

Businesses keep telling us that they can't find qualified workers in this country. Three-quarters of our workforce is qualified for only 40 percent of the jobs. Our students are being outperformed by their counterparts in Europe and Asia. And according to the latest statistics from the federal government, in 1995, the Social Security payment for today's aging population will have to come from five people, three of whom are going to be minority and 42 percent of whom will be poor.

Those who think in purely economic terms understand the immediate consequences—in order to keep the lights shining brightly on our democracy, we can no longer sort and select, track, and decide who can learn and who cannot. We can no longer write off a portion of our society. We need *everyone* learning and producing.

In the next 10 years, the Anglo-American school population will increase by 10,000 students. The number of black, Hispanic, Asian, and Pacific Islander students will increase by 3.5 million students, the majority of whom will be economically and socially disadvantaged. By the year 2020, over 50 percent of the students in the public schools will be minority.

The consequences of ignoring the educational needs of America's children are catastrophic. Dr. Henry Levin, director of the Center for Educational Research at Stanford University, states that the impact will be felt by every American in at least four areas:

- Reduced economic competitiveness of the nation as well as those states and industries heavily impacted
- Higher costs for public services as a response to poverty
- Massive disruption in higher education
- The emergence of a dual society with a large and poorly educated underclass

Many would argue that we already have that underclass and that we must look to not only the education of present and future generations but those who have already been failed by a system that tracked them into a class labeled as "uneducable." Effective Schools begin that process.

Schools reflect our ambivalence as a society toward the poor and disadvantaged. It is the task of Effective Schools to change that ambivalence into a commitment to change. And it is being done, not by fancy rhetoric, a few isolated programs, and promises of better tomorrows but by the force of people who believe in their own viable education as much as their students. They believe that if they don't know how to do it, they will learn. They won't accept a status quo that passes the buck and makes excuses. They welcome accountability because they know they can prove their belief that all children can learn.

The Effective Schools Process is about people—people who have had the courage to change and take a risk; people who say, "You want results? You want proof all these kids are learning? I'd be delighted to give you proof." It is about administrators who apply the same production and management principles to the operation of their districts and schools as do the most prosperous Fortune 500 companies. These are people who do not blink at accountability.

The Effective Schools Process is also about parents who have finally been given a substantive say in their child's education. These parents have been forced to face some hard truths, to give up some old prejudices, to find a concern that goes beyond their front door—not just white parents, but all parents—they have had to drop the ways of the past and start anew.

Because good intentions are never enough, and, in fact, have failed the public schools over and over, the Effective Schools Process sets out a very precise plan for school improvement. And because every school is different and every leader functions in a different style, it provides alternative means of implementation. It is an ongoing process of change that provides a structure for school improvement based not only on the aspirations of a child's parents but the aspirations of the school.

Because of the unique compatibility of Effective Schools with mastery learning, the teachings of James Comer, school-based management, and other improvement and reform tools, practitioners are able to pull together the various ideologies and strategies fighting for recognition in the arena of school reform. Effectiveness does not mean isolation. It means, and requires, collegiality and cooperation on all levels to reach its true potential.

"Initiate, implement, institutionalize," is the cry that is heard from Effective Schools. People who believe that all children can learn are proving that. For these children, who may not have had a shot at the working class, to say nothing of the middle class, there is now some substance to their hope. We all know that education is the bridge to productivity and prosperity. Our history has not extended that bridge to many children. Effective Schools are changing that, and it is to the advantage of all of us. Effective Schools are making equity and quality as American as apple pie.

CHAPTER TWO

Regain Hope, All Ye Who Enter Here

The teacher who walks in the shadow of the temple, among his followers, gives not of his wisdom but rather of his faith and lovingness. If he is indeed wise he does not bid you enter the house of his wisdom, but rather leads you to the threshold of your own mind. —THE PROPHET

I'm just the keeper of the dream. —SUZANNE STILL, Principal

Is it possible for a child not to have dreams? No dreams of becoming a hotshot airline pilot or a daring astronaut? A famous brain surgeon or a professional baseball player? An adored ballerina or a glamorous movie star? No dreams of living in a mega-mansion by the sea or an awesome penthouse in the sky? No dreams of handsome princes and gorgeous children?

There are children in the United States who have no dreams. You can see it in their eyes as they sit in a classroom. Their eyes have no light; they are dark, closed, and they don't let you in. Their faces have no expression. Their hands lay listless on top of an unopened book. Their bodies are limp, their hearts are hard and cold. Nothing excites them; nothing really interests them.

But it's the eyes you keep going back to, hoping you're wrong, that you'll see something in them other than that shadowless darkness. They're too young—this is only the third grade. Could they really have given up hope at such an early age? Are the dreams really gone or were they never there? The answer is in the darkness, and maybe in the movement, for when the eyes move, you sense the child's anger and your fear.

These children without dreams are very real. They are in schools across this country. They come in all colors, and usually, it is by the third grade that their last bit of hope fades out and they surrender to the blackness. The rest of their school days are just a matter of getting by until they can drop out or graduate illiterate with a certificate but no future.

They scare you because you know what they mean for this great U.S. society. You know that they are proof of the promises broken and dreams never dreamed. And you see so many children like this—in Boston, in San Diego, in the mountains of Montana, in the flatlands of Nebraska, in Virginia, Louisiana, Florida, North Carolina, Washington, D.C. The despair fills the evening news and talk shows. It is the subject of depressing documentaries. Books are published that shout the public schools' failings. Everywhere you turn, there is another story of the failure of public education.

And then you find Hollibrook.

"I'm just the keeper of the dream," says Suzanne Still. Her official title—other than dream keeper—is principal of the Hollibrook Elementary School in the Houston suburb of Spring Branch, Texas.

A pleasant, attractive woman who cruises through her school as Commanding Officer, cheerleader, and guru, Suzanne Still—who, when she's not out praising her teachers or working in the classrooms, can be found sitting on the floor of her office alongside a child who is proudly reading a story, and sharing her jelly beans—is the leader of one of the most effective, exciting, inspiring public schools in the United States.

Hollibrook School, known by some children as "Huggibrook," not only proves through climbing test scores that all children can learn but also serves as a shining example of what one woman's dream can do to guarantee a prosperous, fair, enjoyable future for thousands of children.

"These children can go out there, hold their heads up high, and run with the very best of them," she says proudly of her student body where 28 different countries are represented. "And beat quite a few of the best, I might add."

There are 1,004 students in this one-level brick school that was built in 1954. The population breaks down to 74 percent Hispanic, 13 percent white, 7 percent black, and 5 percent Asian. Almost 90 percent of the children are on the free lunch program.

The Hollibrook—where every classroom is filled with energized, respectful, fascinated children—is located in a rancid, decaying barrio on the north side of Spring Branch. The school literally rises like a phoenix out of the ashes of broken dreams. Less than a mile from its front door, the other side of Spring Branch takes over—the Spring Branch that is home to some of the wealthiest oil and cattle barons in America; the Spring Branch of extravagant homes resting behind tall, ornate wrought-iron fences; the Spring Branch home of the "Education President," George Bush.

The President has been invited to visit his hometown's schools, but he hasn't made it there yet. Students at the Hollibrook hope he'll come to see their school. Although it would be a short jog for the President, it would be a long economic journey. He would go from one of the wealthiest neighborhoods in the United States to one of the poorest. This is a community of abject poverty, raped by the demons of drugs and violence—a community where families still live in abandoned cars and burned-out buildings.

The Hollibrook neighborhood was not always like this, however. When the school was built in 1954, the area was a white, middle- to upper-class neighborhood for those who could not afford the real estate on the south side. Today it primarily consists of federally subsidized housing that serves Spring Branch's growing minority, low-income population. And less than five years ago, the Hollibrook was part, and probably a factor in, this neighborhood's despair.

"This was a school that was out of control, to begin with. Parents escorted their children to their classes to make sure they'd be safe," reports Suzanne Still. "It was failing. It was like there was a cloud over the whole school. Teacher morale was bottomed out. The kids were just blank. They would speak but didn't talk. The locus and control of behavior was anybody but themselves. Many had just given up."

Not anymore. These kids are passionately committed to learning and to being responsible for their own actions and behavior. Accountability is part of the mission of this school—accountability for everyone: teachers, kids, secretaries, janitors, parents, and the principal.

President Bush should stop by on a Friday. Fridays at the Hollibrook are "Fabulous Fridays," the day when the faculty has put together special enrichment courses for all children in all grades. The President could come along with some first- or second-graders and maybe take a violin lesson, try calligraphy, learn some secret codes that he may have overlooked when he was head of the CIA, brush up on his public speaking, learn French, discuss the culture of Latin America, participate in the art of pantomine, learn some babysitting safety techniques, or join the jogging club.

There's a school store, run by the students, where the President could ask a student to give him a rundown on recent price changes on vegetables or meat and why that is happening. Perhaps he would like an explanation on the difference in ingredients for biodegradable products. He could stop by the third grade and ask how the Only Popcorn Company is doing now that they're starting to franchise to other schools. A student would be happy to explain the company's profit and loss sheet and what's going on with the company and the local bank.

If he's looking for ways to revamp the Postal Service and avoid any price hike in stamps, the President could talk to the students who run the Hollibrook Postal Service. Their delivery, pick-up, and special delivery services are the best in the area. And they recycle all their packaging material, and most everything else in the school. Hollibrook is an environmentally safe zone, with recycling in classrooms, the cafeteria, and even in maintenance. And the students know why a particular item is recycled, how it is recycled, and the advantages of recycling.

The first-graders are always ready to show off their latest writing project. Each student averages a couple books a year. And check out that penmanship! The President could learn some pointers from the lefties in the class.

And if he looks at the test scores, the rate of achievement for the students at Hollibrook, he will see these students are excelling *beyond* their counterparts on the other side of the tracks (the President's neighborhood). The test scores at the Hollibrook have created no less than open-mouthed amazement from the parents on the south side whose children are attending what have long been considered Spring Branch's premier elementary schools. Not only is Hollibrook going over the top in achievement scores but the opportunities at the school are second to none. In fact, they are unlike anything Spring Branch and the Houston area has seen before.

The President could learn a great deal about education from the multicutural population at Hollibrook. He would also meet some interesting people there: the students, teachers, staff, and parents, of course, but also a variety of visitors—professors and school practitioners from throughout the United States, Europe, the Far East, and Eastern Europe. It seems that there are a lot of people who want to know how Hollibrook did it.

"When I was first assigned this school, I wondered what had I done wrong in my life to deserve this," recalls Suzanne Still. "You just mentioned Hollibrook out there and people would shake their heads and pity you. We were considered the worst."

Hal Guthrie agrees with that assessment. When he came in as superintendent in 1987, Hollibrook was one of ten schools on the north side that were "lousy, rotten schools." His assessment did not win him any friends.

"No one wanted to admit it, but here were these schools that were just disasters. They weren't serving the children. It was time to call them for what they were and say this cannot be tolerated." Guthrie still gets angry when he remembers how poorly Hollibrook and other schools were performing. It was as if these schools, the majority of their populations poor and minority, did not really exist. "They were just written off, forgotten. Students, faculty, everyone. People only cared about the schools on the south side, the white schools."

The Spring Branch Independent Schools District has a long reputation as one of the nation's finest school districts. In 1967, it was designated one of America's exemplary school systems, and no one has ever quite forgotten that. Although Houston's population expanded into the suburbs, in 1985, Spring Branch, with its glass-encased office buildings and expensive, Texas-huge subdivisions, still catered to a school population that was 85 percent white. At that time, only 1 percent of the 26,000 students were listed as low income (based on applicants for the federal free lunch program). But the increase in immigrants to Spring Branch and the movement of minorities out of Houston's inner city was beginning.

By 1989, over 40 percent of the students were listed as low income, and the school population was now 50 percent white, 32 percent Hispanic, 10 percent black, and 8 percent Asian and Pacific Islander. In 1991, the elementary school population was over 50 percent minority.

Hal Guthrie came into Spring Branch in 1987 from Des Moines, Iowa, saying it was time for serious change and he was going to do it with the Effective Schools Improvement Process. After a year of planning, the district drew up its mission statement and began training teachers in the Effective Schools Process. Suzanne Still, then a high school assistant principal, was one of those individuals sent to a seminar in Washington that was headed by Larry Lezotte.

"When I first heard about 'Effective Schools,' it was like, finally, someone had turned me free to be the best I could be," says Still. "Effective Schools begin with a basic belief system, and it's that belief system that I was looking for. And then I looked at the correlates, how the correlates became integrated into the operation of the school, and I saw our blueprint for success."

Still has labored diligently in the education fields. She is a graduate of Michigan State, an elementary school teacher, a junior high school teacher, a special education teacher (all conditions), a coordinator of alternative high school for severely emotionally disturbed students, a teacher-trainer for teachers learning to recognize and deal with handicapped students, a grade-level principal at one high school, and a curriculum principal at another Spring Branch high school.

"People thought Guthrie had lost his mind putting a high school administrator into Hollibrook," says Still. "But they soon realized Guthrie knew exactly what he was doing. And I realized that all my life experiences have been training me for this assignment. I sat down and listed all the things that made a good principal, and all the things that made them rotten. Then with the Effective Schools guidelines, I formulated what I wanted to do. But I never dreamed the changes would come so fast and be so pervasive. I never dreamed of this much success this soon."

At first the teachers were very skeptical. For all its chaos, Hollibrook had been a "technically correct" school, precisely following federal and state policies. Every child and teacher had a slot and a very detailed role to fill. There were the low classes, the low-low classes, the very low classes. The *entire* school was tracked *down.* And now here arrives Suzanne Still (from a predominantly white high school, nonetheless) and the first thing she does is . . . nothing. The teachers saw no set agenda.

But Still was watching and listening. She was also concentrating on discipline, knowing she had to get the school back under control in order to start building trust. Students were wandering in and out of the building, doors had to be locked and equipment safeguarded; there was vandalism, endless student trips to the nurse for nonexistent ailments, and fights in the cafeteria and corridors.

While Still worked on discipline, the teachers and staff were gradually initiated into the Effective Schools Process by the district. There were seminars and special workshops. Teachers took classes in new instructional techniques and learned how to take advantage of the multiculturalism in their school. Teachers, administrators, and even secretaries started to notice that every written communication from the central office referred to "teaching for learning for *all.*" There was suddenly a superintendent who regularly showed up at schools. And everytime he spoke to teachers, he spoke of "teaching for learning for *all.*" And he was saying it was up to them, and he knew they could do it. They had never heard such words before. Support, as well as acknowledgment—it's up to them—and then permission for them to do it? Rather revolutionary.

The district released its own mission statement, making certain all of Spring Branch understood that a new day had arrived. The district was "teaching for learning for *all*":

> *The Spring Branch Independent School District is committed to providing a quality education to meet the needs of a diverse student body. Every learner will have the opportunity to be challenged, successful and prepared for a future as a responsible and productive citizen.*
>
> *The district believes that quality education will provide students the opportunity*
>
> - *to develop the ability to think logically, independently, and creatively,*
> - *to communicate effectively,*
> - *to develop appreciation for self and other people, times, and cultures,*
> - *to develop appreciation for the arts,*
> - *to develop health fitness, and*
> - *to build responsibility to local, state, national, and world communities.*

The schools were basically told: Here's the district mission. You must follow its principles, but establish a mission and an improvement plan that is specific to the needs of your school. It's in your hands.

At Hollibrook, Suzanne Still kept her teachers involved in the district's staff development and then started asking them questions: If you could have three wishes granted for yourself in this school, what would they be? What are the weaknesses and strengths of this school?

The wishes were very simple at first: certain books, a time change in Physical Education, access to the copy machine. The weaknesses were the rigidity and the large number of students. And then the quality of the wishes started developing: I wish I knew more so I could be more successful with the children. The weaknesses became lack of communication and the feeling of no real support from anyone.

Still knew the staff development would address the faculty's teaching concerns in the area of high expectations, but she knew it was up to her to bring back the communication and let the teachers know she was there to help them, guide them, and, most important, support them.

"I am a teacher first. That's it. I am a teacher first," emphasizes Still. "Then somewhere down the line, I'm a principal." It infuriates Still that teachers are not treated with more respect in this country. "We're the only vocation where everyone thinks they can do our job better than we can. I'm sick of it. And I hate it when teachers say, 'Oh, I'm just a teacher.' No! Dammit! You're a *teacher!* You're one of the most important people in this country."

It is this attitude that began to endear her to the faculty at Hollibrook. They were a tough group; they admit it. "We were being blamed for all the school's troubles," recalls a third-grade teacher. "Our self-esteem was at the bottom. We were angry. But then here was this principal who was acting unlike anything we had seen before."

Still says there are two basic parts to her philosophy. The first comes from *The Prophet.* A teacher gives faith, lovingness, and leadership. The second comes from her father, who was the chaplain to General George Patton during World War II.

"He always said that what made that man great was that he never expected his men to do anything that he would not do himself," says Still. "He was always out there in the tank columns. He was a soldier first."

Still worked with her teachers, first individually, and then in groups. She began a dialogue ("I talked *with* them, not *at* them") and slowly these tenacious teachers starting initiating change. And Still was right behind them. They were accustomed to a hierarchy. Still demolished that model, giving each teacher autonomy within his or her classroom and area of expertise. The curriculum was revised, programs within the school changed, and exciting new classes for the students were begun. By the middle of the second year, the school could barely be recognized from what it had been.

There were no locked doors. Computers and other equipment sat out in the open. Vandals and thieves no longer existed. Students sat energized in their classes, giving full attention to a teacher who had a new sense of respect—for herself and her students. The corridors were empty between classes, and when students did move, there were neat, quiet lines, all eyes forward, all hands at their sides. The nurse's office was suddenly empty. Students now came in only when a teacher noticed they were running a fever. Children were upset at missing class.

Still does not say the change has been easy. She talks of the hours and hours of "discussing, envisioning, clarifying, even the smallest things." There were problems with personalities, different agendas, and the fact that they were traveling in uncharted waters.

"We had the district mission statement and our mission statement. We had our plan, and how we were going to accomplish our objectives," says Still. "But so many times, even with this, we were flying by the seat of our pants. We were trying so many options. Options that we suddenly now had. I think I was looked at as the resource center. I'd find the research and data that would either give us the go ahead or push us in another direction. It was constant monitoring and adjusting. That's what Effective Schools is. Change that doesn't doesn't end. And we had that belief system. That made all the difference."

Not only are there the fascinating stories of programs at Hollibrook—a fourth-grader knowing how a CEO operates, with balance sheets and stock offerings—but there are phenomenal stories of success that may seem insignificant but are just the opposite. Children's lives—their futures—were restored.

For example, there was a third-grader who acted out, fought, aspired to be a gang member, and was not interested in reading. One day Still gently pulled him ("I just have one ironclad rule. You raise your hand to a child and you're out of here. I'll personally throw you out.") into the office and gets him to admit to thinking a very long time ago, before he got smart like he is now, that Air Force pilots were cool. Still immediately found a book on pilots then went out to get all the eye-catching, "awesome" literature she could on the Air Force. The kid couldn't help himself. He had to know what these words were saying. Today he is in the fifth grade and is a class leader academically. His vocation now alternates between medicine and being a university president.

There are literally countless stories. Two sisters who had been labeled "educationally retarded" are now winning district science prizes. A second-grader would not speak to anyone, so a teacher began working with her in art, acting just like she was communicating. The little girl went from angry scratches to softer scribbles to still lifes to portraits and is now into clay models. She now helps the teacher lead—with oral presentations—in the Fabulous Friday art classes.

There are many more stories. Actually, there's an amazing story for every child because these children are no longer performing below grade level. Not only are they CEOs and artists and authors and debaters but their basic skills are at the top of the charts.

"I remember when the new scores came in for Hollibrook," says Gary Mathews, associate superintendent of Spring Branch. "We were blown away! We knew they were making progress, but you're talking about a school that went from the basement through the roof. These kids not only collect stamps, learn how to swim, run companies, but instead of being two and three grades behind, they are now phenomenal successes. These are kids who would have been lost. And why weren't they? Because that school didn't dumb down. It created a high-profile, high-status curriculum and said, 'You can do it! You can do it!' And it all started with Effective Schools and the vision and the will of the person called the principal."

Still doesn't like the last part of Mathews's statement. "I didn't do this; the teachers did. By believing in the kids. This is the work of the teachers. They let every kid know they could climb every mountain." She points to an illustration of the working model for the Hollibrook School. At the center of it is the child. "First in this school come the children, then the teachers. Sure, I've had an impact on this school, but I'm not the one in the classroom doing the teaching. *There's* the important person."

The teachers want to give a lot of the credit to Still. It was her leadership, they say, that allowed them to become better teachers and to have a greater influence on the learning process. Like Still, they point to the foundation of the Effective Schools Plan, the correlates that were the school's blueprint. Indeed, a look at Hollibrook through the lens of the correlates reveals important lessons.

Clear and Focused Mission

"Hollibrook Elementary School is a school where students are respected as individuals and accept responsibility for their choices and actions."

"Students are supported by staff and parents who care enough to let them explore, grow, experience, challenge, and reach for personal success and academic excellence!"

You will find these mission statements in hallways and classrooms, and on banners in the front of the school. The statement is often accompanied by the district mission statement and the phrase "Together In Excellence." The key here is respect and accountability. You see it in the way the students act, in and out of class. They are eager but controlled in their classrooms. In the cafeteria, there may be some loud talk but there is no shouting. The object here is to eat and the students seem anxious to get back to their classes. If you ask them, they tell you they have "more fun" in their classes.

The call for respect in the mission statement goes far beyond words. There are specific programs to make sure there is respect. Teachers work on making certain the students feel secure. There are programs for the parents to be involved in that hone in on mutual respect, within the family and within the school. Each student is treated like the most valuable person in the world, and whenever a child has work he or she wants to show off, there is a principal and many faculty members ready to praise.

The students are taught responsibility. No longer, as they used to do, can they blame everyone else and everything else for their behavior. The faculty decided that if the teachers weren't going to have any excuses like "It's the fault of the neighborhood, the state of the world," then students couldn't either. This may seem rough, but when a child comes in and doesn't have the homework done, he or she cannot blame it on the gang fighting outside. It's the student's responsibility to get it done. No excuses for the school. No excuses for the children.

The faculty and staff never forget what their mission is. Still has created another symbol for the school seen on the walls, stationery, and pens: A bridge. Bridges. All types of bridges. "We look upon this school as creating bridges," she explains. "Because that's how we see ourselves. As the bridge to the middle class. We are trying to move all of our families into the middle class. We really don't care what color the middle class is. We don't care what language it speaks. But we feel very strongly that the future of this nation is dependent upon having a literate, employed middle class. And that's what we're all about. We're very focused on children maintaining their culture and, at the same time, getting the skills that they need to be viable in the future as adults. We don't forget our mission here."

Safe and Orderly Learning Environment

Three years ago, the Hollibrook School was not a safe, orderly place. As the teachers describe it: "Back then, this was a scary place."

"It was basically a discipline center," explains Still. "As it needed to be because of the lack of any respect—for anything or anybody. Children just sat in their cubicles and did their work. If they chose to. They could not behave. There was a 104 percent mobility rate (it dropped down to 87 percent and then down to 62 percent). There were fires in the bathrooms being set by the children. Toilets exploding. There were incidences of knives in school, which was the excuse that the Anglo, middle-class parents needed to pull their children out of the school. Staff morale was low. It was a dumping ground. You could not get up and down the halls, and I'm not exaggerating, because of the mothers of the younger children that would not leave the school because they had no trust in what was going on. You cannot treat people as though they are second-class citizens and expect them to trust you."

That's why Still began working right away on discipline. An exact schoolwide policy was set up for what precipitated a reprimand in class, when a child was sent to the principal, and what action was open to the principal. The child and the child's parents knew exactly what was expected of them. And Still added a counterpoint. She put in reward systems—from special trips that often she took the kids on, to books they could take home, to opportunities to hang out with the principal, to jelly beans. Still made it much more enticing to behave and perform well in class than to be disruptive or stubborn.

It took most of the first year to get the school calmed down. Still realized there was more to the environment issue than discipline. "When I began, no one wanted to come here. And who could blame them? This was not a happy place," she says. "Not for teachers, students, anyone. I knew I had to make this a place that people wanted to come to everyday."

She knew the best way to do that was to give the teachers back some pride in their work. The students were beginning to see the benefits of learning, and the teachers were responding, but she knew she had to build that elusive, essential element: trust.

Still began one-on-one meetings and showed she was there for the teachers. She encouraged them to call her at home. Slowly, they started. In faculty meetings, she gave them the floor. She listened, and when necessary, gave direction. She started to support them outside the school. The teachers began hearing how Still would be at a central office meeting and would start praising her teachers. And Still became the buffer between the teachers and the district office, and the teachers and the community, when necessary.

She began the process of restructuring within the school, breaking down, literally and figuratively, classroom walls. She let the teachers try things they previously would have been afraid to suggest. She fought their battles for resources and professional development classes. Slowly, she built the trust. She gave them power, step by step.

"Effective Schools opened the door for us to restructure, for us to have a common language, to pull together as genuine colleagues," says Still. "That's important. You don't get confused about what your mission is. And we took full advantage of our autonomy. I have teachers making decisions out there that other administrators would cringe at. But it's the best way because we're all in this together. We're not isolated."

Still believes that a school is only as good for the children as it is for the adults who work in it. "And to go right along with that," she emphasizes, "is if we are going to be the professionals that we purport to be, then let's be it. Professionals. That's all I did. I treated them as professionals.

"Nobody can find a specific thing and say, oops, this did it. Knowing the Effective School correlates, I'm telling you, does not, in and of it itself, make a difference. It's believing them, putting them into practice, monitoring, adjusting, going through it every day. This faculty is the same faculty that was here before. It's just that now it has a vision. It has respect!"

There is one thing Hollibrook used to have but doesn't have anymore: recess. The faculty and staff voted against "organized time to bash your own head and your neighbor's head," and instead allows "Brain Breaks" for classes at any time the teachers see fit.

On these Brain Breaks the children can go outside and draw, head off on a nature walk, consider the growth of flowers and trees, study insects, have a special reading or theatre class under a shady tree, or just take time to stretch and refresh themselves—just no bashing or organized hyperactivity. There is, however, regular, required physical education classes, where students not only do sports and exercises but learn what the impact is on the body. The students particularly enjoy calisthenics when joined by the principal. They are all eager to check her pulse and breathing, ready with their newly acquired tips for better health.

There should also be a few words here about the physical environment of the classrooms. They are as colorful as an explosion of rainbows. Student work is all over the place (neatly): cut-out paper animals, atoms, and anachronisms hang from the ceilings. There are bookcases filled with children's books and projects. Plants, globes, stuffed animals, bean-bag chairs for reading corners, murals, and sculptures are seen. One classroom is a ship of learning, complete with entry gangplank. And all this, and so much more, does not come via big budgets, but by the simple creativity of teachers and children. Everything is child-made. Wherever the children look, they see examples of their work and that of their friends. Teachers say it is not a distraction—just an inspiration and a constant reminder of how valuable the students are.

Strong, Instructionally Focused Leadership

Hal Guthrie has set the course for Spring Branch. He now lets his principals be at the helm of their own ship.

"The key here, is, I have to trust them. I have to trust their knowledge, their experience, their behavior," he says. "And in turn, they have to trust me."

Suzanne Still believes that one of the most important reasons why Hollibrook has been a success is because of the support and direction from the district office. "I couldn't even begin to do the things I have done here without knowing that the central office was not only behind me but would break down some barriers, or even change old policy when necessary," she says. "Because, let's face it, this school never would have turned around if someone didn't make some pretty drastic changes."

"Larry Lezotte has always described a good principal as being, I'll never forget it, he said, 'You be a loose cannon on the deck of a ship.' And that's exactly what I've been. That wouldn't be tolerated if I didn't have a superintendent who believed in Effective Schools and an associate superintendent in charge of instruction that believed in Effective Schools and empowering people to be decision makers. That has to be there, because if that's not there, it doesn't matter what we want to do out here."

Does Guthrie regard Suzanne Still as a loose cannon?

"Of course!" says Guthrie. "That's why I put her there. That school was in terrible shape. I needed someone who would make changes, who would take risks, who would tend to teaching and learning, who would do what was necessary. The last thing I wanted was someone who was safe with the status quo."

"Guthrie empowered me, and I empowered the teachers. Words are easy, but it's the actions that you take," states Still. "I stuck by my word. I'm out in the classroom. I work with them. I teach with them. You don't coach a teacher by going into the classroom once or twice, writing down what they do and discussing their strengths and weaknesses. If you want somebody to learn how to do something, you model it. You work with them. You work beside them. It took several months because, look, talk is cheap. They've heard talk before. But they had to see that I was who I said I was."

Still says the analogy that works for the most part is that of a parent with children. Although she is nervous about that, because she says these teachers never acted like children. "But they needed nurturing. They needed that type of trust that you have with a good parent. So, yes, it was kind of like raising them, pulling them along."

The teachers don't take offense to this remark. They have nothing but respect for Still—respect for her expertise, her commitment, and her inspiration.

"What this faculty did was build on Suzanne's strength," maintains Gretchen Goodson, a second-grade bilingual teacher. "It didn't take long to realize she is one of the most talented, creative administrators in the schools today. She showed us the way, and then let us take over. But she made sure we were ready."

Still does her homework and then some. She can rattle off information on research and data for her school as easily as she can recite her own address. She also studies any new teaching technique or approach that may be of help to her teachers. And along with that, she works on her own leadership and management skills.

"Suzanne knows how to work with us. She knows how to bring the best out of us," insists Lynne Williams, a kindergarten teacher. "And she has helped us all to be decision makers. Not just in our classrooms, but on issues involving the whole school."

When the teachers are asked how they became such effective decision makers, they speak of specific courses offered by the district and—what they say is most effective—that their principal kept giving them opportunity after opportunity to be responsible decision makers.

"The problem has always been that teachers are isolated," maintains Still. "And at first, they were here. That had to stop. The real power of problem solving comes from the fact that all of us are working together. There is not a problem that comes to this school that we can't solve. That's where I started with this faculty, giving them that same message: You are professional educators; I intend for you to be problem solvers."

An example of major change at Hollibrook that is now being picked up by schools throughout the country is the policy of teachers staying with a class for two or three years. The teachers at Hollibrook had been concerned about the fourth-graders seeming to turn into "little monsters" overnight—specifically, when they entered the fifth grade.

One teacher suggested the possibility of staying with the kids for three years. Still started investigating and found a school in Cologne, Germany, that was doing it. The research, although sparse, held up, and the teachers, after exhaustive meetings, decided that those who wanted to do it were free to try. The result is increased stability for the students, enhanced learning skills, and a decrease in the number of "little monsters."

"But this didn't just happen. We worked very hard on this, and the faculty was split," recalls Still. "Some teachers just didn't like it, and were afraid it would be applied to all before we knew what the benefits might be. We worked it out. Like professionals. And the teachers made the decisions. I just gave them the research and my input."

Suzanne Still spends a good part of her day walking around her school, visiting the classrooms and being involved with the teachers and the students. The students beam when they see her, relax into silly, contented smiles when she places a praising hand on their shoulder. If they are free, they will rush over to hug her. She is careful not to interrupt a class, and treats the teachers with maximum respect. It is clear it is *their* classroom. But is also clear that the principal, and her caring and professional input, is wanted and appreciated.

Still knows the students. They often visit her office and leave her notes. They write little books about her, thanking her for all she does for them. She will work with them on special projects, she teaches a class on stamp collecting, she helps them in the store, she serves on their companies' boards of directors, she takes them to the museum or out to the mall. She is as comfortable on the floor of her office with a child as she is working on a teacher's lesson plan or addressing professors at Texas A & M.

After school hours, you may find her over in the projects, talking to parents, or perhaps downtown convincing a company that it should adopt the third grade and supply the children with computers. Or maybe she's at a social service agency trying to get the back rent paid for one of her families. Or she may be working with a teacher setting up a course for teenage mothers and their children. Or she may be at the central office arguing the need to change old policies. Or she just may be in her office analyzing some test scores, trying to figure out why one student isn't doing his or her best work.

Late at night, when she locks the door of Hollibrook and gets into her car, she puts in a tape that she has picked up from the recorder outside her office. On it will be messages from kids who wanted to see her but missed her while she was busy in another part of the school. And as she heads out of the Hollibrook driveway, she'll listen to a second-grader reading his or her very own short story.

"I'm just the keeper of the dream. And that dream is that this school is absolutely the most exciting learning environment that is absolutely possible to have, and that our children come into this school to learn and they create within themselves a desire to learn, and that our children, no matter what color, no matter what, have an experience base and a background that will carry them through life as winners."

Climate of High Expectations

As soon as you enter the Hollibrook School, you are met by students' artwork that proclaims such slogans as: "I can do whatever I try to do!" "I can climb the highest mountain!" "I am strong, and smart, and kind!" "I love school because it teaches me how to be the smartest and greatest I can be!"

In the classroom, the high expectations are exhibited by teachers who ask a question and, when the student hesitates, does not move on to another student, but pauses and speaks softly, "Come on, Eddie, you know how to do this. Just like those other numbers repeated that pattern, if you add more numbers, but follow. . . ." You see the student struggling, looking from the board to his paper to the teacher. Other students watch anxiously or try to figure it out themselves. Slowly, Eddie begins to do the computation. The teacher walks over, places a hand on his shoulder. "That's it, now keep going. No. Not that one. You were right before." Eddie figures it out, and if it's a big enough breakthrough, he will receive a large cut-out star to display and perhaps get the chance to go to the principal's office where he can show off his new computing skills and get a big hug and jelly beans, as well as another special note to take home informing the home front of his achievements. Then he will be given a short speech on how he can do even better and that there is now another Hollibrook student on his way to the Nobel Prize!

"It's as simple as believing in these kids," explains a second-grade teacher. "Often they have no one at home who ever praises them, who ever tells them they can do something beyond the walls of their depressing neighborhood. We begin by telling them there's no limit."

Suzanne Still believes one of reasons for their success with the children is because the staff never "dumbs down" to the students. They treat every student as a competent, aggressive learner, and never give a child work that would humiliate her or him in front of peers.

"Just the opposite. We're always challenging them. For example, kids love huge words. And we use them here, explaining them, spelling them. We will never dumb down for the children here. That's why we've got every child on grade level. I told them, 'Hey, none of you is retarded. We're going to go for it.' You come in this school, you sweat. That goes back to Edison. He said it's 99 percent perspiration, 1 percent inspiration. That's what makes a genius. So for 1 good thing we sweat 99 times."

But she emphasizes that the essential component in the correlate of high expectations is the teacher.

"The teachers have to believe in themselves. That's why the testing has been such a help. They see the progress they are making. They see how good they are. Last year the momentum came from the teachers, who truly believed and trusted in what they were doing. The momentum this year is beginning to come from the children who are believing in themselves, knowing that its working for them, whether they can articulate it or not. They know they can do it, and they are pushing it. Matter of fact, if they all don't stop pushing so fast, I'm not sure I can keep up with them."

Hollibrook does not do any remedial reading. For a school that used to have classes designated low reading, low-low reading, lowest reading, it now has no differentiations. The difference is that every child is now at or beyond grade level. They are told they can handle it, and what's more, they are expected to handle it.

"What if I came up to you and said you can't handle what you're doing? Pretty tough, huh?" asks Still. "Well, can you imagine how you would feel if you were six years old, in a strange school, having come from a disadvantaged, troubled home, and a big smart teacher comes up to you—you're six or seven—and says, you can't handle the reading like the other kids; you're going to have to be in a class for slower kids?" She pauses, looking sadly at some of her children. "What do you think that does to a child?"

That immediately says to the child: You're a loser. You're not as good as the other kids and probably never will be.

"The analogy I use for that is, you think about when you first learned to ride a bicycle. Nobody took the pedals off first and made you identify all the parts of the pedal and then made you be an expert pedaler, and then moved to the handle bars or whatever," explains Still. "They put you on the bicycle and you got started. When your feet fell off, they held them. They coached you. They helped you keep your balance. They never said, 'Well, if you don't know the parts of a pedal, how can you ride a bicycle?' They just *knew* you could. And they told *you* you could. And one day, off you pedaled! That's the way we teach children."

High expectations is something you can actually see, you can feel, in a school like Hollibrook. Just for starters, you don't see children "of the dead eyes"—children who have been told or who have had it implied to them that they are losers. These kids are happy with themselves. They are involved—very involved—in their work. They are animated and interested. Discipline problems have become nonexistent because the children have better things to do. And they also think more of themselves than that. They believe they are winners.

"These kids know that they are responsible for their own behavior. They have to be accountable," says Still. "I know, it sounds too good to be true, but you give a kid a little responsibility, you respect that child, and you get it back tenfold."

There is no doubt that the teachers' training in Teacher Expectations and Student Achievement (TESA) has had significant impact. As in other Effective Schools Process districts, Spring Branch did extensive work with teachers and staff in high expectations.

"I've been at this for over 10 years, and I thought I had a pretty good handle on what I was doing. Considering all the different situations we were dealing with," explains a fourth-grade teacher. "Well, what a shock, to be honest. I started with the basic Effective Schools workshops. I mean, I thought, what's the big deal, I believe all children can learn." She shakes her head and laughs softly. "I realized that in my gut I really didn't. I was being prejudicial and I didn't even know it.

"I guess it had the most to do with expectations. I just never pushed some kids as hard as other kids. But in this workshop I started looking at all the data, the research, and I realized I was being stupid. Worse than that, I was denying some kids a decent shot by not having the same expectations for them that I had for others.

"It was a tough reality check, and I know other teachers went through the same thing. We just don't like to admit it. But through these workshops we were able to kind of nod and say—oh, we already knew all that—but really, we didn't and we needed help. And, finally, we got it. And now we not only know all these kids can do it, but we can prove it."

Frequent Monitoring of Student Progress

In following its mission, Hollibrook has clear-cut goals: "All students will demonstrate mastery of basic skills at a minimum, on or above grade level by the completion of the fifth grade. Hollibrook will be a school where *all* children accelerate their learning and develop cognitive and social skills needed to participate successfully at school."

The Texas Educational Assessment of Minimum Skills (TEAMS) is the primary state testing tool for the Spring Branch Schools. The Hollibrook test results are made available to the public each year as soon as they are compiled. In most school districts, this means the spring scores are known in the fall. At Hollibrook, the April scores are released by June 1, a little over a month after they are taken. The test scores for third grade, considered one of the most difficult years for children, give a general overview of the performance:

> Math: From 77 percent mastering in 1988 to 96 percent mastering in 1990. This surpasses all the other elementary schools in the district as well as the state/national average.
>
> Reading: From 65 percent mastering in 1988 to 86 percent mastering in 1990.
>
> Writing: From 58 percent mastering in 1988 to 81 percent mastering in 1990.

But the best of test scores often fall apart when you disaggregate them—not so at Hollibrook. In fact, here is where the strength of, and the justification for, Hollibrook's diverse programs is seen.

> Math: The scores for the low SES (socioeconomic status) students went from 87 percent mastery to 93 percent mastering. Scores for the high SES students went from 93 percent to 100 percent mastering.
>
> Reading: The scores for the low SES students went from 60 percent mastering to 82 percent mastering. Scores for the high SES students went from 83 percent mastering to 100 percent mastering.
>
> Writing: The scores for the low SES students went from 69 percent mastering to 76 percent mastering. Scores for the high SES students stayed at 83 percent mastering.

And there are just as dramatic results for the Limited English Proficiency students. Their reading mastery went from 28 percent to *83 percent in one year.*

What these scores show is not only the increase in scores for the low-income children but the increase in scores for higher SES students, thereby negating any charge that the more privileged students suffer when a school moves to the teaching of *all* children.

"I love these scores. We all love these scores," claims Gary Mathews, associate superintendent, not hiding his pleasure. "It's when we get scores like this, and we get them all the time from Hollibrook, and from some of our other schools, that I can say to parents, 'Here is the proof the tracking system hurts your kid just as much as the other kid.' And parents look at these scores, see what exciting things are going on at the Hollibrook, see how happy the kids are, and the teachers, and they have to agree with me. The tracking *was* hurting them. And now, what's even better, is some of those parents who took their kids out of the Hollibrook are now trying to get them back in."

Outcomes drive the process. Still and her staff study the test results and continually adjust their programs and instructional techniques. It is an ongoing process of monitoring and adjusting. Still and her staff never stop working on new ways to enhance their students' learning. Success is its own sweet incentive, and Still has learned her Effective Schools Process lessons well: A school that isn't improving is declining. You can't even get to the point of maintenance; a school must always be monitoring, adjusting, enlightening, and enhancing.

Frequent monitoring at Hollibrook also means asking the students how they like what is happening at the school. Are they happy with Hollibrook? An enthusiastic 93 percent responded yes (the 7 percent who gave mixed reviews were some left over "little monsters" from fifth grade who admitted to being nervous about the transfer out to junior high). The students were also asked how much school work they do at home, whether a parent or friend helps, if they feel safe at school, how much they read at home, and if they feel good when they learn something new. (These inquiries are also disaggregated.)

The faculty is also included in this monitoring process. Each year there is a survey done among the teachers to assess the Effective Schools Process correlates. The survey is anonymous. Teachers are free to make whatever comments they choose. Attitudes and personal performances of teachers, staff, and administrators are expressed in the survey.

Some comments:

> Instructional Focus: "Very clear plan." "Everyone here believes *all* children can learn and we prove it!" "We are much more focused than we ever were."
>
> High Expectations: "We expect all students to master skills and all are willing to go the extra mile to achieve this." "Our expectations have risen greatly. One hundred percent are expected and *will* graduate from high school."
>
> Climate: "A supportive caring place for teachers and students." "Fantastic." "This is a great place to be."
>
> Instructional Leadership: "Excellent." "Could not be better." "We are so lucky to have Suzanne Still." "She always communicates great pride in Hollibrook. Makes us proud."
>
> Major Strengths: "Caring faculty and staff." "The children." "Fabulous Fridays." "Suzanne Still." "Teacher collaboration." "Our nonstop expectations for *all.*"
>
> Pressing Issues: "Home environments." "More time." "Need more space for special projects." "Money." "More bathrooms."

Hollibrook believes that careful monitoring also means keeping the parents closely informed about their child's progress. There are regular report cards for each class done in English, as well as the native language of the child's guardian. There are also detailed notes sent home every six weeks, informing parents how their child is doing and if there is any particular area of concern. These reports are not just glib comments on conduct and coloring skills. For example, the kindergarten progress report is broken up into seven categories: language arts, mathematics, science, social studies, health, health fitness, and fine arts.

Under language arts, the parent is informed at what level their child is performing: communicating ideas clearly identifying main ideas in stories and pictures, following oral directions, demonstrating reading comprehension by recalling important facts and details from stories, and much more for this category and the others.

What is social studies for a kindergartner? It is knowing your name, age, birthday, address, and telephone number; working cooperatively; and completing tasks. Oh yes, and they should also know the major continents on the globe.

Time on Task and Opportunity to Learn

The teachers at Hollibrook knew that there were lessons they could learn about classroom management and how best to handle their heterogeneous populations. They were fortunate that they had a principal who had been a teacher, and since her days in the classroom had made a point of examining and understanding new instructional techniques and approaches. Still also learned group management and interpersonal communication skills so she could assist her teachers without taking control.

"Once I knew that our belief systems were in line, we could go to work," says Still. "These teachers were committed to teaching *all* children, they just were not sure what was the best way." She went through lesson plans and classroom techniques with every teacher. Then she worked with the teachers on the students.

"Every student. That's the only way we were going to get moving," says Still. "I would say, 'OK, let's see what she's done. Here are her strengths, here are the weaknesses, here's how to nurture her, here's a way to challenge her.' We did that with every single child in this school. And we continue to."

But as far as the day-to-day operation of the classrooms and the interaction with the student, Still gives the teachers a wide berth. She says she has "absolute, *absolute* faith" that they are doing the right things for the students now.

It was difficult at first to get the teachers to break out of their molds, to take a chance on a different style of teaching or a perhaps slightly strange way to reach a child. But soon the teachers were comparing notes and working together. As the walls came down and the desks were pushed together, the students became more and more fascinated with their new freedom. The students liked this new atmosphere so much they would do anything to keep it, even behave like studious, responsible children most of the time.

"These kids love being accountable. They also love proving that different ways are often better ways, that change is good," reports a fifth-grade teacher. "And they love helping each other."

That is obvious. The children are always working together, in reading, in math, in art. The only time they work alone, say the teachers, is when they are being tested.

"We have all kinds of cross-grouping. We have English and Spanish together. We have fifth-graders working with first-graders. All this kind of stuff goes on all the time. What more can you say about accountability and responsibility than, we have moved beyond the assembly line where I'll put in the screw this year and you put in the next one next year.

"They're responsible for everything. That's how our curriculum, our teaching and learning works. I'm going to put it on the line. We've created learning, achieving, challenging, exciting families of children within this school. Yes. We have *done it!*"

Still and her staff are vehement believers in staff development. They admit to shortcomings in their previous training, and jump at the opportunities the system offers. And when they want additional seminars themselves, Still works it out with the central office. Some staff courses that are available and attended regularly include behavior management, focused instruction, integrated/accelerated instruction, special education, data analysis, attention deficit disorders, accelerated school model, whole language, cooperative learning, mastery learning, and TESA.

Then there are the classes in leadership training, infectious waste, anti-victimization, recycling, just to mention a few. According to Still, in addition to the professional development through district/campus-based activities and individual enrollment in graduate school, 62 members of the professional staff attended 740 hours at professional workshop/seminars last year.

"I can't adequately tell you the difference the staff development has made in my teaching," begins one fourth-grade teacher. "I hate to think of what would have happened without Effective Schools. I was a good teacher. But I'm a lot better now. Not to brag, but just the difference cooperative learning has made in my classroom. I've made some additional changes in it. You should see how my kids are taking off. Soaring! When I go to bed at night, I know now that I have given my kids the best possible day of teaching and learning. The very best."

When told of the teacher's comments, Still says it doesn't surprise her. "I'm glad that they're now confident enough to admit it. See what I mean? The teachers know that they are respected. They're empowered now. They also know they're damn good so they can admit that maybe in the past they weren't as good as they could be. See? It all comes around. The children get better, the faculty gets better, and everyone keeps moving faster. I can't keep up anymore."

Before, she says, everything was done out of an act of compliance. Now it is done out of an act of passion.

Despite all the activity at Hollibrook—or maybe because of it—the teachers and staff have their eye on the ball at all times. "We don't look at our campus plan once a year," says Still. "We live it. Understand, this school is run by teachers. I have a steering committee of teachers, and then there are four other committees that feed into it. One is in charge of staff development, one is in charge of the grade levels and all the different instructional teams, another one is in charge of curriculum organization, and another one is in charge of marketing the school. And then there's another team that is in charge of documenting, keeping up with all that goes on, letting us know where we are, telling us where we need to go next, and helping us keep focused on where we're going with our campus plan. Now that's intensive involvement by everyone in our vision. They laugh and tell me all the time that my only job is I'm keeper of the dream. I say, okay, I'll do that.

"We have a unity of purpose in this school, and it's not only just me and those magnificent teachers; it's the magnificent parents, it's the magnificent kids. We know where we are going. The school has its mission statement and then it has a pledge that the children say at the beginning of school, every single day.

"They pledge to accelerate their learning; they pledge to be responsible for their actions; they are responsible for their lives; they are going to cultivate their desire to learn; and they are a unique and wonderful person because they are themselves.

"And the kids *love* it! I mean, even though we started it this fall, it's already made a difference. It inspires them. It inspires all of us. Think if you're a parent and you hear your child saying that, wanting and doing all that. Just think how it would inspire you! And when you're a teacher and you hear your kids saying and believing that everyday, you better believe that you know what your task is. And you better believe you want to do it, and do it with all the passion and effectiveness you have within you!"

Purposeful and Supportive Involvement of Parents

There are two stories that explain the involvement of parents in the Hollibrook School. When Suzanne Still had her first PTA meeting, there were 13 parents in attendance. "It just broke my heart," she says. "But then I remembered how difficult it is moving from one culture to another. Coming from a Third World Nation, into this culture with all these aliens. I mean, PTA is alien to Hispanic cultures. There is no PTA in South America. You look at many of the countries where our parents have come from, they didn't even have public education for about 15 years. If you have money, your children go to school; if you don't, they don't. So we're talking about generations of illiteracy.

"We had all the excuses here: Well, these parents don't care, they're not involved, blah, blah, blah. But they do. And I told the teachers, I said, 'These people did not walk thousands of miles with their children on their backs because they didn't care. They care. They just don't understand what we're trying to do, why they should attend these meetings.'"

So Still got her teachers together—everyone picked up tables and chairs, coffee and cookies—and they headed out of the school and across the street to the apartment complex. They gathered in the common room and then branched out, going door to door, some teachers speaking Spanish, others communicating whatever way they could.

"'Please come and be with us,' we pleaded. 'Listen to us. Please, we're here to help.' I call it 'the drums are beating in the community,'" Still recalls. "At first they were very timid, and there were more of us than there were of them. But eventually, we had them playing pool, drinking coffee, having a good time talking about stuff, hugging kids. Then they got to see, hey, these people are human beings. If they care enough to come across the street, we may have something here.

"And the word spread to the black parents. They had to know that we didn't see color in this school. We've told them that from the very beginning: What we want for our very own children is what we want for your child. That's the overriding issue in this school. And the word started spreading to the black parents."

Now there are over 700 parents at Hollibrook's PTA meetings. Parents are in and out of the school whenever they wish. There is now a Parents' Room where parents can go to have coffee, cookies, and talk with teachers or other parents. Here, there is a sewing machine and basic supplies for the parents use. The room has become a gathering place for the community, as well as a place where parents can learn basic skills such as how to open a bank account, how to deal with social service agencies, how to find a doctor, how to care for newborns. Teachers and parents work together, with and without the children.

The school has also started reading and writing courses for the parents as well as a Parents Fabulous Friday, with courses designed especially for parents and community members. Almost accidentally, the school has become multi-generational.

"This is the community's school. The parents have every right to be here," insists Still. "And they have every right to have access to me and the teachers. That is the way it should be, and frankly, we wouldn't have it any other way. We know we need those parents in order to really help these kids."

The second story about parent involvement involves a very quiet mother of four young boys who are enrolled at Hollibrook. Hildana Saldana and her sons live in a two-bedroom apartment in the barrio, surrounded by crime, drugs, and filth. She and her husband moved to Spring Branch from Houston. In Houston, her children were at the bottom of their classes, staying back, labeled as "academically and behaviorally immature."

At Hollibrook, her boys are on the honor roll and have been for two years. And although Hilda is delighted and bubbling with pride, her sons' success comes with a personal price for her. Such success can be tough for a mother who has trouble reading herself, never graduated from high school, and has serious family and marriage problems.

"I am embarrassed that I didn't graduate and I have two kids on the honor roll. They would come home with their papers and I couldn't even read them. I didn't understand what they were doing. But they were good with me, they tried to explain things to me. 'It's OK, Mom,' they say, 'I'll show you how to do that.'

"But it wasn't OK. I couldn't continue my life like this. I went to the PTA meetings and stuff and talked to Miss Still and I got into some courses.

Then I got a type of job as receptionist for the school. Kind of like official greeter. I'm the first person you meet when you come in. Which is really nice because I love that school. I'm really proud of it."

With encouragement from the faculty, Hilda took her GED, passed with flying colors, and is now thinking about further education and putting an end to an abusive relationship. Her husband, according to Hilda, has a serious problem with drugs and regularly beats her. She has arrived at the school trying to hide her injuries.

"My husband, he says it's all because of that school. Sure, when I thought I was nobody, I let him throw me around. But no more. 'I'm somebody,' I tell him, 'I can live with you or I can live without you.' I could never live without him before. But now I can. I like myself now. And I am somebody now. And so are the boys. They know they are worth something now. That they can do something with their lives. We all can. We can get out of here. We can do much better. And we will."

It all began at a local school—a school where her boys moved from the designation of "academically immature" and the bottom of their classes to "polite, terrific kids" at the top of their classes, and where their mother gained the self-respect to get a job, get her high school diploma, stand up for herself and her family, and end 15 years of physical and emotional abuse.

So, this is the abbreviated story of the Hollibrook, just one of this country's Effective Schools. There are many more Effective Schools with programs and attitudes just as exciting as Hollibrook's. These schools are all over the United States—in ghettoes, farmlands, military bases, and exclusive suburbs—wherever teachers and principals believe their children can reach out and grab the brass ring of their lives.

It doesn't matter where the students are from or who their parents are. The family background and the education of the parents is insignificant. The only thing that matters is the will—the will of the people who are entrusted with the educational care of these students. And if the will of those teachers, principals, and superintendents is truly that of desiring to teach *all* children, then those schools have the potential to be Effective Schools, to be like Hollibrook, and to have excited, fascinated, and fascinating children hungry for learning.

The children at Hollibrook haven't been told they can't learn. They've been told they can. The children at Hollibrook have eyes full of light. They believe in themselves. The children at Hollibrook have wonderful dreams for their tomorrows.

Every school can be a Hollibrook. There is no reason why Hollibrook Elementary should be one of a kind.

CHAPTER THREE

The New Paradigm

Escaping Our Psychic Prisons

> *We are witnessing a crumbling of hierarchy, a gradual replacement of the bureaucratic emphasis on order, uniformity, and repetition with an entrepreneurial emphasis on creativity and deal making. But at the same time we are also watching new societal dilemmas arise in the wake of this change. Post-entrepreneurial management is results oriented, rewarding outcomes . . . seeking innovation as well as efficiency.*
>
> —ROSABETH MOSS KANTER, *When Giants Learn to Dance*

The business paradigm in the United States is shifting from the industrial society to the information society, from forced technology to high technology, from centralization to decentralization, from conformity to innovation, from representative democracy to participatory democracy. You see it at AT&T, General Motors, United Airlines, True Value Hardware, Kentucky Fried Chicken. It's happening at your local supermarket, your dentist's office, the corner bookstore, the city taxi company—and the public schools of Spring Branch, Texas, Junction City, Kansas, Frederick County, Maryland, and others you will read about in this book.

Public schools? Yes. It was inevitable that the revolution begun in business in the late seventies would finally reach our public schools. Of course, the first concept that had to cross the schoolhouse threshold was that, in the final and only valid analysis, the public schools are the public's *premier* businesses. And that business is the educating of all students, fulfilling the mandate that every child in the United States has a right to an education—an equal opportunity to learn. It's the business of educating *all* children. There's that phrase again—*all* children.

That is the major attitudinal shift the schools must make in order to fill their public mandate. No longer can we educate just the so-called bright children, the children with special talents, or the children from the "right" families. We must educate all of them: black, brown, white, Asian, poor. And this doesn't mean by throwing them in remedial classes, but by giving them the same opportunities of those blond, blue-eyed children from the "right" families.

To fulfill this mandate to educate *all* children, there must be that major attitudinal shift—accompanied by a corresponding behavioral shift—in the minds of the people orchestrating the operation and learning in our public schools. This attitudinal, psychological, and behavioral shift is the core of the changing business paradigm that is reflected in the research of the Effective Schools Improvement Process. The Effective Schools Process is about a new way for schools to view their mission and teach for learning for *all* students in the nineties.

Since the days of Horace Mann, the public school has been operated much like a factory. The principal did the work of the foreman, the teacher was the worker, and the students were the products, moving along an inefficient assembly line to be molded, adjusted, and added to. There was basic sorting and selecting (tracking). The factory operated on a predetermined bell curve, with some students sorted out as sweepers and some as prospective managers. And some, in particular those with vacant looks or family histories of nonachievement, were for the most part neglected, allowed to collect mind mold at the bottom of the curve.

There were even assigned physical locations for these students. The sweepers were put in dusty, ground-floor basement rooms with worn primers, creaking machine tools, and tired, uninspired teachers. The managers were in cheery, upper-story rooms with brightly colored maps, sparkling test tubes, crackling new books, and energetic, enlightening teachers. And what about the children with special needs or who were offhandedly labeled a "lost cause"? Well, for years, their places were in dark basement rooms, the corners of an empty cafeteria, or sometimes on leftover chairs jammed into a crowded utility room. For some, "classes" consisted of discipline sessions in drafty, echoing stairwells.

The students took their assigned slots. There was no questioning their placement. Others had passed judgment on the quality of their minds. Others had determined their future without even a glance at their present promise.

As the students rolled out of the first school factories, they headed for either the fields, the steel mills and assembly plants, or further schooling that would carry them into white-collar professions. Later, as the millions of immigrants entered this country, the schools equipped them with basic English, simple math skills, a sprinkling of literature and history, and then discharged these new Americans into the economy of the Industrial Revolution. These (for the most part) men were adept at following simple instructions and handling the paperwork of day-to-day living. They didn't need to know how to calculate, process, or analyze.

But the situation in the last part of the twentieth century has changed and many of the machines that have been introduced require employees who know how to read complicated instructions, handle sophisticated computers, and, when necessary, figure out how to stop these machines and computers (i.e., Failsafe). In a phrase, workers now have to *think,* and this is a new concept.

Complicating the changing needs of industry is the changing face of the student population. Unlike any other country, ours is a cornucopia of races, religions, and ethnicities. The United States also brings more women into the working world than other countries. And, as if the heterogeneous face of the population is not enough to deal with, the schools also find themselves on the front line of the ramifications of poverty, drugs, discrimination, disintegrating families, abuse, neglect, and social service and justice institutions that are outdated, overburdened, and inefficient. The children, with their many faces and their many problems, arrive on the school doorstep of the twentieth century. On the other side of the door is a public school system that is trying to figure out how to teach these children to think and to answer the needs of the industrial and business communities that stand at the exit door, demanding an intelligent workforce.

The schools have had to make a major market transition. Many have failed and continue to fail. But they don't blame the plummeting achievement scores and soaring dropout rates on the organization that is the public school. Instead, they place the blame squarely on the only image they can find in the mirror: the children, a lackadaisical teaching staff, and occasionally the parents. In a major statement on education at the beginning of the 1991 school year, President George Bush visited a school in Lewiston, Maine, and spoke of the failure of education in large part because students are not working as hard as they used to, and parents are not involved enough in their child's learning.

But practitioners of the Effective Schools Process insist that students and teachers are not the problem. In fact, they are the solution to the problem, which lies within the structure, culture, and beliefs of the public school. Those school variables have to make an adjustment to the realities of the twenty-first century. They have to catch up with the revolution that is well underway in U.S. businesses.

Finally, that process has begun in many school districts and the change is dramatic. The factory model of hierarchical management, authoritarian teaching, and standardized learning for all is being replaced by a decentralized, shared decision-making model of teaching for learning for *all* that meets the needs of the new age, as well as America's multitalented, very complex, student population.

In the new business and school paradigm, the rigid slots are abolished and the factory becomes an information-age satellite transformation center. Instead of *translating* a child (i.e., a child comes in poor and disadvantaged; is labeled poor, disadvantaged, and difficult to teach; and goes out poor, disadvantaged, and uneducated), a child is now *transformed* from poor and disadvantaged to educated and aspiring. The foreman is gone, replaced by a visionary leader. The teachers are now professional, instructional leaders with high expectations for all their students. There is freedom in the classrooms. No longer forced into a lock-step mentality of teacher-lecture/student-regurgitation, teachers are awakened to new teaching methods that create in their students the power to learn—to *think*. And the students are now the workers—active participants in their school and their future. The product is the new educational program in each school where all students are learning.

There is no bell curve, there is no tracking. Every child gets an equal shot at a quality, inspired, and inspirational education.

The power behind the school has historically come from above—from the school board to the superintendent and the central administration of the school district. Today, that power, or *modeling force* as Effective Schools interpret the position, must still be there. But under the Effective Schools Process and the determined push toward decentralization, the real power of the individual school rests with the principal and other instructional leaders of each school. School-based management and shared decision making at the local level is the new paradigm of the public school. This collaboration in shared decision making recognizes that a school functions best when it relaxes the constraints of behavior that previously kept teachers separated from each other and isolated from other members of the school community.

The school, like most major organizations within a democratic society, is an organization maintained by the norms and behaviors of the players within that organization. Every action, every player, is intertwined with another. An organization's interest, an employee's interest—and, in the case of schools, the student's interest—must coincide.

After all, once the sophisticated rhetoric is pushed aside, an organization is simply, and essentially, people—people working together to achieve certain goals, people working to fulfill themselves, reward their lives, and benefit the organization. Schools are, in that regard, no different from IBM or General Motors.

Organizations (people) receive their direction from leaders and from the interaction of those leaders with people whom they employ. This is not revolutionary thinking, but, because of the heavy political stakes in public education, this thinking escaped the schools. Too often principals and teachers had conflicting visions, or, equally disturbing, had no vision at all. And while businesses in the seventies were looking around saying, "We need a vision here; we need to get people unified after the same goal," the schools turned their sacred-cow shoulder, insisting, "We're different—we're not a business."

However, at the same time that many schools and districts were indifferent to the business renaissance, a few schools were raising an interested eyebrow to the concept of a school with a "vision." They questioned whether shared decision making and an instructional leader whose role went beyond that of a gatekeeper or disciplinarian might get them out of the quagmire they were in. Surely one thing was certain: Whatever they were doing now wasn't working.

So, with an eye to the burgeoning business reforms, the founders of the Effective Schools Improvement Process recognized in the seventies and eighties that it was time for structural and cultural change. If business was succeeding with a new breed of manager, then public education should try to learn a few lessons. The premier management lesson was that the superintendent and the principal, whose powers in the past were often more stated than lived, had to make a new commitment—to the students and the faculty instead of to the bureaucracy and the politics of the central office.

This is akin to the plant manager who realizes the goals of the company are best served by an operation that is supportive of its workers and a business that sees as one of its major responsibilities the creation and sustaining of a cooperative, pleasant working environment.

In the past, it was often a blessing in disguise that an ineffective superintendent was not as dangerous as an ineffective principal. An ineffective superintendent kept to his or her office and own political agenda, letting the school system be run according to the dictates of the status quo and trusted politicians in the central office. An ineffective superintendent was basically "mush" for the system, whereby the effective superintendent (as shown in the following chapters) is a dynamic leader who turns the system on its head and models and executes dramatic change.

Unlike a nebulous ineffective superintendent, an ineffective principal can do great harm to a school. In recent years, the number of effective principals has been rising, due in large measure to the research of the Effective Schools Process and the increased awareness and practice of the skills of leadership as well as good management.

The profile of an Effective School principal evolved in the shadow of the effective business manager. It is important to point out here that this new principal is not "new" in the sense that the species never before existed. There have always been superintendents and principals who walked a different path, who have been Effective. They are just very small in number, considered an alien breed or a maverick in the system, and, overall, a well-kept secret.

This new principal, who is now being recognized as the model for strong instructional, visionary leaders is not a political manager who spends time covering his tracks and counting rolls of toilet paper. The Effective Schools principal models, leads, educates, and inspires the entire school community. And, in turn, this principal is educated and inspired by those with whom he or she works.

By the early eighties, research had evolved to the point that specific characteristics could be used to identify the Effective principal. In a study from 1982 to 1985 of 67 public schools by the Effective School Project of the Seattle School Districts and the University of Washington's College of Education, it was concluded that principals who succeed—in schools with both high and low socioeconomic status (SES) students—have very distinct leadership behavior and strengths in key areas: (1) mobilizing resources, (2) communicating, (3) serving as instructional resources, and (4) being a visible presence.

The Effective principal eschews the safety of the corner office; moves about the corridors, classrooms, and assemblies; and interacts with teachers, students, staff, and parents. This person is a model of the value of an informed, inspired, reflective life. He or she *lives* the mission of the school. This principal is a risk taker, encouraging creation and innovation from the entire school community. Teachers are no longer controlled by assembly-line mentality, but neither are they alone in dealing with complex issues in the process of bringing their students into the twenty-first century. The teacher in an Effective School now has a principal who is informed about changes in instructional learning and is there to assist and enlighten. This principal has knowledge of staff development to help the struggling teacher. If that staff development is not readily available, the principal will seek it out.

The Effective principal still controls the physical resources of the building, but often goes beyond the school boundaries in search of additional resources. This principal is out in the community, and not just with parents, but with businesses, seeking their assistance. He or she also recognizes his or her role as a buffer between the teachers and outside interferences. When parents complain or an associate superintendent has a problem, the principal receives the information first, deflecting and often liquidating the complaint before it can disrupt the teacher and classroom.

A principal who greets parents when they drop off their children and spends time talking to parents or guardians will send a clear message of caring and involvement. This is a very different message than from the principal who walks past the parents in the morning, but nevertheless issues a statement saying that "the door of my office is always open" and "the comments of all parents are welcome."

If this work and behavior of the Effective principal seems familiar to businesspeople, if this goal of operating very openly, supportively, visibly, and collaboratively is familiar to businesspeople—well, it should all be very familiar. It is the management style and structure of successful businesses in the nineties.

Leaders as the Motivational Force

In their popular 1985 book *Leaders,* Warren Bennis and Burt Nanus,* established a model of a leader that matches the effective superintendent and

*Excerpts in this section from *Leaders: The Strategies for Taking Charge* by Warren Bennis and Burt Nanus. Copyright © 1985 by Warren Bennis and Burt Nanus. Reprinted by permission of HarperCollins Publishers.

principal of today. They emphasize that a great leader is a leader with a vision that is the "motivating force for all actions." This perspective has served as guidance and/or confirmation for the visionary actions of many Effective school leaders. Bennis and Nanus emphasize that an effective leader must be like the Zen archer: The desire to hit the target is irrelevant. The leader—the arrow—and the target are all one. They insist that an effective leader pulls rather than pushes.

This philosophy is akin to the Effective Schools Process position that modeling and inspiration accomplish much more than mandates. But it is the act of synthesizing the inspirational direction of the organization with the day-to-day operations that is perhaps the most challenging, the most vital, and the most familiar to progressive school leaders:

> *Leaders require* foresight, *so that they can judge how the vision fits into the way the environment of the organization may evolve;* hindsight, *so that the vision does not violate the traditions and culture of the organization; a* world view, *within which to interpret the impact of possible new developments and trends;* depth perception, *so that the whole picture can be seen in detail and perspective;* peripheral vision, *so that the possible responses of competitors and other stakeholders to the new direction can be comprehended; and a process of* revision *so that all visions previously synthesized are constantly reviewed as the environment changes. (Bennis and Nanus, 1985)*

Whether it is IBM or the Hollibrook School, or a 50,000-pupil school district, the task or the goal is the same: "If there is a spark of genius in the leadership function at all, it must lie in this transcending ability, a kind of magic, to assemble—out of all the variety of images, signals, forecasts and alternatives—a clearly articulated vision of the future that is at once simple, easily understood, clearly desirable, and energizing" (Bennis and Nanus).

Leaders is a book that you find on the bookshelves of many Effective superintendents and principals. Perhaps what makes *Leaders* so appealing is its understanding and acceptance of the idiosyncrasies of the workforce. The authors point out that it is important for all participants within the organization to understand that the sense of community "is not about liking one another, but relying on one another to accomplish a desired goal."

It is difficult for schools—because of the very nature of power relationships—for there to be one big, happy family. But with a strong leader committed to an inspiring vision, there can be the desire to do the best job possible for the students. And, in many schools, that is enough.

Throughout the Effective Schools Process, personal values as well as values shared with colleagues and students form the foundation for professional commitment. Every school superintendent, principal, and teacher will tell you that if you do not have the will to teach *all* children, it will never happen. You have to believe in what you are doing in order to fulfill the promise of the Effective

Schools Process, for fulfilling that promise is very often not so much a technical endeavor as a moral endeavor.

In light of that, Effective School leaders find inspiration from Bennis and Nanus's popular quote: "Managers are people who do things right. Leaders are people who do the right thing." Bennis and Nanus defined four strategies that successful leaders articulate and enact:

1. Attention through vision or "creating a focus"
2. Creating meaning through communication or the "management of meaning"
3. Trust through positioning or "engaging in the actions necessary to implement the vision of the leader"
4. "Management of self"

These strategies involve the direct interaction of a leader with the school. The principal who espouses these characteristics cannot be withdrawn or invisible to staff and students. This is hands-on. And with students, it is often a literal hands-on. At the essence of any talk of "focus," "actions necessary to implement the mission," "management of self" must be concern for the student.

In an Effective elementary school, you will see this with the principal who opens his or her office to second-graders who have finished writing a story and have come to share their accomplishment. At the high school level, you will see it with a principal who joins in the teaching and counseling of an after-school group working on the problems of family interaction. These Effective principals are not afraid to be involved with students. In fact, these principals will tell you that it is the most important and rewarding part of their job.

All this goes beyond the rules and regulations a principal (or a superintendent, or a teacher) will find in a neat packet of do's and don'ts. It evolves from a much more significant, more demanding entity: the human will. Repeatedly, Effective practitioners insist that if you do not have the will to do the Effective work, it just won't happen.

Schools and the Golden Rule

Understanding the importance of the human will in any successful endeavor, Stephen Covey, author of *The Seven Habits of Highly Effective People* (1989),* stated that leadership would never develop effectively unless it came "inside-out." He insisted that the power of leadership must begin *within* the heart, the soul, of

*From *The Seven Habits of Highly Effective People.* Copyright © 1989 by Stephen R. Covey. Reprinted by permission of Simon & Schuster.

the human being. It was fundamental that it begin with the self. Once the vision is within us, he stated, then there were seven basic "habits" that, if performed without fear, would be the tools of effective leadership. As with the lessons of *Leaders,* Effective School leaders saw these habits as touchstones to their own motivating ideologies:

1. Be proactive. Behavior should be a function of decisions, not conditions. Covey urges the use of self-awareness, imagination, conscience, and independent will to lead aggressively.
2. Begin with the end in mind. Have a vision and a mission statement; be "principle centered."
3. Put first things first. Prioritize. Delegate.
4. Think "win-win." Look for the win for all involved.
5. Understand first, then be understood. Diagnose before you prescribe.
6. Synergize. The whole is greater than the parts.
7. Sharpen the saw (renewal).

Although Covey talks of all these steps in the personal sense, step 7, renewal, is a behavior or characteristic that school practitioners and experts believe is one of the most important aspects of Effective Schools. Businesses have been into the work of renewal for several decades, but renewal is just now coming into the public schools, and usually only after an arduous battle.

It is estimated that big business today spends an average of 7–10 percent of its budget on retraining or renewal. In most school districts, the budget accounts for the designation of *less than 1 percent* for the renewal or retraining of staff and teachers.

The very first discussions of renewal brought apprehension from some teachers, and particularly union officials, because of the fear that the call for staff development implied that teachers were doing an inadequate job. But once the nay-sayers realized there were no threats involved, and that state-of-the-art teaching methods could in fact help teachers raise the achievement level and improve the classroom atmosphere, the negative cries soon turned into positive cheers.

When the hurdle of the teachers' insecurities was passed, in quick pursuit came the attitude of the public that they were paying for teachers to teach, in the classroom, and not to attend any courses themselves, or even participate in any renewal activities. Teachers were not practicing teaching unless students were present.

It is hard to imagine a company or business not operating with some kind of renewal. And we usually do not think twice about it. Do we question when First National Bank or IBM sends employees off for two weeks of retraining seminars, all expenses paid, usually in some pleasant resort in a warm climate? Do we argue with the doctor who goes to Paris to attend a medical conference? Do we think it strange when the local department store sends its salespeople out to full-pay retreats to be instructed in new selling techniques? No. Retraining and refocusing retreats are part and parcel of the business world. Check any hotel in any major city on any given day and you will find the billboard listing numerous seminars and workshops for various and diverse groups. From Mary Kay, to Citicorp, to radiologists, to electricians, lawyers, accountants, and surgeons, renewal is not just a given—it is a *must.*

However, only in recent years do we see genuine, thoughtful renewal activities coming into the public schools. Superintendents still report being stunned at the public's extreme reticence for teacher renewal. It's almost as if their children's quality of learning was *not* at stake.

The process of renewal is pointed to by Tom Peters and Nancy Austin in *A Passion for Excellence* (1985)* as very often being the determining factor in a company attaining and maintaining success. A business that does not invest in the development of its own people is a business that becomes stagnant, outdated, and destined for failure. Peters and Austin also discovered through their extensive research that the feeling of support from managers was a major factor in successful businesses. That calibre of support is further explained in their book's leadership chapter, which contains the following headings: "Attention, Symbols, Drama, Vision—and Love." These are extaordinary attributes for business. But they are what one might have expected from a school setting. Unfortunately, in many schools, these attributes—just like renewal—were neither identified nor recognized until the Effective Schools Process integrated staff development with the renewal process in the schools. And only now are they starting to be hailed as proven, powerful characteristics of success.

Along with emphasizing the visible presence of leaders, leader support, and the renewal of leaders and the workforce, Peters and Austin point to three criteria that they call "sustaining edges of excellence":

1. Superior customer service
2. Constant innovation
3. Turned-on people

These sustaining edges of excellence, when applied to U.S. schools, account for the lifelong learning process that is the crux of education—the motive for Effective Schools. Each of the three "edges" must be applied to *every* member of the school community.

On a lighter, but just as relevant note, Peters and Austin created a unique phrase that coincidentally is a mainstay of Effective School leadership:

*From *A Passion for Excellence* by Thomas J. Peters and Nancy K. Austin. Copyright © 1985 by Thomas J. Peters and Nancy K. Austin. Reprinted by permission of Random House, Inc.

MBWA—Management By Wandering Around (or management by paying attention). As referred to earlier, the principal of an Effective School has come out of the office—he or she is no longer invisible. And if this is true for the principal, it is just as true for the superintendent. The days of the invisible superintendent are long past in Effective School districts.

This presence of a leader is important because by "wandering around," a leader acquires a grasp of what exactly is happening. Whether it's the working environment of a factory worker or the quality of a chocolate bar, Austin and Peters say the best way to ensure a product of which you can be proud, is to check out the process for yourself. This doesn't require actually performing each individual task, but *understanding* the work required within that task.

Examples given are foremen being sent out to labor in their own factories. It is amazing how quickly and earnestly the foremen's suggestions for change came in. Then there were the small plane mechanics who were told they would go out on the test flights the next day. That evening the tarmac was spotted with the beams of flashlights as anxious mechanics checked the nuts and bolts of their earlier work.

And so it is now with Effective School leaders checking out the quality of education for themselves. No longer can superintendents and principals get away with putting their own children in private schools. They put their hopes for their own children in the same building from which they receive their paychecks. They ask their teachers to teach the children in their classrooms the way they would want their own children taught, to treat them the way they would want their own children treated. It is the basic theory of the Golden Rule that has come back into favor in the new business and the new school paradigm.

What is coming together here are the basic tenets of ownership, trust, and managerial integrity that reward policy that breaks away from the patterns of the past to more effectively serve the consumer as well as the worker. If you add at the top of this a strong, inspired vision, you have an organization moving into effectiveness.

The Process: An Integrating Mechanism for School Change

How did the Effective Schools Process manage to bring all these basic business principles together, along with the Golden Rule, and pull them into the schoolhouse in a manner that would work for all the interacting parties of the organization? How did the Effective Schools Process become the vehicle in which the public schools could ride the business paradigm into the twenty-first century? Researchers, experts, and practitioners of effective schools pulled together years of intellectual, social, psychological, and emotional training—as well as conflict.

They took the research-based validation and integrity of the basic premises—all children can learn and the means to accomplish that is school-based management based on the seven correlates—and joined them with premier management styles, group-processing skills, and shared decision-making principles.

"Effective Schools (Process) has given the leaders out there a clear vision of what education ought to be about," says Larry W. Lezotte, Ph.D. "It does that in a very simple, sharp way that speaks to the head and the heart.

"It's not just a vision or a dream that cannot be tethered to anything else. It has a map that is associated with it that is based in research. In other words, if you work these fences and fields called leadership, climate, expectation, it will start to yield that vision. What separates Effective Schools from other models is that it has had from the beginning a delivery system as far as the change process is concerned which is the collaborative democratization process. So it has the means to get there. The places to go, the map to follow.

"The biggest problem in pulling administrators into this collaborative way of thinking stemmed from the fact that most were trained as trouble shooters, fire fighters, public relations people—all piecemeal experts with a strong authoritarian bent. For years they have pushed and politicized their way according to the classic bureaucratic map. Now, to suddenly throw the collaborative mode on the table is to do serious disruption to the more traditional style."

Many administrators survive the transition. After surviving the first onslaught of people-oriented instruction, they realize there can be some real advantages to this approach. They get others to share the load and still don't relinquish their own power. They get the opportunity to experiment and to express themselves. They also have, through the Effective Schools Process, extensive research and planning—a distinct "map" to guide them and to help deflect criticism. After dealing with the technical aspects of Effective Schools, they can broach those nebulous areas such as school culture that have always intrigued but puzzled administrative teams. In questions of culture, like so many other new niches of school management, Effective Schools have a research base ready to assist.

"We never realized how very important the culture of a school was," says Kent Peterson, Ph.D., former director of the National Center for Effective Schools Research and Development. "Now we see that we must change some underlying beliefs of teachers and administrators. This gets to the heart of changing attitudes, behaviors, and motivating people out of mediocrity. That's essential, and that's finally what's happening."

The attention to culture is not exclusive to the Effective Schools Improvement Process. Businesspeople talk about it as the one element that is hardest to get a handle on, but the element that, when addressed, often holds the key to a successful workforce.

One of the superintendents who has adopted the Effective Schools Improvement Process for his district is Noel T. Farmer, Ed.D., in Frederick County, Maryland. Frederick County Public Schools serve over 26,000 students in a population that moves from rural countryside to historical Frederick City. As the community becomes a feeder suburb for the Washington area, the population continually shifts. An estimated 30 percent of the students in Frederick County are low socioeconomic status; 8 percent are minority students.

In 1988, Dr. Farmer initiated the Effective Schools Process in his school system. Within two years, the very public process of turning around the troubled school system was showing documented success. Farmer, who came from a district where he had plenty of money, but no Effective Schools, insists it is the Effective Schools Process that pulled together all his aspirations and inspirations.

"I came from a place where there was so much money you could do just about anything (nearby Howard County). But I had in my soul a definite yearning. I knew something was wrong. I couldn't put my fingers on it, but I knew something out there in the terms of how we were doing it was just wrong. We didn't have the proper method. And I personally felt incomplete. Out of focus. I had moved up the ranks, succeeded in the system just fine, but I did not know exactly what I was doing and how to make it better. I knew I was failing at some very important level."

He began reading Effective Schools Process literature and its link with recent management changes. He says that his study finally put his task, his career, and his goals into focus, especially the concept that outcomes drive process. "That was important because up to that point in time, I had spent 25 years letting process drive my entire life as an educator. I didn't have to worry about outcomes. We had a captive audience. You go to us or who do you go to? We're the only game in town. So my whole orientation was on process. I'm not blaming anyone. That's just what happened to me and I didn't change it.

"The second thing that kept haunting me was when I read that structure has to follow purpose. The same thing as saying outcomes drive process. That might sound simplistic, but it did change my way of looking at education from an organizational development approach."

Farmer says that these distinct approaches—based on Effective School principles—laid the groundwork for instructional lessons that previously had been incomplete, if not backwards.

"For example, the emphasis on teaching for learning as opposed to teaching and learning. My whole life had been spent with the conjunctive *and.* A *and* B. Teaching and learning as if they were two separate acts and they weren't married really. Teaching for learning is a more of a focused, directed approach.

"Also, with the question of equity in excellence. Up to that point in time we had married the word *equity* and the word *excellence* with that conjunctive *and*. We had been going 200 years, well, not 200 years because we weren't worried about equity too long ago, but for the longest time, we were worried about equity *and* excellence. The game is equity *in* excellence. That preposition is so powerful."

Farmer points out that educators have always had philosophies of education, but, for the most part, those philosophies have been putting the responsibility on the wrong people. "We kept using that unbelievable tired phrase 'to develop the student's potential.' It hasn't worked for 200 years and that's the truth, and it isn't working now. What we had to do was talk about developing *our* potential—our potential to help students learn because they already can learn more than we know how to teach them."

Farmer has put himself and his leadership on the line. He says the time is past when superintendents and boards of education can continue to blame others, in particular principals, teachers, and students. He says Noel Farmer and Frederick County's Board of Education are responsible and will remain so. He has put his money where his mouth is. He has put his outcome goals into policy, and each year publishes a detailed document informing the county exactly where the schools stand. If businesses can demand and speak of this accountability, so, too, can schools.

His results have been impressive, to say the least. From a district that was down near the bottom in state ranking, Frederick County—in three years,and with an expanding complex student population—has risen to the top. You also see it in the people behind the achievement scores. Faculty and staff are energized, grievances are at a minimum, and the students express their enthusiasm with increased rates of attendance and decreases in the number of dropouts.

"Effective Schools (Process) has given me the tools to improve this district, to serve all children with a quality education," maintains Farmer. "There never should be any excuses and there never will be in this district. This isn't magic. This is just common-sense school improvement."

Noel Farmer has shifted his school district from the old business and factory paradigm of hierarchical management to the new paradigm of visionary leaders, MBWA, the Golden Rule, the power of will, and collaborative decision making. But the change really goes beyond all this, far exceeding the dramatic alterations in rules, roles, and responsibilities within the public school. It goes to the very heart of the way we have regarded our public education system for the last 200 years. It is a change not so much of job descriptions and policies but of a nation's mindset.

"Trapped in Webs of Their Own Creation"

Are the public schools in the United States trapped in outdated, unrealistic, poorly managed, ill-serving webs of their own creation? Are the people within the public schools locked into their own degrading psychic prisons that lock out progress, reality, enlightenment, and achievement?

Yes. The public schools have labored under an image of what they should be, who they should serve, and how—that is basically ignorant, discriminatory, and academically, psychologically, and emotionally crippling.

What practitioners, researchers, and others in the Effective Schools movement are saying is that we must abandon the old image of the public schools and embrace a new, exciting, enlightened vision. Part of that vision must come from the new lessons being espoused by today's successful businesses. Schools must shift the paradigm if they are to serve the new generations.

The school paradigm has some different wiring than the business paradigm. Understand the major changes that Dr. Noel Farmer has just spoken about—changes in the *image* of the task of the public school:

Teaching *for* learning.
Structure *follows* purpose.
Equity *in* excellence.
Teaching *all* children to *our* fullest potential.
Accelerate students, don't remediate them.

Gareth Morgan in *Images of Organization* (1986)* writes of how human beings "have a knack of getting trapped in webs of their own creation." He uses the metaphor that organizations—and here the analogy to the public school system is particularly appropriate—are "psychic phenomena" and that people become imprisoned or confined by "the images, ideas, thoughts and actions to which these processes give rise."

It is Plato's *Republic,* Morgan reminds us, that first explored this concept. It is the allegory of the underground cave where people are chained and cannot move. In front of them is a blank wall. Behind them, at the mouth of the cave, is a roaring fire. The blank wall exhibits the shadows of the chained cave dwellers. And it is these shadows that the cave dwellers regard as reality. "Truth and reality for the prisoners rest in this shadowy world, because they have no knowledge of any other."

Now, according to Socrates, if one of the cave dwellers is freed from the chains and ventures out into the world, he will see that the images of reality held by his fellow cave dwellers are "distorted and flawed."

> *If he were to try and share his new knowledge with them, he would probably be ridiculed for his views. For the cave prisoners, the familiar images of the cave*

ɔuld be much more meaningful than any story about a world they had never seen. ˣ'hey would probably regard the world outside the cave as a potential source of danger, to be avoided rather than embraced as a source of wisdom and insight.

The cave stands for the world of appearances and the journey outside stands for the ascent to knowledge. People in everyday life are trapped by illusions, hence the way they understand reality is limited and flawed. By appreciating this, and by making a determined effort to see beyond the superficial, people have an ability to free themselves from imperfect ways of seeing. However, many of us often resist or ridicule efforts at enlightenment, preferring to remain in the dark rather than to risk exposure to a new world and its threat to the old ways. (Morgan, 1986)

"The Old Ways"

The public schools have, for decades, been trapped in "the old ways." What the Effective Schools Process sets out to do is break that pattern of the old ways, break up that "flawed" thinking, get rid of those dangerous images of the past.

What images? The image that is as old as America: The image of the poor, disadvantaged student with the label across his or her chest stating "Stupid, Uneducable, A Waste of Time." It's the same label we put on the Negro slaves, the southern European immigrants in the 1800s, the twentieth century refugees. It's the same label we put on women.

Every day in U.S. public schools, that image perpetuates itself when teachers and administrators look at a child who may be wearing torn or dirty clothing, speak a foreign language or a ghetto dialect, come from a family on the "wrong side of town," not come from a "family" as society defines it, act out beyond what someone arbitrarily decides as proper behavior, or have a learning disability or physical or emotional handicap. According to the *image* we have for what constitutes a child worthy of our educational expertise and effort, that child is out in the cold, shut out of our image of who the educational system can and should serve.

We have passed laws to build in equality and equity, but as the allegory of the cave shows—and the state of education in this country confirms—it is very difficult to change the views of the cave dwellers.

The image that certain children are just uneducable was confirmed in 1966 with the now notorious Coleman report, commissioned by the United States Congress, which found that "most of the variation in achievement could not possibly be accounted for by school differences, since most of it lies within the school." Policy makers took these findings to mean only family background (socioeconomic status) matters.

It took almost 10 years and the work of such people as Ron Edmonds (Harvard University and Michigan State), George Weber (Council on Basic

Education), John Frederickson (Harvard University), Wilbur Brookover (Michigan State), Madden, Lawson, and Sweet (California State Department of Education), and Larry Lezotte (Michigan State) to compile and present the evidence that effective schools existed where students' learning levels were not dependent (related to) on their socioeconomic status or family background. These schools made a difference; they taught *all* children.

But even though there was now proof that the image of the uneducable, disadvantaged student was the wrong image for the schools, this new image of how a school should function and succeed was not accepted by the community—neither the community within the school nor the community outside.

In 1974, almost 10 years after the Coleman report, Ron Edmonds wrote:

> *The central substantive issue is the community's response to "universally" successful pupil mastery of schooling. That means that no child, free of certifiable handicap, will be expected to acquire less than the community's definition of basic school skills.*
>
> *Rejection by educators of such a notion proceeds from two culturally autocratic premises. First, there is the widespread belief that pupil home life and social milieu are principal causes of pupil performance. Second, educators reject a community's definition of schooling when the community does not fulfill the educator's cultural expectations of what a community should be. Both premises have the effect of placing the burden of performance on pupils with no concomitant responsibility for teachers.*

What Edmonds has described is the blatant juxtaposition in the mind of educators of an image of an uneducable child along with an image of a dysfunctional community that produced the child. These two images combine inside the classroom to effectively cripple any substantive learning process going on there.

The Effective Schools Process holds at its heart a moral imperative: the importance of changing the cultural ignorance and bias of a school. A school that believes the community is as uneducable as the child serves only to further handicap its constituents. An Effective School reaches out into the community to understand its people and to make sure the community understands the school. In every Effective School a major emphasis is placed on increasing the cultural understanding between teachers, administrators, constituents, and especially parents.

A very simple but powerful example again comes from the Hollibrook School in Spring Branch, Texas. As part of its initial registration process, school officials needed birth certificates, Social Security numbers, or passport numbers if nothing else was available. This process frightened many of the parents to the point they backed off from sending their children to school. What the school officials found out was that in many of the South American countries from which these people had fled, the procedure of gathering birthdates and other information was the start of persecution from the government. The school officials discovered the best way to deal with the problem was to send parents whom the community trusted back into the community to inform the new parents that these procedures were not the beginning of a new form of the persecution, but simply a way of identifying and enrolling a child. The school was trying to *help* them, not persecute them.

Along with the cultural changes come the changes in the basic image of the public school. If the school is in a wealthy middle-class suburb, the image of the school is as an educational institution that instructs its students in basic skills and knowledge, as well as socialization techniques, and then sends the majority of its students off to college. If the school is in a poor, or inner-city neighborhood, the image changes. The school becomes a holding pen to keep children and teenagers off the street. The goal is to prevent dropouts, keep the peace, control and perhaps lessen drug use, and train some of the students for blue-collar jobs. If, somehow, a few students head off to college, then it's usually considered a fluke.

The image of Hollibrook School, its mission, its vision, is dramatically different than that of the middle-class suburban school. However, even though the cultures surely differ, there is no reason why the image, the goals, and the role of the school in this Texas community should be so different from other suburban communities. Unfortunately, public education is locked in its psychic prison that dictates that one cannot expect the same from a school serving a disadvantaged population as a school serving the middle or upper classes. "People in everyday life are trapped by illusions, hence the way they understand reality is limited and flawed" (Morgan, 1986).*

Effective Schools raise a loud protest to this discriminatory ignorance. They also offer proof,through the regular testing and monitoring of high and low socioeconomic students, that this image is wrong. What becomes essential at the very beginning is to set strict standards for what an Effective School is:

1. At least 95 percent of all students at *each* level will demonstrate minimum mastery. Students who achieve minimum academic mastery are prepared so that they will be predictably successful in the next grade in either their own school or in any other school building in the nation. Minimum academic mastery is measured by performance on a standardized test, preferably one of the newer norm-referenced criterion-referenced tests.
2. There will be no significant difference in the proportion of youth demonstrating minimum academic mastery as a function of socioeconomic class.

*Excerpt from *Images of Organizations* by Gareth Morgan. Copyright © 1986 by Sage Publications. Reprinted by permission of Sage Publications, Inc.

3. The above two conditions will have been obtained for a *minimum of three consecutive years*.

Following these very strict guidelines, it becomes impossible for a school to garner and keep an image as a holding pen for the uneducable. With these standards and the resulting rise in achievement levels, the teacher, administrator, parent, and community leader are freed from their psychic prisons.

"Oh, there's no doubt that we've been trapped in the image of a school that is just unable to educate certain children because we have believed for years that certain children just cannot be educated like their more fortunate counterparts," explains Dr. Hal Guthrie, superintendent of the Spring Branch (Texas) Independent School System.

"The toughest part of all this is changing the thinking. You've got to rise above the excuse making that is rampant in an ineffective organization. You've got to change that image, the folklore of the board rooms, faculty lounges, teacher parking lots. And if you don't change that image, the public education system is going to disintegrate."

For Guthrie, the finest—and perhaps only—way to change that image is through the Effective Schools Process.

"Effective Schools (Process) says you can't make any more excuses. They just don't fly. Because we've got the proof right here that those kids at the bottom of the socioeconomic ladder can learn just like the other kids. So forget your excuses."

According to Guthrie and other administrators, the image of the public school in the United States is founded on *the excuse:* "Well, these kids can't learn because their parents are not educated . . . or because they live in a housing project . . . or because their homelife is rotten . . . or because. . . ."

"You've got to change that image you've had your whole life," says Guthrie, who adds that one of the toughest things to change is the view that schools are to operate for the benefit of the teachers, not the students. "That's what I found here. Schools couldn't work for the kids, so the next step was to at least make them good for the teachers. But they weren't doing a damn thing for the students. And somehow, don't ask me how, or why, but that was all right. They accepted that as how it should be."

The reason it was accepted in Spring Branch and is part of the psyche throughout the U.S. public school system is because that is the functioning image of the school serving the lower socioeconomic classes. The image, as old as chalk itself, locking teachers and administrators into their psychic prison, is that *some children cannot learn.*

"The thought that all children can learn challenges the belief systems of people that say 'I've worked with these kids and these kids just can't learn,'" says Jean Norman, Ed.D., director of the School Assistance Project for the state of South Carolina. "What they're saying is they can't learn the way I teach them. And that challenges you as a teacher. So, it's threatening. Improvement implies change. And change is an uncomfortable process."

South Carolina has taken on a statewide educational improvement program. The foundation of that program is the Effective Schools Process. Despite a political and financial commitment to improvement, Dr. Norman and other state officials point out that major barriers still exist.

"We have in this state the thinking that education is not that important, that getting a job at the mill with a decent shift is what matters," says Norman. "On top of that, there is the feeling that if education *is* important, it's only important for a certain segment of the population. That's a tough image to overcome." And this is born out by the facts in South Carolina. Although by law every school is supposed to have school improvement plans in place, there is still a fair percentage of the 1,100 schools that have seen no need to change—or even assess—their operations.

"I constantly get phone calls from principals who are new to a school and say, 'Help, Jean, there's nothing here. This school hasn't even thought about change.' It's tough going against the public's idea of what a school should be and who it should serve."

And although there's been desegregation in the south for 35 years, many of the schools in South Carolina maintain a particularly degrading segregation.

"Sure, they all come in the front door together. White and black. But then the black kids go off to the remedial classes, and the white kids go off to the gifted and talented classes," says Norman, emphasizing that it all goes back to the image of the student and the school.

"High expectations is the toughest for these people because it focuses on values. And the question is do you work on behaviors or values? I'm not sure we can wait until we change the belief system. These kids are coming in the front door and we're messing with them because of the values we've got. The values that have been passed down for generations."

Once again, the allegory of Plato's cave returns to the conscious. Cave dwellers regard new knowledge "as a potential source of danger . . . preferring to remain in the dark rather than to risk exposure to a new world and its threat to the old ways."

Dr. Max Heim, superintendent of the Geary County Public School System in Junction City, Kansas, is quick to point out that the biggest problem he had in bringing in the Effective School Process was that it contradicted the image his teachers and administrators had of who their students were. "Their minds," he says, "were locked tight."

"We basically had to open up the minds of our teachers and principals to the fact that these kids can learn. We've made a lot of progress in ten years. Before they just said 'No, we're not responsible. This kid here can't learn, neither can this one, and we're not responsible. And that kid over there, he's black, he sure as hell can't learn.' Now that's a tough image to turn around."

But Heim has managed to turn that image around. It has taken a lot of teacher training and a lot of test reinforcement. And he admits he still has some hard nuts to crack. Junction City is the home of Ft. Riley Army Base. A large percentage of the school children are from military families.

"The military, at least at this base, just doesn't build it into people that education is important. The image is often just the opposite," says Heim, obviously frustrated and angry with the low percentage of parental involvement in the schools. "Last year I went out to the parents meeting at the Ft. Riley Elementary School, which is where all the officers' kids go. And there were more teachers there than parents. The whole thing wasn't more than 20 people. That's pathetic. One time we did get a colonel who made a statement encouraging the parents to get involved, and that helped." *One* time . . . a colonel helped.

Breaking the constraints of that psychic prison is one of the first missions of the Effective School Process. But, as every administrator will admit, all the reform movements and training programs in the world will make no difference if a teacher or administrator is not willing to at least listen.

"When we first started saying these kids at the lower end can do just as well as these other kids, there were some teachers who just looked at us like we were crazy," says Robert Sudlow, Ed.D., assistant superintendent for instruction for the Spencerport (New York) Public School System. "And many of them still look at us like we're crazy. Even though we can pile the desk high with proof that the kids are comparable in ability and achievement."

Spencerport was one of the first white, middle-class suburban school districts to adopt the Effective Schools Process and have the Effective Schools Process adopt them.

"I think Edmonds took us on because of all the things we were not," explains Dr. Sudlow. "We weren't poor, urban, minority, or in trouble." Even though Spencerport looked like a good school system on paper, Sudlow and Superintendent Joe Clement believed it could be better. They believed that not only the scores of the higher socioeconomic students could be raised but also the scores of the lower socioeconomic students (measured by the level of the mother's education) could, and should, be raised. And, in fact, they were right. Not only have test scores risen for all populations but the number of students taking Regents courses and exams has also increased. And the scores on those exams show improvement.

"There's no doubt that Effective Schools has dramatically improved this system. But there's also no doubt that one of the most important things we did was to change the thinking of many of our teachers and principals," says Sudlow.

Teachers don't like to admit that they may have been wrong in their image of their students, and the role of their school. But even the teachers in Spencerport allow that changes in attitudes have been made.

"I don't think there's any doubt that each one of us, some in big ways, some in small ways, had our thinking changed," said a high school teacher. "Remember, we've just about been *trained* to believe some children just cannot learn. It's not like the education schools are pounding it into our heads that all these kids can make it."

The problem is greatly exacerbated when you put the public school in the midst of New York City's Spanish Harlem, one of the country's most violent, drug-infested neighborhoods.

"Hey, I just floated along for the first five years of teaching," explains a middle school teacher who was formerly in an upper middle-class school on New York's East Side and is now teaching in District 6, Spanish Harlem. "I didn't have any problems at all. Then the layoffs came and in order to stay in the system, District 6 was my only choice. When I told my friends I was going here rather than move out of the city, they thought I had lost my mind. They told me I'd either get stabbed, or end up throwing myself out the window. And that's what I was prepared for. That was the image."

This teacher has been in Spanish Harlem now for six years. He witnessed firsthand the changes brought in by Superintendent Tony Amato, and he has no intention of transferring out.

"Before Effective Schools, this place was almost as bad as I feared. But what made it so bad was as much my attitude and the attitude of the other teachers as anything the kids did or didn't do," he explained. "We just thought the kids were losers and our job was to survive. That's it. Did we try? I don't think so. Really. Remember, we had it ingrained in us that it wouldn't do any good even if we did try."

Then Amato started making changes. He decreased the number of students in a classroom and increased the supply of books, paper, and resource materials. He instituted a Golden Hour in each school, every morning, when the entire school does nothing but read—without interruptions. He gave the teachers more autonomy. He increased all teacher and staff training. He made the central office work *for* the schools.

The result has been the most dramatic rise in test scores of any district in the city. District 6 went from the bottom of the city's educational statistical heap to the middle, but the major difference seems to be in attitude.

"We care about these kids, now. We know they can do it," explains the middle school teacher. "We no longer write them off. Every kid gets the same shot and there isn't a day that goes by that one of the teachers doesn't shake his or her head and say: 'Who would have thought?'"

Consultants, researchers, superintendents, and principals say they are all too familiar with this attitude from teachers.

"And sure, you get a great feeling when you break through and these teachers start to understand," says Dr. Lezotte, who began the Effective Schools Process staff development in Spanish Harlem. "The problem is we shouldn't still have to break through to teachers and principals. But we do. Everyday."

The reality is that in order for a school to become effective, the degenerative psychic prison has to be blown apart. *The teacher has to be freed from those shadowy reflections on the cave wall.* That is why staff development is so essential to the Effective Schools Process. Courses and seminars are specifically designed to confront a teacher's biased image of the students. Hours of training, reinforced by stacks of research material, present contradictory evidence to the "old ways."

As a teacher goes through the staff development, it is vital for that teacher to have an instructional leader to look up to and to turn to for guidance in this most complex endeavor. Effective Schools have discovered that, unfortunately, a teacher is unlikely to be enlightened—and carry out the lessons of that enlightenment in the long run—unless there is a commanding, inspirational leader in the principal's office.

Enlightenment without leadership to guide is a very risky proposition. A teacher without the unequivocable support of the principal can find the road to teaching for learning very difficult. Enlightenment often means innovation and risk taking. A principal stuck in the old ways is only threatened by such activity.

Just as in the shifting business paradigm, the image of that principal, stuck in the old ways, must be blown apart—especially if the image is based in reality. In the past, the principal has been viewed as a nebulous, benign individual who orders supplies, deals with disciplinary problems, and speaks at school assemblies. In the majority of cases, he or she is a former coach who has played a competent political game and now rests comfortably in the corner office.

That reality must change. Effective School principals must be a model of wisdom, experience, and commitment. They must know as much, if not more, about instruction than teachers. They must be active in the school, and *welcome* in the classrooms. They must get along with parents, students, and school boards. They must be good managers, manipulators, movers, and shakers. They must be visionaries.

"It's way past time to demythologize the image of the principal," says Jill Hearne, Ph.D., principal of the Adelaide Elementary School in Seattle, Washington. "I have real trouble with the perception of the big, bad principal. The one in power suits. The female-male clone. No thanks. I like being part of the school, an active part, an equal part, in a way. I like joking with the kids, I like calling parents by their first name, and having them call me by my first name. It's important that the bus drivers feel comfortable with me. I don't like these people who agree with me just because I'm the principal. That's not healthy. React to me because of who I am, not because of some phony image."

Hearne, like most Effective School principals, is not like the principal of yesteryear. She is involved in every aspect of her school. She not only knows the teachers who are in each classroom at any time of the day but what will be going on in a given class at a given time. She is welcome, and expected, in the classrooms. She discusses science projects with sixth-graders and music basics with first-graders.

The setup of Dr. Hearne's office area is indicative of the attitude at Adelaide and the changing image. Her office door opens into a short hallway that leads into the faculty area. Faculty come and go freely, stopping to share information or lunch. Teachers work together and work with Hearne.

At times, Hearne's demeanor can be tough or intimidating, like when she is talking about how she hires teachers.

"When I can, I try to find good, highly qualified men teachers. I think it's important to have a faculty that is representative of what is going on in the real world," she says. "And the last thing I'll do is make a positive decision on someone just because they say they like kids. If you just like kids, you should consider daycare. Teaching is a sophisticated, difficult job that takes brains, talent, dedication, a lot of hard work. . . ."

Just when you think Hearne, who is tall, attractive, and elegant, may be just a little *too* tough, she pulls in another side to her character.

On a bright, fall day last year, she was tending to guests in her office when she overheard from the hallway outside that a third-grade student had fallen down in the playground. She had not been summoned; the matter was being handled. But immediately Hearne was up from behind her desk, telling her guests that if they wanted to talk to her, they would have to "run along" with her. And then she was out of her office and out the back door of the school and *running* (fast) across the playground. The child had fallen and hurt her back. Hearne had a stretcher there in seconds and, after comforting the child, personally helped carry the stretcher into the school, the whole time holding the weeping child's hand and assuring her she was going to be all right. While an ambulance and doctor were summoned, Hearne was on the phone notifying the parents. The injury turned out to be insignificant, but for several minutes that playground tumble was the most important thing in the third-grader's life—and in Jill Hearne's life.

"There's no doubt that not only is the old image of a principal wrong, it's dangerous. It doesn't serve anyone other than the system in a real politic type of way," says John Morefield, principal of the Hawthorne Elementary school in Seattle. "To be an educator today, an effective educator, it's a calling, a vocation. It's not just a job. Not any more."

The Hawthorne Elementary School is in Seattle's poorest neighborhood, surrounded by decaying apartment buildings and a conglomeration of Vietnamese, South American, and African markets. This brand new school is being called a "demonstration" school. After years as a successful principal and then a central office administrator, Morefield vied for the principalship of the Hawthorne. He promised parents, in writing, that with the help of the Effective Schools Process, he would make Hawthorne one of the finest schools in the Northwest. And he's succeeding.

He spends several hours every day working with community leaders and associations, drumming up support in the form of sponsorship (as in zoos or businesses), tutors (from retired veterans to local Boeing executives), assistance (from field trip monitors to babysitting help), and resources (after-school jobs, computer supplies).

To help Morefield keep his promise to parents and the community, the Seattle School District let him handpick most of his faculty. He says the most important thing he can do for his faculty is help them abandon an establishment image of what a successful school is.

"When I was principal at the Whitworth (an elementary school in Seattle), we won the National Excellence in Education Award, straight from the President of the United States. We were the first urban elementary school to win. Then, right after that we disaggregate our data. It was one of the saddest days of my life. There it was, staring at us. Disproportionate student achievement. And here we had this image of being so great. Our parents had been so happy." Morefield shook his head sadly as he remembered. "Well, just for some kids it turned out. The image worked for some, but not for others."

Morefield's task was difficult. "Your instinct was to turn away and hope it would all disappear real fast. Or to discount the information—which I know some principals still do. But it was very clear to me that my role as a leader was to keep the information before the eyes of everybody and to keep our consciousness raised. We had to take this information and do something with it. We had to make student outcomes change in the following years."

So, among the other images a school must change is, ironically, often its image as a good school. According to educators in Effective Schools, in the majority of U.S. schools the interpretation of test scores used to evaluate a school or school system can be very misleading. Perhaps that is why it is still the policy in most school systems not to disaggregate data.

Hal Guthrie, Ed.D., superintendent of the Spring Branch (Texas) Independent School System, laughs when you mention disaggregating data, something he has been doing for years. "You should see at these meetings of the superintendents when you start talking about disaggregating data . . . you never saw grown men get so quiet so fast. They don't want any part of it. You start disaggregating data and you demolish their little fiefdoms. No. Disaggregation means telling the truth as to what's going on in the schools."

And the truth is often far from the glowing image of the public school: "Organizations and their members become trapped by constructions of reality that, at best, give an imperfect grasp on the world" (Morgan, 1986).*

There are several images right at the very top of the public school organization that also must be corrected in the Effective School.

*Excerpt from *Images of Organizations* by Gareth Morgan. Copyright © 1986 by Sage Publications. Reprinted by permission of Sage Publications, Inc.

"It's this whole disease of being accountable only for process and procedures," says Dr. Noel Farmer of Frederick County, Maryland. "We don't hold the important central office people accountable. Who gets blamed if something goes wrong in the schools? The teachers and the principals. We hide behind them. We've got to have the superintendent and boards of education held accountable. We haven't done that in our history. Maybe the blight on American public education is the unaccountability that we have held for superintendents and board members."

One of the first things that an observer notices about a school system that embraces the Effective Schools Process is that the superintendent has made certain their respective board is totally immersed in the Effective Schools literature and then the process itself. A board has to understand and accept the tenets of teaching for learning, structure follows purpose, equity in excellence, teaching *all* children to *our* fullest potential.

"At first, the whole board didn't really understand what they (the superintendent and his staff) were talking about," says Gay Lenhard, a member of the Spencerport School Board during the implementation of the Effective Schools Process. "It sounded like more of the same, initially. But then we started to get into it, saw how worthwhile it was, and well, if the superintendent was willing to stake his professional life on it, and the data was there that it worked, well, we went for it. The whole way."

The board must also accept the validity of the changing business/school paradigm and the need to see beyond the shadows on the wall. One of the most dramatic discussions of that as it refers to the empowerment and renewal of teachers—and the accountability of all educators—comes from Dr. Noel Farmer:

"We must remember the basic philosophy that you can never have the outcomes in the industry higher in importance than the development of the worker. Yes. The *development of the worker.* The care and concern that you have for the development of the worker is as important as the outcome. Because we know that one doesn't cause the other. Satisfaction does not cause productivity, but you certainly want both to appear at the same time. Valuing the worker and wanting the worker to have good opportunities for self-development is as important as the outcomes you're after.

"So the system has to be functioning on the concept of helping to support teachers and principals in the quest of improving the probability of students learning. And we're trying to do a major cultural change here so I'm trying to enhance the development of the worker as much as possible. And that worker won't develop if they're stuck in the past."

However, Farmer is quick to add, "If I have a hospital where all the patients are dying, I'm going to shut the hospital down or change the scene in terms of actors and actresses that are in that hospital. I have to do that. I can't—won't—escape accountability."

Under the Effective Schools Process, all the images, all the shadows on cave wall, have to be discarded. Whether its the image of a barefoot, brown-skinned child with torn jeans who some educator has decided is "uneducable," or the history teacher who doesn't know the Constitution and is only interested in summers off, or the principal who spends his days in his office on housekeeping details, or the superintendent who only sees a school at commencement, or the board member whose only educational interest is the election process for county commissioner—all these images must be abandoned. And if any of these images are in fact reality, they must be put aside in order for a school to become Effective.

Outside of the schools, the image of the parent and the community must be an enlightened one. Parents of poor children cannot be described and discarded as ignorant and apathetic. Just as parents of middle-class students cannot be uniformly accepted as intelligent and caring. Communities cannot be viewed with the same monolithic prejudices. There must be cultural growth and understanding in the schools of the middle class as well as the schools of the inner city.

One of the last images that must be abandoned is that image of change happening overnight. The Effective Schools Process emphasizes that change is a *process,* not an event.

"I keep telling my people that good change takes time," says Dr. Farmer. "The good news about school improvement is that you can start tomorrow . . . and the bad news is you really never have it finished. You have to be more concerned with trend line data than you are with one year data. People want it to happen real quick. They want us to correct what we've been doing wrong for 100 years or 200 years, they want to correct it overnight. I have to be aware of that and try to make them understand why it's not going to occur overnight. A lot of stuff we do in the high school is not but two inches away from being labeled a band-aid to begin with. That's why our task is so enormous. We've got so much to correct. For a truly systemic approach you've got to take it all the way down to pre-K and make the difference there—and then carry it through."

Effective/Ineffective: The Differences Are Enormous

If we were to list the strongest images that come to mind concerning the operation of an "ineffective school," whether it's in a middle-class community or the inner city, those images—what we have locked in our psychic prisons and what is the accepted reality—are:

- A school building that is dirty, messy, and disorganized, with an undisciplined, often violent, environment

- A school that has no direction or no idea of its true purpose, its role in today's world
- A principal who has no control over the school and who is ridiculed and incompetent
- Teachers who don't care about students and who don't know what they are teaching or how to teach
- A system that has no way of evaluating itself or of informing parents or the community leaders whether it is doing the job of educating
- A school where students are looked upon as just pawns in the political process because they have no future anyway
- A school that regards parents as worthless as the students—not worth working with or consulting
- A school that has no idea what is going on between faculty members and school administrators, or between the school and central office

If we were to list the strongest images that come to mind concerning the operation of an "effective school," the characteristics are:

- A clean and safe environment
- A clear, strong mission of educational goals and social objectives
- Instructional, respected leadership with a vision
- Staff development and renewal for teachers
- Frequent monitoring of students, faculty, and administration performances
- High expectations for *all* students
- Mutual respect in home-school relations
- A complete understanding among faculty and administration of their purpose, role, and goals, and a strong working relationship with central office

As these two lists demonstrate, the images of the past—the flawed realities of the psychic prisons held by the cave dwellers within and outside the public schools—are in direct conflict with the goals of the Effective Schools Process. The task that public education faces in changing the many images of its organization is indeed great. But the fact that it can happen, and is happening, is the inspiration. Nothing succeeds like success.

Under the Effective Schools Process, the final, important image—the truthful image, the vital image—of schools from San Diego to Seattle to Boston to Miami has changed. The people in the Effective Schools have broken free of the chains in Plato's cave. They have given up the old ways, moved out of the dark into the light that guides prosperous, responsible businesses. No longer trapped in their webs of illusion, their psychic prisons, they have moved out into wider knowledge, and in their journey, they have freed America's schoolchildren from the bondage of ignorance.

CHAPTER FOUR

Leadership as a Moral Act

In Aristotelian terms, the good leaders must have ethos, pathos, and logos. The ethos is his moral character, the source of his ability to persuade. The pathos is his ability to touch feelings, to move people emotionally. The logos is his ability to give solid reasons for an action, to move people intellectually. —MORTIMER ADLER

"I can get paid just as much for not doing this" (that is, turning a school system around from declining scores and morale to ascending achievement outcomes and a rising sense of pride and commitment from teachers, students, and staff). The man talking is Dr. Hal Guthrie, superintendent of the Spring Branch Independent School District, a complex, evolving, conservative community bordering Houston, Texas. "Actually, now that I think about it, the way this country's going, I can probably get paid *more* for not doing this. I certainly know a lot of colleagues out there who are."

Hal Guthrie is into change via the Effective Schools Improvement Process. And because of that, he is both loved and feared. Change is anathema to those who have prospered under the old ways of public education. If anything can be said for certain in Spring Branch today, the old ways of education have no place in Spring Branch's present or future.

To begin with, Hal Guthrie is a far cry from the image of the superintendent of the past. He is not an invisible enigma. It is hard to find someone in Spring Branch, or, for that matter, anyone in the ranks of the business, political, or institutional arenas in Houston, who doesn't know him. At night he's pulling businesses into school partnerships or lobbying for a bond issue. By day, he's in the schools, interacting just as easily with a third-grader, her teacher, and her mother, as he did the evening before with the knights of Texas business. Everyone who knows Hal Guthrie knows what he stands for: the best learning process that he can bring to *every* child in Spring Branch. He's going to accomplish that no matter what it takes. He has a firm, precise vision to which he is passionately committed. If you agree with that vision, and work toward that vision to the best of your ability, enhancing your performance with the growth opportunities Guthrie's administration has made available, you have nothing to fear from Hal Guthrie.

The best example of this is seen when Guthrie enters one of Spring Branch's schools. He is a man who does not ask for more than what he gives. As tough as he is, he is also flexible and as compassionate as he is passionate. The good principals love to see him come through the door. They trust him. They know what he wants and they know they are doing their best to deliver it. They understand the desire—the desire for the children—that stokes his fire. The lesser principals, those working on their own political agendas and not Guthrie's vision (and their numbers are slowly diminishing in Spring Branch), begin shaking and bowing as soon as that strong stride hits their tiles. They fear him. They have reason to. (Guthrie has replaced all but a handful of his 33 principals.)

Hal Guthrie is forthright in his educational opinions, inspiringly passionate in his beliefs, and deeply committed to the research and experience-driven conclusions that *all* chidren can learn. He has little patience for academics and their postulations, and no tolerance at all for political positioning and excuse making. He has, throughout his career, taken on positions where he would be challenged to make a difference. His record supports his reputation as a man who accomplishes his goals.

With his pipe clenched firmly between his teeth, this tough, solid man dares his opponents to challenge him. "Look at the changes in this system. We're giving kids not only hope for the first time, we're giving them a hell of a good learning experience. And we can prove it. Prove it for *all* kids. Not just the kids at the top of the ladder, or the bottom. *All* kids. Look at the scores. Talk to the teachers. This is called progress. This is called realizing what the future is all about.

"And hey, like I tell my board, if you don't like what I'm doing, I'll get the hell out." Guthrie pauses to light his pipe. His voice, still showing his passion, grows softer, but just as determined. "And I will leave. Because I won't change the way I'm doing things. If they want to live in the past—that demoralizing, disintegrating past of myths and lies, excuses, and status quo—then fine, but not with me around."

The Spring Branch Independent School District's Board of Trustees does not want Hal Guthrie to leave. They have shown that by giving him an unprecedented, new (early) contract package. The reason they don't want him to leave is because under his leadership, the Spring Branch schools have been saved from what many believed was certain slippage into the ranks of those school districts judged as failures—for students, teachers, staff.

Failure? In Spring Branch, Texas? The school district that in 1967 was named one of the most outstanding school districts in the United States? The mighty Spring Branch a dismal failure?

"We were in complete denial about what was happening to us, and we were going down the tubes—fast!" Bob Wells would know. Raised in Spring Branch, and pursuing a career as teacher, principal, and head of the teachers' association, he is a self-confessed "good ole boy" and now the executive director of human and technological resource development for the school district (staff development). "We just would not admit that the days of the white, wealthy, west were gone in Spring Branch."

This is the voting residence of President George Bush, which, up until the 1970s, was viewed as one of the wealthiest, per capita, and most conservative in the nation. Driving out of downtown Houston, past the glittering glass of highrises and the polished stucco of corporate condominium complexes, you pass through miles of *huge,* as in "Texas huge," wrought-iron fenced homes of the exclusive Texas bluebloods—the oil and cattle barons of the West.

But if you spring off to the north side, away from where the President lives, you cross over the tracks, literally and figuratively. Here, on the north side of Spring Branch, despair, crime, and poverty rule. Once the home of middle-class whites who couldn't afford the real estate on the south side, it is now populated mostly with blacks and Hispanics, many from South America. Most residents live in dilapitated, drug-infested housing complexes. Some pass time in the junked cars that claim a sidewalk address for the children existing inside. There are few businesses, and instead of elaborate wrought-iron fences protecting multimillion dollar homes, there are the strong steel bars at the windows trying to stop the criminal from destroying lives and livelihoods. In less than a 30-second drive, you can move from one of the most independent bastions of wealth in the United States to one of the most dependent barrios of poverty.

On the south side of the freeway, the children were being dropped off in limousines in front of high schools that had some of the highest reading scores in the nation, whereas the children on the north side were straggling across junkyards and abandoned, burned-out businesses to enter dysfunctional schools that were hiding some of the nation's lowest reading scores. But no one in an educational power position in Spring Branch wanted to admit this. Much like the metaphor of Plato's cave, the characters were convinced of the accuracy of the shadows they saw—those shadowy images they had grown up with that they believed would always represent the truth the way they wanted and perceived it. Even when facts appeared that contradicted their perceptions, facts like population figures and school test scores, the cave dwellers chose what they believed was the safer route—a route of denial. This bold, dangerous denial of reality was choking the Spring Branch Independent School District.

"We were in such a state of denial the central office never even spoke about those schools on the north side. Really, it was like they didn't exist," recalls Wells, who lives in "one of the remaining decent areas" of the north side.

"And if you were a teacher over on the north side, you didn't exist either. How could you? Your students didn't exist. Not in the eyes of the central office—or of course the people with the power in Spring Branch." The result of this thinking was that whole schools were being ignored and neglected. They received inadequate resources, and then were told to just go quietly about their task. "It's like the starving child who should be grateful that the coffee grinds are tossed at them," explained one teacher.

Bob Wells agrees it was far from fair. "Back in the seventies and eighties, the leadership—and I use that term loosely—was really into management, into complete denial about the changing demographics and the kids who were coming here," explains Wells. "They were top down, boss managers, always keeping the lid on, the key philosophy being 'Kids who have different needs must be made the same. And if they're not, we don't want to know about it.' We could not admit we were anything other than a lily-white, upwardly mobile school district."

But the facts became too loud to continue to deny. Like many other suburbs of large U.S. cities, Spring Branch's character was changing fast. The school population of over 40,000 in the seventies dropped to 20,000 in the eighties. (The population, as more and more middle- and lower-income families move into Spring Branch, is now climbing again.) Schools had to be consolidated and some boundaries were redrawn. But the most dramatic change was not in numbers—it was in the color and economic status of children. Suddenly the public schools, which for years were viewed as basically private schools for the very affluent, were seeing children who not only didn't have trust funds but whose parents probably didn't have a bank account.

A Dangerous Denial

In 1983, the population of the Spring Branch Independent School District (26,000) was 85 percent white, 15 percent minority, and only *1 percent low income.* Just five years later, the district was 50 percent white, 32 percent Hispanic, 10 percent black, and 8 percent Asian, and *40 percent of the students were on free lunch.* In 1991, the district is as high as 56 percent minority at the elementary level.

Johnny was suddenly in a class with Jose, and Johnny's parents vented their dissatisfaction in the voting booth, removing the school board in the next election. Then the superintendent resigned, along with associate superintendents and other key central administrators.

"It was a knee-jerk reaction to the denial," says Wells."And of course the plain fact that the school system was in a state of annual decline. Our scores—the ones we even bothered to release anymore—were going down. Morale was down. The community was in an uproar."

There was also a very dangerous process of denial going on in the individual schools. "No one wanted to admit that we didn't know how to teach, really teach, at all well, this new population," says Wells, emphasizing the teachers in Spring Branch were used to a wealthy clientele with sophisticated parents.

The new trustees finally realized the schools were in trouble and that it was probably going to take someone from the outside to even begin to turn them around. In 1986, after all the "rascals," as Bob Wells identifies them, were swept out, the trustees launched a national search for someone to help Spring Branch regain status as a premier school district.

"And along came Hal Guthrie," says Wells, his face slowly lighting with a knowing smile. "And my hunch is, when the school board chose Hal Guthrie, they didn't know what they were really getting."

Hal Guthrie, Ed.D., a man of robust, determined stature who never seems to have a pipe out of reach, laughs easily when he's told this. "Oh, they knew all right," he says, his eyes teasing a wink. "I told them if they chose me they were choosing the Effective Schools Process. In great detail I explained Effective Schools, and that we were going to be an Effective Schools system."

Wells agrees with the presentation of facts. "Oh sure, it's very clear to me why a board that is not familiar with the research would still find the Effective Schools jargon very attractive," says Wells. "Knowing Hal now, I can hear the way he answered those questions. You know, safe environment, instructional leadership, focus on mission, monitoring, teach for learning for all. I think they hired him saying, 'He will turn the district around.'

"And lo and behold, he has done exactly what they hired him to do. But it's thrown them into some philosophical quandaries because I think politically they're having a tough time supporting what is really the driving belief system of the way in which the district was turned around. But you can't argue with the results."

Wells is not the only person who believes the board did not have a full understanding of what the true implications would be when Guthrie implemented the Effective Schools Process. And Spring Branch is not the only board that has accepted the Effective Schools Process and then, when the tough changes started to take place, started asking, "Wait a minute. Is that what this is really all about?" The saving grace is the powerful fact that superintendents are able to back up their actions with research and data indicative of success.

However, the Spring Branch board is still having a few rough times and Guthrie is fighting several battles. As recently as the fall of 1991 there was an uproar when the premier high school took the step of making some advanced classes not quite so exclusively white. Many in Spring Branch were surprised at the degree of heat in the argument, thinking the school system had gotten beyond the hurdle of tracking. Hal Guthrie was not.

"There is always going to be that irrational element out there," says Guthrie. "And that's what it is, it's just not rational because we can prove to these people that their fears are wrong, just plain wrong. They are founded on myth. But you've got to deal with it because until there's true equity in this country, tracking will be a very hot political issue."

While Spring Branch has made some adjustments, setting up a special committee to examine the literature and its impact, Guthrie will not back down. He stands before the parents and the board and takes everything they throw at him. And he talks about research, facts, and experience. What brings his opponents up short every time is the simple record of the school district. Spring Branch has brought its students up beyond the national average, with particularly impressive scores at the elementary level. The downspin has been halted; the rise has begun. But just as important as that rise in scores is the renewal of energy and commitment in Spring Branch. That renewal is ongoing because of a superintendent who stands firmly behind his mission, not allowing the politics, agendas, biases, or fears of others rock him from his position.

Today, one of those schools on the north side that had been abandoned by the district—Hollibrook Elementary (profiled in Chapter 2)—is being touted as one of the most progressive and successful multicultural schools in the nation.

"It is no mistake that we chose Hal Guthrie when we did," says Judy Perkins, a member of the board in Spring Branch. "We knew we needed change. I think Hal saw it a lot more clearly than we did. He convinced the board that we had to take a strong stand for Effective Schools. That stand meant teaching for learning for all, with teachers and parents involved. It was the first time we had been presented with something like this. It was different, and tough. And that's what we needed."

She says that one of the biggest changes she has seen is in the difference in involvement, not just from teachers and parents but from principals. "We just never saw principals as instructional leaders before. In the past they could always look to the central administration building for decisions. Take it upstairs. They didn't have to do it themselves. They were pawns, middle-management pawns. Well, they had to do some relearning. That training has made all the difference. They are finally accountable and that is real change."

What is setting Spring Branch apart and ahead of other school districts is its intense commitment to school-based management and the restructuring that entails. The system is viewed as almost ahead of its time as it lays the foundation work for other effective districts around the country. But it all began, and continues, with the Effective Schools Process and its moral impertive that is its heart. It is around the fire of the Effective Schools Improvement Process that Hal Guthrie has stoked his career.

Guthrie came to Spring Branch from Cedar Rapids, Iowa. He began his education career as a teacher and then as a principal. After receiving his doctorate, he became a professor at Temple University in Philadelphia where he specialized in the study and teaching of organizational behavior. But the college atmosphere did not connect with Guthrie's personality and ambitions. He wanted to take the lessons of organizational behavior on the road. In 1974, he jumped for the chance to be superintendent of the 3,500-pupil school system in St. Mary's, Pennsylvania, a rural blue-collar community in the Appalachians.

He says he began immediately with thinking about administrative function in terms of results of students. At the time, this was a radical thought. Superintendents not only didn't get involved with messy details like outcomes but the educational wisdom at the time—still caught up in excuse making—was far from results oriented.

"It's just common sense," says Guthrie. "You have to look at results in order to maneuver the resources to get the kind of results that you want." He says it all goes back to the belief system that is commonly shared by the principal players of an organization that leads to the creation of a mission and the articulation of a vision. What Guthrie was talking about, and trying to get others to listen to, was the attitude that schools should operate like successful businesses, with a firm vision, a means to accomplish it, and then an examination of whether it was accomplished. Guthrie, sitting alone in the Appalachian Mountains, set up a team to investigate.

"We talked about the kind of outcomes we wanted to produce at the schools, how procedures needed to be changed, but always with a participatory process where you collected the wisdom and vision of those who work there and you guide and steer and encourage and motivate that towards some defined purpose," says Guthrie, adding it just "made sense" to pursue management from the strategic planning perspective.

That meant talking to the area's corporate leaders in the steel business and Mack Truck business, among others. The discussion was about the kind of graduates Guthrie was sending them, and, from Guthrie, the kind of opportunities business was offering for those graduates. After talking about needs and skills, Guthrie went back to the schools and talked about curriculum, goals, and requirements. After seeing where there was alignment and where there were things missing, Guthrie and his staff worked out a plan.

"To tell you the truth, we didn't know what to call it back then," admits Guthrie. "After looking at some high-tech books, we saw that we were doing strategic planning. We're looking at the future. We're writing a plan for the future. And we matched that plan with our objectives."

Those objectives were the attainment of results for *all* students. While Guthrie was plugging away with his strategic planning at the district level ("I'd talk to other superintendents around the country about this and they just weren't interested. They wanted nothing to do with external factors. Fools."), Ron Edmonds and Larry Lezotte were proving the vitality of the Effective Schools Process.

Guthrie began studying the Effective School literature and then started running some comparison programs through his computer. He and his staff looked at results—why a school wasn't succeeding—and then started to analyze why. Once he convinced the union that he wasn't looking to fire teachers, he was able to analyze performance data *on the basis of the strategies that were in place.*

"We were looking at our outcomes and managing our system on the basis of results. That's pretty radical. It's still radical across the country in terms of education," says Guthrie. "We're managing by results, we're working with a few instructional programs that deal with the area of expectation, we want to raise expectation. And all of a sudden, all of the things we're doing are, hey, wait, that's the Effective Schools Process. Here's the package that legitimizes everything we're doing."

Guthrie says that through the Effective Schools Process he was able to fully understand the process he was trying to crack—the process that would bring together strategic planning and all the correlates of the Effective Schools. After attending several conferences on Effective Schools, he found the research base and program that legitimized and supported many of the things he believed about how schools ought to be run and how kids ought to learn.

The problem (at least it was a problem for those defending the status quo) was that the knowledge base Guthrie was building went against much of what he had learned in his educational training—not just the discussion of outcomes, but equity *in* excellence, teaching *for* learning, and structure *following* purpose.

The tensions pulling at him have been described by Donald Schön in *The Reflective Practitioner* (1983):

> *The tensions inherent in the bureaucratization of professional work tend to amplify when professionals seek to become reflective practitioners. A practitioner who reflects-in-action tends to question the definition of his task, the theories-in-action that he brings to it, and the measures of performance by which it is controlled. And as he questions these things, he also questions elements of the organizational knowledge structure in which his functions are embedded.*

Guthrie was questioning not only the *how* but the *why* of his organization, and of public education itself. He began implementing his changes, and in one key area went off in a slightly different direction than prescribed by the practices of Larry Lezotte. Guthrie's experience told him to pursue strategic planning across the whole district. Larry Lezotte disagreed, saying instead that campus planning was where the real strength was. Lezotte believes that strategic planning is still "very much a man thing, right out of the military." He says that for many participants in a school improvement process, the strategic planning doesn't have quite the "passion" of campus planning.

"It's like a night on the town," says Lezotte. "It doesn't generate longstanding passion. It isn't alive. It's very difficult to get people to have a sense of ownership with it. It's without process, without passion. You have to get people to own the dream."

Guthrie disagrees and while he and Lezotte are ready to continue the argument, there are others who maintain there is nothing to argue about.

"Larry thinks that strategic planning leaves out the moral commitment to Effective Schools, and that's just not the way it is," according to Gary Mathews, Ph.D., associate superintendent in Spring Branch. "The essential part of our strategic planning process *is* the mission. Strategic planning insisted from the board level on down that teaching for *all* is what the process is all about."

Mathews, who was the principal of a highly successful Effective School in Jackson, Mississippi, and then an assistant superintendent in Jackson before joining Guthrie's staff, says that although strategic planning does deal with everything from business to buses to budget, its "linkage" to the schools is the Effective Schools Planning Process.

"The districtwide initiatives come out of the strategic planning," allows Mathews. "And the campus planning is a combination of the identified needs of the individual schools with the key improvement priorities set out by the strategic planning. So there is a natural meshing there. And yes, we all own the dream."

The Drive to Be Districtwide

The history of the Effective Schools Process gives some indication as to why individuals like Lezotte and Edmonds may have been skeptical of an across-the-board/across-the-district strategic planning process. The major indication was that it was so difficult to do. Why? Because there were, and still are, very few Hal Guthries around who are willing to risk change, to turn a school system on its head. And until recently, there was a lack of appropriate technical understanding and support. The majority of superintendents still operate in the political realm of the status quo. They are not interested in getting into a fight, or a challenge, over equity. Many believe they can continue to stumble along, getting fat on a patronage-driven system that denies opportunity to students, teachers and staff.

Given this reality, which was even more intense 20 years ago, Effective Schools tried to do an "end run" around the central office, counting on the instructional leadership of a principal to turn a school around and maintain it. This not only worked but, in the majority of school districts, it was the *only* way you could get equity and quality into a school. Superintendents who had ignored the schools in the past would continue to do so. The only time they were visible was when something good was being said about the school, and they were there to take the bows.

But now with what many are calling the "new breed of superintendents," the end run around the central office is no longer necessary. Individuals like Guthrie are proving that it not only can be done across the district but that it is much more powerful, faster, firmer, and cohesive if done with all schools. Tougher, yes, but better, as even the skeptics are prone to admit now.

But whatever ideological discrepancies Guthrie may have had with the initial conceptions of the Effective Schools Process his commitment to the rightness, the need, and the power of Effective Schools has never wavered. "Oh, believe me," he says, snapping his pipe in his palm. "There is no doubt this is the *only* program that's going to change—and save—this country's public schools."

After Guthrie went through the first few months of his first year in Spring Branch, he knew he needed more help at the administrative level. He called Larry Lezotte and asked for names of the best people in Effective Schools. Lezotte aimed him in the direction of Mathews in Mississippi. Mathews came on board in April 1987.

"As soon as I read about Effective Schools, I knew that if I ever got a school under me, I'd go for it," says Mathews. He did with the Callaway High School in Jackson, Mississippi. A school on the decline, Mathews soon had it doing its Effective School paces on the positive side of the school ledger.

"Other school improvement initiatives were just pieces. The Edmonds model brought together the whole picture. Teachers. Principal. Students. Climate. Instructional focus. That was the whole ball of wax."

Mathews is a major proponent of moving the schools from the industrial age to the information age. He believes that one of the reasons the Effective Schools Model flourishes today is because it addresses the changing needs of the population.

"Given the necessity of the information age world, where we have to produce a large society of literate individuals, Edmonds and company make clear that teaching and learning for *all* kids, regardless of the group from which they come, is an imperative," says Mathews. "The country can no longer afford to sort and select its school children, because our competitors in the information age simply would not find us competitive if, in fact, we insisted on the old, industrial age model of teaching and learning—that is, some can and some can't."

Admitting he is a great fan of statistics, Mathews points to the changing U.S. population as well as the changing needs. By the year 2000, the increase in Anglo *middle-class* children in America's public schools is estimated at 10,000. The increase in the number of *Hispanic, black, and disadvantaged* children is 3.5 million. Those numbers of minority and disadvantaged children are going to require services either at the beginning stage of their life or later in life, which will require much more expensive services because they will be dependent on the system. Mathews says that is one of the messages of the need for school improvement.

"One of the questions that anybody out there looking at school improvement is asking themselves is, 'Why bother? It's an uphill battle and what will I get for it?' Well, thank God that people like Hal Guthrie have a moral base, and also a realistic view." Mathews says that once you study the changing demographics and the accompanying needs, a just person is compelled to get on with teaching for learning for *all* children. If we don't, Mathews believes, in the areas of health, economy, of safety on the streets, the prospects for a better life for all Americans, middle class especially, are very dim.

"So what we must create is a motive. Why bother? Because we must and because it's right. It's for that reason that we need moral instructional leaders in the schools. We've got technicians out the kazoo. What we've got to have is moral leaders committed to teaching all the kids and to seeing that the results are produced for all children. We don't have a prayer otherwise."

While Guthrie and his team were busy infusing the motive into the Spring Branch board and the community, along with the Effective Schools Process, Guthrie was also dealing with the administrators in the schools. He had set out a detailed implementation process, with his office expounding on the vision and mission at every bend in the road. He wasn't going to allow people to forget for a moment what they were all about. Plaques were put up praising and explaining the Effective Schools Process. The walls of the administration building and the schools held the framed quotes of inspiration from Ron Edmonds. And on *every* communication from every administrator was a line about accomplishing the mission of teaching for learning for *all.* It was not just part of the vocabulary, but, like other growing effective districts, it was like a religion.

Guthrie was a realist, however. He knew he was going to have some problems that all the finest planning in the world could not erase. And his biggest problem at the start was strangely that no one quite grasped the problem. The district had been in denial for so long that it could not face the truth of what was happening around them.

"I got here and there were 10 schools north of the freeway that the scores were going down, down, down. The people in central office and at the schools said, 'What do you expect? These are poor people, minority people, with problems, etc., etc., etc.,'" recalls Guthrie. "So I said, 'Hey, we're going to take those schools and call them trouble schools and put extra resources in there and really start assessing the results. And we're going to turn those lousy results around.'

"People said, 'You can't do that. You can't point the finger at us. You can't take these schools out and identify them. You'll make us look bad.' I said, 'You *are* bad! So let's admit it and see what we're going to do about it.'"

Guthrie becomes a bit agitated as he remembers the negative atmosphere of many of the schools in Spring Branch when he began. He says there was no mission, no vision, no real desire to improve. It was almost as if, for some school employees, the Invasion of the Body Snatchers had occurred in Spring Branch. There was no feeling—no understanding that kids' lives were not just being damaged, they were being destroyed.

"There were principals where the only concern was really for the parents. They were afraid their parents were going to take over their schools if they didn't do exactly what the parents said. And bowing to the teachers? They bowed, but wouldn't share power. They thought if they delegated, they lost power. That's how backwards everyone was here," says Guthrie.

The other thing about many of the Spring Branch schools that infuriated him was that if they weren't functioning to satisfy the irrational requirements of some parents, they were functioning to keep the teachers happy and quiet. There was more concern given to whether or not a custodian was happy than if a child was learning.

"I couldn't believe it. But this was happening. This is what I saw when I started roaming these streets, examining these schools." (Observers of public education say this is one of reasons why superintendents never get out of their offices.) Guthrie had his contract by the time he fully realized the shape and attitude of Spring Branch. He went to the board and told them they were in for some major changes, that there had to be, and if there wasn't going to be change, "I told them there was no point in my being here."

So Guthrie set out across the district with three goals: communication, participation, and improvement.

"What you have to do when you change an organization like this that was so bogged down in its own denial, is that you have to change what people know and what they value," says Guthrie. "We had to show them that they must come to school with a new understanding. And that understanding is that *all* children can learn. Excuses are rampant in an ineffective organization," he recalls. "The toughest part was changing that excuse riddled thinking. And you have to be careful to change that thinking without telling them they're dead wrong—all the time."

Guthrie and Mathews began intensive training programs throughout the district, knowing that the improvement would either rise or fall on the merits of the staff. They tried to anticipate and provide every developmental need for teachers, principals, and staff. And they were careful not to close any doors. The courses in group process skills and leadership training were as open to teachers as they were administrators. Even secretaries and aides were encouraged to become involved in the learning dynamics of group decision making. Guthrie immediately sought and received funding for leadership training in order to better prepare his employees for school-based management. He was beginning a process of major change that held at its core the transforming of the public belief that all white middle- and upper-class children are brighter than all others.

Building True Empowerment

"Once you begin to expose people to the research, begin to enlighten and inspire them in the area of expectations, show them, prove to them, over and over again if necessary, the educability of *all* children, you can start a Texas wildfire," believes Guthrie. "You establish the mission, then you select and promote people on the basis of their commitment to teaching for learning for *all,* and then you *take the system's shackles away* and you begin to see real good things happen for all the kids."

But seminars, research, training dinners, speeches, good hiring, and pencils with mission statements emblazoned on them can all be for naught if there is not someone at the top who is a true leader—visible, verbal, and vital. Historically, as Bennis and Nanus (1985)* say, "Leaders have controlled, rather than organized, administered repression rather than expression, and held their followers in arrestment rather than evolution." This is the behavior of superintendents tied to the old ways. This is just the opposite of the Effective Schools superintendent.

Hal Guthrie knew from the beginning he was going to have to restructure the Spring Branch school system not only in order to bring it into the twenty-first century but to make it an equitable, quality system. His first acts were to organize people into new roles and responsibilities, providing them with the knowledge to accomplish their tasks. He then opened his doors and said, "Talk to me. What's going on around here? How do we change?" He gave people a chance to learn and grow. But what everyone who worked with him during the beginning stages of the Effective Schools Process keeps coming back to is the fact that they knew exactly what Guthrie was trying to do and *going* to do.

"We all knew what his vision was," remembers Wells. "He let us know that over and over. And he was only interested in people who were committed to it, or willing to learn. He talked about how that vision was going to change the Spring Branch schools. How people believing in that vision were going to change the schools."

This is what Bennis and Nanus (1985) refer to as "transformative leadership—the capacity to translate intention into reality and sustain it." Guthrie presented his vision, backed it up with research and experience, then began what was a very precise process of carrying out that vision. Experts who have watched Spring Branch note that Guthrie and his team have always been one step ahead of everyone else in their planning and execution. He is restructuring the entire school system and the way it operates, not so much by pushing people but by pulling them.

You see this in a meeting with his central office and the principals of the schools. He has their total attention as he goes through the latest statistics and plans. There is a free-wheeling comraderie. He jokes with some and some joke back. He knows each one and the details of their school or task. He raises

*Excerpts from *Leaders: The Strategies for Taking Charge* by Warren Bennis and Burt Nanus. Copyright © 1985 by Warren Bennis and Burt Nanus. Reprinted by permission of HarperCollins Publishers.

and lowers his voice easily as he speaks with passion about what Spring Branch is doing. He is very proud of the accomplishments. He trusts his people. He knows they trust him.

"They wouldn't work so hard, be so committed, if they didn't trust me and what we're trying to do," says Guthrie, adding a phrase that business experts say is one of the keys to a leader's success. "They know what to expect from me. There are no surprises." This is what many call "trust through predictability." You understand a leader's vision, the goals, and how those will be accomplished. You know your own task, so you therefore know what is expected of you.

One of Guthrie's often cited leadership skills is his hiring of principals. People watched with gaping mouths as he bounced principals that first year and put untested principals into troubled but pivotal schools. "It was the action itself that shocked you," says Wells. "Not so much the person. Because you knew what Hal was after, what he wanted, and you also knew these people. And they were the best for those slots."

Suzanne Still was one of those principals. She was brought into the Hollibrook Elementary from a *high school* administrative team ("People thought he had lost his head," recalls Still, "including the faculty."). Linda Watkins was another one of those principals. She was first pulled into Landrum Junior High, then after getting that school on course, Guthrie grabbed her for Northbrook High. He had done a national search looking for the right person, but he kept coming back to Watkins. He knew she didn't want to leave Landrum.

"He's really so predictable," says Watkins. "He talks about the schools, his vision for the schools, how we are attaining it, then your role, and how this is just your *duty* to take on this challenge. Your *duty!*" And this predictable call to duty seems to work. His principals say it has a great deal to do with the trust they have in the man and the trust he has expressed in them. That very first year, he let the principals know he would give them all the tools to fulfill what was going to be *their* responsibility.

"Right off the bat I told them, 'These schools are going to be all yours.' I told them to go out and identify some teachers, parents, people in the attendance area, and together, write down the things that they would like to do at the school to make it a better place for all kids, the things they think the school needs to be effective."

He then met with the principals, went over every plan, every nuance of the plan, then supplied the resources, to the extent they were reasonable and accessible, and then after a few suggestions and a pep talk, sent them on their way.

"We're about campus planning. They know my vision. They know the mission statement of this district. And they've now been trained. They know what they're supposed to do. So I said go and do it. And I keep saying that. I don't care how you do it, but you and that faculty do it!"

And his schools are trying to do it. Each of them varies in its approach. One may have one planning team, another may have three. One may be trying one instructional approach, another a different one. One school's discipline code may be entirely different from another. The only requirement is that the schools live within the correlates of the Effective Schools Process, and that the schools follow the district mission statement of teaching for learning for *all.*

Guthrie combined the campus planning with strategic planning at the community and district levels. There were three distinct areas: the mission statement, long-range goals, and key priorities (the specific things that must be done the next year). Spring Branch finds itself way ahead of other districts in Texas that are now scrambling to comply with a new state law requiring district plans for school-based management in 1992.

But while Spring Branch moves along, it is ever mindful of that problem that stalks the process as fiercely as the enemy of cultural ignorance: time—time to teach and time to plan thoughtfully. "One of the toughest areas is providing time for school improvement," comments Mathews. "Maybe another way of putting it is providing the energy for school improvement. The two are interrelated; energy is a product or byproduct of the time one has." Mathews explains that the issue of time is something Spring Branch has grappled with in numerous meetings with the board. He says it is often difficult to explain to people outside of education the need for time for renewal.

"I find it real interesting in a profession that ought to be among the most reflective in the world, it is often one of the least reflective," says Mathews, adding that one of the reasons for that is the lack of time. "So unless we begin to institutionalize time, when we're not with the kids, we're never going to get it. Without time to reflect, it's virtually impossible to do school improvement. It's like (Larry) Lezotte says, 'We built the American public school without the back porch on it for discourse to take place.'"

But somehow time continues to be found. As the board sees the success that simple allocation of time for planning helps foster, they are becoming less argumentative. The board and the school district have made substantial progress. People remember what it was like those first few years when campus teams were being set up, power was truly being delegated, and morale was once again discovered and even starting to build.

"The winds of change were whistling through here at a good clip," explains Bob Wells. "The dead wood was rolling out fast. People liked Guthrie's choices of principals (even though only 6 of the 33 original principals were still in place); they were leaders. And to the credit of a lot of staff here, they were ready for the wind to change. Nobody wants to work in a district that's declining. To have somebody walk in the door and say, 'We're going to turn this around and this is now,' that in itself is mobilizing. That's what Guthrie did, and now we're seeing the results we wanted."

And back then, just like today, although to a lesser extent, the question uppermost in the minds of the conservative politicians in power was: "But what is going to happen to all our bright kids, the gifted and talented kids, while the school system is spending time on the kids at the lower end of the curve?"

It was in dealing with this fundamental question that coalesced Guthrie's leadership skills. He knew he had to have principals who were devoted to *all* children learning, who wouldn't compromise on that, but who would also be patient and tolerant of other views until Spring Branch's results were in.

"While we were trying to raise all the boats, we had to make sure some of those boats weren't leaking," says Gary Mathews. "And we've been able to prove that to our parents. The kids that were on the top are still on the top. For the last two years, we've been able to show that all the kids are holding their own."

Mathews explains that prior to implementation of the Effective Schools Process, for the four previous school years, the Spring Branch District witnessed declining state skills scores at just about every level. They have now stopped that decline, are holding in many schools, and in many others, in particular at the elementary level, are showing marked, impressive increases.

"Because of these scores, we've been able to sell what we're doing," says Mathews. "More than once I've ended up head to head with a parent or board member who says, 'I may not like what you're doing, but I can't argue against the results you're getting.' So, yes, we're data driven. We love to pull out our data!"

Those data, the successes of the schools under Guthrie's leadership, precipitated another change that no one would have ever predicted. The same population that voted no faith in the schools in the mid-eighties went back to the voting booth in 1990 and approved (80 percent) a $60-million bond issue for the schools. It was confirmation that the denial had stopped. The community had recognized that the change going on was good and that they had to prepare for more changes coming in with the increased population.

Guthrie was a key player in the passing of the bond issue, as were his principals and teachers. They were all out on the stump, talking to anyone who would listen. Guthrie didn't require anyone to do this; he didn't even have to ask. They saw him out there night after night, and they followed his lead. At the bottom of the devotion is the belief that Guthrie is simply doing the right thing for students and staff, and that he is also going about accomplishing it the right way.

The major structural changes now being put into place are a result of the data gathered by the individual schools. The data, after being organized and assessed by central administrtion, are funneled right back into the individual schools where they are used as the basis for ongoing changes.

"Once the Campus Improvement Teams have looked at the data about who their kids are and what the data say about their learning, once they've looked at the research and affirmed their teaching and learning for all, they come to the central office and tell us," explains Mathews. "Then they tell us what they need from us in order to continue improving. And we serve them."

In the majority of school districts, the notion of the central administration working for the schools is still foreign. But at Spring Branch it is just the beginning of the intensive overhaul of the structuring of the school district.

"The restructuring process finds out where the needs are," says Wells. "There are no students taught here at the central office. They're out there, with the teachers. And we have to keep giving the teachers the tools they need to do the best job."

The budget for Spring Branch Independent Schools District is currently $100 million. The staff development budget is only 2 percent. While private industry spends between 7 and 10 percent of their budgets on development of employees, the average for school districts is usually less than 1 percent. Spring Branch comes in high on the staff-development budget scale.

"Is 2 percent enough? I'm not sure any amount could be labeled as enough," says Bob Wells, whose office handles the staff development. "If my budget were doubled, then I'd be able to extend teacher contracts, pay teachers for the whole day. . . ." Does he think the teachers would be willing to go along with that? "No doubt about it. I guess something that bothers me seriously about our current efforts is that we have so many teachers doing so much for gratis already."

Guthrie recognizes and accepts how hard his teachers and staff are working. He says the schools are daily picking up more and more speed, to the extent that he decided to put in place a day-to-day mechanism by which school improvement could be monitored and adjusted. "In the fall of 1990 we started the Campus Leadership Teams. This is a body of five or six teachers, more often than not members of the larger Campus Improvement Team. This CLT has an additional planning period, either for their own classes or for school planning and monitoring. These groups, run by the principal, are the day-to-day operators of the school. They get to focus on a daily basis, monitor and adjust and then go back to report to their colleagues or central office."

Spring Branch believes the instructional leadership of schools and classrooms deserves unique, special attention, and therefore has set up its own leadership academy to handle the individuals at both the campus and district levels.

"If we're going to be serious about this, if we want to make campus leadership a reality, we have to have it in the classrooms, just as much as in central offices as in the principals' offices," says Mathews. "We believe very strongly in that moral commitment. Campus-based improvement has to be data driven, research based, and attached to a higher moral philosophy."

Mathews, who has consulted for the Effective Schools Process in 40 states and in Canada, says that he has discovered six essential elements of the school improvement, under the Effective Schools Process, in Spring Branch.

"First, understand that all people want to succeed, whether its staff, teachers, or kids. Second, know that schools must be for teaching for learning for all. Third, get it into you: *All* kids can learn. Four, realize that teachers cause learning, and that at times is good news and bad news. Five, judge your success on whether or not kids learn. No other criteria. And six, change must be seen as a process, not an event."

He adds that a lot of what he is saying is common sense. "Sure everyone wants to improve, but it's knowing *how* that really separates the winners from the losers."

Each year as Spring Branch pushes its knowledge of *how* in restructuring, the power becomes more decentralized, and more and more people feel a stronger sense of ownership in their schools and their work. This ownership, Guthrie believes, is the real power of the school improvement process. "People are committed, really committed, and they're seeing where that commitment is getting them, and the schools. We have the data behind us now, and we're really catching fire," says Guthrie, smiling as he lights his pipe. "Success, dear sweet success, there's nothing like success to motivate and encourage, to get people involved."

And Guthrie believes, with a passion that fuels him, that if change is not undertaken *now* in the public schools, then the country will be left far behind. "To say nothing of the thousands, no, millions of kids who will be lost," says Guthrie. "If we have to hit bottom before the schools really start to change, you just might have to kiss this country goodbye. Because by then it will be too late, and we'll have to abandon the public schools.

"What is still so disheartening to me is when I go to these superintendent conferences and someone mentions the progress that Spring Branch has made. And no sooner than progress or success is mentioned than all the other guys start with, 'Well, you don't have the poverty, you don't have the deprivation, the crime and drugs like I have, and the teachers union. . . . And I say, Hey, wake up! I've got the poverty and deprivation and crack houses and unions. But what I don't have is excuses. What we will not accept in Spring Branch or anyplace I'm superintendent are excuses why these children cannot and are not learning. Because it has been shown, in Spring Branch and elsewhere, that the excuses are just excuses.'"

Guthrie maintains the bottom line is will. "It's a matter of will. That's the biggest problem I see with American public schools not accepting and working with the Effective Schools Process. Superintendents, principals who are just unwilling," he says, banging out his pipe. "They just plain flat out don't have the will to change and restructure the organization and create this vision and mission statement. They've *got* the resources. They're *too* comfortable. It isn't a matter of resources or money in creating Effective Schools. It's a matter of will."

Superintendents as Business Athletes

When the public reads about leaders in business, they read about a variety of significant people with awesome responsibilities. But some would argue that it is a superintendent of schools who has the most awesome, most important responsibility of all. It is he or she who determines the future of thousands of schoolchildren. Perhaps in the past superintendents have been ignored because, except for middle- and upper-class districts with ready cash and more involved, trouble-free (for the most part) parents, superintendents were a sorry lot. They were political appointees more interested in the maintenance of mediocrity and the status quo. Unfortunately, that is still true in numerous large and small districts.

But it is *not* true in many others. There are some superintendents in this country who are extraordinary, visionary leaders who are helping to make the American dream come true for millions of students. Among them is Hal Guthrie, Noel Farmer of Frederick County (Maryland), Tony Amato of District 6 (Spanish Harlem) in New York, Max Heim of Geary County, Kansas, Joe Clement of Spencerport, New York, Robert Fortenberry of Jackson, Mississippi (formerly), and several others. These are all individuals who fit the description of the "business athlete of the nineties," as described by Rosabeth Moss Kanter in her book *When Giants Learn to Dance* (1989), an examination of America's changing strategies for success. She describes this new business hero as one who eschews the "excesses of the corpocrat and the cowboy," and hangs tight to the "four F's: Focused, Fast, Friendly, and Flexible."

Kanter explains that there are seven skills or "sensibilities" that she believes must be cultivated in order that managers become "true business athletes." It is an interesting and helpful exercise to look at the leadership style and actions of Hal Guthrie (although many of the effective superintendents could also be used as an example) in relation to these seven skills. Business leaders must do the following:

1. *Learn to operate without the might of the hierarchy.* Guthrie took the hierarchy of the superintendent's office and tossed it. He did not, from the very beginning, depend on rules and regulations, but instead relied on his own vision and his own personality. He didn't listen to the dictates of the board; instead, he led and learned with them. He didn't listen to the town managers; he told them what was going to happen. He did not tout the test scores of high-achieving schools because he dismissed them as wrong. In serving just one end of the curve, the district had denied all others. And whether they wanted to accept it or not, the very thing they were proud of—those scores in the white, wealthy neighborhood schools—were the things that needed serious change. In particular, it was the attitude that created them that needed change. That

attitude that said, "I am better than you, I deserve more." So, Guthrie tossed out the hierarchy—the structural, power hierarchy, as well as the attitudinal, behavioral hierarchy.

2. *Know how to compete in a way that enhances rather than undercuts cooperation.* Guthrie started working with other experts and practitioners in school improvement as soon as he began his process. He brought in anyone who could help him and his staff. He didn't get into a race with the next district. He just wanted to do the best job he could for his students. And he didn't compete with those who knew more than he did. He knew that the expertise of teachers was in the classroom, that they knew better how to improve their teaching. He gave them and their principals complete autonomy, after laying down the guidelines. He did what he did best, and let others do what they do best. He worked with anyone, from grounds crews to business leaders, who would help him realize his vision.

3. *Operate with the highest ethical standards.* Everyone in Spring Branch knows how Hal Guthrie operates. It is in his mission statement, written on his stationery, and some say they can even see it across his forehead. There is no guessing as to where Hal Guthrie is coming from. He is predictable. He does not ask anyone to do that which he does not do. He is a model—always ready to be in a school, to listen, to take action. He trusts people and is trusted in return, commanding an intense commitment from secretaries to principals. He is honest, admitting to the mistakes right along with the wiser decisions. But he doesn't believe in standards; he believes in expectations. Expectations have no bounds.

4. *Have a dose of humility.* Despite his bravado, Guthrie admits to much he does not know (that's why he leaves school decisions to those inside the schools). He is a voracious learner, actively pursuing new and better ways of accomplishing the teaching for learning for *all.* And, according to those who work with him, he can and does admit his mistakes.

5. *Develop a process focus, a respect for the process of implementation as well as substance of what is implemented.* The success of the Effective School Improvement Process in Spring Branch is due to the care and attention that went into its implementation. For months (and even today) every facet of the operation was analyzed and involved. Throughout every step, detailed communication was made with all parties. Precise guidelines were set forth and adhered to. Close attention was paid to all staff development. All parties were kept informed of progress as well as pitfalls. He emphasized that it would not be done overnight and that this was a process that would never end. The implementation process, which has been the model for numerous other Effective districts, kept at its heart a respect for everyone—students, teachers, and staff.

6. *Be multifaceted and ambidextrous; be able to work across functions.* Guthrie is a team player. From his first report to the board of trustees, it was clear to observers that Guthrie was putting together a team that would ride Spring

Branch to success. That team has extended into the schools and into the community. Guthrie works with teams on strategy, school planning, instruction, curriculum, discipline, and technique. He reaches far and wide to pull in business, academia, social institutions, politicians—anyone who will be part of his team. In return, he gives his services to other teams, in other school districts, in business, and in social institutions. His knowledge, his responsibility, grows daily.

7. *Gain satisfaction from results and be willing to stake their own rewards on them.* It was Guthrie who, at the beginning of this chapter and at the beginning of his career as a school superintendent, said, "You have to look at results in order to maneuver the resources to get the kind of results that you want. We were looking at our outcomes and managing our system on the basis of results. That's pretty radical. It's still radical across the country in terms of education." He began the outcome cycle then and today he stakes his name and career on the outcomes he is achieving and trying to achieve for the students of Spring Branch.

All this is not to say that Hal Guthrie and superintendents like him do not have their detractors. As Guthrie and other Effective superintendents attest to, they are very often disliked and ridiculed by their colleagues. Many don't like what the Guthries of education do: They rock the boat; they change the status quo. Guthrie is a threat to the "old ways." There are people in Spring Branch who obviously are not pleased with Guthrie. Some say he springs too fast; his decisions and placements are often too risky. There are mistakes. But Guthrie says he has to take risks, that this is what it is all about, that he often does not have the luxury of months of analysis before acting.

The bottom line, of course, is that those who see the schools improving, who feel the empowerment and ownership within the schools, insist that the bravest thing, the most important thing, that Hal Guthrie did was bring the Effective Schools Process to Spring Branch. And now the only fear is that if Hal Guthrie leaves (he has been sought by larger, troubled districts looking for help), the work of Effective Schools will unravel as the district slips back into the dreams of the images of 1967. Of course, 1967 is gone forever. Spring Branch's only hope is facing the future through the Effective Schools Process.

"We don't even like to have mentioned the thought of Hal Guthrie leaving," says board member Judy Perkins. "But if we ever had to replace him, I'm sure we would insist upon someone who was strong in Effective Schools. We know the difference. The parents want Effective Schools. We have a commitment here,and that commitment comes from Hal Guthrie's vision."

Gary Mathews remembers an event that he believes is indicative of the determination of Guthrie. It was during Guthrie's acceptance speech as Texas Superintendent of the Year. He was elected not only by representatives of the school boards but by administrators across the state. "Throughout his acceptance speech, he repeatedly made it clear that the very reason we work towards

Effective Schools, towards collaborative decision making, is so we can successfully teach all children. He kept saying that's what it all boils down to: successfully teaching *all* kids. That's a powerful communication for a superintendent to give to his peers."

What makes it so extraordinary may not be that Guthrie was saying it but that a superintendent was *finally* saying it. And he was saying it, no doubt, to many superintendents who had implemented the Effective Schools Process and *then* realized that *all* children can learn.

Today, Hal Guthrie is leading the way for many other superintendents and for the people in Spring Branch. His critics are still trying to kick him down, but he now has his growing supply of results. He says each day he is monitoring, adjusting, keeping up with the changing forces around him. His team remains strong and committed. The vision is never out of sight, never out of reach.

As examined in Chapter 3, and as related in this chapter and the next, Effective School leaders are taking many of their cues from the strategies and actions of successful businesses. Indeed, in Hal Guthrie's case, it was his affinity toward the evolving business and management arena—in particular its emphasis on accountability and teamwork—that was one of the major reasons the Spring Branch board hired him and continues to support him so strongly.

Guthrie and other superintendents are now on education's firing line. They are being held accountable for the educational growth and the safe, mature development of the nation's schoolchildren. As they continue to refine their art and their leadership skills—motivated by their commitment to learning for all—it may now be time for business leaders to look back to the schools to renew and revitalize their own visions.

CHAPTER FIVE

Leaders Who Took the Dare

It's not the same to talk of bulls, as to be in the bullring. —SPANISH PROVERB

It is the business of the future to be dangerous. —ALFRED NORTH WHITEHEAD

"They thought I was a nut case. I was the joke of the city. Honestly. They thought I'd be out of a job by the end of the first day of school."

Tony Amato, superintendent of District 6, Spanish Harlem, on the upper west side of New York, believes the community and city school officials were justified in thinking he'd be run out of town by his own school buses. After all, he admits, he was making major changes that could permanently alter this school district of 23,000 students (90 percent on free lunch) that sat at the very bottom of New York's district achievement ladder. Spanish Harlem ranked 32nd out of 32 districts.

Tony Amato was also making promises he didn't know if he could keep, but he was going to try. He would give it his best shot. He had to. It was the only chance this school district had. He had to take the risk—not for himself, but for the kids.

Before New Yorkers wrote off Tony Amato, they should have looked at where he had come from. Then they would have known his best shot was pretty good. And he just might make lowly District 6 the most successful district in New York City.

In 1982, he was appointed principal of a public school in the Ocean Hill, Brownsville section of New York. "And I'm talking about the poorer section of Ocean Hill. I kid you not," says Amato, a short, muscular individual. "I'm talking about neighborhoods of crack dens, blocks totally empty except for charred building remains. And I'm talking about my kids walking in that building and turning and looking across the street to an empty lot that was their school front yard and had been an illegal dump site for not only garbage but chemical waste. Chemical waste." His dark eyes grow darker and he clenches his fists. "A gift from other communities with chemical plants to the children of Ocean Hill. I mean, who the hell cares about further contaminating the minds and bodies of the kids of Ocean Hill? It's just Ocean Hill, after all. Dumped basically on the school's front lawn. On a little one-way street. The kids coming and going walked through chemical waste." Amato shakes his head and sets his jaw.

"I told them I'm going to make that infested pit a garden!"

And he did. With the help of faculty and children, the community created a farm out of the chemical waste site. It was not only a learning experience but the school and community takes a thousand pounds of produce out of the site each year.

What about inside the school? The results there were just as dramatic. Inside, learning bloomed. The scores had been among the lowest in the city. Reading averaged at the 22nd percentile. Six years later, it was at the 63rd percentile and still climbing.

"So one day the Chancellor comes by and sees all we've done in Ocean Hill," recalls Amato. "Then three days later he calls, says he's been looking for my type, and says, 'OK, Tony, you ready to rock and roll?' I say, 'Fine, I have nothing to do this week.'" That was on March 23, 1987, and the following months saw the suspension of not only the present superintendent of District 6 but his administration *and* the school board. Amato walked into one of the most politically, socially, and educationally chaotic districts in New York.

"First of all, I told the people of this district *we're* going to do it. *We're* going to make this happen because we *have* to make it happen because these are our children and if our children are not taught, we are all losers. If these were your children, what would you personally want for them? Are you going to just write them off and relegate them to a life of failure or are we going to do something about this?"

That's when Amato started making his promises.

"I told the teachers and staffs, 'You do this for the kids and I'm going to take the classroom size down from 40 kids to 28. I guarantee you that. And I'm going to give you all the materials you need. I don't care how I get them, but I'll get them into your hands. And three—I'm going to give you the training to teach these kids the very best you can.'"

This is where Amato didn't know if he could succeed. In fact, he knew that the odds were against him—that, perhaps, he was a "nut case." But he also knew he had to try—not for him, he insists, but for the kids. However, parents were livid at the thought of their kids traveling out of the district. "I had to guarantee them the same degree of top-notch education wherever they went," says Amato, adding that there wasn't even "a shovel in the ground" for a new school building in Spanish Harlem despite the fact it was the most crowded district in the city. "So, I pulled strings, used every favor I had out there, to get kids into good schools." (District 6 now has the most construction going on of any district in the city.)

The problem of pulling in supplies was a little easier because, according to Amato, District 6 did receive a lot of services and money that "just weren't being appropriately given out to kids." Fighting the internal politics and making a few more enemies in central administration, he rearranged the money and services. He admits it is not judicious for him to say publicly exactly what he did and how he did it. "Let's just say that with a little soft shoe we got everything in line for 23,000 kids and their teachers."

On the first day of school, there were demonstrations and a few near riots, but inside the classrooms, there was a stunned response that bordered on celebration.

"I had basically told the teachers, 'I'll give you these gifts, will you give me your commitment to the students?'" explains Amato. "And when we opened in September, they had 25 kids in class, all their books, and supplies. And training and time off for more training, with pay, coming up. They'd never seen anything like that in District 6."

Amato also started something else that very first day of school. His "Golden Hour" or "Power Hour." Each day, every school starts off with an hour and fifteen minutes of reading—nothing but reading. Everyone in the building participates. There can be no interruptions, not even by loud speaker, not even a parent. This is guaranteed reading time: Power time.

"I had to create a mission for my schools. I wanted them to see where we were all going. This was the beginning." If this was the beginning for the teachers and their mission, where did the mission begin for Amato? Where did the Effective Schools Process make its entrance for Tony Amato?

"I had most of the elements working in my head, and I was constantly talking to my administrators about climate and expectations and all. But we didn't have it all together," states Amato, saying he felt like they were living out a Pirandello play. "We were seven characters in search of an author."

That "author" came along in the form of the Effective Schools Process. After attending seminars and workshops, Amato and his people decided Effective Schools was the vehicle for change for District 6. But it wouldn't be that easy to get Larry Lezotte, the senior consultant for Effective Schools, involved in the notorious New York School System.

"Edmonds (Ron Edmonds, one of the founders of the Effective Schools movement, who became senior assistant for Instruction in the New York Public Schools in 1977 in order to implement the first large Effective Schools demonstration project in 17 schools in Manhattan) had alerted me years earlier that there's no place as cut throat, as difficult, as prone to failure as New York City," remembers Lezotte. "So I went in there with my antenna up and watching over my shoulder."

It was the fall of 1987 and after the shaky start, Amato had District 6 operating fairly smoothly, although he knew it needed a major overhaul and that was why he was looking to Lezotte. But Lezotte was hesitant.

"Understand, I didn't know Tony. I didn't know what Tony's agenda was all about," says Lezotte. "With the board and superintendent before him fired, he was in a very precarious situation. I didn't know if his agenda was school improvement or to shore up his own station. And I didn't want to be used for political legitimization."

According to Amato, there was another factor. "Larry doesn't like to fail, and he wasn't going to take us on if he thought we would fail."

What Lezotte learned was that Amato wasn't about to fail either. "I realized that Tony was authentic about wanting to help kids and improve education," says Lezotte. "I saw him going through and taking all this flak that he could have avoided politically if he backed down on his commitment to all kids learning. But he didn't back down. I became convinced he wanted all kids learning, all teachers teaching. This was not a situation that was preordained to failure."

But it was preordained to a showdown with the eminently powerful teachers' union. There were several meetings where Amato says he could hear the knees of his assistants knocking. He was, after all, going for unprecedented changes in the operation and accountability of this district's public schools. The question of in-service training had ignited a major fuse of the union and Amato was facing a boycott because, according to the union, he had not sought their concurrence. Lezotte had a meeting with the union's chapter chairs, minus any representation from the administration. It was a meeting where all of Effective Schools was up for grabs and Lezotte played a tough, very risky card.

"Oh, I still tremble when I think of how scary that meeting was," says Lezotte. "I told them that from my point of view, if they truly thought Tony had violated the canons of the culture to such an extent that it was going to cause problems for school reform, then they wouldn't have to boycott. That I was sensitive to the needs of teachers as well as administrators. And I would go and tell Amato that I wouldn't be involved."

Lezotte admits he broke out into "big bubbles of sweat," but believes, to this day, it was the right card to play. "I was hoping to God they wouldn't say cancel it. We had done so much work. Tony had gone down the path. Worked so hard."

The gamble paid off. The union came back and told Lezotte they did not want to go on record as opposing this effort to launch school reform. So the union gave the Effective Schools Process their benign endorsement and Tony and District 6 were off.

The most important lesson to impart from Amato's point of view was that everyone in the system mattered, and everyone's opinion and hard work mattered. Then, he put his money where his mouth was and started giving teachers and staff the necessary time, training, and resources to plan the changes for a comprehensive, effective, school-based management system.

Helen Santiago, a former teacher who is now the executive assistant to

Amato, says that right from the beginning there was heavy emphasis on the "teaming aspect": "The first year that Tony was here, he did something that I don't think any other superintendent in New York had done. He took out his entire district level staff for two days worth of team training and team building. We're talking about 25 coordinators, 25 pedagogues. And that continues."

One of the most difficult areas to change was the bureaucratic process that was stifling even the thought of reform in District 6. Rules and regulations sidetracked and bogged down any attempts at change at both the district level and school level. And on top of that was the lack of any group process skills.

"We had to change the paradigm of how we all met and dealt with each other," explains Amato. "When I now look back at the archaic ways we interacted, I say, 'You jerk, how could you have been that way?' But I've evolved. I've learned to delegate responsibility. I don't have to be at the center of the table with 49 other people sitting there passively going uh-hum, uh-hum, uh-hum. Now our meetings flow. And we've pulled the philosophy of Effective Schools into everything we do."

Amato says that one of the "hardest nuts to crack" was the way principals interacted with their staffs and with each other. "In terms of their mindset, 90 percent of the principal conferences deal with instructional issues. Before, if you had 1 percent dealing with instructional issues; it was a revelation."

Amato has been careful in his appointments, especially at the principal level, to place people in schools who are very familiar with instruction and curriculum. There is also now a common language and an understanding of the data that are driving District 6. "It's no longer 50 different systems and 50 different areas and no end receiver," says Amato. "We started speaking the same language, writing it, acting it. And slowly, people started to feel good about what they were doing. Real good. Attitude problems get crunched away when success is out there breeding. And we've had so many kids ringing those bells of success."

That success, according to Santiago, comes mainly from the change in attitude at the district level. What is happening at the central office is considered revolutionary in New York's school hierarchy. "We've reexamined our role and responsibility. Rather than just work with people, we now also work *for* people," says Santiago. "Many district offices out there think the schools work for them. But not here. We work for the schools. We work for the people in the schools. And the schools work for the kids."

Changing the Status Quo

That first year there was the lessening of overcrowding, the presence of necessary books and supplies, the in-service of teachers and staff, the "Golden Hour," the work on the curriculum, the push for high expectations, the calming of the climate, the firming of discipline procedures, the growth of school autonomy, the enhancement of relations with parents and the home, the renewed emphasis on the quality of instruction, the incessant communication of the mission, and the visible presence of a superintendent who was continuing to deliver. Amato was in principals' offices, classrooms, the apartments of parents, social service agencies, the central office, meetings with the faculties, and more.

Leonard Clarke, Ph.D., deputy superintendent of District 6 came to Spanish Harlem after 26 years in the New York Public School System, the majority of them in central administration. "When you talk about establishing a vision and creating goals and objectives that are workable and doable, and re-creating and revising the curriculum in key content areas, it is obvious that where District 6 is heading is where a school district needs to go if you are going to in any way increase the instructional level and the learning achievement of students," says Clarke.

The instructional level and learning achievement was in serious need of help. Only half—55 percent—of the children were reading on grade level. "Things were so bad, the District was in such bad shape, that principals were going around being proud of the 55 percent on or above grade level," explains Clarke, remembering and still horrified. "I kept saying to them, 'What's happening to the other 45?'"

Amato went after that other 45 percent, and it didn't take him long to change the image and statistics of District 6. "Before, the schools in this district were looked on as just babysitting services. I mean 32nd out of 32 districts—that's low. And we were real low. Six points just to get to 31st. We were so far in the sub-subbasement people didn't even want to talk about it. It wasn't even up for discussion," says Amato, his mood brightening. "So the first year we blew them away! We did those six points. The second year we went up five. The third year, four and a half. This last was our lowest, but it's still the highest in the City of New York. Two point seven. The highest gains in the City—not just in reading but in math, too. Now, to my knowledge, that has never happened in the City of New York. You don't get a double bang. You either do one or you do the other. You never do both. But we did. The highest gains in both and we're still climbing!"

He adds those scores are happening despite the fact District 6 has the largest number of bilingual students of any district in the country. The district is also one of the country's most economically depressed.

Clarke remembers the meeting when the scores were announced. "We had principals and teachers, together nonetheless, cheering and clapping each other on the back. Cheering! Together! That's unheard of." Santiago remembers being just as moved by it. "I asked Lenny if this type of enthusiasm happens in other districts, because Lenny's been around a lot of them. And he said, 'No. This is all special to District 6 and the Effective Schools changes.'"

The key that turns the lock, according to Amato, is that he has internalized the Effective School Process right into the curriculum planning process. Through extensive and numerous meetings, including a summer institute just for the teachers and curriculum chiefs of District 6, he has re-created and revitalized the curriculum.

"The whole point of creating the curriculum is to internalize the Effective Schools Process within the framework of that curriculum," explains Amato. "For example, what is the current thinking on social studies? Is it about reading a textbook, briefly digesting it, and spitting it out on Friday on a multiple-choice test? No. It's about problem solving, discussing the issues of the world in terms of environmental issues, social issues, political issues, community, etc. It's about fusing and coming to terms in groups and on teams. It's about getting basic content but within a framework of applying it, not of spitting it out on a test. Application of content."

The teams then put all the information together, then apply the Effective Schools research. The next step is for the teachers is to examine all the material and decide what a program should look like. They hammer it out, working with the mission of the schools and district. They set the goals and objectives, and determine a strategy for implementation. A time line is then set for, say, your typical third-grader in your typical third grade.

"But what about the kid just coming into school?" comments Amato, noting the high rate of mobility in his district. "That's where high expectations come in. We expect so much from each student, new or otherwise. Then we monitor that student. Testing. And within the course of that year, we expect the principals to be totally knowledgeable about this course of study and to be able to discuss it and work with improving it. That's instructional leadership. And also, we expect the parents to be involved in this course of study."

As Amato continues to explain how the Effective Schools Process correlates are embedded within the design of the curriculum, he becomes increasingly excited and animated discussing various programs in language, math, and science.

"In science, we have created this Science Satchel. It has a section for winter, spring, summer. And special projects. The kids create an electrical station. We give them all the supplies: wire, bulbs, batteries. And they do it with their parents." He goes on to explain that they have even designated a special Science Saturday for the entire district. The local cable station is also plugged into their science projects. This becomes even more complicated when one understands there are over 10 Spanish dialects formally recognized in District 6.

That may be one of the reasons why the central office for District 6 is cluttered with boxes, piles of paper, and stacks of books and other reading materials. Very often the superintendent is out delivering the supplies to a school that may be short.

"We produce a lot of this stuff ourselves because otherwise it's too expensive. And yes, sure, I end up doing some of the delivery. We all do. That's the difference. This district works together," say Amato, adding that in two weeks' time, his district makes a million and half copy runs off their machines—which is more than all the other districts in New York combined.

The push for high expectations for each and every child is particularly significant when you look at the student population of Spanish Harlem. "A lot of districts do a lot better than we do, and that's fine. My hat is off to them. But they have kids from middle-class backgrounds who come in the door reading," says Amato. "Our kids walk in at the age of 12 and have never had a pencil in their hand except maybe to throw it. We have over-age kids that are not even illiterate, they are preliterates. They are not even ready for readiness."

For these children, District 6 has adopted an Israeli model used with children living in the West Bank who, at an older age, are getting their first taste of education. "You can't treat them as kindergarten kids, because they have a different mindset by the age of 12, 13," says Amato. "So we did the research, found what worked, and its's working. And these kids are turning out to be some of our most incredible success stories. And why? Because we expect just as much from them as we do from the others. Because we believe they can do just as well. And instead of shuffling them off to remedial classes or special ed, we work with them. We give them that chance."

Amato pauses, thinking. He grits his teeth. "These kids have been screwed by the system for years. They come through that school door and get screwed over by us. So, too, with their parents. It can't continue. And it won't. Not here. Not as long as I have something to say about it.

"If I admitted that there was a line where we couldn't handle it, that there wasn't a solution for that child, then I cannot profess to be for children and education. Because we have to be for the least likely successful child in this city or we're not for anybody. We have to aim for that child. And in doing that, we catch every child in between. It's a captive audience in between if we shoot for that child."

Lenny Clarke sees the direct impact of this thinking out in the schools as a result of the disaggregation of data. "Before we disaggregated, teachers would get a printout of their scores and look to see how many kids were on grade level and who they were," says Clarke. "Then those kids would be grouped homogeneously, put the bright kids in one class, then there would be the two class, the three class, and down to the four class that would have the worst underachievers."

But that has changed. "All of a sudden with Effective Schools thinking, they started saying, 'Well, I have 30 kids out of 120 at grade level. Let's look at that second 30 and see where they're lacking,'" explains Clarke. "Then you keep going and by the time you get to that last group, you have a series of different strategies. And for that group at the top, now they get the enrichment they need. You enrich the curriculum. And you bolster the services for the others. Everyone, *every* kid gets what they need. And the scores don't get put away and forgotten."

One of the reasons a teacher or principal doesn't want to forget those scores is because there's a superintendent afoot who also has a copy and studies that copy. "I've been with Tony when he sits down with principals and teachers and whips out those scores and starts asking them, 'Well, what about this group of kids? What are you doing for these kids?' says Santiago. "Then the process begins of everyone working together. Tony comes in strong with the support effort. 'Now what do you need from me to help these kids?' They know they're not alone out there. Not the faculty, staff, or kids."

With this style of operation, the old cracks in the school system of District 6 that used to swallow up hundreds of school children each year are far less.

Because of the problems that come with some students, Amato says he spends a fair amount of time seeking the additional help for them and their families. Often is it raising money for a family that has been burned out or finding hospital care for a pregnant mother with a crack addiction.

"It is astounding what can happen if you give people a chance," says Amato. "I am constantly inspired by these people."

He admits his time is also filled with personnel matters. He is not afraid to take on a teacher or principal who has become slack and is not adequately serving the children. "Just last week I stumbled across a child's folder. Now we're really insistent upon writing assignments for our kids. And this folder doesn't have the right number of themes in it," explains Amato, his voice beginning to wear a sharp edge. "Now this teacher should have been on this student, and the principal should have been monitoring that teacher. The old instructional leadership. It wasn't happening. I blew up. I just blew up."

Amato says, and this is backed up by those around him, that he rarely "hits the roof" about anything other than the bottom line of educating the children.

"I'm proud of the fact that the union and I have evolved to the point that we are comfortable with each other," says Amato. "I now really feel like the union for the most part and the educational agenda of this district can be aligned. The last thing that I ever allow myself to get into is a war. I never allow that. It's misguided energy. If I'm going to spend energy, it's on kids, on education, and making things happen. I'm not going to spend it on language trivialities."

Building Blocks for Accountability

The education watchers have been very surprised—perhaps *astounded* is a better word—over the development of trust between Amato and the teachers. The motivating factor for that trust has been, according to Dr. Clarke, genuine empowerment of the teachers through additional training.

"If we're not prepared to teach teachers how to be prepared in the nineties, and how to teach in the nineties, then we have no right to hold them accountable for learning in the nineties," maintains Clarke. "But what we try to do in Effective Schools, is not just say you're accountable, but you're accountable once you've mastered or been exposed to as much training as possible. That's the important thing. Training and resources."

But there are politics larger than even the teachers' union in New York, and Amato insists that it is a quagmire that once he steps into, not only will he lose out but so will the children—and for that matter, so will sincere teachers and administrators.

"I'm smart enough to know that politics and education are well-embedded, but if I don't emulate the model of keeping the politics out of interfering with the kids, then I'm not making it. I'm very consistent. I go to a school and look at the education and the kids. I don't fall into the trap of who's kissing whom in terms of the politics and did you see so and so and will the board vote for me," he shakes his head disgustedly. "That's politics. That should be extraneous to education."

The proof of that statement came in the summer of 1990 when Amato's contract was up for renewal. He didn't play the political games and the word was that he was out. The process was opened up and was very competitive.

"Why am I still here? Because of the kids, the community. They came out and said, 'Hey, are you crazy? Look what he's done for us!'" He ended up receiving a unanimous nine votes for reappointment.

Like other Effective superintendents, his days are never ending. He's usually at the schools around 6:00 A.M., when many of his schools open for their first shift of children, and he will be in his office or out in the district or, unhappily, at central headquarters, until 10:00 or 11:00 at night. His weekends are spent on school business. The only time he gets away from it, somewhat, is on a summer vacation when he tries to "do something as physically challenging as possible without killing myself" (such as mountain climbing). But his real job is with the children in his district and the educational journey they have begun with the Effective Schools Process.

"Do you know we even use some of our programs, like the science and math, for disciplinary purposes? As in, 'If you don't behave, then you're not going to have science.' I've never heard that in my life. And I hear it here regularly," says Amato, delighting in his own excitement. "The kids love the learning. Love it! And that's what's driven us, the program. It's a lot of hands on, a lot of teaming, kids working with each other. Because the whole thing is, hey, in the future, if you're not a team player, a team member, that's it. You can't survive standing out there as a crazed rebel all alone. You've got to work with others, and you've got to be a problem solver, so you can prepare for your future. You've got to be flexible, know how to think. And you've also got to be technologically oriented.

"Those are the big three pieces in terms of our vision manifesting itself. We set the vision so everything else becomes the mission and then everything else becomes the goals and objectives. It's all the Effective Schools, the teaming, the thinking, the believing in a vision."

Tony Amato loves walking through the schools in District 6. He says he enjoys appointing "daring, dynamic" principals and working closely with principals and teachers on the educational future of the children.

He knows that many Americans, thanks to the media, ignorance, and bias, have an image of Spanish Harlem that is probably a little bit of Dante's *Inferno* and "New Jack City." He admits it's tough on the streets, but it's very unfair to put any labels on the schools.

The schools in his district may be crowded, and there may be classrooms that are in need of fresh coats of paint, but the schools are clean and, for the most part, safe. (High schools in New York City are a separate jurisdiction, not part of the "districts" per se.) There are no metal detectors; no frightened teachers packing cannisters of mace. The mood is calm, the teachers are busy, and the students are energized.

It would be difficult for the schools in this district to be in chaos, simply because there is a very conscientious man watching over them. Teachers talk about looking out their classroom doors and seeing Tony Amato just "checking to see that everything's OK." It is not unusual to see Amato having lunch with the kids in the cafeteria, talking with parents before and after school, or just listening and talking to the students. He is a brave, honest man—a leader who does not stoop when he bends to tie a child's shoelace.

"Come on, face it, we've got one shot with these kids and during their years in school, in our hands, is that one shot. That's it. If we don't do it here, it's never going to be done for them," says Amato, his voice strong, uncomprisingly. "So, if you work for me, and you don't do it, I'm going to be mighty upset. We've got to do it for these kids because it's got to happen. That's it. I don't deviate from that. We know how to do it now. We've got to do it!"

Amato has no tolerance for excuses—and in New York City, of all places, you would think a few excuses would be thrown around. But no. Like the other Effective superintendents, it is as if he who excuses himself accuses himself.

Larry Lezotte says it is mind boggling that Tony Amato has stood the political battles of New York and, at least so far, has come out victorious. "Tony is doing amazing things. He should be giving that whole city hope," says Lezotte, adding that the very system he's making look good is looking down on him. "A lot of his colleagues are very envious of what he has done. Unfortunately, he's been isolated for being so successful. He's an outcast. That's one of the tragedies of this. A superintendent starts to move a system and he becomes persona non grata. That's a sad commentary on American education."

In the process and politics of education, it often seems like the human mind is designed to accommodate mediocrity.

"Once you get a stone in your shoe," says Lezotte, "it's pretty hard to walk comfortably. But you adjust. You forget about taking out the stone. That's what it's like in the ineffective schools. These people are strutting around like those stones don't exist. But then along comes an Effective leader, someone who does real well, takes that stone out and takes off running, and everyone looks down on them."

This is a phenomenon that happens not only to superintendents who succeed but also to principals who pull their schools into the winning column. The political bureaucracy is still so strong and still so involved in the maintenance and protection of the status quo, that anyone who tries to change the way of doing things is looked upon suspiciously, if not negatively. For this reason, and obvious others, Effective School practitioners repeat that if you do not have the *will* to make the changes, if you do not feel the vision within, if it does not "grab" you and you cannot "grab" others with that vision, then improvement for *all* will never happen.

The Power of Will in Maryland

Effective superintendents believe unanimously and fiercely that the major reason change has not occurred in all public schools is because of the lack of will.

"Once the problems set in, no one had the will to change," says Noel Farmer, Ed.D., superintendent of the Frederick County (Maryland) Public School System. "Then they became entrenched and everyone was too threatened to do anything about it. And if you're threatened, or just don't care enough, then you can kiss school reform goodbye.

"And you cannot do school reform without the will. Sure, you can start it and you can make all the fancy speeches, but it's never going to get off the ground if you don't put your heart and soul into it. People have to see that commitment from you. They have to see how much you believe, and how much you want better schools."

Farmer is a former teacher, football coach, and principal, who bears the physical presence of a tall, large, tough linebacker who isn't going to be bounced around. But that first image is misleading. He is, say those around him, very flexible and very understanding. Any pretense about him as an all-powerful authoritarian leader who takes advantage of the trappings of his position couldn't be further from the truth. He can be the most understated appearing person at the regular principal meetings. His large bulk will be folded and squeezed into a student's desk as he eats the school lunch of tuna fish and potato chips, listening calmly but intently to the various progress reports and problems.

"Everyone in this district knows the greatest model for what we are doing is the superintendent," maintains Kevin Castner, Ed.D., associate superintendent in Frederick County. "We have a superintendent who is never going to be outworked by anyone in the field. As a role model, they don't come any better. The honesty, integrity, drive. He's here at seven in the morning and is working out in the schools or community four, five nights a week. He's not asking anymore of anyone than he gives himself. And when we have a meeting, he's right there teaching. Not ordering us. Not shouting commands. He's teaching, instructing. That makes a big difference. Higher expectations. Right from the top."

Farmer is careful not to talk about the Effective Schools Process as the "magic" that is going to reform all public education. He says it has been this feeling that the other reform movements were "magic" that has led to their downfall. Instead, he looks on Effective Schools as the legitimate "process" by which school improvement can be realized.

He admits that prior to the Effective Schools Process, he knew something was missing in his understanding and work of education. It was Larry Lezotte and the Effective Schools Process that brought his training and knowledge into focus. It has also renewed his faith in the public schools and been the impetus for all his school improvement endeavors.

"The key is that the whole system must understand it has been in the dark," believes Farmer. "And the way into the light is, I believe, through Effective Schools. But it's no magic. I would rather refer to it as school improvement via the Effective Schools research because I think it more appropriately identifies what we've done or what we're doing if you look at school improvement as the real focus."

Farmer also believes it is very important to keep in mind that the phrase, *all students can learn,* should not be standing completely alone. "We need to say that *all students can learn provided we give them the appropriate time and assistance.* Now I think most educators understand that implicitly, or at least they should. But some may thing this just happens. It doesn't. You need that time and assistance."

Farmer is very critical of the way children have been assessed in the past. He believes that the old intelligence tests were actually "about an amoral business" because they judged not a child's capacity to learn but the rate of learning. This led to the creation of the bell curve and an educational setup "that guaranteed that some kids just don't get any of the good stuff."

That policy has reigned for 200 years, even in Frederick County, and it is that policy, that mindset, that Farmer is breaking with the Effective Schools Process. It is a risky position to take in the middle-class community of Frederick County.

Farmer's district is dramatically different than that of Tony Amato's. The area runs from historic Frederick City to the rural countryside, complete with rolling hills and farms, to the bedroom communities forming the Washington-Baltimore Beltway area. It is moving from an agrarian-based economy to a

Beltway bedroom community. There is a student population of 26,800, with 6 percent black and 2 percent other minority. Less than 10 percent of the students are low socioeconomic status.

Farmer said his task began and continues with the simple but difficult problem of communicating the need for change and how that will be accomplished. It is "talking the talk, and walking the walk" of the Effective Schools Improvement Process.

"You've got to change a lot of people who have had a whole career of education doing it the other way," says Farmer. "I haven't done it, yet. I'm just chipping away at it by saying it over and over again. You've got to keep saying it. You've got to live it. You've got to put it into imagery. You've got to communicate it in as many different ways as possible and you've got to constantly be consistent with what you're saying and don't deviate from the path. And be willing to stick there with the county for a long period of time.

"You cannot be a vagabond superintendent. You've got to stay there for a long time to get it to occur. And make it become a *religion* and have all your disciples saying the same thing. And get everyone all the way down to the community member talking the same talk. Once we've got that language established with those who have to implement as well as those who talk it in the central office, I think we'll be moving in the right direction."

If anyone even remotely involved in the Frederick County Public Schools is not aware that the county is undergoing school improvement via the Effective Schools Process, they have been existing with their head firmly imbedded in several feet of sand.

It began on October 5, 1988, with the Frederick County Board of Education adopting the Effective Schools Improvement Process. Like other superintendents, Farmer is a firm believer that the board must be informed and "on board" from the very beginning (and must take the responsibility for the failures as well as successes). In fact, very much like Hal Guthrie (Spring Branch, Texas), Farmer let his board know when they were hiring him (from the nearby affluent Howard County School District) that his goal was school improvement via Effective Schools.

Rallying Around Effectiveness

Next came a pep rally—not for the football team but for the Effective Schools Process and school improvement. In a foot-stomping, cheering, banner-raising rally, the superintendent and his staff told school department employees what was going to be happening to the schools over the next four years. There was excitement and, according to the teachers, a sense of "togetherness and pride" for the renewal that was happening in Frederick County.

Once the pep rally and dinner to celebrate the school improvement process has been held, the work began to bring school-based management to the 46 schools. Despite the enthusiasm and research-backed statements from central office, people at the schools were very skeptical.

"You have to realize that like every district, we had gone through school reform programs before," explains Sherry Collette, supervisor of the elementary schools in Area II of Frederick. "The teachers would give a yawn and go 'Oh, wow,' and that would be it. But then, I think we all started to look closely at Dr. Farmer and what he was doing. He wasn't letting up. Not for a second. He was dead serious about this. Everyone was forced to take a second look."

Collette notes that one of the aspects that struck the faculty and staff as different was that "Farmer was so public about this." She said that everywhere you went in the district you encountered Effective School signs, plaques, and literature.

"And the whole central office was talking about it. And putting out all these reports and copies of research reports about this improvement process," says Collette who was already familiar with Effective Schools. "Many of us started to realize that this was going to be different this time, that Dr. Farmer was going to improve the schools. And he was also going to keep us informed every step of the way."

If there is anything that is throwing the old guard in Frederick County off step, it is Farmer's openness, his keeping in the public eye at all times, keeping everyone informed. His office is regularly putting out material on the implementation process, from guidelines to problems to progress. He says as long as people realize this improvement process is going to take time, and that he's going to give it all the time it takes, then there is nothing to fear—or hide.

Like every superintendent, one would think that Farmer might want to hide a few facts about his school system, like how poorly the Chapter 1 children were doing. But he did not. He let the county know right off that only 2 percent of the Chapter 1 children were performing at the accepted level.

"Only 2 percent! Can you believe that?" asks Farmer, who is reminded that in many school districts prior to Effective Schools, the Chapter 1 program is performing at abysmal levels. "And the disaggregation? Sure, that was a shock, too. But you've got to make all this public. You've got to show where the starting point is."

That starting point for Frederick County was the establishment of eight systemwide improvement goals that are boldly displayed, along with all other elements of the school improvement process, including test scores, in the hallways of the central administration building in Frederick. The eight goals for the time period (school years) 1988–89 through 1991–92 were:

1. Criterion-referenced standards will show annual increases in the percentages of students at the respective grade level who attain essential objectives of the curriculum.

2. State functional test scores for Frederick County Public Schools will show annual increases in the percentage of students at grade 9 and 10 who reach or exceed criterion for mastery.
3. Standardized test scores for Frederick County Public Schools will show annual increases in the percentage of students within the fourth quartile, and annual decreases in the percentage of students in the first quartile.
4. There shall be no significant differences in the proportion of youth demonstrating minimum academic mastery as a function of gender, race, or socioeconomic class.
5. The percentage of student attendance will increase annually.
6. The percentage of student drop-outs will decrease annually.
7. Ninety percent of all students will complete the equivalent of Algebra I before graduating.
8. As overall achievement scores rise, outstanding individual achievement will also increase.

These goals do not just sit staring out from the walls at the central office. By his own hand, Farmer has directed that each year his office must issue a report on how each individual school is doing in the achievement of these goals. A detailed report is released giving the evaluation of progress as well as all test scores, disasggregated by race, gender, and socioeconomic status.

In that report, Farmer reminds his constituents exactly where Frederick County stands in the national school improvement process. From a national perspective of school improvement, Frederick County is among the top school systems:

- 42 percent of more than 16,000 school districts have a program of school improvement. *Frederick County is one of them.*
- 27 percent of these school districts require collaborative planning for school improvement between teachers and principals. *Frederick County is one of them.*
- 11 percent of these school districts routinely disaggregate student outcome data. *Frederick County is one of them.*
- 1 percent of these school districts annually evaluate progress and publish their results. *Frederick County is one of them.*
- 0.1 percent of these school districts placed the goals of their school improvement programs into policy. *Frederick County is one of them.*

Just Doing the Right Thing

"We've opened the system up and we're proud of that. No question," says associate superintendent Castner. "But we're not doing anything that shouldn't be done in every school, every school system. This is the way we achieve the focus we want. And this is the way we maintain the focus.

"If there's any problem here it may be, it *may* be, that Dr. Farmer sometimes wants too much. For example, the SAT scores. He wants us over 1,000. The state average is only 910." The 1989 class of Frederick County seniors—63 percent who went on to postsecondary education—scored an average of 438 on the verbal SAT and 486 on the math SAT. The state average is 434 and 480. The national average is 427 verbal and 476 math.

"Of course I expect a lot," says Farmer, "And that's the last thing I'll ever apologize for. High expectations is what we're all talking about here. Look at the Chapter 1 kids." The Chapter 1 students went from 2 percent on grade level to over 70 percent on grade level in three years.

In the 1990 Maryland "Report Card" (Maryland School Performance Program Report), Frederick County scored second in the state, hitting five of the seven standards. (Howard County, the county Farmer had just come from, scored first.) The schools are especially proud of this fact, given that Frederick County rates in the middle of the 24 counties in Maryland in per pupil expenditure. Frederick County has a per pupil expenditure of $4,397; Howard County, $5,549.

Overall, Frederick County's scores sit above the national and state averages. That certainly isn't enough for Farmer—nor is the fact that Frederick County is number one in the state in the Maryland Writing Test: 90 percent is satisfactory; Frederick County scores 95.9 percent. In the Maryland Functional Reading Test, satisfactory is 95 percent; Frederick County scores 96.1 percent. On the Maryland Functional Mathematics Test, satisfactory is 80 percent; Frederick County scores 78.5 percent. This mathematics score has already been turned around according to the most recent scores. Frederick County reports a score of 86 percent, a climb of almost eight points. Asked if they were now first in the state in mathematics, Castner said, "Well, we've been told there is no one ahead of us."

It is the disaggregation of some test scores that causes concern for Farmer and his staff. On the reading test, low SES students declined from 90.9 to 89.4 percent. Black students declined from 90.9 to 87.4 percent. On the math test, black students fell from 61 to 49 percent, whereas low SES increased from 55.5 to 55.8 percent. On the writing test, black students increased from 80 to 90 percent; low SES students also increased from 84.8 to 88.6 percent.

"We've got some problems and now we see where they are," says Farmer, pointing out that just about anything can look good at first blush. "Look at our dropout rate. It fell from 3.2 percent to 2.2 percent. Looks pretty good doesn't it? Well, it's not, because we had 30 more black students drop out. That's unacceptable." He goes on to note that the number of low SES students dropping out also increased. "So remember, this is not a matter of race. In 90 percent of the cases, it's a matter of class."

But as each year's reports come in, Farmer sees the fruits of the system's labors. The 1991 report card was even better than the 1990 card for Frederick County. "We're doing a good job," says Farmer. "We're one of the top two school systems in Maryland. This wouldn't be happening without the changes. And what's really astounding is that we're outperforming counties that are spending 26 to 50 percent more than us."

But there are still many attitudes that need to be changed in Frederick County—most of them not any different from those found in other counties in other states. "We blame the students. Always, always, blame the students," says Farmer. "We think there's something wrong with them if they don't learn, if they don't stay in school. Well, we've got to stop blaming the student for what he or she can't do and look at it as our potential, not theirs."

Once you start to examine student performance from the vantage point of the teacher's degree of expertise, you start to understand how essential staff development is.

"Working from the outcome perspective forces you away from seeing teachers as pawns. You really have to value your employees and give them the opportunity to have a real major role in helping you hit the outcomes," says Farmer. "The problem is that teachers have been trained to blame the student. They have a hard time accepting that the potential is with us and not with the students. They have to believe that those kids are doing the best job they can do under the conditions that they find themselves in and with the knowledge that they have."

Staff development in Frederick County not only involves the basics of improving teaching techniques through the expanded base of higher and higher expectations but also supplemental courses in all levels and areas of curriculum. One of the most important concerns for Farmer is leadership and decision-making skills.

"I devote about 25 percent of my time to work in this area," says Farmer. "Not just in meetings but in teaching. My goal is to make sure I keep the true mission in front of the eyes of the constituents at all times. We are all here to lead in the mission of teaching for quality learning for all students."

Farmer says the school district is at a point where he can see the genuine leadership skills building throughout the system, throughout the schools. It is a difficult process of unlearning old habits at the local level and building value-added power relationships. "I have made it a job description for everyone in this district to be a leader. I want the teachers leading as much as anyone." Farmer says he knows the school improvement teams can, and do, make the right decisions for their schools. "We're finally seeing that you cannot put the burden on one teacher here and another teacher over there. They must all work together. You put the burden on the back of the entire school."

In reality, however, Farmer won't let it stop with the school. He talks of the concept of "collaborative institutional response" as the impetus for the change in the attitude and function of the central office. As in the other Effective Schools districts, the central office is beginning to work for the schools.

"The only reason the central office exists is for the sake of the schools," insists Farmer. "When the schools have been in need in the last few years, the central office has come through. And we're taking a lot of pride in the fact that the county has come from the back of the pack to the front."

But there are still struggles. "Time is the most powerful, manipulative variable that we have. It's easy to misuse and abuse. What we have to concentrate on is deciding what time is best spent in in-service training and what type of training is going to do the best for both the teachers and the kids. I've learned it doesn't matter how much money you have," says Farmer, noting that education has been famous for wasting in-service funds. "We know what our goals are and we know our money has to go toward those specific goals. It's that easy, that difficult, and that mandatory." He says he will continue to fight as much as necessary for the right training and development opportunities for his teachers and staff.

"You're dealing with a major cultural change here, so you have to be careful that no one sees what you're doing as a threat," explains Farmer. "I want each individual to see himself or herself as a primary delivery system for the quality teaching of *all* children. Yes, it's hard and it requires more energy, more time. But if you make the goals clear, inviting, and doable, attainable, then the goals themselves will drive you, they really drive you.

"Teachers and principals that buy into it, into the invitation, the inviting aspect of it, the doability of it and the clearness of it, they eventually get to the point where they say, 'Hey, what's happening here? I'm in a whole new ballgame.' And you see now that people are finding it very rewarding."

However, associate superintendent Castner points out that there are many teachers who are feeling the stress of these changes. "As the bar of success changes, as you incrementally get better, then you're doing more for kids than you've ever done before—and that's great, but you also have some weariness, as well as anxiety where you still know there's more to do. That's tough and that's something that has to be balanced—that if you get 90 percent, well, you want to get a little more, because truly you can't say you've been successful to every kid until you've done that. And that's what we have to work on, is balance."

Farmer and his staff prevented a major impasse with the teachers' union that could have affected the progress being made with the Effective Schools Process. The contract was up and there was word that negotiations would be difficult, at best. But Farmer and the union settled ahead of schedule, with three 6-percent raises. But then the state stepped in and froze all wage hikes. Farmer then took the unprecedented step of appealing to the county for a tax increase to cover the pay raise. It was not a surprise to those who knew Farmer and his track record that the tax increase was passed.

"What we've done is we've shown the faculty how much we value all the work they're doing, all the work they've done," says Castner, "This has a message to the teachers that we are proud of them, their work, and that we realize they are the ones who are responsible for the progress that has been made."

What Farmer is hoping is that as time moves on, more and more teachers will see the Effective Schools Improvement Process the same way he does. "This approach allows me to have a good litmus test for keeping my sanity and knowing that I'm doing the right thing," he explains. "There are three basic questions that you have to answer with Effective Schools that for me keeps everything in focus: What is your mission? That's number one. You've got to spend time deciding what your mission really is. Second, what evidence are you going to collect to see whether or not you're hitting your mission? And third, how are you going to evaluate it? Mission, outcomes, evaluation. Sure, it's tough. Because now at last teachers, principals, and superintendents are feeling the full burden. They're trying to teach all children, which they haven't tried to do before."

Changing Culture in Kansas

If Noel Farmer was having a tough time breaking through 200 years of ideology in the rolling hills of the allegedly progressive East Coast, you might expect it would be even more difficult for a superintendent in the flatlands of mid-America.

Max Heim, Ph.D., is the superintendent of the Geary County School District based in Junction City, about 100 miles west of Kansas City. Although Heim won't take any bets on where in the United States it may be most difficult to bring about change in schools, he does look back on his district's school improvement process and believes that the one area where he and his staff fell short was in acquainting the people with the promises and pitfalls of the process of change itself.

"I look back and I see that one of the things we didn't do well in our district was talk about change and what change does and what change means," says Heim, who in 1990 was named the Kansas Superintendent of the Year. "We needed to do that. We've not done enough about change with our teachers and administrators so that they will finally, intellectually, come into this and buy into the things we are saying. Every district, every school must explain the process of change if you're going to make this work."

Although Heim, like a loyal disciple of the Effective Schools Process, refuses to make excuses, he does maintain that his district has at least one more major obstacle than other districts. There is a mobility rate of over 60 percent because most of his students are children of military personnel stationed at Fort

Riley in Junction City. They don't stay in one place longer than two or three years.

Out of 750 Junction City kindergartners, only 235 will still be around to be seniors in Junction City. "I'm not using it as an excuse," insists Heim. "I'm just saying it makes our job a little more difficult. Because it's not like we don't have all the other problems."

And Geary County does have all those other problems. Although it is a rural district, just outside Manhattan, Kansas, and down the road from Lawrence (in the center of the state), the majority of the students come from urban/suburban environments. There are the problems of drugs, crime, and poverty.

The district is the ninth largest of 304 school districts in Kansas. There are 7,000 students, with 45 percent minority. Over 60 percent of the students are on free and reduced lunch.

Heim came into the district in 1980 from a position as Dean of the College of Education at Mississippi State University. He admits that he came into Effective Schools later than he should have. He first started reading about it in 1983 and began the process of change in 1985.

"Our children were not achieving, were not learning, and we had a lot of excuses to why that was happening," says Heim, not hiding his sadness. "My regrets are that I did not seize Effective Schools earlier and do something about the education here. I'm ashamed of myself."

Heim admits that his own personal recognition of learning equity came later than others. Or perhaps he is one of the few superintendents who will admit it. "I started this game in 1957 and I have to tell you that in the early days, I don't think I believed all kids could learn. I don't really think I felt that," he says. "I was compassionate, but I don't really think I felt that. And then I started to read and study. And here, finally, in Geary County, I got a chance to make it happen."

But Heim had more than the mobility problem working against him. In this military community, which teachers refer to as "home of the garage sale economy," right down the road from President Dwight D. Eisenhower's home in Abilene, there was an American obstacle as old and dangerous as military might itself.

"This pond of tranquility that we live in out here has just below the surface terrible, terrible racists—whole racist organisms living," maintains Heim. "In communities out here you look and you think no. But no. It's a terrible, rotten problem. And I don't care how much the people out there smile and say we all get along. We don't. And many of them out there don't want us to."

Heim says that attitude in the community was harbored in the schools. "You've got to be able to get teachers and principals to be openminded, at the least, about what they can do for minority and disadvantaged kids. Instead of saying, 'No, we're not responsible and no, they can't learn, and if you're black, you sure as hell can't learn.'"

Heim tells the story that is often repeated by Lezotte and other experts about this "Elmer" that school districts are in need of. "Elmer is this person, a farmer, who is pretty successful and people look up to him and he tries new things from time to time," begins Heim. "So these folks come out with this new fertilizer, say preemergent herbicide that is supposed to kill all weeds. Well, the farmers don't even try it. They immediately say it won't work. But this Elmer gives it a try, puts it on his land, raises his corn. All the other farmers drive by in their pickup trucks. No weeds. What did the farmers say? Did they accept the herbicide? No. They concluded that there wouldn't have been any weeds anyway.

"So the makers of this herbicide surrender. A bit. They say, 'OK, we'll just put a little bit of preemergent herbicides on and the weeds will come up a little bit—so they can see that they were there, but they're just not going to make it because they were stunted.' And so, the farmers drive by and say, 'Boy, there must be something to that.' And so now everyone uses the herbicide.

"What we're looking for in Effective Schools is that 'Elmer' who will try these things and isn't afraid of being successful."

In the early eighties, Heim began studying the Kansas state test scores of his students and saw that only 55 percent were performing on grade level. Already aware of the Effective Schools Process, he sent his Director of Elementary Education to an Effective Schools conference in Phoenix. "Now this is one of the most conservative faculty members we have," explains Heim. "And she came back so excited about Effective Schools. She kept saying, 'We have to do this! we have to do this!'"

So Heim and a group of teachers and staff went up to a longer conference in East Lansing, Michigan, with Lezotte and Ron Edmonds. There, the fire was ignited, and the process was begun.

"School improvement is like working on a railroad when a train is coming down the track at 60 miles an hour. You can't stop the train, but somehow you've got to fix the track," says Heim.

"You keep hearing two words—*restructuring* and *empowerment*. And the trouble is you can't do one without the other. And how do you do them? With time. And where does time come from? Sure, I can give mine and the staff can work their overtime, but what about the teachers? Their time has to come from money. And where does that come from? The board."

And where does the board take its cues from? The community—a community that Heim claims in its gut was not, and still may not be, interested in educating minority children.

"I think we have consistently gone out of our way to see that the minority children get every chance the other kids do," says Mark Edwards, president of the Geary County Board of Education. "The problem with any changes—and believe me, most of us have been behind Effective Schools 100 percent—is that it costs money. And we don't have any reserves."

That first year of planning costs between $20,000 and $25,000, says Heim. To many that was too much to spend on an "experiment to help black kids."

"Maybe I'm getting weary of the fight, and that's why I call it as I see it, but that was the situation," says Heim, some of the old anger returning. "Sometimes you can throw all the research data you want in front of people . . ." but if they don't want to change or learn, they're not going to. And there isn't a whole lot more you can do about it.

The budget for the 7,200 students is $23 million. The valuation of the school district is placed at $81 million (Spring Branch, Texas, is valued at $8 *billion.*) Heim says in 1989, the district spent 0.7 of *1* percent on staff development. "And I get a lot of heat for that lousy seven-tenths of 1 percent," says Heim, noting that the detractors of the school improvement process ordered a complete examination of the budget. After 15 months, they could find nothing wrong.

"Staff development is the key to this," insists Heim. "If we didn't have the backing of the board back in the mid-eighties, we never would have made it. But now it seems that people are forgetting how important that staff development is."

That staff development in Geary County is regarded, even with the small financial expenditure, as one of the finest in the state. In fact, as an observer travels around the schools and talks to the teachers, the overwhelming majority will say they either stay in Geary County, or came to Geary County, because of the opportunities for renewal and development. They say there is very little reason otherwise to come to this district. Out in the middle of the state, with any significant culture 30 miles away in Lawrence, Kansas, they say there is little to do unless you are interested in watching downtown Junction City and some poorer neighborhoods decay.

The salaries are 102nd in the state for teachers (out of 304 districts) and 183rd for administrators. ("How do I keep them?" asks Heim, "Thank God for staff development.")

"At first, we were suspicious," says Pat Anderson, who was a high school English teacher and president of the Teachers' Association when the planning for the Effective Schools Process began. "Max was talking about some very foreign things. School-based control. Staff development. Increased resources. It sounded too good to be true."

What also sounded too good was the research showing the progress made by minority students under the Effective Schools Process. Teachers and administrators just weren't buying it. So, Heim pulled the fancy football bus into service, loaded it with the skeptics, and drove down to St. Louis, Missouri, to one of the earliest Effective Schools programs to be successful. There, they visited schools far worse than any within the wheat fields of Geary county. "They came back saying, 'If they can do it, then we can do it.'"

Geary County has made significant progress under the Effective Schools

Process. Test scores for all groups of students are climbing. There are improvement teams in every building. Morale of teachers and administrators appears good.

"There is no question that there is a growing cooperative spirit," says Pat Anderson, who now works out of central administration. "There is a sense among the staff, and it has to be among the teaching staff in particular, that they are the closest to the situation, they are the ones who can do the most, and therefore need some development in problem solving. To empower these people is to understand their tremendous role in identifying and coming to terms with the problems these children bring."

Heim looks on it as the process of "tapping into the potential of the teachers. You can't just say to the teachers, 'All right, you're going to teach all children and all children can learn.' And the teacher says, 'OK, I buy that. I'm a pretty good teacher.' And then I come back at the end of the year and say, 'Hey, why haven't you done this and this?' And you say, 'Hey, wait a minute, buster, I agreed with you, but you did not provide me with any help in how to accomplish this.'

"The school is where we make the difference. We have to work with the teachers. As soon as we prove it to the teachers, then these kids begin to emerge and to learn and to demonstrate that they want to learn and can make a difference," he insists. "It's slow. Incredibly slow. But we're making it."

A Matter of Trust

Heim explains that his major impetus over the years through the Effective Schools Process has been to convince the teachers that he and the staff are there for them. "You've got to have some trust," says Heim.

Pat Anderson agrees. "Oh, if this faculty didn't trust Max, we never would have jumped forward. And at first it seemed like he was just giving more of the same old answers as the ones before him. But then we realized he was sticking with what he said. He meant it. When he said he'd fight for a pay raise, he fought for a pay raise. When he spoke about renewal, he was serious. He wanted us to have ownership."

Dave Flowers, Ph.D., assistant superintendent for instruction, says the change has been dramatic in many schools. "And that is because of the teachers. There is now effective teaching going on. You can notice the difference. The kids are being reached, and they're learning. You see it in the classroom, you see it on the tests." Flowers also notes that in the last year, 26 schools and 19 school districts have come to observe the changes being made in Geary County. "And what they see is enhanced performance because of improvement in teaching practices."

There is very little talk among teachers about the problems of the mobility of students. Instead, in every school you will find teachers working overtime either alone or in cooperative learning teams with other teachers, diligently trying to raise their students scores and get them on a path of improvement before their parents are transferred to another base either in the states or overseas.

With so many of the students' parents heading for the Gulf War in 1990 and 1991, teachers found an additional burden: the emotional trauma of dealing with long periods of separation and sometimes death."These kids really get the very short end of the stick," said Pat Anderson, watching a young girl carefully, passionately, tying a yellow ribbon in her pigtail.

At 3 o'clock in the afternoon, as you stand outside the Custer Elementary School, the "innocents" of the first, second, and third grade, an occasional teddy bear head sticking out of the top of a backpack, walk past the military crossing guards, down the cracked sidewalks to the military bungalows or crowded apartment complex. This military housing is not in good shape, but these children are the lucky ones. Children of military personnel of the lower ranks live with their parents off base, usually in run-down crowded apartment buildings or in deteriorating shacks and old rusted trailers that in the summer roast their inhabitants in the 110-degree heat, and in the winter freeze them as the prairie winds whip through.

"It is military, government subsidized poverty," said one school official. "I don't know how some of these kids survive."

But if the spirit of the child can stay alive in Spanish Harlem, it can stay alive in Kansas.

"One of our biggest problems is that we cannot get parents involved," says Heim. "Too often the teachers and the kids end up out there alone." He says that once he managed to have the Colonel order his people to be involved in the schools, but that that was years ago and there has been no recommitment to the educational process. Heim admits part of the problem is that the military is constantly moving the parents, but "we can't use that as an excuse and neither can the parents."

What frustrates Heim and his staff is that in many instances, they have identified the "at-risk" children and begun extensive programs to serve them, only to have a child pulled out of school at some crucial juncture.

"One of the things we know in helping at-risk kids is that early intervention is critical," says Dave Flowers. "We know, for example, that we can predict within 70 percent accuracy which kids are going to drop out. There is a strategy called *recovering* that works much better than the old remediation. We know what to do to help these kids. And often, just when we're about to turn the corner, they move from us."

But even for those students, Heim says the school district has served them "far better than it would have served them ten years ago." He says the schools prove to the children that they are not in any way inferior.

"You see, I look at every child, every child, and say, 'That's the kid who's got the cure for cancer,'" says Heim. "Sure, it's simplistic. But the bottom line is it is our absolute obligation to treat that kid like he or she has the cure inside their head."

Given the problems of trying to change a very conservative community (Max Heim himself is a friend of Bob Dole and believes the biggest problems facing children today are drugs and television), trying to convince the skeptics on the board, a lack of parental involvement, and mobility, Heim believes he and his teachers and staff have done a remarkable job.

"You look at the other school districts around here. They're terrible, just terrible," he insists. "And we're not as good as we should be. I'd probably give us a C plus. But that's only because we're still in many ways in this change process. I mean, you see conservatism, but this faculty and staff is just the best one around. Ten years ago, this school district wasn't even in the same ball park that it is now. We've made progress—a lot of progress."

But can a superintendent report this same type of progress in a school district that is not fighting problems such as poverty, racism, crime and drugs, mobility, and lack of parental interest? In short, Can a superintendent lead the way to success in a white, middle-class district that is already regarded as successful? Can the Effective Schools Process improve on middle-class success? Yes.

Improving a Good School System

Spencerport, New York, is a white, middle-class, conservative town of 19,000 people located in the quiet hills along the Erie Canal outside Rochester. The Spencerport Central School District has an enrollment of 3,300, with 95 percent white, 2 percent black, 2 percent Asian, and 1 percent Hispanic. Some 6 percent qualify for free or reduced lunch, although Spencerport disaggregates its scores according to the level of the mother's education. There are three elementary schools, one junior high, and one senior high.

The Spencerport School District was rolling along like most other school districts in the early seventies when Robert Sudlow, Ed.D., assumed the position of Assistant Superintendent for Instruction. His assignment was the curriculum. It didn't take him long to realize all was not well in suburbia.

"A lot of the basic curriculum work just had never been done at the elementary level," says Sudlow, a man who often wears the frustration of pushing uphill through two decades of school improvement. "They had no syllabus. The math program at the secondary level was a disaster. There were no honors programs of any nature anywhere in the district. No advanced placement."

And there were the political problems. "The school district basically consisted of five independent empires (the five schools) where they lowered the flag and charged for the sheer joy of battle," recalls Sudlow, noting that it did not take him long to realize there was a need for change in Spencerport—if anyone was willing to take the risk.

Joe Clement, who was then serving as assistant superintendent in charge of business matters, was appointed superintendent.

"Despite the fact that it was clear that our strengths are the exact opposite of each other, Joe decided to keep me on," explains Sudlow. "Over the years, we've learned to complement each other."

But how and why did the Effective Schools Process come in?

The district was experiencing declining enrollment, teachers were being laid off, and, according to Sudlow, "we were without any new ideas, and we knew we had to systematically infuse new ideas and new research into this settling environment." Sudlow said he was also interested in the aspect of the new research that spoke of *all* kids learning, and given the fact that Spencerport had just gone through a particularly bitter teachers' strike that had closed schools for two weeks, the necessity for cooperative, collegial, collaborative behavior.

"I had been sending out a lot of different articles that I came across and one day Joe says to me, 'You know, Bob, there's a theme in these articles and its called Effective Schools.'" Clement then told Sudlow to look into Effective Schools and gave him a full year for the research," which was atypical of Joe."

Sudlow discovered there were two places doing work with Effective Schools: the research Center for Better Schools in Philadelphia and "this guy named Ron Edmonds."

"This was like '81, '82, and I don't know why, it was just a hunch, but I called up Edmonds and Lezotte and told them I wanted to talk with them about Effective Schools. They said to come on out. I think they wanted to inspect me. And so I climb aboard one of those puddle-jumping airplanes and get to Michigan State. I guess I said all the right things because they agreed to work with us," says Sudlow.

Spencerport would be the first K–12 system to ask for their services. Prior to that, all the Effective Schools work had been at individual buildings, primarily at the elementary level.

"We were a lot of things other districts were not. We were not urban, we were not black, we were not poor, we were not a school system in crisis, either with the community or in terms of student achievement. By all traditional criteria, we were a good school system," explains Sudlow. "Ron said they were interested in us for the things we were not. In other words, we provided a great test tube for them to see whether these ideas, which were researched and developed primarily in an urban environment, would be applicable in a very dissimilar environment—but typical of the vast majority of school systems."

Edmonds and Lezotte then came to Spencerport in January 1983 and met with the Spencerport Board of Education. The board approved the launching of the Effective Schools Process. "I think they realized we needed something," recalls Clement. "Our staff was getting real set in their ways. We needed to revitalize them. And as for me, I was getting real tired of just moving from one crisis to another. We needed something so encompassing for the school district it would drive us and sustain us for a long time."

But why take the risk? No one in the community was complaining about the schools. They appeared to be operating smoothly. "Sure, they appeared just fine. Just as they had for years and years," says Clement. "But no. We had to take the risk. The board members would ask me, 'Do you really want to take that kind of risk?' and I would say, 'We can't afford not to.'"

After the board's approval, Edmonds and Lezotte began a series of meetings with administrators and then teachers and staff. One of their first obstacles was the reform attempts that had gone before.

"In all fairness to the teachers and principals, we had made skeptics out of them," says Clement. "We, like so many districts—and I suspect that a lot of them are still in that mode today but that's their problem, not ours—went from one fad to another. We went in one direction, then we would switch gears for whatever reason and go in another direction. And the people who had stayed around and watched this over a number of years would say, 'We'll just wait this out because we know Clement's going to have a different idea or the board will try something else.'"

Clement and Sudlow both remember an interaction early on between Edmonds, Lezotte, and the administrators of the schools.

"A classic example of what happened was this good principal, dedicated but very skeptical, made the mistake of raising a lot of issues with Ron and Larry," recalls Clement. "Really going after them and their research. But Ron and Larry were ready. I mean they knew what they were talking about. And finally the principal realized he was going down a path that he shouldn't, that he couldn't win, and he reached into his pocket, took out his handkerchief and waved surrender. And that guy is one of our greatest supporters of Effective Schools today."

A districtwide leadership team consisting of two key teachers from each building, the building principal, a district testing expert, the union representative, and Sudlow was established. By June 1983, a master plan had been developed and approved by the superintendent and board. (Edmonds called this master plan "outstanding" and it has become the model for numerous other school districts.)

At the same time the individual buildings were selecting members for the building planning teams, needs assessment data were being accumulated from the teachers' questionnaires, and the results of the New York State achievement tests were being released.

"We disaggregated the data according to the level of the mother's education and we saw, right before us, that kids were learning as a function of socioeconomic status," says Sudlow, adding that it came as a surprise to many teachers. "I think that if I had even hinted at this before, they would have driven me out of town and had a good time doing it. But this way, we had the research data to help us, and overall, I think a lot of people did some private reassessment. The issue of the dialogue on a clear school mission became very helpful."

Sudlow also points out that the disaggregation of data was not that popular with many conservative, middle-class people in the district because "basically, they didn't give a damn that anyone other than their kids were doing OK."

That's when it became so essential that Clement was willing to take the strong stand in favor of disaggregation.

"You can't do this without the superintendent standing up there saying this has to be done because we have to teach *all* children," says Sudlow. "And that's what Joe did. He spoke to the people on the board, the community, telling them it was essential that this school district be here for *all* the kids—not just the middle and upper classes. And he also had to convince them of the validity of the data that it wouldn't hurt their kids. Without that, we never would have made it."

Clements admits that at times it was difficult to convince people of the "rightness of what we were doing."

"But I wasn't about to back down, and they knew it. I was putting everything—my name, my reputation, my job, my family, my future—behind Effective Schools," says Clement. "And why? Because I believed it was right. And it *is* right."

It was during the summer of 1983 that Ron Edmonds died suddenly. According to Sudlow, "The last thing he was working on was the plan for Spencerport."

"A lot of people here were really devastated by his death," says Sudlow. "We had become very close to him. We respected him immensely. He was the most brilliant man I've ever known. Utterly brilliant."

But then Larry Lezotte and others picked up Edmonds's unfinished work and diligently helped Spencerport stay on the path to school improvement. The building planning teams went to work.

The summary of Spencerport's implementation of the Effective Schools Process is:

- Create extensive awareness.
- Have a representative group of teachers and administrators write a master plan for the district that is approved by the superintendent and board of education.
- Administer a needs assessment instrument that measures the presence of the correlates.
- Disaggregate student achievement data.

- Have a building planning team that represents the faculty and administration. The team annually develops a proposed school improvement plan based on the needs assessment data and works with colleagues to implement it.
- Have faculty review and approve the proposed plan.
- Evaluate the effects of the building's plan by readministering the needs assessment instrument and by disaggregating spring testing data.
- Prepare a new or continuing plan of school improvement based on the spring evaluation data.

Like all other school districts, Spencerport faced the problem of time and money. The district ranked 14th in wealth per pupil and 16th in per pupil expenditures ($5,577 for 1988–89) out of the 18 school districts in Monroe County. It spent $20,000–25,000 each year to initiate and support the Effective Schools Improvement Process.

"I kept hearing a lot of 'Well, if we had more money, we could do this.'" says Clement. "Not only from our teachers but from other school districts. That always seems to be the line. The educators' appetite for the dollar is insatiable. We have for far too long just thrown dollars at the problems and, doggone it, I'm not going to be a part of it. We keep saying, 'Give me some more dollars, we'll do a better job.' That's just a cop-out in my judgment. Districts put in more dollars, and somehow it doesn't make a difference with the kids."

One area where Clement will spend money is on staff development. "I'm tough on a buck, but when it comes to staff development, I will spend that money," says Clement. "We will spend money in this district where we know it's going to be effective in improving the abilities of teachers in instruction."

Spencerport decided the best way to handle the process of training teachers in such areas as the elements of instruction, cooperative learning, TESA, classroom management, and other instructive procedures was to train one individual and have that one person handle the workshops and seminars for the faculty. According to both the administration and the faculty, this approach has proven very effective.

"I think there's no doubt that it helped that it was one of their own who was teaching them and working with them," believes Clement. "Yes, we have an older faculty, some of them are very set in their ways, and it was difficult to light a fire under them."

One of the problems, of course, is when anyone suggests that a teacher change their teaching approaches, the implication is that the teacher is not doing an adequate job.

"Hey, I get a lot of flak about not being behind the teachers, but I am the biggest proponent of these teachers in the district," insists Clement. "They have made it happen."

And what has happened with the Effective Schools Process is that there has been significant improvement in test scores at both the elementary and secondary levels, for all groups of children.

"Kids are achieving more all the time in this district," says Clement. "I mean, I keep hearing this nonsense that we've got to have homogeneous grouping, that we've got to isolate kids. But I don't think so. Look at the difference between a system that was very compartmentalized to a system that is opening up to more and more kids all the time.

"I'm a bug on results, on data, and when people start throwing their perceptions at me, and that's all they are is perceptions. I love to hand them the data. Now isn't it interesting, I say, that Spencerport back in 1980, for example, used to have 5 to 6 percent of our kids who won New York State Regents Scholarships? And in 1989, 21 percent of our kids won Regents scholarships—that's third highest in the whole county. And they said, 'It must be that Spencerport is getting some bright kids these days.' And I said, 'No, we're not. We're getting a lot better teaching, we're getting a lot more commitment from people and as a result, kids are in fact learning more and doing better.'"

Teachers/Administrators: Antagonists to the End

Because of the presence of such an active union and entrenched, older faculty (it is not unusual; in fact, it is the norm to encounter teachers with a minimum of 20 years' experience), and a history of mistrust between the administration and the teachers (often the norm and not the exception in school systems), the central office had to move cautiously but deliberately through the stages of school improvement.

"The board was real anxious to just push this through," maintains Clement. "I kept saying we had to be patient. And so we took our time in bringing the staff along. And, believe me, the use of consultants, especially Ron and Larry, was essential. I don't know if we could have done it without Ron and Larry."

Clement admits they made some mistakes, mostly in the area of relationships with teachers.

"Oh, we made some good mistakes, no doubt about it," he says. "But if you're going to make mistakes, make them on the side of the teachers. I mean we gave them full rein. There were times, especially in this one building, where I knew they were going to stumble, but it wasn't like they were going to listen to me. They had to find out for themselves. I just have to be supportive. I have to be a cheerleader and let them decide their own destiny."

There are numerous teachers in Spencerport who believe that the school system has gone too far in its emphasis on both the New York State Regents Exams and the grade-level testing programs. The teachers maintain there is too much teaching to the test, and that is not good for the students or the teachers.

Both Sudlow and Clement disagree. "There can be no question in anyone's mind in this district that Joe Clement has been, is, and will be a strong supporter of the New York State Board of Regents and Regents Exams," insists Clement. "Now, when somebody says, 'Well, you teach to the test,' I say, 'Wow, let's think about that. If you mean teaching to the test because you're testing what the youngster is supposed to learn, well, what's wrong with that?' Teaching to the test is a phony issue. It truly is a phony issue."

Sudlow, who has watched this argument grow over the years, believes people don't even understand what they're arguing against. "What's the purpose of testing?" asks Sudlow. "Is the purpose of testing to trip up a kid or show a kid how much the kid doesn't know? Or is the purpose of testing to find out whether or not a kid has learned the curriculum that you want the kid to learn? Every teacher who gives a local, teacher-made test on a Friday morning has been teaching to the test all week. Now you know what your objectives are and you teach the objectives."

"The bottom line," says Sudlow, "is that you need a test as an objective piece of feedback to help you know whether you're achieving what you want to achieve, whether you're teaching all the students."

Larry Lezotte says he has heard the grumblings on both sides of the testing issue in Spencerport, but says he and his people have not been officially called in to examine the situation. When asked whether it is possible for there to be too much testing, Lezotte says yes.

"Sure, it is possible to push too hard on monitoring, but I really wonder if that is the real problem in Spencerport," comments Lezotte. He notes that historically the relationship between the teachers and Clement has been rocky at best, tumultuous at worst. He suggested that if the teachers are really questioning the school improvement process it should be put to a referendum.

In early 1991, the districtwide planning committee met for the first time in several years. Administrators as well as teachers admit that progress was made in getting issues on the table and finding a common ground for discussion. Overall, there have been no major confrontations on Effective Schools itself.

Yet there are still teachers unhappy with the administration, and Clement, himself, is growing weary of the talk of incompatibility. "I'm getting real sick of this," says Clement. "Intelligent, professional people cannot live in the past. I mean, these union problems, as far as I'm concerned, are in the past. That thing was done a long time ago and now I can point to some of my best friends and best supporters among the teaching staff.

"And for those teachers—or members of the community for that matter—who are having a tough time dealing with the Effective Schools, then I say to them, look around you—why is it—with changing populations, our increased minority enrollment—why is it with these changes there is a larger percentage of kids performing at higher levels? Why is it that we've been able to move from a comfortable district to become more inclusive, to reach out to kids and their parents and offer them a better shake?"

Another criticism that is coming to the Effective Schools Process in Spencerport is that there is not enough emphasis on the "affective" growth of the child, that there is too much emphasis put on the academic growth.

"The last time I looked, that's what the schools were here for," says Clement, although he does admit that he would like to see more extracurricular activities in the schools. Spencerport does not have a major sports team.

"I think it would help a lot if we had a football team," admits Clement. "I don't think we do a good job in this district in providing the wide range of extracurricular activities for kids. I really don't. But it's more than sports. The kinds of extracurricular we need are a chess club, newspaper club, and different studies seminar. And we're working on that. But our teachers are awfully busy doing what they're supposed to do.

"And I believe the best thing we can do in public education is make winners of kids. Nothing succeeds like success. When we have a successful guy or gal, you're taking care of the affective side of the kid."

Sudlow says that this year his office is working with principals to develop more extracurricular activities. But he says it's not just a matter of extracurricular, but a matter of attitude—an attitude that may come with such an entrenched and, in many ways, conservative faculty.

"Personally speaking, I think things are too boring. It's too comfortable here. There are no risk takers, either in the principals' offices or in the classrooms," believes Sudlow. "They don't do enough things to make education better for kids and teachers. One of the things Joe and I have asked principals to do is to explore how to make school more fun for the kids, how to improve school participation. It's not that we're completely boring, it's just that there should be programs out there that really get the kids' blood running. Like I've seen in other Effective School districts."

However, given the facts that this very conservative, middle-class community took on such a massive school improvement program, and they are continuing it—well, many believe that just might be risk enough.

"Oh, there's no doubt that Effective Schools is in this district for the very long run. It is part of us, now," says Clement. "An essential part of us. The journey, the process, continues. There is still a great deal we can do, that we need to do. The important thing is to stay in focus. To stay focused on that big picture of teaching and learning for all kids. And as long as we keep doing better and better at that, well, only a fool would try to go in some other direction. The proof has arrived."

Courage and Determination

What has happened in Spencerport, New York, Junction City, Kansas, Frederick County, Maryland, Spring Branch, Texas, and Spanish Harlem, New York, is that the Effective Schools Process has become part of the culture. And being part of the culture, it is in every school, every classroom, every teacher's head, and every student's work.

Although it is essentially a bottom-up operation, it always begins in the top-down motif, with a strong, determined, committed administrator. It is that individual who begins placing the language of Effective Schools into the vocabulary of the district. Slowly, the Effective Schools Process becomes part of the fabric of the district. Inevitably, with a true leader, the process becomes *the* consistent brightly colored thread running throughout the entire tapestry that is the school community. It is the thread that all others run off of. It is the strongest, brightest thread.

The attributes required in order to be a successful superintendent, an Effective leader, for a school district going from translation to transformation in the Effective Schools Process are many and complex. To list just a few that the superintendents in this book possessed: sensitivity, honesty, self-knowledge, keen intelligence, ability to "feel" the vision and get others hooked on it, a sense of humor (able to laugh at themselves), gentleness with people, toughness with people, a lifelong learner, and a lifelong teacher.

Then there are those qualities of determination and courage. The leaders in this book—whether they are superintendents, principals, or teachers—are no saints. They have their faults and they know it. But they also know exactly what they believe, why they believe it, precisely what they want to accomplish, and how they are going to accomplish that. On this, they are determined. They will not be deterred or even slowed. They will take the dare and place their personal and professional ego and name on it. They are not frightened of failure because they know that, very simply, if the children are given the equity and quality they deserve, and if the system implements that change through the proven process of Effective Schools, there will be no failure. The dare doesn't frighten them. It is those who do not take the dare that feel their wrath—those districts not concerned with equity that frighten and anger them.

What about politics and the superintendency? It has always been assumed that, in order to survive, a superintendent must be politically astute. That is no less true with the Effective Schools Process—the difference is that the political motives are not the same. In the past, it was the superintendent's survival that was the dominant motive. In Effective Schools, it must be the educational growth and achievement of all students that motivates. Anything less is not enough, it is not right, it is not acceptable. And in Effective Schools, where teaching and learning is a moral as well as a technical endeavor, doing the right thing always ranks first—doing it in the right way is second.

These superintendents began by telling their bosses—the boards of education—that this was how they were going to do it. There was going to be change. There *had* to be change. After they explained it to the boards, the boards said, "Hey, this is common sense—go for it."

It has not been easy. There are still problems and controversies. But the research and outcomes are with these individuals, and the districts are improving for students as well as teachers and staff. There is ownership at all levels. And there is pride.

These superintendents believe that what they are doing can be done *anywhere.* It starts with the will and the Effective Schools Process. It is carried on by honest, hard teamwork, with the leader, waving a bullhorn and a spotlight, not a switch and a cloak, urging the forces onward and upward.

It takes its toll. In these districts profiled, there were many aspiring leaders who said their goal had, until recently, been to be a superintendent of a school system. But now that they had seen what it really takes to do the job effectively, they have decided to stay in lower management positions. There's living your job, they say, having the superintendency be your life—then there's what these people do. But each leader said it was worth it. When it gets too much, they head into a classroom, take a seat, and watch the children and teacher. Then everything falls back into perspective. It's just like Amelia Earhart said: "Courage is the price that life exacts for granting peace."

CHAPTER SIX

Walking the Walk

We have found schools that had strong instructional leaders that weren't effective, but we've never found an Effective School that didn't have a strong instructional leader.
—RON EDMONDS

It's real easy for the principals to just talk the talk. But that's not enough. It never is. You have to walk the walk. —LAWRENCE LEZOTTE

When I first heard about Effective Schools, it was like, finally, someone had turned me free to be the best I could be. —SUZANNE STILL, principal

Larry Dixon remembers very well his first day in freshman English at Kansas State University.

"Near the end of the period, the teacher tells the class, 'I want you to write a theme about yourself, giving us some information, and turn it in tomorrow,'" recalls Dixon. "Well, I was the last one to leave the room. Finally I walked up to the teacher and said, 'Ma'am, could you tell me what a theme is?'"

It's a long way from that question to being Lawrence Dixon, Ph.D., principal of one of the largest high schools in Kansas, and one of the most respected school administrators in the Midwest.

"That professor did not put me down," recalls Dixon. "She didn't say to me, 'You're in college, young man, you should know that.' She sat down and explained it to me and worked with me, every day. I think if she had said to me, 'Young man, you should know that by now,' I would have packed my bags and gone back to New Jersey. And who knows, I might be sitting alone in the ghetto right now. But that teacher changed the course. She believed that I could learn just like the other kids." He leans back in his crowded office in the Junction City High School and smiles.

"That was the first time anyone had ever said that to me. That I could learn just like the other kids. My whole life the teachers and principals had let me think I was just plain dumber than those white kids. And they treated me that way. Gave me the stupidest work. So you can bet when Effective Schools came along I perked up my ears. 'Say what?'"

Despite desegregation, Dixon never received equal learning opportunities when he was attending public school in the East. He was bused to an "integrated" school, then, on the basis of skin color and economic status, he was tracked directly into remedial classes where he learned how to memorize. He was a wiz at learning vocabulary and grammatical terms, but he never actually learned how to write. His teachers didn't think writing was important for the low-level classes. After all, why would a poor black kid ever need to know what a "theme" was?

"I knew I wanted something better for myself, so I tried for college," explains the tall, lean Dixon. "But I couldn't get in because my SAT scores were bad. You don't learn much in those remedial classes. So I went to work for AT&T, but I knew I didn't want to do that the rest of my life. I tried for college again. This time it was Kansas State and they took me, I guess because I could play ball. And I could also take the SATs *after* I got out there."

Once Dixon had his English composition class under control, and he learned how to write, other classes fell in line. It wasn't long before he had his master's degree and knew he wanted to devote his life to giving kids the education that he almost missed. "And the best way, the only way for me, is through Effective Schools."

Junction City, Kansas, is a military town two and a half hours west of Kansas City in the middle of the state. The school district has a population of 7,200 students, the majority of them connected to the Fort Riley Army Base in Junction City, which is home to some 20,000 soldiers. In years past, Junction City was best known as the Kansas town that imported the prostitutes from Denver on weekends to entertain the troops. The city has since cleaned up its act, but if you are looking for that idyllic farm community amidst the waving fields of grain, this is not it. It has, according to the teachers, a "garage sale economy" and is "one of the most boring places except for maybe Uranus."

The high school students reinforce that sentiment. When asked what they dislike most about Junction City, they answer: Junction City. When asked what they like most about Junction City High, they answer: Larry Dixon. Both white and black students see him as a model of proof that you can overcome adversity. And, with a little hard work, anyone can escape their beginnings—even in Junction City.

"Sure, there were some people who were a little surprised to see me end up in the principal's office," explains Dixon. "But I had been working in this district for 12 years, and this is my third year as principal. They know what I'm about. They know I treat all the kids the same. I don't take any guff from the white kids and no rap from the black kids. And the teachers? They know I'm here to help. They know I'm not going to hide anything, not going to protect anybody."

Dixon admits he remains a little angry over the short shrift he received in education. He also has some unpleasant memories of the way he was treated by his colleagues and peers. It has not been an easy climb for him; he is constantly having to prove who he is or who he is not. To this day he still gets criticism on his language skills. His speech still has a twinge of the past—that past where teachers and community did not think it was necessary for an athletic black kid to learn language skills. He says he's "always working on it."

If there is any chip on Larry Dixon's shoulder, the edges have been smoothed by his professional growth and maturity. His focus is directed almost exclusively to Junction City High School, the 1,500 students (54 percent white, 34 percent black, 12 percent other), and his own uncompromising commitment to the Effective Schools Process and school-based management.

"The support that I have is just tremendous. If I need something, I go over to central administration, and if I can justify it, they get it for me. I know you don't find that in many school districts. We make the decisions here, in this building, for us."

The Effective Schools Process has not been painless for Dixon and Junction City High School. When they first disaggregated their test scores on the California Achievement Test and the Kansas Minimal Competency Test, they realized what so many school districts have to come to terms with: They were not adequately serving the lower socioeconomic kids.

"Here we were, opening these doors every day, thinking we were giving everyone a good education and bang! Look again." That second look showed that large numbers of the low socioeconomic students were performing in the 25th percentile, the lowest quartile. In the last two years, they have started to turn those figures around. Where they had 22 percent of the low SES kids in the lowest 25th percentile, they now have less than 15 percent, often 10 percent in key areas like science, math, and language.

"Tell me that's not improvement! And while we're lowering the numbers there, we're putting more and more kids up in the top percentiles," says Dixon, stern with pride as he points out the growth on the detailed charts he is displaying. "And look at the white kids. No one is getting hurt here. The higher SES kids are going up also."

Dixon loves to show off the progress of his students. Black males up, females up. And he doesn't hesitate to point out that black students do better than white students on the CAT in spelling. "See, just like me. They've been tracked before they got to Junction City. They learn how to spell words. They don't learn much about writing, but boy, can they diagram sentences!" For these reasons, Dixon says writing is one of the most heavily emphasized skills at Junction City High School.

Although Dixon is a big proponent of the Effective School correlate calling for frequent monitoring, declaring that the data give him the chance to "prove to the nay sayers how good our kids can be and are," he insists there is one other correlate that is the key to all success.

"The main reason I like the Effective Schools program is because it doesn't draw any lines across a student's ambitions," says Dixon. "If God came down and said, 'Dixon, I'll give you one missing ingredient in this school to help you become an Effective School. Which do you want?' High Expectations. Period. Every time. Every place.

"Standards don't work. I don't like standards. Regular standards make you lazy. Then you have minimum standards and those only hold you back. Expectations are *growth*. Give everyone an equal chance to live up to our expectations. So we work with everyone. Everyone gets the same shot. The same belief. From there, the cream of the crop will rise to the top. That's why we say our minimum expectation in our mission statement is that all students will learn the essential objectives to assure that they all have equal choices upon graduation from Junction City High School. That means if I choose to go to college, I should be able to do OK on the SAT so I will be accepted."

But Dixon is a realist. He knows this isn't going to happen overnight—or over a period of a few years. "It takes a lot more than just telling teachers all kids can learn," says Dixon. "We've got to help them do it. And that's not an easy task, especially at the high school level."

Dr. Max Heim, superintendent of schools for Junction City, believes he couldn't have picked a better person for Junction City High. "Dixon not only runs that school effectively, he's the finest role model those kids could ever have." But, explains Heim, Dixon came into the position at a particularly difficult time. "Larry came in as principal just when we started disaggregating the scores," says Heim. "So he's got this new responsibility plus now here's the proof out in front that we're falling short and the lower socioeconomic kids are not doing well. So he had big problems to face right at the beginning. Those scores were also made public."

Dixon says that although he was upset at what the scores showed, he was probably the only person in town who was happy about the process of disaggregation. "Finally, thanks to the Effective Schools Process, it's out in the open. We see it right there. What we've always suspected, and what some of us have always known. The lower SES kids—the black kids, the Hispanic kids—aren't making it. And it's right there. We can't turn our backs on the facts. Now that it's out in the open, something is going to be done about it. I'm happy," affirms Dixon.

In a school district that, because of the high mobility of its students, has few constants, Larry Dixon seems to be a very dependable, consistent factor. He regularly patrols the halls, visits the classrooms, and attends to some of the discipline problems himself. ("I refuse to let any child infringe on another child's learning time.") He gets along as well with teachers as with students, with parents as well as with other administrators. He has two daughters attending the high school and says he takes very personally the motto: Teach every child as if she is your own.

Teachers support him because he has brought empowerment to the school. For the first time, they have a say in school operations and policy. And students, white and black, are not hesitant to say they see Dixon as a role model. Even the white kids, who have watched some of the battles Dixon has fought, say they are inspired by the man.

Running a large high school with a changing as well as extremely mobile population is difficult. And Dixon admits he has made mistakes. It's tough, he points out, knowing how to balance the different factions that operate within a high school. But it is also a matter of being proactive, of knowing how to *direct* and, at the same time, delegate. That, says Dixon, echoing the sentiment of all Effective principals, is the toughest balancing act of all.

Despite the growing pains of transforming a high school bureaucracy, Larry Dixon has learned how to "walk the walk" of the Effective Schools Improvement Process. In its most precise but all-encompassing terms, walking the walk—*effectively*—means:

- Attention to detail
- Attention to the needs of people—the teachers, staff, and especially the students
- Dialogue to demonstrate the mission and articulate the issues of change
- Confidence in staff to solve problems with the principal and parents
- Reconfiguration of school according to the correlates—changing the way things are everyday, with an eye on the goal of teaching all children

Dixon does not feel like a lonely black man standing amidst the blonde wheat fields of Kansas. "Hey, I feel wanted here. This is where I belong. This is where people gave me a chance. Not back in New Jersey. It was here that someone said a poor, black kid can learn just like a white kid. And there is a challenge here, and I care about the people. I know I can make a difference."

Dixon is also a realist, however. "Reality is that we're not going to save all kids, so I don't lose any sleep when I have to put a kid out of here. Because I can say pretty much that we've given every kid that we have an opportunity to make it here. We may do it a little differently than the next place and yes, we take some risks, but we give them all the same chance, a good chance," says a proud Dixon.

It is that characterization as the risk taker that sets the Effective School principal apart, whether he or she is in the wheat fields, among the New York tenements, or the barrios and corrals of the southwest. The problem is: There aren't that many risk takers in the public schools.

"We only find about a third of the principals out there willing to take risks," says Lawrence W. Lezotte, Ph.D. "Just a third who even begin to be that kind of charismatic, leading principal you want at the school level. The others are all looking for guidance from elsewhere, and too often, it's just not there."

What happens in most Effective School districts is that a superintendent steps in and gives control to the principals. Those principals are either already trained in Effective Schools philosophy or are eager for the opportunity. But there also has to be that other factor—the ability and courage to take the right risks, to shoot your cannons at the right time.

Having the Guts to Do the Right Thing

It has become very comfortable, and, for some, fairly profitable, to continue the status quo, no matter what level of mediocrity and/or failure is reached. What school districts need is someone willing to take a chance, or as Tony Amato, superintendent of District 6, Spanish Harlem, in New York, says, "Somebody who has the guts to do the right thing. No matter what."

One of those people in Spanish Harlem is Mirian Acosta-Sing, principal of the Mott School, a very old, crowded, five-story, former convent, without cafeteria or gymnasium, on the corner of 131st Street and Convent Avenue. It is P.S./I.S. 223, and in 1988 it had the highest reading scores in New York City.

"Oh, this didn't happen overnight," explains the vibrant Acosta-Sing. "We had to shake this place upside down, inside out. I'm sure people thought I was out of my head. Nuts. But sometimes you just do it because you have to."

The Mott Hall School, which is a school of Mathematics, Science and Technology for the Gifted and Talented, was not giving out many gifts a few years ago. According to Acosta-Sing, it was a disorganized, confused school with no focus. "None of the Effective School correlates was in place," says Acosta-Sing. "The school needed so much. There was no handbook about the school, no teacher bulletin. We didn't even require a writing sample before allowing kids in. Although we had a very committed faculty, there was no direction. The classes were not organized in any way that would lead to enrichment."

She pulled the teachers and administrators together and started to work out a plan—collaboratively. This was the first time many of these teachers had ever been consulted on how to improve the school they were part of. They responded with insight and enthusiasm. First, they built a structure for enrichment, then planned courses, then a handbook, then instructions for admission, then staff development and programs to motivate teachers.

While the teachers worked on their courses, Acosta-Sing stepped outside the school and started to beat the drums of the community—across the street and on Wall Street. She went to nearby City College and got her students involved in pre-med and other programs. Then she tackled the business community: Coopers and Lybrand, Morgan Stanley & Co. She pulled in lawyers, architects, loan officers, hospital administrators, doctors, marketing executives, environmentalists. Anyone who expressed an interest? "No, anyone I could get to listen." There are poets, artists, musicians, actors, journalists. Among the Enrichment Programs: Architects in Residence, Poets in the Schools, Urban Woodlands, Symphony Space, CNN Newsroom, Harlem School of the Arts, Street Project.

The tired walls of the old convent have never held so much activity. You walk into the school and a subtle buzz of excitement is heard. Everyone is busy. Everyone is energized. The chipping plaster and crowded library and the cramped-upper story rooms used as a cafeteria are unimportant. What matters here is the energy and desire of the students and their teachers.

"Before Effective Schools (Process), we didn't even have a mission," says Acosta-Sing. "We didn't know where we were going. Now we know we can go anywhere. And we do! Our teachers are accountable, just as our students are. We expect a lot from all of us. The tools of Effective Schools are the tools we will all need to be better, to be the best we can be."

Acosta-Sing knows what she's competing against. You just have to look out her office window. Her kids are not coming from Riverdale and Park Avenue. They are coming from the street—from one- and no-parent homes, where often instead of breakfast cereal on the kitchen table, the children see the dirty brown streaks of cheap heroin or the cloudy vials of crack. Unlike the troubled middle-class family that litters the rooms with empty bottles of scotch and gin, here the decaying apartments hold the refuse of drugs. Children live an X-rated existence. Often the only escape they see is the bribe of the drug pusher—or hopefully the school.

"I know what I'm up against," says Acosta-Sing, showing her anger as she gestures towards the street. "The offers they get out there can be very, very appealing. Very! When you're that poor. We've got to offer them something better."

What she offers them is a way out—and proof it can be done. That is why, she says, she works so hard putting together the enrichment programs—to show the children there is someplace else, something better than the streets.

"We give them the best we have, then we hold them accountable," says Acosta-Sing, adding that the overwhelming majority of the students not only live up to the challenge, "they go beyond it."

Tangible evidence of the success of the changes at Mott Hall is seen not only in the rise in reading and math scores—that put Mott Hall on the front page of *The New York Times*—but the consistent 98 percent or better attendance record. And now that the school has this special energy, and apparently a principal who is willing to take risks for her school, the teachers now give her "125 percent—yes, they give me an extra 25 percent in time and energy every week."

Is Acosta-Sing a loose cannon? Her eyes circle around her school and she laughs, happily. "Do you know a better way to get things done?" But she is quick to add this would not be possible if it were not for Superintendent Tony Amato and the Effective Schools Process. "Effective Schools gives me the tools. The central office gives me the power," says Acosta-Sing.

This sentiment is repeated in the northern part of District 6 in P.S. 152 where another young principal begins her days at 6:30 A.M., and does not leave before 7:00 in the evening. Mrs. Felicita Villodas is the tough but loving principal of 1,500 elementary students, 93 percent of whom are Hispanic and are crammed into another ancient five-story brick building. This one, however, does manage a small cafeteria, and despite all the bodies flowing through in shifts, there is a clear sense of order and calm.

"We teach our children that control, politeness, manners are very important," says Villodas, stopping to hug a third-grader and congratulate him on a science project. "They see enough of the other behavior outside these doors. We're an oasis here, in many, many ways."

As she walks proudly through her school, she stops to corner a central office administrator about crossing guards that are needed and then turns to deal quickly with a contractor who, with his crew, is putting on a much needed addition.

"We have to fight to keep everything going here," she says. "But we do it. We have to. It often means pushing people who don't want to be pushed, but, well, I have my priorities."

Despite the age of the five-story building (built in 1927) and the numbers of children, the hallways are immaculate. The walls have new coats of paint and the floors are freshly polished. Within the classrooms, there is a keen attentiveness as teachers work excitedly to kindle the fires of learning. Bright, eager faces follow every word, every stroke on the blackboard.

The majority of the children are in green and blue plaid uniforms. Yes, this is a public school, and yes, the girls are in jumpers with white blouses, and the boys are in pants with blazers or sweaters, white shirts and ties. And there are not many pairs of sneakers. Most children are wearing loafers or tie shoes. And outside this school is the community with the highest crime rate and drug rate of any neighborhood in New York.

"We do the uniforms for the obvious reason of pride and neatness," says Villodas, adding that not all parents approve. "But many see it as a plus. It's expensive to keep a kid in school clothes today. Especially when you have to compete with what your neighbor is wearing. But for $84, they get a couple uniforms, blouses, jumpers, shirts, blazer, sweater. It can make life much easier."

Villodas, like other Effective School principals, knows what is happening in each classroom, and is quick to show it off, always eager to express her pride for the children and the teacher. And the teachers do not hesitate to applaud their principal. "Look at her, look at her energy, look at how she cares," exclaims a fourth-grade teacher. "How can you not be inspired by that? Who could ever do a mediocre job when she's out there working like she does?"

Villodas says it's important to her to set a strong example and to be a role model for teachers as well as students. But, she adds, she always feels like she's not doing enough. However, the shortcomings of P.S. 152 appear to be more a fault of the system than anything that is happening within the school.

For example, Villodas points to the reading resource room. It is, very simply, a converted shower room, with the spigots still protruding from the peeling walls. Every inch of space is taken with small reading labs, bookshelves, electronic equipment, desks for the students, and a cramped corner for the teachers. But for the 11 women who work in this overcrowded atmosphere, you would think, listening to them and observing their energy level and degree of excitement, that they were in a spacious state-of-the-art reading resource center at a major university. It is obvious that what matters to them is the children, not the room they're in. They are proud, dedicated professionals. "We show off our kids, not the room," says one teacher.

"I don't know how they keep their spirits up day after day," says Villodas. "No, I take that back. I do know. It's the kids. They work hard with the kids, but they see how it pays off."

Like the other schools in District 6, the change with the Effective Schools Process has been dramatic at P.S. 152. The teachers talk about being involved for the first time in the school's decisions. They say they feel like they "really matter"—not just for what they do in the classroom, but for what they contribute to the operation of the entire school.

Like Mott Hall, P.S. 152 brings in other professionals from outside to tutor the students and help in the classrooms. Parents are now a major factor, often showing their appreciation by holding celebratory breakfasts or teas for the teachers and administrators.

The school itself has become a strong, independent educational facility. Because of school-based management and its visionary, determined, and committed principal, it operates much like a business. It has thrown away the old paradigm of the inner-city public school. It is not an expensive babysitting service with metal detectors at the doors and uniformed police in the corridors. It is a calm, controlled educational business. With climbing reading and math scores, it is a successful business.

These school "businesses" in New York have to fight daily against the pull of a much glitzier business—a business that, in its own bizarre way, is an equal opportunity facilitator. As expressed in the movie *New Jack City:* "Drugs are not a black thing. Drugs are not a white thing. Drugs are a death thing." And principals all over the United States are realizing they have to make the learning options greater than the money and hazy euphoric fix of drugs. It is a challenge that is requiring the pulling in and processing of every available resource.

What Larry Dixon has done out in the wheat fields of Kansas, and what Mirian Acosta-Sing and Felicita Villodas have done in the dangerous and tragic neighborhoods of New York, is be *change agents* for their schools. They took on their leadership responsibilities just as the Effective Schools Process was gearing up in their district. The lines were still very hazy, but they grabbed hold of the process, set themselves out as the visionary leader, brought their "business" together, brought their teachers together, and then marched around on the deck doing whatever was necessary to serve the constituents in the best way possible.

In *The Transformational Leader* (1986) by Noel M. Tichy and Mary Anne DeVanna, leaders are described as being change agents, lifelong learners, courageous, value driven, visionaries, and people who believe in people. These are the characteristics that you will find in the Effective principal.

As Tom Peters and Nancy Austin (1985)* state, "Leaders create a 'place to go,' a 'place to be.' They have commitment, passion, zest, energy, care, love, enthusiasm that they readily express. And that is their distinction."

Because the Effective School Process is based on decentralized school-based improvement, or management, the ability of the principal to work with people is a vital factor. A principal needs to have not only the trust but the respect of the school community. And, according to Kouzes and Posner (1987), they must also have the capability to inspire people, by their own free wills, "to climb the summit." Considering the diversity of needs and wants of a public school, this encouragement of staff is not only vital in assisting a school in achieving its goals but it also makes the job less demanding for the principal.

Kouzes and Posner list five principles of a leader that they believe achieve the purpose of getting people to "climb the summit." When you examine each one of these steps, you see that they integrate that delicate balancing act of *directing* and *delegating*:

1. Leaders challenge the process.
2. Leaders inspire a shared vision.
3. Leaders enable others to act.
4. Leaders model the way.
5. Leaders encourage the heart.

Daring to Guarantee Success

For John Morefield, principal of the Hawthorne School in Seattle, the first step, and the most important part of the job when he began, was communicating the vision and seeing who really understood what Hawthorne was out to do.

*From *A Passion for Excellence* by Thomas J. Peters and Nancy K. Austin. Copyright © 1985 by Thomas J. Peters and Nancy K. Austin. Reprinted by permission of Random House, Inc.

"It all begins with the principal having a vision of where the desired future state is. That vision has to be presented and understood by the faculty," says Morefield. "So, I begin by telling them, 'This is the vision. Now some of you were here before I came. Some of you think you will be here after I leave. But I'm in this thing for the long haul. This is the direction the train is going. If you want to get on this train, great. If you don't, then you need to make some choices.'

"This is not to say the leader must be an autocrat. That is the last thing I am. I am incredibly inclusive in what I do, but it's very clear to the people in the schools where I am that I have a vision of what a school ought to be and I communicate that vision in a regular way. Effectively. That is something strong leaders need to be able to do. Not only to the teaching staff, but to the parents, the community, and to the kids. There has to be a unity of purpose. We are all in this thing together to accomplish the same goal."

Morefield says he makes the vision of success for *all* children a part of every communication. Research shows that this is essential at the school level and the district level. But right now, for Morefield, the concern was his elementary school campus. He knew that in maintaining an ongoing discourse on school improvement, there were three things he must do:

1. Establish a language of school improvement.
2. Create organizational structures.
3. Dedicate time to the discourse of school improvement, introducing ongoing and current research.

Morefield deals with the communication of school improvement not only in individual teacher meetings and faculty meetings but in special staff development seminars and regular faculty retreats. "We are constantly affirming who we are and why we are here," says Morefield. "This isn't a job, this is a vocation, a calling. This is serious business here."

The business is so serious for Morefield that he worked out a unique deal with the Seattle school board: If the board allowed him to work with the teachers' union so that he could staff the school in a way that core teachers came there by choice (after extensive interviews with Morefield and making a commitment to the mission), he would guarantee that within six years, the entering kindergarten class—each and every one of them—would graduate from the fifth grade at fifth-grade level or better.

"If that doesn't happen, then they fire me," says Morefield. "And if they don't fire me, I'll quit. I'll resign."

The board and the union bought it and now Morefield says he has a faculty that is dedicated to the mission and to the Effective Schools Process. And just two years into his guarantee, Morefield believes the school is a "phenomenal success." In 1989, 32 percent of the black students were in the lower quartile on the California Achievement Tests; in 1990, that was reduced to 19 percent. In 1989, 8 percent of the white students were in the lower quartile in reading. There were none in 1990.

The Hawthorne School, opened in 1989, is in a tired, inner-city neighborhood of Seattle. There are 430 children, 60 percent are minority, with 65 percent on free or reduced lunch. Twelve different languages (dialects from the Pacific Rim to East Berlin) are spoken at Hawthorne. There are 85 students who are classified as non-English speaking.

Seattle is a city where parents can choose where to send their children. In the last year, there has been an increase in the number of white parents who have chosen to transport their children across town to the Hawthorne School. The parents say they send their children for three reasons: the quality of the learning, Morehead and his staff, and the diversity of the students.

Morefield seems to have taken to heart the leadership principle of "challenging the process."

"We apologize a lot around here," he says. What he means is that the school is forever overstepping the bounds that have been drawn by central administration. For example, when Morefield and his staff discover a new way of teaching special needs children that has not been approved (or perhaps even realized) by the central office, Morefield will go ahead and institute the program. And when central office comes down on him, he starts apologizing: "Oh, I'm so sorry, I had no idea. I should have asked, but, well, I'm really sorry." Or when he goes out and pulls in 30 new computers from private business and is informed he didn't do the proper central office paperwork: "Oh, I'm so sorry. I should have known. It will never happen again. So sorry."

Morefield maintains it has been the added support of the community that has made Hawthorne as strong as it is. That support and involvement is something Morefield seeks diligently, often urgently. And when he says "community," he means *community*—not just parents.

"I know how much we need everyone out there," he says, giving the impression that the involvement of the community may be the deciding factor in the success of Hawthorne. Rather than establish a PTA, which Morefield believes excludes many people because it has the stereotype of white, middle-class power in the schools, he has set up Friends of Hawthorne, a tax-exempt, nonprofit organization with its own 501(c)3 to keep Uncle Sam happy.

"Yes, it raises tons of money," says Morefield. "But more importantly, it is the outreach to traditionally less involved parents, those who tend to be poor and minority, or single parents. Part of what we do is find ways that will hook and engage parents, always being aware of the needs that they may have. Every event that we have has childcare; every event that we have invites people by telephone, utilizing the oral tradition in the black community; every event that we have attempts to have something in it for parents, something that either their child is doing or something that they can do for their child."

At the first session in October, there was an evening with "lots of food and lots of childcare" with parents making reading and math activities directly related to what their kids were doing in school. They could all do these activities at home together. It was a "phenomenal success."

Unfortunately, for many of the disadvantaged parents, the public schools have already failed them one time and they are wary of any potential for success their children may have. For those parents, Morefield assigns a "buddy" to be with them at all school meetings. Teachers and staff regularly visit the home so the parent at least knows that the school cares.

"While these parents have the wish that education will be different for their child, for most black parents, they have given up hope that the public schools can really do it," explains Morefield. "Part of our task is to ask them, first, to suspend their disbelief one more time, and then, see if we can help them find hope by the end. And we will do it. We are doing it. I have 100 percent support from every black parent I work with."

But Morefield also has a secret weapon that other principals would beg for. She's up in her own bright, inviting room on the second floor, holding court for whomever comes in, whether they want something, have something to give, or just need a hug or a boost to keep them going.

She is Lea "Mom" Wilson, a bold, loving, retired school teacher who greets friend and stranger with open arms. She has what amounts to a veritable department store in her room—from sacks of rice to diapers to jeans and sneakers. Whatever needs the children may have, she can fill.

"I'm just here to help," she says, daring you with a smile. "Look, this morning I was able to get all this fresh fruit from the guys down at the warehouse. I just told 'em we needed some up here and they said, 'Sure, Mom, whatever we can do to help out.'" She proudly displayed a bushel basket of oranges, apples, and melons. From other merchants around the neighborhood, she will get the other goods.

"You never know when a child is going to have a little accident," she says, running her hands along a shelf of different sizes of pants, shirts and sweaters. "This way they don't have to interrupt their day by going home, by us trying to find the parent, getting the parent out of work. And it's appreciated. We always get everything back. Usually the next morning that child has it back to me all cleaned and pressed."

But Mom Wilson's greatest role at Hawthorne is getting parents to do something they may not think they want to do. "If we call these parents and they still don't show up, then I just get myself over there," she explains. "I pick up that mother or father, bring them over here, and make sure they get to see that there is a different reality in this school than perhaps their historical reality."

Although the major emphasis of Hawthorne is on academics, a considerable amount of attention is given to the social behavior of the students.

The atmosphere is very strict. Morefield emphasizes there is "absolutely no backtalking allowed."

"We're a very warm, nurturing, loving environment, but our discipline is very tight," he says, pointing out the cafeteria where students are not only quiet but take extra time to wipe down their tables with a sponge. "At the beginning of the year we always have disruptive behavior because we have kids coming from other schools that must be zoos. They have not only been passed by academically but they haven't been taught basic manners, behaviors, issues of politeness and courtesy."

Morefield believes one of the reasons for the legacy of bad behavior is because many of the liberals of the sixties thought the bad behavior was something that should be tolerated, and not stopped. "Now I'm just as liberal as I ever was," says Morefield, "but that has nothing to do with the fact kids should have respect for each other, respect for their parents. It's a must in this school." He says he believes you do the kids a disservice to expect anything less.

Watching the students file through the corridors, or go to lunch or assembly, it is obvious that the correlate of a clean and safe environment is taken very seriously. But because the students are quiet does not mean they are lacking in enthusiasm. In the classrooms they cannot wait to demonstrate their knowledge, their hands striking into the air like swords seeking stars.

The variety of outside businesses and organizations involved with Hawthorne grows almost daily. The city zoo, banks, legal offices, museums, and colleges are among the groups that have "adopted" Hawthorne. Morefield talks of getting businesses involved to the point where they support, pay for, and end up chaperoning field trips for different classes. He is just as successful in getting individuals involved with Hawthorne. He has tutors ranging in age from the teens to the nineties, from sea captains to city councilors to surgeons to artists and musicians.

"And each person who comes in the door knows exactly what this school is all about. They know the mission, the vision, and they know we're going to succeed," says Morefield, who hastens to add that he is also clear in telling his people that the improvement process is going to take "just as long as we are here."

This acknowledgment that improvement does not stop when the programs are in place and the first test scores are read is essential to the growth of the Effective School. From his very first discussion with prospective Effective principals and teachers, Larry Lezotte pounds home the theme that the principal must constantly be refining the school organization. "The principal must convince all members of the school community that there are only two kinds of schools—improving and declining," says Lezotte. "An improving school lives by the belief that a school must continuously adapt its organizational practices, continuously improve."

This means different things to different schools, depending on the degree of progress being made, the level of collaboration, and the overall amount of change taking place within the school. What every principal depends on, though, is the research and data available through the Effective Schools Process. The principals are able to discern where their school is in the improvement process, and what they can anticipate. There is always more information on programs and progress available—information that is expanding and evolving.

Many Effective School principals say there are three questions that they keep asking themselves throughout the school year: What business are we in? How well is business doing? What can be done to improve business?

If these questions sound a little too "business for profit" oriented to a principal new at the task, then Effective School practitioners say that individual may not quite understand the task. The bottom line for every principal is to carry out the mission of educating *all* students. That is the business they are in. And the most important time to keep reminding the school community of that is when the school is going through a difficult conversion or adjustment.

"Nothing serves an organization better—especially during times of agonizing doubt and uncertainties—than leadership that knows what it wants, communicates those intentions, positions itself correctly, and empowers its workforce," state Bennis and Nanus (1985).*

The authors explain what they believe are the four best strategies for accomplishing and maintaining this posture:

1. *Attention through vision:* "I see a durable future state."
2. *Meaning through communication:* "I can convey that future state clearly and forcefully."
3. *Trust through positioning:* "I can take action to make the vision happen."
4. *Development of self:* "I behave in ways that best promote the best efforts of self and others."

The essence of this consistency of mission and ongoing improvement is *stability* for the school. A strong, instructional leader will leave no doubt as to the course the school is on. Yes, there is collaboration, but a truly effective instructional leader is always guiding, always directing. The analogy of a sailing ship is particularly helpful here. The mission can be viewed as the rudder. The principal, captain of the ship, tending the wheel, keeps the school balanced and on course, but is not ostentatious in that accomplishment. You know

*Excerpt from *Leaders: The Strategies for Taking Charge* by Warren Bennis and Burt Nanus. Copyright © 1985 by Warren Bennis and Burt Nanus. Reprinted by permission of HarperCollins Publishers.

the principal is there on the bridge, and the mission and goals, right below the surface, are directing the course.

Directing Quietly, Below the Surface

Dr. Jill Hearne personifies the mission and goals of the Adelaide Elementary School in the Federal Way District of Seattle. On all surveys of the school, she receives very high marks from faculty and staff on the integrity and conduct of her instructional leadership. Hearne comes right out and pushes aside any glorifications of her job. It is not an easy one in the nineties, if you are going to do the job right, "but once you bring the school community together, everything is possible."

Hearne spends considerable time working with her teachers, in groups as well as on an individual basis. There is a strong collegiality evident to even the most inexperienced eye. The teachers' lounge is just a few steps from Hearne's office, the doors are always open, and interaction is steady and respectful.

"I trust her," explains a third-grade teacher nodding towards Hearne's office. "I trust her leadership, I trust her skills with curriculum and teacher development. I trust her with parents, with the kids."

Hearne agrees that the trust element is one of the most essential at Adelaide, as well as the free flow of information and feelings. "I respect these teachers and, yes, of course I trust them. Very, very much," says Hearne. That trust has not just increased the collegiality at Adelaide, it has laid the groundwork for substantive changes in teaching for learning.

"In the past we used to teach according to the Betty Crocker approach," explains Hearne. "You do this and the kid will come out like that. And everyone was to act accordingly. I don't like that. I prefer, let's say, the gourmet approach where I trust the teacher to do the best for her class. They have the knowledge to know what their students need."

This is a process that does not, to the confusion of some, leave out the principal; quite the contrary, it involves the principal even more directly in the classroom activity.

"What they need from me is two things. First, the expertise that I can bring in the area of instruction and curriculum. And if it's an area that I don't know, I better find out about it or be able to point the teacher in the right direction," emphasizes Hearne. "And second, they have to know that I believe in their abilities, that I have absolute faith that they are doing the right thing for their students. You can't always follow a textbook curriculum. The teacher has to know that I trust them if they are going to take the risky step of deviating from the textbook curriculum."

One of the examples of that is the Adelaide class dealing with the education of students on the subject of AIDS. The class, developed at the Adelaide, has won national recognition and praise. The quality and value of the course—along with the Adelaide's close work with the community—negated the threat of any controversy.

The success of that "gourmet approach" to teaching for learning shows up with all work scoring far above average on basic skills tests for the children of the Adelaide. And the trust shows up on the staff assessment questionnare where teachers applaud Hearne's leadership. They say she has brought an openness and stability that allows them to do their best work.

Hearne realizes that a vital part of operating an Effective School is the ability to hire good people. This has not always been possible, given that in the past, teacher assignments were made by central offices with little regard to the needs or sentiments of the school. But now, with school-based management, principals, along with their teachers, have greater say.

"Of course I'm very careful in whom I hire," says Hearne. "And if they don't make it, I remove them. It's difficult, especially with all the paperwork today, but it has to be done. What I need in teachers is creativity, flexibility, and intelligence. You give me that, and I'm usually happy."

Although Adelaide has a minority population of only 11 (out of a student body of 525), the community is changing with the influx of more Hispanic and Pacific Rim families. The faculty and staff say they have been preparing for the change with numerous multicultural programs and specific staff development seminars. They say they look forward to serving more new students.

"Let's face it, this is America today. This is our future. We've got to remove this hesitancy, all these preconceived notions," says Hearne, who also teaches education at Seattle Pacific University and feels very adamantly about the term *at-risk* students.

"I don't like that term," says Hearne, as she pauses in a classroom to hug a student and talk with him about a reading test. "As soon as you use that term, you give an excuse why a child is going to fail. In talking with my staff and in my mailings, I use the term *school dependent*, because it sends a message to the staff that the success of this child is dependent on the school and you can't be sitting around waiting for that parent to come home or for food to get on the table or for the clothes to get bought. What happens with these kids depends on what we do here at school. And the buck stops here."

Changing a Tough High School

The inertia on that buck can be pretty strong when it rolls into the office of the principal of a large high school—especially when that high school is located in a traditionally working-class community where it has "not been cool to be bright."

So when the buck stops in the office of Cathy Davidson, Ed.D., there can be the loose change of many different and strong agendas tinkling around it. For that reason alone, Davidson believes it is absolutely vital that she keep the mission of her school in the forefront of everyone's thinking.

"We are not here to keep the past going. Not at all," says Davidson, a former physical education teacher and business teacher. "We are here to educate *all* the kids. Not just the ones that want to graduate with the skills to do auto repair or landscaping (a major business in the Seattle area), but the kids who also want the liberal arts and the chance at a college education."

Tahoma High School has a student body of 1,500 students with only a handful (8 or 9) minority. It is in Maple Valley, a 45-minute drive from downtown Seattle, and a community known for its "toughness." There are a lot of cows (a fair amount of ranching goes on in the area) and trucks are more often than not wearing a gun rack. Nearby, coal is being excavated.

For years, the high school reflected the community. A tough school with discipline problems is not found only in the urban sprawl. In fact, Davidson thought her experience in physical education may come in very handy.

"Principals before me often spent their time breaking up fights, tackling fleeing students in the hallways, and dealing with the toilets blowing up," says Davidson, who has been principal for four years and says it has "been a while" since the huge four wheel drive "monster" trucks drove up on the grassy knoll by her office, their bumpers within inches of the window, usually when she was seated at her desk talking with a board member about how the school had calmed down.

But Maple Valley is quickly changing. It is fast becoming a bedroom community for Boeing and Nordstrom's. Larger homes and housing developments being built, and along with this population influx is coming the demand for change at the high school.

"Just as we started to change with the Effective Schools and I came in, it was clear the needs of the community were also changing," explains Davidson, as she hurries to an all-school assembly on drug and alcohol use. The precariousness of her situation is not something she dismisses. As Davidson oversees and directs the change in this high school, she says she is very aware of the fact that before her, Tahoma High was a revolving door for principals who, she said, managed with a tight autocratic style.

"And it obviously wasn't working," she says, climbing up onto the bleachers in the gymnasium as a rock band begins to play. She pauses to talk with students and teachers and is very comfortable, rocking and clapping to the loud music. "As soon as I arrived here, I knew we had to do something to get this faculty and staff together. We needed help. I had read about Effective Schools and in my gut, I knew that was our best bet."

Davidson began by contacting the University of Washington and Jerry Bamberg, Ed.D., about a special school survey he was conducting to assess different schools' needs. The faculty and staff of Tahoma High took the survey and found considerable divisiveness, no clear mission, and a lack of understanding as to how the school should be functioning, philosophically as well as physically.

"It's that thing that Effective Schools talks about all the time," says Davidson, trying to be heard above the rock music. "Student outcomes should drive your programs and you cannot, as educators, punish your kids for not coming to you with all the skills that you think they should have." She smiles at a group of students off to the side and continues. It is very clear that she has no intention of letting the students think she doesn't care about this assembly and the topic just as much as they do.

"By God, these kids are coming to us with whatever they have, and if you're a teacher, your responsibility is to help them learn, not to measure them according to whatever standard you arbitrarily selected as being tenth-grade level. That was hard for us. It still is, and I'm not real proud of that."

But she is proud of the progress the school is making. The environment is now calm, clean, and safe. Even on this particular day, with all the grades crowded into the gymnasium rocking and stomping to a rock band screaming against drugs, there is no sense that the crowd is not in control. Davidson remains energized and involved throughout the entire concert, joining in the singing and clapping, general good time, and comaraderie.

"That would have been a real zoo five years ago," she says after the concert is over and she is outside on the school grounds, showing off the expansive and very impressive track and athletic facilities. "We wouldn't have been able to do it. But now we have a sense of pride in the school, and stability."

Staff development has come in strong. Each year there are more courses offered for teachers and staff on and off campus. And each year more people become involved. There are also programs, retreats with students, and a major push to involve parents, who were neglected in the past.

"One of the most important things for us as an institution is that kids and staff and parents know that I'm here, not just mentally but emotionally here," explains Davidson. "And because I'm committed to whatever it is that we decide that we're going to do, it's something that other people can hook onto and they can trust and they can become energized and they know we're going to get on with it together. Nobody's alone.

"If they want to throw their hat in a special ring and it's of value, then I'm right there with them. They have to feel safe to do that and I try to make them feel safe. I like to trust people. And for me leadership comes first from personal qualities. They've got to trust who I am, what I stand for."

Davidson is as excited in her description of the mechanics shop and weight rooms as she is the library and computer room. She is just as at ease in a class for the behaviorally disturbed as she is talking to the football players in the cafeteria. ("There hasn't been a food fight all year, thank God.")

And she is not afraid to be honest about the problems facing Tahoma High. The problems are serious; Davidson's honesty about them is disarming in its bluntness.

"I think one of the most exciting things about what's going on in this district right now is that there are a whole bunch of people who understand the need for change—and change meaning that it's not working for kids. It's not working for kids so is there an answer? No. And are you afraid that you don't know the answer? Well, kind of. But are you willing to venture into the discussion? Well, sort of. And will you go with me? Yeah. And so there's an esprit de corps, that comraderie that makes it safe for people to say, 'It hasn't worked, but we're going to change that.'"

Davidson says she's a devout believer when it comes to the tenets of the Effective Schools Process—from modeling for students and teachers to regular visits to the classrooms. She says she doesn't visit the classrooms as much as she would like because she is afraid of interrupting. But unlike many other high schools (effective and not effective), the teachers put on the assessment surveys that they would like to see her in the classrooms more often. It's obvious they respect and desire her input.

"They're starting to be very proud of what we're doing here," says Davidson, who is quick to admit this change is going to be difficult and may not please everyone. "We are in a crucial stage of transition here. We're going to look very different at the end of this than I think many people out there suspect, and I don't know if they're ready for that," says Davidson, not masking her concern.

"But the real issue is whether or not we can get off the dime, whether or not we can make the changes, and are we ready for the changes. People are committed, but they're also tired. Do we have the strength for the changes?"

Davidson says she has the strength, and the fact that it involves risk doesn't bother her. "You have to take risks; it's too important not to." She says she only has to look at the past, in this school and other schools, to see what happens when a principal becomes content doing technical maintenance on the status quo.

The risk-taking component continually rears its head in discussion of the Effective Schools principal. And it is not only in a school on the edge that the principal need be a risk taker. As demonstrated by the work of Jill Hearne in a fairly stable, upper middle-class community in Seattle, it is just as important for her to be a risk taker. In Hearne's situation, it is, among other things, the willingness to place the ultimate decision making in the classroom in the teachers' hands.

For principals in inner city, at-risk schools, the risk taking can be very dramatic because bold moves are needed there to precipitate change. Principals often say that, despite the backing of research, they are "flying by the seat of my pants" in implementing change.

Bennis and Nanus (1985)* list ten dominant characteristics of a leader:

1. Risk taking
2. Clear sense of purpose
3. Persistence
4. Self-knowledge
5. Perpetual learners
6. Love of their work
7. Ability to attract and energize people
8. Mature in human relationships
9. Fail-safe (do not believe in failure)
10. Ultimately followers

Because of the significant amount and degree of interaction in the school setting, the importance of being "mature in human relationships" is often pointed to as not only one of the most important characteristics but one of the most difficult to achieve. There are at least three identifying features of individuals possessing this "maturity":

1. They accept people the way they are.
2. They are centered in the present and not the past; they do not dwell on mistakes and they give people several chances.
3. They do not take people for granted, treating those close to them with the same attention they would a stranger.

A Matter of Trust

"Oh, I have absolutely no doubt that the quality of the interaction, the mutual respect, the values of the relationships in the Hollibrook are the major reasons it is so successful," says Hal Guthrie, Ed.D., superintendent of the Spring Branch (Texas) Independent School District.

He also has no doubt that the reason for that quality, respect, and value is the principal, Suzanne Still. But the process of developing that has not been easy. When Still first took over the 1,000-student Hollibrook (74 percent Hispanic, 13 percent white, 7 percent black, 5 percent Asian) in one of the poorest, grimiest, troubled parts of town, she didn't think she had been done any favors.

*Excerpt from *Leaders: The Strategies for Taking Charge* by Warren Bennis and Burt Nanus. Copyright © 1985 by Warren Bennis and Burt Nanus. Reprinted by permission of HarperCollins Publishers.

"My first reaction was 'What did I do wrong to deserve that?' Really. This was a school where teachers said they didn't like to say they were teachers because then someone would ask them where they taught and they'd have to say Hollibrook," says Still, who grimaces at the thought of such sentiment.

She goes on to say she finds it abhorrent when a teacher introduces himself or herself as "just a school teacher." "That's terrible. Where is society without teachers? It's nowhere. Since the beginning of time, the teacher has been the essential element."

Still believes that it is her attitude toward teachers, coupled with her belief that a school is "for the kids, not for the adults, the school board, the state, just the kids," that has made her leadership so successful at Hollibrook.

"You see, I'm a teacher first. I will always be a teacher first. And as a teacher, I have always resented people who thought they knew more about what I should be doing than I did," says Still, who adds that that type of second guessing just doesn't go on in other professions.

Believing in the knowledge of her teachers, Still's first acts were to ask the teachers what they thought was good as well as bad about Hollibrook, and how they thought it should be changed. It was the beginning of a heretofore nonexistent foundation of trust between principal and teachers. "We have trust here. That is a key to it all. Trust," she explains. "I trust the teachers, students, parents. They trust me. They have ownership of the school. And the more ownership, the better job they do."

Still's enthusiasm for Hollibrook is not only contagious—it is exhilarating. Whether she is explaining the daily health fitness classes where the children take their pulse before and after ("We work on the development of the whole child; they learn about nutrition, exercise, how to maintain their health") or discussing a child with a learning problem ("He just didn't see why reading was so vital. Then he told me he wanted to be an Air Force pilot. Well, that's all I needed. He's now reading everything we have on flight and the military, working on plane models . . ."), there is a relentless building of joy in her manner. Unashamedly, she admits that the only workdays she is unhappy are when she has to be out of the school, away from the children.

Unfortunately, that seems to be happening more often as the bold success of the Hollibrook spreads and Still is called on to lead lectures and deliver speeches. More and more schools want to be Hollibrooks.

"I think we've found the key. And that is so many things, but it starts with keeping the child as your focus. Only the child. The growth of the child," she explains. "I tell people not to be frustrated, don't give up, you can make a difference.

"The nicest compliment Hollibrook ever received was not all about this school reform stuff, but very simply—Hollibrook is the way every school can and should be."

The approach that Still took, right at the beginning, is now being documented as one of the most efficient ways to initiate change in a school. In Still's case, she was changing a school that previously had been run "technically correct." Everyone knew their place and function. There were exacting operating procedures followed to the letter. Students and teachers were arranged in neat cubbyholes, such as low reading group, low-low reading group, and lowest reading group.

Still, like other Effective practitioners, discovered that technical success just didn't make it in the eyes of most teachers. They felt hemmed in, too controlled. They didn't think they had the power to try new approaches. Until Still came along, no one had asked the teachers what they thought or what they wanted.

"We have found in our research in the last couple years that the ideal way to get change moving in a school is to appeal to the teachers for what they intrinsically know a school should do," explains Dr. Edie Holcomb, associate director for training and technical assistance for the National Center for Effective Schools (see Appendix B, page 423). "You ask the teachers what would be the ideal for the school, and what they believe are the best ways to accomplish that. We know what you don't do is come charging in and say, 'Hey, I know a lot about Effective Schools and this is what we're going to do.' You have to remember, labels turn most people off." Still discovered that the means and type of communication were very important. "You don't talk *at* people, you dialogue with them. You make them feel involved."

Effective Schools research has found that the "positioning" of a principal is carefully watched by faculty. "Teachers want to see where a principal really stands—on the side of really wanting that active involvement, or just giving it lip service," explains Holcomb. "I don't think people build their belief in a process alone. They build their belief in a person or people around them. Then progress is made, and it can grow, based on trust.

"When you think of someone who has had an influence on you, it may not have been only because you thought they were smarter than you so you should listen. It was probably because in some way you trusted them and believed in them as people. I don't know if it's realistic enough to be practical, but I don't know any other way."

At Hollibrook, much of that trust was built by Still's insistence that "I wouldn't ask the teachers to do anything I wasn't willing to do." They always knew exactly where she stood. And at the beginning, when they were just initiating the changes in the classrooms that would make Hollibrook one of the most progressive schools in Spring Branch, it was Still's job to come up with the research and data to help them find their way.

"I worked individually with each teacher, and we worked individually with each student," says Still. "Then we all worked together. Discussing, envisioning, clarifying." Still approaches the paperwork of her job with the same excitement that identifies her style when she works one on one with a child.

She is constantly reading, studying, and searching for more ways to reach her children and give them the very best her teachers and she have to offer. When she finds something outside the school that can also help them, she jumps for it.

"The Houston Museum is having the Pompeii exhibit. I went and saw all these Yuppie mothers with their kids and I thought, 'Hey, our kids are going to do this.' So we've redone my office into a Roman school and we have days when we dress in togas and play all the Roman roles. For the last five weeks they've been researching Pompeii. *Really* researching. We've mapped out the city, literally every street. And we're ready." She goes on to explain, her voice rising with excitement, that the coming Friday the class is climbing into a bus and going to the museum for the exhibit. "They are going to love it. It's going to be marvelous. I can't wait!"

At the heart of Hollibrook is the Effective Schools Process. The correlates and lessons of instructional leadership are followed devotedly. The mission of the school is never far from the lips or the eyes of faculty and staff. The communication of the school is in the language of effectiveness. The pronunciation for that language comes from the top, from the central administration in Spring Branch that began the Effective Schools Process in 1987.

"We couldn't do what we are doing without the Effective Schools changes in this district," says Still. "And it goes beyond staff development and leadership training. It's what's at the core. Effective Schools is about a mindset change. It is a belief system. We never forget that."

Whenever a compliment is tossed in the direction of Still, she catches it, puts another spin on it, and sends it right back. Her message is always the same: The reason this school works is because of the teachers. "I'm just part of a phenomenal community."

That community extends literally into her community. And when the school is not reaching out into the poverty and despair of the neighborhood, the school is making a place for the parents inside. There is a parents' center, equipped with washing machines, books, and daycare resources. Parents come in not only to get help with basic learning or nurturing skills but recently it was the major gathering place for a family going through a sudden death. With the help of the school, the family planned for the funeral, joined with friends in grieving, and was able to bring together the necessary social services.

"This school is multigenerational," explains Still. "A school has to be today. We want the values that we teach to go out beyond our children, to the family, the community. We want that trust and accountability, that sense of self-discipline, to be cultivated and grow far beyond our classrooms."

Suzanne Still, former special education teacher, former Detroit inner-city teacher, seems to encapsulate the cultural dimensions of instructional leadership as set out by Kent Peterson and Terrence Deal in *Symbolic Leadership and the School Principal: Shaping School Cultures in Different Contexts*:

- The principal as *symbol*, affirming values through dress, behavior, attention, routines
- The principal as *potter*, shaping and being shaped by the school's heroes, rituals, ceremonies, symbols
- The principal as *poet*, using language to reinforce values and sustain the school's best image of itself
- The principal as *actor*, improvising in the school's inevitable dramas
- The principal as *healer*, overseeing transitions and changes in the life of the school

A Loose Cannon with Central Office Support

Still agrees that she is a "loose cannon," stating that it is the only way Hollibrook could even broach success. "We had to do things differently," she affirms in a statement that manages to sum up much of the process.

But along with a committed faculty, Still had another thing going for her. She was placed at Hollibrook to create change. As Superintendent Hal Guthrie said, "Of course she's a loose cannon. That's why I put her there." But Still was also part of a district that was undergoing the Effective Schools Improvement Process. There was, and still is, very vigorous districtwide staff development going on, leadership training opportunities for principals and teachers, and an insistence within the district to go for change and the teaching for learning for *all*.

"I don't think I would have been able to get through half the changes at the Hollibrook, had it not been for Gary Mathews," says Still, referring to the associate superintendent for instructional services. "He helped pave the way. He supported not just me, but the teachers."

And in most school districts, there is a person who fills the role of Gary Mathews in Spring Branch—someone at the central office level who is not only a buffer but a facilitator. This type of person is a "must" because so many school systems have an investment in maintaining the ways of the past, even if there has been the order for change made up in the superintendent's office.

"Guthrie can't be everywhere," says Still. "And he really has a lot more demands on his time than dealing with what every principal may want. No. The important thing from Guthrie was the philosophy of Effective Schools. He got the Spring Branch schools moving in that direction. But if it hadn't been for Gary Mathews, so much of what happened at the Hollibrook never would have happened. There were people between me and Gary Mathews who made my life miserable." Those were the people who were, at best, obstructionists, and at worst, cruel, vindictive, and dangerous. "The problem people in the schools today are those who are just clones, stuck in some lockstep, with no creative thinking. Those are the dangerous people in education."

One of the examples where Still and her teachers went up against people "stuck in some lockstep" was over the issue of a language arts curriculum. Attached to the curriculum was a very strict testing component whereby students would be shuffled down to lower clusters within a grade when they failed a mastery test, but they would not necessarily be held back from moving up to the next grade level when the time came.

"There were many problems," explains Mathews. "Instruction was slowed to a snail's pace, and the false assumption was made that these kids were ready to move on. The result was that these kids got further and further behind. When they got to the fifth grade, they weren't close to mastering their work. But this system was continuing. Now we have some excellent people in central administration, but we also have some people who insist that kids jump through hoops whether they can or not. And those people were sanctioning failure."

What Mathews did was not only work with Still to prove the system was failing students, and causing serious repercussions down the line, but approved a policy where Still broke down the rigidity of the clusters, worked with students more independently, and started almost immediately to turn around the low achievement ratings. Mathews then sent a memo to the other schools, saying they should support the new direction Hollibrook was taking. Superintendent Guthrie backed Mathews and Still, and Hollibrook was on its way, breaking out of the clusters and the failing scores.

Mathews now looks back on that as another example of the central office syndrome of "If you're not part of the solution, you're part of the problem." There are people in the central office and in the schools who are not ready for change and simply don't want to change. Their reasons range from political—protecting themselves and their patronage opportunities—to ignorance—they just don't know anything other than the "system," to defending the status quo: This is the way we've always done things; this is what I'm used to.

Because there is this element in every school district, it is particularly helpful to have an individual like Gary Mathews for principals to go to. Mathews, a major proponent of the Effective Schools Process, who has devoted his professional life to the teaching for learning for all, says that he is more than willing to be a lightning rod for not only principals like Still but, in a negative sense, for those who are out there to oppose change. The reason he does it is, quite simply, because change and principals like Still help the students much more than the defenders of the status quo. Suzanne Still cultivates that change and has produced some extraordinary results.

The fruits of Still's cultivation are seen in the behavior of the students—polite, interested, disciplined—and in the test scores—equal to and better than many of the schools in the "better part of town." Reading, writing, and math scores prove that Still's approach of trusting the teachers to make the right decisions and placing the child at the center of all those decisions is working. The bonus comes in with all the additional programs: Fabulous Friday with 42 different classes ("We're now going to have one for parents, the Parent University") and the programs at the school's general store, the Only Popcorn Company, the school postal service, involvement of businesses (Shell, Chevron, among others), writing, and research challenges.

"The most important thing we give these kids? The dogged determination that they know they can tackle and accomplish any task life is going to toss at them. That we equip them for that. You know you can do it, you know how to do it, now go show 'em."

What is Still's role? "I'm just the keeper of the dream. My dream as the administrator for this school is fourfold. One is I want the children in this school to be able to hold up their heads and say, 'This is the best school in the district and I am lucky to go here and I am a wonderful human being. Smart.'

"Two, I want the parents to say, 'I could not have picked a better school. If I had a million dollars a year, I could not have provided my child with a better education.'

"Three, I want this to be a school where teachers hold up their heads and proudly say, 'Hey, I teach at the Hollibrook.' And that's happening.

"Four is that if I should ever leave this place, I want the next person who comes in to think 'I must walk on water to be even thought of as capable of being the principal of that magnificent school, and an instructional leader of those magnificent teachers, and the caretaker of those magnificent children.'"

One of the administrators in the Spring Branch system who receives memos from Suzanne Still is Linda Watkins. She is the principal of the Landrum Junior High School, which is a couple blocks from the other side of the housing project that serves as the backyard for Hollibrook. The two women are holding up the two main educational institutions for the Hispanic community.

After Watkins and members of her staff made a special visit to Hollibrook to talk with the fifth-graders about their transition to junior high, Still sent Watkins a memo about the calibre of students she will be receiving.

"We would like to share some good news about the children we are passing on to your 'tender loving care,' which should only add to everyone's anticipation for what the next year will bring!" begins the memo. It goes on to discuss that, unlike in previous years, the percentage of fifth-graders passing the TEAMS went up dramatically:

"Math: 82 percent passed (up 11 percentage points).

Reading: 72 percent passed (up 11 percentage points).

Writing: 73 percent passed (up 16 percentage points).

Math: Of the low SES last year, only 67 percent passed. This year, 82 percent passed.

Reading: Of the low SES, only 53 percent passed last year. This year, 70 percent passed.

Writing: Of the low SES, only 51 percent passed last year. This year, 70 percent passed.

Math: Of the LEP students, last year only 59 percent passed. This year, 78 percent passed.

Reading: Of the LEP students, last year only 31 percent passed. This year, 64 percent passed.

Writing: Of the LEP students, last year only 36 percent passed. This year, 64 percent passed.

"We are sending you a bunch of cuties . . . really neat kids . . . who are more responsible citizens and who know how to do the 'Hollibrook Hustle.'"

Linda Watkins smiles and laughs slightly when asked if there has been a difference in the type of child who is coming to Landrum Junior High from Hollibrook. "Oh yes, there's been a change, a major change. Thank goodness."

Landrum Junior High not only used to receive the students from Hollibrook when it was producing the toilet blasters, but it was also a school that the district regarded as the "dumping ground" for students—and faculty—that no one else wanted. It had gone through 5 principals and 14 assistant principals in 11 years, all experiencing varying degrees of failure. The school was in such disarray that some of the students were unclear about what grade they were in, and the only way the district could keep peace was with police officers and principals from other schools patrolling the halls.

The teacher population turnover rate was so high that the *majority* of the 75 teachers each fall were *brand new*—never having taught before. One of those brand new assistant principals suddenly found herself in the superintendent's office getting some rather surprising news.

"It was one of those good news and bad news things. 'The good news is we've promoted you to principal. The bad news is you start tomorrow at Landrum,'" says the young, petite Watkins who graduated from a genteel women's college before going to the University of Virginia, and then on to teach and serve as a principal in parochial schools before Spring Branch.

Delegating While Staying in Control

Watkins would be one of the youngest principals in the Spring Branch system, and she was getting one of the most troubled junior high schools with the largest non-English population. She also would have the highest number of students on free and reduced lunch: 75 percent.

It was three years ago and the beginning of the Effective Schools Process.

Now, when you enter the front door of this sprawling one-level gray brick school that houses over 1,000 students (63 percent Hispanic, 7 percent Asian, 6 percent black, 23 percent white and *72 percent* with English as a second language), it is as quiet as a monastery.

Behind the classroom doors, there is a firm, uncompromising learning process going on. The basic scores are moving upward. There are programs in and out of the school that have the students involved and excited. The faculty is no longer transient. Last year, there were only 12 new teachers and they filled spots for faculty whose families were transferred out of the Spring Branch area.

"In the last three years, I don't believe one faculty member has left because they did not like Landrum," says Watkins, sitting in her Texas-style spacious office. "From the moment I came in with Effective Schools, there has been constant change—for the better," explains Watkins. "When I first came into this job, I knew they needed someone to make decisions. I did really take charge for a while and slowly I've been able to let up on that and hand it over to teacher decision making."

Watkins said she had no trouble realizing she had to *delegate* in order to do the job effectively. She says she is delighted with the new Campus Leadership Team. "A lot of principals were concerned about giving up control. I never looked at it that way. I looked at it as someone to help me," she adds, pointing out that just recently she has stopped running the meeting. She is now "just a participant."

"Now that the structure is there, the teachers can make the decisions on what our priorities are and how we are going to implement them. They are essentially the ones that end up having to do it. I can do my part, but I certainly can't direct it all. It's a tremendous help to me."

This mode of operation is essential for the school, she says. "It's the only way the teachers and staff are going to support me and make everything work right around here."

But it was not all that easy, and when she was confronted with the problem of considerable arguing among some of her faculty, she decided to have a professional do a "personality style inventory" for her. Now she is able to group people according to their personality type: aggressive, passive, dominant, technical, theoretical, and so on.

What Watkins, Still, and most Effective School principals have mastered, in varying degrees and ways, is the concept of *shared leadership*—something that all Effective School principals are working toward.

"I envision a school as a community of leaders," writes Roland Barth, former Co-Director of the Principals' Center at Harvard University. "A place whose very mission is to ensure that students, parents, teachers, and principals all become school leaders in some ways and at some times." Barth lists nine steps to the accomplishment of shared leadership:

1. Articulate the goal.
2. Relinquish power.
3. Entrust.
4. Involve teachers in decision making.
5. Assign responsibilities wisely.
6. Share responsibility for failure.
7. Attribute success to teachers.
8. Believe in teachers.
9. Admit ignorance.

Educators say that once you get involved with shared leadership, once you start to delegate, shared leadership almost takes care of itself. However, the hardest part is starting that ball rolling. The step of *relinquishing power* is the most difficult because principals in the past have been trained to "accumulate and consolidate."

"They don't realize that in the process of delegating, they are actually gaining *more* power," explains Dr. Lezotte. "The stronger the school community becomes, the stronger their leadership becomes." This is because, in the final analysis, leadership remains very personal. It all comes back to the principal—how he or she articulates the goals for the school and how he or she lives a personal and professional life. As Roland Barth states, "Leadership is making what you believe in happen."

Principal Linda Watkins says that so far she is making progress in her mission of "providing students an education that accommodates their academic, social, emotional, and physical needs" but admits there are still some problems with discipline and getting parents involved. When all other tactics at drawing in parents failed (only 150 at PTA meetings and just a handful at teacher conferences), Watkins told the students the only way they would get their report cards was for their parents to pick them up during parent conferences. The parents arrived—over 900 of them to get the cards and ask about their children.

"Sure, we have to be different at this junior high, but then so does any school today if it wants to succeed," she says. "I think what happens at other schools with low SES kids is they want it to be like it used to be. And it's not going to ever be that way again. And if you always look at it for the old days, you're not going to do anything with what you have."

With pride, she talks about how the majority low SES kids at Landrum score "better than most every other school now" on the basic tests. "It may not look good over all, or as well as I'd like to, but I look at that and I think we're doing a good job."

She points to the problem of working with a child who brings so much baggage from the street with him or her. Watkins believes it is the school's responsibility to help balance children, help them deal with the social problems, so they can settle down to learning and build their self-esteem. She believes strongly in rewarding children, "especially these children who have to struggle so—we have no idea", and says the shortcoming of her job now is that she doesn't get to spend that much time with the students.

"I enjoyed being an assistant principal because I spent more time with students. But now . . . ," she shakes her head, admitting to some weariness at the 15-hour days (12 hours at the school, another 3 working at home). "This isn't a job, it's a way of life. It's something I have to be thinking about and doing all of the time. At this time in my life I'm willing to do that and make sacrifices, but some day I won't be willing to. It would certainly be impossible with a family."

But for now, she is content where she is, although there is no doubt there is pressure on her. Even the central office admits it. "They want this school to be the biggest and the best and the shining example, which is what I want to do, but sometimes I don't think they realize the odds over here." But Watkins admits she is fortunate to be in a district that is undergoing the Effective Schools Improvement Process. Another principal who benefits from that district-wide involvement can be found up north with the Yankees.

Needed: Someone Teachers Can Trust

Bonnie Seaburn is principal of the Munn Elementary School in Spencerport, New York. She is regarded by everyone—and it does appear to be everyone—as one of the fairest, kindest, most intelligent, sensitive principals within the Spencerport School District.

Ironically, she has one of the angriest faculties in the system. Her teachers are known as the "Munn militants," and even admit that they not only do not respect the central administration but they often do not have respect among themselves within the Munn School—except for Bonnie Seaburn. They agree she is the finest principal for the school and is the major reason for the school's academic and social success.

Seaburn, of course, says the success is due to the teachers—naturally. Prior to taking on the Munn School, Seaburn was in charge of Spencerport's staff development, where she organized and ran the various renewal programs within and outside the system. She believes it is this staff development process—the further education and often the reeducation of teachers and principals—that has made Spencerport Effective.

"The process of educating the teachers and principals so they could promote the achievement of the child better is the heart of this," says Seaburn, a young, petite brunette who does not do summersaults of glee when talking about her job. She is very pragmatic, very careful, and can be disconcerting. It's easy to think she's a pushover. And that's a grand mistake.

"You can't just encourage a child to do something, you have to know what to do with him or her," she says firmly.

But what do you do with a divided, divisive faculty when you're trying to implement the Effective Schools Improvement Process? There were no easy, quick answers from Seaburn. She responded by letter very late one Friday afternoon:

"I am the type of person who needs time to think and I wanted to write you with my insights on my own behavior:

"I wanted to establish a trust relationship with the teachers so they would enable me to move the school in the direction I think we ought to be heading. Someone once called this *vision* or (I like this better) 'moving the herd roughly West.' The behaviors I chose to try and establish this trust relationship were:

1. Opening the storeroom for their supplies (The teachers could go in and get whatever they needed, whenever—"What were they going to do, steal construction paper?")
2. Participating in parent conferences to model appropriate behaviors with parents
3. Holding staff development type faculty meetings (focus is on improvement of instruction)
4. Holding many informal discussions with teachers in the faculty room on improving instruction
5. Teaching in the Reading Center so the Reading Specialist could meet with classroom teachers to coordinate their programs
6. Doing "fun" activities with the staff
    - organizing a shopping trip to Toronto
    - holding a Holiday get-together at my house
    - holding a Teacher Appreciation day with food and a small token for each teacher
    - putting Payday candybars in their mailboxes on payday
    - giving them a small gift on the day before the children arrive in September
7. Talking informally with the children and trying to get to know as many as I can
8. Sending positive letters to the teachers at home related to their teaching skills and sending a copy to the superintendent
9. Encouraging teachers to try new strategies and helping them process what worked and what didn't
10. Praising the teachers at every opportunity, publicly and privately

"These are a few ideas I had in the past. I also have been working directly with the teachers on improving the curriculum, analyzing test results, etc., but I think that the above behaviors paved the way for me to work effectively with this staff."

And it has worked. But there is that one bit of concrete that holds the entire foundation, if not the whole building, together: trust. The faculty at Munn, despite their distrust of each other, trusts Bonnie Seaburn. It is that trust—between faculty and principal—that paves the way for success in *every* Effective School.

"Knowledge in Action"

When you ask a principal what is providing her or him with the personal/professional foundation for the change process he or she is directing, the answers are varied and intriguing: The way I was raised; My own high school experience; My college training; Watching my grandparents run their farm; The lessons of Kahil Gibran's *The Prophet*; My spirituality. Whatever these professional and personal motivators are, they are seen in the daily activities of the principal: how a principal interacts, directly and indirectly, with the teachers and students, parents and central office; how an operating procedure is enforced; how the principal monitors and models. Some people refer to it as the principal's *karma*—the assembled results of their life experiences and how they choose to put them into action.

It is complex and unique, but every Effective principal has a very powerful way of displaying his or her "knowledge in action"—the term set forth by Donald Schön (1983). And it is the brand and calibre of the "knowledge in action" that so often sets apart an Effective principal from other principals. The difference can be seen in the most simplest but dramatic of examples: when a principal enters a classroom. By observing the interaction with the teacher and students—the principal's knowledge of the classroom itself, the students, the method of instruction, the principal's ease or lack of ease, the rapport, the excitement and warmth or lack thereof. These are the details that say so much about a principal's motivations, goals, ethics, leadership skills, and personal and professional security. There are few careers where the "knowledge in action" is so explicit.

All Effective principals display their "knowledge in action" in ways that further direct and motivate the school and its change process. But just as the principals cannot name one precise reason why they lead the way they lead, there is no set style that says this is the "best way" to change or improve a school. What *is* known, as stated by Dr. Barbara O. Taylor (1984), is that there are certain managerial strategies that form the framework for strategic action within the schools. Taylor identified four strategies, or frames of reference, that the Effective principals work with while leading their school's change process.

The first is the school's *criterion of effectiveness*. This is where the principal begins the change process by setting out the mission and goals of effectiveness. The atmosphere for change is set by the correlates and *all* children learning. Here, the principal is following a district mission statement, but also making certain that the school has ownership of its own very distinct mission and objectives. Like the other frames of reference, the criterion of effectivesness is spread throughout every activity and operation in the school.

The second frame of reference is the *working relationship* between principal, teacher, student, and parent. Here, the principal deals with the working rules, operating procedures, the "buffering" policy, the new curriculum programs, scheduling, grouping changes. Through this frame of reference, the principal establishes the manner in which she or he works with the school's constituents. There is a form, a predictability to the principal's manner.

The third frame of reference is setting the *professional standards* for the school. Here, the faculty and students learn exactly where the principal is coming from, and where the principal stands. The monitoring system is set up, as well as the evaluation process, the staff development program, and the discipline procedure.

The fourth frame is that of the establishment and enforcement of an *equitable discipline code*. Despite critics who say there is too much emphasis on discipline, there is not an Effective principal who doesn't walk into a chaotic school and make the first priority the discipline. Teachers cannot teach in confusion, and students cannot learn. The discipline code influences the teaching-learning process at all levels. Teachers and students must know where they stand and what they can expect.

Each of these frames of reference works with the forces and tensions within the school to give the principal distinct compass readings on the change process. The frames are used by the Effective principals to chart their way through these unknown waters.

Take the example of an elementary school student who is falling behind his class in reading. From the first frame of reference, *effectiveness*, this simply isn't allowed. *All* children learn in this school. From the second frame, the *working relationship*, the principal and teacher talk about possibly changing instructional techniques, or the child's class, while the principal works with central office and the parents. The third frame, *professional standards*, sees the application of the established, curricular and academic standards, monitoring and evaluation system, and, if necessary, an additional development class for the teacher in order to help her children. And last, the *discipline code* is a valuable frame because the student, administrator, teacher, and parent know what is expected, what type of self-discipline is appropriate and rewarded, and this makes for a consistent and more equitably run educational program.

All of these frames are part of that "knowledge in action" that on the one hand seems so elusive, and on the other hand becomes almost programmed over time.

Beware the Knife in the Back

It would be very nice to leave the discussion of new principals plunging into Effective Schools here, on a positive note. But then we would leave part of the truth lurking between the pages of this book. That truth is not pleasant, and principals still active in their districts are not anxious to talk about it, but it is real and it is a problem that diminishes all Effectiveness. It is the animosity, jealousy, and negativity of the peers of Effective School principals. It happens to each of them.

"Face it, if you're trying to make changes, you're pretty much isolated," says Suzanne Still. "Out of the 30-odd principals in Spring Branch, there are not that many who were real healers and supporters. Too many principals and assistants either kept to themselves, or would just go in wounding and pouring salt on that wound. And they made some of those wounds pretty deep. My own peers made my life miserable!"

It's not just Spring Branch, Texas. It happens everywhere: New York, Kansas, Seattle. And the victims of it still aren't really sure why. They talk about the protection of the status quo, the attitude of "me, my, mine," the jealousy, the feeling that it's not important to teach all children.

And it happens to a certain extent among superintendents, board members, and between and among teachers and staff. And of course it happens in the central office. What is most obvious is that those creating the problems for others are more interested in the perpetuation of those problems and their own private agenda than in teaching for learning for all children.

"Yes, we know it happens. And it turns off a lot of principals. No one likes to work and take the abuse some of these people are taking just for trying to help children," says Edie Holcomb of the National Center. "I have a plaque on my wall, and I think it explains Effective Schools on many levels: We will be able to work together when our love for children is stronger than our differences."

Holcomb says that one of the major reasons why school improvement is so difficult and not as widespread as reformers would like, is because of the difficulty in building communities, in building trust—not just between principals and teachers in one school, but among teachers throughout a district, as well as among principals.

"I'm discovering that the people are finding the job harder and harder out there. You would think that because of the more we know, the easier it would get. But no. It's the trust that is always the sticking point. And this competition thing."

That "competition thing" is something principals will quietly talk about as they shake their lowered heads. "I don't know what this is all about. You would think we would be beyond this, but we're not," explains one principal embroiled in a district battle with other principals. "It's like everyone wants to be valedictorian of the class and doesn't want anyone else to even score in the eighties or nineties. They alone want to succeed. Which means on the other end, they want everyone else to fail. Isn't that a great way for principals to feel about their work? About the kids?"

The pity of it is that this sentiment is repeated in district after district. It is something the Effective Schools Process is trying to break through, but it is difficult because of the turf being protected and the fact that no one wants to talk about it.

"We have to get to the point of putting the kids first," reminds Holcomb. "Obviously, we've got a ways to go." There is also 200 years of hidden and political agendas to dissolve. While some say it is just human nature—people don't like the rate busters, they don't like people who suggest they do something different, or go against the status quo—there is speculation that change may be more difficult in education than other professions. Change has been a long time coming to the schools, and accountability has rarely been part of the fabric. Perhaps in seeking change and accountability, Effective Schools practitioners are going against the major subliminal reasons why some have sought a vocational haven in education.

And why, during this time of change in the public schools, are so many of the principals who are being appointed women? Some superintendents will openly admit that they prefer to appoint women. The reasons they give are the strength of women's dedication to children, the belief that they stick with a job until it's accomplished, that they will work longer hours than men. But there are other more subtle reasons.

"Women have never been part of the network, and so they don't have lots of loyalties and allegiances and people they don't want to make look bad," explains Holcomb, adding that the Effective Schools emphasis on group decision making and team efforts are also factors. "You have to know how to work within a team, and women are better at that than men, in most cases. And I think you cannot forget our affinity for the child. Helping children, nurturing both children and adults, is something that seems to be a part of the very marrow of most women."

But in the end run, the Effective School principal is of no particular gender, race, or religion. In this chapter (although completely unplanned), the principals have been black, Hispanic, white, male, and female, with backgrounds running from East to West, from poverty to privilege. There is no give-away background key, no education requirement. They are found from Spanish Harlem to Kansas to upstate Washington. Each person has his or her own trigger, from a personal drive from childhood to an adult mission for social and economic equity. Some are fighting drug gangs, some are fighting the old ways of school committees and parents groups. And unfortunately, they all seem to be fighting their peers to some extent. They all want the support of their district, but some must go it alone. And every single one of them fights every day to put down another building block of trust, to empower her or his teachers just a little more, and to spread ownership of learning throughout the schools.

They are dedicated to their mission with a consuming fervor. They are people who do not run from accountability, but rather feed off accountability. It is the fuel that motivates them, keeps them driving on course. It is the source of their inspiration to themselves and others, and, in the end, it is the source of their success. It is also the reason why they are feared, and, in some cases, vilified by their peers.

But they know this. They are also realists. They know what they are up against, whom they are up against, and they know they must at all times be ready to defend themselves, their teachers, their schools, and their students. Their armor is their belief, their mission, and hopefully the support of their district leaders. Their weapons are the most current, substantive research and data. These men and women are directive, giving opportunity and insight. Often their power escapes the cursory glance; it glides so effectively below the surface.

They walk through their halls warmly greeting the children, often with hugs and personal knowledge of each child's needs. They feast off the achievement and joy of their children. They are gentle, but don't let this warmth, this lovingness, fool you. They are no pushovers. They are tough. They are people of vision. They are people of the warm heart, the hard eye, and the stirring word.

CHAPTER SEVEN

Changing Reasons and Seasons with Seasoned Principals

I had long since abandoned hope of getting my teacher leaders to share any responsibility for anything. But the structure with Effective Schools gave us a different perspective.
—BILL SELANDER, principal

There's a lot to learn in this process. I hadn't realized how much the role of principal had changed. —MARTY KAY, principal

You're not going to be able to talk your way out of the problems you behaved *your way into.* —LAWRENCE LEZOTTE

There's a story told in Spencerport, New York, about a principal who had been at his post for several decades when the Effective Schools Process came rolling into town. At a meeting with Ron Edmonds and Larry Lezotte, he fired out the verbal bullets of "hogwash," "nonsense," and "a waste of time." Edmonds and Lezotte hit him right between the eyes with their research data. Near the end of the session, the principal raised his white handkerchief in surrender.

That principal is now one of Spencerport's biggest proponents of the Effective Schools Process. "Yes, I certainly have changed from how I felt at that first meeting," admits Bill Selander, principal of Wilson High School. "And it's a change I'm proud of. I've grown, and so has the school. The whole community has benefited."

Spencerport, New York, near Rochester (and Kodak), is different from most other Effective School districts because of what it is *not*. It is *not* regarded as a school district "in trouble" and it is *not* overwhelmed with the problems of facing a growing disadvantaged population. In fact, Spencerport, a middle-class suburban town disaggregates its data not according to race but according to the level of the mother's education. The Effective Schools Process was brought in to see if an average, fairly good school district could be improved.

The consensus—from the superintendent and his staff, to the faculty and individual school staffs, to the school board and parents—is a resounding *yes*—the Spencerport Public Schools have improved with the Effective Schools Process. There are some problematic points, many of them rising from the historical antagonism between the administration and the union, but putting aside those differences of opinion, Spencerport is a school system improving. It has been improving for the eight years the Effective Schools Process has been in town.

"I remember that first meeting, listening to Edmonds and Lezotte and I just thought, 'Here we go again,'" says Ed Pyzybycien, who has been principal at the Cosgrove Junior High for 9 years and in the Spencerport system for 32 years. "Those of us who have been around for a while see reforms come and go with superintendents, school boards, the latest politican. There are a lot of one-shot deals."

Selander agrees. "I had some major doubts. At first I thought it was all a bunch of hogwash. But then I found myself saying, 'Well, if it's a lot of hogwash, it's really too bad, because there are things they're saying that they think they can do that are things I sure want to do.'

"And really, how do you argue with the major thesis?" asked Selander, who has been principal at Wilson for 22 years and before that was a high school principal in New Jersey. "What are you going to say? We believe all kids *can't* learn? We want to have a disorderly school? We don't think we should be evaluating kids but once a year? How can you argue with these? These are like motherhood and apple pie correlates. And that's the way we eased into it."

It was the concept of school-based management and shared decision making that most intrigued both the administration and the teachers in Spencerport. The teachers saw it as an opportunity to have a say in the schools. The administrators saw it as a way to ease their burden.

"I had long since abandoned hope of getting my teacher leaders to share any responsibility for anything," says Selander. "Undoubtedly it was my shortcoming, but I just couldn't get them past the point where they felt they wouldn't get credit, they'd just get the blame. But the structure with Effective Schools gave us a different perspective. It enabled us to have specific goals and a structure to work together. We finally had a shared commitment for leadership. To me, that was a real breakthrough. I wanted that kind of help. For me, Effective Schools was a Godsend in that sense."

Spencerport Teachers Union President Pete Randozzo admits that the atmosphere in the schools, concerning management and the teacher's role, has indeed changed. "And the strange thing is that some of the principals who you never thought would be interested in working collaboratively are now the *most* collaborative. Genuinely collaborative."

Ed Przybycien admits that he had some "trepidation about sharing power with teachers and whether they'd handle it responsibly." He said he moved slowly, carefully. "But Effective Schools provided a vehicle for really responsible building ownership," says Przybycien. "People could share ideas *and* the commitment." He points out that one of the first tasks to be tackled was the curriculum of the junior high schools. It turned out to be a four-year process of rewriting the curriculum—"a big, heavy frustrating thing to do because people didn't want to do it, didn't know how to do it, but knew it had to be done."

Both principals emphasize that the biggest help to the Effective Schools Process was the fact that the central office didn't try to "cram it all down our throats overnight" and that they were given time to make the adjustments.

Joe Clement, superintendent of Spencerport Public Schools, says he was always aware of the depth of change he was asking the system to go through. "This is an old system. The teachers and principals have been here a long time. They've seen a lot of theories come and go. We had to make sure they knew this one was going to stay. And that it was going to make a dramatic change in the operation of this school system, but that it wouldn't *hurt* anyone. This was to help us all."

Spencerport has been in the Effective Schools program for eight years and there are still some faculty and staff who haven't quite caught on to the fact that this is an ongoing process, not an event with an end date.

"There are some people who wonder when will we ever reach the so-called promised land," says Przybycien. "I've been telling them this is an ongoing dynamic and we just have to keep studying, keep moving, and trying to do it better and better."

If there was concern about accountability, both Przybycien and Selander insist that they never felt personally threatened by the increased push to accountability that is demanded with the Effective Schools Process. One of the reasons for that, they say, is because Spencerport had a history of accountability through the emphasis on the New York State Regents Exams, the number of students taking those exams, and the scores of those exams. "There was always the accountability with the Regents," says Selander. "But there should be, and yes, now there's more of a push. But look at the numbers. We're much better than we were. No comparison almost! And because of that, I think everyone's happier. We're all getting much more positive feedback. Not just because of the scores, but because of the whole attitude of the students and the community."

This is a case where the facts speak for themselves:

English Regents: Proportion of students taking the exam increased from 53 to 93 percent, percent passing from 95 to 93 percent (much higher than the state average).

U.S. History and Government Regents: Proportion of students taking the exam increased from 53 to 93 percent, percent passing from 95 to 88 percent (higher than the state average).

Math Regents: Proportion of students taking the exam increased from 55 to 67 percent, percent passing from 89 to 83 percent (higher than the state average).

Biology, Chemistry Regents: Proportion of students taking the exam increased from 42 to 72 percent, percent passing from 90 to 82 percent (same as the state average).

Earth Science Regents: Proportion of students taking the exam increased from 53 to 83 percent, percent passing from 94 to 84 percent (same as the state average).

Reading Regents: There has been eight consecutive years of "Effectiveness"—95 to 100 percent of the student body passes.

The proportion of seniors receiving Regents scholarships increased from 10 percent in 1983 to 22 percent in 1990. The average for all of Monroe County is 13 percent receiving Regents scholarships.

Spencerport is also very proud of the fact that when the scores are disaggregated (according to the education level of the mother), there is very little variance and in some cases the low SES exceeds the upper and middle SES.

"What we've done," explains Selander, "is say to *all* the kids, that passing the Regents level curriculum is now a *minimum* standard. That's a big change, in attitude and expectation. And there's no doubt that that makes the teachers job tougher. And the teachers often have a problem getting the kids motivated, getting the kids to feel accountable. But we're working on that. We're all working harder, and with Effective Schools help, we're working smarter."

The staff development in Spencerport is one of the most aggressive staff development programs in the country. Teachers and principals are quick to point out it is one of the most positive things about the Effective School Process in Spencerport. It begins with the basics of high expectations training, and moves into the elements of instruction, cooperative learning, and classroom management courses. From these first courses, teachers can branch off into their specialties or move into areas involving instructional leadership and group process skills. The teachers say there is a direct link between the staff development and the improving scores because they have now found the firm, research-based foundation for the instinctive beliefs they had held for years.

"I'm convinced that our teachers work harder here than the majority of other districts. I really believe that,“ says Ed Przybycien. "I think much of that comes from Effective Schools. They see the success they're having and they want to do even better. Everybody wants to be part of a winning team. I tell the teachers, 'You and I both know we're not going to get rich doing this, but if we can do it a little better each year, we can hold our heads up, be a little prouder, and that's worth more than the extra coins.'"

There is also a new calibre of teacher/principal conferences. Because both parties have expanded their knowledge and are more aware of the changing dynamics in the classroom, the evaluations are elevated beyond personalities and into instructional concerns. And this doesn't happen just between teachers and principals. Principals report that at conferences with their peers, they now spend 90 percent of the time dealing with learning and leadership issues, where before the time was spent on the petty concerns of dealing with central administration.

The First Priority: Changing School Climate

In the past, when principals thought about climate, they thought about the discipline of the school in terms of how many infractions landed a student in the principal's office and when the principal should contact the parent. But now principals are learning that climate goes far beyond black and white suspension of the rules; it deals with the behavior and attitude that is expected from students. This comes from the policies as well as the modeling of teachers and staff.

Climate also deals with issues of vandalism, school maintenance (how often the gym floor is waxed and the bathrooms are scrubbed), tardiness, and absenteeism. Principals report a change in atmosphere as soon as the rules of tardiness are set out with the clarification that teachers are also expected to be on time. Students like the fact that teachers are also held accountable for their time, and that when the reports come out on absenteeism and tardiness, there is also a column marked "Faculty and Staff."

Climate also has to do with the atmosphere of the school in regard to how the students are developing socially as well as academically. In Spencerport, although there are few complaints about academic progress, there is concern over this "social" development of the child.

"They always use the illustration in the schools that the way you change school climate is to have a principal who walks around picking paper up off the floor," says Selander. "Well, I've strengthened my back considerably over the past six, seven years, but we still have a problem with school climate. I don't deny the importance of modeling, but this is a tough one. We've got to get the kids motivated better and there's also that problem of development of the 'whole' child."

The "whole" child controversy comes from the feeling of many students and teachers that there are not enough extracurricular activities and school spirit. One of the reasons for that is because athletics is not very big at Spencerport. There is no major team, not even a football team.

"There's a problem that I have as principal of this school that if it weren't so focused on student achievement we would have teachers we could throw out there to do extracurricular. But we're working so hard here, and getting those marginal kids up to speed takes time," explains Selander. "So I'm trying to work on the things that are going to help me achieve a positive school climate without telling the teachers, 'Look, instead of correcting those themes tonight, I want you to go out to East Oshkosk and check out a debating club and start one here.' When you have so much focus on academics, the principal has to learn to balance."

Both Selander and Przybycien say they have little patience with those who criticize Spencerport for being too academic, for pushing the kids too much into Regents and off to college.

"Hey, isn't that what a school is supposed to be here for? To get these kids educated and on their way?" says Selander. "I admit, we used to have it backwards. We used to say you can't get into Regents unless you have an IQ of at least 150 or whatever. Now we say—I say—you can't get out of Regents unless you convince me, really convince me, you're just incapable of making it. And there are very few kids who can't make it if they try."

For Selander and Przybycien, the Effective Schools Process has given their jobs more focus, and in doing that, the direction of the schools is now firmly set where they believe it should be—pointing straight to academic excellence and lifelong learning.

Both principals talk with enthusiasm about the changes in teaching because of the high expectations work of staff development. Not only are teachers' intuitive feelings about achievement now reinforced by research but they are given the instructional tools to apply that research to the benefit of the students.

And outside of the classroom, teachers are making decisions on the daily operations of the schools, the changes in curriculum and monitoring, and on their own future development courses. There is a level of involvement—at all levels—that is unprecedented in the Spencerport Schools. "Effective Schools has given us structure and a continuous goal," says Selander, who shakes his head as he recalls his initial skepticism about the Effective Schools Process. "Our strongest asset has been able to come to the forefront, and that is tenacity. That's the thing we've got. Parents come, parents go, students come, students go. We may lose a battle with a parent, or board member, but we'll hang in there, we've got success on our side."

The faculty and administrators in Spencerport emphasize that the fact that school improvement was happening districtwide, with strong, committed leadership coming from the superintendent's office, made the transition easier in that they knew there was a strong support network. That is not the case with a school that more or less stands alone in its implementation due to either politics of the school board or the fact that the district is just too spread out to feel any cohesiveness.

Struggling to Be a Leader

Marty Kay, principal of the Jefferson Elementary School in Mount Vernon, Washington, is stuck in the lonely reality of both those worlds. Mount Vernon is migrant farm country about two hours north of Seattle. The policy of the school district encourages school-based management and Effective Schools reform. But Marty Kay, who admits he is still getting acquainted with all the Effective School literature, says he often feels he's out there all alone. It has not been easy for Kay. He and his school are struggling and have a ways to travel before anyone is going to be satisfied with Jefferson.

"We're certainly no longer in the category of a declining school," says the gentle, soft-mannered Kay. "But we're also not improving as rapidly as I would like to see us. We've got the Effective Schools correlates in, but it's taking time and a lot of additional work."

One of Kay's complicating factors is the community that Jefferson serves. During the fall harvesting season, as much as 25 percent of his population is from the migrant camps that harvest broccoli, cauliflower, and cucumbers. Then the families leave to work the crops in Eastern Washington, returning in the spring.

"So, there's a lot of movement," explains Kay, whose own children attend an elementary school in another part of Mount Vernon. "It takes a huge commitment on the part of the migrant family for a child to be successful in a school."

Kay says the usual pattern is that although the law protects most children from working in the fields, they are needed to take care of their younger siblings while their parents are in the fields. He believes the ideal situation would be to have a mobile classroom set up near the migrant farmers, but "this community isn't ready to make that kind of investment."

"These migrant families value learning and education," says Kay. "But when you are offered a choice between putting food on the table or getting your children into a school, it's hard. And right now the county does not have the resources to get the children into the schools. And once again, there is a legacy of neglect for migrant workers that holds those parents back from bringing their children to the schoolhouse door."

Within the Jefferson Elementary School, an old brick building scarred by broken windows and surrounded by scraggly bushes and torn-up lawns, there are some 600 students, with up to 40 percent on free and reduced lunch. The atmosphere is very conservative and very traditional. Although there is some cooperative learning, Kay maintains the majority of teachers stick to "their own style." Reading scores are "average but lower for the low SES kids", according to Kay.

"I believe in using the Effective Schools research," says Kay. "But I'm not sure you can assess a school's effectiveness on the way, for example, the principal is viewed by the teachers. I think it's more than the principal, it's the energy of everyone."

Kay honestly admits that one of the problems in the school—according to him and the needs assessment—is the instructional leadership. Of all the correlates of Effective Schools, the leadership correlate came up the weakest.

"I'm very disappointed because I think I try. But there's a lot to learn in this process," says Kay, who concedes that when he took over the job at Jefferson he did not realize "how much a principal's role had changed." He had been part of the "old school" and found himself coming in with the Effective Schools Process and, according to his own admission, "wasn't quite ready; it's a lot more work than you think."

Kay talks about the "old days" when the principal's role "seemed more defined" and one knew what everyone's task was. The principal merely carried out the directions from the central office and kept the operations smooth and steady. He says that now, with the push for collaboration, the lines are blurred. The indication from teachers is that those lines are blurred because Kay has not provided sufficient instructional leadership.

Kay says he is just beginning to build a stronger rapport with his faculty. "At first I had this meeting explaining how we were going to work on an improvement plan and really get up to speed, and after I get through, what's the only question I get from a teacher? 'Is there any way we can get roll paper in the rest room rather than the tissue kind?' Now, how's that for concern for the students and school?"

As inappropriate as that question may seem in this context, practitioners hasten to point out that when teachers are first presented with the opportunity to have a hand in the school's operation, they often fall back on minor complaints. It is not uncommon for teachers to first come up with mundane requests, almost like they are testing the premise itself.

But there has been progress at Jefferson Elementary since those first days. Kay says that he and his faculty are now working together—with significant help from staff development programs—to improve not only the leadership and communication within the school but the quality of teaching and learning. The teachers know that they still have things to learn, but, for now, the major part of the school improvement plan addresses the weaknesses in instructional leadership.

There is a call for Kay to become more involved in staff development and the latest instructional techniques—to be able to work with teachers and students on specific teaching and learning problems. There is the sentiment among teachers that Kay does not express a strong belief in the school and the teachers—that his pride, like his leadership, is weak.

Teaching is a complicated task that takes knowledge and experience to be done well. At an Effective School, that statement is almost an understatement. What many teachers look for in their principal is someone who can work with them in areas such as classroom management and issues of time on task. But many of the "old line" principals have not been trained in the latest research in these areas. Their experience did not involve knowledge of the intricacies of teaching for learning for *all*. So Marty Kay is certainly not the first person to be overwhelmed with the leadership demands of the Effective Schools Process.

"Because there is such a need for that strong leader at the top, and because in many ways you have to undo the practices of the past, you have to have leadership training academies, special seminars, workshops," explains Larry Lezotte. "It's not fair to expect principals to grab a hold of the theory and new responsibilities overnight."

Many states, with the help of the National Center for Effective Schools, have established such programs, and in districts such as Spring Branch, Texas, leadership academies have been set up. There are also regional labs such as that set up by Jerry Bamberg in Seattle.

As in all learning, one of the initial aspects of the reeducation or enhancement of a principal's education is the debunking of the accumulated myths about leadership. Bennis and Nanus (1985)* list five of the most popular myths:

1. Leadership is a rare skill.
2. Leaders are born, not made.
3. Leaders are charismatic.
4. Leaders exist only at the top.
5. Leaders control, dictate, prod, and manipulate.

Once you remove these myths, the mind of the potential leader is freed to pursue his or her own strengths. One of the first components of this leadership must be not only the will to change and to provide quality learning for all children but the will to face the needs and problems honestly.

"You're not going to be able to talk your way out of the problems you *behaved* your way into. You're going to have to get beyond conversation," states Lezotte, emphasizing the phrase of not just "talking the talk, but walking the walk."

Changing the School and the Leader

"Sure it's tough, extremely tough, but what do you expect? This job itself is tough, and anyone who says it isn't, or anyone who has just cruised through it,

*Excerpt from *Leaders: The Strategies for Taking Charge* by Warren Bennis and Burt Nanus. Copyright © 1985 by Warren Bennis and Burt Nanus. Reprinted by permission of HarperCollins Publishers.

hasn't been doing it. It's that simple," believes Sue Galletti, principal of the Islander Middle School in Seattle. The energetic, fast-moving principal moves proudly through her 800-pupil school, stopping frequently to watch a teacher or assist in a lesson.

"The key to this school is community and respect. There is a unity to this school, a strong sense of togetherness," says Galletti, as she stops to talk with a pupil working on a computer program. "Everyone here, from the kids to the top administrators—and especially the teachers, has a sense of ownership, a real sense. The ownership is very real."

That ownership is one of the reasons why Larry likes his job so much. Larry is the head custodian. "I've been at other places where the kids trash the school, and in some ways, even the faculty and staff trash it, but look at this place—it's clean, it's beautiful," beams Larry. "Everyone's a part of this school, and everyone respects everyone else. It's a big happy family and everybody cares about everybody."

It wasn't always like that—not by a long shot. Mercer Island, along with Bellevue, is one of the wealthiest communities in the Seattle area. Years ago the island was just summer cabins that vacationers traveled to by ferry. But with the construction of bridges, Mercer Island became an upper middle-class community, home to many of the area's top Boeing executives.

Five years ago, the 30-year-old building housed the junior high school. "It was a very, very unhealthy place," explains Galletti. "There was a lot of vandalism, the programs were not that good, and there was an active parents' movement to pull kids out and send them to private schools." The school district decided to make changes and one of those changes was to make Mercer Junior High a middle school.

"I came in as a change agent—me and Effective Schools research. Before, this place was very autocratic, no site-based management, no involvement of the faculty, kids, parents," says Galletti. "We now have strong, shared authentic decision making. Interdisciplinary programs. Representatives of the parents, faculty, students all working together.

"We all share our ideas; we listen to each other, we reach concensus, and we're involved in everything from designing the budget in the spring to putting together the master schedule." There are also the meetings on curriculum changes, setting up the testing schedule, planning for special events and projects, and the manner of dealing with parents and businesses.

Galletti admits that at times she has to take the predominant leadership role that she has personally studied and researched. She gives as an example a recent decision to expand a humanities program from a single honors class to a program for all seventh-graders.

"Some parents and teachers didn't like that at first; they were threatened by their preconceived notions of what we meant by expanding it," explains Galletti. "But I'm a firm believer in the more information you give people, the more power people really receive themselves and the more professional they are going to behave. It's simply a matter of giving people information and being strong enough in your convictions to say, 'This is what I believe.'"

At the core of the controversy over the humanities class is the issue of tracking, and Galetti did not hesitate to let the school community know her feelings and beliefs. "It's ludicrous to pick 27 'exceptional' children and tell all the others that they're not exceptional," says Galletti. "This is a very exciting program that does away with labeling." It is also a program that was made possible because of the teachers' growing knowledge of heterogeneous grouping.

Galletti's excitement for her school is seen among the faculty and students. Wherever the students are—in the common area working on projects or just talking among themselves, in biology class where they are putting together nature videos using laser discs and other state-of-the-art equipment, or language arts where they are discussing the cultures of the Middle East—there is an active involvement in the learning process. "I stay in this school because of that excitement," explains teacher Annie Hall, whose mother was one of the first southern black teachers in the state of Washington. "And because we are all involved in this school. We are all respected, our opinions, our feelings."

"In the other schools, you see the administration imposing on the teachers what the administration thinks should be taught," says Hall. "But here, they listen to my 15 years' experience. They know I work hard at my teaching." And it's not only the activity in the classroom that Annie Hall and the other teachers talk about. It is the ongoing staff development plans, the ongoing improvement process.

"Of course we're always changing," says Galletti. "A little here, a little there. You have to. You're always monitoring and improving. We look at our scores, which are excellent, but can always be improved, and we look to how we can do it. You must. This process doesn't end." Galletti spends as much time watching and talking with her teachers as she does studying their classroom reports. She follows one struggling student as carefully as she follows a sixth-grade trend.

She says that this process of monitoring and improving is something that she is always doing with herself, with her own leadership. She assesses the strong and the weak points, not afraid to ask for help, and always on the prowl for programs or research that will improve her leadership and the school's level of achievement.

Seeking Change with the Good Old Boys

Northbrook High School in Spring Branch, Texas, has just been named a National Exemplary High School, and although Jim King, principal, is proud of the recognition, he says that given the "odds we work with," there is still a long way to go. One of those areas still changing at Northbrook is in instructional leadership.

Jim King has seen a lot of changes and attempts at changes come and go in Spring Branch. He says the Effective Schools Improvement Process, brought in by Superintendent Hal Guthrie, is the most substantive, "and it looks like it's going to stay." He's not sure what exactly will be the long term effect on Northbrook High.

Northbrook has over 1,800 students that King says total a representation of over 50 countries. Among the population of 43 percent white students, 36 percent Hispanic students, 10 percent black students, and 10 percent Asian students, there are over 40 languages spoken. The curriculum boasts of hundreds of different course offerings. Over 400 students are in vocational education.

"The neighborhood and school have gone through a lot of changes," says King, who has been in the Spring Branch system for most of his academic life. "Ten years ago we had less than 3 percent of the kids on free lunch. Now that's up to 47 percent."

He also points to a major curriculum transition taking place. Despite the fact that 75 to 80 percent of the students go on to some higher education, there is an increasing demand for vocational courses. "Our population now would be better served by more vocational offerings," says King as he walks around his 40-acre campus (300,000 square feet inside the building itself). "We still have the three levels—honors, academic, and essential—but we need more base-training courses in industrial arts, auto shop, things like that for these kids."

The school is calm and King says there is very little need for the Spring Branch police officer stationed at the school. "We still have a cowboy kicker element, but it's pretty quiet now." The dropout rate at Northbrook is close to the national average: 20 to 25 percent.

The biggest change that King has seen with the Effective Schools Process and Guthrie is the switch from procedural emphasis to instructional emphasis. "If you have instruction in line, then procedure, discipline, all else, will follow," explains King. "I have always felt that if instruction's all right, procedure will fall in line, so we're pretty stable here."

The teachers say that Northbrook has always been one of those schools that was "technically correct," but that it lacks any real creative drive. It does what it needs to do for the students on a very basic level, but does not inspire any real enthusiasm. The slogan of "TLC, Teaching, Learning, Caring—All Northbrook students will learn," is seen throughout the school and on all school material. The students move throughout the school calmly, mixing in different groups without any apparent notice of racial or ethnic diversity.

Like all Spring Branch schools, there is an ongoing improvement process, a school improvement plan always being adjusted and revised. "The teachers here are excellent, and we work together very well," says King. "I have to admit I don't spend that much time with the students. I don't interact with the students that well. My strong point is the teachers. I interact with my faculty more and better."

The scores for Northbrook are good for such a large, diverse population, but King admits there is too big a spread between the high and low SES students. And the white students fall a few points below the white students at Stratford High on the other side of town. But then Stratford High is a school of a different color. Literally and figuratively. Instead of driving across the rutted ground of burned-out gas stations like you do in the Northbrook neighborhood, in the Stratford High community, you drive past the wrought-iron gates that surround and protect the sprawling mansions of the old Texas cattle and oil barons. There are a few older apartment complexes in the district and school officials point out that it is from these homes that the majority of the lower-income students come.

Only 22 percent (10 percent Hispanic, 8 percent Asian, 4 percent black) of Stratford's population of 1,700 students is minority, and only *6* percent are on free or reduced lunch. Just a few years ago, the school was over 95 percent white. "Our neighborhood has been changing gradually, so I think the transitions have been easier for us than for those schools where the population has changed quickly," believes principal Fraser Dealey, who in 1990 received his 25-year pin from the Spring Branch system.

"Our faculty, staff, parents, everyone, are aware of the changes taking place in this community," says Dealey, noting the closing of schools in the mid-eighties that hastened the integration of some high schools. "And I think for the most part, those changes are being accepted and we're all working with them."

The large, expansive school, which offers most of the same courses as Northbrook but does not have any increased emphasis on the vocational arts, operates quietly and efficiently. It is much more "mainstream" than Northbrook, with the majority of students involved in clubs and sports and cheerleading. You walk the corridors and see notices for school elections, rallies, football games, and cheerleading clinics.

"The major change with Effective Schools has been the increased involvement of the faculty," says Dealey, adding that he has always believed that shared leadership was essential, especially at the high school level. "But we now have a basic terminology for all of us to work with. Correlates, leadership, climate. The whole campus planning process has been new. And it's good for us. We now make the decisions here, on campus, where they should be made.

"There's an awareness of the need to work together, to increase the opportunities for teachers. I guess I pride myself in being open to the teachers and shared leadership right from the beginning. I've always had an open door policy for teachers to come in and make suggestions, complain, whatever."

Dealey explains that the Effective Schools Process has "added a structure without burdening us with a structure." He points to the increased flexibility and control that has come in with Superintendent Hal Guthrie and the Effective Schools program. "It's like they say, the decisions should be made by those who have to live with them. And that's us, here on the line."

Overall, this school-based (or, in Spring Branch, campus-based) management appears to be working at the high school level, just as at the elmentary and junior high levels. Basic scores are going up, although the lower SES students still fall behind (there is a slight increase in the lower grades). SAT scores in 1990 are above the national average:

	Math	***Verbal***
National	476	424
Stratford	515	448
Northbrook	471	402

Northbrook is still below the national average, but school officials point out that Spring Branch has been into the Effective Schools Process for only three years and at the high school level the fruits of the school improvement process do not appear as readily as they do in the elementary schools. Northbrook is still a school undergoing transition to effectiveness.

Effectiveness, Southern Style

When the governor and legislature of South Carolina made an unprecedented commitment to education in the mid-eighties by approving a 1¢ sales tax with all proceeds going to education, it was done with a firm eye to the Effective Schools Process. The goal was for the schools to create school planning teams and improvement plans and goals, and for the faculty and administrators to work together toward their accomplishment.

Some districts have made progress; others, as explained in Chapter 13, still have a very long way to go. One of the problems is that the state has not provided the necessary support systems for the districts. There is also the sentiment that the additional funds have come with the price of reams of paperwork for principals and their teams. But in some areas, Effectiveness is very real. That is due, to no surprise, to the instructional leadership of the principals involved.

In Landrum, South Carolina, it is the day after National Boss Appreciation Day, and Janie Summers's office is filled with cards, banners, flowers, and gifts from her faculty, staff, and parents. Summers, the principal of the O. P. Earle Elementary School, does not mask her gratitude. "I knew I had a thoughtful faculty," says the tall, impeccably dressed black woman as she looks at the dinner gift certificate that was also a present from the faculty. "But who would think I would get all this? I am overwhelmed. They are just too good to me."

The faculty would argue—as do the faculties of other Effective School principals—that Janie Summers gives far more than she takes and whatever appreciation is shown her is never enough. In an Effective School, with a strong instructional leader, that appreciation keeps moving through the school in a never-ending cycle.

"The teachers know that I am here for them. And they are here for me. And we're all here for the children and parents," says Summers, as she moves through her 550-student school in Spartanburg County, north of Greenville. As she enters a classroom, she will nod to the teacher, receive a welcoming smile, then after pausing to hug a waiting child or two, she will move to the back of the room and quietly watch the activity.

"Only by spending time in the classroom and seeing how the teacher interacts can I really be of any help to her," says Summers. "And how else do I know how the student is doing? When the parent comes in first with a complaint or whatever, I want to be able to protect that teacher."

This act of buffering, or "screening out the static," is one of the most important functions of an Effective principal. Not only does it save the teacher from unnecessary disruptions but it also serves as a reinforcement, a support, for the teacher from the school administration.

There are no fancy management strategy books found on the bookshelves of Janie Summers's office. Her style of leading comes from the heart more than any strategic, management analysis. "I would never ask these teachers to do anything I wouldn't do," says Summers. "On the other hand, they know I expect great work from them. I model hard work, good work. I believe in that."

Summers's appointment as principal of the primarily white Earle School (86 percent white, 14 percent black, 150 students on free and reduced lunch) in the primarily white middle-class community of Landrum came after almost 30 years of diligent, uphill toil in the South Carolina educational system. She graduated from college in 1954, taught in segregated schools, then in 1969 came to Landrum for her first teacher assignment in a desegregated system. Then, eight years ago, after considerable urging from mentors and colleagues, she took the courses for her management certificate and applied for the principalship of the O. P. Earle School.

"Everyone knew how sincere I was about giving these children the best," explains Summers. "And I don't mean just academically, I mean the total child. There's no doubt that my background helped me in the development of my views. There have been a lot of struggles in my life. I easily could have given up, or just retreated to being a full-time wife and mother (her husband is also a principal). But I knew I could do more. I look upon those stumbling blocks not as obstacles but as stepping stones. It's not where you are but what you overcome, and that has helped me give courage to these children, and, when they need it, the faculty and staff."

Summers grew up in a poor, working class family. Her father worked two to three jobs to send his children on to college. Summers herself worked in the fields picking cotton or in the hotels as a chambermaid in order to help with the load.

"Oh, I think it may have been a little tougher for me than for some," she says quietly. "But I've never been angry. All the farms I worked for were owned by whites and I learned long ago, 'You get what you give' in this life. Whatever I send into the lives of others, I'll get back."

She admits that she had to work very diligently to attain the position of principal in Spartanburg County, one of the state's more prosperous districts. "I had to be super good, much better than most candidates. Everyone's eyes were on me." Summers says there are still times when a parent comes up to her, thinks she's the secretary (or custodian one day when she was out sweeping the floor) and asks for the principal. "I think it hurts them more than me.

"It's hard. It's still difficult. My rewards don't come from my paycheck. They come from helping others. When I see good teaching going on, when I see an Effective teacher really enjoying her work, when I see a pleased parent, and especially, when I see a happy child."

Very often, it takes a hug or two to make a child comfortable and happy, and Janie Summers is always available for that. In fact, she cannot walk across the lunchroom without hugging several children. And it is not unusual to see a group of children smothering her in hugs and then, at her command, politely heading off to class, bright smiles leading the way.

Although Landrum is a middle-class community, it is a different middle-class community than that found in the suburbs of San Diego or Rochester. There are no Champion sweatshirts on these children. Very often the clothes are ragged, obvious hand-me-downs from siblings or church clothing drives. Whether the children are blonde haired and blue eyed or dark haired with coal black eyes, there is a need visible in many of them to be recognized with an affectionate hug and some encouraging words.

This affection is clearly the essence of Janie Summers's leadership style. She believes the key to her being an Effective principal is, very simply, her caring. "I love each one of these children. I love every teacher." And with that attitude, that very genuine caring, she doesn't believe she can fail.

But anyone who believes Janie Summers's strength as a principal comes from her ability to wrap her arms around a group of children (and to remember all children's and teachers' birthdays with a card and small gift) is missing the larger picture. "Janie is committed to educating the whole child, just as she says," emphasizes Phyllis Crain, a former teacher at Earle and now the Coordinator of Instruction in the district. "And where with some people it's just words, not so with Janie. There is a commitment here to not just the basic skills but the arts and humanities—the programs where you really have to work hard in this state to get any resources for."

She explained that Summers has, like other Effective principals, pulled in the community for additional help, be it local artists and musicians, businesses to supply computers, or writers to handle special language arts projects. And with the help of her "extended family" and a borrowed auditorium, each year the school writes, produces, and acts in their own play.

"The state just gives us the basic instructional supplies," says Crain. "All the enrichment material has to come from outside. Other schools just don't bother. Janie does. No matter what it takes, she'll do it for the kids."

And when she's not out pulling in people and resources for enrichment programs that principals in other states take for granted, she may be out in the hollows, explaining an educational program to a parent, or paying an electric bill, or bringing food to a family in need. "I just try to do everything I can," says Summers. "As I said, what I give comes back to me. That's my reward." All that she gives also comes back in the form of achievement scores for Earle. In the first grade, 84 percent of the students were above standard. In the fourth grade, 61.5 percent of the students were above standard. In the fifth grade, 60.6 percent of the students, and in the sixth grade, 87 percent of the students were above standard.

Although the majority of her students are above standard, Summers allows that the percentage of prospering students varies from year to year, depending on "the type of student body we receive." With the state's ongoing reorganization, there is frequent shift in district lines. Just recently, the school stopped receiving children from nearby towns in North Carolina.

"I'm not making any excuses," she is quick to add. "I'm just saying there is a lot of mobility and that mobility is a factor. It does not make any difference in how we treat our children or what we expect from them." She smiles. "We expect the world, of course. From each and every one of them!"

Summers has the apparently unconditional support of her school's parents. Literally on a few moments' notice, they (all white parents on this particular occasion) will gather at the school to sing her praises:

- "If there is any problem, any problem at all, Janie is there tending to it personally."
- "She always lets you know you are welcome in this school at any time, *any time.*"
- "I have had children in other schools in this district, and not in one of them was the principal as competent, as caring as Janie."
- "Janie has the teachers going to these special staff development classes (the state of South Carolina allows 10 days per school year; Summers manages additional time for her staff) and they are now better than ever.

I can't believe the things my son is learning. In science, my husband and I can't keep up with him."

- "I love to tell parents in other schools the programs that Janie has brought in here. Artists, poets, even architects. Other principals don't even try."
- "I had Janie Summers as my teacher. She was the best teacher I had. She was loving and caring then. She's even more loving and caring now. I know my children matter here. They matter to Janie."
- "Janie is on call 24 hours a day. If there's a field trip, she's here waiting, even into the night, for those kids to return. She calls us on weekends. If anyone's in the hospital, she's there with flowers and gifts. She's at every funeral. . . ."
- "There is nothing not important to her."

Summers has the support of the community and takes advantage of resources from local drug programs (there have not been any drug-abuse incidents at the Earle since Summers began), hospital check-up activities, the Lions Club, and anyone else she can pull in. Because of South Carolina's reticence in the past to appropriate significant funds for education, Summers often has to rely on her PTA and the community for help with even the most mundane supplies, like extra paper for the children or books for the library. And last year, with the help of bake sales and carnivals, they were able to purchase a copier for the school.

If anyone wonders just how far you can take the theme of caring about your school, they should have checked the Spartanburg local paper on Valentine's Day. Summers and the District Superintendent declared it "Hug Your School Day," and Summers and her staff took it literally. They had students measure the area around the school (metrically, of course), and number and measure students, faculty, and staff. Then when the big day came, the students, faculty, parents, and community officials gathered around the school, holding hands, forming a heart. It took less than 10 minutes. Summers had found a willing soul with a plane, another with a camera, and at the right moment, the picture was taken. The caption was "A School With A Lot of Heart." Nobody could remember the last time they had seen 600 children and adults hugging a school. "It's about climate," says Summers. "I want the children to care about their school and know that the adults really care about them learning inside this school. That's important. Just as I want the teachers to know I care, the parents to know we all care about their children. And I guess if you want to be dramatic, you could say it's caring about education and the future of this country." She smiles and nods, then, feeling a pair of blue eyes on her, looks down at a waiting second-grader and, with a wink, immediately reaches down to hug.

A High School Is a Great Place to Live

If Janie Summers has the caring, hugging style of leadership, Russ Lessmeister, principal of the Rock Hill High School, in the middle of northern South Carolina, has the style of nonstop positive reinforcement.

"You get a lot more from kids with a pat on the back than a blow to their ego," says Lessmeister, who was an assistant basketball and football coach and history teacher before smoothly moving into the principalship of Rock Hill 12 years ago at the age of 32.

"You have to accentuate the positive, let these kids know when they've done something good, when they're on the right track," he says. "So often they never get any encouragement. And without that encouragement, they don't have the desire to push on. We give them encouragement."

Rock Hill, despite being the home of Winthrop College and York Technical College, is still a predominantly textile and printing community. Located 25 miles south of Charlotte, North Carolina, the population of 52,000 is increasing with the number of business commuters. Rock Hill High, with a population of 1,800 students, a third of them minority, is one of two high schools. The other high school, Northwestern, deals with "more upper middle-class kids." "Although we've got our fair share of doctors and lawyers, our kids are really more working class," explains Lessmeister, a tall, thin, very confident man. "Our kids need that extra boost, and we try to give it to them."

That "extra boost" comes in the form of congratulatory letters from the principal, "Happy News" postcards from faculty members, numerous assemblies and school activities organized to demonstrate pride, and a "family atmosphere that lets the students know they count."

"I say to my teachers, 'Treat these kids like they're you're own, and you'll see results,'" explains Lessmeister. "Sure, we do a lot of stuff that may look like its major purpose is just public relations for the school, but that's not it. These reinforcements are instruction oriented, to get the kids moving in their classes, for them to see that good work in class brings rewards. And those rewards are then also felt by the teachers.

Lessmeister asks each of his 100 teachers to send at least two postcards of Happy News home every week. "At first the teachers were hesitant, but then they started to get feedback from kids. You know, 'Thanks for the note you wrote momma.' That type of thing. Sure, we're putting hay in the barn for the rough times. We don't want these parents to only hear from us when things are bad."

He is careful to spend as much time on his teachers. He does not wait for formal review occasions to let the teachers know how he thinks their classes are going. He daily writes letters and memos to teachers, expressing interest or applauding their efforts.

"To be a good principal, you have to let everyone know you're involved with them. Everyone," says Lessmeister, who in 1989 was named the South Carolina Administrator of the Year. He believes very strongly in maintaining the family atmosphere of the entire school and making sure everyone is involved. He refers to it as "The Bearcat Family" after the bearcat mascot of the school. The "fighting bearcat" head or paw is a familiar stamp around the school. And athletics—football, basketball, soccer, wrestling, track, golf, tennis, and a large marching band—are major elements of Lessmeister's "Bearcat family".

"Sports and the extracurricular activities are not just important here, they are essential to what we are trying to do. All our programs have at their base the motivation of students, teaching them the value of honest competition, of working together, of seeing how much they can push themselves and how good they can be," says Lessmeister, who sees to it that the community leaders have tickets to sports events so they, too, can be part of the "Bearcat family."

"And I see to it that these kids are rewarded. Just as I see to it that the kids are rewarded for their academic excellence." Lessmeister keeps up with the progress of as many kids as he can, and he stays involved with them, which may account for what some faculty and parents refer to as Lessmeister's "sixth sense" about the students.

"There's just something about him," says Eleanor Porter, a parent. "He seems to know what the kids are up to at every minute. And he can talk to them about anything. He has an excellent rapport with the kids. It's a very comfortable atmosphere." It is because of that "comfortable atmosphere" and the "excellent discipline" at Rock Hill that Porter chose to send her children here rather than across town.

"I'm very flattered that the parents think I do a good job," says Lessmeister. "But all I'm doing is having a great time with the kids. I enjoy being with them. I always have." And when he walks through his high school, Lessmeister's free style and friendly rapport with the students is obvious.

"Hey, hon, how ya doing? How'd that test go the other day?" he asks a young girl who is waiting outside a classroom. Or he tosses 25 cents to a student having trouble with the soda machine, and after a friendly jab on the shoulder heads on his way. As he walks through the lunchroom, faculty and students alike are anxious to talk with him. He has some students he will joke with, others require his more serious side. There's no doubt he knows not only the students but their parents.

"I know it seems to look like I interact more with the white kids, and I guess that's so, but everything takes time," he says, emphasizing that he goes "out of my way" to make everyone feel at home. One of the students he doesn't go out of his way to pay attention to is the president of the sophomore class—his daughter. "No favoritism here," he says, smiling.

"One of the best things about being principal of a high school like this is that the high school atmosphere is a great place to raise kids, to have a family grow. Whether we're piling in to head to a football game or going to a dinner downtown, it's great, and it keeps getting better."

Lessmeister says that the Effective Schools correlates have always been something he has believed were important, especially when dealing with school climate, discipline, and faculty involvement. "I'm kind of stunned here. How do you run a school without faculty involvement?" asks Lessmeister. "Isn't it just common sense that if you want to run a successful school, you involve those people who are responsible for doing that? I don't really need a big university study to tell me that."

Lessmeister admits he does not spend equal time on the matter of student monitoring. He says he has an assistant principal who handles the details of that. "I'm more student oriented. I don't spend a lot of time fussing over tests. I just know we're doing better and we've received recognition for that.

"I'm not a percentile person. I don't lay any claim to that. I'm here for the leadership. The teachers handle the academics in their classrooms. That's their job. I handle the students and the school overall. It's not do as I say around here. It's do as I do. The teachers with the students. Me with the teachers and the kids. Our effort here is in terms of the family setting, the family atmosphere of the school. We give all we can to take the kids as far as we can."

Rock Hill sends between 35 and 40 percent of its graduates on to two- or four-year colleges and technical schools. The dropout rate averages out at between 6 and 7 percent. For the 1989 Basic Skills Assessment Program (all subtests) for grade 10, Rock Hill averages 67.8 percent above standard. The district averages 71.9 percent above standard, the state 66.1 percent above standard. That trend of being ahead of the state but behind in the district continues on other basic tests. On the SAT, Rock Hill falls behind the state on the verbal (393 for Rock Hill, 399 for state, 409 for district, 427 for national) but stays ahead on the math (450 for Rock Hill, 439 for state, 462 for district, 476 for national). In 1984, Rock Hill High was recognized by the United States Department of Education as a "School of Excellence."

Official disaggregated scores are not available at Rock Hill. But an in-house analysis of reading levels shows that although 47 percent of the white students read below their grade level, 70 percent of black students read below theirs. Also, 16 percent of white students in grades 9–12 read below the seventh-grade level; 34 percent of black students in grades 9–12 read below the seventh-grade level.

"Remember, academic excellence was never a high priority in this state," says Lessmeister. "Much of the state is just now getting on the bandwagon and we're receiving some of those kids who have never had an equal chance. We're doing everything we can. We won't allow them to stay behind."

It is for these students who Lessmeister refers to as "those on the margin" that he believes the positive atmosphere can best serve. "These kids have to know we believe in them. That their education is just as important as the education of my own daughter. And it is. I tell them that. I show them that the best I can. That's what I believe effective leadership is."

For some of the principals who were in the trenches for a long time before the Effective Schools Process came along, the changes were not earth shaking. They already had in place many of the correlates that are now part of a mandated system. For others, with very active teachers' unions and a dynamic, persistent leader in the superintendent's chair, those changes have brought some strains and some getting used to. It is not easy to change authoritarian ways, especially when that change means more active involvement by teachers and parents in decision making. Those principals who have not adapted to the changes, or not changed themselves, have been removed by Effective superintendents. It is a common phenomena in Effective districts.

But for those principals who remain, those principals who always held accountability—their own and their school's—as the motivating factor, the Effective Schools Process was nothing to be feared. Perhaps the changes took some adjustment, but they were never opposed to the changes. And they were impressed by the accountability and renewed enthusiasm it brought to their teachers.

The major difference between a seasoned principal moving into Effectiveness and that of a principal with not as many years in the system, seems often to be a matter of style and not of substance. These seasoned principals have seen many reforms come and go, they have their own established ways of doing things, and are not interested in rocking the boat of 200 years of educational policy. They move cautiously, always aware of the political ramifications of any change.

When asked about the animosity of their peers who are not into Effective change, they admit it exists, that often they have been surprised by how vitriolic the criticism can be. But they say that over the years they have grown hard shells—shells all the more impermeable because they have paid their political dues.

"So I'm not going to get it, or at least it's not going to come back to me, as much as the person who is new to the game," explains one veteran principal. "You have to understand that what may be being thrown at the other principals is not so much a personal thing. It's not even so much a thing against Effectiveness. Right now many of us are losing our positions, we're getting hit from all sides—from the press, the politicians, even foreign countries that say they do it better than us—so when one of our own ranks breaks ranks, well, it's sometimes more than you can take sitting down. I don't approve of it. And I've had to take a lot of below-the-belt punches myself. But let's just say I understand it."

The last frontier that these principals are having to cross is the delegation of power, and their own directiveness. They talk of reading the latest books, diligently attending seminars and workshops, but in the end they realize that knowledge and intention are sometimes not enough. "There are principals leaving the field now. These are men and women who have been running schools for a long time," explains a principal who was talked out of resigning by the superintendent. "Some of them are being urged to leave. The others just don't think making the change will be worth it. And I think the reason for that is because of the trust issue. In the past, it was politics. You didn't need trust to survive in your school. You do now, especially with districtwide Effectiveness and the pressure from the top. You can't fake the trust. I was lucky. Over the years, I had built up trust with my teachers. What almost got me was the parents. It wasn't so much that I didn't trust them. Well, wait a minute, I didn't. I barely spoke to them. I didn't bother with them. I thought they would just interfere. Well, I had to change. And I'm doing OK now, but I gotta tell you my first instinct was to say the hell with it."

Those principals who do make the changes and are successful in raising achievement scores as well as teacher and parent morale report that their jobs now bring them a much greater degree of satisfaction. They also admit—just as do superintendents and teachers who embrace the Effective Schools Process—that their own level of self-esteem has grown along with the knowledge that they are doing a better job for their entire school community.

The knowledge that their performance is better, and the appreciation they now feel from the teachers as well as the community, becomes its own motivating force. The accountability, something that many looked upon as a threat, is now welcomed, even by the oldest of the "old line" principals. As one principal said, "This isn't the demon I thought it was; these changes have improved me as much as the school."

That improvement is what matters. Unlike the other reforms they have lived through, the principals can see the improvement in scores, attitudes, and teaching skills brought about by the Effective Schools Process. The principals know that they are no longer losing as many kids as they did in the past. Even though principals talked in terms of excuses ("It's the home, the community, the drugs, etc."), it still bothered those who held a sincere commitment to the children. And today, although they say they still lose some, they are losing far fewer, and finally, they say, now it is not for lack of trying. With the help of the Effective Schools training in instruction and leadership, the accountability, the school-based improvement, they believe that they are doing the best they can. And in some schools, that best is producing extraordinary results.

CHAPTER EIGHT

Teachers Making Dreams Come True

Maybe I'm too much of an idealist, but I really believe we can change these kids' lives. I believe we can be that one person who makes a difference. You know, later in their life, when they say, 'If it hadn't been for my sixth-grade teacher . . . .'

—LESLIE MYERS, teacher

In this chapter, we look at the classrooms of yesterday and today, examining how the inspirational teaching for learning values of a half century ago can be found in Effective School classrooms of the nineties. Here, we join the insight of the Effective School literature and research with the observations, reactions, and beliefs of those Effective School teachers who daily confront the dreams, dramas, fears, and disappointments of the children who are America's future.

Images of Classrooms of the Past

Coauthor Barbara O. Taylor, Ph.D., presents her "best" teachers at Irving Elementary School in Alton, Illinois, in the early forties: Emma Muser, Mildred Geltz, Alma Bremer, and Dorothy Ells. With the writing of each name, pictures of their classrooms come into focus:

Miss Muser's First Grade

Twenty-four children sit at individual desks, each consisting of four rows divided into reading groups of six students each: Brownies, Elves, Leprechauns, and Fairies. The Fairies are the best readers; the Elves the slowest readers. Reading lessons are assigned by row, and yet all children receive the complete and intended curriculum. The slower students receive smaller doses, with more "hands-on" techniques. Whole class sessions are held, in dialogue, with every student called on to recite at least once or twice a day. Miss Muser teaches art and music, along with reading, writing, arithmetic, and the daily bulletin board. Miss Muser is also principal of the school.

Miss Ells's First Grade and Second Grade

A very structured classroom of 35 students, all sit at tables of 5 children. Miss Ells teaches reading and writing across the curriculum (as we say in the nineties). She is a stickler for good penmanship and spelling. There are four groups for reading, each with a different text. Miss Ells teaches art and music, arithmetic, and language arts. She is also a gifted story teller, which is her strategy for introducing literature to the class.

Miss Geltz's Second Grade and Third Grade

The class consists of 40 students. The day is divided into study, exercise, recitation, oral reading, quiet reading, arithmetic, social studies, art, music, and literature. Each day is different and Miss Geltz works her teaching plan by naming objectives for two weeks, rather than the typical one week or one day. (The coauthor knows this because she visited Miss Geltz when she was attending college. She asked Miss Geltz how she planned her schedule, remembering that there was no set routine in her classroom.) Miss Geltz is able to work more effectively with both the quick students and with the slower ones, if she allows herself this flexibility.

Miss Bremer's Fifth Grade

Lots of independent work is given to all 40 students in geography, civics, and literature. Assignments are made according to past performance and talent. There are two reading classes and two arithmetic classes: "A" for faster students and "B" for more average students. Students may move from one group to another, depending on their comfort with the topic. All receive the same content and texts, but work at different speeds. Miss Bremer uses a variety of teaching techniques to engage students and keep them on task. She loves to teach art, and teaches her students how to create and letter posters, as well as how to illustrate themes written for independent work. Miss Bremer grades the student against himself or herself; she does not believe in the validity of the normal curve.

The socioeconomic background of the children in Alton ranged from small-town poverty, through poor working class, to middle and upper class. No blacks went to Irving School in those days of segregated schools, but many children were from immigrant families, largely Eastern European, Italian, and Greek.

In 1940, it was a different era, a typical small town (33,000 inhabitants) where "community" still existed, before the "knowledge explosion", Sputnik, desegregation and diversity, drugs and spreading teenage crime. More families were composed of two parents, and, in many homes, three generations lived together. Often three generations shared one or two large rooms and one bathroom.

Times have changed in 50 years. Still, it is interesting to note that these teachers were able to teach all children in their classrooms, as long as they were able to enjoy flexible classroom arrangements and share decision making at the school site. They were allowed to adapt the curriculum to each child. They had no bells ringing to separate periods and distract them and their students (except at recess, lunchtime, and dismissal) and no intercom systems. When teachers wished to communicate with each other or with the principal, they sent students to each other's rooms with written memos. In short, these teachers took responsibility for their students' learning and were allowed the discretion to make decisions that helped achieve this goal. This is what empowerment is all about.

Examples of empowering actions and activities abounded at Irving School. As a group, these teachers and their building colleagues formed their own rules for student discipline, within state and local codes. Award ceremonies, "socials" (yearly gatherings where games, food, and fun were enjoyed by all generations on an afternoon in the late spring), field trips, and visits by the local fire and police departments were planned and carried out with a minimum of paperwork and permission from the superintendent. In these programs Irving School was very different from Washington School (in the best part of town), from Rufus Easton School (a progressive school), and from the Lincoln School (where a few blacks from that neighborhood attended, by special permission). All of these programs suited the neighborhoods they served and represented the cultures of the childrens' families.

The superintendent was a kindly man, not professionally trained in education but more of a business manager. The principals in all the schools, except for the two junior highs and high school, were women. The principals reported to the superintendent the absentee and tardiness numbers, ordered new texts and materials, and reported grades. Each year each principal drew up a financial report and a financial plan for the next year that was passed on to the board of education.

There was no doubt about it—these teachers ran Irving School. Here was school based management without all the fancy rhetoric, detailed plans and calculations, and self-protecting politics. Today, the Effective School Process exemplifies many of these tried and true, common sense school and classroom procedures.

What happened in the intervening years to the school system to make effective classroom teaching more difficult, if not impossible, for the typical public school teacher?

In general, most of the blame can be laid at the feet of growing educational bureaucracies at the state and local levels that began at the turn of the century and continued after World War II to increase in size in medium-sized districts as well as large urban districts. Large cities had to cope with monolithic bureaucracies all through the twentieth century. These bureaucracies attempted to standardize everything about the delivery of educational services. Teachers' associations and unions grew powerful as they attempted to protect teachers from the encroachment of policies that would lessen the teachers' say about working conditions as well as salaries.

The history of public school education in the late fifties and sixties in the United States showed that less and less professional (discretionary) decision making was given to the classroom teacher. In fact, many policies and bureaucratic procedures at the state and local levels were counterproductive to effective teaching practices.

Effective Schools and the Teacher of the Twenty-First Century

Many teachers today emulate these earlier, gifted teachers in their determination to teach all children. Most teachers begin their careers by wanting to reach all of their students and to teach them to their (the teacher's) highest potential. But then rules and bureaucratic procedures often get in the way. A bell rings every 25 minutes, startling the classroom of students, announcing a stringent schedule that does not take into consideration the needs of slower or faster learners. A text is chosen because it has the best coverage of all the topics needed to satisfy diverse and highly organized special-interest groups. Recess is deemed necessary, even when the school day shrinks to five hours.

All of these traditional procedures omit important considerations, as we know the needs of students today. *The needs of students:* This is what the best teachers have always considered first. Their own needs are next, and the needs of the parents, community, and the teacher's colleagues follow close behind. But the needs of students come first.

Yet in most schools, many decisions about curriculum, reporting decisions, and evaluation of programs are still made solely by administrators to answer to the bureaucracy's needs: standardized procedures, paperwork, superficial evaluation that has its eye on public relations, not rocking the boat. What is important here is maintaining the school to serve the best interests of the bureaucracy. These are administrators who, in thought and deed, do not have as their priority the learning of children (and certainly not the learning of *all* children). These are administrators who do not *want* change. They do not seek it; in fact, if they were honest, they would say they fear it.

For the teacher in a school with that type of administrator, there is going to be little change. There will probably be no staff development. The maintenance of the status quo is the rule for the past, the present, and the future. And as we know from the reports from U.S. public schools, this is not enough. It is not only not enough but it dooms the school to failure, with only a small percentage of the students achieving adequately. A school that is not improving is a school that is declining.

In schools going through the change process that produces Effective Schools, allegiance to the status quo is buried with nailed-down desks. The needs of the students are uppermost in the principals' and the teachers' minds. However, in order to adequately serve the needs of the students, Effective School districts admit that first the needs of the teachers must be addressed.

Teachers: Life-Time Learners or Assembly-Line Workers?

There is a cavern in the instructional landscape of teaching techniques, behavior, and attitude today. That cavern comes from the failure of many schools of education to teach teachers to accept the fact that, given an equal chance with equal resources, one child can learn just as much and just as effectively as the next child. This is difficult for a teacher who has been processed through typical teachers' colleges to accept. For many teachers, this is a cultural, ideological, and emotional change that does not come easily. It is very often a struggle that requires courage and involves risk to push through to the light on the other side. Some may believe it emotionally and intellectually, but discerning how to make it happen within their present systems is a huge task.

"Do you think that *all* kids can learn? Come on, if I put you in front of a class of 30 kids, boys and girls, a mix of whites, blacks, Asians, Hispanics, some dressed nicely, some in dirty dungarees, some smiling, some scowling, some sneering, some nodding off, some speak English, some don't. Are you really going to stand there and believe—in your mind and in your gut—that each and every one of those kids can learn?"

That question was asked by a teacher in the Olive Peirce Middle School in Ramona, California, a calm picturesque town an hour north of San Diego. The teacher believed that it was part and parcel of growing up in America and attending America's public schools to believe that some children just cannot learn.

"I know when I was going to school myself, there were kids who were just considered the losers. The teachers didn't even bother dealing with them.

And even in college, it was very subtle, but there was an underlying sentiment that there are some kids you just can't do anything with, that you just bring along for the ride. Then of course the Coleman report justified that thinking. So, I'm afraid, like so many teachers, I just wrote off some of my kids, just figured they'd never make it. Then this Effective Schools literature comes along and you're first reaction is a polite, 'Sure, sure.' Then you start to look at the research and get a little nervous. Is there something here? Then you can either start to try to change your attitude and your teaching—or you can continue to live in a dark hole and screw over a lot of kids."

The initial shock is not unusual.

"When we first heard that statement—any child can be taught to learn when we choose to teach that child—well, we all had to jump back," recalls Fred Cardella, a teacher at the Bernabi Elementary School in Spencerport, New York. The district has been implementing Effective Schools reform since 1983, and represents one of the longest ongoing K–12 Effective School Improvement Processes in the country. Spencerport's program was recognized in early 1992 by the National Diffusion Network.

"I'll be real blunt. I think we looked at some kids and said, 'This kid is a loser. This kid just can't make it. So I need to ease off this kid and just really kind of back him down, because he's struggling. He's just not going to make the curriculum,'" says Cardella. "Now we're not doing that. Now we're trying to take these kids and identify them as quickly, as immediately as we possibly can, and we're trying to bridge the gaps."

Tony Marcello, also a teacher at Bernabi Elementary School in Spencerport, who has been instructing children for over 30 years, recalls it was not just the values of the Effective Schools Process that were troublesome to many.

"I started on the groundfloor with this, and I remember when they first held the meetings on Effective Schools. I jokingly said to a fellow teacher, 'Why don't we go to this meeting? We can get a couple days off.' But the longer I sat in on those meetings with Edmonds and Lezotte, the more I was convinced that probably, for the first time, based on the studies, the evidence, we could improve the kind of teaching that was going on, the focus of teaching," says Marcello, maintaining that he was convinced "right off the bat" that this was the way to go.

"But I was also a little dubious in another way, only because I felt this was maybe another thing that we're going to try for a couple years and then quit," recalls Marcello.

The skepticism was felt by administrators as well as teachers. They had all seen plans come and go in Spencerport. Even the administrators thought it was just another gimmick, another game that would be played until someone turned their head and changed their mind. "You have to realize we had gone through a lot of reform schemes. It was like, 'Was this the new flavor of the month?'" recalls Bill Selander, principal of Spencerport's Wilson High School.

Not even the needs assessment surveys, even though they were more thorough than anything they had seen before, made any impact in the beginning stages.

"We were all skeptical," says Pete Randozzo, president of the Spencerport Teachers' Association. "They had tried surveys of the staff in the past to try to get a feeling of what's going on and none of those things ever materialized into anything constructive or positive, so my first reaction was, 'This is just another gimmick, and we'll sweat it out. It'll be the educational word for the year, so to speak, and then we'll be hearing from someone else.'"

But the approach was different this time. There was research and additional literature that began to interest and excite teachers and administrators. The process started to look comprehensive and long term. The questions probed where other surveys had not, and the teachers found themselves dealing with issues on a gut level.

"One of the statements on the surveys asks if you believe all kids can learn," recalls a Spencerport teacher. "So you answer, 'Sure, all kids can learn.' But on the other hand, there was a great number of teachers who had some reasons why all kids couldn't learn."

"I think that whole statement for me was, well, yeah I believe all kids can learn, but I look at my class and say, 'But that kid, well, I may have one or two who will not achieve at the same level as other kids.'

"So it was a mental exercise in 'Do I believe it or am I going to accept the fact that two aren't going to make it?' Or do I get beyond that feeling and think, 'They all can learn and I'm not going to expect any kid not to make it.' So it was real gut level.

"I think that was the crux of the whole thing with Effective Schools because if you can't believe that all those kids in your classroom can learn, then are you going to work as hard on that one or two who you've already thought, well, because of family background, or poor skills, they just won't—so what you believe has a big affect on how you're going to teach."

This was considered dangerous thinking, although teachers knew in their hearts it was true: *What you believe has a big affect on how you teach.*

So with the research in hand proving this point, Spencerport began the arduous process of doing something about it. The first step was to introduce teachers into the Effective Schools Research and let them see for themselves the accumulated data on teaching for learning for *all*.

The next step was to subtly but very seriously address the issue of changing teacher attitudes and teaching techniques. They knew the past practice of having teachers attend random college courses or local seminars would not work. It had to be systematic retraining. With the support of the teachers' union, Spencerport did a thorough assessment of attitudes and faculty needs, and then began systemwide staff development.

Once the teachers understood the Effective Schools Research, the task was to translate that research into practice. Recognizing that it is in the classroom where change must be most significant to affect systemwide improvement, the Spencerport administration set out to instruct teachers in how to take actions that promote learning.

That was touchy. Was the inference from this action that teachers were *not* doing a good job? "Yes, I think we were threatened at first," recalls a teacher in Spencerport. "Wouldn't you be if someone came to you while you were working and said, 'Hey, I want you to take a course so you can learn to do your job better'? Sounds like they're saying you're not doing your job right."

Robert Sudlow, Ed.D., assistant superintendent for Instruction in Spencerport, says one of the keys was to make sure the teachers understood that the change process was meant as an improvement, not a punishment.

"Some of our teachers took this personally, and that's the last thing it was," says Sudlow. "Yes, we were talking about changing belief systems, and when you do that, that's tough, but it wasn't meant to be negative towards teachers. Quite the opposite. We were saying 'Let's just improve something that is already very good.'"

Larry Lezotte agrees there can be a "bad attitude" around staff development. "The whole culture around in-service is very poor," insists Lezotte. "It's a very interesting irony that the schools are really very poor examples of learning organizations."

One of the problems, according to Lezotte, is the intensive screening process school districts go through before bringing in the staff development programs. Districts can spend an entire school year studying different proposals and bringing them before teachers' associations and boards. Then there is the problem that communities believe teachers should always be in the classroom.

"There just has never been the *time* given to properly do staff development," says Lezotte. He believes the problems of released time, compensation for teachers (for staff development courses), and the failures of higher education in the initial instruction of teachers are still major hurdles for reformers in public education to face.

"But there is movement," says Lezotte, hopefully. "I do see more teachers, more principals, more school people saying we know that we didn't learn everything when we started this job."

Ron Edmonds recognized this problem with his first work on Effective Schools and staff development. "We tell them: 'We are not going to ask you to do anything that we can't teach you how to do, if you ask us,'" said Ron Edmonds. "We teach that there are no instructional problems that have not already been solved. The only issue is whether or not the organization makes available to principals and teachers the extraordinary repertoire of school behaviors that will produce mastery for the full range of the population."

The administration in Spencerport emphasized that the staff development was to *help* the teachers teach more systematically, to help them examine their own skills, and "to strengthen and reinforce the ones which are effective and to enlarge their repertoire of effective teaching practices."

Bonnie Seaburn, now a principal at the Munn Elementary School in Spencerport, but initially one of the key staff development instructors, said getting teachers to make a commitment was not that difficult. "Once they saw that the administration was serious, and that this was a serious, well-thought out program, they were fine," she explains. "Remember, teachers want to do a good job. They want to see their students succeed. Most believed all kids can learn when they started teaching. They knew that there had to be better ways to reach these kids to improve their performance."

Spencerport emphasized that the last thing staff development was, was "remedial." In communicating to the teachers, the point was made that "staff development is the ongoing, job-related, research-based activity provided for employees to maintain their competencies. It is designed to maintain and improve staff proficiency."

The presentation of the staff development was essential. In-service days with their "listen and then go back and do as I say" design were dismissed as too brief, too fragmented, not necessarily job related, and lacking a follow-up component. In order for the Effective Schools staff development program to have a sustained influence, Spencerport officials, in coordination with the research of Edmonds and Lezotte, insisted that certain components be in place:

- Job-related content is useful to the employee. The content must be oriented to answering the question "What can I do to increase student achievement?"
- The program must be planned and coordinated. Evidence of this guideline can be obtained from answers to questions such as:

  Are there objectives for the program?
  Where does it fit into the school's and district's goals?
  Is participation mandatory or voluntary?

- District-level support is essential. Money must be budgeted annually. "Even more important than money is continued positive publicity from those in power such as the Board of Education, Superintendent, central office staff, and teachers union." All groups must work together.
- Is time provided for a program to develop and then prove its effectiveness? There are no "quick fixes." Experienced teachers and administrators don't change overnight.
- Is there a follow-up component? "If there is none, then the staff development program might as well be cancelled!"

High Expectations for Teachers and Students

Spencerport chose two specific staff development programs to introduce the findings of the effective teaching research: Teacher Expectations and

Student Achievement (TESA) and the Essential Elements of Effective Instruction.

"These are basically unlike anything we had tried before," explains Sudlow. "TESA really got to the heart of what Effective Schools was all about."

TESA was a six-session monthly program where teachers were taught to demonstrate "fifteen specific, supportive and motivating behaviors equitably among the students in a class. TESA helped to make teachers aware of their unconscious discriminatory interaction between their perceived high achievers and their perceived low achievers. *The rationale for TESA is that teachers can directly affect the quantity and quality of students learning by the expectations they hold for pupil performance and how they manifest those expectations"* (Spencerport Staff Development materials).

TESA goes right to the heart of the Effective Schools in addressing that all-important high expectations correlate. TESA has become the staff development program that is used in most Effective Schools Processes, and is one of the most highly respected instructional renewal tools in the country.

In the TESA program, a teacher selects from one class five students viewed as high achievers and five seen as low achievers. These are the "target students" who are then closely observed.

Each month, the teachers learn the research for expectations and are taught three new behaviors to accelerate learning. (These workshops in Spencerport were held in local hotels, accompanied by dinners paid by the district.) The teachers put the behaviors into practice, at the same time being observed by four others in that group. The frequency and distribution of specific behaviors is recorded.

The results are powerful. Teachers learn firsthand the impact that high expectation behavior can have on the entire class. Not only do most student scores improve but the attitude and increased participation of students, especially those designated as "low achievers," is dramatic.

"Some teachers were clearly stunned," says Seaburn. "That's how impressive some of the results were. We knew intuitively, but now we had the proof. What was fascinating to me was how excited the teachers got, how they couldn't wait to expand the program, to bring it into more classes."

TESA brought a common language to the teachers in Spencerport. They also now knew what was fair to be expected of them in the classroom, and they were getting support to reach, to attain, what was expected of them.

Spencerport also discovered another plus, and that came from the impact of the peer observation. Before the Effective Schools Process, teachers would have been nervous about this peer observation. Now they refer to it as one of the highlights. It not only helped to develop collegial relationships but it helped teachers appreciate the talents of teachers throughout the school system.

The major impact, however, fell on the students. Tony Marcello talks of how today students are amazing the faculty members who in the past gave little thought to expectations for their students. "I think our expectations overall were pretty vague," he says. "We weren't concerned with the higher end of the range of kids, and then I think we were just kind of lackadaisical about the other kids. We had the impression that some kids just aren't going to be successful.

"But since we've initiated this project, well, it's had a tremendous effect on upper-end kids. They've progressed as much as kids at the lower end. We're zeroing in on the lower end of the socioeconomic scale now because of Effective Schools, whereas before we had a very poor attitude about them and a biased attitude about them. Our expectations continue to go up and up, and with our expectations go the learning levels of all kids."

Mirian Smith has been a teacher in Spencerport for 22 years. She is now at the Town Line Elementary School. "In the past I believe there were many of us who allowed ourselves to say 'This kid can't learn.' But now, if we see a kid not doing well, we know how to balance what is happening with what can happen. And we move from what *can* happen. We expect more—and we get it."

Larry Trippodo, who is team teaching with Smith, admits to a major change in attitude and in expectations. "You have to make every kid feel like he can do it. And that's not the way it used to be. It was so easy to throw out the excuse. But now, I don't allow myself any excuses. When that kid comes in, he's mine. He's my responsibility."

The three basic behavioral strands for high expectations have been broken down into Student Response Opportunities, Teacher Feedback, and Personal Regard for Student (see Table 8–1). In addressing these areas, teachers learn the most effective way to accelerate the students' learning through each student's own expectations of himself or herself.

But are there basic assumptions and actions for a teacher encouraging high expectations? Researchers believe there are, and these guidelines are reproduced in Figures 8–1 and 8–2. One of the key components in both figures is a change in the classroom atmosphere (or climate) with the increased interaction between teacher and student—not only the amount of interaction but the *kind* of interaction. The student is given a more equitable role and is given more opportunity to ask questions and seek insight. *There is an observable, dramatic shift in the power relationship within the classroom.*

Seymour Sarason (1990) talks about the need for change in the behavior of the classroom, paying particular attention to the importance of student-teacher interaction through question asking. He notes that students often do not feel secure enough to ask questions. And while recommendation after recommendation for educational reform discusses a student's perception of the "rules of the game" in the classroom, none of these recommendations discuss question asking.

TABLE 8–1 · *High Expectations for Diverse Student Populations*

BEHAVIORAL STRANDS		
Student Response Opportunities (R)	*Teacher Feedback (F)*	*Personal Regard for Student (P)*
1. Teacher solicits individual student participation.	1. Teacher extends student response/ contribution.	1. Teacher seats and groups students to facilitate their learning.
2. Teacher provides ample time for student to respond to question or solicitation and to consider content as it is presented.	2. Teacher reinforces correct response or performance.	2. Teacher uses appropriate technique to prevent off-task behavior.
3. Teacher solicits responses or demonstrations from specific students for assessment purposes.	3. Teacher provides corrective feedback or clarifies.	3. Teacher uses appropriate technique to redirect/stop inappropriate/disruptive behavior.
4. Teacher challenges individual student.	4. Teacher reteaches consistently and fairly.	4. Teacher applies rules.
	5. Teacher reinforces desired behavior when appropriate.	5. Teacher relates content to student interests/ experiences.
	6. Teacher reinforces/ praises the learning efforts of students.	6. Teacher establishes climate of courtesy and respect.
	7. Teacher encourages slow and reluctant students.	7. Teacher maintains a positive rapport with students.
		8. Teacher maintains a respectful proximity to student.

The explicit ultimate goal of all of these recommendations is to improve educational outcomes. The assumption undergirding these recommendations seems to be that those outcomes can be achieved without any significant alteration in the behavioral-constitutional-social regularities of the modal classroom. It is an assumption as obfuscating as it is invalid.

FIGURE 8–1 · *What High-Expectation Teachers Believe*

- They tell themselves, their students, and others that they believe their students can learn regardless of difficult circumstances.
- They refuse to believe that family background is the principal cause of low academic achievement.
- They believe that their work with all students is important and meaningful, and they talk about it a lot.
- They believe they can be successful with even the most difficult students they have.
- They believe it is their responsibility to see that students learn; and, when the students experience failure, they examine their own performance for ways they could have been more helpful.
- They plan carefully for student learning, set goals for themselves and their students, and identify strategies for achieving them.
- They feel good about teaching in general, about their particular students, about themselves, and they are enthusiastic about their students' progress.
- They resist expressing a sense of futility; even when they feel overwhelmed, they don't admit defeat.
- They see themselves as involved in a joint venture with their students, pursuing goals that they share in common.
- They think students should be involved in academic/affective/behavioral goal-setting and strategies for achieving them.

Distributed to participants in Staff Development in Spring Branch, Texas. Compiled from "What's the Truth About Teacher Expectations . . . Really?" Paul S. George, The University of Florida, 1986.

> *One can change curricula, standards, and a lot of other things by legislation or fiat, but if the regularities of the classroom remain unexamined and unchanged, the failure of the reforms is guaranteed.*

Gary Mathews, associate superintendent in Spring Branch, Texas, says that the issue of classroom behavior was one of the key problems he addressed as principal of a high school undergoing the Effective Schools Improvement Process in Jackson, Mississippi. "We knew the dynamics there were wrong, that they had been for years," explains Mathews. "And there is the research to show that you have to get the kids more involved. It's no longer a story of lecturing all week and having the kids cough it all back up for a quiz on Friday. No. You have to involve them. And yes, you have to let them feel secure. Make sure they feel secure."

Mathews says that once his teachers began changing those power relationships in their classrooms, the students became more involved. They also started working with each other more. And with the introduction of cooperative learning, the students saw it was all right to help each other. The adversarial

FIGURE 8–2 · *What High-Expectation Teachers Do*

- They make standards and expectations clear to the students.
- They return a student's work because those standards have not been met.
- When introducing an assignment, they might stress that, of course, hard work is expected, and that it will result in success.
- They praise students for their accomplishments and they explain that they expect them to continue their progress.
- They are more likely to visually display student work because they assume that they and other students will be interested in it.
- They "push" students to get going, to do their work, and are less likely to tolerate silent off-task behavior in exchange for peace.
- They are more likely to be found engaged with students in warm greetings and casual discussion before the class period begins.
- But they spend a greater percentage of their time in class actually engaged in instruction, no matter which students they have.
- They often have a formal signal that tells students that it's time to get down to work and that no further unbusinesslike behavior will be tolerated. It may be as simple as announcing that the bell has rung, or it might be a daily ritual like a quote or thought for the day.
- They also tend to have a formal procedure for signaling the end of class, which discourages students from quitting before quitting time.
- They understand the power of "wait time" and give all students time to think, to respond carefully to the teacher's questions.
- They seek out the low-achieving student for academic assistance.
- Sometimes, in order to manage the class effectively, they feel they must call on low-achieving students less often. When this happens, the high-performing teacher compensates by increasing the number of private contacts with slower or less successful students.
- They treat all students courteously and refuse to tolerate students' mistreatment of each other.

Distributed to participants in Staff Development in Spring Branch, Texas. Compiled from "What's the Truth About Teacher Expectations . . . Really?" Paul S. George, The University of Florida, 1986.

relationships were gone. And once the adversarial relationships lessened between the students, so, too, did they between teachers and students.

"What Sarason is talking about is students taking more responsibility for their learning," says Mathews. "And if you look at Spring Branch's high expectations material and our emphasis on interactive learning techniques, you will see that at the heart of it is the student taking this responsibility. And the teacher having accountability. You see this in our mission statements, and you see it in the classrooms. It's what our staff development is all about."

This is the process of bringing that all-important correlate of high expectations down into the classroom. It's vital that a school district function with high expectations for administrators, teachers, and even (and especially) the superintendent, but where the water turns into wine is in the teachers' belief in high expectations for the students. And what teachers are learning is that with the proper training and insight, they can realize the revolutionary ramifications of high expectations.

Staff Development in Effective Instructional Skills

The second major staff development tool used by Spencerport and many other Effective Schools Process districts is the Essential Elements of Effective Instruction program that is based on the Madeline Hunter model of the teacher as decision maker. It is twofold: an intensive, 5-day workshop for teachers and an 11-day workshop for principals and supervisors.

Once again, according to Spencerport staff development findings, the teachers' workshop "strengthens skills which teachers intuitively know are effective by giving them the research based rationale for their behavior, and emphasizing research regarding how children learn and translating this research into teaching practices."

In Figure 8–3, Spencerport has illustrated how it views its staff development process. Staff development is, in the symbolic sense, the handle to the umbrella of Effective Schools correlates. New teaching techniques are continually being added to the staff development program, from mastery learning to cooperative learning to classroom management skills. For most teachers, these are exciting times. The staff development, no longer a threat, is the means to professional fulfillment.

"I don't know how a teacher can think that they don't need the staff development," says Larry Trippodo, a sixth-grade teacher at Town Line Elementary. "You're not going to pick up all you need to know about cooperative learning, TESA, mastery learning, to say nothing of the different methods of dealing with children of different cultures, by reading a few brochures. I've grown a great deal in this process. There's no doubt about it. I'm a better teacher because of the staff development and Effective Schools."

Mirian Smith agrees. "Through the entire process, from the staff development to our roles on the building teams, we have been allowed to become better teachers. I've been teaching a long time. I see the changes."

Bonnie Seaburn emphasizes that in many instances, the staff development is just building up around what the teachers already knew. "In the classroom today, what they're finding is a lot of support and reinforcement of processes they already had," believes Seaburn. "They're saying, 'Oh, that's what I do in the classroom, now I know the reason behind it. I always did it intuitively, but now I know why, and now I can continue to do it and do it better.'"

FIGURE 8–3

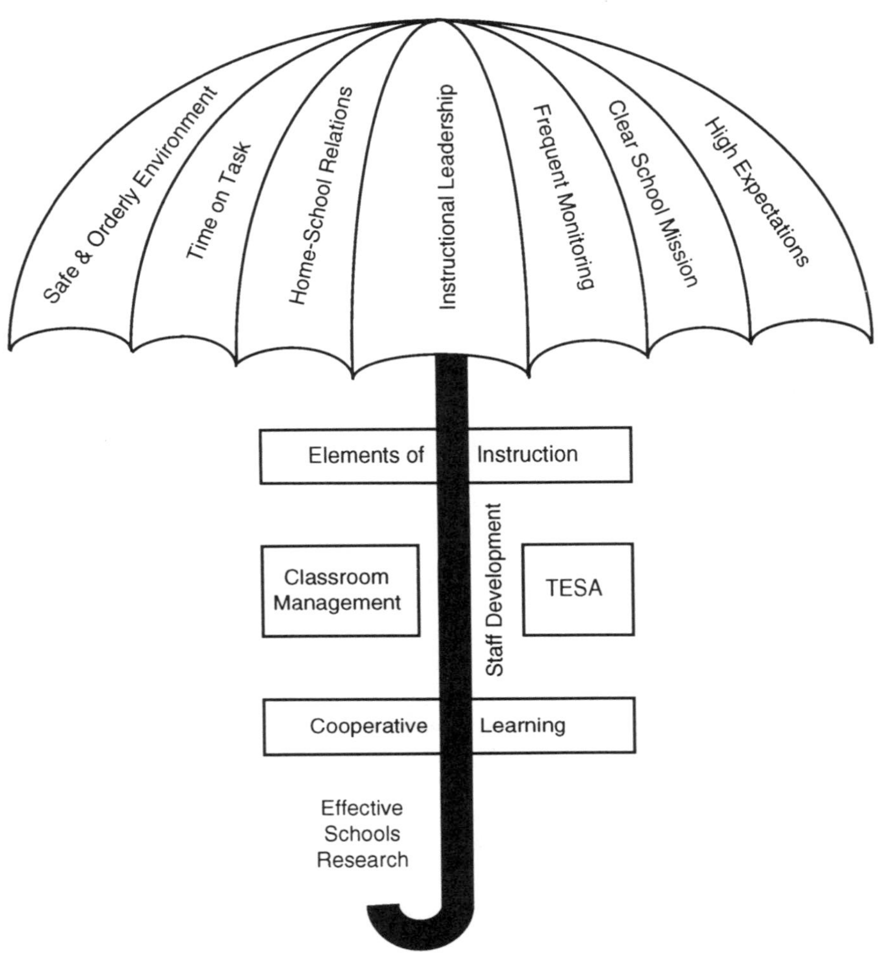

Spencerport's Wilson High School principal Bill Selander can be as excited about staff development as his teachers. "There is no doubt in my mind that the teachers in this town are working smarter. They may be working harder, too, but they're definitely worker smarter," says Selander. "This staff development is one of the best things that happened. I am envious of the teachers.

"I observed a new biology teacher yesterday, actually we stole her from the junior high. She was doing just a cracker-jack job of using those elements of instruction. When I taught, which was obviously a long time ago, I thought I was a real hot shot. But compared to her, I didn't know what I was doing. I was stumbling around in the wilderness.

"She used three different ways during the course of one lesson of having kids respond so that she could check out how they were doing. Just like there was nothing to it, and the kids responded like there was nothing to it. I'm saying to myself, 'Boy, I wish I had the chance to practice that enough to get that good at it.' I wish I had had the chance to learn the stuff she's learned. And what the other teachers have learned. It's incredible how they're teaching today. And the success of it shows!"

Ed Przybycien, principal of Spencerport's Cosgrove Junior High, remembers having no desire to go to a course on the elements of instruction. "I spent the first morning complaining and not listening," recalls Przybycien. "Then I woke up and couldn't get enough. After five days I came out of there and I was as excited as I was the first week I had started to teach. It kindled that kind of enthusiasm, because it was the first real thing I had heard in education about how people learn and how people should teach that made sense to me in many, many years. I knew that other teachers would be fools not to be just as excited.

"I believe that school reform in a building or district begins with how teachers can help themselves to teach better, how they can size up their children and help them to learn better. As teachers get better at what they're doing and analyze how children learn, the results get better, across the board, from the school to the district. And then teachers feel better about themselves. For the last 1,000 years, teaching has been a solitary, behind-the-doors profession. You closed the door and you did what you wanted behind that door.

"Well, the doors have been opening a little at a time in this Effective School Process. Staff development is bringing people together, starting dialogue. Everybody wants to be on a winning team, and they see that things are getting better, they can be proud, and their kids are really getting stronger and smarter. Everyone's holding their heads up a little higher around here.

"And you know, once you reach one level of success, you want to go higher, you want to feel even better. You want even more students to succeed. The goals get higher and higher."

A Tough Fight Needs Support from Above

The influence of staff development on the quality and quantity of learning proves that good intentions are just never enough in the classroom. Teachers need knowledge of teaching techniques that will help them address and deal with the problems of heterogeous classrooms.

And they need something more. They need the guidance and support from a strong administrative staff. The overhaul of a school system is going to have its greatest impact in the classroom. But as that impact is felt, the teachers must know they are not alone, that what they are going through is being experienced by many, and whether they are stepping forward or making a slight slip backward, they are under the protective understanding of their administration.

Noting the importance of this, Spencerport mentions in its staff development materials that everyone from the Board of Education to all echelons of the central office must be out on the hustings endorsing and explaining the staff development and school improvement process. The teachers must not feel that they are working in a vacuum.

"I'll tell you, I didn't think that Clement (superintendent of Spencerport Public Schools) was interested at all in educating all children," says a teacher at Wilson High in Spencerport. "One of the big things that happened here was that we saw how committed the central office really was to the improvement plan. We saw that they were willing to take a risk. Frankly, a risk with us, the teachers."

This is a significant observation because what is very often lost in any school improvement process is whose shoulders it all falls on in the end. It is the teachers' shoulders—in the classroom. A school improvement process does not succeed or fail in the superintendent's staff room. It succeeds or fails in the classroom. A good, Effective superintendent will repeatedly tell you that, yes, changes are being made at upper levels, but what this is all about is the support of good teaching and innovation in the classroom.

Although it is essential to have the backing from the central office, there is yet another level of support necessary, and that is the principal, or adminstrative staff, of the individual school. Teachers must feel and know they have these two levels of support and guidance standing above them and with them.

"Let's get this straight," begins a teacher for the Munn Elementary School in Spencerport. "The teachers in this district would not be so concerned with teaching for *all* kids if we didn't have a central office that was telling us this was the way it should be done. *And* it would never be going forward to such a degree in this school if we did not have the model of our principal (Bonnie Seaburn) to follow. And, not just to follow, but to protect us, and encourage us."

Seaburn believes that the staff development has helped bring out the best in the teachers in Spencerport. She says the teachers have learned how to tailor their own behavior to get the student behavior they desire.

"It was the process of educating the teachers," explains Seaburn. "Not that they ever thought, 'Gee, I never expected him to achieve.' That's not what they said. What they said was, 'Gee, now I know how I can promote her achievement better.' *You can't just encourage children to do something. You have to know what to do with them.*"

Seaburn says her role as one of the trainers in staff development has helped her in understanding the problems and changes her teachers are going through. But, she adds, the fact that she was a trainer is not the only reason she understands the trials in the classroom.

"Remember, *all* staff went through this. And continue to go through it. It was very important right from the beginning that this retraining not skip over anyone. It just wouldn't be enough if it just went to the teachers," says Seaburn. "We all had to understand how the brain works, how children are really learning today. It's essential that principals understand the behaviors, that they know just as surely as teachers, that you can't just encourage children to do something, you have to know what to do with them."

That line—you can't just encourage, you have to know what to do—works between principal and teacher just as it works between teacher and student. Principals must know what mastery learning, cooperative learning, is all about. They have to understand the role of high expectations so they can be there to assist a teacher. If they don't know the specific answers, they at least have to know where to refer the teacher.

But teachers also point out another role of the principal in all this classroom change. This role doesn't come with a precise definition. It's a role of strong mettle, of constant mental and emotional interaction, but not physical intervention. It's the process of letting a teacher alone to do what is best in the classroom. It's trusting a teacher to know, basically, what he or she is doing.

"I'll be very honest," begins Suzanne Still, principal of the Hollibrook School in Spring Branch, Texas, that has made such dramatic strides under the district's Effective Schools Process. "I have stopped in some classrooms and wondered what that teacher was doing, where she was taking her students. I mean, sometimes it might just seem a little off the wall."

But Still explains that is because she is not in that classroom every minute of every day and does not know that class like the teacher does. Whenever Still has been stumped by what a teacher is doing at a particular time, her reaction is never to call the teacher in and demand what was going on.

"Oh, never! Never! That teacher knows what she's doing. So do the kids. I just don't!" protests Still. "These teachers are so creative. You wouldn't believe what they can do. They just may not do it the same way that you remember being taught in school. But look at their results. These teachers, these kids, are cooking! So now when I see a teacher doing something that I just don't understand, I get excited. Because I know she's onto something new. Nine times out of ten in the next few days, she'll come up to me and say, 'Hey, Suzanne, I'm trying this new approach and you wouldn't believe how these kids are . . . .' Sometimes they learned a new approach from their own studies. Sometimes it's from something I give them. Sometimes it's instinct. But do I question it? Never. These teachers know what they're doing and I'll fight to the death for their right to do it whatever way they feel will work best."

Not every principal will say that they will fight to the death for their teachers, but they will say they have total confidence in those teachers. The days are past, they insist, when a principal can shuffle the blame down to the teachers.

"These teachers are mine. I'm not firing these teachers so therefore I must believe in their abilities, right? Right," says Jill Hearne, principal of the Adelaide Elementary School in Federal Way, Washington. "If there is something these teachers want to try, I say fine, try it. I know because of the way we work around here that it will be set up in such a way that we know when we come out the other end just how effective it was. I trust these teachers. I want to increase their self-assurance that they can look at a child, figure him or her out, and then use whatever they feel is going to work. And if they feel it's going to work, it most likely means it's going to work."

This trust for the teacher in the classroom is a new phenomena in many schools. Teachers talk of never feeling that the administration trusted them before. They talk of "always feeling like big brother was just waiting for you to slip up." Now they talk of the "comfort" in the classroom—the comfort of knowing that your principal not only trusts what you're doing but will leave you alone to do it, and if necessary, go to the mat for you.

"Do you know how different that is from the way we've been treated in the past?" asks a teacher at Bonnie Seaburn's Munn Elementary in Spencerport. "I mean, I have felt for years that I've been all alone out on a very shaky limb—no matter how I was teaching. But no more. With Bonnie, we all have a solid support system. She gives us the utmost respect and dignity, which we can then pass on to the children. This dignity has a snowball effect."

The "snowball effect" is why the founders of the Effective Schools Process built into the original framework the importance of *modeling* from the superintendent, to the principal, and into the classroom. That modeling—that trust—that knowledge—is as vital in Spencerport as it is in Spring Branch, Texas.

"This school was a dump—a dumping ground for kids and teachers—before Linda Watkins came in (principal of Landrum Junior High)," explained a veteran teacher. "But immediately, we knew we had a leader, a real leader, who would fight for us. And she reported to a guy whom we were quickly gaining a lot of respect for (Hal Guthrie, superintendent). To put it simply, we could trust them. And if you trust who you're working for and what they're about, you work a lot harder, and you're much more conscientious of your own actions."

In Frederick County, Maryland, teachers say that even after three years, they are still being surprised by the behavior pattern set down by Superintendent Noel Farmer.

"When he first came here, there were stories, all true, of how he was all over the district all hours of the day and night. Really, intensely involved, and really giving teachers, especially teachers, it seemed, a lot of support," recalls a high school teacher who admits to having been very skeptical at first.

"But he's still doing it. I have run into this guy at 6:30 in the morning, checking to make sure a science lab has the stuff it needs. Apparently, he had heard there was a problem and he said fix it and now just wanted to make sure. When was the last time you saw a superintendent out in the schools making sure a classroom was ready for the students?"

What about New York City?

"I've been short of books and one day I had it, so I passed by everyone and called the superintendent's office (Tony Amato). He was out, but I told his assistant, 'Hey, he promised us these books and supplies. Where are they?'" recalls Mirian Acosta-Sing, principal of Mott Hall School in Spanish Harlem. "And the next morning, I'm coming into school and what's happening? Here's the superintendent hauling the books out of a car, hauling them into the school. So, hey, if he can be there for me, I can be there for my teachers."

It's important to keep in mind that all this change and support, trust and modeling, just doesn't occur by happenstance. It is all part of a research-based approach to school improvement. The lines drawn are very precise. The actions required are very specific. The *structure for the process* is laid out right at the beginning.

As Effective superintendents have explained, they are not working and planning on the basis of whim. They are not "flying by the seat of their pants." When they create the master plan for the district, they know exactly what the focus and goal of staff development is to be. In Frederick County, Maryland, there is not only a mission for staff development, there is a philosophy:

"Staff development for Frederick County will encompass an organizational development model with a strong site-based management component. Planned interventions based on diagnosis of the organization and the people within the organization will result in collaboration for problem solving and decision making. Formative and summative evaluation of planned interventions will allow for continual staff development."

The ongoing aspect of staff development should keep the program fresh, with the overseers always on the lookout for more and better teaching programs. But all of this takes a commitment beyond just a mindset. There must be a significant allocation of time.

"There's never enough time," says Tony Marcello. "There are review sessions, awareness sessions, half-day, full-day, two days, five days, all over the board. Summer, winter, you name it. And we're still asking if there is more needed. And of course there is, and so far the central office has been good at providing it. But it's tough.

"Before this, staff development was a joke. You know, you'd get a brochure in the mail from some place and then put in a request and if you were lucky after weeks of waiting and paperwork," continues Marcello. "But now, the teachers request it through their schools, and once the time is cleared, they're usually on their way and the program is integrated with what we do."

Teachers are discovering that although their district may be immersed in staff development, it does not necessarily mean that development is going on across the district boundary line.

"I bump into a teacher from another city, say on vacation or something, and we'll get to talking and staff development courses will come up," says Fred Cardella. "And I'll ask them about cooperative learning, or something, and they'll just say, 'Oh yeah, heard of it, and they're talking about having some courses in it, but I hear it's a waste.' And I can't believe it. Not only that these people are in the dark ages in their thinking but that they haven't even gone to one staff development course. And these people are often from decent places making big money. But when I read a report that their scores are way down, I know why. I'm not surprised."

There are now at least four levels of staff development for teachers going on in the United States. There are the basic courses in high expectations and the research-based advantages of equity in the classroom. Then there are the courses in the day-to-day learning dynamics, such as cooperative learning and mastery learning. The third level represents those courses that may currently be looked at as more experimental in nature—those courses offering an examination of presently controversial learning and testing strategies where the data are still being gathered. On the final rung are the courses in school organization, teacher leadership, and teacher decision making (the process that is examined in the next chapter).

"As far as I'm concerned, you can't get enough," says Tony Marcello, asking the familiar, "Aren't we all supposed to be into lifelong learning?"

Marcello continues, "The difference is major. Anyone who doesn't see that is kidding themselves. I have learned that my expectations of my kids will *definitely* have an influence on their productivity in the classroom. The elements of instruction? I've seen that by providing a better design, by being more organized, by knowing the focal point for each lesson, I do a better job and the kids benefit from it.

"I'm a better teacher and I can prove it to you that I do a better job in the classroom. I can verify that. No question about it. I'm spending more time in the classroom, and I'm more conscientious. The staff development ideas have proven to me that they work.

"Before Effective Schools, I'd say, 'Yeah, I thought I was doing a good job.' But I wasn't able to prove it to anybody. Well, I can prove it to you now that I'm doing a good job. I used to look at my kids and say, 'well, some of you just won't make it.' I don't have that idea or opinion any longer. I have 29 kids in my homeroom right now, and I expect all 29 to be successful!"

Just as the integrity of the intitial staff development programs has progressed, so has the means of choosing those programs.

"Two years ago, I created trainings, districtwide, for all teachers and administrators, and everybody got the same dose whether they needed it or not," explains Bob Wells, executive director of human and technological resource development for Spring Branch, Texas. "It helped build a common language, helped people see where we were going. But it's losing it's meaning.

"A year ago we shifted so that now schools tell me what they think, what they want. We talk to principals about how they believe campus needs assessment should be done. And they discuss it with their staffs. That's the people who know the needs. Not us here. They collect the data relative to their schools, have their teams examine it, then they call me up and say 'We've got such and such phenomena at our school.' Say their seventh grade writing is an area of student outcomes that is least successful. What can we do about that? What I do is try to keep a portfolio of promising practices, so as people from schools call me and say, 'Is there anybody around or anything that can help us teach writing more effectively?' Well, I need to be aware of the resources out there that could maybe be of help. I'm more and more a supply center."

There are some critics of the teaching force who still argue that teachers are not interested in taking additional courses, that they want to—and will—teach just as they have for years. The facts show that teachers know that hanging onto the ways of the past will not serve them well in the future.

Sam Humphrey, now an administrator with Geary County Public Schools central office, explains that the staff development is the draw for many teachers in this Kansas community. "My wife and I are both teachers, and when we were looking for placements, we kept coming back to the idea of Junction City, Kansas," explains Humphrey, who came to Kansas from Colorado. "We knew that the way education was going today, it was essential to know all the very latest and most sophisticated teaching techniques. And Junction City had the reputation of the best staff development in probably the whole Midwest."

Many teachers in Junction City came for the staff development, and, as they have stated, it has been one of the biggest bonuses of their employment. "There's no question that I have learned a great deal," says Greg Lumb, a fifth-grade teacher at Custer Hill Elementary School. "But it goes beyond that. You get the feeling here that the administration has a vested interest in our growth as professionals. I have friends who have worked in this district and stay here because they are proud to be a part of the growth of the district."

Jan McNeefe, also a teacher at Custer Hill, says one of the best aspects of the staff development is that it is designed by the teachers. "We decided what we need. We tell them in town what is necessary," explains McNeefe. "Which is how it should be. No one else knows our needs better than we do. We get to make the plans according to our decisions as a faculty, as a school."

McNeefe talks about the exhiliaration teachers feel after attending special workshops for a week in Minnesota or after being part of a seminar in Kansas taught by one of the leaders in mastery learning.

"For some of the teachers who have been in the classroom for 20, 30 years, all this stuff was a little too much at first," says McNeefe. "Like when we first came back from some of the classes and knew that the tracking system was all wrong. The other teachers thought we'd just eventually get this out of our system and they didn't go along with us. We had to make sure they got into the Effective Schools classes so they could understand what was best for the kids. Now we're all in line and it's OK. The faculty in this school has accepted the fact that we're going to be openminded and grow."

McNeefe also makes a statement that is very familiar among teachers of Effective Schools, but something they are usually hesitant to say on record. "I learned more in Effective Schools than I learned in my entire master's degree program," says McNeefe, who received her degree from a nationally recognized teaching institution.

At the Ft. Riley Middle School, four teachers gather after school to work on the lesson plans for their sixth-grade classes that they team teach. Cathy Hall, Shirley Simmons, Carol Ohm, and Leslie Myers point to the administration and the staff development as the reasons why their classes are so progressive.

"We have all learned a great deal," explains Leslie Myers. "We've been able to go after the development courses that each of us was interested in. And it makes a big difference. We're doing things team teaching that I know other districts have never even heard of."

"Not only that, but I'll put these kids up against any group," says Cathy Hall. "These kids love to be taught. And they love this idea of having the four of us. It keeps an excitement going. You can see it. And look at the work they do. It's amazing! They love learning!"

"We're consistent, and that makes a big difference," adds Shirley Simmons. "We keep giving out the same message. They have to be responsible. They deserve respect. There is a lot of limit setting, a lot of responsibility training."

"The team rule is to help, don't hurt," explains Cathy Hall. "We never attack them. We're always positive. We do a lot of modeling."

"I think we've all learned different things from our development courses," says Carol Ohm. "And so we all bring some little extra that maybe the kids would miss otherwise. And we know how important this is. This has to be good. This has to be a wonderful place. This is the best that they have."

"If it were not for the advances I think we've all made in our teaching over the years, these kids would not have the success they're having," explains Leslie Myers. "You have to remember that in many ways, a student's success can be directly related to the success of the teacher."

Teachers remember when staff development was not always held in high regard. "You used to get the evil eye when you mentioned staff development or—God forbid—renewal," recalls a teacher from District 6 in New York. "If you were in favor of staff development, that meant that you accepted the assumption that teachers didn't know everything—or, worse, that we were doing something wrong, that there was need for change. Well, there *was* need for a change."

That need for a change goes back to the statement, *What you believe has a big affect on how you teach.* Never forgetting that and mindful that teachers are constantly moving in and out of school districts and that their resolve can weaken, or their ideological edges grow rusty, the Effective Schools Process keeps reminding staffs that their first loyalty is to teaching for learning for *all.*

"The belief that some children *cannot* learn is part of our culture. It doesn't matter if you're a teacher or a corporate president. As a society, we don't believe all children can learn," says Lezotte. "But thank God there have always been some teachers out there who have always believed every kid can make it. I mean *really* believed it."

Larry Dixon, principal of the Junction City High School in Geary County, Kansas, says it is the *all children can learn* value of Effective Schools and its disaggregation process of scores, that is the primary appeal for him, and something he keeps pounding into his teachers.

"Never mind the poor white kid with the torn clothes, what about the kid with the dark skin? Do you think teachers believe that kid can learn? Oh, he can maybe memorize some spelling words and do some simple arithmetic, but that's it," says Dixon, a black man who attended public desegregated schools in New Jersey. "But do teachers believe that child can think? Can calculate? Can reason? Can write? No. No to all the above."

"I think Larry's right," agrees one of his teachers at Junction City High School. "We can say the words *all children can learn*, but it's tough to believe them in the gut. I'm ashamed to admit I was not a believer. But now I see what is happening when we just try. Kids who I never thought had a prayer are now doing beyond our dreams. And we see the proof in the testing."

A teacher in New York City's Spanish Harlem sees the Effective Schools Process as making a major change in the way teachers see the students assembled before them.

"There was a time when, because of a number of factors—poor administrators, no supplies, violence, rotten morale—that you'd just sit at your desk and look out and think, 'What a bunch of losers; how quickly can I get through this day?' And you'd just do the minimum to get by. I know it sucks, but it's a fact.

"However, having said that, I've also got to say, 'Come into our classrooms now. Look at what we're doing. We're not defeated anymore.' What made the difference? The new superintendent (Tony Amato), for one, and the Effective Schools Process. For the first time, we started to look at the scores and see what we were doing—and also how other schools, with kids no doubt as tough as ours, were doing incredible things. And so we began trying. We started thinking the kids weren't losers. We gave them a chance."

A high school teacher in Spring Branch, Texas, agrees that there was a time when you "just went through the day anyway you could, not getting concerned about the kids who couldn't learn."

"But we started to see that you could turn around a few kids here and there—kids who you thought were destined for the streets or worse. So we started to make a real effort, I mean, thinking we could make that difference. And some kids, yeah, you've got to get them into special programs. But other kids—you start to believe in them, push them, even challenge them—and they surprise you. I think these kids have surprised a lot of us."

Every teacher can speak of extraordinary stories of extraordinary turnarounds. It's old hat now to talk of kids who go from the bottom of the roster to the top, to talk about the third-grader who hated reading and is now reading at the sixth-grade level, or the young girl who they thought was learning disabled until they started treating her like the others, and encouraging her, and now she has among her trophies the first prize in the Science Fair.

These stories, which teachers say no longer surprise them but which they can never get enough of creating, are made all the more powerful when one thinks of what would have happened to these students if the teachers had *not* applied the lessons of high expectations research. And teachers say that although the results themselves no longer stun them as much as the fact that in some cases it takes so little—a few extra questions, a pat on the shoulder, a curiosity in a student's interests—to flip a child from the loser to the winner column.

So, whether surprising teachers or challenging teachers, children in Effective Schools programs are being looked at differently. Fred Cardella of Spencerport talks about one of his young charges: "Myself, in kindergarten, I already have a kid that before the end of September, I had identified, and said, 'This kid is really in deep trouble, and I want something done, and done immediately.' So we're testing and working with him and he's getting the help. I don't want this kid out of the normal classroom setting. I firmly believe this kid can learn. I couldn't have said that 10 years ago. That's the difference. This kid could have gotten lost in the old system very easily.

"Lezotte says this over and over again: 'What's the issue that wakes you up in the middle of the night?' The issue that wakes me up in the middle of the night is the kid that comes into kindergarten that really has severe language problems that needs to catch up on those language problems before anything else. We have to identify him immediately and get resources to help, or the kid will fall by the wayside. So I sleep a lot better at night knowing I'm doing everything, everything within my power to do."

Just as It Once Was, Only Better

In the Effective Schools Process, teachers believe all of their students can learn the intended curriculum. The responsibility for learning lies with both the teacher and the student, but the teacher has the primary responsibility to make learning appropriate and exciting for each student. Primary motivation for learning comes from the teacher, no matter what the climate for education is in the student's home.

Teachers alter their behaviors, professional procedures, and pedagogical practices in the classroom so that each child receives and learns the intended curriculum the district has laid out. High expectations for all players (teachers, support staff, administrators, as well as students) in an Effective School is demonstrated daily, hourly. Teachers plan their lessons so that they can monitor all students, and expect the principal, support staff, and central office staff to align policies, programs, and practices to afford enough classroom time and opportunity to teach all students well. Scheduling and grouping designs become more flexible and under the teacher's control. Teachers plan with other teachers and with the principal to make the best use of every hour of every school day, so that all children have the opportunity to learn their lessons. Finding time for the planning and implementation of the Effective Schools Process makes up the major reallocation of resources, which occurs in improving schools to teach *all* children.

Just as the best teachers in the forties planned and ran their school by collaborating with the principal teacher, Effective teachers and principals today hold themselves accountable for what happens to their students in the classroom and the progress students make. School improvement happens first through the school planning teams and the faculty. Then teachers feel empowered, ready to take the risks involved in organizing their school and classrooms to teach all children.

The students are motivated in an equitable school because they know they are important and will get a fair shake. Students perform and achieve better, and their self-confidence is increased so that they are ready for the next level of learning.

Schools should be places of learning. It is up to the teachers, administrators, support staff, parents, and the community of a school to see that they are. It begins at the top, with Effective leaders in the central administration and in the schools. Then, given the opportunity, without threat and with support, to enhance their own learning process, teachers will train hard in order that they may step up to the bat prepared to take on the complex teaching challenges of America in the nineties.

"I think we're making some progress in those schools with staff development and real school-based management," says Jan McNeefe of Junction City, Kansas . "I just don't know if the public realizes how much more the teachers are giving. And I don't know if it's all fast enough, or in time."

CHAPTER NINE

Teachers as Instructional Leaders

Decision Makers Outside the Classrooms

An Effective teacher is an Effective leader and vice versa. One of the false distinctions which I wish people would get off of is who's more important in the schools? The principal as a leader or the teachers? And I say if we're all doing our job well we're both leading and teaching. —LAWRENCE LEZOTTE

For 200 years we have ignored, or dismissed, the leadership talents of the teachers. And that's a major reason why schools fail. —NOEL FARMER, superintendent

We were given the opportunity to lead. That's all we needed. Just the opportunity.
—MARIA FERNANDEZ, teacher

Equity is the word most often associated with the Effective Schools Process. But it is not equity that stops with the student—it is the equity of the entire school, the entire staff. In recommending school-based management, the Effective Schools Process calls for the equitable treatment of teachers in not only matters of the classroom but in the day-to-day operations and the atmosphere of the school as a whole.

In the Effective Schools staff development courses, teachers are instructed in the need to change the power relationships within the classroom. Students must be allowed to participate actively in their education, to feel that they have a responsibility for learning. This is done by drawing the student out in conversation and inquiry, encouraging different ways of accomplishing tasks, and creating group learning situations where the student can explore interpersonal skills.

The greater participation of the student goes beyond the classroom. An Effective administrative team is trained to be open to students' inquiries and concerns. Students will be asked how they feel about their education, the daily routine, and the atmosphere of the school. The students' responsibility to contribute on many levels is greatly enhanced.

This is what Effective Schools is about. But the philosophy also says that teachers can't give what they don't have themselves. A teacher cannot give children greater responsibility for their learning if that teacher does not feel that he or she has any say or power over the climate, ideology, and operation of the school in which he or she teaches. It's a lesson from the beginning of time: You have to have power to give power. And, like the student, the more responsibility you are given, the deeper your personal commitment.

School systems have always flirted with the notion of empowering teachers. There would be talk, especially at contract renewal time, of teachers having increased input in school matters. Superintendents and principals would hold forth on how much they respected their teachers' opinions, how much they wanted that input. But after the contract was signed, or the faculty meeting was over, the principal would return to her or his corner, and the teachers to theirs. Schools were (and many still are) little fiefdoms. The superintendent or principal rules and the teachers work in their little corner plot, like little farmers sowing seeds, rarely seeing their fellow farmers, never encouraged to get together with those farmers to discuss the harvest, and not even having a say over so much as how much fertilizer they may need for the new season.

In some school districts in recent years, there has been the establishment of school-based management and school improvement teams. But, unfortunately, in too many locales it is being done on a school-by-school basis. There is no uniform policy from central administration, no mandate to the principals to make school-based management work, and no staff development to assist teachers in their new roles. The result is floundering, confusion, bickering, a lack of cohesiveness, and a bureaucratic nightmare. Where there is no set policy, no specific guidelines, the schools are left to request "waivers" of the central office policy in order to accommodate the changes desired. But who decides and how do they decide? Without a set policy, the system is ruled by whim and the desires of the political hierarchy. The teachers lose again.

"We've been hearing this teacher empowerment stuff for years," says Pete Randozzo, head of the Spencerport (New York) Teachers' Union. "But it never came to anything. Just a lot of words. The power stayed where it had always been."

The Effective Schools Process stopped that. No longer placating teachers with empty rhetoric, Effective Schools makes the statement at the start that the strength of the improvement process is *dependent* on the empowerment of the teachers. The philosophy of Effective Schools calls for a concrete process whereby the teachers are given significant power in the day-to-day operation of the school, curriculum decisions, and matters of testing, parental involvement, discipline, and school mission and goals. Specific guidelines are to be drawn up, voted on, and distributed.

The empowerment of the teachers—their renewal—is written into the superintendent's master plan. That plan, which is to be drawn up with the assistance of teachers, is usually unequivocating on the matter of school-based management. Through school-based management, the board of education then *requires* teachers to be major players in any and all school planning teams. These planning teams are not to be nebulous nabobs discussing cafeteria conduct. These planning teams are to set out precise objectives and strategies for improvement. Teachers are *required* to be decision makers dealing with matters ranging from grading criteria to the hiring of staff and allocation of resources.

But how do teachers go from that corner plot to the corner office? They go as planned. The Effective Schools Process demands a firm framework of staff development to train the teacher in not just the principles of effective teaching but group process, management, and leadership skills. It is just as Ron Edmonds initially said: "We are not going to ask you to do anything that we can't teach you how to do."

The fact that the increased responsibility (and accountability) of the teacher is written into the correlates of Effective Schools, and the subsequent planning process, is the major difference between Effective Schools and other reform movements. The fact that it not only makes a place for the teacher in school planning but prepares that teacher to assume that planning position to the very best of his or her ability is the factor that draws in even the skeptics.

"My first reaction was that it was just more empty talk about getting teachers involved," recalls Randozzo of Spencerport. "But then I looked more closely and started to ask some questions. I learned it was a genuine effort to really involve staff in trying to improve education. I actually wrote a letter to the membership, saying let's not be afraid of it, let's give it a try.

"And my reason for that was that I saw an opportunity for teachers to have some say in the running of the buildings. And this was before any of the national phrases like *teacher empowerment* and *shared decision making* hit this area. This was brand new here, although we had heard it from the unions. Over the years, teachers had been offering suggestions to administrators, to the district, and it was falling on deaf ears. And I thought, 'Well, here's an opportunity to give our teachers a say in what's going on.' Now how much a say nobody knew. But that's what I said to people: 'Let's not be afraid of it, let's give it a chance.'"

The Effective Schools philosophy recognizes that *empowerment*, the granting of increased authority and responsibility, is an empty phrase if it is not accompanied by retraining. And that retraining is never going to be meaningful if the district does not commit a certain amount of time to it. This cannot be time that is captured between classes or after a long day of dealing with students and administrators. It has to be separate time devoted exclusively to retraining. And you can't ask teachers to spend Saturdays or vacations doing this out of the goodness of their heart. There has to be a commitment of not only time for retraining but money to pay for that retraining. The teachers must be paid, just as experts and outside practitioners must be paid. What makes this issue of time and money outside the classroom so controversial and politically sticky is that many parents believe that teachers should not have these renewal days, that they are a waste, and that the taxpayer should be paying only for the time the teacher spends in the classroom with students. The burden of dealing with this falls, as it should, on the shoulders of the individual at the top of the organization.

"You have to have a leader who is willing to just about institutionalize time to reflect, plan, and change," insists Larry Lezotte. "If you don't have someone up at the top who believes in that, you're in tough shape."

In every one of the Effective districts profiled in this book, the superintendent was waging battle every year with his or her board for more money for staff development. And while the boards recognized the need for it, they repeated what a hard sell it was in the community. Because of our ingrained culture that says a teacher's place is *only* in the classroom, even businesspeople, who regularly attend, at full pay, retraining sessions and elaborate retreats, did not see the need for teachers being paid for a few days of staff development. And if the public had trouble with teachers attending classes on teaching techniques, they were apoplectic about teachers taking courses in leadership and group process skills. In the end, it came down to superintendents just getting the most public money they could, and, in some districts like Spring Branch, Texas, and Spencerport, New York, supplementing the cost with private funds.

"We know that we live or die by the quality of our teachers and staff," says Hal Guthrie, superintendent of Spring Branch. "And because of that, I'm going to do everything I can to make sure they get every chance to be their best. How do they give the kids the best if they don't have the best?"

Even up in Spencerport, New York, where Superintendent Joe Clement has an adversarial relationship with some factions of the teachers' union, and is known throughout the district for being "very tight on the dollar," teachers insist when it comes to staff development, Clement finds the money.

"I have to admit that the one place where this district seems willing to spend money is in the area of staff development," says Union President Pete Randozzo. "And it's quality staff development. They do a good job."

Behind a superintendent's commitment to staff development is that individual's attitude toward the teaching staff. For years, throughout this country, teachers and central administration have been at loggerheads. It was often hard to believe that these two entities were supposed to have the same professional mission. But just as in the business world when managers realize they defeat their purpose by being authoritarian rulers over the workers, so, too, are school superintendents realizing that the degree of teacher discord and disillusionment is linked directly to a school's image of itself, and its standing as either a successful or failing school.

"Effective Schools has everything to do with how you treat the faculty," insists Noel Farmer, superintendent of Frederick County, Maryland. "You must value your workers. The care and concern that you have in the development of the worker is as important as the outcome. Satisfaction does not *cause* productivity, but you certainly want both to appear at the same time, and valuing the worker and wanting the worker to have good opportunities for self-development is as important as the outcomes you're after."

Not only is the staff development in Frederick County expansive (and well thought out; Farmer planned for a year before beginning Effective Schools implementation) but the administration has put its money where its mouth is. In strained economic times, it negotiated a contract that boosted workshop pay and also gave the teachers three 6-percent salary increases spread across three years. This was approved, but then the state stepped in and said because of tough times, this wasn't going to happen. Farmer stuck to his word and said it was. He convinced the county commissioners to raise taxes to pay for the teachers. There was some adjustment made in the timing of the raises, but the bulk of Farmer's negotiated contract stood. It is hailed as unprecedented that a county would actually raise taxes in this anti-tax time in order to increase teacher salaries.

The reason it happened was because Farmer was able to show to the county the incredible strides the district had made in the last three years. Under the Effective Schools Process and Farmer's leadership, Frederick County has moved from close to the bottom to the top in state ranking. When faced with the outcomes the teachers had produced, the county said yes to the pay raise.

"It's the old line: You get what you pay for. We are expecting a great deal from our teachers. And in the past few years, they have given us a lot," explains Kevin Castner, Ed.D., assistant superintendent in Frederick County. "We believe it is essential that the teachers know how much we recognize all the work they have done. That we don't take it lightly."

Farmer lays it down flatly: "I know the value of these teachers. I know the value of treating them with respect and intelligence."

And Farmer is not alone. Hal Guthrie in Spring Branch has pushed through the first bond issue for schools in years. Tony Amato in New York finally has new construction happening in his district. And Max Heim in Kansas went to bat and received one of the biggest pay raises for his teachers in that district's history.

These superintendents are doing it on the basis of the outcomes they are receiving, and those outcomes are a direct result of the staff development and the school-based management that is giving new and genuine power to the teachers.

Power with Responsibility

One of the major clues that the atmosphere and attitude within the school are destined to change comes when the individual schools begin doing a needs assessment. In this, the teachers complete an assessment on how their school operates with regard to school mission, instructional leadership, environment, outcomes, support mechanisms, staff development opportunities, and parental involvement. The assessment tools vary, but overall they are an inquiry into every aspect of the school's operation.

"I was filling that assessment out and I looked around at my fellow teachers, and I thought, 'If we all fill this out truthfully, there's going to be some bombs dropped,'" recalls a teacher in Spencerport, New York. "And then the administration was going to have two choices: Ignore it or do something about it. And if they were going to do something about it, given what we had been learning from the Effective Schools Process, the matter of doing something about it was going to involve the teachers. Not just in the classroom, but making decisions that affected the whole school."

In discussing power relationships, Seymour Sarason (1990) states that a major problem in education is who makes the decisions: "The definition of power as 'the ability to act or produce an effect' was one that in practice applied only to a small number of school personnel and that did not include teachers. The reformulation clearly suggested that the educational decision making process ignored the creativity and experience of people with an obvious stake in improving our schools."

No one will argue with that statement, but Effective Schools practitioners do cast a wary eye on Sarason's conclusion that: "I am aware that there are schools in which teachers participate in decision making in regard to the classroom and the schools generally. With few exceptions, teacher participation was not a consequence of a system-wide policy proclaimed by the superintendent or the board of education. It was a consequence of a school policy intitiated and supported by the principal."

The Effective Schools districts must be those "few exceptions" of which Sarason writes. However, the numbers are quickly going beyond the "few"; today, districts involved in the Effective Schools Improvement Process numbers over 400.

This school-based management, this increased power of teachers in decision making, must involve districtwide restructuring, not only to bring consistency and cohesion to the system but to increase opportunities for learning in the classroom and to give every teacher and staff member a common language—not just throughout the school, but throughout the system.

Teachers support the systemwide approach, saying that it helps them in drawing up school improvement plans ("We can discuss it with other schools, look into the solutions they've used") and in the feeling of comaraderie ("We know we're not alone, not as teachers, and not as schools"). It is this feeling that the entire district is working together for a common goal, but with the option of each school to approach and accomplish it differently, that builds collegiality as well as self-esteem. The teachers are making new policy on district level as well as school level, aligning that policy between school and district.

The Effective Schools districts are very careful to offer the necessary courses and options for staff development, not just in teaching but in decision making. In most districts, these decision-making skills come straight from established, successful business practices and actual hands-on workshops.

"In our leadership workshops, we take our teachers and, just like our administrators, put them through simulated work situations," explains Gary Mathews, associate superintendent of Spring Branch. "They spend all day with real-life situations, and, in a group, work out different options for dealing with the problems." Mathews explains those "problems" range from curriculum decisions, hiring and firing controversies, allocation of resources, even how best to deal with the central office. Group interaction is emphasized because the teachers will always be working on teams to accomplish the changes they seek in their schools.

Is it necessary for every teacher to attend these decision-making workshops, empowerment classes, retraining in effective instructional techniques? "There are some people in those classrooms who have been leaders in teaching and school operation since the ark landed," says Lezotte. "They decided that they were going to decide for themselves what this thing called education is all about. And they've been doing it."

Lezotte says he gets frustrated with the notion that teacher empowerment is new to the block. "If we took all these definitions of empowerment and went out to school districts around the country, and asked 'Do you have someone in your school who fits this set of empowered behaviors?' they'd immediately say, 'Of course, right down here is Mrs. Jones . . . .' And of course Mrs. Jones has been doing the right thing for kids for years. She's learned how to work around the impediments, treat all kids equally . . . .

"You see—*you can liberate teachers but you can't free them*. Those who would be empowered are. Those who aren't would rather not be.

"When you see an unusually Effective teacher, look closely and watch what that teacher is doing in the classroom. You put on the lenses of leadership and you're going to come out and give her a high mark on anybody's definition of leadership. An Effective teacher is an Effective leader and vice versa. One of the things that is important to teach them is followership, they're teaching the community how to proceed *with* them. That's what they're doing. One of the false distinctions here which I wish people would get off of is who's more important in the schools? The principal as a leader or the teacher? And I say if we're all doing our job well we're both leading and teaching."

The problem arises when you have a principal who just has never been a leader, isn't interested in being one, and will forever remain a political bureaucrat. Schools need risk takers — men and women who are willing to put their integrity on the line just as is happening in the superintendent's office.

"You've got to have the same leadership and the same skills of leadership at the top that you have at the teaching centers," says Lezotte. "And unfortunately, we can only find about one-third of the principals willing to take risks, make school policy, and be willing to be the kind of charismatic, leading principal you want at the school level. And if you don't align the rest of the organization with the values and the vision, then you're not going to make it for the kids. If you have a principal who doesn't have a sense of vision or leadership, even if you have a superintendent who is skilled at it, that doesn't make those principals skilled at it."

"I think some of the biggest holdouts were in the administration," believes Pete Randozzo, president of the Spencerport Teachers' Association. "For the most part, the administrators have improved drastically. Ten years ago they were just awful to work for. But there's been a substantial improvement in their relations with staff — how they manage people. Things aren't perfect, but they've improved. Then there are others who definitely haven't reached that level yet. They are still trying to be very dogmatic and authoritarian."

Randozzo's belief that some administrators lagged behind and still lag behind, is held by other faculty members.

"We've made progress, but in other instances, they just haven't caught onto shared leadership. And I think there's one or two who haven't caught onto *all children can learn.* And you can really feel that. That makes it tougher all around," says one Spencerport elementary school teacher, who adds, however, that each year it generally seems to get better.

"It's difficult in an entrenched school system to make the changes you need to make at the principal level," explains Spencerport Superintendent Joe Clement. "You have to hope that people will come around. Give them the chance, and if they don't, you either work around it, or move them out."

Effective Schools districts are marked by major changes in the administration of the schools. In some districts, as many as 70 percent of the principals have been transferred or replaced. Superintendents say they just don't have time to waste seeing if a recalcitrant principal will come around. They have to take action, and most do.

"It really comes back to that building principal," says Randozzo. "How secure and how strong he or she is. If they're still living in the fifties, forget it, in most cases. I say in most cases because we do have one principal who has really come a long way. There is serious trust building where you never would have imagined. Principals are building trust."

Without a principal who builds trust, without a principal who is an Effective leader, most schools and teachers are left in the lurch. In some instances, an assistant principal, if strong enough, can step in and take over. But in most cases, the viability of school-based management and teacher decision making is tied with a very strong rope to the principal.

"How did we learn how to make the right decisions about this school? Simple. We were given the opportunity to make the decisions," explains Lynne Williams, a teacher at Hollibrook School in Spring Branch, which has gone from a school where teachers shamefully hung their heads to a school where teachers now shout with pride. "Suzanne (Suzanne Still, principal) said she trusted us to know and do what was right for this school. And those turned out not to be just pretty words. She did trust us. We decided we were going to lead this school into real success."

The district supplemented Still's trust for her teachers—as they did with all other schools—with every major development course she and her staff might need in order to accomplish their objectives. The courses were wide ranging and open to whoever wanted to take the opportunity to accelerate and expand their learning. (Many noneffective districts only allow administrators in management or leadership classes.)

"I remember, if five years ago you mentioned you were going to a leadership workshop, people would look at you like you were some narcissistic pig with illusions of grandeur," says a teacher in Spring Branch. "And you'd be taking this course on your own time with your own money. But now it's an accepted thing—you're even encouraged to do it, really encouraged. And of course it's all paid for. To say nothing of the fact, you'll actually need and *use* what you learn in the course."

What matters just as much as the central office support for teachers who want to take leadership and development courses is the strong push from the superintendent's office for teachers and their schools to improve. Teachers say this sounds simplistic, but emphasize its importance. In the past, in some of these districts, schools like the Hollibrook were written off. The central office had just decided the school was in a lousy neighborhood and was performing as a lousy school, so why even bother to try to change it? Instead, the central office would concentrate on the more promising schools.

"Sure that's what was going on," admits Still, who, when told she was given the principalship to Hollibrook, wondered what she had done wrong in life to deserve such a task. "Now I wonder what I did right. That's how terrific this school is. And yes, it was lousy, and that was the status quo to be maintained. But the teachers changed that. Those same teachers who felt powerless to do anything have turned this school around."

Still and the teachers—and to some degree, central office—say it is the teachers who run Hollibrook. And when you look at the planning team, leadership team, and steering committee, it is clear the teachers have significant power. However, you would be hard pressed to find a teacher who does not say that the reason the teachers have been so successful in their operation of the school is because of Suzanne Still.

"Suzanne gave us the strength, the insight, to do what we needed to do," explains Gretchen Goodson, a second-grade teacher. "She was always there with the additional information we needed, with the process skills we needed. She kept us on track. She supported us."

Still insists, "I just helped show them the way. And they didn't need much help. Just the opportunity." But Still was also doing something else. She was setting a powerful example within the school that was not missed by anyone. "Let's put it this way. If I didn't trust that Suzanne Still was working her butt off to the best of her capabilities and if there was anything we wanted she wasn't going to go out there and fight for, I wouldn't be working as hard as I am," insists a teacher, expressing a very common sentiment.

Honest, Emotional, and Professional Support

Teachers at Hollibrook School in Spring Branch say that Still acts not only as a mentor, a leader, a motivator, and a buffer, but also as a cheerleader.

"I can't count the number of times I have introduced myself to someone in this district," begins a teacher at Hollibrook, "and as soon as I say where I teach, they start telling me how they just heard Suzanne Still out at a seminar or whatever saying how incredible her teaching staff is. It happens all the time."

"I used to work for principals who were very nice to your face, but then you never knew what they were going to say once they entered their office, or once they went up to the superintendent's office. In many cases, you could count on the principal to blame the teachers for whatever was going wrong in their school. That just doesn't happen anymore. For one reason, if they even tried that, I think Guthrie would tell them to . . . . For another reason, they've learned. They know better."

The vehicle that is bringing teachers and their principals together is school improvement teams set up under Effective Schools. These teams are sometimes chosen by the principal, sometimes elected. They work diligently on the needs of the school, setting out objectives and developing strategies and activities to achieve those objectives. They then report to the entire school on their work. These teams are their own bosses. They set their own goals, parameters, and means of accomplishment.

"We all work very closely, and we all have very specific tasks within our teams," explains Maria Fernandez, a member of Hollibrook's Steering Committee. (Hollibrook has gone beyond just improvement teams and now has a steering committee and, like other Spring Branch schools, a campus leadership team.) "This is unlike anything we've done before, because we really do have power here."

"Of course they have power," says Hal Guthrie, Spring Branch's superintendent. "As I keep telling them, 'You know what your school needs, you know what your kids need, now just do it. I don't care how you do it, just do it!'" And that was possible because of the procedures, practices, and channels available for problem solving.

Down the rode a bit from Hollibrook is Landrum Junior High, a school that was also viewed as a lost cause until Hal Guthrie, Effective Schools, and Principal Linda Watkins arrived on the scene. The school is now making major strides in achievement, and Watkins places all the credit with the teachers and says she increasingly steps back from the head of the table.

"So many principals think they're losing control by giving the teachers this empowerment. I never looked at it that way. I looked at it as someone to help me," insists Watkins, who says the teachers now run most of the team meetings. "These teachers know what they want, know what they need. They're the ones with the students. I trust them, and that's very important. I know their concerns are for the children and I believe they trust me for the same reason."

Watkins has formed a teacher advisory group. She and the department chairs choose six representatives of the faculty, and those teachers, during a six week period, take written input (anonymous) from teachers on the areas they believe need improvement. It can be as minor as the duty roster or as major as suggesting that an administrator be removed.

"I meet with them once every six weeks and we go through every concern that's been raised. I give them written feedback, explaining what is going to be done about it. Action is taken," explains Watkins, who says she now wants to get the faculty more involved. "So now we're going to take these concerns and divide the whole faculty up into four or five small groups and we're going to discuss it within groups, rather than just me with six people. Again, I'll have more teacher input and more teacher decision making, which is what I'm after."

This collaboration between principals and teachers is causing culture shock for teachers across the country. It doesn't matter if it's rural Texas or New York City, the fact that a principal not only wants the teachers' input but acts on it is revolutionary to say the least. The schools are getting better because of it, but the atmosphere is also changing.

"Many of us are discovering for the first time what our principals are really like," maintains a teacher from the Sheridan Elementary School in Junction City, Kansas. "All over the district we're sitting down with people who are our bosses and discussing how to improve not only the teaching but the leadership of the school."

"One of the best things is the trust that the principals are showing in us as far as making decisions on what is best for the school," explains a teacher at Landrum Junior High in Spring Branch. "Before, if a teacher even suggested to a principal that there may be better ways to solve a certain problem, the principal would ignore you and usually let you know you were out of line. That was *their* jurisdiction, but in most cases, they didn't know how to improve a situation."

Or, as many teachers attest to, principals just were not interested in many of the teachers' concerns.

"It may seem like a little thing, but it proves the point," begins Tony Marcello of Bernabi Elementary in Spencerport. "We have had a problem at this school with parking. The school buses parked up here, taking half the spaces. People were having to park all over the lawns, the street, wherever. And for years, we've been talking to the principal about it. Nothing ever happened. We ask her to talk to the superintendent about it. She just shrugged her shoulders and said there was nothing she could do.

"So we circumvented her and went through the Effective Schools Process and the building planning team. And almost immediately, the problem was solved. Just like that. Central office responded. And there have been other instances where in the past, we wouldn't have gotten anywhere, and bang! Things are getting done."

"There's a whole foundation of trust building that just was never here before," says Fred Cardella, also of Bernabi Elementary in Spencerport. "We have teachers working with other teachers, and teachers working with administrators. The things we have been able to accomplish are absolutely amazing."

In Kansas, some of the teachers talk about the importance of trust among themselves, not just with the principals and central office. "I know that I can count on my fellow teachers to help me out if I've got a problem," says Leslie Myers, sixth-grade teacher at Ft. Riley Middle School in Junction City. "And I know they're here for me in the classroom. We're all fighting for the same goal. And that's to give these kids the best chance in life we can. You push a little harder if you feel trust around you. If you feel safe where you are."

"I think there is much more collegiality now than there was," says Randozzo. "There are not so many distant units anymore. The schools and the teachers have come together for the most part. Because we all know what the mission is, because we all have basically the same vision, and because we all end up in the courses together, there is a lot more unity," explains Tony Marcello of the Bernabi Elementary. "We know why we're here. We're in this thing together. We work together on the needs assessment and on the building teams. Before you would just see people when you were going in and out of the building, or maybe in the lunchroom. Now we're much more of a group."

The teachers agree that there has always been more collegiality at the elementary level than the secondary level.

"I think that's just the nature of the beast," explains a teacher at Junction City High School in Kansas. "High school teachers are more categorized. We have specific areas that we teach in: English, biology, math. We've been referred to as little cottage industries, and I guess to some extent, that's true. If we got together with colleagues in the past it was only with colleagues in our field. Maybe the biology teachers would go to a special biology seminar or whatever. But now we find ourselves in courses together, talking about elements of instruction or on improvement teams for the whole school, talking about things like discipline, climate, and scores."

Jan McNeefe, a teacher at Custer Hill Elementary who has taught for 16 years, maintains she has never before experienced the collegiality that is now part of the fabric of her school and district. "In the past, you never saw the principal. He never came into the classsroom. The teachers just kept to themselves. Did their own thing. Just followed instructions," McNeefe recalls. "But now, since Effective Schools, it's all turned around. We now all work together, inside and outside the classrooms. And for the first time since I've been teaching, I feel like I'm really valued. I'm valued for my opinion now instead of just being told what to do. I know I speak for many of my colleagues when I say we feel respected, not just by the principal but by the superintendent."

Teachers at the Adelaide Elementary School in Federal Way outside Seattle, Washington, say the push to empowerment has helped them realize how fortunate they are to have the principal they have, and how important her ideology on management has been to their learning process.

"It's not like we didn't have power before. We did to a certain extent. But now you can see, especially at this school, and I would like to think throughout the profession, there is a greater degree of respect. Certainly not enough as there should be, but it's growing," says Patty Fedler, a fifth-grade teacher at Adelaide. "The good teachers have always had control and power in their classrooms. That wasn't a problem. What you see now is those teachers who maybe didn't have the confidence or skills coming in, and well, now they have that confidence. And if they don't, there is a structure and channels to help them get it. And we'll help them. The teachers, the principal, will work together.

"We're lucky here. We know we have a principal (Jill Hearne) who not only trusts us but wants us to be leaders," adds Fedler. "When you don't have that, it can be be awfully lonely."

Teachers at Landrum Junior High in Spring Branch, Texas, expressed enthusiasm not only over their increased role in school decisions but in the fact that now there is stability at Landrum and the teachers now know the people behind the faces.

"Prior to Effective Schools, the teachers just rotated in and out of this building almost as fast as the students—sometimes faster," said a teacher at Landrum Junior High in Spring Branch. "Now not only are the teachers staying but we're meeting together, first in larger groups, and now in smaller groups. But it's amazing. We now know each other. For some of us, we're not only no longer isolated but it's greatly improved our social lives."

"It's very easy to start out as antagonists," explains another teacher from Landrum. "It's almost as if it's in our blood to be suspicious of each other. I don't know why. But that's all stopped, or at least slowed down, with Effective Schools. We now have a common language, communication channels, and a real goal. We really want this school to succeed, and it's starting to. That's bringing us all together. Join that with the feelings of success throughout the whole district, and you've got a lot of teachers building collegiality for the first time."

Hiring has always been a major area of contention with teachers and now, under most Effective Schools Improvement Plans, teachers are given a say in who is hired. Principals laugh at this, saying that in the past, *they* never even got a say in who was hired. Teachers were just sent down by central administration. "It used to be that you got stuck with whatever teacher was sent down to you from the central office," recalls a teacher in Spring Branch. "And many times that teacher was a friend of some board member. You had no control over the quality. That doesn't happen anymore—at least not that I notice."

Spencerport Teachers' Association President Randozzo admits that even he has seen a change in the hiring practices.

"There have been times in the past when someone would slip in someone who you had concerns about," he says. "But for the most part, and especially with Effective Schools, we're seeing very, very strong teachers. And if you're interested in accountability, I think our teachers have always wanted to produce. In the eyes of the district, they want to be considered good teachers. And so they bend over backwards to do what the district is asking them to do, which is to bring up those test scores.

"I think the district over the years has done a commendable job in hiring very good people, which has just improved the ranks of our teachers. And if there are some people who are ineffective, I think those people are weeded out during the probationary years."

The importance of good hiring cannot be underestimated. Larry Lezotte says that executive studies show that 75 percent of leadership skills are in hiring the right people. And finally, teachers are having a say in trying to choose those people with the leadership skills.

A Feeling for Fairer Evaluations of Teachers

The process of teacher evaluation has always been a troublesome one. But now, with the Effective Schools Process and the increased collegiality among faculty and staff, there are reports that the evaluation process is not as harrowing and schizophrenic as it once was. Because of the increased trust and the specific guidelines of master plans, teachers no longer feel they will be judged by a principal's whim or pressures from a political interest group in the central office. In fact, in many districts, teachers referred to the evaluations as helpful, rather than "second guessing" or "just looking over our shoulders." Programs, courses, and workshops are in place to help the struggling teacher. The emphasis is a positive pressure for improvement, and even with a focused eye to outcomes, teachers overall are not feeling a negative pressure.

"The big difference that I notice is that with the Effective Schools, the principals really have their act together. The whole teacher evaluation process is much more a professional undertaking," explains a high school teacher in Spring Branch, Texas. "In the past, it was so much politics. How cozy were you with the principal? Did you respond to every little request from the principal? Did you play all the necessary games? In many instances, and not just here, in other school districts I've been in, the evaluation process depended on how well you got along with the principal and his staff.

"That's just not the case anymore—at least not in most schools in Spring Branch. The principal now does a very thorough evaluation, and I tell you I trust this a lot more than I trusted the other process. This evaluation is done on my competency. Not on how much I kiss ass. I think one of the reasons for that is because the principals now know someone who also knows what he's doing is watching over them and looking at these reports when they come in."

"I tell you, I have worked for principals who wouldn't know how to properly fill out an evaluation form if their life depended on it. Seriously. Thank God they had decent secretaries that could handle it," says a teacher from the Seattle Public Schools. "And it was a scary time when those evaluations came out because if you had done something that just didn't please your principal, it would manage to show up somehow on your evaluation."

"The difference is you're getting fewer ex-football coaches and more and more qualified teachers and instructional leaders in the principal positions," claims a teacher from District 6 in New York. "And if you see a principal who has a qualified district superintendent, you can be sure you'll get a professional evaluation. Why? Because they're getting one. The principals are being forced to clean up their act."

Jill Hearne, Ph.D., principal of the Adelaide Elementary in Federal Way outside Seattle, says that teacher evaluations are one of the most sensitive and important tasks of a principal.

"This is where the keen expertise of a principal comes in," she explains. "You find a teacher who just isn't making it. You know right off they're not making it. And so the process begins. You start talking and try filling them with additional courses. Sometimes they're willing to improve; sometimes they think nothing's wrong. But you can't keep them at the head of a class and have the kids suffer. You move them, put them with another teacher. Maybe you convince them to go into support staff briefly. Maybe you get them to take some time off.

"But throughout it all, you accumulate your papers, your documentation.

And you bring in other people to give other opinions or substantiate your observations. All along this teacher knows exactly what's going on. And the paper trail builds. I have file drawers full of material just to remove one teacher."

Not only is the paper trail long and detailed, but so is the cost. Depending on the involvement of unions, administrators, even board members, the costs can soar. Some large urban districts have put the costs in excess of $300,000.

"When I realize someone has to go, I just groan," says Cathy Davidson, Ed.D., principal of Tahoma Senior High School in Maple Valley, Washington. "Because I know it will entail years of work. We're talking years. And it starts out real simple. Like asking, 'Do you like coming to work? Are you happy here?' Then you begin the process of looking for alternatives."

"I really believe that you work with the people you have and you don't enter into this saying, 'OK, you're a rotten teacher and you're going to be out of here in two years.' The person isn't doing a quality job and so you say to the person, 'How do you feel about what's going on in your classroom?' 'Well, I think it went OK'. 'Gee, I didn't feel that way. I saw . . . . Did you see that. Do you think that was right?'"

Davidson believes that because of the increase in collegiality among the staff, it is actually easier to work with a teacher who may be in trouble.

"Other teachers can see when there's a problem. And they want the school to improve. They don't want to see the teacher and those students dragged down," maintains Davidson. "If you say to a teacher, 'Do you want to improve?' and he or she says yes, then you're on your way. Everybody wants to improve. Or at least they should. And the other teachers will help their colleagues become better teachers. I've really seen that recently. That's called *investing in your staff* and that's called *lifelong learning*. And isn't that the model you're trying to give to the kids?"

Davidson emphasizes that is is very important to carry that push for excellence right into the school's central office. "I have had a vice-principal here who just wasn't doing her job. I did everything I could. Put her on a growth plan, the whole thing. Now understand this is all going on confidentially. No one else in the school is aware of it. A very professional process. This woman wasn't being assaulted by rumors. And that's the way it should be," says Davidson. "But what kept coming back to me is that these administrative offices here are modeling growth and competency. If they're not, we're doing something wrong," she says. "It's OK to come and grow here, as long as you're pulling your weight. And as long as you're accountable. But will we carry somebody for life? No. Will I do everything that I can to help that person? Yes. And so I think that's why staff is willing to help. They see I'm up here doing the best and always reaching out to help and learn more. And they know they can trust me. They know I'm fair. And the teachers see that. In the end, all the teachers and staff really want from you is competency and fairness. And honesty. They've got to be able to trust you."

The Troubles of Testing

Since the first schoolhouse opened its doors, there has been someone questioning the need, validity, and integrity of testing. Some say there is too much testing, some say there is too little. In the Effective Schools Process, testing and monitoring the evaluation of outcomes is a major tool in the functioning and analysis of the school itself. Practitioners and experts see testing, both norm-referenced and criterion-referenced testing, as essential to improving the learning of *all* children. Indeed, the measurement and monitoring of outcomes is one of the correlates of Effective Schools. But rather than being viewed as a tool for improvement, some teachers and some teachers' unions have taken the position that this increased emphasis on testing is meant as a judgment on the teacher rather than the child's level of learning. And therefore, the test—this correlate—is a threat to the teacher's career. However, a study of the research and the employment actions going on in Effective Schools belie this.

"The true instrument of empowerment is to be able to stand outside yourself and see observable results," says Larry Lezotte. "I don't think you can empower people by just letting them *feel* as if they're doing a better job.

"I like to draw the parallel between an educator and others. If an educator were being a consultant to somebody who wanted to lose weight, the educator would say, 'Now if you're going to do weight loss, here's what you have to do. You have to have a clear goal. Okay, 10 pounds. You want to lose 10 pounds. So we have a clear goal. Now we've got to have a curriculum. You've got to go out and read the different weight loss books and so forth and then you'd adopt one.' Then you have to implement the curriculum. Of course, that is to say you have to eat proper foods and do exercises and all this and that.

"Now if you're an educator and you have clear goals and you've adopted a curriculum and you've implemented it, from the educator's standpoint—up until very recently—*there was absolutely no reason why you have to stand on a scale!*

"Why? Because if you did everything, you had a goal and curriculum to implement it, obviously you were going to lose weight. So, if everything's as it should be, what's the big risk in confirming the weight loss? Everything was in the process, but no one measured the outcome, the actual pounds lost!"

It is this issue of accountability that has become a major point of controversy in the Effective Schools Process. While some teachers insist it is a paper tiger—that good teachers have always been accountable and there's no problem—other teachers insist the rush to accountability, carried out through testing, is doing more harm than good. One place where the faculty seems divided about the issue of testing is in Spencerport, New York. "You end up with teachers teaching only to the test, and the kids are hurt by that," says a teacher at Spencerport's Munn Elementary School. "And that's all we do now. We teach to the test! Our major goal is that kid passing the test."

There are numerous teachers in Spencerport who agree that the accountability issue is forcing teachers to teach to the test. In Spencerport, there is considerable weight given to the Regents tests and the Regents classes, leading to a Regents diploma. The Regents classes are generally regarded as the upper-level classes and the Regents diploma is the highest grade of diploma a student can receive in New York state.

Since Spencerport began the Effective Schools Process, the number of students in Regents classes and exams has, in some instances, doubled, with the high percentage of those passing remaining the same. For example, the percentage of students taking the English Regents has gone from 53 percent of the students in 1983, with 95 percent passing, to 93 percent of the students in 1990, with 93 percent of the students passing. The number of students receiving Regents scholarships has grown from 10 percent of the senior class in 1983 to 21.8 percent of the class in 1990.

"We always got good results on the Regents exams, but we got those good results in the past by weeding out the marginal kids, by not letting them into the courses," explains a teacher from Wilson High. "Now we don't let those marginal kids out. We expect them to work. We expect a lot of them. So, yes, we're more accountable now for more kids."

"And it's too much," insists one teacher. "They are not giving us the necessary resources to deal with all these kids. And if you've got a kid who doesn't make it, that looks bad for the teacher."

Wilson High Principal Bill Selander and Superintendent of Spencerport Schools Joe Clement disagree that it ever falls back on the teacher. "We know some kids out there just aren't motivated, and if the teacher does his or her best to get them motivated, and can't, well, there's nothing more they can do. But they're never, never held responsible in a negative way," says Clement, who is button-bursting proud of the gains Spencerport has made in Regents Exams.

"If there is a kid who can't make it," explains Selander, "we'll let him out of Regents. But that kid and his family and the teacher are going to have to make a real case to get out of it. It's not like it used to be. Easy to get out of Regents, hard to get in. Now, you're in, and it's almost impossible to get out."

The president of the Teachers Association says that's exactly the problem. "We've got a lot, no, some kids who just don't belong," says Pete Randozzo. "But we can't get them out. I've had one kid who has failed over and over again, and it's ruining the kid's self-esteem. This just isn't right. And it keeps putting unnecessary pressure on the teacher."

Randozzo continues, "I'll agree that there's more learning going on in the classrooms now with Effective Schools. But we judge that solely by how well the students do on these tests. My problem is I think the district has pushed too far.

"If we were to go back 10, 12 years ago, very few of the kids were encouraged to go into the Regents program. If a kid didn't want to, fine, that's his choice, freedom of choice. And we let the kids be too lazy. That was a decade ago.

"With Effective Schools, we're putting more of an emphasis on academics, and so we're making kids more and more aware of their responsibilities and we're encouraging—demanding I guess is the better word—we're demanding that they get these high scores. And they take these more difficult courses. And again, I think we've gone overboard. Somewhere in there there's a happy medium. I think somewhere along the line the pendulum has swung too far. It has to begin swinging the other way."

Larry Lezotte admits there is "always the possibility of going too far" in the testing of students, but says he has no idea if that is the real problem in Spencerport. "There are many different personalities at work in Spencerport," says Lezotte. "What they need is a comprehensive evaluation of teacher attitudes and that just hasn't been done."

Spencerport has a history of faculty and administration mistrust. Many believe that the concern over testing is just another excuse to dig at the problems between the union and the administration. But others insist there is a legitimate concern over the degree of testing.

"I think we teach to the test, and it puts an unrealistic amount of pressure on the teachers and the students, to say nothing of the parents," maintains a teacher from the Munn School. "I know teachers who just teach for the passing of that test. And then I think the school district just pushes the tests because the more tests we pass, the more money and prestige the district can get."

Administrators insist there is no connection between testing and money in the district. There are many teachers who disavow such a connection and believe it is all much ado about nothing.

"I don't understand what is wrong with teaching to the test," says another Munn teacher. "We do that when we present material and then quiz the kids at the end of the week. How else do we know if they're getting to know the curriculum?"

"I think it's just more whining on the part of some to try to get more money out of the administration," claims another teacher. "They say, 'Hey, we brought up the test scores, so give us more money.'"

Randozzo admits there are some teachers who believe the administration does not truly appreciate the hard work done by the faculty. "I think the district has too much emphasis on trying to save money," says Randozzo. "Everything is equated to money and there seems to be a feeling coming through that there's not as much to the teaching staff as we'd like. There are also those people who believe that there is a lack of respect coming from above. So, if you put those two things together, you can understand why we have contract troubles."

The teacher salaries in Spencerport run from $25,000 to $60,000, with over 50 percent of the teachers earning more than $40,000.

"I really don't understand all this talk about teaching to the tests," says Mirian Smith, a teacher at Town Line Elementary. "How else do you determine if a kid knows the work? How else do you know if you're teaching for learning? The kids don't feel pressure from the tests. They feel pressure from me. I don't teach to the test. I teach to the curriculum. These kids are tested a lot, but it works out for them. This is how we find out how best to teach them, how to keep them going. If there are problem areas, we can pick them up immediately and work on them."

"I think one of the problems is that the teachers were first concerned that the tests and test results were going to be used against them," says Fred Cardella. "That was a real worry."

A worry written in the sand, says Larry Lezotte. "One of the greatest myths that is a social control myth is that if we look at results and they're not what we want them to be, then you'll lose your job, you're going to be fired," explains Lezotte. "That's just not true. This isn't how it happens. Teachers do not get fired on the basis of how their students do on tests."

In fact, there was not a teacher interviewed in any of the Effective Schools districts that knew, or had even heard about, any teacher who had been fired because of a problem with their test scores. Lezotte uses as an example of the irrationality of such an argument the story of the state of Texas adopting the state policy Teacher Performance Appraisal Process. It was alleging a tough, standard-oriented process, and after three years less than 1 percent of the faculty had been dismissed.

"And I would be willing to think that that 1 percent would have been counseled out anyway," says Lezotte. "The myth that's out there is that once a month a big truck comes along and takes all the incompetents off. That just doesn't happen."

The teachers in Spencerport were not alone in their initial concern as to whether or not the testing would be used against them. In New York's District 6, teachers saw the "frequent monitoring" as perhaps another ploy by the administration to impose on a teacher's autonomy.

"We feared the worst. You know, that someone would be sitting in a corner office going over these scores and saying, 'Oh, look at this class, 30 percent can't read, better get rid of the teachers,'" says a teacher in Spanish Harlem. "But then after talks with the administration, and after a couple terms, we saw that the tests were being used for the kids. To help form curriculum for the kids. To actually *help* the teachers."

"It really all boils down to what the teacher and principal want to do with test scores," explains Leonard Clarke, Ph.D., Assistant Superintendent for District 6. "Instead of teachers saying 45 percent of my kids passed, we now have them saying 55 percent of my kids are in trouble and we've got to find out ways to help them. It all depends upon the attitude of the principal and central office. You can ignore the scores or use them to help the kids."

Some teachers just do not understand the controversy over testing. "How else are we going to find out how our kids are learning?" asks a teacher at the Adelaide Elementary in Federal Way outside Seattle. "If we can't monitor them, we'll never find out if we're being effective. It's that simple. And I really don't want to walk through my life not knowing if I'm reaching these kids."

As far as firing a teacher on the basis of test results, Adelaide Principal Jill Hearne just laughs. "You don't need test results to know if a teacher is doing his or her job," maintains Hearne. "If you can't tell within five minutes in that teacher's class whether or not they are an effective teacher or have it within them to be effective, then you have no right to be a principal." She adds that she has never heard of a teacher being dismissed on the basis of students' test scores.

Many teachers believe that the controversy over testing is just a cover for a greater concern—the issue of accountability and the belief that *all* children can learn. If you honestly, totally believe that all children can learn, and that you are a good teacher capable of teaching for learning for all, then you invite the test to prove that all your children are learning. And the test validates your accountability and the belief that all children can learn.

"One of the statements of Effective Schools that I really like is that 'Effective Schools makes teaching more accountable, so it will make learning more predictable,'" begins Fred Cardella from the Bernabi in Spencerport. "I don't mind being accountable for my teaching and I don't believe any other good teacher minds being held accountable. We are accountable. We like believing in ourselves and we try to do the very best for the kids now that we have the better tools to know we can help them. We try to get them over every hurdle we can. I'm not so sure we did that as effectively before. I think we always tried to do it, but we didn't have the direction. I don't think we had the vision. And I certainly don't believe we had the belief that *all* kids can learn."

Tony Marcello believes it all goes back to the onset of staff development. "It's like I thought that I was accountable. I thought I was doing the best job for the kids," says Marcello. "And I was doing the best I could do at that time. But I wasn't doing the best that I was capable of. Through the different courses, I've learned to be a much better teacher, so I can give more to my kids. And yes, I now have the proof that by expecting more and using these various techniques, the kids are learning more and better. And sure, for that alone I'm more accountable."

The more common complaint about accountability in Effective Schools districts was not its presence but instead the fact that it rarely reared its head in their college education training. Teacher after teacher talked of how professors "seemed to avoid the word *accountability*."

"It was almost like—if they taught us to be accountable to our students, then they might just have to be accountable to us, here, at the college," maintained one teacher. "And God forbid that those professors for one minute would be accountable to the high-priced, alleged education they're spewing out. I guess you have to give them credit for that. They didn't want to say: 'Don't do as I do, do as I say.'"

For some teachers, the push to accountability in Effective Schools is something whose time is past due. The threat that the testing would be used against them has never materialized. Those teachers who complain about the testing say they are complaining only about what they see as too much testing and too much emphasis on the tests, and not a question of how they feel about accountability. They maintain they are accountable and have always been accountable.

This phenomenon of a vocal, strong concern on behalf of some teachers for testing was found only in Spencerport, New York. The majority of teachers in all other districts involved in the Effective Schools Process found the issue of testing a nonissue. However, it should be noted, as explained in Chapter Thirteen, that there are instances in school districts purporting to be effective, where testing is clearly not accomplishing the goal of directing and enhancing the learning of all students. These are districts where teachers teach to strict essential skills with weekly criteria, and then test those students at the beginning of each year and at the end—with the *same* test. This is clearly a scandalous use of testing to judge a district, and defeats the purpose of testing to enhance and enrich a child's learning. But, as stated, these are districts that say they are effective but are clearly not and only demean the work of truly Effective practitioners. It should also be emphasized here that in those ineffective districts, there is no real school-based management. This type of testing is being done at the administration's request, and is, for the most part, deplored by the teachers. Unfortunately, they have no say and must teach to the skills, and, at least in these cases, to the test. It's their required lesson plans, which are ordered and enforced by the superintendent.

Decision Making in the Future

The empowerment of teachers, resulting in increased responsibility for decisions at every level of a school's operation, is becoming more the rule than the exception. Many thought school-based management would never succeed because of the concerns of the unions, which are, ideally at least, about giving teachers power.

"Unions get control through centralization. You push a few key buttons and the whole district jerks. But Effective Schools is talking about *de*centralization," notes Bob Sudlow of Spencerport. "The other thing is the unions, they want the faculty to come to them so they can solve the problem through the union so that the allegiance of the faculty is to the union. Whereas in Effective Schools, you have people in their own buildings solving their own problems, that will draw the allegiance away from the union . . . and that will be a loss of power."

The power base that both teachers and unions now look to is the district mission statement and the school mission statement. With a district and school in alignment in their task and objectives, teachers can anticipate fairly accurately what procedures and policies will follow. The mission statement is also the union's best assurance that the decisions affecting teachers will be equitable and not political.

For the most part, major teacher organizations in the United States are supporting school-based management. They certainly are supporting the empowerment, the renewal, of teachers. And the results of this empowerment—when it is not an empty word and is accompanied by the commitment of time and resources—is the more successful, harmonious, enlightening, operation of the public school. The examination of Effective Schools districts shows that where teachers have true empowerment, and the ongoing staff development courses to expand and enrich their knowledge, schools are not only becoming better but, as profiled here, schools are pulling themselves out of the mud and mire of defeat. Teachers, given more responsibility, now show much more pride in and commitment to their students and school.

It is happening because policies are set from the superintendent's office that establish specific, thoughtful guidelines on school-based management and school improvement. The resources, along with the autonomy, are given to those schools. The superintendent says 'Go, it's all yours, I trust you.' The principal says, 'OK, we'll go, I trust my teachers.' The result is the trust is returned, and the teachers, now empowered, can give to all of their students their own power to learn.

The one variable that makes it impossible to make a blanket assertion about teachers and decision making is the principal. The degree and atmosphere of the empowerment is dependent—good and bad—on the personal and professional interaction of the principal with the staff. In the matter of teacher empowerment and renewal, as in so many other factors of school improvement, the way in which the game is played and whether or not the school and students win, is greatly dependent on the character and professional insight of the principal.

But what can be concluded, without doubt, without question, is that the more genuinely involved teachers are in the operation of the school, the climate of their environment, and the instructional decisions affecting their classrooms, the more committed they will be to the task before them. The more committed the teachers are, the harder they work, the more fervent their desire for success and personal accomplishment.

Once teachers have this responsibility, once the school is "theirs," once they have ownership and are rightly held accountable, they can no longer reach out and point the finger at someone else. The Effective Schools Process proves that in many schools, teachers, given an equal chance and ownership in their schools, will rise—much like children who are given that equal chance and ownership—quite impressively to any challenge put before them.

CHAPTER TEN

Implementation

First You Must Have the Will

If you don't believe it in your heart, if you don't believe the basic premise that all youngsters can learn, and want to see that survive, and want *to see the youngster prosper, then you'll never recognize that it* can *be done. Because you don't* want *it done.*

—NOEL T. FARMER, superintendent

We know it can be done. We've proved it. At all levels. But you must have the will.

—HAL GUTHRIE, superintendent

Skeptics of the triumphs—no matter how exactingly documented—of Effective schools and districts often say that these successes are just a flash in the pan, that they are the fruits of the labors of innovative and dedicated people and not the results of a cohesive, research-based planning and implementation process. Although they commend some individual programs in schools, the critics nonetheless maintain that there is no process to bring these successful programs together. The country lacks a "vehicle" for reform, they say. And in fact the President has proposed a several hundred million dollar study to try to discover this "vehicle."

"The good—actually very good—news is that the president of the United States has proclaimed that comprehensive and structural changes in our system of elementary and secondary education are a national priority," writes Edward Fiske (1991) in *Smart Schools, Smart Kids.* "The not so good news is that while the Bush plan talks a lot about successful new schools, it does not say much about a successful new system of education."

In fact, notes Fiske, some education experts believe the United States is wasting time if school renewal does not address this void.

"'Bush has proposed a giant demonstration project and a new examination system,' said David Hornbeck, the consultant to Kentucky. 'It's fine to generate a lot more Comers and Levins and Sizers, but there is no vehicle to organize them into a system other than choice, which is not a powerful vehicle'" (Fiske, 1991).

This sentiment that there is no vehicle in which to travel from a deteriorating, failing, or even mediocre school system to an improving, thriving school system comes as a surprise to those who have been on the carefully mapped out Effective Schools journey to equity and excellence for the last several years.

It does not come as a surprise to those who watch the power politics in elementary and secondary educational reform. Since long before the days of Horace Mann, those who have the power at the moment receive the spotlight for their own agenda, casting shadows on all others. In the eighties, the "power" talk was of excellence and restructuring. In the early nineties, it moved to choice and national assessments.

Effective Schools practitioners hope that now the focus will move to that which is working—that which answers the call for comprehensive and structural changes in the individual schools and districtwide.

One of the reasons the experts believe the spotlight has skipped over the Effective Schools Process is because it requires not only a change in philosophy (that *all* children can learn) but a commitment of time and energy that many superintendents just do not have the political inclination to endorse.

"Effective Schools is no quick fix, and today we're always after the quick fix," says Dr. Noel Farmer, superintendent of Frederick County (Maryland) Public Schools. "People just don't want to take the time to do it right."

"And remember," adds Hal Guthrie, superintendent of Spring Branch (Texas) Public Schools. "This is still a hot political issue. Equity. You have to have the will. We know it can be done. We've proved it. At all levels. But you must have the will."

Spring Branch and Frederick County are not alone in proving that the Effective Schools Improvement Process works. There does exist a valid, successful, research-based vehicle for school improvement. It has been shown in this book's compilation of facts, interviews, and observations in districts as widespread and diverse as Frederick County (Maryland), Spencerport (New York), Junction City (Kansas), Spanish Harlem (New York), and Seattle—big/small, black/white/Hispanic, rural/urban/suburban. It works. (Appendix C contains names of some districts that have successfully implemented the Effective Schools Process, according to criteria of the National Center for Effective Schools.)

What is being discovered in school after school, and in district after district, is that the Effective Schools Process—based on the belief that *all* children can learn—is the moral imperative for a school improvement journey that dramatically restructures the rules, roles, and relationships of America's schools and districts. That restructuring is not only helping to solve many of the problems of today's diverse and complex student populations but that Effective

Schools Process for restructuring is laying the foundation for some of this country's most exciting, progressive, and successful schools—schools that are viable, equitable centers of learning for students, teachers, and the entire school community.

What sets it apart, and perhaps gives it its unique strength, is that the Effective Schools Improvement Process begins in the heart, maybe even the gut.

"It all goes back to belief," says Noel Farmer. "If you don't believe it in your heart, if you don't believe the basic premise that all youngsters can learn, and want to see that survive, and *want* to see the youngsters prosper, then you'll never recognize that it *can* be done. Because you don't *want* it to be done."

But how is it done? What is this process—this structured process for school reform?

It begins with a superintendent who believes—in his head and in his gut, as Farmer says—that *all* children can learn. He or she embraces the Effective Schools research, which often includes a renewal of personal priorities and management style. The superintendent commits to it, totally. The Effective Schools Process becomes a way of life for the superintendent and the district. Change is in the wind, but it is a carefully executed change.

"Remember, it's not just changing a school system. It's *improving* that school system," emphasizes Hal Guthrie. "You can change a system and it can actually end up worse. That's why you have to know what you're doing. You have to have a plan."

Gone are the days when superintendents and principals can "fly by the seat of their pants." Not only is it essential to have a plan, an implementation process, but you also must have the research to back up every step you take. The Effective Schools Process provides that research. It is a data-guided improvement process.

If we were to sketch out the first steps of that improvement process, in the *simplest* terms—for the district and the schools—this is what that time line would look like:

- The superintendent accepts the Effective Schools Process and philosophy.
- The superintendent explains Effective Schools to the board.
- The board and top administrative staff meet with Effective Schools experts. The superintendent submits a "rough plan" for implementation.
- The board approves Effective Schools planning.
- The superintendent forms a districtwide planning committee (composed of all stakeholders in the schools and community).
- The districtwide planning committee creates a master plan, including district mission, goals, and objectives.
- The board approves the master plan.
- The planning committee spreads the word to the schools (staff development in Effective Schools is underway).

- The school principals meet with staffs for further Effective Schools orientation.
- The principals/schools form school improvement teams.
- Needs assessment of the entire school is conducted.
- The teams analyze the assessment results, identify problem areas (on basis of the correlates), and adopt strategies of action.
- The teams report back to schools on strategies and activities for improvement.
- The teams draw up a mission statement for individual schools—as well as objectives, goals, and means to achievement.
- The teams report back to the schools. The teams receive consensus on mission, goals, and objectives from the faculty.
- The teams and schools adjust, then approve the annual action plan.
- The plan is approved by the superintendent and board.
- The plan is implemented and monitored.
- Planning/development continues at school and district levels.

Communication and Involvement

The superintendents who have had the most success with the Effective Schools Improvement Process began their journey by laying their Effective Schools cards on the table right at the start. This means that while interviewing for the job they said they were proponents of Edmonds's and Brookover's Effective Schools research and would implement that particular school improvement process. And then, once in position but before so much as even thinking of a time line, they made sure their board (or school committee) understood exactly what was about to occur.

"The first thing we did was get the board together for a long Saturday session and then have them spend the day with people from Effective Schools who outlined the correlates, what they meant, and what the original and present research shows," recalls Guthrie. "You've got to have your board of trustees supporting you, so you have to make sure they understand this research and what it means for your district."

Spring Branch, Texas, just outside Houston, and until recently the haven for the southwest's oil and cattle barons, was undergoing radical changes in its schools. Its student population was growing increasingly disadvantaged, with a large influx of black and Hispanic children. Indeed, this previously elite white enclave had in 1991 a minority population of 47 percent in the high schools, 52 percent in the middle schools, and 56 percent in the elementary schools.

But the power remained where it had always been and it was up to Guthrie to convince that conservative board that Effective Schools was the right thing for *every* child in Spring Branch and for the future of Spring Branch itself.

The board examined the Effective Schools correlates. This essential step goes far beyond a simple listing of the correlates on a blackboard and a corresponding piece of paper. The correlates were *discussed.* For example, what is really meant, in terms every board member, parent, and teacher, can understand and relate to, by the phrase *safe and orderly environment*? Indicators of such an environment were identified and explained: No student shall have to be concerned for personal safety in the school; the school is neat, clean, attractive; an atmosphere of pervasive caring exists; students are placed in appropriate instructional settings that provide both success and challenge; positive self-disciplined behavior is recognized and reinforced; a school discipline code is equitably enforced; there is a high rate of attendance and no tardiness among students and staff.

Fine, says the board. That all makes common sense. But how do we go about doing that? It is at this point that the board is given some possible strategies for both planning and action, such as: A code of student conduct is established and communicated to students, parents, and the community; alternative programs are provided for children with special needs; central office collaborates with schools to help them develop and maintain preventive maintenance programs for school buildings.

Each school district's means of enacting a correlate will be different, depending on its experience, culture, and infrastructure, but the basic outline of planning and implementation remains the same. The better a board understands the correlates—and how all planning rotates back to and around those correlates—the easier it is for a district to keep its "Effective" focus.

The correlate that often causes the most concern is that of *high expectations for success for all students.* This is an essential tenet in the belief that *all* children can learn. However, as the research and schools have found, believing that *all* children can learn and having high expectations for *all* children goes far beyond a creed on the wall.

The board and community should examine the indicators for high expectations: Teachers believe they are the most important determinants of student achievement and demonstrate professional and personal behavior in accordance with this belief; all staff members act on the belief that all students can learn curriculum identified as essential; student placement in courses and temporary instructional groups reflects high expectations for success for all students.

If the board understands and accepts these indicators (just as later on the faculties and staffs of the schools must) it is laying the foundation for a long-term, ongoing improvement process.

Once the board comprehends the correlates' meanings and implications (in this example the high expectations correlate), the superintendent can set forth a plan of action, such as:

- The school system develops improvement goals that clearly reflect quality and equity; for instance, staff development programs are established to help principals and teachers carry out a curricular alignment process, which sets standards of academic achievement that are appropriate for the students and the community.
- Teachers design ways to communicate high expectations, and strategies to help different types of learners succeed.
- Teacher recruitment efforts focus on identifying prospective teachers who have or wish to develop proficiency in assuring that *all* students learn the essential curriculum.

In dealing with the correlates in detail like this, superintendents and their staff can apprise boards of specific issues that will be faced in dealing with these correlates and prospective problems that come with those issues. The most common controversy that raises its head under *high expectations* (and stems from the original premise of all children can learn) is, of course, the issue of tracking. School officials find it essential to come right out with the changes that will be required as the system disengages from tracking, and deal with the ire those changes ignite in certain pockets of the community. This is the time for delivering the first onslaught of data relating the impact and benefits of moving out of the tracking system. Here, as in the discussion of other correlates, the board members will see how data will drive decisions and decision making in the Effective Schools Improvement Process.

"We have found that right from the beginning, the more information you give the board, and everyone involved, the better off you are," explains Dr. Gary Mathews, associate superintendent of Spring Branch. "We knew that the tracking issue was going to be a problem, and we assembled our data right at the beginning. And three years later, there are still holdouts and we are still distributing data to justify our position."

But the important point is, says Mathews and other school officials in the Effective Schools Improvement Process, that the board and the community knew at the start where they were going with Effective Schools and all it meant. There were few surprises. It was all communicated to them and discussed. So when a board member was hit with the issue of tracking from a constituent, the member could step into the equity and high expectation discussion with ease and conviction.

Of the remaining correlates (clear and focused mission, instructional leadership, opportunity to learn and time on task, frequent monitoring of student progress, positive home-school relations), the characteristic *frequent monitoring* may cause the most confusion (whereas *high expectations* causes the most concern). Once again, indicators explain and draw the parameters:

- A variety of assessment techniques is used to check student progress.
- Results of assessment measures are systematically analyzed and used for instructional decision making.
- Student achievement data are disaggregated to assure quality and equity across all subsets of students in instructional programs.
- Instructional adjustments are made on a frequent basis.
- "Reteach" is identified as one of the most powerful variables, so that no child falls behind.

The board is again walked through potential plans for action: Curricular alignment is initiated by teachers, principals, and central office staff; criterion-referenced tests based on essential curricular objectives are developed and used in a manner designed to enhance the learning process; data are collected and prepared in disaggregated form to facilitate planning for program development or adjustment; data are provided to assist local school personnel in analyzing relationships between student achievement and the instructional delivery system within the school.

For most board members, the concept of disaggregating scores will be, at best, a foreign one. And for most school systems, the practice of disaggregating will come only *after* the Effective Schools Improvement Process begins. But it is right at the beginning, when superintendents are first informing the board about Effective Schools, that the discussion of disaggregation is initiated. Superintendents can safely predict—on the basis of Effective Schools research—what the disaggregated scores within their system will show, and therefore can enhance their argument for the need of Effective School reform. This explanation lays the groundwork for the rebuttal that will be needed later when segments of the community start the rumblings of the "teaching to the test" controversy.

The emphasis on the board's understanding of the correlates is stressed here because as the improvement process progresses, participants will see how each manuever evolves from and returns to the correlates. They are the strong threads of major improvement designs and planning. What is contained within them are the basic means and philosophies of school-based improvement. The correlates all work together with school-based management to create successful organizational dynamics in meeting goals. Not only must the board understand this but *everyone* involved in the district's planning.

Demanding Accountability and Taking Time

There are other key areas of emphasis in school improvement planning. The work of the correlates cannot be done overnight, nor can it be done without a firm commitment to responsibility. "What we're talking about here is accountability. Right from the start," says Noel Farmer of Frederick County, Maryland. "And this is new. For boards, for superintendents, for principals and teachers. In the past, if a student didn't do well, it was the student's fault. No more. You have to put accountability where it belongs."

Farmer believes that accountability belongs with those who are making the decisions. For that reason, you must give those decision makers all the information available when they begin the Effective Schools Improvement Process. Farmer, like Guthrie, made sure his board knew when they hired him that they were bringing in Effective Schools.

"It's accountability at the top and it's the only way to do it," says Farmer. "I don't know if they understood completely what was going to happen then. But they certainly understand now."

Frederick County is one of the first school boards in the United States to translate its outcome goals into policy and then from the beginning, publish an annual public document saying exactly how the schools are doing in attaining those goals. It is a dramatic change, but nothing that the school board did not see coming.

Fairness would stipulate that the school boards would be well informed, given the change in their role from blame sender to blame accepter. What is being discovered is that boards do not mind accepting the accountability that comes with Effective Schools because it not only increases their knowledge of what is happening in the system but, for the most part, the changes have led to serious improvements, bringing new life to mediocre or decaying districts.

"And don't forget time. If you've got a board that thinks this is all about a quick fix, then you've failed in your explanation," insists Farmer, who planned for a year before taking the first school improvement steps. "This is something that takes years. They have to understand that. You're talking about valuing people—students, teachers, administrators, board members. The whole way up. And that takes time. Time to build new relationships. Time to *improve* relationships."

So, in that initial meeting or meetings, when the board hopefully attains a firm grasp on the meaning and implications of the journey it is embarking on, it is essential that everyone understand that this is going to take time. Time to do it right. You have to plan, diagnose, and implement. If the board accepts—truly accepts—that school improvement is about a process, not an event, then the board and the community should give the superintendent and staff between three to five years to travel a course that will begin to show positive results. In fact, as has been described in this book, districts like Frederick County and Spring Branch showed dramatic improvement in less than three years.

That improvement, for an Effective Schools district, comes in the form of attaining and passing specific goals based on student outcomes. The board, the community, and the staff must understand that these goals are not written in sand to be washed away by the next tide of changing school populations or decreasing budgets. There can be no hedging, no waivering down the line. Student outcomes must improve and that improvement must be distributed across the entire student body.

This first stage of informing the board and garnering its support can either be easy or very difficult, depending on the makeup of the board and the political realities within a given district. Although all superintendents and boards vary, the one constant in their relationship seems to be that the more open the communications and the more sincere and active the involvement, the more productive and less acrimonious the interaction.

Many superintendents find it advantageous to put the rationale and implications of school improvement into writing and make that document available to the community. Dr. Farmer, as seen in his introduction to Effective Schools in Figure 10–1, believes this black and white presentation leaves no room for misinterpretation. He explains exactly what the mission of the school system now is, the background of the strategic planning assumptions, the implementation of school-based management, and the philosophical basis of this particular school improvement process.

Farmer emphasizes the "school-by-school focus on school improvement" lest anyone become confused as to exactly how this reform will be accomplished. He also makes sure the community understands this is a *process* that will take *time* in order to "institutionalize school improvement for enduring change."

Farmer believes the release of straightforward, detailed explanations such as this not only reduces the probability of misunderstanding but further infuses the "religion" of the Effective Schools Process into the community.

The District Role

Although the goal of Effective Schools is an effective *school*-based management process, that process cannot operate with equity throughout the system unless there is a districtwide mission statement, districtwide goals, and a matching basic master plan etched in stone and bearing the impramatur of the community as a whole.

The process begins in the superintendent's office, where a team is assembled that reflects the administrative and instructional factions in the district. This means the assistant superintendents, curriculum heads, specific teachers, union representatives, and key principals. In small districts, it can even include all principals. In Spencerport, New York, it included the district's Teachers of the Year. Some districts include parents, but most believe that because the master plan is so closely reviewed by the school board, there is sufficient parental input at that level.

This team goes by different names. In some districts, it is the steering committee, in others, the district planning team, in yet others, the district

FIGURE 10–1 • *An Introduction to the Effective Schools Improvement Process*

From Dr. Noel T. Farmer, Jr., Superintendent,
Frederick County, Maryland, Public Schools

The primary mission of the Frederick County Public School System is to teach for quality learning for all students. This mission is best accomplished in an environment characterized by strong instructional leadership, high expectations for success for all students, sufficient time for teaching for learning, a safe and orderly school environment, frequent monitoring of students' progress, and effective home-school communication.

As a means to accomplish its mission, the Frederick County Public School System will use the principles and procedures derived from the body of knowledge known as the "Effective Schools" research. For an entire school system to improve its schools, all the policies, personnel and non-school based resources within the system must be employed toward the goal of school improvement. The focus on school improvement at the school-building level will be guided by the Organizational Development (OD) principle of directed empowerment.

The strategic planning assumptions which were used for the purpose of implementing the Effective Schools process are as follows:

1. All schools will be required to focus on the primary mission of teaching for learning.
2. In the future, all schools will be held even more accountable for measurable outcomes.
3. Equity will receive increasing attention as the proportion of minorities and poor people increases.
4. Decision-making will become more decentralized, and the school will become the production unit and the center for change.
5. Models of collaboration and directed empowerment will increase building level teacher and administrator involvement.
6. School improvement will be data-driven and will utilize the research for the basis of planned change.
7. Instructional monitoring systems will incorporate technology such as computers to accelerate the feedback loops which are currently utilized by teachers.
8. New and veteran administrators will be expected to demonstrate skills as managers and as visionary leaders of instruction.
9. By emphasizing results or outcomes, schools will be able to loosen the emphasis on process, thus causing a restructuring at the school level.
10. The school improvement process will be institutionalized so that any "work-to-rule" strategy could never stop it.
11. The old model of instruction (teach; test; grade; go on) will be replaced by the new model of instruction (teach; test; adjust and teach/enrich; retest; grade; go on).
12. The only reason for monitoring student progress is to adjust instruction.
13. There is room for school improvement in the district and in every school in Frederick County.
14. The potential for school improvement resides in the school.
15. There are only two types of schools and school systems: (a) improving schools and school systems, and (b) declining schools and school systems.
16. School improvement is a process, not an event which represents an endless success of incremental adjustments.
17. The client system in the district is changing, and the schools and school system will adjust.
18. The nature of what subject matter ought to be taught is changing.
19. The essential prerequisites for internal school improvement are time, organizational place to meet, and a common language.

FIGURE 10–1 • *Continued*

Using the above strategy planning assumptions, the Frederick County Public School System and each individual school must ask and answer the following major questions which will launch the journey of the Effective Schools process:

1. What is the primary mission of the school system and the school?
2. What will we accept as primary evidence for judging school improvement?
3. How will we evaluate the evidence or outcomes of school improvement?

In order to answer the above three questions, it is important for a school system to agree on its belief system. The following statements represent the philosophical basis for answering the above three questions:

1. The toughest part of doing school improvement is finding a motive to do it.
2. Schools are for teaching for learning.
3. All students can learn.
4. Teachers cause learning.
5. All students will learn when those around them want them to learn.
6. The school mission can be different from the district mission, but it cannot be contradictory.
7. School improvement is a code word for working smarter, but not harder.
8. What gets measured and published, gets attended to.
9. Who gets measured, gets noticed.
10. All teachers should teach all children first, about content second.
11. Work should be fun.
12. All educators should realize the limitation of doing something alone.
13. The school improvement process should include the concept of organized abandonment.
14. The Effective Schools process is not just about teacher competence; it is more about problem solving and organizational change.
15. The algorithm for effectiveness is: quality and equity equals effectiveness.
16. Effective teaching leads to improved identified student outcomes.
17. Effective administrators do the right thing (effectiveness) right (efficiency).
18. Teachers and administrators are already doing the best they can. The change has to be in knowledge and working conditions.

As a final note, the Superintendent and the Board of Education will have institutionalized school improvement for enduring change when the following four elements exist in the Frederick County Public School System:

1. Discernible, describable new competence of the school and school system.
2. Discernible, describable new confidence in the school and school system.
3. Discernible, describable new changes in the level of collaboration in the school and the school system.
4. Discernible, describable new changes in the culture of results in the school and the school system.

The document describes how the school-by-school focus on school improvement will be realized within the larger context of a school system. It is designed as a guide for the Frederick County Public School System implementation of the Effective Schools Process.

leadership committee. The name is not important. What matters is that the group has the respect of the school system.

Although the identification of the participants will vary according to the district, there can be no doubt as to who is the leader of this group. The superintendent is the final arbiter and determines the agenda, time line, activities, and final wording of all communication. Right here—if not before—all correspondence from the administration should include a reference to the district's commitment to teaching for learning for *all.*

The fact that such a districtwide team exists and is working on a master plan should be common knowledge in the system. People should be impressed with the calibre of participants and the time, seriousness, and resources given to the team's work. The last thing a superintendent wants is for this district team to be looked upon as consisting of a group of the superintendent's "pets" who are just shuffling test scores and spending a few days out of the office.

During the time this district team is drawing up the master plan, the rest of the school system should be moving ahead with a general initiation into the Effective Schools research. When the plan is released, the process used in setting goals and objectives will not be totally alien to the school system.

This strategic planning process will be new to most districts. It will involve both an external and internal planning process (see Figure 10–2). The external involves social, economic, political, and demographic trends. The internal analysis looks at student achievement, dropouts, the climate, and standards. The mirror is also turned to include a review of the strengths and weaknesses of the central office.

After analyzing the conclusions from these data, a mission statement and general objectives are developed. From there flows the development of specific action plans, a schedule, and resource requirements.

The final components of a master plan include an introduction to the Effective Schools research and a brief synopsis of the correlates; the mission statement for the district; the goals and objectives for the district; the new roles and responsibilities of the superintendent, board, and central office; the guidelines and timetable for individual school improvement plans and recommended makeup of the school improvement teams; the allocation and/or increase in resources; and time for future planning for the district as a whole.

The plan should bring together a framework for top-down, bottom-up management. The superintendent must get on the speaking circuit in the community as soon as the team starts to meet. He or she must prepare people for what is coming, as well as build enthusiasm for the work being done and the changes anticipated. There is no question that there will be opposition at different levels of the planning and implementation. The more the community knows and understands, the less strident that opposition will be.

Noel Farmer took a very bold step when he put his accountability on the line and announced specific objectives and goals for the Frederick County

FIGURE 10–2 • *External/Internal Analysis*

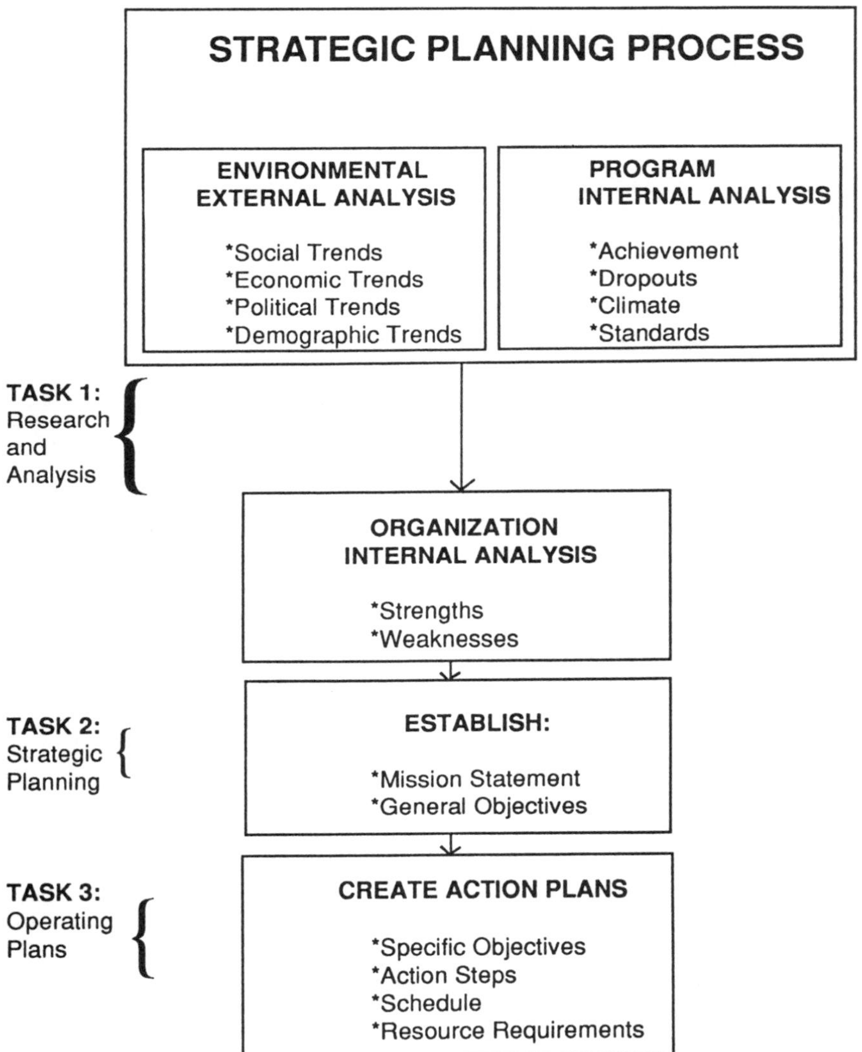

Spring Branch Independent School District.

School System. He not only made them part of the master plan but he released annual reports on the status of achieving the goals. Some of those goals are: Criterion-referenced tests will show annual increases in the percentage of students at the respective grade level who attain essential objectives in curriculum; the percentage of student attendance will increase annually; ninety percent of all students will complete the equivalent of Algebra I before graduating; there shall be no significant differences in the proportion of youth demonstrating minimum academic mastery as a function of gender, race, or socioeconomic status.

"Some of my colleagues think I'm crazy to do this," says Farmer. "But I have never regretted it. Outcomes are what we're supposed to be about, so why hide it? The best run businesses operate by measuring what they're trying to do. And if you let people know, you get them behind you. You get them on your bandwagon. And that's what I want. Informed people succeeding with me."

Farmer and others say they also learned that important players in this process are members of the media. School officials should begin early in the process explaining to newspaper editors, television reporters, and news producers exactly what this Effective Schools research is and the impact it will have on the community. The press should not be regarded as an adversary here. They can be the best friend the superintendent will have in this process. Yes, they can also be troublesome partners, but the odds of that are lessened if the superintendent deals with the media openly and honestly from the very beginning.

Once the districtwide planning team has released its master plan and achieved the support of the board and schools, its duties are not over. In some districts, this team stays in place to review the incoming school improvement plans. In other districts, they move on to future planning and changes in the organizational structure of the district. Although the roles differ in every improving school district, this team stays actively involved. It is the conduit between the schools and the superintendent and board. As time moves on, it will be their responsibility to organize and analyze the data from the schools in order to report to the board and community the progress of school improvement.

As the master plan and individual school planning progress, the central office must make certain that no one thinks the entire burden for improvement has been passed to the school themselves. The central office has very specific opportunities to enhance the progress and quality of school improvement. The Spring Branch district office details its "opportunities" (or "responsibilities") in Figure 10–3. They include curriculum review, staff development, and the institution of an administrative leadership academy to train staff in their new roles.

The superintendent and the districtwide team will set the first example that school improvement is a process—not an event, but a living, breathing process. The district is there to set the pace, set the guidelines, offer whatever training and resources are required, and then review and report the progress. It's up to the schools to make it happen.

Accepting School-Based Management

Once the school district understands that school improvement is based on the premise that *all children can learn,* it must now accept that this improvement is going to be accomplished via school-based management—across the district—no exceptions. Each school will develop its own planning team and its own plan.

There are school districts throughout the country that believe they are implementing the Effective Schools plan and have endorsed "decentralized decision making," but they have not implemented school-based management. In these districts, all decisions continue to come from the top. These school districts are *not* participating in Effective Schools. They are continuing the safe, status quo.

It is in the schools where the work of education is being done. It is the schools, the principals, and the teachers who know the needs and expectations of their students. So the schools must decide what action should be taken for improvement. As Gary Mathews, associate superintendent in Spring Branch, says, "We don't teach one single student here at the administration building, so why should we be making those teaching decisions?"

The board can approve the Effective Schools Process—the goals, objectives, accountability procedure, training, time line—but it is the *schools* themselves that have to make the plans and process work. As Hal Guthrie states, "I put up the framework of the house. They go in there and finish it off, from the wiring to the plumbing to the interior decorating. It's up to them."

It is essential that the superintendent prepare his or her district for what will no doubt be a major change in thinking. For 200 years we have believed it is the central administrative office that runs the schools. It's the schools' turn now. "It's a major cultural change, but there's no two ways about it," says Farmer. "We're accountable up here at the top for providing the means and framework for the schools to do whatever they must to attain the goals. That's it. And the support. We've got to be there with all the support we can muster."

As the Effective Schools Process continues, practitioners see the school district organizational paradigm shifting: The central office is now working for the individual schools. This is illustrated in Figure 10-4, created by the administrative team in Spring Branch, Texas, which is moving toward the new paradigm.

It has become fashionable for educators, researchers, and often practitioners themselves to talk about the need for a tightly defined *structure* for school improvement. Indeed, some structures have been tried and are still floundering within districts. The complaint often leveled at Effective Schools research is that there is no structure. In the literal sense, that is true. Each school district is slightly different. It would be impossible to develop one structure that would work for all districts. What Effective Schools research has developed is a *structure for a change process* for school improvement.

FIGURE 10–3 • *District Opportunities to Enhance Effective Schools, Spring Branch Independent School District*

MONITORING	FOCUS	CLIMATE
MAP: Monitoring Academic Progress	**CR & DC: Curriculum Review and Development Cycle**	**Multicultural Education**
*To assist in the improvement of district programs of curriculum and instruction	*To assist in accomplishing the District Mission (i.e., Thinking Skills Communication Skills, Interpersonal Skills, Civic Responsibilities)	*To create greater cooperation and understanding between teacher and student among students
*To assist in the improvement of campus programs of curriculum and instruction (i.e., building implementation of district curriculum and instructional practices)	*To create a curriculum concept (i.e., Common Skills, Common Content, Individualized Learnings, Co-operative Learnings)	*To promote interpersonal skills (i.e. positive view of self and balanced view of others)
*To assist in the improvement of classroom intruction and student learning	*To define a curriculum design (i.e., philosophy/ goals, program guidelines, learning objectives, assessment/ evaluation, reteaching, suggestions, enrichment)	*To promote a "personalized" education for all students
*To assist students and parents in the improvement of self-understanding and individual development	*To define and implement components of CR & DC (i.e., Develop Adopt; Implement; Monitor/Maintain/ Revise; Research; Evaluate/Recommend)	*To improve student achievement through improved self-concept
	*To identify subject areas to be reviewed/ revised according to a Five to Seven Year Schedule or Cycle	

FIGURE 10–3 • *Continued*

EXPECTATIONS **Teacher Expectations for Student Achievement**	**LEADERSHIP** **Administrative Leadership Academy**
*To increase teacher behaviors which promote student achievement	*To create a new source for administrative selection in the district
*To decrease teacher behaviors which decrease student achieve-ment	*To strengthen existing ranks of school administration
*To promote the responsibility for the learning of ALL students	*To strengthen understanding of the District Mission, Strategic Planning Mission, Classroom Strategic Planning and Effective Schools
*To develop reteaching/ retesting (reassessing) for student mastery	*To strengthen understanding of the role of the Board of Trustees, Superintendent, and the Divisions of Instructional Services, Personnel and Management Services, and Business Services

FIGURE 10–4 • *School District Organization Charts*

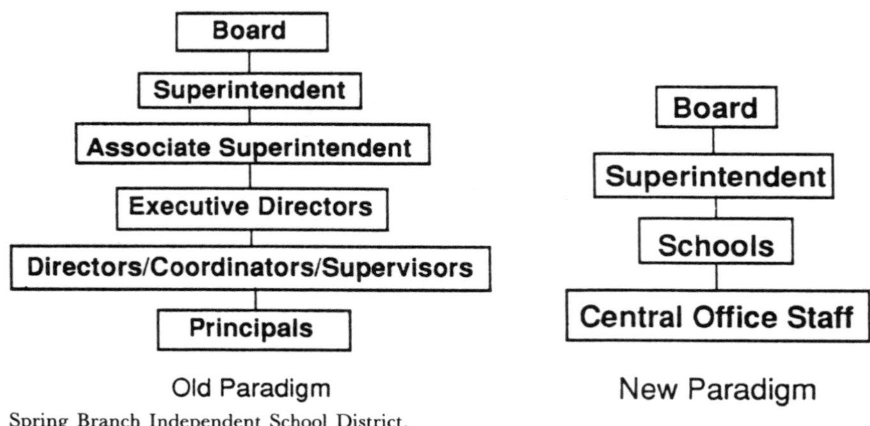

Spring Branch Independent School District.

There are five "guiding statements" given by Lezotte and Bancroft (1985) as key elements of the school improvement planning process: (1) a focus on the single school as the strategic unit for school improvement; (2) a recognition that change is a long-term process and not an event (3 to 5 years); (3) a belief that change is possible without infusion of major resources or personnel; (4) an acceptance of the idea that effective schools and effective teaching research provide a useful framework for school improvement planning and implementation; and (5) a representative team of administrators, teachers, and parents who can provide the leadership and inspiration needed to plan and implement the design of school improvement. (See Appendix A.)

After accepting these "guiding statements," districts move on to the four research-based steps for school improvement. As shown (in more detail) in Figure 10–5, these four major steps or components of the school improvement process are:

1. The foundation of Effective Schools research for the achievement of quality and equity
2. An assessment and analysis of the needs of the individual schools and school district as a whole
3. The identification of strategies and activities (interventions) that make a difference in teaching for learning
4. The organization and empowerment of staff to initiate change and innovation

FIGURE 10–5 • *Steps to Systemwide School Improvement*

As a means to accomplish its mission and reach its improvement goals, the Frederick County Public Schools has adopted the principles and procedures derived from the body of knowledge known as "Effective Schools" research. As helpful as that research is, its focus is primarily on the school building level. Therefore, the school system has gone beyond that research to develop a process for system-wide school improvement. It is clear that for an entire school system to improve its schools, all the policies, personnel and non-school based resources within the system must be employed toward the goal of school improvement.

The School Improvement Process, when implemented system-wide, has four steps or components:

Step 1: *Establishing an organizational context for achieving quality and equity.* The Effective Schools research provides an organizational context for achieving quality and equity. It offers evidence that schools can achieve quality and equity, and identifies specific school-based, organizational characteristics that effective schools share. The research establishes a foundation on which schools can create a vision, develop a mission, and define goals and objectives for school improvement.

Step 2: *Assessing needs to determine priority areas for school systems — and local school improvement.* The Effective Schools research emphasizes the importance of using data to determine priority areas for school systems and local school improvement. Types of data useful in such a needs analysis include information on student outcomes, results from staff surveys and archival information.

Although the Effective Schools research provides clear guidance for steps one and two in the School Improvement Process, it does not include specific strategies for reaching agreed upon goals and objectives. Thus, a broader research base must be consulted to progress toward step 3.

Step 3: *Identifying the strategies or interventions that make a difference in teaching and learning.* After needs are identified and goals and objectives determined, it is important to select those intervention strategies that will be most useful and productive in meeting those goals and objectives. These "high yield" intervention strategies should be selected after reviewing relevant research literature. For example, if a priority is to "maximize engaged learning time," the "time on task" literature should be reviewed to identify which intervention strategies are most likely to yield desired results.

Step 4: *Organizing and empowering staff to bring about change and innovation.* Because the School Improvement Process focuses on the local school as the unit of change, local school staff must be empowered to bring about the needed change. If the School Improvement Process is to work, teachers must be actively involved and have direct and ongoing input in the functioning of the school. This involvement includes a broad range of activities such as needs identification, selection of strategies and activities, and evaluating school effectiveness.

Each school, as it considers a school improvement process, might wish to reflect on the comment of J. Mark Lubbers who says:

> . . . *a unique culture exists in each school. No recipes can be applied to "fix" all schools. Any innovation carries with it assets and liabilities. Each innovation must be approached as a process and altered to maximize its strengths while minimizing its weaknesses. The key element of the innovation must be molded and fitted to meet the unique qualities of each school.*

"School Improvement," *Effective Schools Research Abstracts* Vol. 1, No. 6, 1986-87 Series. Reprinted with permission of Frederick County Public Schools.

These research-laden steps and guidelines are the original blueprint of the Effective Schools *structure for a process*. The advantage of having this *structure for a process* instead of an iron-clad, prescriptive structure is that the implementation remains flexible. It not only grows with the district and schools but it also can be adjusted to the demographics, culture, history, personalities, and idiosyncracies of a school district and a school. The particular management style of one superintendent or principal may suggest a completely different implementation process from another superintendent or principal. But there are specific steps within the structure for the process that have been proven to be most effective and the least disruptive to the operation of a school system.

The process is not easy, however. It is appropriate to remember here the comment from Superintendent Max Heim in Geary County, Kansas: "School improvement is like working on the railroad when a train is coming down the track at 60 miles an hour. You can't stop the train, but somehow you've got to fix the track."

This is true at the district level and it is just as true at the school level. You cannot send teachers and kids home for three years with "Hey, kids, we're going to make some changes. Come on back in three or four years."

Again, just as dealing with the board, the two constants required at both the district and school levels are *communication* and *involvement*. The more ownership individuals feel they have in any plan, the more pride they will feel and the harder they will work on its implementation.

Getting to Know Effectiveness, Spencerport Style

It was the fall of 1982 when Dr. Robert Sudlow, assistant superintendent in the middle-class suburban district of Spencerport, New York, traveled to Michigan to talk with Ron Edmonds and Larry Lezotte about their Effective Schools research. For several years, Sudlow had been gathering literature on different school reform movements and he and his superintendent, Joe Clement, decided it was the Effective Schools Process that made the most sense. After meeting with Edmonds and Lezotte, Sudlow told Clement that Spencerport, already a good school system, could become much better and more effective if it went through this improvement process. Clement agreed, and Edmonds and Lezotte began to work with Spencerport. It would be the first suburban district in the nation to take on the Effective Schools Process.

Spencerport, a town of 19,000 near Rochester, New York, has a school population of 3,300, 95 percent white, with 6 percent of the school population eligible for free and reduced lunch. Because of the low number of students on free lunch (the usual indicator for low socioeconomic status), Spencerport chose to disaggregate its scores—after studying extensive research—on the basis of the mother's education level.

The following is the detailed time line worked out by Sudlow, Edmonds, and Lezotte for the beginning stages of the planning process. It is instructive because it shows the unrelenting communication and insistence on involvement at all levels. And, because it is the time line drawn up by Edmonds himself, we can see exactly what the founder of Effective Schools had in mind. The Spencerport Effective Schools Project Flowchart, blocking out these general time periods, noting additional planning time at the beginning of the cycle and after board approval, is shown in Figure 10-6. Specifically, the following occurred:

Fall, 1982: Sudlow meets with Edmonds and Lezotte and the three agree on a time line for development and implementation.

January 26, 1983: Edmonds and Lezotte meet with the Spencerport Board of Education. That evening the board approves a project to investigate research on Effective Schools in cooperation with Edmonds and Lezotte and the Michigan State University College of Education.

February, 1983: Separate, day-long awareness sessions are held between Edmonds, Lezotte, and the Spencerport Schools Administrative Council, Curriculum Council, K-12 Teachers of the Year, and the Executive Council of the Teachers' Union.

March, 28, 29, April, 19, 1983: The districtwide leadership planning team—consisting of two teachers from each school, a principal from each school, a district testing expert, the president of union (or designee), and the Assistant Superintendent—is formed and meets with Edmonds and Lezotte to draw up the master plan. The schools also form planning teams and Edmonds and Lezotte do in-service staff development for those teams.

May 20, 1983: Districtwide Superintendents' Day—a full-day workshop for teachers and administrators. Edmonds and Lezotte administer a needs assessment school interview (at that time the Connecticut assessment instrument was for only elementary schools; it was amended to include secondary schools) in the morning and more in-service in the afternoon.

June 14, 1983: The master plan for Spencerport is submitted to the superintendent. He approved and recommended the plan to board.

June 22, 1983: The board approves the master plan.

Late June: The building planning teams begin to meet. Teams consist of principal, two teachers from district leadership team, and four to six teachers from school. Additional training begins on data analysis and plan development.

Early July: Socioeconomic data were gathered for district (based on level of mother's education), then disaggregated student achievement data were compiled on that basis.

July 15, 1983: Edmonds dies. His last work was a profile of Spencerport's Cosgrive Junior High based on disaggregated scores. Lezotte finishes the school

FIGURE 10–6 • ***Effective Schools Project Flowchart***

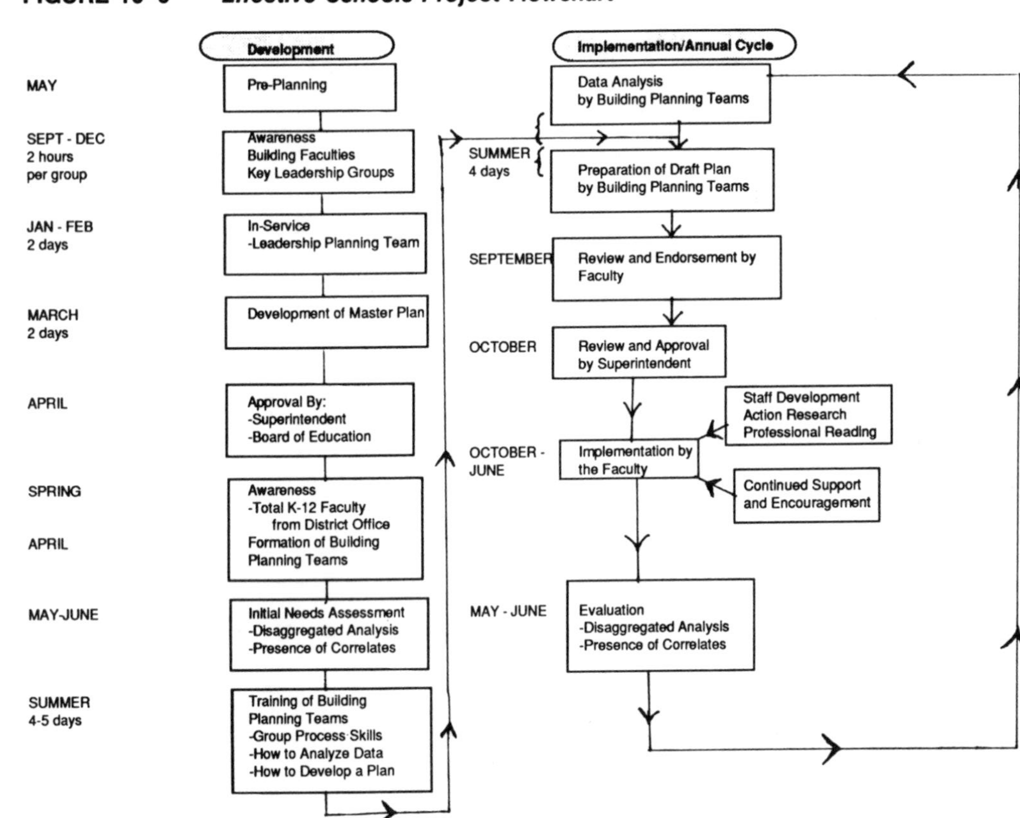

Spencerport, New York.

profiles (profiles were the analysis of each school, what the needs assessment and disaggregated data indicated about an individual school).

July, August, 1983: The building planning teams meet to go over data and Lezotte profiles, and draft plans for school improvement.

September, 1983: The plans are submitted to school faculties at the opening of school and are discussed and approved in successive meetings, then sent to the superintendent for approval.

September 23, 1983: The superintendent gives final approval of the last plan for school improvement.

October, 1983–June, 1984: The plan is implemented by the faculty. Staff development begins. Central office gives strong support.

May–June, 1984: The plan for implementation is evaluated and disaggregated analysis is reviewed in relation to correlate strength. Draft planning for next year begins.

Unlike the more flexible, expansive flowchart, Figure 10–6, the actual time line for Spencerport gives the schools very little time to disaggregate scores, analyze the needs assessment data, and develop the school plans. Ideally, the schools would have six months to do their planning following board approval. However, in Spencerport, the board approval did not come until late June, leaving the schools only two months to develop the plans. This was also complicated by the sudden death of Edmonds. It fell upon the shoulders of Lezotte to complete the analysis of the school data in order that the teams could tailor-design their plans.

"We worked hard, and we worked very, very fast," says Sudlow. "In looking back, it is rather amazing that we accomplished all we did in that amount of time." Amazing indeed, when you keep in mind that Spencerport was not a declining school system. It was not "in trouble" and many of the people in the town, and in the schools themselves, wondered why such a process was being initiated when there had been little or no complaint about the performance of the school system.

"We didn't think there was any need for a radical program," recalls Gay Lenard, a member of the Spencerport Board of Education when they approved the Effective Schools Process. "We also thought this may be just another one of those alleged reform programs that's over in a couple months."

But those perceptions changed the more the board listened to Edmonds and Lezotte, and the superintendent, and the staff. Board members saw that the schools needed improvement and that the Effective Schools research provided the structure for that process. What was radical was the new belief that all children can learn, and the Effective Schools Process or restructuring, itself. "It was all new to us, and in many ways to Edmonds and Lezotte," says Sudlow. "They never had done a suburban district like ours—or an entire K–12 district. So we learned together."

What helped the process move quickly and efficiently was the constant communication between all those involved.

"The board knew and understood—thanks to all the time given us by Lezotte and Edmond and later Bob and Joe—exactly what was happening," recalls Lenard. "And we were able to keep the community informed. We were also able to discuss what was going on with the teachers and administrators. That was important. Believe me, we know these correlates and indicators inside out, and that's made one huge difference."

There were many different personalities coming together in Spencerport. It was, in many ways, an "old" school system that hadn't officially investigated school-based management. The faculty and staff had been in place for many years. They had seen numerous reform programs and attempts at staff development come and go. They were skeptical. (For further detail on teacher reaction in Spencerport, refer to Chapters 8 and 9.)

"And you can't blame them," admits Sudlow. "What we had to keep telling them was that this was not just another fly-by-night program. This was serious. We were going to stick with this. For the long haul. And that's the difference. You have to let people know this is going to take time. And you have to take the time to plan it right, and implement it wisely." And thoughtfully.

Creating and Sustaining Respect

One of the crucial steps in spreading the Effective Schools Process word from the superintendent's office and board room into the schools is the districtwide planning team. Practitioners say the manner that the word is given and received by this team can set the mood for the beginning stages of school improvement.

This team must be given *time*—just as the planning team within the school must be given the proper time to do an effective job. Each superintendent handles team planners differently, but one constant is that time is built into the planning. Teachers and administrators are not expected to do this on top of other duties in their "free" time. It is always a working day (or days) in the sense that the participants are compensated at the district rate. Meetings are usually held away from the schools, very often at the district office itself, in order to allow teachers and principals to free themselves from duties and interruptions. There is a congenial atmosphere in these meetings; people are served meals. (The cost has been worked out far in advance, given that the average superintendent in this position has been in his or her own planning stage for six months to a year.)

What can set this school improvement process off from other attempts is *attitude*. From the first day, there must be an atmosphere of mutual respect—an understanding that we are all in this together and it is going to make life better for not only our students but for teachers and staff also. In dealing with districtwide planning teams and school planning teams, the administration should go out of its way to encourge collegiality and build trust. This is often accomplished with small gestures.

In New York City, a group of teachers and principals went on a retreat to become acquainted with the Effective Schools Process. This shocked teachers (and still does because it still happens for major planning sessions) who had never been treated this way in the past. But it set the mood for how Superintendent Tony Amato was going to go through the Effective Schools Process. He was going to listen to and respect his teachers and administrators—an essential maneuver in a strong union town.

In Frederick County, Maryland, after a year of planning, Superintendent Noel Farmer set up special workshops throughout the district, working out a very satisfactory compensation plan for the staff. At the end of that planning stage, a huge dinner and pep rally for school reform (it's believed to be the first pep rally for such a cause) was held where every member of the faculty and staff was wined and dined and given souvenirs of the first night of a new day for Frederick County Public Schools.

In Spring Branch, Texas, a group of 25 people—teacher representatives, central office personnel, and principals—traveled to Washington, DC for a conference and seminar with Larry Lezotte. It was a conference where they were instructed to "learn and enjoy yourselves."

"How people are treated in those initial stages sets the tone for how the district is going to plan and implement," says Lezotte, who is usually the common denominator in the district initiation process. "They have to start right from the beginning, saying this is going to take time, but we trust you and we're going to give you the time to do it right. If they don't, central administration is in for rough going."

If a team does not travel to a location where Lezotte is speaking, or to one of the training conferences conducted by the National Center for Effective Schools, then Lezotte or representatives of Effective Schools travel to the district. Once again, it is important that the teachers and staff are treated to a day away from their school site, and that the teachers are able to see the *active* participation of their superiors.

"I've been in districts where the superintendent or principal will introduce me, then they slowly sneak out of the room," says Lezotte. "That immediately tells me these are not Effective Schools leaders, and it tells the teachers that the district is really not committed to Effective Schools."

In most instances, and especially in the larger districts and schools, the superintendent and principals have met with the Effective Schools practitioners before the initiation begins with other faculty and staff. Ideally, a superintendent will have the plan and time line on the drawing board even before the orientation begins. And as the districtwide planning team is handing over the gauntlet to the individual schools, the staff in those schools is already into its Effective Schools research.

"We took it one step at a time. First, the board of trustees," explains Guthrie. "I knew I had them when they started saying, 'Hey, this makes sense. Why didn't we do this before?' Then the administration met with people in districts across the country that had already implemented this. They learned from the practitioners. At the same time, we're holding community meetings making sure everyone knows where we're going. Then we build a leadership cabinet of teachers. Now we're all talking the same language. And then I say to the schools: 'OK, now you know what you have to do. Get a team together and you start telling me what you would like to do at your school to make it a better place for kids. And I really don't care how you do it. Just do it.'"

Planning at the School Level

It is when the process moves down to the individual schools that "the rubber meets the road." There are three recognized major stages: Preparation, Diagnosis, and Implementation, as illustrated in Figure 10-7. Once again, although the details of the enactment and processing of these stages will differ from district to district, and school to school, the structure for the process remains constant.

Philosophically, the schools are dealing with the Effective Schools Research Process and the research on strategic planning and organizational behavior. Different superintendents and principals may choose various tools, from popular business and planning texts to fine-tuned academic research. But whatever planning and instructional tools are used, the basis is always the Effective Schools research.

In this process of pulling the entire school together in planning and implementation, practitioners have learned that there must be, as Larry Lezotte describes, "three prerequisites for successful school improvement efforts":

1. A common language—Effective Schools
2. A place to meet—the school or campus improvement team
3. Time to meet—uninterrupted, usually compensated

In documenting their school improvement process, Spring Branch officials say they have learned there are two additional prerequisites: a shared understanding of the process and products of campus improvement planning, and a shared vision of what the school *could* be juxtaposed with an accurate picture of what the school *is*. The vision is necessary for any progress to take place.

FIGURE 10–7 • *Developing Campus Improvement Plans*

Overview of the Process

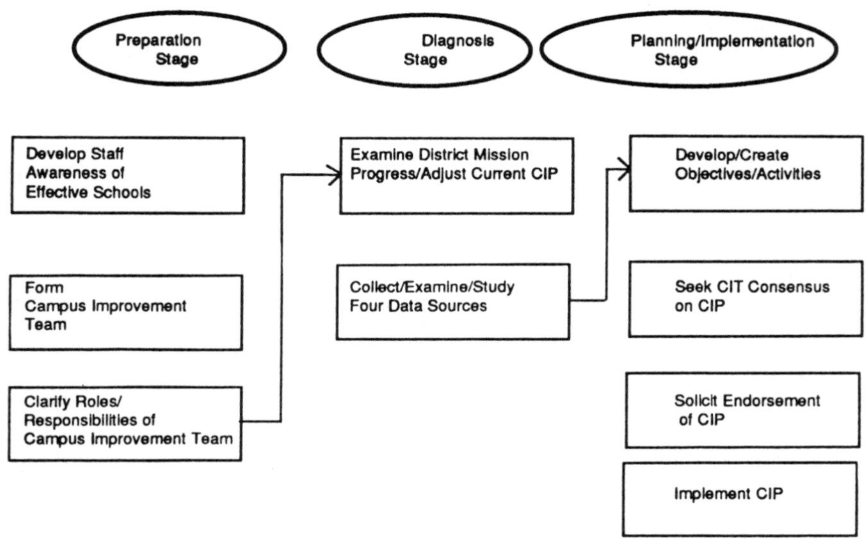

Spring Branch Independent School District.

A written overview of the Effective Schools Improvement Process, following and explaining the three stages of Preparation, Diagnosis, and Implementation, is offered in materials circulated by the superintendent's office in Frederick County, Maryland, and reproduced here in Figure 10–8. In this document, Farmer lets the community know exactly what will be taking place, and informs the schools and their planning teams what will be expected of them. Farmer's specific guidelines for the development of local school improvement plans are reproduced in Figure 10–9.

Farmer, along with other superintendents, believes this presentation of guidelines gives the school planners a concrete beginning for their individual process. Although the planning and implementation will differ at each school, the questions and concerns about how to begin school-based management are often the same in each district.

With the circulation of memoranda from the superintendent's office giving guidelines, procedures, and outlines, each school is again reminded that this is a *districtwide* process. There can be no room for thinking, "Well, this really doesn't apply to us." Nor is there any reason for staff and teachers to ponder,

FIGURE 10–8 • *An Overview of the School Improvement Process*

Frederick County Public Schools

Implementation of the Effective Schools/School Improvement Process at the local school level is under the direction of the principal, who heads the School Improvement Team (or Campus Improvement Team). The implementation process can be accomplished through the steps listed below:

Preparation

1. Orient Staff
   The entire staff should understand major findings of the Effective Schools research and implications of the research for school improvement. Additionally, the staff should understand the commitment of the entire school system to the Effective Schools/School Improvement Process and the nature of local school involvement in the process in relation to the system outcome-based goals.

   They should also be very familiar with the Maryland School Performance Program (MSPP) data-based areas for student performance, as well as the implications for the school and the School Improvement Plan if a school does not attain a satisfactory standard in one or more of these data-based areas.

   Procedures must be in place to orient staff new to the process and to define their role with respect to the process.
2. Form School Improvement Team
   The School Improvement Team should be representative of all components of the staff. Parent involvement is highly recommended. The Team has as its primary responsibility working collaboratively with the principal and staff to guide school improvement efforts through analyzing needs and initiating schoolwide discussion on school improvement issues related to the school's improvement plan.
3. Mission of School
   The faculty must embrace a clear, attainable, and attractable school-wide mission in order to indicate who they are serving and what business they are about.

Diagnosis

4. Conduct Needs Assessment
   The development of the School Improvement Plan is based on the following needs assessment process:

   a. Review and analyze student outcome data for each of the system goals and indicators.
   b. Identify areas where established system goals and Maryland School Performance Program standards have not been met, particularly noting areas of improvement or decline from past years.
   c. Analyze results of Effective Schools Surveys to ascertain the degree to which staff, student, and parent perceptions support the outcome goals.

Planning and Implementation

5. Establish Goals and Develop School Improvement Plan
   Each school, working through the School Improvement Team, identifies school improvement goals unique to that school. The School Improvement Team identifies strategies and actions needed to reach established goals. A School

FIGURE 10–8 • *Continued*

Improvement Plan is developed which includes goals, objectives, actions to address goals, persons responsible for implementing the actions, materials and resources needed and formative and summative evaluation strategies.

The plan must include objectives/goals for addressing those MSPP data-based areas in which a satisfactory standard was not attained. NOTE: the overall goal should be attainment of all data-based areas within five years. In addition, two elements are essential: (a) helping parents/students/community understand and use outcome-based education and (b) involving parents and community in improving a school's performance in the data-based areas.

School Improvement Plans, as they focus on attainment of satisfactory standard in MSPP data-based areas must address the following items, at a minimum:

- Needs in data-based areas
- Objectives to achieve standards
- Activities to achieve the objectives
- Resources and sources
- Time lines for each data-based area
- Monitoring procedures
- Evaluation measures

Additionally, the school may opt to include in its individual School Improvement Plan items related to a variety of system initiatives, based upon its assessment of the school's and community's needs. For example:

- Multicultural Education Implementation Plan
- Values Education Implementation Plan
- Technology Education Implementation Plan

The school should develop only one School Improvement Plan. Schools involved in special programs such as Chapter I, Maximizing Achievement Potential (MAP), etc., should use subsections in their School Improvement Plan to identify specific requirements or strategies.

6. Review School Improvement Plan
The Division of Instruction and School Administration will review each School Improvement Plan. As part of the review process, schools will receive a written review with suggestions and questions about the contents. Schools will then make necessary adjustments to the plan or react to questions. After a second review by the division, plans receive approval and can be implemented.
7. Disseminate School Improvement Plan
The complete plan is shared with all members of the school staff and with parents. Appropriate aspects of the plan are shared with students.
Support, endorsement, commitment and ownership of the plan by all school-based staff are needed for successful implementation of the plan.
8. Implement School Improvement Plan
Adjustments to the School Improvement Plan should be made, as needed, by the School Improvement Team. Use of the formative and summative evaluation strategies identified for each goal or objective will signal when adjustments may be needed.

FIGURE 10–9 • *Guidelines for Development of Local School Improvement Plans*

A School Improvement Plan is a document developed by the School Improvement Team which states the specific goals and activities the school will implement to assure that all students within the school learn the essential curriculum. The plan is based upon an analysis of school needs as reflected in disaggregated data from student outcome measures, results from the Effective Schools Survey given to all staff within the school, and a variety of archival data. The principal is responsible for assuring that the School Improvement Plan is developed, monitored and updated as needed.

A. Components of the School Improvement Plan

Each School Improvement Plan should include the following components:

1. Goal statements related to Effective Schools characteristics and evidence that the goals represent problem areas that require improvement.
2. Specific activities or strategies designed to achieve the goals, including staff development plans.
3. Personnel responsibilities for implementing each activity.
4. Resources and materials needed from within the school, as well as from area and central offices.
5. Formative evaluation strategies such as timelines or checkpoints to assess progress throughout the year.
6. Summative evaluation strategies, expressed in terms of student outcomes whenever possible, to determine if goals have been reached.

Each year, at least one of the school improvement goals should focus directly on instructional improvement. By continuing to highlight improved student achievement, school personnel demonstrate that high levels of learning for all students are the school's major priority. Because each Effective Schools correlate relates to the goal of improving achievement for all students, the plan should indicate how each focus area contributes to this goal.

The Effective Schools Process is an ongoing process for the system and for each school. Some aspects of implementing the process will be short-term in nature, while others may take three to five years to fully implement.

B. Suggested Questions to Generate Information and Discussion Needed for Development of School Improvement Plans

The following questions are provided to help generate the information and discussion needed to develop the School Improvement Plan:

1. What were major areas of focus indicated by the needs analysis process? For example, what areas of need were identified through an analysis of the Effective Schools Survey Instrument? What needs were identified through the disaggregated analysis of student outcome measures, including results from standardized and criterion-referenced tests?
2. Has any action already been taken to address these identified needs? If so, what has been done? Based upon the needs analysis process, what priorities should be addressed during the next school year?

FIGURE 10–9 • *Continued*

3. How will goals, objectives, and strategies needed to address those priorities be identified?
4. Who will be responsible for addressing each activity or strategy?
5. For each activity or strategy, what benchmarks will be used during the year a) to determine whether or not each strategy is being implemented appropriately and b) to determine whether or not the strategies are having the desired impact or effect?
6. What human and other resources will be used to implement each strategy?
7. How will you know at the end of the year if objectives have been met?

C. Additional Information to Include with the Plan
Prior to submitting the School Improvement Plan to the Area Superintendent for Effective Schools, check to be certain that the components listed above have been addressed. Additionally, the following information should be attached to the plan.

1. How was the School Improvement Team involved in developing the School Improvement Plan?
2. What strategies were used to obtain staff input and consensus?
3. What sources of data were used in establishing goals and priorities?
4. Which types of data where disaggregated?
5. How will local school staff development occur (if not specified in the plan)?
6. What steps will be or have been taken to disseminate the School Improvement Plan?
7. Who will serve on the School Improvement Team for the new school year? How will the community (and students at the high school level) be represented?
8. What will be done to acquaint new staff and community representatives with the Effective School Research and Process?

D. Final Note
All schools must consider themselves guilty on the seven correlates and the eight school system improvement goals until data proves otherwise. Therefore all principals will need to submit to their Area Superintendent for Effective Schools the data which they used to make decisions on each correlate and each system improvement goal.

Reprinted with permission of Frederick County Public Schools.

"What is going on up there in administration?" Or even to think, "Well, this too will pass." These superintendents are serious—the schools had best be too.

School Orientation

There will be no Effective Schools improvement unless the *entire* faculty and staff—and this means substitutes that are usually called to fill in, as well as secretaries, aides, nurses, and custodial staff—are instructed in what exactly is going to transpire in the school in upcoming months and years. This is done in most cases with the use of reading materials, available videotapes on the Effective School Improvement Process, and outside or local experts.

Spring Branch, Texas, used a campus team of administrators and teachers to train other groups who then trained those on the various campuses throughout the district. As explained by Gary Mathews, associate superintendent of Spring Branch, "The training of the campus teams was accomplished by much attention, fanfare, and excitement, so that even though the model was comfortable and familiar, the message was clear: This is new, this is important, this is not going away."

Right from the beginning, dialogue must be encouraged in order that a thorough understanding of the process is achieved. At no time should the school feel under any unrealistic time constraints. The initiation must be thorough and involve everyone in the dialogue. This way the entire school will develop the *ownership* that is so vital to any planning or implementation process.

The school should also be made aware at this stage that the changes that will be coming are not aimed exclusively at the schools, but that the changes are coming for the organizational arena of the school system, including the roles and responsibilities within the central office.

The overview of this staff awareness process, as illustrated in Figure 10–10, includes not just work on the correlates but on the principles of Effective Schools: quality/equity; teaching/learning; school based/district supervised; schoolwide staff development; collaboration/collegiality; celebration of student/staff success; a process, not an event.

As the staff awareness proceeds, a change will start to occur within the school. People will see by the research the change and progress that have been made by many schools. As more than one teacher has reported after studying the data, "Well, if they can do it at that school, we can certainly do it here."

For some teachers, this will be their first acquaintance with the new research. They will be awakened into the changes that can be made at not only the school level but, most importantly, for them, within the classroom. Principals report that excitement begins to grow as the teachers study the data. They soon begin asking for more, and are anxious to try out the new instructional techniques in their own classrooms.

FIGURE 10–10 • *Developing Campus Improvement Plans*

Overview of the Process

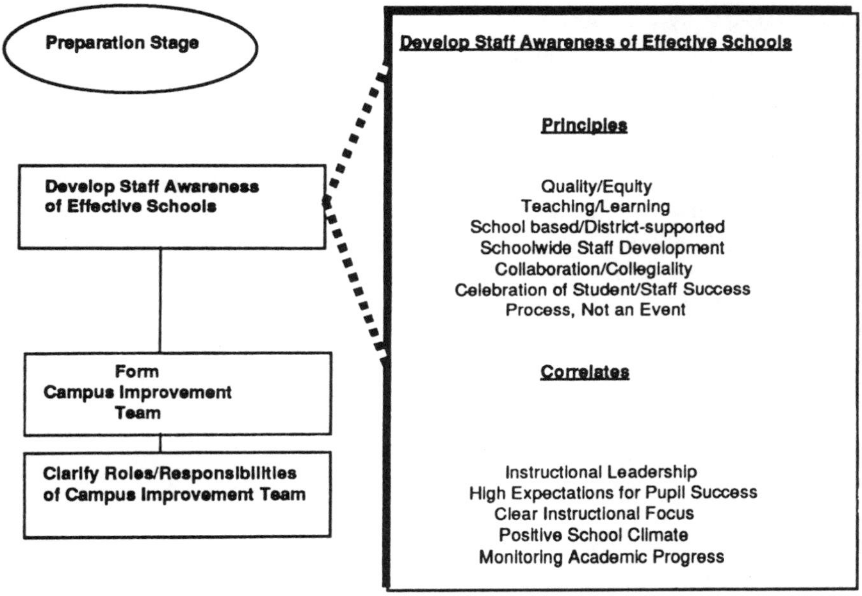

Preparation Stage

Develop Staff Awareness of Effective Schools

Form Campus Improvement Team

Clarify Roles/Responsibilities of Campus Improvement Team

Develop Staff Awareness of Effective Schools

Principles

Quality/Equity
Teaching/Learning
School based/District-supported
Schoolwide Staff Development
Collaboration/Collegiality
Celebration of Student/Staff Success
Process, Not an Event

Correlates

Instructional Leadership
High Expectations for Pupil Success
Clear Instructional Focus
Positive School Climate
Monitoring Academic Progress

Spring Branch Independent School District.

Forming the School Improvement Team

Each school varies with how it chooses its school improvement team and who is on it, but there are some *essential* members. The principal, of course, has been involved from the beginning, as either a member of the districtwide leadership team or as a member of a special principals' committee that was initiated into Effective Schools as the process moved out from central administration. It may be decided that the principal chooses this team. Other schools do it by election, although they must be careful to include a cross-section of the entire school community.

Teachers are the core members. The number and identity of the teachers varies along with the school's instructional needs and demographics.

Most school improvement teams will include a parent or another active member of the outside school community. In some schools, secretaries and custodians are on the team. Consideration should also be given to the inclusion of support personnel from the central office. At the secondary level, some teams have found it beneficial to have a student representative.

The important criteria here are simply that the team is composed of members who not only have the support of the rest of the school community but who are representative of that school community. This means looking at gender and race, as well as a cross-section of the instructional components within the school (see Figure 10–11).

"The most critical attribute of the CIT (Campus Improvement Team) must be that it is perceived by the entire faculty as a representative body. Every school has trend setters, attitude shapers, power brokers, 'priests and story tellers.' The degree of campus endorsement and commitment to the eventual plan can be greatly enhanced by the membership of the CIT. A wise principal will seek to make the CIT a team comprised of staff that cannot be faulted as being 'in,' 'do-gooders,' or generally the 'favorites.' The team should include those members of the faculty who will be in a position to pass informal judgment on the plan, and/or shape faculty attitudes regarding the plan" (Guthrie, Mathews, and Wells, December 1990).

The time given to this team to organize, assess, and plan is essential to its success. This is difficult and there must be coordination from the central office to allow the proper time and compensation. Many schools have found it advantageous to have meetings away from the school. In some districts, these

FIGURE 10–11 • *Developing Campus Improvement Plans*

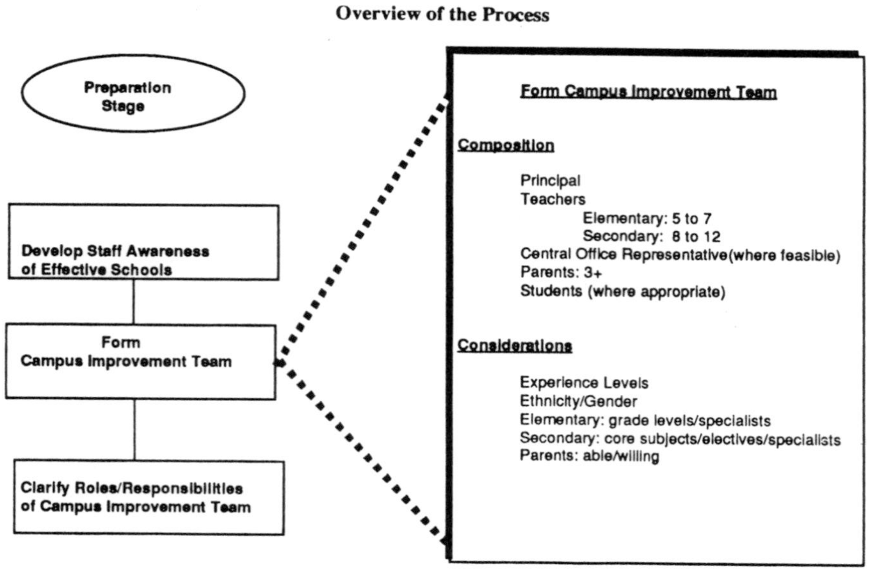

Overview of the Process

Spring Branch Independent School District.

teams have gone on weekend retreats, using a team member's nearby vacation home. Other schools set up a conference and planning day at a local hotel.

Each district and school works out its own compensation procedure depending on time needed and contractual requirements. It is usually estimated at a minimum rate of 20 hours of summer work during that first planning year.

The team should be careful not to be secretive or aloof from the rest of the school. Regular communication should take place, both in the form of written matter and reports at faculty meetings. The team therefore works on the basis of two time components: the time to do the work of the planning itself, and the time to report back to the school community.

"The one area that we are constantly having to work on is feedback time," explains Noel Farmer. "The team must have the opportunity to make connections with the rest of the faculty. We've found we do fairly well in capturing planning time, but we're always being challenged on ways to find feedback hours."

For this reason, the school district must build feedback time into the schedule right at the start. Not only does it pave the way for those necessary interactions but, by planning it ahead of time, the district is sending the signal that these planning teams will not be working in a vacuum, that the input of the entire school is requested and needed.

The Principal Takes the Helm

There must be an immediate clarification of roles and responsibilities within the team (see Figure 10–12). The leader of the school improvement team is the principal. This team is immediately in trouble if the school does not have a strong instructional leader at its head. There has to be someone who will guide the team, who will set up the collaborative strategies, who will run interference when necessary, and who will be heard when help or support is sought from the central office.

The leader of the team must *lead*, showing the faculty where they have to go and the best way to get there. A strong principal will delegate as easily as she or he rules, and will instill pride with the same finesse as he or she strikes out for hard work and accountability.

The principal is a director, coach, facilitator, and delegator of responsibilities. The principal must encourage and demonstrate collaboration and trust—but never abdication.

The principal will be learning right along with the campus improvement team. Principals who are true instructional leaders in the Effective Schools Process emphasize that the beginning months of work with the improvement team are some of the most difficult and challenging in their careers. For too many principals, being an Effective leader means changing the way they have done

FIGURE 10–12 • *Developing Campus Improvement Plans*

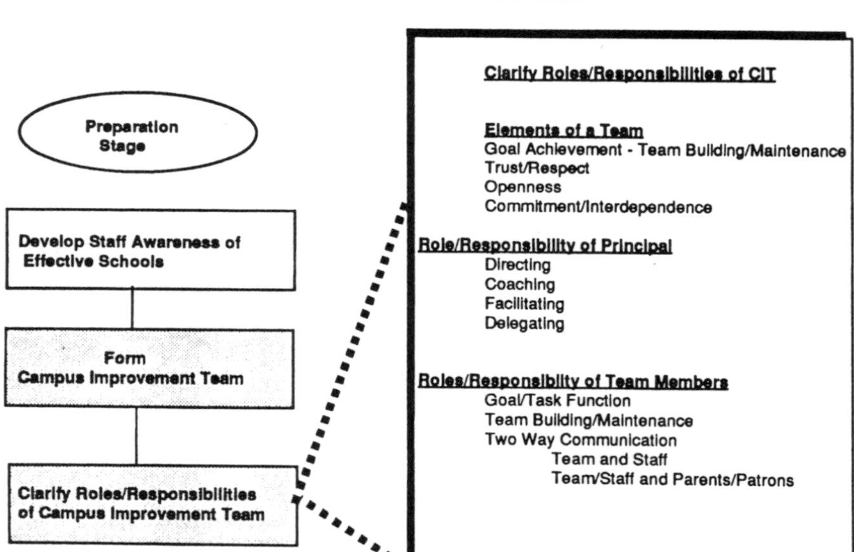

Spring Branch Independent School District.

business for many years. They must now learn the fine art of delegating and collaborating and, at the same time, staying on top of every aspect of the planning and implementation process.

"While my team was taking courses in decision making, I was taking courses right along with them in leadership and management skills," said Suzanne Still, principal of the Hollibrook Elementary School in Spring Branch, Texas. "It wasn't easy, for them or me. But I was lucky. I had a dedicated team that would do anything—anything—to improve their school and bring in teaching and learning for all. They wanted it!"

While Still plays down her role in her school's dramatic improvement, giving the credit to the teachers and the team, her faculty points to the evenings when Still would burn the midnight and early morning oil, analyzing data and studying behavioral management. "Sure, we had a good team," insists one teacher, echoing the sentiment of many. "But we would have been nowhere without Suzanne. She gave us power, but we never forgot who was in charge."

The Effective leaders find it difficult to put into exact terms what they do at this stage to convince their teachers that they have a legitimate, very real say in the improvement process for the school. In examining the steps the principals take, one maneuver keeps asserting itself. The principals do not *give* the teachers empowerment; they *create the conditions* for the empowerment of the teachers.

Gary Mathews, associate superintendent in Spring Branch, says that throughout the improvement process it was important for the entire system to focus on the "people" dimension in planning, rather than just the "task" dimension.

"We were very fortunate to have strong leaders like Suzanne," says Mathews, noting that Still was among a handful of principals who were moved into their positions just prior to the beginning of the Effective Schools Improvement Process. "We knew there were some schools that would be better off with a brand new leader in there. A leader who wasn't bound by the old ways of doing things."

Mathews said the role of the central office was always to provide support and insight, making sure schools did not take steps that would lead to disruption or failure. "In some schools we took a very low-key role," said Mathews. "Other schools we had to be very involved right from the beginning. And over time, it was mostly in those schools that you would see a replacement of the principal."

What Spring Branch and other districts have discovered in undertaking this planning process is that no matter how excellent the school improvement team is, the team can go only so far without an instructional leader. And if a leader is not interested in collaboration or delegation, the team members may start fighting amongst themselves and destroy any chance for progress or school improvement. School planning is synonymous with team building.

The specific functions of the school improvement team include: Serve as key leadership group; develop two-way communication structures with entire school staff; collect, organize, and assess school data; reach consensus on needs and objectives; target and gain staff acceptance for improvement; develop and review plan; monitor plan; evaluate progress and strategies; prepare ongoing strategies and activities.

While the improvement team will be receiving ongoing training in group processes and group skills, it will also be taking on its own individual leadership training. The goal here is to continue to build leaders within the team.

When teams have been asked why they succeed, they usually point to the calibre of training and the degree of collegiality (and, of course, the leadership from the principal). Why they fail may be even more constructive, given the range of personalities and behaviors in a school.

The National Center for Effective Schools has identified five major reasons that teams fail:

1. Members do not understand the function, purpose, or goals of the team effort.
2. Members do not understand what roles to play or what tasks are their responsibility.
3. Members do not understand how to do their tasks or how to work as part of a team.
4. Members do not accept or believe in the function, purpose, or goals of the team effort.
5. Members reject their roles or responsibilities.

To add further insight to the group process, and hoping to build stronger collegiality, Frederick County published a compilation of the characteristics of productive and unproductive teams (see Table 10–1). Out of these characteristics of productive teams, teachers have commented that one of the most helpful is knowing exactly what your role is within the team itself.

Missions and Goals

This stage of planning is one of the most important because here is where the blueprint for the future of the individual school is created. According to Lezotte, the school team must now ask the question: What will constitute evidence of school improvement in our school?

This question will initiate a discussion on the present functioning and future needs of the students and the school as a whole, as well as how the school fits in with the district's mission and goals. The mission statement must now be examined with an eye to the individual school. How is the mission being carried out and how is it reflected in what we expect in outcomes? (See Figures 10–13 and 10–14.) As the discussion continues, the input from the various members and their constituencies within the school will begin to form an outline of the prospective mission for this school. This mission statement usually involves the educational, emotional, philosophical, and social development of the entire school.

The mission can be as simply stated as "Every Child Will Learn" or can be a longer, more detailed statement emphasizing key areas of concern in the school against which progress will be evaluated. Many schools form a mission statement that is very similar to that for the Spring Branch Independent School District: "S.B.I.S.D. is committed to providing a quality education to meet the needs of a diverse student body. Every learner will have the opportunity to be challenged, successful, and prepared for a future as a responsive and productive citizen. The district believes that quality education will provide students the opportunity

TABLE 10–1 • *Characteristics of Productive and Unproductive Teams*

Productive Teams	*Unproductive Teams*
All members are working together toward common goals which are well understood and accepted.	Members are unclear of their and other's goals and priorities and what the overall goals of the team are.
Clear assignments are made and accepted.	There is unnecessary duplication of effort. Some things just don't get done, they seem to "fall between the cracks."
Team leader encourages a supportive and cooperative versus competitive relationship among members.	Team members seem to be pulling in different directions. Team productivity is low.
Frequently the team will examine and discuss how it is functioning.	Decisions are not followed up as well as they could be. Meetings are ineffective, dull, and get off the subject.
Team has high participation in discussion. Communication takes place. Members listen to one another, do not topic jump and are free in expressing feelings and ideas.	Communications are blocked, messages are not received—some people don't know what is happening. Communications are primarily up and down, little laterally. People are very careful about what they say.
People are involved and interested and the atmosphere is informal and relaxed. The team is comfortable with conflict and carefully examines and resolves it.	Members of the team are frequently in conflict and conflict is suppressed. Team morale is low, people are grumbling.

Reprinted with permission of Frederick County Public Schools.

- to develop the ability to think logically, independently, and creatively,
- to communicate effectively,
- to develop appreciation for self and other people, times and cultures,
- to develop appreciation for the arts,
- to develop health fitness, and
- to build responsibility to local, state, national and world communities."

FIGURE 10–13 • *Developing Campus Improvement Plans*

Overview of the Process

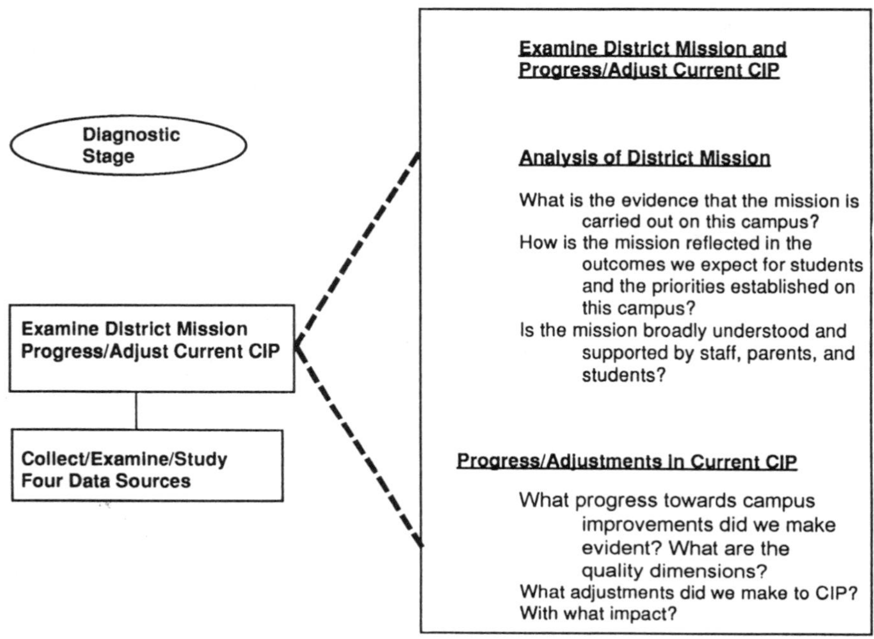

Spring Branch Independent School District.

At the Hollibrook Elementary School, the campus improvement team thought the district mission statement covered the issues of equity and quality for their school and decided their mission statement needed to be more personal—perhaps what might be referred to today as more "user friendly":

"Hollibrook Elementary School is a school where students are respected as individuals and accept responsibility for their choices and actions. Students are supported by staff and parents who care enough to let them explore, grow, experience, challenge, and reach for personal success and academic excellence!"

And the team developed a set of goals for the 1989–1992 time period:

"Hollibrook is a school where children feel they are respected. As respected individuals, students therefore learn and achieve at their maximum level in a safe, orderly, and caring environment.

"Hollibrook is a school where ALL children accelerate their learning and develop the cognitive and social skills needed to participate successfully in school.

"Hollibrook is a school where teachers feel supported and competent and make decisions about what is taught, how it is taught, and how the school is organized for learning.

"Hollibrook is a school where ALL parents feel welcome and respected and join as partners with teachers to support the learning of their children."

The goals at Hollibrook address the correlates of the Effective Schools Process as they relate to this individual school. The focus or mission: Respect for children. The environment: A school where *all* children accelerate their learning. The teachers: Teachers are supported and have a strong role in decisions. The parents: Respected and welcome.

The progress, or lack of it, at the Hollibrook will be described in terms of its mission, goals, and objectives. Everyone knows what policies, procedures, and practices they can expect at Hollibrook; it is all in the written statements.

A visit to Hollibrook proves that this mission statement and goals are

FIGURE 10–14 • ***Developing Campus Improvement Plans***

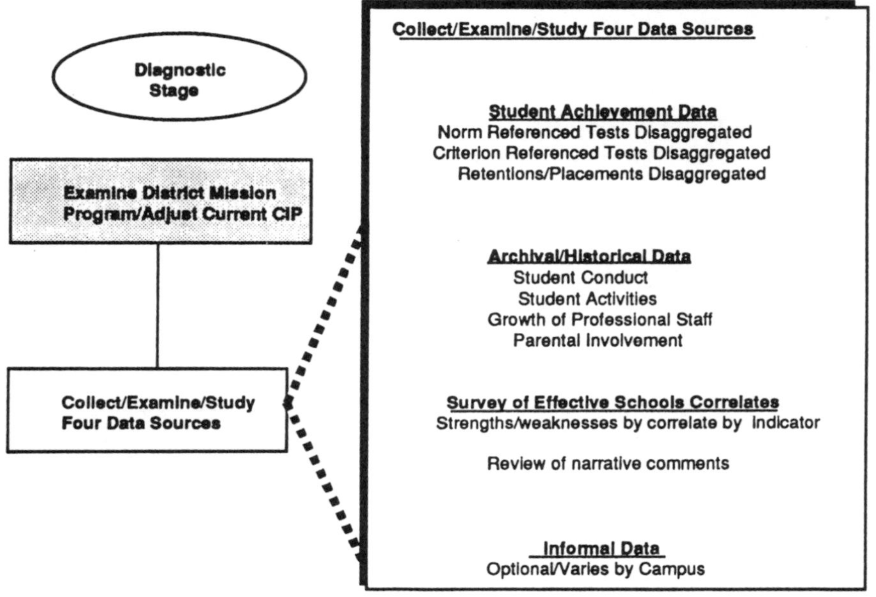

Spring Branch Independent School District.

not just a group of nice sounding words. The mission and goals are at work constantly. The children are respected and they return that respect. They accept responsibility for everything, from breaking into a run in a corridor to helping a classmate. Discipline problems are almost nonexistent. You won't even find a locked door at Hollibrook. Computers and supplies are out in the open.

Children at Hollibrook work at their own level, earning placement into special programs and rewards and incentives from faculty and staff. Cultures join, not collide. Creativity and imagination abound, from students and teachers. The faculty has considerable power in the instructional focus of their classes as well as in the day-to-day operation. Parents *are* welcome. There is a special parents' room and they are encouraged to meet with faculty or the principal whenever they desire.

"We have a different student body than schools on the other side of town (wealthy, predominantly white). And our students have different needs," said Still. "In teaching those students, our teachers were taking on responsibilities they never had before. For that reason, we had to make sure the teachers knew they had the power they needed to make the necessary changes. And we had to make sure the community knew that, above all, this school was for their children. And their children deserve our respect." She adds, "And we wanted to make that known in our mission statement and objectives. It's important that everyone knows and understands what we're about. And it helps us to be reminded of that as we work together to renew the school."

Once the mission and the goals of the school improvement team have been agreed upon by the team itself, the results must be shared with the entire school to seek their unanimous support. In many schools, teachers have reported that they were initially shocked at the work of the improvement team—shocked for the better. They were surprised at the degree of insight and hard work that had gone into the mission and goal-setting process. Many who may have still been thinking this improvement process was to be another nebulous flash in the pan realized that the team was serious, that Effective Schools research was making a difference in the future of their school. A sense of sharing and cooperation was growing stronger throughout the school. The school became even more enthused about their improvement process and were eager for the team to move onto the next stage, which would take a fine mirror to the school and its educational process.

Diagnosis: What's Really Going On Here?

The diagnosis phase of the Effective Schools Improvement Process is one of the most distinguishing features of the structure. School reform cannot be done adequately without a close examination of the school itself, and this goes far beyond peeking into test scores and the cleanliness of the bathrooms. Along with examining the school's commitment to the district mission and goals, this diagnosis includes a very intense analysis of the functioning of the school and the students, faculty, and staff.

Practitioners point out the importance of individual schools analyzing their own compliance with the district mission statement because schools can very often become so involved with their own distinct problem areas that they overlook the main objectives of the district. To bring all schools into alignment—and to have the teams working on the same goals—builds unity within the school system. It also gives ready reminders that this school improvement is districtwide. It gives teachers and principals common areas of discussion. A principal at one school can say to another, "We're having a terrible time finding a program to help us build responsibility among our students to their local and state governments." The other principal can offer help by mentioning programs initiated on her or his school site.

The district mission is usually broken down into key areas, and different members of the team analyze a given area, like policy changes, curricular development, or professional standards. This helps the team begin the early assessment of activities of its own campus, and it also gives the team concrete objectives in the disposition of their analytical process.

One of the common areas needing help in many district plans is the call for an appreciation and development of programs in diverse cultures. The emphasis on multiculturalism is considered so important that districts place it in their premiere statement, rather than wait for schools to endorse it. And many schools, especially those with predominantly white, middle-class enrollments, are not quite ready for this emphasis on multiculturalism. Many districts find themselves conducting special workshops and seminars to handle the concern over multiculturalism and to present individual programs in a way that is responsible and effective.

"What happens when you review mission statements and improvement plans is that you find areas where you need help," explains Bob Wells, head of staff development in Spring Branch. "So the teams come back to us and say, 'How are we supposed to know how to handle this? We've never faced this before.' And instead of just saying, 'Do the best you can,' we look into where we can get information on this and how we can get it to our people."

Effective districts emphasize that this process is research based and data guided. No programs are put in just because they sound good or fill a gap; they have to have the reason and research in back of them. Many teams find that in this analysis of how their schools fit in with the rest of the system, they enter new areas of learning for themselves and their students. This stage, as in the others, should reinforce for faculty and staff the feeling that this is a process that is affecting every corner and crevice of the school system—that it is a process, not an event.

As the implementation moves forward through the years, this will also become the stage where the school improvement team will look at its own, current improvement plan and decide where the school is succeeding or falling short in its objectives and goals. Figure 10–13 shows how, at this stage, annual adjustments are made in the plan, as well as assessments of the plan's overall impact.

Self-Analysis: The Needs Assessment

There are four types of data that are used in this assessment: student achievement data, archival/historical data, survey of Effective Schools correlates, and informal data based on the needs of the individual campus (see Figure 10–14).

For most schools, this needs assessment will be a new process, and it is often one that creates considerable acrimony among the faculty and staff. Here is where a strong leader keeps firm hold of the helm, making sure that factions are not created within the school, and that everyone knows this is not a process of pointing fingers of blame but simply and essentially an improvement process.

Schools will have their achievement data on hand, but most schools will not have entered into the process of disaggregating that data. The data must be disaggregated in order for the school to determine how effectively it is serving the *entire* student population.

Most schools disaggregate on the basis of low and high socioeconomic status, gender, and ethnic group. The socioeconomic status is determined by one of two main factors: whether or not the child is on free or reduced lunch and/or the level of the mother's education.

Once these scores are disaggregated, the school can see exactly how it is serving its population—and not just the school in general, but individual classrooms. Depending on how the disaggregation is presented, this can come as either a threat to the teachers or an opportunity for improvement for their students. Here, once again, if the district leadership and the school leadership have done their job in convincing the district that this is a process of improvement for *all*—administrators and faculty as well as students—the disaggregation will cause some anguish but not revolt.

The first time principals and teachers look at their disaggregated scores, there is shock and dismay. The usual comment is "We thought we were doing a much better job than this. We had no idea we were not serving those kids at the lower socioeconomic level."

This disaggregation is difficult because teachers are forced to realize that they must alter their instructional methods and often their attitudes. The school district must be ready with funds for staff development programs in place and welcoming—not threatening—to teachers and staff. The principal must ensure the faculty that "we are in this together and together we will change this."

The disaggregation must be at all levels, not just within the school but within the data itself. The school's norm-referenced tests, as well as criterion-referenced tests, must be analyzed. Also, data on school dropouts, discipline infractions, student retentions, truancy, and absenteeism must be included in order to get a *complete* picture of the school.

Along with the disaggregation of the scores comes the assessment of how the school does in providing and living up to the seven correlates of Effective Schools (safe and orderly environment, focused mission, climate of high expectations, opportunity to learn and time on task, frequent monitoring, instructional leadership, and home-school relations). These assessments are given to *every* member of the school community. Secretaries and custodians would, of course, not answer those questions that directly involve teachers.

The most common instrument for this is the Connecticut School Questionnaire, one of the first needs assessment instruments developed for Effective Schools. There are others now, including those created in New York, San Diego, and the University of Washington in Seattle. And some schools, after being involved in the process for as little as a year, find it beneficial to create their own questionnaires. Many districts find it most productive to bring in a professional facilitator to deconstruct the responses.

But all of these questionnaires are similar and the questions are broken up into the areas of the seven correlates. For example, in the area of instructional leadership, some sample questions to be answered (by strongly agree, agree, undecided, disagree, strongly disagree) might be:

- My principal is an important instructional resource in the school.
- My principal communicates clearly to me regarding instructional matters.
- My principal's evaluation of my performance helps me improve my teaching.

Concerning staff, some questions might be:

- People in our building seek out training experiences that increase their ability to educate students.
- We are committed to working together as a faculty.
- Staff in our building have a great deal of trust.

Concerning high expectations, questions might be:

- Nearly all of my students will be at or above grade level by the end of this year.

- Teachers in my school generally believe most students are able to master the basic reading/math skills.
- Most of the students in my school will ultimately graduate from high school.

The assessment, always anonymous, never fails to cause concern, even rancor, among faculty members and the principal. In fact, the results have been so devastating for some principals that they have responded with resignation, believing they could never work in a climate where they are held in such low regard. Other principals, after swallowing some bile with their pride, set out to make the necessary changes. But district officials are always quick to point out that a principal is never removed on the basis of the needs assessment questionnaires. It is up to the principal to improve and bring back the trust of his or her faculty. If that trust cannot be earned, the failure shows itself in many areas other than just the questionnaire.

The results of the questionnaire come to the principals first. There are stories of principals wanting to burn the results, lock them away, lose them, change the name to another school and send them to that principal, or simply ignore them. The needs assessment brush is broad, and the teachers also take their blows. It is one thing for an individual teacher to think that her class will not make it to grade level, but what if that teacher finds out through the questionnaire results that the majority of teachers think that? Or what if that teacher sees that only *one* teacher thought that?

"Oh, we had some tough times going through those assessments," recalls Bob Sudlow of Spencerport, New York. "This was the first time we had done anything like that, and the results were shocking. It proved that no one, the teachers or the principals, had the school that they thought they had."

Because the questionnaires are broken down into specific areas (the correlates), the team can see where they have to do their work. They can also see where there is need for basic attitudinal changes by comparing student test scores with the questionnaire results.

If you have 70 percent of your low socioeconomic students performing below grade level, and your questionnaire shows that the majority of your teachers don't believe *all* children can learn, then your school has a lot of staff development ahead of it.

The questionnaires, especially those developed by individual districts or schools, often enter areas that go beyond the specific parameters of the seven correlates. For example, many schools now get right into the multicultural arena:

- The teaching styles in our school are sensitive to the ethnic and cultural diversity of our students.

Or gender equity concerns:

- Staff members of our school have the same expectations of academic achievement for both female and male students.

The results are shared with the entire school community. Positives are emphasized and a strong leader will present proposals for improvement at the same time that leader releases the assessment results.

The analysis of the school does not stop with the needs assessment and the test scores, as depicted in the outline for data collection for the Spring Branch School System in Figure 10–15. The improvement team must look at how the school is functioning behind and beyond scores and assessments. What is going on in student activities? How are the students doing in communicating with faculty? What role are the parents playing in the school? Is the school involving itself in necessary business or university partnerships, state and federal multiculturalism? Is the school acting creatively in the development of programs to involve *all* students (such as school businesses or school fairs)? And if the school is having a problem in communicating with parents who may have already been failed by the educational system, is it recognizing it, and is it trying to do something about it?

What about the history of the school? Does the archival data on students or faculty give any hints about how to handle present problems? And what about the teachers? Have they been served adequately by staff development in the past and is there a way to make that development more effective in the nineties? Are the teacher evaluations being done effectively? What about faculty daily attendance? Is it as strong as it should be? And what about this thing called the community or neighborhood the school resides in? Is the school an active, positive element of that community? Are there ways to further involve the community with the school? What are the neighborhood's concerns?

There are also informal surveys that can be used in this analysis of the individual school. Some schools send out parent surveys to inquire what the parents really think about their local school. What do they think about bus service, guidance counselors, report cards, homework, the discipline code, instruction, curriculum, health services, the principal?

Ironically, despite the fact that parents are affected daily and dramatically by the ongoings of their child's school, very rarely are parents asked to comment on that school. The next time you're at a gathering where parents of schoolchildren are in attendance, ask them if they have ever answered a survey on the performance of their child's school, its faculty, and principal. Yes, parents are welcome at PTA meetings, but schools seem to be frightened of having a written record of exactly how parents feel about their child's school.

FIGURE 10–15 • *Outline for Data Collection*

Campus Improvement Plan

Three kinds of data are collected and used in the needs assessment process associated with effective school planning at each campus site. These data are:

- Student Achievement Data
- Archival or Historical Data
- Survey Data Related to Effective School Correlates

I. Student Achievement Data
disaggregated or sorted according to Socio-Economic Status (SES) based on meal program or mother's level of education or father's level of education if mother's is unavailable.

   A. Tests
      1. Norm-Referenced
      2. Criterion-Referenced
   B. Other Learning Outcomes as Available
      1. Grades (A–F), Overall Grade Average in Core Content Areas
      2. Percent of Retention by Grade Level

II. Archival or Historical Data
at least one previous school year prior to implementation of the Campus Improvement Plan
   A. Student Conduct (may be disaggregated by SES and/or Ethnicity)
   B. Student Activities (may be disaggregated by SES and/or Ethnicity)
   C. Professional Growth of Staff
      1. Staff Development Participation
      2. Teacher Appraisals
      3. Staff Attendance
   D. Parental Involvement
      1. PTA Membership
      2. School Volunteers
      3. Parent-School Activities

III. Survey Data Related to Effective School Correlates
focus on school performance related to the "correlates" or characteristics of "effective schools" as discovered in the research by Edmonds, Lezotte, et al.
   A. Elementary: use a version of the Connecticut School Questionnaire (i.e., SBISD Survey of Effective School Correlates)
   B. Secondary: use a version of the Connecticut School Questionnaire (i.e., SBISD Survey of Effective School Correlates)

   OUTPUT DATA = Student Achievement — (I)
   INPUT DATA = Archival/Historical and Survey — (II & III)

Both Student Achievement Data and Archival or Historical Data should be updated at the end of each school year by the Campus Planning Team and other appropriate school staff members. Survey Data Related to Effective School Correlates should be updated one year following the first administration of the instrument and every other school year thereafter.

IV. Informal Data

Spring Branch Independent School District.

And what about the students themselves? Some schools are now asking the students what they think about their school. Principals report that the results are very often illuminating, even when done at the elementary level. They can show biases felt by students, as well as lapses in instructional practices and desires for additional programs.

In analyzing these data, the principal must, right from the start, look at the glass as half full, not half empty. There will be things to celebrate as the data begin to roll in, and the principal should give as much time to the positives as the negatives—not just for the sake of morale, but because there will be important lessons within those areas of success.

What all these surveys accomplish is bringing the school community together. Participation builds *ownership* in the school and its improvement efforts. The more involved everyone feels—from teachers to students and parents and secretarial staff and custodians—the more Effective the school will be. Indeed, telltale signs of the effectiveness of a school can be detected as soon as a visitor enters the front door. If the school is clean, it shows a pride from the custodial staff, a sense of ownership. They treat it like their own. And the secretaries? If they are energetic, proud of their school, and gladly welcome parents, it shows their sense of ownership. On the other hand, if you walk into a school with littered hallways and a secretary that sits behind a glass wall and mumbles something about how busy everyone is and acts unhappy and bothered by your presence, it is obvious there is little or no pride, and no ownership, real or desired.

Practitioners emphasize that it is for reasons like these that the *entire* school be involved in the diagnosis stage of the school improvement planning. And through adequate feedback sessions, the entire faculty can be involved, to a much lesser extent than the planning team, in the analysis of these data. The more ownership people feel they have in their school, the harder it is to ignore the call for improvement, and the harder they will work to improve that school and themselves. Also, when the positive results start to come in, it means that everyone can take a bow and know they deserve it.

"What we're talking about here—disaggregation, needs assessment—it all makes great common sense," says Noel Farmer, superintendent of Frederick County Public Schools. "What doesn't make sense is why schools are not doing this. We've proven that these steps form the structure for an Effective School Improvement Process. The tools and the research are all right there."

As Farmer points out in his annual report, very few districts take the necessary school improvement steps. Only 42 percent of the nation's more than 15,000 school districts have programs of school improvement, and only 27 percent of those do collaborative planning between teachers and principal. Only 11 percent of those disaggregate scores, and only *1* percent of those evaluate progress and publish their results.

Creating the Plan

Once the school/campus improvement team has met with the entire school community and received their reaction and input on the information garnered in the data collection stage, it is then time for the team to regroup and decide how they are going to make that information go to work for the sake of school improvement. But before the team goes off into their separate rooms and meetings, it is important that they let the rest of the school community know that they will be doing nothing without the school's approval, that they will be sharing in planning and reporting back to the school in search of additional input. At no time should the school community think they are not involved in the creation of this improvement plan. They are as much a part of it as the team itself. They must feel they have as much ownership as the team; otherwise, the implementation of the plan will be difficult and spotty.

Staff development is continuing and expanding as the improvement process moves along. The school team should still be in leadership training as well as courses in organizational and group process skills and the ongoing change process. Because the entire district is moving along on the same time line, this staff development will be up to date and accessible for all.

Faculty and staff outside of the school improvement team should also be attending development classes. These can range from additional work in the Effective Schools Research Process to workshops in elevating teaching skills for diversified student populations. And once the schools see their needs assessment, it may be necessary for the principal to bring in experts on behavior, multiculturalism, and, of course, new instructional techniques. The important thing here is that no faculty or staff member feels that he or she is "out of the loop"—that if there are problems, he or she cannot receive the necessary help and guidance. It becomes a responsibility of the principal and the improvement team to make sure there is always the necessary support structure for any and all faculty and staff members. Although the team is working to improve the school for the students—this being its first priority—it must keep in mind that no school is Effective unless the teachers also feel that they are growing and improving along with their students.

The school improvement team now has a large pile of data concerning the individual school. There is much to work from, distinct directions to be taken, and, in many areas, already obvious goals that must be reached no sooner than yesterday.

There are some districts purporting to be "effective" that have never gone through a needs assessment. Data may have been disaggregated, but teachers have never seen a survey on their feelings toward the school. How these schools then put together a worthy improvement plan intrigues effective practitioners. The reasons for failure seem obvious.

The advantage that the needs assessment questionnaires give the improvement team is that they break down the potential problem areas into distinct categories — namely, the correlates and additional survey arenas. As illustrated in Figure 10–16, the team can look at the evidence before them and ask: OK, so where are we, where would we like to be, and how do we get there? And if we get there, how will we know if we arrive?

The best way to tackle the task of creating the plan is to once again divide the team into correlates and specific problem areas. One group, for example, would work on the *frequent monitoring* characteristic, another, on *high expectations* or *school environment.* Each group would look at the mandate and research of the correlate, the district's philosophy for that correlate, the school's mission statement, and then the information received from the various data sources.

The *high expectations* group would look at the disaggregated test scores, the attitudes of teachers and principal (and staff), and, if available, any archival data, as well as dropout rates, absenteeism, and student surveys. After reviewing this material as it directly relates to high expectations, the group then offers its analysis of exactly where the school sits.

The next step would be for the group to decide where the school should be in dealing with high expectations, taking into consideration school and district mandates as well as Effective Schools research. It is now that the vision for the new school must be clearly articulated. Only then does the group begin to set down objectives for the school in the area of high expectations. By working

FIGURE 10–16 • *Developing Campus Improvement Plans*

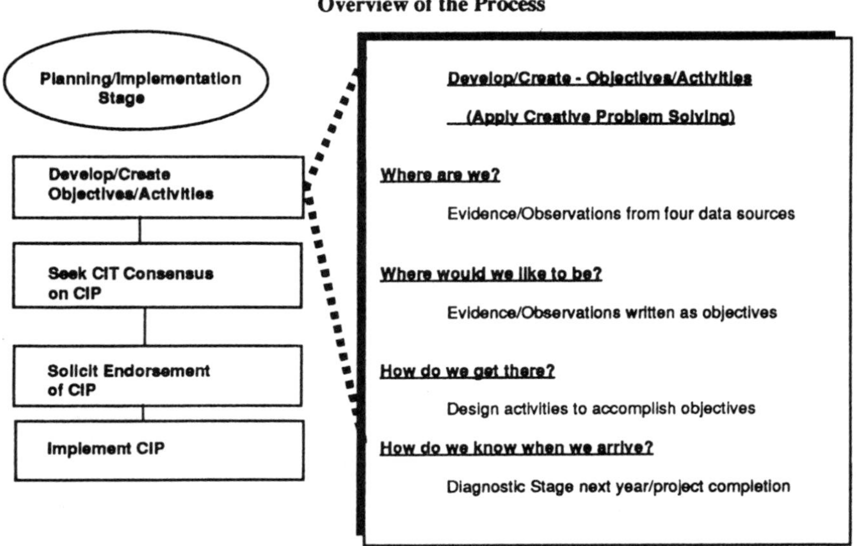

Spring Branch Independent School District.

this way, the group, and therefore the entire team by the time the work is done, achieves a thorough working knowledge of this correlate.

Every group submits its objectives to the improvement team as a whole. The objectives are discussed again, with a review of the correlate and the school data. The entire team then gives its approval to the objectives of improvement for that correlate. And now the group goes back into its corner to determine the best way to accomplish the agreed upon objectives.

"It looks like a very 'task-oriented' process," explains Gary Mathews from Spring Branch, the district that works with such a plan. "But in fact, it is very 'people oriented' and that is its strength. You have constant discourse among the subgroups, the larger team itself, and then the school community. People understand exactly where they are going, from the correlates to the objectives to the means of accomplishing those objectives."

This discourse is essential, says Mathews, in order to expand the process beyond the creation of simple activity-based improvement plans. He recalls that in Spring Branch in the first year of planning when the teams did not use this systemic approach, the plans were marked by "multiple, nonfocused events." Planning systemically has created activities that are data based and objectives based, and from which priorities can be set. The source of these activities, or strategies for improvement, is once again the data and research available in the Effective Schools Process. The days of gimmicks are over in this district. When the group presents its strategies to the team, and the team to the faculty, there will be no room for, "Well, it just feels right."

Selling the Plan

The first people who have to agree with the smaller groups' means of achieving its objectives are the other members of the improvement team. They have already approved the group's objectives. Now they find the road to accomplish those objectives (or, as Spring Branch refers to it, the "do" part of the plan). This process is depicted in Figure 10–17.

As the group explains the activities or strategies to the entire improvement team, they must at the same time present data supporting the proposals. This allows the time and opportunity for team members to become immersed in additional research that may be useful in accomplishing other improvement objectives.

Spring Branch has discovered that as the group presents each activity, it should request that the team assess that activity on the basis of the following three criteria:

- Will the activity become practice? (i.e., What will be the impact? Is this more likely to be an event rather than ongoing?)

FIGURE 10–17 • *Developing Campus Improvement Plans*

Overview of the Process

Planning/Implementation Stage	Seek CIT Consensus on CIP (Apply Criteria for Decision Making)
Develop/Create Objectives/Activities	CIP reflects input from a variety of sources
Seek CIT Consensus on CIP	CIP reflects objectives/activities judged as having the greatest impact, quality, and immediacy while supporting the district mission
Solicit Endorsement of CIP	CIP consistent with effective schools principles and correlates
Implement CIP	CIP is supported by research
	CIP is clearly formated

Spring Branch Independent School District.

- Is the activity important? (i.e., What is the quality dimension?)
- Is the proposed activity consistent with Effective Schools practices?

The entire improvement team should judge the activities on this basis. Figure 10–18 is an example of this judgment procedure. As the criteria for change are discussed and the checklist is put together, the growing dialogue again works to pull the entire team into alignment. Also, by using specific criteria for judgment, there are no personality squabbles. Team members do not get into a battle over personal ownership of an activity. The process remains professional and objective.

Once the criteria have been analyzed, it is then up to the team as a whole to either accept, amend, or reject the suggested activities. Some strategies may be delayed for six months or a year, or merely postponed because certain members of the team would like to see more research before making their decision. Whatever decision is made, however, must be unanimous or at least consensual. There can be no division among the team members. Each and every member must agree with the means of accomplishing the objective in order not to create rifts in the faculty further down the road. And an approach must never be taken because, "Well, we just did that because the principal wanted it."

In the final written plan to be presented to the faculty, the team must be precise in its action plans. Each call for change should include:

FIGURE 10–18 • ***Examining the Procedure***

Correlate: Expectations **Rationale:** Although student achievement is improving, no improvement was shown in retention, expulsion, and dropout rates. The gap between SES groups remain the same.	Analysis Criteria		
	Will it become Practice? (Impact)	Is it important? (Quality)	Is it consistent with effective school Principle/research?
Idea 1 Objective: To increase the number of students who are successful in school Act. 1 - Use incentives and rewards to improve attendance in tutorials. Act. 2 - Form a discipline management committee to monitor discipline referrals and find ways to decrease them. Act. 3 - Form a committee to improve the honor roll system to include more students and improving students. Act. 4 - Give students who master unit tests a class period of free time as a reward. Act. 5 - Begin the school year with stress on the importance of grades in student assembly.			

CAMPUS IMPROVEMENT PLAN

____
SCHOOL

CORRELATIVE: ____________________

OBJECTIVE: ____________________

____

RATIONALE: ____________________

____

ACTIVITIES	RESOURCES & STAFF	COMPLETION EVIDENCE/DATE	PROGRESS &/or ADJUSTMENTS

APPROVED: ____________________ DATE:
Executive Director

- The rationale for identifying it as a priority (with reference to mission, goals, and correlates)
- The strategies or activities selected to meet the improvement objective
- A flowchart, table, or narrative description of the implementation plan for each strategy
- Procedures for monitoring progress toward the objective

And before the plan is presented to the entire school, the improvement team must have answered the who, what, where, when, how, and why of each step of the plan:

- Persons responsible—who prepares, plans, leads, coordinates?
- Persons involved—exactly who does it affect?
- Resources needed—will they be provided?
- Time line
- Indicators of progress and procedures for monitoring

School Approval

If the lines of communication have been open throughout the improvement team's planning process, the task of achieving the backing of the entire school will not be difficult. The school should have been kept up to date on the team's machinations, including regular reports of the team's efforts and progress.

The principal also is key when it comes to winning school approval. Throughout this process, an Effective principal would have fostered and maintained an atmosphere of true collegiality and collaboration. The school should be excited about its improvement efforts. And the faculty and staff should be anxious to get started and help out their colleagues.

The plan should be presented in a manner that invites and encourages feedback. At the same time, the plan should be very specific. In every area of concern (the correlates), there should first be the statement of the improvement objective which can be operationalized. Then comes the rationale for the need for action. This will involve the school in the same data and needs assessment that they were a part of in the earlier stages of development. The activities and strategies should then be mapped out, along with a flowchart and procedures for monitoring.

Hopefully the improvement team and the entire school now see the improvement process as something that is not going to go away and is not going to be dealt with by a few patches of fix-it programs here and there. The faculty and staff should see the improvement plan as a living, breathing process that will grow with the school and the available knowledge. It is something that involves *everyone* and is a threat to no one.

Faculty feedback should lead to adjustment of the plan. This is something that should not be dreaded by the improvement team, but anticipated positively. This is not the "pet plan" of a chosen few; it is the plan for the entire school community. The planning team could not have anticipated every problem with an activity or strategy. As seen in Figure 10–19, the team must be ready, with plans in place to overcome some of the anticipated obstacles to the finer nuances of implementation.

Implementing the Plan

Once the faculty and staff have approved the plan, there should be special meetings held with parents and/or community leaders to inform them of the improvement changes. The central office will have been involved throughout the planning process—in either a minor or major role depending on the vitality and strength of the improvement team itself. But now that the plan is approved by the school itself, it can be made public to anyone in or outside the school system.

The objectives and strategies of the plan should be written in a simple, straightforward manner that can be understood by all members of the school community (this must also include translation into Spanish, Vietnamese, etc.). Examples of how one school in Frederick County presented its plans and

FIGURE 10–19 • *Developing Campus Improvement Plans*

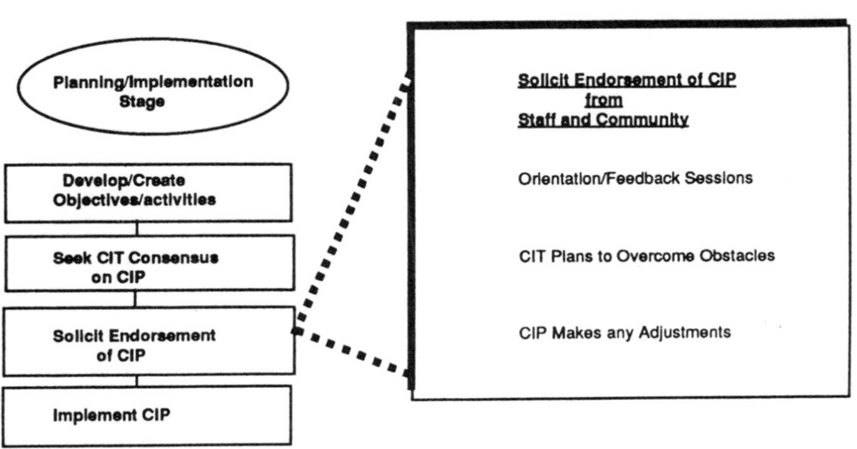

Spring Branch Independent School District.

FIGURE 10–20 • *Frederick County School Improvement Progress Report (1990–1991)*

School: Hamilton High School DATE: March 14, 1991

SCHOOL MISSION STATEMENT:
Teaching for Quality Learning for all Students

STUDENT DEMOGRAPHIC INFORMATION:

TOTAL ENROLLMENT: 924

GENDER %		RACE %		SES %	
MALE	51%	WHITE	85%	LOW	13%
FEMALE	49%	BLACK	12%	MIDDLE	58%
		OTHER	3%	HIGH	29%
				NO RESPONSE	0%

SYSTEM GOAL/CORRELATE:
GOAL E. The percentage of student attendance will increase annually.

SCHOOL GOAL/CORRELATE:
* Increase student attendance

SUMMARY OF STRATEGIES:
Lottery for perfect attendance rewards
Daily phone calls to verify absences
Saturday school for unexcused absences

OUTCOMES:
- Schoolwide attendance increased from 89% to 92%.
- White students, female students and mid/high SES students have met the 95% goal.
- Male students improved from 87% to 90%, black students improved from 84% to 87% while low SES students remained at 82%.

*Eventual system goal is 95%

STATUS OF SCHOOL GOAL/CORRELATE:
____ ACHIEVED
_X_ IMPROVEMENT NOTED
____ NO IMPROVEMENT/DECLINE
_X_ GOAL CONTINUED NEXT YEAR

COMMENTS:
Next year's School Improvement Plan will have to concentrate heavily on improving attendance for low SES students.

FIGURE 10–21 • ***Frederick County School Improvement Progress Report (1990–1991)***

SCHOOL: Hamilton High School

SYSTEM GOAL/CORRELATE:
GOAL A. Criterion reference standards will show annual increases in the percentage of students at the respective grade level who attain essential objectives of the curriculum.

SCHOOL GOAL/CORRELATE:
Increase the percentage of students with grades of "C" or better.

SUIMMARY OF STRATEGIES:
Student advisement program
Increased use of computer-assisted instruction in mathematics and science classes
Math "walk-in" clinic
Staff development training in
TESA
GESA
Mastery Learning
Mastery Teaching

OUTCOMES:
Percentages increased from 78% to 81% in total grades for all courses with all student sub-groupings showing increased percentages.
Specific course grades improved for
Male students in math and science
Female students in English, social studies, math and science
White students in English, social studies, math and science
Black students in math and science
Mid/High SES and Low SES students in math and science
Some narrowing of gender differences is evident in English and math, but course grades in all subjects continue to vary by gender, race and SES status.

STATUS OF SCHOOL GOAL/CORRELATE:
_______ ACHIEVED
___X___ IMPROVEMENT NOTED
_______ NO IMPROVEMENT/DECLINE
___X___ GOAL CONTINUED NEXT YEAR

COMMENTS:
Improvement is noted with all student sub-groups showing increased percentages, but emphasis needs to be placed upon providing consistency in course grades in all subjects.

strategies for change—and then how the team perceived the school's progress in key areas—are shown in Figure 10-20 and 10-21.

With its tasks laid out, the improvement team must now implement the plan. As seen in Figure 10-22, the actual implementation of the plan is just another beginning in the ongoing implementation process. The team must continue to meet regularly to monitor and report on that school's progress, as well as any changes being made at the district level. A time line will have been established and the team must not slouch in its monitoring. It must look for specific results as well as keep its ears open for negative feedback.

It may be that one or more activities just do not work out at this particular time and have to be withdrawn. The team has to be careful here to make sure they continue to do everything by a consensus, among themselves and with the rest of the school. Any modifications in the plan must be approved by the team as well as the rest of the school.

When progress starts to be shown, the principal and improvement team members must be ready to sound the call to the entire school community. Everyone must be continually reminded that school improvement is not static but ongoing. Progress in one area can lead to progress in another area. Lack of progress means another thing: Try harder, and perhaps try harder with a

FIGURE 10–22 · *Developing Campus Improvement Plans*

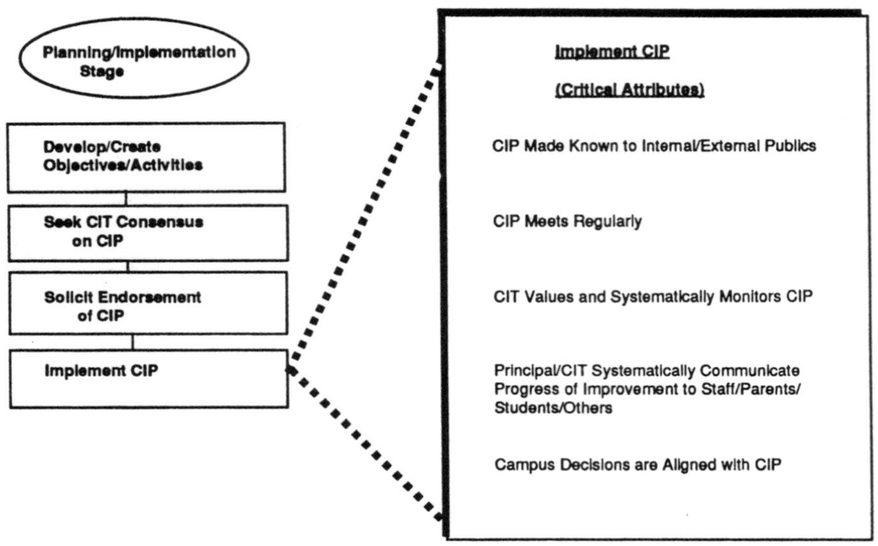
Overview of the Process
Planning/Implementation Stage
Develop/Create Objectives/Activities
Seek CIT Consensus on CIP
Solicit Endorsement of CIP
Implement CIP
Implement CIP
(Critical Attributes)
CIP Made Known to Internal/External Publics
CIP Meets Regularly
CIT Values and Systematically Monitors CIP
Principal/CIT Systematically Communicate Progress of Improvement to Staff/Parents/Students/Others
Campus Decisions are Aligned with CIP

Spring Branch Independent School District.

different approach. The objectives of the school plan will not go away until they are met. And the only way they will be met is through effective strategies based on the correlates that have the support and involvement of the entire school community.

When the school scores, there should be a celebration. Some schools have special parent nights or teacher banquets to celebrate when they have achieved an objective. The school spirit around an improvement plan can be, and should be, as important as any spirit around a winning sports team. As Effective Schools research has shown, when one child loses, the whole school loses. So when a group of students starts to fly high, that entire school should be airborn.

The school should be well aware at this point that school improvement—at the district and school levels—is an alive, ongoing process. Time lines should be drawn up at both the school and district levels with the school improvement team in tight step with the district process. Figure 10–23 reproduces the time line of Frederick County, from the core initiation in 1987 to full-blown school improvement planning—and its coordination with central office planning—through 1992.

This review of the *structure for a process* for implementation of school improvement via Effective Schools reminds one of that slogan often heard around improving districts: "It's simple, it just isn't easy." It's simple in relation to the fact that every step of school improvement stems from, and returns to, the heart of Effective Schools—the correlates. And the correlates are purely and simply organizational design variables to be manipulated in the strategic planning and implementation process. (Organizational theory has addressed organizational design for over 40 years.) It isn't easy because it requires at its essence two commodities that are in short supply in U.S. education: time and will.

But the hopeful aspect of all this is that it has been shown that whether you call it a *structure for a process*, a *reform plan*, or a *vehicle for school improvement*, the means to successful school improvement—at the district and school levels—does exist. There is no need for multimillion dollar studies—just the need for committed, informed people with the will to make a difference.

FIGURE 10–23 • *Time Line for Effective School Improvement Process, Frederick County, Maryland (1987–1992)*

1987–1988
SEPTEMBER–APRIL

- System planning year with System Steering Committee to review and organize the Effective School/School Improvement Process for implementation.
- Establishment of 8 student outcome-based system goals.
- Board of Education adoption of policy to support the mission of the Effective School/School Improvement Process and 8 outcome-based system goals.
- Arrangement for administration and supervisory staff orientation to Effective School/School Improvement Process.

1988–1989
SEPTEMBER–APRIL

- Central/area offices will identify strategies and resources for correlates
- Training of principals
- Training of SIT (School Improvement Plan)—Lezotte
- SIT's develop tentative plans
- Involvement of total faculty

FEBRUARY

- Identification of strategies due to schools

MARCH

- Schools submit plans to area superintendents for Effective Schools

JUNE

- SIT's complete rewrite with pay (1–2 Days)

1989–1990
AUGUST

- School plans to faculty for consensus

SEPTEMBER

- Final plan due to area superintendents for Effective Schools/implementation of school plan

JUNE

- Results of plan to area superintendents for Effective Schools

FIGURE 10–23 • *Continued*

Revised August 1989
1989–1990
AUGUST-SEPTEMBER 1989

- School Improvement Teams will revise the SIP.
- SIP revision will be reviewed with the total staff and suported by the staff.
- Applications for 2 + 2 Grants due September 8, 1989.
- Principals present 2 + 2 Grant applications to committee on September 13, 1989.
- Schools informed of grant awards on September 15, 1989.
- SIT begin monitoring and implementing the SIP.

OCTOBER-JUNE 1989–1990

- School Improvement Team is responsible for monitoring the goals/correlates assuring that objectives, strategies and measures are progressing according to the planned time line.
- Perception surveys will be administered as determined by the systemwide Steering Committee.
- Staff perception surgery will be administered in May, 1990.

JUNE-AUGUST 1990

- All data will be disaggregated and analyzed.
- Results of the process toward each of the goals/correlates will be determined.
- Results of the progress toward each of the goals/correlates will be submitted to the area office on the appropriate forms. This will be the end-of-year report due to the area office in late July or early August. (Exact date to be determined.)
- The SIP will revise the SIP for 1990–91. It will be completed using the same guidelines. These guidelines are found in the *Master Plan* on pages 45–52 and in *The Training Manual* on pages 6–69. The SIT will meet during the summer, analyze the data and revise the SIP for presentation to the staff.

SEPTEMBER 1990

- SIT will present and discuss the end-of-year report during a meeting(s) with the entire staff.
- SIT will present and discuss the revised SIP with the staff. Staff support will be obtained for the revised 1990–91 SIP.
- Revised SIP will be forwarded to the area office on September 28, 1990.

OCTOBER 1990

- Area staff will analyze SIP and return a reviewed report to the school by October 31, 1990.

NOVEMBER-JUNE 1990–1991

- Revised SIP will be implemented.

Continued

FIGURE 10–23 • *Continued*

Revised August 1990
1990–1991
AUGUST-SEPTEMBER 1990

- School Improvement Teams will disaggregate and analyze the student outcome and school improvement data for the 1989–90 school year.
- School Improvement Teams will examine the student achievement in comparison to the revised system goals A-H/correlates.
- School Improvement Teams will revise the SIP.
- SIP revision will be reviewed with the total staff and supported by the staff.
- Revised SIP will be forwarded to the area office by September 28, 1990 (Plans must be completed according to the 1990–91 format for SIP included in the notebook provided.)
- Applications for 2 + 2 Grants due August 15, 1990.
- Principals present 2 + 2 Grant applications to committee on August 21, 1990.
- Schools informed of grant awards on August 24, 1990.
- SIT begin monitoring and implementing the SIP.

OCTOBER 1990

- Area staff will analyze SIP and return a review report to the school by October 31, 1990.

NOVEMBER-JUNE 1990–91

- School Improvement Team is responsible for monitoring the goals/correlates assuring that objectives, strategies and measures are progressing according to the planned time line.
- Perception surveys will be administered as determined by the systemwide Steering Committee.
- Perception surveys may be administered in May, 1990.

JUNE-AUGUST 1991

- All data will be disaggregated and analyzed.
- Results of the progress toward each of the goals/correlates will be determined.
- Results of the progress toward each of the goals/correlates will be submitted to the Area office on the appropriate forms. Progress Report #3 will be submitted to the area on July 5, 1991.
- The SIT will revise the SIP for 1991–92. It will be completed using the same guidelines. These guidelines are found in the *Master Plan* on pages 45–52 and in *The Training Manual* on pages 6–69. The SIT will meet during the summer, analyze the data and revise the SIP for presentation to the staff.

SEPTEMBER 1991

- SIT will present and discuss the end-of-year report during a meeting(s) with the entire staff.

FIGURE 10–23 • *Continued*

- SIT will present and discuss the revised SIP with the staff. Staff support will be obtained for the revised 1991–92 SIP.
- Revised SIP will be forwarded to the Area office on September 27, 1991.

OCTOBER 1991

- Area staff will analyze SIP and return a reviewed report to the school by October 31, 1991

NOVEMBER-JUNE 1991-92

- Revised SIP will be implemented.

Frederick County Public Schools.

CHAPTER ELEVEN

The Parents and Students of Effective Schools

I don't depend on parents organizing politically. If they did do that, I think it would be a fringe benefit. I don't depend on their spontaneously doing that. —RON EDMONDS

Any parent that has a choice between a school with a mission statement on the wall and a school with a blank wall has a choice between a realistic, productive future for their kid or a future of laziness and ignorance about people. I know. I didn't have a choice for one of my kids. —SPRING BRANCH (TEXAS) PARENT

I have a brother who went here before it was an Effective School. Boy, was it easier, and you could get away with anything.
—JUNCTION CITY (KANSAS) HIGH SCHOOL STUDENT

When Ron Edmonds first started gathering information and research on the Effective Schools Process, he saw that one particular variable was parental involvement. It was the factor over which the school and the research design had no control. It was also the factor that, if you made it an essential link in the school improvement process, could be used against you.

"I just am unwilling to put forth a design for school improvement that depends on parents," said Edmonds. "Because the scenario I envision is one in which the school people say, 'We tried to get parent cooperation but we didn't get it, therefore . . . .' I stick with what is inside the school because there is no way to avoid that."

This attitude from Edmonds has opened the Effective School Process up to some controversy concerning whether parents are a necessary, or even a desired, participant in the school improvement process. As more information on parental input becomes available, experts such as Larry Lezotte have been re-examining the parental component.

"I think one of the criticisms, and it's a fair criticism, is that in the initial years, we did not pay enough attention to the parent role," says Lezotte, adding that he has found it necessary to develop some "very definite language" to discuss it. "I always say that parent involvement ought to always be aggressive—if true partnerships are to be built. But I also say that no effort at school improvement can *depend* on it. In other words, you use it, but you can't use its absence as an excuse for not going forward."

So, although Effective School researchers have accepted the value of "aggressive" parental involvement, they have not moved from the position that it's still a variable, a fringe benefit. "One of the underlying principles that is buried in Effective Schools literature is that the school must have control over the necessary variables it chooses to manipulate to change the outcomes," insists Lezotte.

There is no means to discover how active a community is going to be in its school, or even what type of activity the parents will bring to the school. Principals report anticipating apathy and getting hit with rampant enthusiasm, and others say they were sure the parents would be involved, but only a handful showed up at parents' night. When parents do arrive at the school door, they can be a beneficial or a disruptive force. So much of the parental role depends on the interaction between the leaders of the school and parents, as well as the history and culture of that school. It also depends on what signals are being given by the superintendent and the board.

In school districts where the Effective Schools Process has been brought in by a new superintendent, the policy of encouraged parental involvement exists from the beginning. Parents are expected to be involved in the forming of a districtwide mission statement and districtwide plan. Parents are inundated with material about the new Effective Schools Process, its philosophy, and what it will mean to their children. The first thing they learn is that Effective Schools means more and better communication between all participants in the school district.

For a truly Effective School system, this increased communication is a must. *Everyone* must be kept informed, and that means parents, too. It is interesting that in the Effective School districts where there has been greater communication, parents are not aware of Edmonds's reticence about parental involvement, but instead hear only the call for their increased involvement.

"It was the parental involvement that mattered to so many people," explains Judy Perkins, board member in Spring Branch, Texas. "Sure, we had schools where principals did work with parents, but it wasn't the accepted policy. This was going to make principals reckon with parents. Now they can't shut them out."

For changing, improving districts, there are changes of which parents need to be informed. There will be adjustments in curriculum and testing, as well as in discipline and tracking. There will be increased districtwide activity, at all levels.

The area affected the most will be the individual school as it grows toward school based management. Parents will learn of their opportunity to serve on school planning teams. They will also be kept informed—and have a say—as a school improvement plan moves forward. Now for some districts and some schools, these are not earth-shattering changes, but for others, this is a whole new way of doing business.

Lezotte points out that increased parental involvement often does not live up to its advertising. Some districts and schools will put forth a strong public relations campaign to get parents involved, and then, once they appear, the school only gives them lip service. "It's the problem of the walk not matching the talk in that one," says Lezotte.

That is an occurrence found more in middle-class school systems than inner-city districts. Lezotte refers to a study of parental involvement that reports the emphasis in the suburban schools is on "how to manage parental involvement, how to control it, how to keep it at a distance," whereas in the inner city, the emphasis is on "how to get parent involvement, how to increase it, how to sustain it."

Whether it is a suburban school outside Seattle, or an inner-city school in Spanish Harlem, teachers and staff consistently report an increased involvement with the community and the parents under the Effective Schools Improvement Process. And those who feel the brunt of the change are the teachers.

For years, teachers and parents seemed to be at loggerheads. Teachers say this comes from the fact that parents usually fall into two categories: They either trust you or they don't. If they don't, they believe they can do the job better and don't hesitate to tell you that. This doesn't set the groundwork for peaceful interactions, or even welcome interactions. Therefore, teachers did not actively encourage parental involvement.

But as mass media has brought more electronic learning into the home and the classroom, and as *both* parents and teachers have found themselves overwhelmed with the problems of today's students, there has been an easing of attitudes. Many parents now realize that teachers are faced with an Herculean task. On the other hand, teachers are now seeing that parents can be very helpful to them, and not just in providing cupcakes on birthdays.

"I don't think there's any question that the parents make this a stronger, better school," maintains Sue Galletti, principal of the Islander Middle School on Mercer Island in Seattle. "Sure, they can be a real pain, sometimes. They often think they know more than we do. But at least you're in a dialogue and you know someone's paying attention to what's happening to the child. The school isn't alone."

That "attention to what is happening" is regarded by administrators in Spanish Harlem as the factor that can make the difference between a child's success or failure. "We believe very strongly that the parent, or some guardian, must take an interest in the child's school work," says Felicita Villodas, principal of P.S. 152 in District 6. "We are constantly trying to build up our parent strength. That's one of the reasons this school is always open to parents. We don't want them to feel like they're not wanted. We want them to feel that they are essential to their child's progress."

Tony Amato, superintendent of District 6, not only believes that the parents are important to his schools' success but he goes out of his way to get them involved. "We have science projects, math projects, social studies projects that are specifically designed to involve the parent and, if necessary, to improve the parent's level of education," says Amato. "I can't imagine not reaching out to the parent. We've already failed many of these parents once. Maybe we can get them the second time around. At any rate, you don't *not* try. If you pull in just one for one kid, it's all worthwhile."

It seems that since the first schoolhouse opened its door, the process of pulling in parents has not been easy. The theories of why parents don't bother becoming involved with their child's education range from not caring, to being intimidated, to believing the school knows best (and doesn't want them involved), to telling themselves they have done their duty by just getting the child into school.

Accountability in an Expanding Role

The Effective Schools Process has two secret weapons that appeal to parents: *improving* the school and making teachers and staff *accountable*. Improvement and accountability are concepts that parents understand and welcome. They hold teachers accountable, and are encouraged to do so. Unfortunately, teachers cannot hold parents accountable. If parents do not know how to be cooperative, or are not interested in cooperating, teachers know that they are still held accountable for student progress. Cooperation from parents makes the going easier. If parents are absent or not up to the task of parenting, then the school becomes an oasis for learning, a place where children feel secure in what they often see as a more orderly and perhaps more just world than the one at home.

Teachers' responsibilities keep on expanding. They are finding that more and more they need the support of someone from the home environment. In Effective Schools districts, the call for increased involvement is being answered.

"I've had instances where I've taught three kids from one family and never seen a parent. Now, all of a sudden, here comes the fourth child, and I'm seeing the parents," says a teacher from Cosgrove Junior High in Spencerport, New York. "The reason, I think, is simple. There is a different push from this school district. A push for real quality learning, and I think the parents are seeing that. They see it in the press reports. They see it in the information that their kids bring home. And they see it in the learning that their kids are doing. And now they realize this learning process can and *should* involve them."

"There are some teachers, I think, who are threatened by the increase in parents around here," a teacher from Munn Elementary School in middle-class Spencerport believes. "We're working so hard to pull them in, some people are saying, 'Why?' It's like we were happy working alone. But I think now many of us are seeing that the parents can be helpful."

"In the past, we often saw parents as a burden. They either thought they knew everything, or they didn't know a thing and knew that, too. Either way you couldn't work with them," says a high school teacher in Spring Branch, Texas. "We used to grouse at just the thought of parent conferences. But I think with this whole emphasis on teaching for learning, we see the parent as someone we need. And really, as someone the child needs in their corner. So, although it takes time, we're working with them as best we can."

"I think parents saw us as the enemy, someone to be feared," says Shirley Simmons of Fort Riley Middle School in Junction City, Kansas. "They thought the only time they'd hear from us was when their child was in trouble. We've had to turn that perception around. To let the parents know we want to talk to them about the *good* things."

"And that we need their help to continue to do the good things for their kids," adds Carol Ohm, also a teacher at Ft. Riley Middle School. "They don't have an easy job and we don't have an easy job. If we work together in the right way, we make it easier for all of us."

Leslie Myers points to a note she received at the bottom of a notice sent home to parents. It was a notification of some additional work a child needed to do. "Look what this parent wrote: 'Thank you. Parents and teachers need to continue working together.' Now you don't get many of these, but you know that many of the parents out there feel this way."

"It's very easy to be frightened of the educational process," believes Myers, who is a sixth-grade teacher at Fort Riley. "We tend to forget that for some of our parents, the schools were not a nice place, especially if you are a minority. I've learned to be very conscious of that fact."

Teachers maintain that thanks to much of the Effective Schools training that deals with parental involvement, they have learned how to bring the parents into the learning process. "The key is to help them realize you're on their side," says Simmons. "That you are not their adversary. Your interest and their interest are one."

Principals of schools in middle-class suburban neighborhoods are quick to point out it is a myth to think that the more well-to-do parents care more about their child's education than the parents of a disadvantaged child.

"I've been in schools with the rich kids and the poor kids, and the only constant I'm really sure of is that rich or poor, it's amazing how difficult it can be to get parents involved with their child's education," says Suzanne Still, principal of the Hollibrook School in Spring Branch, Texas. "It's as if some parents just believe it's not their business to be involved."

Still experienced this feeling head on when she had her first parents' meeting at Hollibrook (a school of 1,000 students that serves a predominantly Hispanic population, but because of its high scores is now pulling in Anglo children from across town) and only a handful of parents attended. For the next meeting, she and her staff took chairs and coffee and cakes across the street to the apartment complex and "dragged" the parents in. She now has over 90(parents at her meetings.

"I have no patience for those who say these people don't care about education," says Still. "These people have struggled to get to this country. Have struggled and fought for their freedom and this way of life. It's not a matter of not caring. It's a matter of not understanding, and being scared to death."

There is also the language problem. Still, who is fluent in Spanish, conducts all of the school's business with the children's homes in two languages.

"I know of schools where they just forget about the parents if they don't speak English," says Still, clenching her teeth. "I mean, literally, forget! Slam the door in the parents' faces if they won't bow to the English language. And what do you think that means for the kids?"

This is unfortunately a common phenomenon in the country's public schools. In northern Washington, Gene Medina, Ed.D., assistant superintendent for the Mount Vernon School District, says that he has known principals who don't even bother trying to communicate with parents if they think they may encounter a foreign language.

"A lot of our parents are migrant workers, and aren't exactly tied into our public school process," explains Medina. "And we have principals who that is just fine with. They don't want to be bothered. And where they don't talk to these people, they don't have any idea what they are like, what their homes are like—and you can imagine what that means these guys are really thinking."

What they're really thinking, says Medina, is that the migrant workers are dirty, unhealthy, ignorant parents who don't care about their children's education. "Once I was so furious I made this one guy go into the migrant community with me. I made him see that all his stereotypes were wrong," says Medina, who also speaks Spanish. "He came out talking about how devoted these people were to their children, how industrious and hard working they were, and how they were getting screwed by the system."

"So, sure, it's fine now. He's asked for a translator for his district and we've given him one and now he's really doing something for not only the kids but the parents." Medina pauses. "But it really makes you mad because this guy has been in the system for a long, long time. How many hundreds of kids have gotten the short end of the stick because this guy didn't believe their parents were worth a note home?"

Many principals believe that if you follow the Effective Schools mission to teach for learning for *all* children, then you must also make the sincere effort to reach out for *all* parents. It was this belief that had Suzanne Still and her faculty out in the neighborhood barrio preaching the Effective Schools mission to *all* parents. One of those parents who heard the call, and knew it was different from anything she had heard from any other school, was Hilda Saldana, mother of four boys attending the Hollibrook.

"I know that no one ever tried to pull in my own parents, and when I had the boys in the Houston schools, I mean, they didn't care at all about us parents," recalls Saldana, who wonders if maybe her lack of involvement in the Houston schools had something to do with her childrens' performance.

"My boys were failing in Houston. They had to be kept back," says Saldana. "And I never really understood why because no one at the school bothered to explain it to me. I would talk to them, the teachers, but they would just say the boys weren't 'mature enough.' I would ask, but I never understood what that meant." The staff at Hollibrook doesn't quite understand what that means either, especially considering that Hilda Saldana's boys are now on the honor roll in a school with rapidly ascending achievement scores and a challenging multicultural curriculum.

Saldana believes that prior to sending her children to Hollibrook, she was looked down on by teachers because of her own lack of education. She did not graduate from high school and married very young.

"I just wasn't treated like I mattered. Like anything I said mattered," says Saldana, a warm, open woman who admits to being very insecure in the past. "And if they didn't treat me like I mattered, I couldn't help but think they didn't really care about my children. At least I never got the feeling they really cared." The reason she believes that is because she now knows what it is like to be around a faculty and staff that does care.

"You wouldn't believe it. I am listened to here. The teachers realize I am the boys' mother and I know my children. And that I can help the teacher if we work together," says Saldana. "And they are really interested in anything that will help my boys learn. These are Anglos who want my boys to be something when they grow up."

The light that Hollibrook shines casts a wide glow. It has managed to pull Hilda Saldana out of the dark.

"For years I have just been known as 'Joe the roofer's wife.' I had no self-esteem. I didn't think I was worth anything," she says. "And my husband, he has a problem with drugs, and he beats me. I was the punching bag, always wearing black and blues. But I thought that was just the way it was. I didn't think I deserved any better."

The Hollibrook School changed that. It started with Hilda getting involved with the parents' meetings. Then she became bold enough to tell the boys' teachers that she didn't understand the work her sons were bringing home. The teachers and Suzanne Still found Hilda some academic help and started her on the path to her GED. Then she applied for and received the job as "official greeter" (receptionist) at Hollibrook. She passed her GED with "flying colors," reports a teacher. However, the changes are not going over well with her husband.

"He says, 'Ever since you became involved with that Hollibrook, you have changed,'" she relates. "And he's right. I have. I have my self-respect. I am somebody now. I can do something with my life. I don't have to sit around and be treated like trash by my husband. I can live without him. All of us can. Because we all have our self-respect. We're all going to do something with our lives."

These are not idle words. Hilda Saldana is preparing the course to leave her husband and support her children on her own. "And it never would have happened without the Hollibrook," she insists. "If they hadn't thought that my children were important. That I was important. Look. My children are going to go on and do something very good with their lives. They're going to be lawyers and maybe doctors. And they can be. This is one of the best schools and they're on the honor roll. And they love school. If they are sick, they hate to miss a day. If we were back where we were, they'd be failing, not wanting to go to school, and we'd be fighting and I'd still be black and blue."

The Saldana family progress is dramatic and inspiring. What makes it even more powerful is that the story is not one of a kind. Many of the Hollibrook parents who live out in the barrio say that the school has given their lives purpose and direction. The proof of this is seen not only in the enthusiasm of the parents meetings but in the parent activities where mothers and fathers crowd into the school to take special language and math classes, or learn about nutrition, parenting, or the finance and banking system.

You can see the excitement on their faces and feel the sense of belonging as they give a teacher a thank-you hug. "So many of these parents were completely lost before the Hollibrook. They didn't know how to get any help. They were all crowded into one room, trying to live off a few pesos," says Saldana. "They were embarrassed and didn't think anyone wanted them at the school. They didn't even think their children were welcome."

Now that the word is out that children are welcome at the Hollibrook—and that parents are also treated with respect—Hollibrook has another problem. "People will do anything to get their children in there," says Saldana. "And the school insists on Immigration papers or a birth certificate or a passport as proof that they are legal. Many don't have it and are frightened to go into the Amnesty program. So they will go out trying to buy someone else's papers, for $500 or more, just to get the papers so they can get their children into Hollibrook."

The Hawthorne Elementary School in Seattle, Washington, faces many of the same dilemmas as Hollibrook. Residing in a neglected, deteriorating neighborhood of Seattle's inner city, the school serves 430 children, 60 percent minority, 65 percent free and reduced lunch. The reading scores of the Hawthorne have climbed above average and Principal John Morefield, who has promised parents and the school board that all children will be reading at or above grade level by fifth grade, finds himself in a potentially unpleasant situation.

"We're now at the point where more and more white kids want to come in," explains Morefield. "In fact, my white population goes up each year. It doesn't bump anyone out, but it precludes a minority kid coming in." What Morefield finds interesting is that this is happening despite the fact that the school emphasizes in its mission the educating of minority children:

> *Mission: To ensure the success of all children,* particularly those from ethnic minority groups not previously achieving as well as other groups, *and to demonstrate and communicate the educational practices that have been successful with students from those groups with other educators in Seattle.*

"So we're finding that a school that has taken on the mission of educating minority kids effectively is getting an increasing number of white kids," says Morefield. "It's like the white folks, the middle class, always know where the good stuff is. We sniff around until we find it."

Working on a bulletin board in the Hawthorne front corridor are two white, middle-class mothers who have moved their children over to the Hawthorne from other "predominantly white" Seattle Schools. Their reasons for placing their children here are to the point: Hawthorne is "a much better school—the kids do things here you won't even find in the advanced schools" and "the principal makes sure all these kids behave."

The mothers maintain that the discipline aspect of Hawthorne is just as important to them as the academic growth. "You're not going to have a quality school if you don't have a disciplined atmosphere. It's that simple," says one mother.

The Hawthorne Elementary School can be very strict. You see that in the way students file down a corridor or interact with their peers. There is no pushing or shoving, no loud voices. But the atmosphere is also not that of a military school. The behavior here is based on respect, not fear of punishment. The students like the way they are treated, and treat others in the same way. And that's the way John Morefield wants it.

"We're very strict. Our discipline is very tight. Parents see it in their kids skills and manners," says Morefield. "We're a very warm, nurturing, loving environment, but you walk in line in the hall, and you never backtalk an adult, and every adult is responsible for every child."

Morefield insists that in the past, and even today, administrators are harming children with their leniency. "We too often allowed kids to do things that we never would have allowed them to do had they been a different color. And black parents know it," believes Morefield. "I am a white liberal, and I know it was done with the best intentions, but it hasn't helped kids."

Morefield sends home with his children a detailed accounting of his schoolwide discipline plan and procedures. It covers not only his perspectives and the teachers' but what is expected of every child. There are specific instructions on when to use "quiet voices," how you are to carry your bathroom pass, what you can and cannot do on the playground, how you are to clean your table in the lunchroom, the proper bathroom procedure to follow, and many other rules as well as information on reward and penalty systems.

"Mom" Wilson, a warm, loving black woman who is a former teacher and now works as a community liason for Hawthorne, agrees that the behavior management (discipline) system is a major draw for both white and black parents. "Many of these parents are sick of having their children in schools where they just learn how to be irresponsible and rude," she says, straightening her shelves of additional clothes for the children. "Sure, we get some kids who are very poorly behaved. But they just don't know The Hawthorne Way. We teach them the proper way."

The big plus of the behavior management program is that the children soon start to feel better about themselves and are given additional responsibility. "And it's not as if it's only the black children who cause the behavior problems," points out the mother working on the bulletin board. "In fact, my son's problems have all been with white kids from those families that are supposed to know better. The kids with the superiority complex can be a real problem."

Morefield says that whatever discipline problems the school did have, they are decreasing. He believes that the combination of good academics and good discipline not only draws in parents but keeps them involved. "It becomes a community thing. Everyone begins to grow and learn under this process. We started out with only a few parents, but thanks to people like Mom Wilson and this staff that just won't allow parents to stay away, we now have four-fifths of our parents represented."

And what happens when you put the parents from the neighborhood with the parents who drive up in their Mercedes'? "You know, I wondered about that, and I was nervous," begins a white mother. "But there is so much going on at the school. And the teachers get us all involved so much working with our kids and each other, I know it sounds like a cliche, but you don't notice it."

The black parents, for the most part, agree. The troublesome areas come with those parents who have not themselves received a good education and have trouble understanding the material. In those instances, a "buddy" is assigned to help the parents through the maze of services and resources in order that they may receive the necessary help for themselves and their children.

"Those are the parents we don't have much interaction with," admits a white mother. "Although, you know, now that I think about it, there have been times in the meetings where a young mother will come up to me just so excited about something and we'll actually begin discussing what's going on."

But, in general, principals admit (although they don't like to) that parents usually behave very much like their children. Black parents stay with black parents, white parents with white parents, and Hispanic parents with Hispanic parents.

Answering the Call for Multigenerational Schools

The Effective Schools Process offers advanced training for teachers in dealing with parents—not only the eager, educated parents but the reticent parents who may be lacking in their own communication skills. Schools are finding that they have to serve not only the present and future generations, but often the past generations that were already passed over in their chance for a quality learning opportunity from the public schools.

At many schools there are specific activities designed to involve parents in the learning process. In District 6 in New York's Spanish Harlem, parents and children receive special science, math, and social studies packets involving projects they can do together. They are invited to special school activities, including field trips.

At the Hawthorne School in Seattle, where parents are brought in for special learning nights and where they are often paired with a "buddy" if there is anything they don't understand or may be suspect about, teachers make it a goal to make contact with every parent, often setting up home visits. If parents don't show up for these functions or parent conferences, someone from the school's staff goes out and brings them in.

At the Hollibrook School in Spring Branch, a special Parents' University Day is held where parents can take courses in anything from computer techniques to amnesty programs, nutrition, or how to look for a job. They have their own parents' room at the school.

"I can't imagine not involving our community," says Suzanne Still, principal of Hollibrook. "This, after all, is their school. I think there was a time when we thought schools just belonged to teachers, and maybe students. But that can't be. This school belongs to the community. We have to reach out to them and allow them to use us. That's what *public* education is supposed to be about."

"It has to be equal sharing, or at least a sincere effort towards that," maintains Larry Lezotte. "In the past it was always that the schools saw themselves as the authority and the professional. The parents were the patients and the professionals would write the prescription and expect them to follow it.

"You have to move to the parent partnership model, not this professional/client relationship. The school as base is a community of shared values, of teachers in the school and outside the school. I don't have much antipathy for this role differentiation of I'm the professional, you're the parent."

However, Lezotte says the reality of the makeup of the parent population today creates some second thoughts. "Here's the problem on the other side of it, the paradoxical nature of it," says Lezotte. "I'm not sure the unwed 18-year-old with a 5-year-old child has many resources to bring to the situation. So, even if you say we're going all out to prepare an involvement, and that becomes a percentage of your parent constituency, what have you got when you get there? As somebody said, you've got children having children. It's a tough one. I always say parent involvement will make all of this work better and easier and more powerfully and so forth. But I don't know."

Teachers say that the lack of education, and often basic English skills, is one of the biggest barriers to school-home relations. Teachers must often use the children as interpreters, which seriously limits a straightforward conversation on that particular child's progress or lack thereof.

As Effective Schools open the doors to the community and come face to face with the problems therein, many of them are moving toward becoming multigenerational learning centers. It is a step that districts hesitate to take because their resources are already strained, but a step that they say someone, somewhere *must* take.

"I'm a stickler for concentrating money on the basic skills and all that," says Spencerport Superintendent Joe Clement. "But it seems to me this is something the schools are going to have to do. You can't have kids running home everyday to parents who can't read. And it's not like you're taking a course of action that's going to break the bank."

Educators agree it is not, in most cases, the money for such programs that is the problem, but the motivation of the school district and the parents. "I think that's why we have to let the communities know that these schools are here for them," insists Suzanne Still. "Sure, we're here for their kids. That's our first mission. But these kids don't live in bubbles. They interact. And now we have given our teachers—for the first time—the skills to interact and help these parents, and these kids. We have to let the community know we are here for them."

In talking about the role of parents in the Effective Schools Process, teachers also note that for the first time, they must be involved with parents who are emotionally and physically doing harm to children. Teachers say it is essential now for all schools to have a psychologist on staff full time.

"Ten, twenty years ago, you didn't get involved when you thought something was very wrong with these kids' homelife," remarks a teacher at Custer Hill Elementary in Junction City, Kansas. "The most you could do was report something suspect to a principal or guidance counselor, but that was it. The police, or social services were never called. Well, that's changed. Thank God."

Teachers are now being instructed in how to recognize and deal with the emotionally and physically abused child. "We had an instance just the other day of a little boy in the second grade, the son of a doctor, who came into school very upset and still wearing his father's shoe imprint on his cheek," explains a principal in the Frederick County Schools. "The teacher came to me immediately and we started getting that boy some help. And we reported his father. The authorities pursued it. That wouldn't have happened years ago."

Schools take up more and more of the custodial slack in U.S. society. They are opening earlier in the morning and closing later in the day to provide care for latch key children. They provide breakfast, lunch, and often, for the kids who stay late, an afternoon snack. The schools are also becoming a place of refuge for many children.

"There's this wonderful little girl," begins Lee Sharp, principal of the Fort Riley Middle School who has seen all manner of neglect in his years in education. "Her mother died and her stepfather didn't want her, so she was sent to her grandfather. Her grandfather beat and sexually abused her. We got her back home, but it was with her stepfather who just doesn't care for her—barely feeds her and clothes her. So, we've gotten our resources together. Clothes and extra food for the family. And we'll get her out of that situation and into a decent home. But right now this school is her 'safe place.' This is where she knows she is cared for, where she is safe. And that's the way it should be for now. I don't want her hurt anymore."

Although there are critics who insist that this caregiver role is not the role the schools are designed or prepared for, they do acknowledge that the schools are nonetheless perhaps the best equipped to handle it. The school is a learning, caring environment, with shared values and a mission of the betterment of the human mind and spirit. For now there doesn't seem to be a better "safe place" for the needy or neglected child.

"It's getting to the point where we don't have a problem handling the needy child," says Suzanne Still. "It's the needy parent with whom we have some catching up to do."

Facing the Terror from the Extremist Students

Unfortunately, the problem of race relations is something that Effective Schools can work at with its mission of teaching *all* children, but it cannot immediately alter the racial sentiment of millions of America's schoolchildren. The fact is that racial tensions among America's young are on the rise (Gallup Poll, October 1990).

At the elementary level, you will see white, black, and Hispanic children working and playing together in classrooms, in the cafeteria, and on the playground. The old saying that children do not see other children in color tones is still true.

But once you move to the high school level, in most cases the colors of the United States keep to their separate places. Yes, there are students of different races talking and interacting together, but if one were to take an overhead picture of a cafeteria or a high school during class change, one would see the different colors sitting and moving together.

Nowhere is that more blatant—especially when referring to literal colors, like red and black, blue and gold—than in the schools in the gang territories of the West Coast. In San Diego's Morse High School, a school of some 2,500 students that has won a national reputation as a good, progressive learning institution, faculty and staff openly admit there is a major problem with gangs.

"We're like any other school in this area," says Rudy Aleman, assistant principal of Morse High. "You see the guys out on the streets, the older guys, into the drugs, the weapons, the prostitution. Then there are the 17-, 18-, 19-year-old kids who are their lieutenants in the school. You know, a day here, four days absent. Typical dropouts, troublemakers. Then all around them is the 'wannabees.' The kids that 'wannabee' part of a gang for safety reasons. They wear the colors, the blues or the reds, just to be safe."

You see them in the classrooms, changing between classes, wearing red sneakers and black t-shirts, or blue pants, and gold sweaters. What is forbidden is wearing the colors on your head. But the wearing is more common than not among many groups.

"It's easier this way because I live in a gang neighborhood," explains one sophomore who is wearing a red shirt, red socks and black pants. "This way they don't bother me. At first my parents were upset, but then they saw it was a way not to be hassled. And I'm trying to stay clean."

He says everyone is very careful around the school. "You know your place, you know? And you don't mess outside your place."

At first glance, the changing of the classes can seem unruly. Teachers and staff keep a close watch on the different groups as they pass through the courtyard. Off to the side, an armed San Diego police officer looks sternly through mirrored sunglasses. And as the seconds tick down, adult voices are heard telling students to hurry. The students usually ignore the warnings, bumping into the classrooms in the general vicinity of the ringing of the final bell.

"The thing is, if your kid doesn't want to be in a gang, he doesn't have to be. Not on this campus, anyway," insists Aleman. "We've got eight security guards whose job it is to keep the peace, to make sure everyone gets into class without interfering with the other kids. You're safe here."

Discipline codes are strict, and the attendance of the students is followed diligently, as it is in most schools today. There is one staff member whose only job is to log into the computer the daily attendance and tardy records of each child. At any time, a staff member can call up the attendance status of any student.

"And then we call home," explains Aleman, "and say to the parent, 'Do you know your kid hasn't been in school in two weeks?' Most of the time the parents have no idea." Of 100 students absent on a fall day, over 80 of the parents were not aware their children were out of school. In those cases, the school staff asks the parent to come in and discuss this problem. Sometimes they show up; many times they don't. Administrators say there isn't much they can do after that.

"The key is keeping the kid in school as much as possible," says Russ Vowinkel, principal of Morse High. "And if we can get them into the classroom work and some of the sports teams and clubs, then they've got a connection. We work hard to solidify that."

Vowinkel, who is a Naval reserve intelligence officer and who has sent both sons to West Point, spends a lot of his time working with the different sports teams and clubs trying to build school spirit. "One of the reasons I wanted this school is because of the school spirit," says Vowinkel. "The kids are really involved in their school and, believe it or not, so is the community. Many community groups come in here and work with the kids. They often take the place of parents. They support these kids and work with them. They help them stay away from the gangs."

Morse High sends 70 percent of its students onto higher education, either two- and four-year colleges or advanced technical school placement. The faculty and staff say that's what they shoot for: to get the kids out of the neighborhood and into an atmosphere that isn't as racially and ethnically divided.

It is a mistake to think that it is only southern California and large urban high schools that have a problem with gangs. The gang colors are now showing up in places as remote as Idaho, Tennessee, and West Virginia. But there is another problem that is perhaps not quite as visible, but just as vexing and frightening. It is a problem that schools everywhere know exist, but a problem that teachers and principals only whisper about: skin heads, white supremacists, the Aryan Nation, the neo-Nazis, the National Association for the Advancement of White People (whose teenage members in Dubuque, Iowa made the front page of the November 3, 1991, *New York Times*).

Very few educators want to face the truth, but the numbers of students involved in racist and anti-semitic activities is growing faster than anyone can figure out how to stop. Because it is such a potent emotional issue, many school administrators choose to ignore it.

"It's a problem that's growing, and all the progressive educational programs in the world are not going to stop it," says one principal of a high school in northern California. "And if we don't start to face what's going on here, it's going to blow up in our face and we can kiss the concept of educating *all* the children goodbye."

Those principals who do face the problem do not like to give it attention by discussing it publicly. They say they simply cannot allow such activity, emphasizing how it goes against their personal and professional beliefs. "Remember, I'm for *all* children learning," said one middle school principal.

"I even get a whiff of one of those groups in here and I'll put an end to it overnight. And I have. I pull in the kids and the parents and just lay down the law. The kid is out of here if he or she continues. And I've got a superintendent who backs me up."

But in many schools, the action is not blatant with specific groups and slogans. It's more an undercurrent, slowly building. Students at the Junction City High School in Kansas note, sadly, that there is such a rising undercurrent in their school. "There are some pretty violent kids out there that just weren't out there before," says one senior. "And I think it makes all of us nervous because the leaders try to get everyone divided up, and most of us just don't want that."

Larry Dixon, principal of Junction City High School, a black man who has come up through the rocky ranks of a discriminating society and is respected by both white and black students in the high school, just nods silently when asked about the increase in racial tension. He and his staff are trying to quell any talk of tension and instead increase the academic power of the school. "But we're also keeping a very strong hand on discipline," says Dixon. "We know there are problems out there, and we're not going to ignore them. You dig your own grave if you ignore problems like that."

The students notice the heavier hand in the area of discipline, and say it doesn't bother them. It is just another change that they have seen as the Effective School Process comes more intently into Junction City High.

"I talk to kids who used to go here and it seems real different," says a senior who hopes to attend an Ivy League College. "One of the things is the teachers. They seem to care a lot more. They're here for you before and after school. And they do a lot more different stuff than they used to."

Other students agree, adding that the teachers "don't complain as much as they used to." "And we have a lot more classes than before. You know, more options, I guess. And the teachers do push you harder," believes a junior. "And everyone agrees that Mr. Dixon makes this a better place. He cares a lot. Always listens to us."

When asked how involved their parents are in the school, the students just shrug their shoulders. "They look at my report card and go to some of the games. That's about it. And that's fine with me." Another student tells how her mother is "real involved, real rah rah education—it drives me crazy."

Dr. Max Heim, superintendent of Geary County Public Schools, which includes Junction City, wishes there were more parents who were "rah rah education." "We have tried everything to get parents involved. Black, white, it doesn't matter. But it just doesn't happen. I don't know if it's because 60 percent of our kids are military (Ft. Riley Army Base is in Junction City) and there's so much mobility, but we can't draw them in. And if we can't get them interested at the elementary level with the little ones, I don't know how we get them involved at the high school level. It just doesn't happen."

Heim says that with the advent of the Effective Schools Process and the school improvement teams that give parents a larger voice, there has "naturally been an increase in involvement." "But once again, you tend to get those parents that were always involved in education," he says. "There are a few new ones, but for the most part, we're seeing the parents who we knew would be there."

Many of the Junction City students said that as long as the teachers and principal were on their side, they didn't think it was essential that their parents be involved. And they agreed that, from what they had heard about the high school just five years ago, there had been a significant increase in concern from both faculty and staff.

"You know, some teachers are always there for the students," relates a senior. "But most of 'em? Forget it. At least a couple years ago. Now, I think we all get the feeling there's more teachers who are pushing for us."

All students in a group of 12 agreed, except for one student, who believed it was still the "better" students who got more attention. The other students thought about this, and allowed that she may be right. "But I still say all someone has to do is ask for help and you're going to get it," countered another student. "And if you don't, all you have to do is go to Mr. Dixon. He'll make sure you get the help you're looking for."

This belief in and devotion to the principal is a common theme in Effective Schools, be they elementary or secondary. In Landrum, South Carolina, at the O. P. Earle Elementary School, parents say it is the principal, Jamie Summers, who has inspired the teachers to be so effective, and who has won over the confidence of the parents, almost singlehandedly.

"It's not easy to be against Jamie. Even if this is the South," protests one parent as she talks openly about the black principal of her daughter's school. "Jamie is loving, and competent, and caring. You couldn't ask for a better principal. And we wouldn't want anyone different."

This group of parents, which has been very active over the years with the school improvement council for the Earle School, is all white, despite the fact that the school has a significant black population. "There are some black parents at the meetings, but not many," comments one parent. "I don't think they feel they can get involved. They don't have the education we have and I don't think they're used to being involved. I mean, their parents probably weren't involved in the schools."

The parents also point out that because of the nature of the South Carolina Public School System (that of low funding and providing only minimal services), parents are forced into a very active role. The parents at the Earle School have raised money for a copy machine, playground equipment, books, and even paper to get the children through the school year.

"I don't think that many of these black parents would feel comfortable going around to the white houses up here and asking for money," says one parent, adding that unfortunately, many of the white parents wouldn't be happy seeing the black parent at the door. "We just wouldn't be comfortable."

Administrators agree that in many communities the PTAs, or now the school improvement councils (or teams) are regarded as one of the last bastions of white control. Black parents are not eager to be involved; in fact, many believe that their presence is not wanted or needed. What you see is a more one-on-one relationship with individual teachers than the minority parents becoming involved in the group PTA.

The Appeal of a Call to Teach *All* Children

In typically middle-class communities like Spencerport, New York, the relatively small black population is attracted by the tenets of the Effective Schools Process.

"I think that the Effective Schools concept excites the parents. They want to be part of it," believes Bonnie Seaburn, principal of the Munn Elementary School in Spencerport. "The idea of the mission, of *all* children learning, the climate, all the correlates that they can see and understand. They know what this school is about now. They can *trust* it. I think this makes a big difference. And for the first time they can feel a part of the decisions that are made."

For Margie Fears, the parent of two boys in the Spencerport Public Schools, there is no doubt in her mind that the schools are doing something right. Not only is her youngest son, Landon, in all the advanced classes (he has missed one day of school in five years) but her older son has gone from a shy, confused youth to one of the academic leaders of his class.

"Daniel had an attention deficit and just wasn't doing well in school," explains Mrs. Fears. "We even sent him off to private school for two years to see if that would help. But it didn't and so he came back here. And then this one teacher got him involved in singing. His self-confidence started to grow. Then he got into swimming, and was made co-captain of the team. His self-esteem soared, and so did his grades."

Daniel achieved a score of 1240 on the SATs and is heading to college with a National Merit Scholarship.

Did Effective Schools make the difference? "These are good schools. There's no doubt about that," says Mrs. Fears. "And because of Effective Schools, I know exactly what's going on, what they're trying for, and the fact they're giving everyone a chance. I have friends with kids in other schools. Those schools aren't effective, and those kids are suffering because of it. My kids are lucky."

But how do the students of Spencerport feel? "I don't know if I feel lucky," says an eighth-grader at Cosgrove Junior High. "I know this is a good school and all that. But it's also kinda hard. I don't think kids in other schools are pushed like we are." That appears to be the only serious problem the students have with the Spencerport Schools. And it is the same problem that many teachers have. "It's like you don't have any choice anymore," complains a junior at Wilson High School. "You have to take the Regents courses. You have to take the Regents exams. You can't get out of them."

The administration proudly admits that there is more emphasis on the Regents courses than in the past. When criticism comes from either the students or teachers, they defend themselves by pointing to the rise in test scores and the rise in the numbers of students receiving Regents scholarships.

"Sure, I guess we're all doing better than we would," says a senior. "But it makes you wonder what would have happened if you hadn't been pushed like this. I mean, maybe I didn't want to get into the advanced stuff. But now it's too late."

Whether talking for their own defense or their legitimate feelings, the students, almost unanimously it seems, believe there is too much emphasis on the Regents scores and the general testing program. "Sometimes I think that the only reason the teachers push us is to make sure we get those scores so they look good," says a junior, who also admits to "a lot of tension around here because of the testing."

But other students, although admitting there is considerable emphasis on the testing, wonder if that really is good or bad. "I mean, like what are we here for? Are we here to just screw around and not work, not get into college?" asks a senior who is enroute to the state university. "You know, if you want to just take the gut courses, you really can. It's tough to get out of Regents, but you can. And before, it was just the opposite. Before you couldn't get into the Regents course. Now you can't get out." And that is defintely the biggest change that has been brought with the Effective Schools Improvement Process for this middle class suburban town. Although some students may think that leads to more tension and harder work, the proponents of Effective Schools say that that harder work, better grades, is what school is *supposed* to be all about.

Students will always complain about their schools. What is thought provoking, to say the least, about the students in the Effective Schools, is that there was a general feeling that the teachers and staff *cared* more, were more involved, and had a better understanding of the students' needs.

Compared to students at other schools who often complained of "lousy teachers who leave when the bell rings," principals who "I never even see; I don't think I'd know him if I stepped on him", classes that "are a joke, they're beyond gut", a climate that is "out of control," the students in the Effective Schools—whether in California, Texas, Kansas, Maryland, or New York—had complaints like teachers "who refuse to let up on you," principals who "show up at your door on Saturday to talk to your parents," classes that "have us working with all these outside businesses," and climate problems like "they've changed to a no-bell system and although it's better, it's confusing."

It's not just test scores and college acceptances that indicate whether or not a school is succeeding, it is the attitude, behavior, and emotions of the students themselves. That difference, from apathy and discontent, to concern and attention, is visible at school plays, at football games, in biology labs and English classes, on the playgrounds and in the parking lots.

The jury is still out on how important the parents are to the success of the Effective Schools Improvement Process. Some schools obviously fluorish without great parental input. Other schools say they would be nothing without their parents. However, as schools undergo the school improvement process and the role of parents is expanded, new data are being accumulated. Researchers report that evidence is continuing to grow in support of the assumption that parental involvement is necessary to support school improvement on a long-term basis.

Dr. James Comer perhaps states it best and most succinctly: "You can do without parents. It will be easier for you. But it will be better for parents and children in the long run—with parents."

Anne Henderson, of the National Committee for Citizens in Education, an organization that spearheaded parental involvement since the early seventies, found that the degree to which parents are involved depends almost exclusively on the strength, the professional and personal security, and the desire of the leadership on top. If the principal is threatened by parental involvement, or is not sure of his or her leadership skills, parents will not be encouraged. But the secure principal, who invites opinion and discourse, will open the door to parents. Like so many things in public school, it comes down to leadership style. A principal who is not collegial is just not collegial, on any level.

In some schools, parents are actively recruited for school councils and can wield considerable power. In other schools, the councils are kept in the hands of a select group approved of by the principal and key teachers. Teachers and principals remain the controlling forces on the school improvement teams, often not even giving lip service to parents.

In some of those schools where parents play a lesser role, or no role at all, a familiar but unfortunate misconception on the part of both parents and teachers is often at fault.

"Some teachers believe that many of the parents, especially parents of poor and disadvantaged kids, know what to do and are not doing it," believes Larry Lezotte. "They think they're almost deliberately withholding competence as parents. Say in the area of getting kids to do homework.

"And on the other side, I think there are an awful lot of parents—and this comes through oftentimes very loud and clear with minority parents—who believe that the teacher is withholding competence for their kid. In other words, they think the teacher has in his or her repertoire strategies of instruction that will get this kid excited about school, but is not choosing to use those tools because he's black or poor."

Lezotte believes that these assessments are "at least in part" a myth. "Most parents I know, middle class or disadvantaged, are not withholding parenting competencies," affirms Lezotte. "Many of them are doing the very best they know how to do. And they just don't know what to do different. They're just as desperate about this.

"And teachers, administrators, they're doing the best they know how given the conditions. They are hard pressed to try other ways to do things even when they know how. If you want to change what they're doing, you've got to change what they know."

This, once again, says Lezotte, comes back to the need for additional training—renewal—for both teachers and administrators in order to find the best means to help the child.

One of the most interesting phenomena happening in Effective Schools is the *contract*—literally an agreement between the principal and parents that the principal will be held responsible for their child performing at grade level. John Morefield in Seattle has done this, going so far as to say the board can fire him if he fails. Often the teachers are involved in this contract. It stipulates, however, not just the work to be done by the school but the work to be done by the parent as far as overseeing homework, working on projects with their child, and supporting school activities.

All this leads to serving that population that has been neglected in the past by public education. The time for the multigenerational school—a school that serves not only future generations but past generations—has arrived in many districts. Even conservative communities like Junction City, Kansas and Spencerport, New York, admit that they must move in that direction if they are going to serve their changing communities adequately.

"I don't think that any of us saw the Effective School as a multigenerational school when we began," says Larry Lezotte. "When the school began to experience success and the adults began to feel more confident in themselves, to take control of their destiny, that's when we saw how very exciting it could be. But I don't think that Edmonds ever envisioned that the Effective School would become a kind of virus that would spread throughout the community, enhancing the lives of everyone it touched." Lezotte believes that many of these Effective Schools have become "the very finest human resource development models."

Dr. James Comer sees this interaction between the schools and the families as beneficial to all parties. "We can't change what goes on in families, but we can bring those parents who can cope reasonably well into the system together with principals, teachers, and others who can cope reasonably well, and help them create effective schools," believes Comer. "And I like those terms, *school effectiveness* and *home effectiveness*. Combine them and let everybody grow and fluorish. You can do that in a reasonably short period of time, and it does not require sophisticated skills. What I hear is: You (Effective Schools) are in fact doing that."

CHAPTER TWELVE

Getting the Monkey Off the Back of School Reform

Transforming the Role of the School Board and the Central Office

> *Teaching all the children must become part of the culture. In most school districts it is not part of the culture and it never will be unless the people at the top, the school boards, believe in the mission of teaching all children.* —LAWRENCE LEZOTTE

> *This school board has come the whole way with Effective Schools. They know and understand this school improvement. And that board, and this superintendent, are accountable for every success or failure along the way.*
> —NOEL FARMER, superintendent

> *It's very different around here now. This central office works* for *the schools of the district*—LEONARD CLARKE, assistant superintendent

Historically, the boards of education in this country have been political playpens where aspiring politicians began building the patronage and payback network essential to seeking higher office. In many cities, such as Boston, the powers overseeing the school system were known more for their sensationalizing, self-promoting speeches to the cameras than for any knowledge of how the schools operated. Boston, like other cities, had a school board interested only in protecting the status quo and their own political posteriors. It just may have something to do with the recognized fact that Boston can claim ownership to one of the worst urban school systems in the United States.

School committee and school board members may not know a whole lot about education, but many do know the process for placing a friend or constituent's son or daughter in a plush, well-paying (but never intellectually taxing) school department office or in the union-protected alliance of school custodians. Many are also very good at putting unqualified teachers into tenured positions and promoting former coaches and campaign friends up to the principal's office.

Because of their ignorance about school policy and school operations, their power is often dangerous and injurious to their community's schoolchildren. In the city of Boston, the school committee's trail of graft, corruption, patronage, ignorance, and meanness (as documented in numerous court cases) has inarguably led to its downfall. The erosion of public confidence climaxed in 1991 when the voters rejected the continuation of an elected Boston School Committee and gave the mayor the authority to appoint a new seven-person school board.

"I'm afraid Boston, like so many districts, is stuck back in the Dark Ages of education," says Larry Lezotte, who admits Boston is one district that has shown no interest in the Effective Schools Process and the concept of educating *all* children.

Fortunately, not all school boards or committees have been as entrenched in the old ways of patronage and politics as the Boston School Committee. Many boards in less politically motivated school systems tackle the problems of school management with conscience and care.

In the past, a school board's agenda was primarily that of representing its constituents, either by policy action or job placement. The boards set minimum standards for operations and student and teacher performance. Other functions included:

- Create policy within the constraints of the state code.
- Assist in the drawing up and approval of the budget.
- Decide on plant expenditures and allocation of space.
- Participate in negotiation of teachers' contracts.
- Hire and fire administrators, teachers, and staff.

Although many of these activities involved the work of the superintendent and his or her staff, the board's primary function was either to veto the actions or place on them their stamp of approval. In some cities, the boards encountered opposition from mayors, selectmen, or the courts, and this precipitated renewed rounds of press conferences and speech making. Unfortunately, in the more "political arenas" the welfare of the schoolchildren slipped lower and lower on the board's agenda.

The advent of pluralism in the United States and the increased regulation and legal processes have forced many educational bureaucracies to abandon their dysfunctional monolithic governing structures and embrace the concept of progressive administrative networks. This change is coming slowly and not without confusion as previously disenfranchised groups are now earning appointment on school boards.

And as school reform movements take hold in large and small communities, it is becoming increasingly important that school boards take an active and informed role in demonstrating not only their interest in improving the schools but their commitment to a process that will ensure the education of *all* children.

School board members who are leaders of a district undertaking the Effective Schools Improvement Process find themselves adopting the role of *stewards* to the teaching and learning of all students. Much like the central office that now finds itself working *for* the schools and students, the board also must alter its thinking that the school system operates for the purpose of enhancing the absolute power of a school board.

Under the Effective Schools Process, the school board looks to site-based, school-based management as the structure that best serves students, teachers, and staff. The board approves a mission statement and then with the correlates setting forth specific objectives, it finds before it a detailed role:

- Monitor and appraise school improvement progress.
- Support the superintendent in his or her program.
- Make adequate resources available to the district.
- Align reward and incentives with goals.
- Integrate teachers' contracts with program goals.
- Oversee the curricular alignment process.
- Set standards of evaluation.
- Keep channels of communication clear.
- Report to the community the status of school improvement.
- Hold the superintendent accountable.

While the board of a school system under the Effective Schools Improvement Process must have some basic understanding of sound educational practices, its task is very straightforward because of the steps laid out by the Effective Schools Research. Its focus is also very different from in the past because of school-based management. No longer can school boards get involved in the day-to-day operations of an individual school. If a district has true school-based management, enforced by the office of the superintendent, there should be no interference from the boards in the schools' operations.

If a school board member is holding tight to the principles of the Effective Schools Process, there are at least four changes of mindset demanded from a board member who may still be stuck in the status quo: (1) the position can no longer be viewed as a job placement service for friends and constituents; (2) there must be a sincere commitment to the education of *all* children via the network of the seven correlates; (3) he or she must feel a direct accountability to the quality of education; and (4) the job is now one of determining the best way to produce the outcomes to support stated goals and objectives.

Because it is the board that the community depends on to represent its values and concerns, it is often difficult for board members to take that final ideological step that will commit them to the Effective Schools Process.

"One of the biggest demons that's out there as an obstacle to quality education for all children is that time-worn demon that you never have to scratch the surface very deep to discover," says Larry Lezotte. "There are an awful lot of people who don't want all kids to learn because of the social and economic implications of that. If they all learn, what is it that one person can use to say that they're better than somebody else?

"It's the class struggle. It's not just a race struggle, it's the class struggle. And the board members are the ones that have to confront that problem head on."

In the school district of Spring Branch, Texas, where Hal Guthrie, Ed.D., went to the board and said, basically, "If you hire me, you hire the Effective Schools Improvement Process," many observers do not believe the board completely understood what Hall Guthrie was saying. It was not that Guthrie did not tell in detail that he was interested in educating *all* children, it was simply that the board members did not comprehend just how determined Guthrie was and how the acceptance of this mission would create serious changes in their public school system.

"The rhetoric sounds wonderful, and I believe the board basically believes it," says one veteran Spring Branch principal. "But I don't think they saw that down the road this school district would never be the same again."

School Boards Must Dare to Change the Status Quo

Judy Perkins, who is now a member of the Spring Branch board but was not when Guthrie was chosen, believes the board knew as much as they needed to know. "We were in trouble and we needed someone to come in and make dramatic changes," says Perkins. "I remember sitting in the audience when Guthrie was presenting Effective Schools. He told us what it would mean. He really convinced the board and the board took a strong stand in backing him. He was talking accountability, business strategies. We had never heard that before."

Spring Branch, in its fourth year of Effective Schools, is still monitoring and adjusting its restructure. Guthrie has made significant changes there, not the least of which is the new leadership at the principal level and the focus on school-based management. There is still controversy, but Guthrie and his staff are able to counter that with the achievement scores that are steadily and consistently on the rise. And this is the saving grace for many districts. After a few years, when people are starting to pick at the process, the administration now can produce the early results of the Effective Schools Process. It is difficult to argue against success. School districts not only have the Effective Schools research reinforcing and championing their district mission but they now have their own district scores that say all students are being served and served well.

"Hey, you can't argue with success. Look at the strides this district has made," exclaims Gay Lenhard, who has been a board member throughout Spencerport's lengthy (since 1983) Effective Schools Improvement Process. At first, she recalls, the board was very skeptical when Superintendent Joe Clement started talking about the Effective Schools Process. After all, it wasn't as if the white, middle-class schools of this suburb of Rochester were in trouble. Students were going off to college, parents were happy, there didn't seem to be any major reason for launching such a broad-based improvement process.

The reason that Clement and his staff kept repeating was: Spencerport can be better. Larry Lezotte and Ron Edmonds met with the Spencerport board and explained the Effective Schools Process and what it could do for Spencerport—not only in the coming years but further down the road when the demographics of the school district would more than likely be shifting.

"What intrigued me, and I know intrigued the other board members, was as soon as we met with Ron and Larry and started to understand the needs assessment part of the project, we realized that Joe and his staff were taking a risk," recalls Lenhard. "Now why, we asked, were they so willing to take this risk?"

The risk in the needs assessment, of course, was asking the teachers and principals what they really thought about the schools they taught in. "Yes, I know the board was intrigued with the risk of it," says Superintendent Joe Clement. "What we tried to explain to them was that there was more of a risk in *not* doing something, in *not* taking a risk."

Robert Sudlow, Ed.D., associate superintendent for instruction, recalls the effort in convincing the board to not only agree to Effective Schools but to *believe* in Effective Schools. "We knew we needed more than just a nod from them," says Sudlow. "After all, they had seen reforms come and go. We had to convince them this was the one—the one for Spencerport for the long run."

Gay Lenhard agrees that at first the board suspected that Effective Schools was just another fad. "But then we kept hearing how this had to be a long-term commitment. And I can't impress upon you how insistent Joe and his staff, and of course Ron Edmonds, were," recalls Lenhard. "I personally started to wonder what this was all about. What was really going on in the schools. And I wanted to find out."

Although some Spencerport board members ended up voting against it (those members now endorse it), the majority felt the Effective Schools Improvement Process was a worthwhile endeavor. And then once the district initiated the process, the role of the board began to change. "All of a sudden, here we were examining mission statements, looking at what the teachers really thought about the schools. Whew! We had never seen anything like this before," says Lenhard. "And we became very excited. Here we were doing education. We were really involved. Sure, we were giving the schools the site-based management, but we were overseeing it."

The board became immersed in mission statements and schools' goals, wondering if mission statements should be alike, and how varied school goals should be. Debates lasted long into the night, and many members found it inspiring to be spending hours on educational objectives and not personnel placement.

"Oh, did we get into the instructional leadership thing," says Lenhard. "We started coming down hard on our principals, pushing them to be instructional leaders. In the past, we had seen them only as managers. That was a sign that we were beginning to really understand what we were doing."

When the board moved on to the considerations of teaching for learning, their lack of expertise reared its head. They had felt somewhat comfortable dealing with principals and the new expectations for them. After all, that was still in the political arena. However, to understand what was going on in the classroom—which some would argue is what school boards should know the *most* about because it is there that quality matters most—was an entirely new and perplexing challenge.

"What did we know about teaching for learning? That wasn't a requirement of running for the board. We knew nothing, or close to nothing, really, when you think about all it takes. Oh, sure, like everyone else, we thought we knew, but . . . . So, all of sudden, here we are studying these position papers, and slowly, our attitudes about teachers started to change. We started to see what the role should be for teachers."

Teachers find this revelation on the part of boards rather fascinating. For decades, boards have been telling teachers how to do their work, when, in essense, they did not know what was actually going on in the classroom. As teachers and principals have said in this book, teaching is the only profession where everyone—from the floor scrubber to the landscaper to the poet to the banker—knows how to teach better than the ones presently doing the job.

The revelations taking place on the Spencerport board were no different than the revelations on other Effective Schools boards. Spencerport is unique because it was to some degree hesitant about the Effective Schools Process. The district was not in trouble like the districts in Spring Branch or even Frederick County, Maryland, where the board saw the need for change and went with a superintendent who had hitched his wagon to Effective Schools.

But all this new-found knowledge on the part of boards is not always to the benefit of teachers and administrators. In Spring Branch, principals found themselves on the hot seat, being pushed to a level of accountability heretofore nonexistent in this community outside Houston. All of a sudden, the board was looking closely at leadership skills, the strength of a school's improvement team, the steps schools were taking to reach their objectives. Where so much depended on school-based management, and therefore the board could not directly interfere, their only source of power came in their interaction with the reports of the principal and the school team, and dialogue about results.

"We had principals who just weren't interested in leadership. They'd always look toward the administration building," explains Judy Perkins of Spring Branch. "And then we had the problem with the central administraiton. People are good at politics here. This is Texas politics, and it gets down and dirty. Well, that type of fighting had some of our people kicking and screaming into the twenty-first century. It hurts us all. That's what we're trying to stop, and we are. We are getting some good, strong leaders in our schools. Principals who work with people, who are eager and willing."

The significant amount of staff development for teachers in Spring Branch seems to be keeping problems with the teachers to a minimum. But in upstate New York, the Effective Schools Process helped rekindle some antagonism between the board and the teachers union.

"I really got sick of listening to teachers complain," says Lenhard. "I'd say to them—and now I knew what I was talking about—for years you've been crying, 'I want input, I want control.' 'Well,' I said, 'here's the opportunity for the very things you've been hounding us about.' They're the ones who know how to run a school, they're the ones who know about education. Here was a great opportunity. I really got sick of them harping when here it was for them and all they had to do was accept the responsibility."

Some observers maintain that it is precisely because the board in Spencerport is now doing its homework on teaching for learning that many of the contract negotiations have gone less than smoothly. Previously, the board was always looking to the superintendent, but now the board was doing some independent thinking.

"There's no doubt the board has grown quite a bit," says Superintendent Joe Clement. "They understand so much more of the process and operation now. Not just the superintendent's responsibilities, but the teachers' also. And they can see the holes in the arguments now. And they should. Their role has changed along with everybody else's. They're accountable just like the rest of us."

While Spencerport was designing its districtwide plan, the board became involved in each of the correlates, discussing school climate, the monitoring process, and staff development. "We got very excited. It was an exciting learning process. We could see how this would improve our schools," recalls Gay Lenhard. "I think we all had our favorite correlate. Mine was, and is, *high expectations*. I've even been able to take that one and apply it to my own life."

Lenhard has become so committed to Effective Schools, so pleased with the successes that keep growing annually, that she often finds herself arguing the casue of Effective Schools outside of Spencerport. "There is this supervisor of this town nearby and he was complaining to me about how low the SAT scores were and all. They have a fair amount of money. And I asked him why the scores were so low. He says, 'Gay, the kids just don't have it.'" She pauses and shakes her head. "Can you believe that? This is an educated man believing this. And there was nothing I could say to convince him otherwise. He was so stuck in all his excuses of broken homes and alcoholism. I think we all get educated with that thinking. But it's just not true. Those kids *can* learn."

Lenhard isn't sure how much the community understood about the Effective Schools Process at the beginning. Explanations were made and material was sent home, but it was not until the first scores started coming in that the community started to take genuine notice. "I think we have all seen that this is a progressively improving type of thing. Sure, there are going to be a few setbacks here and there. But that happens in any program. The important thing is that there is a commitment to learning for each and every child. And this community is behind that commitment."

What about the concerns of increased accountability for the board? Lenhard says she welcomes it, that it is past due. "Isn't that what public service is all about?" she asks. "Yes, the board is accountable for the education of these kids. And that's the way it should be. We deserve that accountability, and you know what? We earn that accountability. And we earn the community's respect. Because through Effective Schools, I believe they receive a much more responsible, involved board."

This renewed, or new, accountability on the part of board members is an aspect of public education that many believe has not only been missing but has been responsible for the poor condition of many public school systems.

"In the past, we blamed whom if the students were not succeeding?" asks Dr. Noel Farmer, superintendent of Frederick County (Maryland) Public Schools. "First we blamed the students, then we blamed the teachers, then we blamed the principals. We never got around to blaming the superintendent or the board itself."

Accountability Must Start with the Board

Noel Farmer believes that in order for a school system to succeed today accountability has to first start at the top. "Sure, you can ask your teachers and principals to be accountable," says Farmer. "But what about me and the board? We never get any of the blame? We're not significant players? We're always jumping right in there to take the credit if something goes right, how come we manage to avoid all responsibility if something goes wrong?"

This professional and moral accountability, which must be woven into the fabric of school improvement from the very first day and from the top on down, is for many the motivating factor of the Effective Schools Improvement Process. To those truly committed to teaching for learning for *all* children, accountability is not feared. Accountability leads to good performance, honest leadership, and rising test scores. If you believe in accountability and the teaching of *all* children, and you teach *all* children, then the test scores will prove your effectiveness.

"What you are seeing in these schools is a welcoming of responsibility," says Lezotte. "The teachers and principals are willing to be accountable. And why? Because in the good districts, they have people at the top who are also taking responsibility. They know they're not standing out there alone."

A board that has made some extraordinary maneuvers in the field of accountability is the Frederick County (Maryland) School Board. In 1988, Superintendent Noel Farmer encouraged the board to adopt policies that would bring strict accountability into the board room. Farmer did not want any waffling on what his administration was all about. He wanted the public to know and understand a new day had come to the Frederick County schools.

The Frederick County Board adopted the following mission statement, known as Policy 100.11: "The primary mission of the Frederick County School System is to teach for quality learning for all students." It backed this up with Policy 100.12, which took the unprecedented step of adopting eight very specific school improvement goals. It also announced that it would annually report the progress on those goals. Policy 100.12 states: "An effective school in the Frederick County School System is one which achieves its teaching for learning mission by demonstrating quality and equity in its program outcomes . . . and that an effective school system is one in which resources are organized and delivered in such a way as to ensure that all students within the system (regardless of race, gender, or socioeconomic status) learn the essential curriculum as defined by the system."

The goals that the board set in place are very specific. Among them: Criterion-referenced tests will show annual increases; there shall be no difference in mastery as a function of gender, race, or socioeconomic status; percentage of student attendance will increase; 90 percent of all students will complete the equivalent of Algebra I before graduating. And Farmer is very prompt with his annual reports on the progress of accomplishing these goals, even publishing a special, detailed document listing the progress school by school. If the goal isn't being accomplished, he comes right out and states it.

"These reports say what we are about. Not just what is happening, but that we are accountable for what is happening," says Farmer, who sets out in his public material the functions of the Board of Education. He states their role in developing policies, promoting community involvement, describing school system mission and goals, and seeking resources to support the mission. He also discusses, for all to see, the role of the specific committees that board members serve on: Curriculum Committee, Audit and Finance Committee, Enrollment and Facilities Committee, Technology Advisory Committee, Minority Affairs Committee, and Vocational Advisory Council.

"The Superintendent and the Board of Education are responsible for selecting the end results that the school system should be pursuing," states Frederick County's "Course of Directions for Policy Makers." "Since they have the power to pursue and enforce these decisions, these policy makers are, in the long run, the *primary accountability points for such end results, just as corporate executives are the primary accountability points for long-term growth and profit.*"

The Frederick County School System works on the premise that what gets measured gets done. This is not only understood by the board but reinforced. A recent example was the case of a board member concerned about the representation of minorities in extracurricular activities, including areas such as homecoming queen. Under the Effective Schools Program and Farmer's eight goals, the most efficient way for the matter to be investigated was by addressing it through the appropriate goal and then seeing that it was measured.

"Everyone working in this school system is aware that if something doesn't get into the book to be measured, it won't get done," says Kevin Castner, Ed.D., associate superintendent. "Measuring is a different way of doing business, but it's the right way. And we're finding that we're breaking a lot of stereotypes this way."

Consider the stereotypes such as the belief that minority children don't excel in the sciences. As soon as they started measuring it, teachers discovered the minority kids often flew right past other students. One of the problems was that because of the stereotypes, minority children were not being nominated for certain programs.

The Frederick Board is not only watching some stereotypes fall by the wayside but they are also seeing a whole new way of doing business. The operation is much more professional than it once was. Administrators maintain that mediocre reports and requests for funds that previously would breeze past the committee now don't even receive a moment's consideration, and are sent back to be redone with proper documentation.

"Everything is related to outcomes," says Castner. "When we present something now, we must justify the cost by relating it to the desired outcomes, based on one of the eight goals. It's a very precise process, and it's very different, based solely on cause and effect."

Sue Rovin, president of the appointed Frederick County School Board, believes she and her colleagues are discussing the right questions. "Yes, it's the old 'what gets measured, gets done.' And that's how it should be. We look at those eight goals and know exactly what we have to do, and what we aren't doing. It keeps us focused, which is what every board needs."

She recalls that when Farmer first started talking to them about Effective Schools, they knew he was on the right course. But Farmer never let up. "What Effective Schools did was put a working plan to good common sense. It was all encompassing. And Noel kept pounding it into us. How important it is, how essential that the board be supportive and make a strong stand. I finally said, 'Enough, Noel, we've got it.' And I think we did have it. But I don't think any of us realized how right he was about the importance of the school board being involved and being accountable. That has made all the difference."

Rovin says that due to Farmer's sincerity, there is a genuine involvement of the board, a genuine sharing of decisions. The board is kept informed and they work closely with the superintendent and his staff. And although the district is very proud that they now rank at the top of the state on the performance tests, Rovin fears the ramifications of the ongoing recession.

"We have some major problems coming. We're increasing a thousand pupils a year. That takes teachers, buildings, resources. We have already stretched and pushed our people so much. They have risen to the challenge. But the future looks very difficult. We're going to have to cut down on the extras, some programs. And it's a shame because we're really on a roll. These people love their work and believe in it. They just wish they didn't have to hold a second job to keep their families afloat."

When asked if she believes Effective Schools was the right choice for Frederick County, she is emphatic. "You bet I do. Everyday I see the difference, and not just in the students, but with teachers and principals who have grown. The whole district is rejuvenated. There is positive movement in self-esteem, self-improvement."

Rovin does admit that change did not come easily for some employees. Frederick County is a system of over 3,000 school employees, and there were factions that wanted very much to protect the status quo. But in time, even those who initially held back, became involved, and, according to Rovin, "We just about worked them to death, and they rose to the occasion."

Because of all that hard work, the budget cuts are being met with some bitterness. And, for the first time since Effective Schools came in, the board is becoming more political. Observers say it is because of the problems with the economy, and the pressure budget cutting is putting on everyone. What Farmer and his staff are hoping, and counting on, is that the foundation of Effective Schools will carry them through the turmoil.

That spirit of cooperation began several years ago with Farmer demanding that the board be accountable, involved, and as excited about Effective Schools as he was. Once Effective Schools got underway, he realized he didn't have to demand the enthusiasm. And now, with the district outperforming districts that spend almost double what Frederick County does, that *esprit* is even moving into the central office. School officials just hope that *esprit* is stronger than the budget woes.

Central Office Serving the Schools?

Another major, almost revolutionary, change in the functioning of school districts undergoing the Effective Schools Improvement Process is that the role of the central office is dramatically changed from a haven for those whose mission is the maintenance of the status quo and the servicing of the political and public relations whims of the superintendent and board. Instead, it is a revitalized operation whose function is to provide skills and services directly to schools and children.

"I'm telling you it's really rather amazing," maintains Suzanne Still, principal of the Hollibrook Elementary School in Spring Branch, Texas. "I say that I want something, or there's a problem with a policy, or that I want to start this new program, and suddenly there are people in the central office doing research for me, investigating ways to change an outdated policy, or trying to find the resources I need. And this isn't just once in a while, this is becoming the way we operate."

Still expresses the feeling of many principals in Spring Branch who now feel they are not "out on a limb all alone." There is support for the innovations they want to do. Often it comes through the actions of individual people in the central office. However, those people are now acting according to a new policy that fosters this new involvement.

"That's what we are here for. The schools. The kids. That's it. Not to take care of politics," says Gary Mathews, associate superintendent in Spring Branch. "We try to make it as easy as posible for the principals to get what they need, be it supplies, resources, staff development programs, or the waiving, changing, of a policy that probably should have been changed a long time ago."

Although this seems like the way that central offices should ideally work, principals are quick to tell you that this is not the way it was. "It is a delightful change to know you have the support and help of the central office," says Still.

What Still is part of in Spring Branch is one of the most progressive restructurings going on in the Effective Schools Process. Spring Branch, Texas, is proudly rewriting the book on how a school department is supposed to operate.

"In the past, say, if Suzanne wanted to start her Fabulous Fridays program (Friday is devoted to special classes ranging from violin lessons to book writing to stamp collecting, along with basic skills tutoring), she would have had to begin by filing mountains of paperwork explaining what she wanted to do, how she was going to do it, and on and on, and maybe after six months, a year . . ." begins Bob Wells, a Spring Branch veteran who now serves as Executive Director for Human and Technological Resource Development. "But now, Suzanne and her school decide to do it. Suzanne talks to central office and receives their support, then the school comes to us if they need anything to get it going or make it better. And then we accommodate them as quickly as we can. Like immediately!"

As the administrators say in Spring Branch, "No children are being taught in the central office." All emphasis is directed toward accommodating the schools.

One of the areas of concern for Wells is staff development. It does not operate as one might think. If a teacher at a school decides that he or she would like to take a course in "Advanced Science for Fifth Graders" and the principal agrees it is a worthwhile endeavor for the teacher, Bob Wells's office is notified. "We then go out and try to find such a course," explains Wells. "Then once we do, we contact the teacher and line her up with it. We will do whatever we can to expedite funding and time off. We are not here to block such movements, but to make sure they happen."

This is indeed different. In the past, teachers would refer to getting something through the Spring Branch central office as "the time when you knew the idea would be killed." Principals say they often just gave up on some teacher initiatives because they knew they'd either be refused by central office or lie around in a paper pile until the words faded off the page.

All this change does not come easily to many people in central office. Their job was to protect the status quo. And they thought the status quo protected them. They saw these changes as not only wearing away at their power but also their job security. Just as in the schools where some teachers were criticized for encouraging change, and some principals were ridiculed and blackballed by colleagues for attempting to change the ways of the schools, so, too, in the central office did many administrators oppose anyone rocking the boat of the status quo.

"It was like there were teams up here," reports one Spring Branch administrator who had been in the system for 22 years. "There was the Effective Schools team and the ones who had no use for Effective Schools. At first, most of your people were on the opposing team. They saw all this change as a threat. And there was some active sabotage. You know, things that should have been done but weren't, some communications that may have gotten a little twisted. But soon people realized the change wasn't going to go away, and neither was Guthrie. And Guthrie wasn't opposed to rolling some heads. So people slowly started to get with the new system."

But wasn't there any recognition of the declining school system and the need for change? "No. Sorry to say that wasn't a concern. Jobs and promotion and hiring and keeping things as they were was important. I think that's finally changed a lot. But it took time."

This involves not just changing a political bureaucracy, but Effective Schools, because of its heavy reliance on data, research, and the process of constantly monitoring and adjusting, requires a streamlining of functions. For some old-line central office personnel who may just be discovering the self-correcting typewriter, all this streamlining is to be feared. Larry Lezotte looks at this as major culture shock for school department employees. "Many people in the central office are going to have to undergo a heart transplant," says Lezotte. "Because what's going to have to happen to people in central office is they're going to have to go to their local cardiologist and turn in their conformity, compliance, and control . . . and ask for a service license."

Much of the "serving" of the schools is going to be done through high technology. Central office personnel will have to be computer literate to handle the processing needs of schools evaluating tests, correlates, and changing needs. That compilation and integration of material will be a major task for central office. The days of central office administrators spending their hours handing out boxes of pencils to schools is slowly passing.

Competency and accountability just may reach the central office. The fact that it is going to come by way of school-based management, and not because of central office political control, will be most vexing to protectors of the status quo. According to Lezotte, in order for people to keep their jobs, they must "figure out new ways to ask the question: How can I help?" Wells and his staff development people in Spring Branch regularly ask that question and have been receiving a question in return: Is there any way we can find out what resources we have available in the system so we don't have to look elsewhere? I mean, if we have the talent here, why pay people from the outside?

So, Wells and his staff went to work. They are now compiling a detailed accounting of the talents of all the teachers in the district—be it hybrid rose gardening or advanced computer science. All these talents are being placed in one large manual that individual teachers and principals can consult to enhance their classes or programs. "That way we can give the work to people within the district," says Wells. "And the teachers don't even have to deal with us."

The end result of ideal school-based management would be a lessening of the need for large numbers of central office personnel. Spring Branch doesn't argue this fact. Indeed, if the Spring Branch restructuring moves along as it is planned, many people in the central office will be reassigned.

"The schools are where many of these support personnel could do the most good," explains Gary Mathews. "Yes, the way I look at it, if I do my job properly, and if all the right training is in line and effective, I'll make my own job unnecessary."

Mathews believes that the only way a school district can move from the old custodial school design of the past to a completely restructured system is to first move through the Effective Schools Process. "You cannot move into the twenty-first century without Effective Schools," believes Mathews. "You must first have that realignment starting right at the top. The Superintendent, the board, all key personnel must be totally committed to Effective Schools. Then you have to empower the schools, let the teachers and principals take ownership. Central office must realize it doesn't work for the board. Over time, the schools will see that the central office is there for them. And then once you have the alignment, you can move into the restructured school."

Most school districts today have as their organizational chart what Spring Branch refers to as the "old paradigm":

Board
Superintendent
Associate Superintendents
Executive Directors
Directors/Coordinators/Supervisors
Principals

The "new paradigm" of school district organization:

Board
Superintendent
Schools
Central Office Staff

"It's much cleaner, more efficient, and it is the only practical way for school systems to operate once you are into Effective Schools and campus planning," says Hal Guthrie, Ed.D., superintendent of Spring Branch. "I believe that unless the old bureaucracies give up their political ways, recognize that they must give up control to the individual schools, and work within the framework of Effective Schools, well, I don't think those school systems will survive," maintains Guthrie. "Oh, they'll be there. It's the kids who won't survive."

Effective Schools advocates agree that the bureaucratic control from a board of politicians only interested in their own political agenda has no place in the Effective Schools Improvement Process. The commitment to teaching for learning for *all* must be woven into the tapestry from the very top. And then every thread must carry and display boldly that devotion.

Once a board accepts its new responsibility and accountability in the Effective Schools Process—and once it understands what Effective Schools is all about and is not threatened by the campus ownership—it can easily give up its power over personnel and petty budget matters. And once the board has lifted its own heavy hand off the schools, then the yoke can be pulled from the central office. No longer will administrators and staff personnel believe their first objective is to keep the board members happy. Instead, they shall serve the schools.

This is happening in Spring Branch, in Spencerport, and in other Effective districts. In Frederick County, Superintendent Noel Farmer talks about the "ownership" now being felt by the central office personnel for the successes in the system. "They know that they are a part of the schools' progress. They are helping, from the expertise of their own areas, to the personal reaching out to the schools, for tutoring, for special seminars. These people are sharing in the pride, as they should."

It is a matter of the entire school district being aware that major change, in this case major improvement, is underway. The people in Frederick County know their system is going through a period of adjustment as they figure out the finest ways for all children to be served.

"Everyone in the central office knows what we're about, and the foot dragging is finally stopping," says Castner, associate superintendent of Frederick County. "We know that our job isn't just to teach for kids. We can't guarantee kids being successful. But we can increase the predictability of students' success. We must do that by finding the best practices, by varying the time and processes. And everyone is involved in that."

And everyone is celebrating Frederick County's success in tying for second place in state performance tests. It is tied with Howard County, a county that spends almost double what Frederick County spends per pupil. When Effective Schools experts are told of this, they are not surprised for two reasons: the recognized power of Effective Schools, and Noel Farmer. "If anyone could do it," says one expert, "it's Noel Farmer."

But Farmer and his staff are quick to say, "It's the teachers who did it—with some help from the central office." At any rate, it's a nice change to see a district passing the praise back and forth, instead of passing the buck and making excuses. As Noel Farmer and other superintendents keep saying, with a smile, "Nothing succeeds like success, and then it just breeds more success."

A New Role for State Education Departments

When Horace Mann set the wheels in motion for the establishment of the Massachusetts State Board of Education in 1837, he saw the state's role as one of providing information and guidance to public school systems. Initially, historians say the idea worked. But as other states created their monitoring bodies and as the bureaucracies grew, state education departments often became more of a hindrance than a help to local school systems. Superintendents spoke of miles of red tape, stacks of outdated rules and regulations, and interference from authoritarian bureaucrats who were only interested in their own survival and the maintenance of the always safe, very reliable, status quo.

Practitioners say that it is now changing in many states. Much of that change they believe is due to the impetus of the federal legislation endorsing Effective Schools (Hawkins-Stafford Act, P.L. 100-297 passed in April 1988) as well as the work of individual school districts with the Effective Schools Improvement Process. Governors and state legislators saw the same thing in Effective Schools that first pulled in change-oriented superintendents: accountability. And while some states do not broadcast the name *Effective Schools,* but call their operations *school effectiveness* or *school improvement,* many of the changes being put in place come out of the Effective Schools research and literature.

Many states now are calling for school improvement plans based on school-based management, outcome-based policies, and increased staff development. It is not unusual to see school districts out ahead of the state's initiatives. In many cases, the state education leaders are taking their cue from what has been happening in certain progressive districts. And while this bodes well for those districts undergoing the improvement process, it does not settle well with those still steeped in the status quo.

"We're very happy with what the state is doing," says Dr. Gary Mathews, associate superintendent of Spring Branch (Texas) Schools. "They're getting right into the school-based management issue, examining all the outcome-based programs, and I think they're going to be taking a very strong stand for accountability." Indeed, in the spring of 1992, all Texas school districts must have filed a school-based improvement plan. The monitoring and testing program for the state is being revised and expanded. Teacher and administrative training and accreditation are being evaluated.

One of the states being very closely watched by educators is Maryland. A 1987–88 report by the Governor's Commission on School Performance asked the question of whether or not the state was preparing its school children for a high quality of life. The answer, in a word: No. Since then, the state has made some dramatic changes in programs as well as approach.

"We have a more active role because now we're outcome based," explains Bob Gabrys, assistant state superintendent and director of the Maryland School Performance Program. "We've shifted from process oriented to product. The big difference from before is we are looking at how a student applies what he or she receives in the public schools. Is the education really working for that student?"

The Maryland program is comprehensive and systemic. It is not only pulling together business and community resources but also the various state agencies that have jurisdiction. "We don't believe you can do it in bits and pieces," says Gabrys. "It's not just a matter of working with teachers and administrators, but the entire community that the child comes from."

The state has adopted 10 goals that run the gamut from health and hygiene, drugs, academic performance, and career training. Several pilot programs have been set up that bring the different agencies together to serve children. There are two staff development centers that deal with school-based instructional decision making. There are also guidelines and procedures for school improvement planning. There is a comprehensive testing program—called the Maryland Report Card—that rates districts in statewide testing and categorizes schools from excellent all the way down to heading for receivership. And, like other states, Maryland has set up comprehensive criterion-referenced testing in language, arts, math, and social science. These tests, which are task oriented, and not multiple choice, are designed to analyze the thinking skills of students.

To assist teachers with the new monitoring procedures, Frederick County has brought together a consortium of over 100 people from 16 different counties to create a lengthy notebook to assist teachers in dealing with the assessment. Over 1,000 teaching and performance objectives are addressed by the teachers, giving them a greater sense of ownership in the entire process.

Overall, the state has become more outcome based, and while this doesn't bother districts like Frederick County that have been working in that direction for several years, it is not sitting well with many other districts. Some superintendents believe the state is pushing too hard and its time lines are unreasonable.

"But for us, it's actually been a help," explains Kevin Castner of Frederick County. "The state's push for higher-level performance goals is just like ours. They are putting instruction and assessment into one, something we've been doing for years. This actually gives us more credibility with our people. We think they're moving in the right direction; they're right on top of all the research."

In pushing its outcome-based, results-oriented approach, Maryland is examining not just academic scores and dropouts but the career paths of students—where they started and where they ended up. Practitioners say it is a necessary assessment of the performance and the needs of the public schools. One of the areas being studied is the eleventh grade.

"Suppose you have one student on an academic course," says Gabrys. "And you have a second student on a career track. Well, the last week of school they decide to switch tracks. Does that mean they have wasted their entire public school education? And if the answer is no, then what is it that they now know and are supposed to be able to do?"

It is this close look at the tracking system, and the aligning of instruction with assessment, and making the product, and not the process, the focus that is exciting educators throughout the United States. But as Maryland and other states move down the path of outcome-based improvement, experts as well as the practitioners say they are all going to end up at the same place—having to address the question of equity in district funding.

And that question is just going to become more complicated because of the performance of districts like Frederick County that have proven they can outperform the higher-priced districts. Even the argument over funding discrepancies may have to wait for another day. Right now the problem for the nineties seems to be figuring out how to survive the currently crippling federal, state, and local budget cuts.

State-Mandated Effective Schools Improvement

Some states have been forthright in their endorsement of the Effective Schools Program. South Carolina adopted the Effective Schools correlates and Improvement Process statewide. Once again, this was based on the business community's appreciation for the motivating factor of accountability. The implementation process has not been without problems, and those problems—and remarkable successes—are examined in Chapter 13, which discusses the struggles and illusions of Effective Schools.

The state often viewed as a front-runner in at least establishing statewide opportunities for participation in Effective Schools is Connecticut. As far back as 1979, the State Board of Education included the philosophy of Effective Schools in its goals for the upcoming decade. However, it took 10 years before the major tenets of Effective Schools actually showed up in state policy. These were addressed in four "themes": focus on equity; resources for professional development; school as a unit for change; and accountability and new age measurement.

The Connecticut process of working within the Effective Schools philosophy was voluntary and at first only 5 schools were involved. That has grown to over 125 schools in 45 districts, with the state actively involved as consultants, trainers, and facilitators to the process, working with the schools in orientation, assessment, planning, and implementation.

The Connecticut Effective Schools Process has been carried out solely on a school-by-school basis, viewing the school as the essential unit for change. The state has been under some pressure to require its schools to report disaggregated data to the state, and is now rewriting its procedures for measurement and reporting, using a school profiles format. While the state is holding fast to its commitment to Effective Schools philosophy, the financial problems within the state are forcing a severe cutback and realignment of all personnel and resources.

Whatever the future holds for Connecticut, it will always be regarded as the home base for one of the most comprehensive needs assessment tests used in the Effective Schools Improvement Process. The Connecticut School Effectiveness Interview and Questionnaire, and the Secondary School Development Instrument, drawn up in the early eighties, were major contributions to the developing research base for Effective Schools. The questionnaires became essential components of school effectiveness programs throughout the country.

Whether it is at the state level, or involving the central office or the district boards of education, the advent of Effective Schools has precipitated some major changes in how school districts operate. There is still politics, as there always will be with public bureaucracies, but there is proof that at least in some instances, and perhaps where least expected, politics is taking a back seat to school improvement.

One of the more stunning examples comes from District 6 in New York City, Spanish Harlem. This district—the worst of New York's 32 school districts before Tony Amato and Effective Schools came in—was also regarded as one "the most political, and the most unmanageable."

Three years after Amato began, District 6 (26,000 students, 90 percent on free or reduced lunch) is topping the charts in the city's reading scores. Union unrest is at one of the lowest levels of any district in the city. Campus planning is the order of the day. Central office works for the schools and the schools know it and take advantage of it.

When Tony Amato's contract was up after three years, there were three other people in line for the job because Tony was known in District 6 for "not playing the political game"—and the board members apparently didn't like that. He was going to be replaced; it was just a matter of choosing his successor.

So, Tony Amato, who didn't play games with or bow low to the board and simply rode on his record as superintendent, was unofficially informed his services wouldn't be required any longer. While Tony packed his belongings, the board's agenda was suddenly changed by quite a few parents, teachers, administrators, and community officials who had some things to say. They started talking about Effective Schools and what Tony Amato had done. They pointed to scores, increased attendance, new teacher involvement, heightened morale, the *esprit*, the fact that everyone was "pitching in for the kids," and that the success was starting to show.

The board listened, looked, and voted—nine to nothing to renew Tony Amato's contract. Amato's comment? "There is hope for this country's public school systems," he says quietly.

CHAPTER THIRTEEN

Money, Vision, and Illusion

The Promises and Pitfalls of Effective Schools

You see, we are not what you think we are. —RUFUS YOUNG, assistant superintendent

There are schools in the United States that wear the stamp "Effective School" that are not effective, efficient, or anywhere near excellent. Despite what appear to be the best laid plans and the finest of intentions, these school districts and schools are failures—failures for the students and failures for the faculty and staff.

The problems can usually be traced back to those "best laid plans" and "finest of intentions." In this chapter, the plans and intentions of bureaucrats, businesspeople, politicians, and educators are examined in three very different profiles. The first is the state of South Carolina, which is struggling with a mandate of effectiveness from the state legislature. The second is the city of St. Louis, Missouri, which initiated one of the most successful Effective School Improvement Processes, only to have it fall to political gamesmanship and administrative ineptness. The last profile is a composite of several districts that call themselves effective but are frighteningly ineffective. The only effective part of these districts is the superintendent's public relations team.

These three profiles do not tell nice stories about Effective Schools, but they are important stories about the power of the status quo, of the political bureaucracy, and of the fears and biases of many Americans. They have important lessons for all of us.

South Carolina: A Penny for Your Thinking Skills

Who would ever think we could do so much for so many with so little? This state government, thanks to the prodding of business, has finally done what it should—give people a life. —ELLEN HAYDEN, vice-president, South Carolina Chamber of Commerce

In the spring of 1983, South Carolina Governor Richard W. Riley studied the latest stack of reports on the economic progress of the people of his state and realized it was past time to address some of the state's most fundamental problems.

The illiteracy rate in South Carolina was climbing. The dropout rate in the high schools was one of the highest in the nation, fluctuating between an astounding 33 and 40 percent. Less than half of the parents of school-age children had a high school diploma. Less than 10 percent had ever attended college classes.

With a starting salary of $18,000, the state was having trouble bringing in qualified teachers.

South Carolina was leading the nation in infant mortality. Other health problems, from heartworm in children to veneral disease in teenagers, were on the rise (South Carolina ranked first in syphilis and third in gonorrhea).

And business leaders were complaining that they couldn't find qualified South Carolinians to hire for their shops and mills. At a time of increased technology, managers were looking for workers who could at least read the manuals for the new equipment. But those workers could not be found in sufficient numbers—not in South Carolina, anyway.

Governor Riley, who had garnered considerable education good will in his election campaign, went to business leaders and proposed a one-cent increase in the then four-cent sales tax. He wanted one-third of it to go to education. The business community said no. However, they said that if he did it next year, they would back him 100 percent. Governor Riley took them up on the deal and designated that all of that one penny would go toward the 1984 South Carolina Education Improvement Act.

The trick was to get the state to accept it. That required the most powerful grassroots campaign in the history of the state. It also fostered the creation of a highly successful partnership between education, the Effective Schools philosophy, and the business community. That partnership sustains educational improvement in South Carolina to this date.

Two blue-ribbon committees were formed, each consisting of 32 members. The first committee was made up of big business, a few senior legislators, and the governor and his people. The other committee (which did the majority of the grassroots work) consisted of one third educators, one third legislators, and one-third business leaders.

"We basically pulled out all stops," recalls Terry Peterson, Ph.D., executive director of the South Carolina Business Education Committee, who worked hand in hand with Governor Riley. "We knew we were talking about the economic survival of this state. We pulled in all the business heavy hitters, the education leaders, and said, 'Hey, we have no choice, we've got to make this work.'"

On these committees, there would be the CEO of a major South Carolina business sitting next to a third-grade teacher. Initially, it seemed they had little to talk about, but as weeks turned into months, the CEOs and teachers became aligned. The business leaders wanted to know why high school students couldn't handle the new automation in the plants and mills. The teachers told them. Meanwhile, the legislators listened.

One of Terry Peterson's first tasks was to analyze and report on the latest thinking on educational reform. "That's where the Effective Schools literature came in," explains Peterson. "Not only did the basic terminology with all the correlates seem to be just what we were looking for and needed but there was also restructuring implicit in the changes, and we knew that was something we had to go for."

Those restructuring changes and the demand for accountability caught the eye of the business community. This was the first time they had heard about schools being operated as businesses, with visionary leaders and an emphasis on outcomes. The business community staked its existence on outcomes. It was the inability to do anything about results, or complete lack of concern on the part of educators for results in the schools, that had so frustrated the business community in recent years. Now, finally, here was a reform package that addressed what they saw as the greatest need in the schools: getting good results.

"Effective Schools has a lot of common sense built into it. Business likes common sense, especially when it boils down to getting a decent product," says Ellen Hayden, vice president for Education for the South Carolina Chamber of Commerce. "We also knew that the schools needed management changes. They needed leadership. The principals needed direction on how to produce the best product. And make the most of that raw product."

In the past, businesses had resorted to holding their own literacy classes on plant and factory sites. But the number of employees in need was growing to a point where it was more economical for business to hire from out of state or overseas than retrain South Carolinians.

"Textiles have diversified. Work in the mills is very different today from what it was," explains Hayden. "The machinery is complicated. We need a skilled work force out there."

Textiles is still the leading industry in South Carolina. Tourism ranks second. But with the ascending inflation in the north, more and more businesses are moving into the Sunbelt. The state advertises a willing, hungry workforce. Business leaders and politicians are concerned that they will slip back on their promise to provide a qualified, ready to go, ready-to-train workforce.

So, the more the business community studied the Effective Schools literature—its emphasis on outcomes and accountability—the more they believed this just might be the answer for the ailing South Carolina schools. "It was the accountability we knew the schools lacked," says Peterson. "There was no surprise when we saw these committees coming back with the accountability push. They wanted Effective Schools. They just wanted to make sure we were going for the whole package. It was like they were asking, 'OK, we'll go for this if you're really sure you're going to get that accountability in there.'"

In that sense, the South Carolina schools were no different from schools in San Mateo, California, or Plymouth, Massachusetts. The history of public education is one that avoids the word *accountability*, does not understand an outcomes-oriented operation, and is mired in the political comfort of maintaining the status quo.

Business leaders in South Carolina were not about to bend on the issue of outcomes. Riley and his staff agreed. As they campaigned throughout the state, they emphasized, over and over again, that the key component of the Education Improvement Act (EIA) of 1984 would be accountability for student outcomes. Pursuing this line of thinking, the EIA called for mandatory exit exams for high school graduates. This was the first time there had been anything like this in South Carolina's history.

"Business was really very sick of seeing these high school graduates who couldn't read the first line of the work application," says Ellen Hayden, adding that the business community had become almost numb with frustration over their inability to do anything about the abyssmal state of the public schools. "So now that the governor comes to us and we finally have a say, well, yes, we took our role very seriously. These kids are the future of this state, and we knew that we were losing them. And with them, we were losing much of the hope for this area's prosperity."

The proponents of the Education Improvement Act knew all efforts would be futile if there was no consideration given to teachers, their salary, and their training. So, under the EIA compensatory education programs were created along with two incentive pay programs for teachers. Staff development was doubled from 5 days a year to 10 days a year.

"We knew we had to do something about salaries," says Peterson. "And that's a lot of what that sales tax increase was about. But the business leaders wanted something in return. They weren't going to approve anything unless there was some guarantee that the schools would be forced into accountability, that they wouldn't just continue as they were, with just more money in the coffers. That's why the concise thinking of Effective Schools and accountability came in."

Very simply, the business leaders wanted a return on their investment. Riley and his staff agreed that that was what they, too, were after. The vehicle for accountability was the Effective Schools Process. So, with the Effective Schools criteria, research, and planning in tow, the coalition of business leaders, legislators, and the executive branch of government started hitting the hustings to sell this one-penny tax for education.

"We knew it would be tough. This is not a state that has regarded education as a priority," says Peterson. "But I don't think any of us knew quite how tough it would be. There was a lot of opposition to this plan." The opposition came from people who believed the state was already spending enough on education. They also didn't believe that the educators were doing an acceptable job with the money they had. They saw the schools as safe little enclaves where the inefficient and lazy could receive a paycheck. After all, they asked, what was the guarantee that more money would make a difference? In many people's eyes, enough money was being spent.

The average per pupil expenditure in South Carolina is $3,465 a year. Over 40 percent of the students qualify for free or reduced lunch. There are 617,000 students in South Carolina's 1,107 public schools. Total expenditures in 1988, including debt service, capital outlay, adult programs, community services, and pupil activities, were $2,430,359,289. Although $3,465 seems like a great deal of money to South Carolinians to spend on education, it is a far cry from the $5,276 spent in Chicago's elementary schools, to say nothing of the $11,000 plus spent in some secondary school districts on Long Island, New York. That average of $3,465 grows even smaller when you consider some districts spend as little as $1,600 per pupil in South Carolina.

"Education has not been a priority. It's that simple and that sad," explains Ellen Still, assistant to the Education Committee for the South Carolina General Assembly. "The problems in this state are very serious. Education and health problems. And one of the reasons for that is because so many of our schools are isolated, far away from resources and services."

Breaking through the Apathy

The problem of apathy toward education is a reality that South Carolina cannot continue to ignore. Ellen Still tells of an incident that is particularly condemning. In the early eighties, there were 350 schools that qualified for free food for their children, but the administrators of the schools never followed through on any of the steps to receive the free food. "They said it was 'too much trouble,'" says Still.

Thus, 350 schools—one-third of South Carolina's public schools—did not receive the free food for their children that they were entitled to. It was performance like this from educators in the schools that made people think twice about the efficacy of any sales tax for education.

There are also stories of special health and education programs funded by the federal government going into particularly needy communities. But because of a failure of local officials to get the word out or to provide a basic environment where the programs could be administered, less than 50 percent of the funds from those programs were used. One of the major reasons given by local officials as to why the benefits of those programs were never received by many in need is the fact that the people in charge of administering them were white, and many of the recipients were black.

"You have to understand," said one legislator, "that there is still a very segregated poor community out there, not all of them black, but all of them dirt poor. And the more well-to-do folks just believe those people like living that way, and if they wanted to change, they would. They don't see that these programs could help. They think those people should do it themselves."

This attitude was displayed in many communities when it came to the Education Improvement Act. Many saw it as a program that would just help blacks, that it was the blacks that needed the most help but were also a drain on the educational system. When asked, business, education, and legislative leaders admit that there are still lingering pockets of racism and that animosity toward the black community is a factor that cannot be denied. "Hey, remember this is a state that still refers to the Civil War as the 'War of Northern Aggression,'" said one businessman, commenting on the lingering segregation and racism.

Another legislator was more forthright: "Many people looked on the EIA as just another program to throw money at 'those lazy blacks.' Riley had a heck of a job convincing them it was for *all* kids. Just as much for 'white trash' as it was for 'lazy blacks.'"

The EIA also had another problem. Some people thought it was another communist conspiracy. "Sure, as soon as we started talking about higher-order thinking skills," explained one businessman, "they thought we were talking about a 'new wave conspiracy' to take control of their kids' minds."

Along with dealing with the concerns of racism, communism, and general antieducation sentiment, there was the psychological problem of whether or not the state could even do any better in the educational arena. Many thought that however South Carolina students were performing now, well, that was as good as it was going to get.

"Believe it or not, one of our biggest problems and it became the major hurdle for passing the legislation, was people's expectations," explains Terry Peterson. "Never mind the expectations within the schools. We haven't even gotten there yet. We're talking about the average Joe on the street. No one felt the schools could do any better."

This is where Governor Riley put his greatest efforts—in convincing the people of South Carolina they *all* could do better. "You have to be very careful not to blame anybody, but at the same time tell people they just haven't tried their best," says Peterson. "That's where the business community came in strong. They pushed this whole development of human potential aspect very strong. And slowly, very slowly, you could tell the general feeling was starting to turn in our favor."

But it was far from easy. Observers say it never would have happened if not for the commitment of Governor Riley and his wife to the betterment of life for all the citizens of South Carolina. They traveled throughout the state, talking to PTAs, garden clubs, police and fire departments, neighborhood watch groups, teachers groups, anyone who would listen. "I don't know how they kept going. I think they were fueled exclusively by the mission," recalls Peterson. "It almost killed some of us. But we knew it *had* to pass, it just *had* to."

And in June of 1984, the Education Improvement Act for South Carolina passed. The sales tax went up one penny, and that one penny went to improve the thinking skills of the state's 617,000 students.

The analogy that is used by many education observers of what has happened and what is now going on is that of an 800-pound elephant slowly sitting down. "It's like there is this 800-pound elephant that is slowly, but inevitably, sitting down," explains one legislator. "And what we've been able to do is get under this sucker and stop it from sitting down. And we've done that. Now we're trying to push it back up. But there's a lot of inertia to turn around."

Those who fought the fight for EIA continued their struggle in 1989, achieving passage of Target 2000: School Reform for the Next Decade, which continued the basic themes of the EIA. Those themes for Target 2000 are the same as those at the heart of that historic Education Improvement Act: the tenets of Effective Schools.

The EIA called for the development and implementation of School Improvement Plans based on six "Effectiveness criteria: (1) positive school learning climate; (2) strong instructional leadership; (3) emphasis on academics; (4) frequent monitoring of student progress; (5) high expectations; (6) positive home-school relations."

The entities for creating and implementing these School Improvement Plans were the School Improvement Councils. The School Improvement Councils were first established in South Carolina in 1977 as part of the Education Finance Act. The councils were then responsible for reviewing annual expenditures to ensure that finances were being used for improved schooling. The responsibilities and power of the councils were greatly increased under the EIA. There was also to be no fudging; this time the councils were to be taken seriously.

Ideally, these councils not only developed, implemented, and monitored the new school improvement plan but also conducted a comprehensive needs assessment of the individual school (prior to creation of the plan), advised on school incentive cash awards from the State Board of Education, and assisted with any special problems.

It sounded good in theory and looked good on paper, but there were a few problems. "The law was passed saying, basically, 'Go thou and do.' But nobody had any idea how to do the 'do,'" says Jean Norman, Ed.D., director of the School Improvement Assistance Council, the office (Norman, an assistant, and a secretary) set up to assist the councils in their school improvement planning and implementation.

"Here come the Effective Schools correlates, and yes, the correlates make sense, it all makes sense, but those people out there in the schools had absolutely no training in Effective Schools," recalls Norman. "What it boiled down to is On-the-Job Training. And that's what it still is. It's just that some people are getting better at it than others." This combined with the lack of training was the usual sentiment that "this too shall pass," that the EIA and the school improvement plans and the councils were just another reform movement—and reform movements come and reform movements go.

"There was the attitude of just wait and see," says Norman. "There had been no training, no preparation of teachers and principals and superintendents and boards as to what was expected of them to put all this into effect. So how else could they feel other than that no one was serious about this?"

The legislation had passed in June and by September the schools were supposed to be into their school improvement plans. Many of them did initiate plans, but many more just took advantage of the increased funding, did the necessary paperwork, and carried on as usual.

"There are many who would rather see this school improvement process just go away," says Norman. "They don't want to share their power with councils, they don't want improvement plans, they say, 'I'm in charge here and everybody works for me and end of discussion.' Then there were those who genuinely wanted to change and saw the councils and us as a means to that. They took advantage of the few programs available at the beginning."

The prospect of regular teacher, principal, and superintendent evaluations caught many people off guard and frightened them. The new accountability aspect of the reform was a change that was new to the South Carolina schools. "This was teacher and principal evaluations for the first time. That threatened a lot of people," says Norman. "Slowly people started to realize this wasn't a fad. This was not going to go away. The evaluations were for real. So was the school improvement plan. This was going to last. The legislature was serious. This was real money here. And eventually, they started taking advantage of our services and reorganizing and rethinking what they were doing."

Principals and teachers realized they needed more training in order to carry out proper evaluations, and that began a long-term process of improvement. There were some teacher-oriented training programs made available and under the progressive principals, faculty and staff received training previously nonexistent.

"Once you had an evaluation process, you could create an incentive process," explains Norman. "And so we had principals and teachers who said, 'Now that I'm doing well, I should be recognized for it. There should also be financial recognition.' That's something that is still being worked out.

"We also need to be looking at those Effective Schools' criteria, and giving acknowledgment or recognition for the kind of programs people have in place that do accomplish their goals. Test scores are going up. You see that across the state. The reason for that is the Effective Schools criteria. Test scores are moving up, kids are doing better, they're staying in school, there's more parental involvement."

Norman says that one of the major problems in South Carolina remains a bureaucracy that does not believe in school-based management. By its very setup, the South Carolina schools run counter to Effective Schools in that respect. All major decisions are still made by the State Department of Education. "And for the last five years, they have been running a leadership academy for principals that has not even mentioned, formally, school-based management," says Norman.

As in many other states, there has been a void in the role of higher education. Ironically, the School Council Assistance Project, which operates out of the College of Education at the University of South Carolina, receives very little input from the University.

"They (University of South Carolina, Columbia) sit just two blocks from the General Assembly," says one legislator, "living off the money we give them. Supposedly training teachers for our schools. But do they even come and see what this school reform is all about? Do they even show any interest? No. We have to tell them what's going on. Then, like your usual academic, they act like they know everything, turn and walk away talking about what important things they have to do. Then we see their teachers in the schools, and they don't know a thing about what we're really trying to do and how it's to be done. Effectiveness, evaluations, cooperative learning, instructional leadership . . . the university just doesn't address these things seriously. And so then we have to start spending more money *retraining* these teachers from the University, whom we've already spent a lot of money on!"

Norman just nods when told of this comment. "I think it's important to keep in mind who engineered and who backed and who fought for school reform in this state. The governor, the legislature, and business. The grassroots," she says, adding that it is unfortunate that when change finally reached the schools, it was the people in the schools who "once again" had to assume the whole burden—alone.

The Penny Made a Difference

Those carrying the burden of the Education Improvement Act—those principals and teachers who have worked diligently on the Effective Schools Process—have scored impressive victories for the state of South Carolina. Some of the more significant gains include:

- Substantial increase in SAT scores (+36 points)
- Higher achievement in basic skills (125,000 more students meeting minimum standards)

- Increase of 18.9 percent in students scoring above national average in basic skills
- Reduced student and teacher absences (20 percent less absenteeism by students and 7 percent less absenteeism among teachers)
- Improved student writing performance (+ 11 percent)
- Increased number of students heading off to college (+ 7 percent)
- More students taking advanced courses (+ 250 percent)
- More students meeting high standards for high school graduation and college entrance (i.e., 132 percent increase in students taking two or more years of foreign language and a 75 percent increase in students taking chemistry)
- *Many* more students meeting Exit Examination requirements for graduation (+ 40 percent)
- More students being trained in vocational programs for which there are jobs (9.7 percent)
- Increased business/education partnerships in schools (+ 800 percent)
- More teachers and principals meeting higher standards (i.e., 10 percent more teachers meeting higher initial certification standards)
- Increase of teacher salaries by 47 percent

These successes do not put South Carolina near the top of the national heap when it comes to school effectiveness, but given how low scores were in the past and how abysmal was the teacher and student morale, the victories are a giant step forward. However, the success does not transfer to all schools. Indeed, the success is proving less of a catalyst for change than people had hoped.

Because of long-held attitudes and biases, and a penchant to protect the status quo no matter how devastating that status quo is, Dr. Norman observes many schools that just have not moved to improve. And there are many schools where principals are apparently very reticent about sharing their command with the school improvement councils.

In a 1990 report of 397 school improvement councils (survey questionnaires were sent out to 600 of the state's 1100 schools; 397 responded), the following assessments were reached:

- From 70 to 80 percent of the councils appear to have the basic structures in place to function effectively.
- From 70 to 80 percent of councils reportedly assist the principal to set school goals/objectives; however, 20 to 30 percent are *not* involved, and 20 to 45 percent are involved in assessing the school but are not involved in making recommendations about the school program.
- Generally, principals report support for the concept of councils; however, 20 to 30 percent of the principals surveyed indicated *an aversion* to even *minimal* compliance.

- Approximately half of the teachers surveyed perceived councils as important partners in school improvement; 25 percent do not support the roles and responsibilities given to councils.
- Council members and principals perceive a *lack of support* for the council's function in the improvement process in 30 to 60 percent of the schools.
- School-site councils that are perceived by principals and council members as having a high impact in the school tend to be in schools that have high expectations for students, frequently monitor student progress, and have significantly positive home-school relations.

There is clearly a direct link between the effectiveness (perceived or not) of the improvement councils and the degree to which the correlates of the Effective Schools have been implemented. The extent to which the councils are having a say in the schools is also open to conjecture. The report notes that 64 percent of the principals in the schools responding to the survey reported their schools had won a school incentive award at least once. "However, only 53 percent of them said they have ever involved their school improvement councils in deciding how to utilize the reward. This is clearly not in compliance with law and regulation," states the report.

Norman says it is still a daily struggle, and the state still has a long way to go before it approaches anything that could be called statewide effectiveness. Frustrated and angry, she talks about the calls to her office from principals who are taking over a school and who discover that there has never been a needs assessment done, no call to set up an improvement council, no real push for teacher training programs.

"There is a large number, clearly at least 25 percent of the principals out there who would be pleased if the councils went away," she says. "But those schools that have implemented plans and change—there is another 25 percent who are doing an incredibly good job—are showing progress in not only test scores but in teacher and staff morale.""

The one area that South Carolina is still having major trouble making a dent in is the dropout rate. It remains at over one-third. In some schools, as many as 40 percent of the high school students drop out before they enter the twelfth grade.

"It all goes back to attitudes, and to a lack of expectations," believes Norman. "I say to these teachers, 'Well, do you expect . . ?' and they say, 'No, of course we don't expect these kids to graduate from high school.' 'Well, why not?' 'Well, because some kids just cannot make it.'

"And unfortunately, considering the system they're working under, that's probably correct. The problem is they've never thought about changing the system, about approaching kids in any other way. Remember, this is a society—a southern society—that has some very firm ideas on who succeeds and who doesn't.

"High expectations is the toughest because it focuses on values. And the question is: Do you teach behaviors or do you teach values? At any rate, the dialogue has at least begun."

The dialogue for school improvement for South Carolina was just a whisper in 1983. By June 1984, with the passage of the Education Improvement Act, that dialogue began in earnest and is now heard throughout the state. Thanks to the EIA, the legislators, and businesspeople behind it, and the Effective Schools research, change for the better has come to many South Carolina schools. A penny on the sales tax has kept the 800-pound elephant from sitting down.

The question that now remains is whether the inertia is indeed broken and that elephant will rise up from its squat and *really* lift the shadow off the children of South Carolina. What needs to happen is that the very same impetus that directed the businessleaders to Effective Schools must now push the people in the schools toward Effectiveness. It is the matter of acountability. The motivating factor for business to choose Effectiveness was accountability. Now it is up to the schools to be motivated by that same drive for accountability. It is accountability that will give the people of South Carolina the just return on their investment.

Cheat Me in St. Louis: Testimony to Effectiveness (and Political Betrayal)

Teachers, principals, and school superintendents come from across the country to sit in its classrooms. Mayors, governors, congressmen, and federal officials walk its corridors. Leaders and educators from Eastern and Western Europe as well as Asia stare out its windows in horror, then turn and gaze, almost unbelievingly, into the vibrant, determined eyes of its pupils. When they leave, they all say the same thing: IF IT CAN HAPPEN THERE, IT CAN HAPPEN ANYWHERE.

The "there" is the Laclede Elementary School in St. Louis, Missouri. It is on the north side of St. Louis, an area known more for its drug trade, violent crime, abandoned buildings, burned-out cars and businesses, and burgeoning gang problems than for education.

But the block that houses the Laclede breaks the pattern of disintegration. The old, brick, Gothic-style school building rises on a small hill like an Eton building on England's playing fields. The lawn is small but immaculate, and the bricks and glass display a clean freshness that stands in glaring contrast to much of the neighborhood.

There is another building that competes for this stand-out attention on the north side of St. Louis. Strangely enough in this time of graffiti-stained, cracked and crumbling inner-city schools, it is another institution of learning: the Harriet Beecher Stowe Middle School.

These buildings rise like phoenixes out of the ashes of despair, decay, and death. Although their exteriors are testimony to the pride of the inhabitants, it is the work going on within that is testimony to the power of Effective Schools and the teaching and learning of each and every individual.

In 1981, Laclede Elementary (K–5) registered less than 20 percent of its grades at or above grade level on the California Achievement Test. In 1987, 93 percent of the grades at Laclede were at or above grade level. The number of students scoring in the bottom quartile had been cut in half, from 19 to 10 percent.

For those who say it is easier to turn around an elementary school than a middle school, the scores at the Stowe Middle (grades 6–8) are even more impressive. In 1981, there were no grades at the Stowe School performing at or above grade level. In 1987, 100 percent—every grade in the school—were performing at or above grade level. The number of students performing in the lowest quartile had fallen from 28.3 percent to less than 8 percent.

In 1981, only 14 percent of the students at the Stowe Middle School passed the state-mandated eighth-grade competency test. In 1987, *95 percent of the students passed all sections of the exam.*

When and how did this transformation begin? It began, simply enough, with a wife prodding her husband to attend a panel on a new brand of school reform. "I was one of the people who edited Ron Edmonds's article on Effective Schools," explains Dr. Savannah Miller-Young, principal of the Shepard Elementary School, as she refers to the now famous article in *Educational Leadership*. "I spent a lot of time on the phone with Ron, so when I heard he was speaking at the Conference of the National Alliance of Black School Educators in the fall of 1979, I knew it was a must for Rufus and me." Rufus is her husband, who is presently the assistant superintendent of the St. Louis Public Schools, and was then the city's Executive Director of Personnel. Rufus, a determined man with a tall, commanding presence, had grown up in the St. Louis schools as a boy and as an educator. He began his career teaching in the classroom and, although his "classrooms" have changed, Dr. Young has not stopped teaching since 1945. As one of the few blacks in the St. Louis School Department, he began making his mark early.

In 1955, following the 1954 Supreme Court desegregation ruling, Young was the first minority principal in St. Louis with Caucasian teachers. He began numerous programs in curriculum development, staff development, counselor training, and community relations (involving the city's numerous social service organizations) that had the heretofore unseen impact of increasing pupil attendance and test scores while decreasing suspensions and disciplinary problems.

In 1967, Young was promoted to district administration where he served as Director of Education. In 1969, he was appointed director of the Title VIII Dropout Prevention Program. And in 1971, he made the leap into central office in the appointment of Executive Director of Personnel.

By this time, people in the St. Louis School community were aware that Rufus Young was a man who was going to ruffle a lot of feathers during his career. He had a reputation for putting children first and politics second (although he always got the job done "trying to keep everyone as happy as possible"). In his role as director of personnel, he walked the heavily mined path between the unions and management.

In July 1979, he became district superintendent for Area 1, one of the most diverse populations within the City of St. Louis. With the responsibility of 16,000 students and over 2,500 teachers, administrators, and staff, he was one of the highest ranking black educators in the United States. It was at this point, later that year in November 1979, that he agreed to attend the Black School Educators conference with his wife.

"We were standing out in the lobby of the hotel and Savannah introduced me to Ron and we started talking," explains Young. "Well, he talked, I asked, and he talked, and I listened. And three hours later, still standing in that same lobby, still listening, I knew this man had it all. He had in his mind the only hope—or maybe the greatest hope—we have for the schools today. It was all right there, from start to finish.

"Along the way in my career I had put together some of the pieces. I knew some of the elements. But here it was—the process. That's the most important. You have to have the process. And Ron Edmonds had it. And I knew right then St. Louis was going to have that process. No matter what." And that's where Effective Schools and St. Louis began.

But Edmonds's research was just breaking out then, and St. Louis was not about to spend a whole lot of time and money on what they saw as an experimental program designed exclusively to benefit the minority student (that's how the Edmonds research was viewed). The administration blankedly refused Rufus's request, insisting then in 1979 that Edmonds's findings were premature.

So, Young went to Dr. John Ervin, vice president of the Danforth Foundation, a national educational philanthropic organization whose activities have emphasized the theme of improving the quality of teaching and learning. Ervin studied the material and became a strong supporter of Effective Schools. With his help, an educational intervention project involving a cluster of schools was finally funded.

Young chose four schools in Area 1 that were "nothing if not miserable—they just weren't making it," says Young. In fact, the four schools were performing at averages more than two years below grade level. The four schools were the Laclede, Hempstead, and Arlington Elementary Schools, and the Harriet Beecher Stowe Middle School. The effort was called Project SHAL, an anacronym using the initials of the four schools. The schools, with populations of around 300, served black students from low socioeconomic backgrounds. Over 90 percent of the students were on free and reduced lunch.

Project SHAL—with its motto, Every Child Can/WILL Learn—was developed around Edmonds's original five correlates of the Effective Schools. Young made certain right from the beginning that everyone involved in Project SHAL, which became the model that was replicated in 117 St. Louis schools over a seven-year period, was a believer, an enhancer of the Effective Schools Improvement Process.

Training and Leadership

"The school staffs would learn the philosophy, tenets, and practices of Effective Schools and institute school programs in keeping with the correlates," wrote Rufus Young. "Through participation in Project SHAL, the minds and hearts of the school staffs would be changed."

"No longer could school improvement be dependent upon the acquisition of new personnel, materials, or prepackaged programs. The staffs would have to rethink, design, and redesign existing services as they learned the research and research implications of Effective Schools. Project SHAL, where every child can—*will*—learn, translated the practices of Effective Schools, eroding traditional beliefs and eradicating failed educational methods to come upon different ways of believing and educating those students whose failure had been previously accepted" (Paper presented to International Congress for School Effectiveness, 1989).

With Young's Area 1 office providing strong support for the project, work began on the establishment of structures, in-service programming, and planning. The general time line set aside a full year for "readiness":

11/80–9/81: "Readiness"—establishing councils and task forces, visits to other exemplary schools and orientation activities, faculty and staff training

2/80: Initiation of community meetings and orientation
9/81: Implementation of SHAL activities in the classrooms of the original four schools

9/82–8/83: Second year of operation (4 original schools); 12 new schools in first year of activity

9/83–8/84: Third year of SHAL activities: first 4 schools in third year; next 12 in second year; 3 additional schools added

In the proposal funded by the Danforth Foundation, there were two basic SHAL goals: (1) to work with children so that they would eventually attain and maintain grade level as compared to national norms, and (2) to develop a plan or model to track the implementation of SHAL and aid in evaluation of the implementation efforts.

An Executive Council (principals, project coordinator, manager of the Management Academy, Danforth Vice President John Ervin, and Rufus Young) preceded the birth of a larger Administrative Council, which had the actual responsibility to plan the activities of the project. This Council included teachers, administrators, and parents. There were also Task Force Groups, which included technical assistants from local colleges and universities.

"Every Council, every group, had a specific task," explains Young. "Everyone worked for that group's immediate goal, which fed into the long-range goal of enacting, maintaining, living by the correlates. And that long-range goal was never, never out of mind."

Young says that by focusing on administrative leadership, school climate, high expectations, instructional programs, and ongoing assessment, each school understood exactly what it was trying to accomplish and how. "Everyone knew the process. That was the key. That, and . . ." Young hesitates, but finally says what most people involved in the St. Louis SHAL project believe, "leadership. We had the leadership." There was the leadership in the individual schools, and there was the leadership from the man who started it all.

"It was incredible what that man did," states a teacher who worked at the Stowe Middle School. "From the very beginning, you could see the fire in Dr. Young's eyes. He really believed, and he had us believing. We just *knew* we could do it. But that doesn't mean we could have done it alone. We knew the people way up at the top didn't really care that much. But Dr. Young did, and he made it possible for the rest of us."

When asked about this, Young just says he did it because he knew it could work, and he knew "it was the only chance those schools and those children had."

"Those schools had been forgotten. I was trying, but there was only so much I could do. I needed Effective Schools and John Ervin and the Danforth Foundation," maintains Young. "John used to say 'Leadership has to be infectious.' And it's true. A staff will go to no end if they believe in, and trust, their leader. They want to be winners. And with Effective Schools, you have to live it every day. And yes, I lived it."

Those were the days when Rufus Young would hold an in-service for teachers and have 100 percent of the staff show up. At times, there wasn't even a reimbursement. Teachers and principals came because they believed in the leadership and the vision. And soon, through that leadership, they believed in Effective Schools. They also liked the idea of accountability. They were not afraid of it, simply because they believed in themselves and their students.

It did not take long for the results of the turn to Effective Schools to start to come in. By 1983, the percentage of students in the initial tier of Project SHAL reading in the lowest percentile had dropped from 33 to 19 percent. By 1986, it would be down to 6 percent. The results were just as dramatic in language. In 1981, 27 percent of the students were in the bottom quartile.

By 1983, it was down to 10 percent; by 1987, 4 percent. In mathematics, the drop was from 21 to 4 percent in five years.

But there was much more to the success story of these schools than test scores. There was now an energy, a vibrancy, a desire to excel in the schools that just was not there before. The climate of the schools was dramatically different. It was the climate of winners. Posters on the walls talked of success, self-discipline, and respect. Faculty and students spoke with pride of their schools. Parents, who before felt unwelcome in the schools, now actively participated, exhibiting as much pride as their children.

Word of success spread across the country and soon the visitors arrived, loaded with their prejudices and suspicions. "I remember looking at that neighborhood and wondering how people got in and out of there alive," recalls Dr. Max Heim, superintendent of the Geary County School District in Kansas. "That area around there is tough!"

But his first impressions vanished as he walked up the front steps of the Laclede Elementary School. "You knew as soon as you walked through the front door that this school was something special. It was the look of it, the feel of it," remembers Heim. "The halls were showcases of cleanliness and talent. In every classroom, there was some new, different teaching technique taking place. And the kids mastering things beyond their grade level. And the kids were so enthused with the teacher and their work, they didn't even notice visitors."

Heim was one of many superintendents who was so impressed with the SHAL project that, when he began implementing Effective Schools in his district, and there was some opposition to the reform, he put his teachers on a bus and sent them to St. Louis.

"That's all I needed to do. I knew that once they saw what was going on in Laclede or one of the other schools, they'd be behind Effective Schools 100 percent," says Heim, adding that was indeed what happened. "They walked out of that school and said, 'If they can do it here, we can do it back home.' And they have."

Over the first three years of Project SHAL, the Danforth Foundation gave $164,000, and the Parsons-Blewett Foundation gave another $52,955 in support of programs to improve teaching skills. During this time, St. Louis was in the midst of its numerous court battles over desegregation-related issues. Initially, U.S. District Judge William L. Hungate ruled Project SHAL was eligible for 50 percent state financing as a "reasonable and appropriate" effort to improve education in nonintegrated schools. That was in 1982, and the state, as a result, paid half of the $410,572 tab. In 1983–84, the state paid half of the tab of $298,507. By 1985, the state financing source had diminished and the courts set limits on monies to be spent on enrichment and remedial programs.

While the federal, state, and city ranglings were going on, Rufus Young and his team were facing some opposition by those who did not agree with the work that was going on. "Some people just didn't like what we were doing," says Young. "Whether or not they didn't like the fact we were educating lower-income children, or that they didn't approve of us spending any money to do it, I don't know. But there were rumblings out there."

The rumblings were not loud enough to stop Young from rising within a political wink of the superintendency of the St. Louis Schools. In 1982, he was one of the top three finalists of 75 applicants for the position. In fact, he had been told by board members that the job was his. And all the reporters in town also had sources revealing the same information.

"The television stations had even told me what color shirt to wear and all for the interview after the board vote. It was all set," recalls Young.

But it wasn't. At the last moment, he heard that some behind-the-scenes backstabbing and political personnel negotiating was going on and, when the votes were counted, Jerome B. Jones was first and Rufus Young was second. "To this day, I still don't know what exactly happened. I can only speculate about the politics of it," says Young.

A few months later, in May 1983, he was the top-ranking finalist for the superintendency of Baltimore, Maryland. He didn't take the job because he was concerned about the brevity of the initial contract (one year) and his own commitment, and what he believed was Jerome Jones's commitment, to the St. Louis Public Schools.

"I made a mistake," says Young. "I should have taken the Baltimore job. I shouldn't have believed that the administration of the St. Louis schools was really interested in the education of all children. They never had any commitment to Effective Schools. Never. Not even close."

Political Dismantling Begins

Over the years, Young's team has gone from 44 people to less than 10. Although the different tiers of Effective Schools were extended, the monies and support from central administration diminished, and by 1990 the program had been watered down to the point that Young and his small but determined staff oversee the "Effectiveness" of school improvement programs in *all* of St. Louis's 117 public schools.

"How do a handful of people, with no money, and no resources do school improvement programs for 117 schools?" asks Young. "It's impossible."

"Over the years, the administration has just beaten down Dr. Young," is the common refrain from those in Young's district. They see him continuing to fight with central administration to gain the funds and resources to continue the school improvement, but they say that Young keeps getting kicked in the knees. "It's like they keep knocking him down, but he keeps bouncing back up. He just won't stop," explains one principal. "And I think the rest of us just say, 'Well, if he can keep fighting, then so can we.'"

Meanwhile, the superintendency of Jerome Jones ended under the shadow of a dark cloud. An investigation of Jones's expenses revealed some alleged irregularity and before there could be further discussion, Jones resigned. His proponents say Jones accomplished his work in St. Louis, his main legacy being a $300 million rebuilding and renovation program for the city's schools.

Concerning the quality of education in the schools, it varies greatly depending on what school and what district you are in. One thing is for certain: Much of the staff development and renewal of teachers and administrators that was going on in the growth days of Effective Schools has stopped. And that, according to principals and district superintendents, is hindering the upgrading of teaching and learning throughout the city.

"You see, we were up against a lot. Not only was there the ingrown biases against teaching all children, but the people in charge wouldn't allow any of the outside money for Effective Schools," explains Young. "They didn't like the fact that we were getting all this recognition, in the states, in Europe, for the work we were doing. People were coming to see Effective Schools, not the rest of the system, which was in trouble. They didn't like that."

What would have happened if Rufus Young had been appointed superintendent of the St. Louis Public Schools? "This school system would have been second to none!" says Young, matter of factly.

What's going on now in the schools? "Well, we're spending $300 million renovating old buildings," says Young, shaking his head. "And you wouldn't believe the waste that is going on!" It's no doubt that comments like this have accounted for some of Dr. Young's rocky sledding with the central administration.

"I really don't care anymore," says Young. "This school system could have been the best for so many. If they had just let the Effective Schools Process continue. Let the renewal continue. But no. For whatever reason—you decide—it wasn't in someone's best interest to keep quality education. They can't hurt me too much anymore. I'll just continue doing the best I can."

Over the years, Young has assembled a detailed procedure for the Effective Schools Process. There are graphs, guidelines, procedures, instruction manuals, and guidelines for seminars and workshops. The entire process is all there for the using. "But the point is you just cannot have an Effective Program if you don't have the top leaders backing you," insists Young. "Yes, we did this school by school. And the schools knew they had my support 150 percent. We hoped we had the support from above. At least they weren't actively fighting against us.

"But Effective Schools must be top down and bottom up. The optimum results will come when there is a superintendent who has the vision of what he or she wants the system to look like. And therefore, all the persons who are in that school system will be moving in the direction of that vision. It will have been communicated to all persons. The school board will have given their commitment to that vision and where they want to go. And there is ongoing in-service. From the superintendent on down. Every school. Every individual.

"Face it," says Young, his voice rising with the passion of his commitment, "we cannot afford medicocrity in the schools. Kids can't afford it, teachers can't afford it. And if you have teachers or principals who are not interested in teaching and learning for all kids, then you've got to separate them. Teachers are the most important ingredients. You've got to put money on them. And you've got to make sure they understand and believe in the vision." He pauses, tightens his lips. "And you must—you *must*—give them good leadership."

Juanita Doggett is the principal of the Sherman Elementary School in what is known as the Shaw neighborhood of St. Louis. The neighborhood around the school consists of many single-family homes with neat lawns and trimmed azaleas. It is a naturally integrated community and the Sherman is one of the few naturally integrated schools remaining in St. Louis. It has not been touched by any of the numerous desegregation orders.

"This school is special," says Doggett, who has been working in the St. Louis Public School for 40 years. "We have everything from partnerships with the Botanical Gardens and Sports Arena, museums, to tutoring four days a week by students from St. Louis and Washington Universities. We have computers, career exploration, reading programs funded by Chrysler, drug and consumer programs . . ." as well as the daily class programs of reading, writing, science, math, and so on.

The Sherman is an old school, with a million-dollar addition under construction. It has the "leftover" basement room now used for a cafeteria; the all tar, frost-heaving playground; and hot, crammed rooms with a lot of ancient-looking desks; but it also has a level of enthusiasm and a learning "high" that is indicative of the Effective Schools' climate.

"Oh, this school would be very, very different without Effective Schools," claims Doggett. "This whole district would be just . . . just . . . well . . . , " she pauses, smiles, and moves on to "safer" comments. "From an administrator's view, Effective Schools was a shot in the arm. It brought together people who were willing to work together to make our school what it is.

"After we would have our training sessions, the teams would come back to the schools, discuss what had taken place, begin to brainstorm, and in a very short time, things were happening that you never dreamed of. People got involved that you didn't think would ever make a move. It was almost like magic, and it has continued, despite everything, thanks to Dr. Young and his people, throughout the years."

There have been monthly meetings with the Effective School coordinators (Young's staff), which Doggett believes are extremely helpful, especially for new people who may be coming in and are not familiar with Effective Schools.

"You have to get everybody in line," says Doggett. "That has become a little more difficult. You really have to hold it together yourself now. With assessments and planning and all."

Doggett notes that many teachers coming into the schools now are just not prepared for the leadership changes brought about by Effective Schools. Nor are they prepared for the necessary staff development programs that are essential to Effective Schools. "I think one of our problems, and our assessment shows this, is that in recent years, our teacher expectations have been down," says Doggett. "That's very disappointing to me. If you don't have high teacher expectations, you know . . . ."

But the assessment of her leadership continually ranks very high. She points out what she believes is the "real value" of Effective Schools: "I'm always looking for help. You need it to do a good job as principal. So anything that could help us—principal and teacher—to lighten our load, I'm for it. I saw that as a real advantage right from the outset. I, at times, would be overwhelmed, you know, I'm one of those dreamers, and I have so many things I want to see happen for children and for teachers. So when I have a group of teachers working together for a common goal, well, the load is lighter, and more is accomplished. Many of the dreams start to happen."

Doggett finds all the politicking around Effective Schools, in and out of St. Louis, a little comical, but also disheartening. "I was at this conference last weekend. On school improvement. And I bought this big thick book on the latest and best of reform. And you know what it is? It's all Effective Schools! They just changed some of the names. But it's Effective Schools. Right down to the correlates and management style. You can't get away from it. It's what works. No matter what name you're hanging on it this season."

One of the most successful middle schools in St. Louis, and one with a long waiting list, is the Mason Middle School, with its main focus on science and math. Doris Reece, principal of the Mason Middle, has been working within the Effective Schools philosophy for many years. "In 1982 when this school opened, we began by setting forth the tenet that all children can learn and they will in this school," says Reece, a veteran of the system. "We are comprehensive. We deal with all kinds of kids."

Students are admitted into the magnet schools through the lottery system. Parents submit the names and the names are separated into two piles, one black, one white, and then the appropriate number of students is chosen. "So we get kids with IQs from 48 to 148," says Reece. "And we don't have a big shiny building and bright new science labs. But we have the right people. I'll put my money on people rather than on those expensive resources anyday."

The Mason Middle is not a showcase of expensive science and math equipment. It has its computers and it has a very old science lab. It is an old school, with cramped classrooms and a tar playground that is its athletic field. Despite this, Mason Middle attracts students from far into the South County, away from the spit-polished, shiny new schools with their fancy equipment and multimillion-dollar athletic fields.

"Sure, additional money would be nice," says Reece. "But the most important thing in any school is the vision, and the people believing in that vision. I'm a strong believer in services, and I think that's the strength of the program Dr. Young provided. It's given us direction in a kind of structured way, and we sit together and talk about the direction of the school, what we want to accomplish, everyone here knows. We have a cause, and we have a structure."

What it all goes back to, according to Reece and her teachers, is the "process" of Effective Schools. They all know the direction to go in, and have the tools to accomplish their goals. "And we have support from the area office," adds Reece "That's important. You can't feel alone out here."

The students don't let Reece alone. Whether she is in her office or walking down the corridors, students eagerly ask her questions, inquire about programs, and make pitches for concerns on their own agendas. You can literally grab hold of any student—any student—in the Mason Middle School, ask him or her about the school, and he or she will elaborate freely and enthusiastically about the school, the teachers, and the tough lady in the corner office.

"She knows her stuff and she really cares," explains one white student (Doris Reece is black) from the South County whose goal is to be an aeronautical design engineer. "I know kids in other schools and they never see their principal. Mrs. Reece is always there to talk to and it's great when she shows up at the stuff outside of school. She cares. That's one of the reasons my parents wanted me in this school."

Reece is known as a tough administrator, a woman who demands a great deal from her teachers and staff. In St. Louis, the central office handles the assignment of all teachers, so Reece and other principals must deal with everything from the extremely competent to the potentially harmful political appointment.

The Need to Reform Teacher Education

Reece does not hesitate to join other principals in St. Louis—and for that matter, brave principals from throughout the United States—in talking about the quality of the teachers coming along.

"I am concerned," admits Reece, noting how politically unpopular it is to say anything negative against the teachers. "But people should know that some of the teachers coming into the schools now just do not have it. I have criticized teachers' colleges, and even though I understand some teachers' colleges have a good reputation and all that, but based on some of the substitute teachers that they send in here, well, I fear for children in the next classes. I fear for them because what I see coming in here is unbelievable."

In the past in St. Louis (and other cities involved in Effective Schools), many of the teachers who may have been short on adequate training had access to courses to supplement their learning and teaching skills. In fact, many teachers, including those interviewed for this book, said they often learned more in the supplemental Effective Schools courses and seminars than they did in their college education courses.

Due to the cutback in the St. Louis program of Effective and Efficient Schools, much of that additional training no longer exists. And where it does exist in St. Louis, there just isn't the drive anymore to become deeply involved and committed.

"In the past, there was a real desire to learn and improve on tne part of the teachers," explains a principal in the St. Louis system. "That was when Dr. Young was just beginning. Everyone was fired up and we filled seminars and workshops with teachers willing to give their time to improve their skills."

"Well, then we had this infusion of money, and all of a sudden, teachers are getting paid for these extra workshops, which is fine. But now that we don't have those boatloads of money, the teachers, who have been spoiled, just aren't interested in attending unless there's payback.

"Now there's nothing wrong with making money, and teachers are underpaid. Well, many of them, at least. But there's also nothing wrong with professionalism, and wanting to better yourself and do the very best for your students. Teaching has changed. We have to stay up with it. The concept that you need to know, want to know, should be the heart of a teacher's commitment. We're losing that by losing Effective Schools. And when you lose that major link . . . ."

In St. Louis as in all school districts in every corner of the globe, it is what goes on in the classroom that counts. And what you see in one classroom can be very different from what goes on in another. For example, one seventh-grade English class was giving book reports. Two out of the seven students who gave their reports in front of the class used bad grammar. There were many sentences like: He didn't know nothing about the dance. She don't want to work after school.

Although the teacher was quick to correct points like posture, eye contact, and placement of hands, there was no correcting of the improper grammar. When asked about this afterward, the comment from the young teacher (two years in the system) was, "Oh, I usually do, but today, I just kinda let it pass. It's a Friday." So, on Friday bad grammar will be allowed in the St. Louis seventh grade.

But it is not allowed on the floor below, in a sixth grade class where students were talking about the writing of the Constitution. One student made the statement, "The Declaration of Independence weren't written by the

Congress." The teacher quickly stopped the comments and asked the class what was wrong with the last statement; while one student pursued the role of the Congress, most students jumped on the grammar issue. The teacher left it up to the students to correct their fellow student, let them explain why it was wrong, what was right, and then confidently moved on to the writing of the Declaration of Independence.

As a good teacher will allow, the key to success in the classroom is not just in informing or correcting students—in knowing what is right and what is wrong—but in how the teacher goes about giving out that information and, when confronted with misinformation, how the teacher corrects it.

The question of language and the proper use of grammar is a common one in schools working with students from the lower socioeconomic classes. For many students, a bastardization of grammar is almost a badge of defiance against the establishment. Teachers recognize this and have different ways of dealing with it. One of the most effective—at least it appeared to have the strongest impression on the students—was a technique used by a teacher in St. Louis.

The teacher played two videotapes. The first was an interview with boxer Mike Tyson talking about beating some "little girl's head (another boxer) to pieces." He was illiterate, crude, stupid, and insulting, stumbling all over the simplest of sentences. The second was an interview with writer/essayist/poet Maya Angelou and her son talking about their experiences in West Africa. It was brief, very dynamic, and elegant. The simple grace and courage of Maya and Guy Angelou, using the passion of very proper English to talk of the inconsistencies and cruelties of life, the strength of kindness and caring, had an intensity that reached black, white, Hispanics, and Asians. The teacher accomplished her mission and then some.

It is because of learned innovations like this that staff development is so important, especially for a younger teacher who is just learning his or her way through the maze of classroom behaviors and techniques.

"You cannot keep a staff fresh and moving and up to date without the use of learning and teaching seminars. That's why Effective Schools is so important," maintains Doris Johnson, the principal of the Hickey Middle School, a nonintegrated school on St. Louis's north side. "You *have* to get these teachers into advanced learning about how to teach these kids, about how to motivate them—and really, about how to motivate themselves and keep their own experiences and expectations up and running."

Johnson says that motivation is essential in her school because in many cases, she's dealing with students who come from single-parent families where there just isn't the motivation to excel, or even participate, in school.

"Kids from our generation had parents who believed in school, who believed in the benefits of school," explains Johnson. "These kids are different. They just don't see the good in school. They don't see the value. No one's teaching them at home. We've got to teach them the value here."

"Before, we had parents who saw education as the way out. But not anymore. These kids are into instant gratification. The drugs, the crime, they believe that's the way to be. We have to teach them otherwise."

That task is made more difficult by the fact that many of the students at the Hickey Middle School never get out of their own neighborhood. They don't see the good that can come from an education. For that reason, Johnson tries to get her students out "into the real world" as much as possible. And if she cannot take them all out, she brings role models in. "These kids don't have dreams," says Johnson. "What do you do when a child doesn't have dreams for himself or herself?"

Can you *give* a child dreams? Can you teach a child to dream who doesn't know what dreams are? "I wish I could say that all our teachers are up to par, that they all believe that all children can learn," says Johnson. "But they do not all believe that. For two reasons. One, they aren't receiving any training that would get rid of their biases. And I'm not talking about white teachers here. I'm talking about black teachers, too. And second, they know if they believe all children can learn, and state that, then they have to teach all children and all their children *must* learn. And that's not so easy if you're a lazy or below par teacher."

Johnson says it can be very discouraging watching the St. Louis schools. One minute they're up, one minute they're down. "For a while there, it was like we all had this unified direction, this goal, and we had the process, and the means to do it," says Johnson, referring to Effective Schools. "But then the focus seems to change. New people arrive. The unity cracks."

Despite this, and the fact that she is one of those principals who goes into a school, turns it around by making it Effective, and, before she can take a proud breath, is moved on to another less than effective school, Johnson doesn't lose stride. She's a tough disciplinarian who at times becomes exhausted with frustration but never stops believing.

"You see I do believe that every child *can* learn. And I see the proof of that everyday," she explains. "And as long as I see that happening, whether its in small steps or large steps, as long as it's happening, as long as some kids are seeing the light that will lead them out of here, then every bit of it is worth it."

Although schools like the Hickey, Mason, Sherman, Shepard, and many others continue to move along in the path of Effectiveness, there are other schools, some within the original tiers of the effectiveness project, that are now slipping into the depths of ineffectiveness. Much of that slippage has to do with the loss of Effective School development for teachers, and some of it has to do with administrative appointments.

Two small examples that happened in two of the first Effective Schools manage to explain it all. One very successful school, with scores well above the national average, had a collaborative, extremely energetic faculty. A new principal came in who started to pit one teacher against another. Division flared up where there never was any dissension before. Teachers gradually stopped working together, suddenly distrustful of their colleagues.

In another school, the appointment of a new principal brought a change in a fundamental unwritten routine of the school. Some of the teachers used to stay after school and work with students who needed additional help. The custodian, who had also been a part of the Effectiveness workshops, willingly stayed on those days to close up after the teachers finished. The teachers did not get paid extra, and neither did the custodian. He received his rewards from the teachers and students who appreciated his time.

Suddenly this new principal tells the custodian he cannot stay late anymore. He wants the school closed up tight by a certain hour and no later. There were no particular reasons—such as increased crime in the neighborhood or the union coming down on anyone (in fact, the union knew this happened in several schools and never voiced a word of opposition). The teachers pleaded with the principal to alter this strange mandate, explaining it was the only time they had to work with some students and these students would be lost without the help. The principal held strong. He wouldn't even allow it for one day a week. And it wasn't as if he had to stay for the closing of the school. He just didn't want the teachers and students there after school and that was it! That was also the beginning of many such rules that did nothing but flex the principal's muscles and harm the teaching and learning.

"Yes, I know things like that are going on," says Dr. Young, not hiding his irritation and anger. "There was a time when that would be unheard of. There was a time when teachers *not* working after hours with their students would be unheard of. We had a real 'esprit' here. We were doing it for the kids, and we had the results to show that what we were doing was working."

He admits that those successful results are not as forthcoming as they should be now, that some schools have slipped, and the major reason for that is that the assessments—the major link in Effective Schools—just aren't being done. And in many schools where they are being done, they are not being done as conscientiously as they should. There are no followup plans.

"There's got to be assessment that's ongoing, for kids as well as teachers," insists Young. "You can't have an automobile and run it without making some assessments along the line. If you don't, it will fall apart. That's what we have done with these children. The schools keep dropping and dropping."

He agrees with members of his staff who say it is just impossible to monitor and assist over 120 school buildings. "They handle as many as 40 schools a piece. Now how are you supposed to physically be in all those places, overseeing all the correlates, the leadership, the quality of teaching and learning? It's impossible. And the central office knows it's impossible."

What distresses Young the most is the firm belief that if the schools themselves do not come to the aid of the low socioeconomic child, then no one will. "We have let poor people's children go to schools that just weren't making it. Schools that we never even assessed to begin with," believes Young. "You have to understand that poor people don't go in to the authority figures to protest achievement, or lack of achievement, in a school. They'll go in and say, 'You pushed my child' or 'You cursed him,' but they rarely go in and talk about achievement."

"The middle-class people demand that you teach their kids. They'll take them out and stand on the superintendent's doorstep. Middle class people and above demand that their kids be taught. Poor people demand that you treat them right. And if they are being threatened, to protect them.

"Now that may be an extreme, but the point I'm trying to make is they allow their kids to go year after year and get into the twelfth grade and can't read. That's incredible to me. It's also incredible to me that these black children will opt to get on a bus at 6:00 in the morning to go to the country or a voluntary desegregation program to get a better education, and there's a school across the street that they could be going to, but no one cares that it's not teaching kids. It's embarrassing to me.

"That's why we've got to upgrade *all* the schools for *all* the kids. And the Effective School is the only hope we have. It offers the greatest hope. We see it in the results. And it's like Ron Edmonds said: How many do you have to see to know it works?!"

When asked why he thinks the Effective School Process was not popular politically in St. Louis, Young shakes his head. "I can only speculate, but I think one of the problems is that people think you are teaching the poor at the expense of the kids who are doing well. We know that's not true, but people have a problem accepting that," says Young. "We have difficulties getting people to buy into Effective Schools because it has a connotation when you say *poor*, it means *black*. It's a black *person*. It is not black. We have poor whites. And I've got the slides of the whites and the blacks working side by side. And I've got the scores. People say they accept the facts, but they don't. This city is the proof of it."

The facts that people just are not willing to accept are shown in at least three independent studies of the Effective Schools Projects, which have shown marked improvement in the majority of grades examined and a dramatic increase in teacher and staff involvement in and enthusiasm for the schools.

"How can you argue against these type of results?" asks Young, pointing to charts showing whole groups of elementary level Effective Schools moving from zero grades at or above the national norm to 83 percent of the grades at or above national norm (five years later). Then there are the middle schools that go from zero grades at national norm to *all* grades at or above national norm six years later.

Even a 1988 central administration study (separate from Young and his staff) of the new "Effective and Efficient Schools" project could not find any fault with the program. They concluded that "teachers rated the E&E practices as quite helpful in improving classroom instruction"; "cost of the program is reasonable"; and that "both administrators and faculty felt that they had benefited from participating in the project."

"Central administration and board members have tried to discredit the program and Rufus (Young), but they've failed," observes one veteran principal. "The reason they've failed is because you can't change the good numbers. You can't argue with success. The problem is, many of them don't view that, necessarily, as success."

You Can Take Away the Job but Not the Beliefs

The belief of many observers is that now that central administration has managed to cut down Dr. Young's staff to just a few valiant, struggling, and overworked people, and where there just is not the push for Effective Schools outside Young's office, that the "Effective and Efficient" program will be watered down to the point that principals and teachers will become demoralized, test scores will reflect a lack of improvement, and any remaining enthusiasm for the Effective Schools will fade away (except in those schools with the Effective principals).

And indeed, in June 1991, that prediction came true. The Effective School Program was shut down. This system that is in a $300 million renovation could not afford the $350,000 cost. Young says the closing has a lot to do with "professional jealousy." His salary has been cut and he is now in a position he held 20 years ago in the St. Louis Public School system.

"The system is now working on different improvement plans," says Young. "They say they'll 'sprinkle the correlates around.' Well, you can't 'sprinkle' and there is no program anymore." He says the school system is "groping for their own image" away from Effective Schools.

Is the bottom line that the city of St. Louis is not interested in teaching *all* children? "Of course," Young answers. What is it interested in? "What every school board and school department is interested in: politics. Getting themselves ahead. Politics is strangling education. It creates all this professional jealousy. This professional back-biting, climbing over each other," says Young. "It's all reward systems. Everyone's in it for their own rewards. Everybody's going out to be the saviour instead of being on a team, instead of following a superintendent's vision. Top administrators only rally if it benefits them personally. They don't work together."

But why? Dr. Young shook his head. He had been a part of this city school system for 50 years—even longer if you count his years as a student. "Money. I suspect money. There's so much of it to be had in school systems. So many people who can be taken care of. So much room for abuse and waste."

Does it have nothing to do with racial biases? "Oh, sure, there was a time when it did. But the courts have straightened a lot of that out. The kids who are hurting aren't white or black, they're just flat out poor. Disadvantaged in every way. Parents. Homes. Schools. White poor girls get pregnant just like black poor girls. You look at the scores of any city—or any suburb that has a portion of their population that is poorer—and there you'll see it, too. The poor just aren't served. Look at your school boards today. You have blacks, Hispanics. But do you have *poor* members?"

He hesitates, lowers his voice. "Then again, maybe I'm just being naive. Maybe it is race, but I lean more toward class and economy. And remember, when you get to the lower classes, you get away from the votes. And board members want votes. So you serve those who shout—and vote."

Why does someone like Rufus Young keep fighting? "I know it's old fashioned," he explains, "but I really believe in what I do. In getting schools to follow the correlates, to have a mission, to have strong leadership, to push the teachers to be their best. I don't care if you call it Effective Schools. Just do it. It works.

"And I see kids who go through our schools. Who go to college. Or kids who just get good jobs. Have good values. Good families. And I know that the big reason why is because they had a *good* school, with *good* leaders. Because they got an even chance."

He pauses and looks out the window, beyond the parking lot, to the decay and despair of the north side of St. Louis. You can see from the pain, the sadness in his eyes, what he's thinking: Have you seen what is happening to our children who are not being served and challenged in our schools? Do you understand what we're talking about here?

Young admits that at times his disappointment may slow him down for a couple days. And he knows that although he has more energy and more on the ball than many half his age, retirement will soon take him away from his long days with the St. Louis Public Schools.

"Sure, I wish I had made superintendent," he says. "Because like I told you, then this school system would be second to none. We have the capability. We have the people, the resources, the structure, and, with Effective Schools, the process. All we needed was someone with a vision at the top. We came *so close. So close!* If we just had a superintendent with a vision who people would rally around. I did the best I could in my area. But you needed the vision, the Effective leader way at the top.

"I'd bet you that every school system you go to that has Effective Schools really humming along . . . kids doing well, teachers energized, staff pushing and pushing . . . I'd bet you there's a strong Effective superintendent at the top."

Meanwhile, the SHAL schools struggle along, some of them already slipping below mediocrity. They were *so close*. The planners didn't know it when they built the Harriet Beecher Stowe Middle School, but the namesake of that school had a clear understanding of good education, the driving essence of Effective Schools, and life and dignity itself:

> *Treat 'em like dogs, and you'll have dogs' works and dogs' actions. Treat 'em like men, and you'll have men's works.* —H.B. Stowe, *Uncle Tom's Cabin*

District of Liberty Bell: The Illusion of Effectiveness

Many of the best lessons in life grow out of failure. Because of the increased emphasis on Effective Schools programs, at both the state and national levels, many more school districts are becoming involved in this improvement process. As demonstrated in this book, numerous school districts are making impressive strides in their journey to equity and quality. That progress is not only documented with the student outcomes but, just as important, it is visible in the day-to-day operations of the district and the schools. An observer sees improvement along with change, and a revolution in the attitudes and behaviors of faculty, staff, students, parents, community leaders—everyone who comes in contact with the school system. There is genuine effectiveness, seen on paper and in the eyes of the students.

Unfortunately, now that effectiveness is the call of many state governments, there are districts out there waving the banner of effectiveness that give less than audible lip service to the moral imperative of teaching for learning for *all* children. They say they are effective, yet they have no school-based management, do not disaggregate scores, provide little staff development, fail to empower anyone other than the usual pets of the administration, and continue to operate dual school systems—one for white students and one for minority students.

It is these school districts that besmirch the name of Effective Schools, distort and manipulate the research, and diminish the dedicated work of the thousands of Effective administrators and teachers. By showing the actions, behaviors, and policies of those who fail in effectiveness but claim success in Effective Schools, the power of the difference of *real* effectiveness is demonstrated. One sees how extraordinary Effective leadership and Effective teaching really is, and how *honest* the Effective Schools Improvement Process is in its dealings with all people within the system. (The capital E designates the comprehensive process has been implemented. See Appendix A.) There are indeed important but sad lessons to be learned from those who manipulate the Effective Schools Process just to foster their own ego.

How do these districts get away with this? In the past, inadequate school districts survived because the public and the teachers were locked out of the decision-making process and no one in the central office wanted to disrupt the lucrative patronage system. Although some of that still exists today, the major reason these districts get away with this illusion of effectiveness is because the superintendent has put together a top-notch public relations effort. This effort is so successful that it fools the public, the press, and many people within the school system itself. In researching this book, the authors were stunned at how cities, towns, districts, and local and national education writers have been fooled by a superintendent's PR machine.

How can this happen? Easy. Observers—parents, businesspeople, reporters—are shuffled off to the showcase schools and then overburdened with material that purports to reveal an open and effective school district. They never take a close look and, more than likely, they have never been in a real Effective school system in order to draw the proper comparison.

In the following pages, there are specific examples given on school systems claiming to be effective, but in fact the effectiveness is a mirage. This district is called Liberty Bell because it screams that it provides liberty for all, but it fails because, in its heart, the system still believes in the Bell curve: Some students must be kept on the bottom, where "they belong." There is no J curve in this district, no real belief that *all* children can learn and excel.

The following examples that prove the existence of districts like Liberty Bell are *true*. Documented here are specific actions and behaviors of administrators, teachers, and parents from a handful of both large and small school systems from different parts of the country. Many of these comments and actions will be very familiar to people in other districts who may think their "effectiveness" is ringing a little hollow—just like Liberty Bell.

Rotting from the Head Down

The first clue was easy. A mother was sitting on the steps of the administration building of a fairly well-respected, large school district in the upper midwest. Next to her was her eight-year-old daughter. The mother was not pleased.

"I went in there to start the enrolling process," she said. "Well, not only was I treated rudely by the receptionist—like, what was I doing bothering her—but she also wasn't sure where I should go. Then I finally found the right office and they didn't seem to really care. Then when we went to the bathroom it turned out to be one of the dirtiest bathrooms I've ever been in. If this is how they treat the school employees, I don't know if I want to see what they do to the children." This woman had just moved from Chicago. "I thought it would be better here. Now I'm not so sure."

Central office procedures can tell you a lot about a school system. This one certainly did. In an Effective School system, you are immediately met by receptionists who not only know what they are doing but like what they are doing. The pride in the system is obvious. You will also see within the walls of central administration constant reminders that you are in an Effective School System. The district mission statement will be on the walls, along with quotes from Ron Edmonds and other Effective leaders. You will see student work proudly displayed, along with the slogan *"all children can learn."*

At Liberty Bell, the central office walls were bare. The bulletin boards contained notices of meetings and nothing more. Inside the administrative offices, there were pictures of the administrators with politicians, but little or no student work, and no slogans about equity.

In true Effective districts, you can't turn around without seeing a sign or slogan about *all* children learning. It is displayed, written on letterheads, and included in all written material, from master plans to homework directives for parents. The call for equity and quality is, as many have said, like a religion. It's the belief that moves the district and you cannot get away from it. At Liberty Bell, you don't hear equity talked about. There may be slogans about excellence, but not equity.

The superintendent of Liberty Bell is very affable but also very defensive. If even the slightest criticism is given, he begins a diatribe on the danger of anonymous critics. When asked where the reference to equity is, he tells you his school district doesn't need to be reminded about that. "And we do talk about it," he says. "Even if my people don't believe it, I still insist upon them saying it."

This statement—direct from the mouth of a superintendent who gets national press for his school system—runs contrary to the beliefs of Effective Schools. First, a true leader of Effective Schools would not have people around him who didn't believe in equity. And second, true leaders don't force others to speak that which they don't believe.

The Effective Schools superintendents previously profiled in this book emphasize the *modeling* and *personal leadership* style that is directed toward centering the community around the belief that *all* children can learn. It is as much a part of them as their pen. They are also not afraid to talk about how they have had to change over the years, and that before they were introduced to the Effective Schools research, they were less than effective. They had much to learn. They still do.

The superintendent of Liberty Bell says he has not had to adjust his management style, that he always knew the Effective way to lead. He "always kept up with the literature" and has never had to make any changes. But he is quick to point out that others around him have had to do a lot of changing.

This superintendent's vita is interesting not for what isn't there but what is. You will find every award, great or small, and every listing of even the most remote *Who's Who* publication. You won't see too many national boards, and the employment record shows that this individual does not spend a lot of time in one place. The maximum is usually three years. This is a short amount of time for anyone to achieve any real ownership—or leadership—in a district.

The staff of the Liberty Bell superintendent also tells a story. Key positions do not belong to the local constituents. Many employees are brought in from other areas of the country. This is true also with principals and assistant principals.

Certainly, many superintendents will pull from a national field, but they also rely heavily on local expertise. They know they must hire locally because it makes the community happier. The problem is that many of these local people have to be retrained and do not slip right into the administration's hip pocket.

The Liberty Bell superintendent has encountered considerable opposition in his community for hiring outsiders and paying them very high rates (he is also one of the highest paid superintendents in the country). When asked why not go to the local pool, he says there is not the quality and "by hiring these people, I know exactly what I can expect."

Control is very big with the Liberty Bell superintendent. In fact, when asked about the push to empower principals and teachers, he immediately dismisses it as "overrated—you have to be very careful who you give power to."

His power, however, seems almost absolute. He controls all information going in and out of the central office. Even the smallest data sheet has to be approved by him. The staff hustles at his slightest throat-clearing and rarely offers opinions of their own. He will also tell you exactly which schools you may visit, what information you are entitled to, and to whom you may talk.

Every Effective superintendent profiled in this book has a standard line for visitors wishing to see the schools: Go wherever you want, talk to whomever, all the files are open. Just keep in mind we're still growing in this process and still have a way to go.

But beyond issues of staff and control, there is something else the Liberty Bell superintendent lacks. There is no "fire in the belly." Every other superintendent becomes animated and empassioned when he talks about his schools, his work, and the Effective Schools research. The *will* to improve the schools for *all* comes at a visitor like a heat wave. And behind that will is a constant stream of facts and research into how the Effectiveness Process is working and *must* work if this country is going to pull its schools out of the mire of the past.

In Liberty Bell, the superintendent is very careful politically. He knows his constituents are not ready to deal with *all* children learning, so he doesn't push it. When teachers or parents were asked what the superintendent stood for, they responded with blank stares. Even the mention of Effective Schools did not prompt recognition. In other districts, there was no doubt that everyone—teachers to principals to parents—knew exactly where their superintendents stood: on the side of all children learning, a believer in Effective Schools.

Policies that Deceive

In Liberty Bell, just like many school districts, there has been an added push for essential skills. These are the basic skills that the school system believes every child should learn at a given grade level. Teachers are told to concentrate on essential skills, often following an "essential" curriculum. This procedure (or *device*, as some practitioners refer to it) helps to build structure in a failing school system. All this is fine and good, but in Liberty Bell (and remember there are many Liberty Bells), the essential skills are etched in stone and woe to any teacher who doesn't follow the granite path.

"OK, here they are," begins an elementary teacher in Liberty Bell, as she pulls out a heavy sheet of paper. "You see listed here the essential skills. This is what we do. Here's the math part. The first week we concentrate on their capacity to do the basic multiplication tables. Two weeks from now, that should be mastered and we move to division."

She produces these thick sheets of paper for all the major learning areas: social studies, reading, science. Every week, or two weeks, there is a specific area of concentration and room to make a checkmark as soon as everyone in the class has mastered it. These lists are broken up into grading periods, so the teachers know exactly what they will be doing and where their class is supposed to be.

What Liberty Bell has done is step back into the time of the "factory model" of public education. Children are being "trained" by authoritarian teaching. They are being taught to regurgitate, not think. There is no learning from others, no range of learning levels. Teachers are kept in line to teach. Students are kept in line not to learn but to regurgitate.

"And we don't move on until everyone in the class has it down," explains the teacher. "Those are the rules. No one *doesn't* make it. At the end of the year, everyone in your class has mastered the essential skills for that year. Or is supposed to."

The problems begin when a student just isn't making it. "You can hold back a whole class for a long time, and then that puts everyone else off for the future," explains one teacher. "But at the end of the year, you better have them all mastered," adds another teacher.

But what if you don't? "Then it really gets to be a mess for next year's teacher. Like it is for me this year. I have some kids who have been pushed through to the fifth grade but can't handle the fifth-grade textbook. So what I do is I record the textbooks onto tape so the kids can then take those tapes home and read along and play catch up. Sometimes it works."

But wait a minute. How can there be some kids who are falling behind in essential skills when the test scores for this district show dramatic changes in the last few years? The teachers smile. "Because of these," they say, pointing to the essential skills lists. "These follow the tests."

And you don't have to master something to pass it on the test. All you have to do is memorize it. "We really, *really* teach to the test," explains a teacher.

It is very easy in this district to *really* teach to the test because this district gives the *same* test in the fall that they give in the spring. "So we know what's on them," says one teacher. "We even know what students are having trouble where. So you can make sure a student gets the information into his head. But does he understand it? Does he master it? No. Not always."

Of all the Effective School systems profiled in this book, *none* of them give the same test twice—only in Liberty Bell.

"And sure," says a teacher, "we fool a lot of parents, even some principals. But the teachers aren't fooled. And neither are the kids." But it looks good on paper.

There is also the problem of creativity. A teacher is not allowed to do anything other than the essential skills until they are all mastered. And that doesn't leave much room for studies outside the skill sheets.

"Last year, with Desert Storm and all, I had my class studying the Mideast, some of the politics and the religions," explains a teacher. "I thought it was important. Maybe more important that learning about the flora and fauna that doesn't grow in Antartica. But when my principal found out I was not on essential skills, well, the Mideast and Desert Storm got canceled. And the kids were upset. For the first time they were really excited about something. We had special projects going. Some of the kids who had relatives over there were having them send back newspapers and magazines. But no. No more. It's not in the essential skills we dictate for them."

But there is room in this district for that type of enrichment—if you're lucky enough to be in a class for the gifted or advanced. In Liberty Bell, those students who score above a certain percentile on the tests (and there are different standards for white and minority children) are enrolled in special classes. These are not just specific classes like reading or science, but *whole grades*.

In most schools in Liberty Bell, there are whole grades for those who are regarded as above average. "What they've done is just taken the cream of the crop and put them off into a separate part of the school," explains a teacher. "And sure, sometimes those classes are good. But sometimes the kids don't get any enrichment, they just get more homework. I feel bad for them. They have a lot of pressure. But I also feel bad for my kids. I have no real 'peer teachers' in the class, no one to help the slower learners. We're just all huddled here in mediocrity."

And for those kids who don't fit into the advanced or average (mediocre) classes, there is another level—again, entire grades where the slower learners are.

"And those kids really suffer," says a teacher. "And we all feel sorry for them because these are often the poorest kids. You know, the parents can't afford to get involved. They don't have the right supplies. No extras. We often take up collections so these classes can still have birthday cupcakes and all that. But the kids know what's going on. They know only the other kids get to go on field trips and have guest speakers and all."

This policy of outright tracking is anathema to the Effective Schools Process. But in this conservative district the tracking goes forward because it keeps apart the socioeconomic groups and therefore keeps the parents of faster students happy.

When the superintendent of Liberty Bell is asked about this, he defends the classes for separate learning speeds, saying there is more and better research supporting the tracking. Most experts will tell you this just is not true.

"And the teachers here know it's wrong. We see what's going on in other districts. We know the success they're having," explains a fifth-grade teacher who has taught for over 20 years. "And we also know what's right in our classrooms. Ever since they've taken away the top kids, our classes have suffered. Let's face it, it doesn't take a genius to know that homogeneous grouping belongs in the dark ages."

In Effective Schools districts, blatant tracking like this that divides the socioeconomic groups is denounced right at the beginning by the superintendent. In Liberty Bell, not only are the tracks defended (and there are also strict tracks at the high school level) but the majority of the grades for the advanced are located in the majority white schools. The less advanced grades, for after-school and Saturday programs for the slower learners, are found in the black schools.

"We're right back at the dual school system that the desegregation was supposed to stop," comments one teacher. "And these kids on the bottom rung are really being hurt. And worse, it feeds all of today's prejudices."

Bare School Walls

Effective Schools have banners and artwork portraying the school mission and expounding on the pride within the school itself. Students' work is up on the walls, along with slogans like: "We're the best." "We can reach the stars." "I believe in me." "All of us win together." In Liberty Bell, the walls in many of the schools are barren. And there is no sign of a district mission statement or school mission statement. When principals and teachers are asked about this, the principal can usually pull out a statement of philosophy. But, even at those schools that the superintendent touts as "most effective," the teachers have never worked on a mission statement.

They also have never worked on a school improvement plan. However, the teachers in some schools say they do have input into some school decisions, such as the discipline code and lunchroom procedure.

The teachers are all supposed to have gone through the effectiveness training that is done by separate firms throughout the United States. This is a 20-hour program and the teachers, who get paid extra for taking the course, say it is is helpful. But the teachers are stumped by this news that under Effective Schools there is to be school-based management and the teachers involved in decision making. The phrase *needs assessment* is something only a few teachers have even read about.

Indeed, the way the staff development is set up in Liberty Bell, the major training is done by "outside trainers." There is no means for the teachers to become more intensely involved in their training: no school planning teams, no leadership seminars or workshops. A look at the staff development courses lists absolutely no classes in leadership skills or decision making for teachers. Those classes that do deal with management or even planning a schoolwide discipline program are marked "for administrators only." There is one course of study on the school improvement process. And nowhere in the staff development literature for Liberty Bell do you see any reference to *all* children learning—Not one quote from Edmonds or Brookover or Lezotte.

Those principals that do have plans for their schools are quick to say they are not improvement plans. "Certainly not improvement plans the likes of which I've seen in other districts," admits the principal of a school that the teachers identify as the most progressive in the district. "We just haven't done what they do other places. Like the needs assessment. I'd love to do a needs assessment with this faculty and really get going, but it's just not going to happen here. Not yet, anyway."

The so-called plan for this school is in fact a faculty and staff handbook that tells the teachers what the policies are for recesses, absenteeism, teacher evaluation, discipline, and so on.

The teachers at this school remark that the changes that have been made came because "the principal was willing to go behind (the superintendent's) back."

"I know she trusts us, so she lets us have as much input as she dares," says a teacher. "For example, we go through our disaggregated scores here. I mean, the faculty too. That just doesn't happen in most of the schools. And our principal just can't let on that we're all that involved. Remember, we're just lowly teachers in this district."

And that may be one of the saddest truths of Liberty Bell. In Effective districts, the administration is continually touting the strengths of its teachers. In Liberty Bell, the superintendent didn't have one positive word to say about his teachers.

"I guess what hurts the most is that we're looked upon as a bunch of mercenaries," explains a math teacher who says she transferred here because she heard it was a good system, but is now transferring out. "You can get a bonus, extra pay, if you teach in one of the schools that's regarded as in trouble. And if you bring up your test scores, you get an additional bonus.

"Let me tell you, when you're making only $20,000 a year and your family is eligible for food stamps, then you can be sure you're going to have your kids memorize those tests so you can get a bonus."

Controlled, Not Empowered

In one Liberty Bell elementary school that has a record of low performance, a new principal is residing. She is an import from another state and is highly praised by the superintendent. She is black, but has never before been in a predominantly black or low-income school. "I don't think that (background in white schools) makes any difference," she says. "This school is just like another school. These kids just like any others. You run them the same."

Practitioners who have spent years in multicultural schools say there is a big difference between predominantly white and predominantly black schools. While theoretically it is justifiable to look on the schools as similar, students from a low economic background bring very distinct differences and needs to a school. However, in Liberty Bell, where all minority students learn the same essential skills and the same curriculum, those differences do not have much room to surface.

"The important thing in this school is that the teachers are always kept in line. That's priority here," explained the principal, as she noted that she had hired five new teachers this year—teachers right out of college—teachers who had never taught before.

"No, I don't think I would have been better off with more experienced teachers," she insists. "When you deal with teachers that have been around for a while, you have to deal with their agendas. It wastes time. I'll always go with a new teacher over one who's been in the system. Unless, of course, that older teacher is really something. But the newer teachers you can teach the newer techniques to. They're not set in their ways. You can mold them. It's imperative in this school that we have new teachers."

The superintendent agrees. "To reform a district, you have to create a climate for change," he says. "You have to disrupt the status quo."

The principal says that she will closely monitor her teachers. "I will be making certain that they follow their lessons plans to the T," she says.

Does she think the school can turn around? "Absolutely," she affirms. "And we'll do it in one year. We can't fail if those teachers just follow the essential skills." However, the principal, who insists that people address her "Dr. ______," says there are already a few problems rising in these first weeks of the school year. She points to problems with parents, the equipment, her presence being required outside of the school, the unemployment around the school, and on and on. This is the first time *excuses* have been voiced in an allegedly Effective Schools district. But then again, this is no Effective School.

When the principal is asked what specific changes she has planned for the school, she mentions that she's going to try to get the parents more involved "and we've got a lot of coupons coming in. You know, coupons for pizzas and meals at McDonalds, we'll be giving those out to the kids who do good work."

The classrooms being overseen by the new teachers are either out of control or the students are bordering on sleep. The teachers yell to try to control the children (really yell!). The children are nonplussed. A few children sit in a corner, leafing through brand new library books. The teacher is on the other side of the room trying to control a group working with clay. Two boys are throwing paper airplanes.

In another classroom, a group of kindergarten children draws wild sketches on large sheets of white paper. Crayons are occasionally thrown. The teacher is writing at her desk, no students around her.

A first-grade class is being read to. The students are lying on the floor. Some are asleep. The teacher reads in a monotone, never looking up at the children, never asking a question. It's almost surrealistic, as if the children are not even there.

Upstairs in this school, a fourth-grade class is completing their fall standardized test.

"I'll be honest with you," begins a teacher who is in her ninth year in Liberty Bell. "I came to this school because of the bonuses. But don't get the wrong idea. Most of the teachers in this school will use their bonuses to put right back into their classrooms. We have to supply a lot of our own additional materials. From posters to reading cards." She says she knows it's not the best thing "to be teaching to the test this way, but hopefully some of the kids will remember something. That's a start for some of them."

This school, like many in Liberty Bell, is not in good physical shape. The corridors are cluttered and the bathrooms dirty. The custodians are not interested in talking about any pride in the school: "I just get paid to try to keep it clean."

But it's in the eyes of the children that the failures of Liberty Bell are most visible. There is no spark of excitement, no enthusiasm for what is being taught. And this school, like others in town, doesn't even seem particularly friendly. The students don't go to the principal's office to show off reading skills, and they rarely receive a warm hug or encouraging pat on the back. And when the final bell rings, the students and teachers do not linger. The school is almost completely empty in a matter of minutes.

So how does this district get away with saying it's "effective" when there is no school-based improvement planning, no needs assessment, and no leadership training and empowerment procedures for the teachers? "I guess because we go through the effectiveness training," answers the principal of the "progressive" school. "Remember, most of us don't see what's happening outside the district, so we don't have anything to compare ourselves with. Even I couldn't tell you what the basic correlates are. I know I knew them a couple years ago, but, well, today, you just never think about them."

In the future, with more and more emphasis being placed on the Effective Schools Improvement Process, there will be many Liberty Bell districts—districts that say they are Effective, but whose policies divide a multicultural student body and exhibit a lack of trust and respect in teachers and administrators. They will be districts where there are a few bright lights, a few progressive schools, and a few areas where the essence of Effective Schools is sincerely practiced. But overall, the districts are an illusion of effectiveness. They are frauds.

The experts and Effective Schools practitioners who have watched districts like Liberty Bell say that most, in the end, fail. Teaching directly to the test only makes you look good for a few years. Eventually, all those students who have been memorizing reach a level where they cannot function because they have memorized and not learned. Eventually, parents see that their children are back in a dual school system. And eventually, the board becomes suspicious of all the grandiose claims.

But by that time, the administrators who have been running Liberty Bell will have satisfied another ego chase. Holding the test scores up high, and their public relations team in check, they will have moved on to another district.

Everyone likes to be part of a success story. And with the Effective Schools proving to be a substantial, long-term success in those districts that undertake it honestly, there will always be charlatans who will try to hang onto the coattails of those who are truly Effective.

For the fortunate districts, a key player may come stumbling across the chess board. This player may have the political clout—or simply the strength of vision—to start to make changes, to build on the disparate stilts of Effective Schools that are already stuck in the ground. This player—once he or she starts to build respect and pull in people to commit themselves to Effective Schools—can turn the system around.

It is like a breath of fresh air. The leader comes in and says to the courageous principals: Do a needs assessment, study your test scores, create real improvement plans. I'll defend you. As for essential skills, those can be taught through creative instruction. Here, let me give you the staff development courses that show you how.

With the conditions for empowerment being created, teachers and principals will feel a sense of ownership in their schools. Respect will flourish along with shared decision making, and slowly, but not easily, change will grow into improvement.

But this is a difficult process in an often desperate atmosphere. With luck, the superintendent pursuing accolades through superficial test scores and change that only protects the chosen few and the politically correct status quo will either depart, "see the light," or dissolve into a political waterboy with no real power.

It has been known to happen. It is hard, but as this book and history prove, it just takes one person to start to make a difference, to turn ineffectiveness into the beginnings of Effectiveness.

CHAPTER FOURTEEN

Keeping Dreams or Treading on Dreams

We can, whenever and wherever we choose, successfully teach all *children whose schooling is of interest to us. We already know more than we need to do that.*
—RON EDMONDS

We must not cease from exploration and the end of all our exploring will be to arrive where we began and to know the place for the first time. —T. S. ELIOT

This book has discussed the school reform process now taking place in schools across the United States. It has examined the changing culture, the shift in the management and operational paradigms from the factory model to the information age model, the reassessment and revision of the roles and responsibilities of public school practitioners, and the call for accountability that is changing the professional image of the entire school community.

After studying this garden of hopeful change, with its myriad bright flowers and satisfying yields, it seems obvious that it all springs from two very distinct seeds: leadership and expectations. When you weed out all the rhetoric, plow through all the research, data, and analyses, you find these two seeds from which everything grows.

Leadership and expectations are the major reasons why public education has in many instances failed. Our schools have been underled. Most administrators have not been properly trained. They are products of political opportunism and an anchronistic system and do not have the expertise or leadership skills necessary for the task. There must be more moral will in leadership to restructure the schools. Our culture has not held high expectations for large numbers of schoolchildren. Because of cultural biases and economic expediency, we have expected poor, disadvantaged children to fail. We got what we expected.

In the future, whether or not we succeed in public school education will depend on the leadership of those in our schools and the expectations of the entire school community. One without the other will not be enough. We must truly *lead* and we must expect the very best. No longer can we use the excuse of students not having the potential. We know now that is a red herring. All students have boundless potential. We must now look to our own potential, as teachers, administrators, and parents.

Effective Schools has shown through the data derived from urban, suburban, and rural school districts, that it is a valid, vital improvement process. It has demonstrated that its belief system provides the moral imperative for change that transforms discriminatory and mediocre school systems to equitable and excellent ones. The Effective School Process is the school reform process that works. It works because of the people who make it work: the superintendents, principals, teachers, support staff, parents, citizens, and Effective Schools consultants and facilitators. They are the ones who stood up against the status quo, who took a chance, who believed *all* children could learn, and changed the school systems to prove it. These are the heroes and heroines of the twenty-first century. These are the people who, through their leadership skills and high expectations, have brought applicable hope to thousands of school children. And it will be the lessons and examples of these people who will direct the effective public schools of tomorrow.

Larry Lezotte, who began so long ago traveling from district to district with Ron Edmonds and sharing his dream, refers to these years in the early nineties as the Silver Anniversary of Effective Schools. When asked the status of Effective Schools, his response is, "Alive, well, and going for the gold!"

The correlates continue to build a substantive and substantiating body of knowledge around them. As more data and experience come in from schools throughout America, the correlates move on to what is referred to as their "second generation." Effective Schools are continuing to improve as they monitor and adjust their never ending change process. Many schools have already successfully moved into this second generation.

Clear and Focused Mission

In the first generation, the mission of teaching for learning for *all* drove the process. Schools now move into the learning for *all.* This implies a higher level of curriculum development, a reallocation of resources to assure good monitoring systems for teachers so they can plan lessons better even as they acquire new skills: visioning (where are we headed), strategic planning (how will we get there), backward mapping (where did we come from and what did we learn), and task analysis (what do we do next?).

Instructional Leadership

The original emphasis was on enhancing the principal's skills. Now, the leadership must go beyond the principal, be more diverse. The teachers are empowered, the principal is seen as a leader of leaders, and the schools are learning centers of shared values. The superintendent's leadership is also crucial for sustained success.

Safe and Orderly Environment

In the first generation, discipline was about the *absence* of undesirable behaviors. Once those undesirable behaviors are removed, the school now concentrates on the *presence* of desirable behaviors. This implies democratization through decentralization, empowerment throughout the collaborative workplace, and dignifying diversity through a multicultural ethos. A consistent and equitable school discipline code is essential.

Climate of High Expectations for Success

Directing initial teacher behaviors was the primary emphasis for first-generation effectiveness. Now, the school must move on to developing responsive organizational behaviors. This involves making the school organization even more collaborative and with a higher sense of efficacy. Extensive reteaching and flexible regrouping must be available to the entire school community.

Opportunity to Learn and Time on Task

Here, the schools began with an emphasis on the learning of the basic skills. Now, the students must move to greater emphasis on learning the larger content that is covered. This requires the "organized abandonment" of the old school teaching practices, with greater flexibility in time allocation (Accelerated Schools) and a core curriculum that includes the teaching of higher-order teaching skills.

Frequent Monitoring of Student Progress

This began the process of the early and regular monitoring and adjusting by teachers. It required the disaggregation of student scores on standardized norm-referenced tests. Now, with those scores in hand, the second-generation correlates call for weekly criterion-referenced tests scored by computers, student profiles and portfolios, and encouragement of the students to monitor their own behavior. This implies increased emphasis on authentic assessment, curriculum alignment, and the clarification of educational values. Computer software, such as the Management Information System for Effective Schools (MISES), will relieve the teacher of the burden of record keeping.

Positive Home-School Relations

This correlate, although a little controversial its first time around, always emphasized parents as political allies. In the second generation, schools push now for parents to be true partners. This means increased communication, regarding parents as teachers, and having the practitioners strive for "authentic partnerships."

Just as with the first generation of correlates, the application of this second generation is not simple. So much of Effective Schools goes back to common sense that the mistake is made to think that the process can be done quickly and easily. The schools in this book—as directed by their districts—have demonstrated that this change process often takes at least a year of planning, and then a careful, step by painful step, structured implementation.

As we move into the second generation of correlates, the complete restructuring of the school system becomes even more important. As many school districts have demonstrated, the best way for the public schools to move from the old factory model to the information model is through the comprehensive planning and implementation of the Effective Schools Improvement Process.

The cultural change inherent in the shifting public school paradigm must be complete. It goes to the heart of personal and professional values, as well as the organizational structure of the school systems. Rosabeth Moss Kanter (1989), in an article titled "New Mangerial Work," maintains that with the "old motivational tool kit depleted" (the ways of hierarchical management), require "new and more effective" incentives. She lists five new "tools" to encourage high performance and to build commitment. To Effective School practitioners, they may sound a familiar chord:

- Mission: "Good leaders can inspire others with the power and excitement of their vision and give people a sense of purpose and pride in their work."
- Agenda Control: "More and more professionals are passing up jobs with glamour and prestige in favor of jobs that give them greater control over their own activities and direction."
- Share of Value Creation: "Entrepreneurial incentives that give teams a piece of the action are highly appropriate in collaborative companies."
- Learning: "'The Learning Organization' promises to become a 1990s business buzzword as companies seek to learn more systematically from their experience and to encourage continuous learning for their people."
- Reputation: "Reputation os a key resource in professional careers, and the chance to enhance it can be an outstanding motivator."

The leaders of Effective Schools not only understand the value of these tools but are applying them, taking full advantage of the results they produce. Today's schools—at the leadership level—are proving that they are not that different from prospering businesses. Kanter's (1989) summation applies in Effective Schools just as in business:

Leaders in the new organization do not lack motivational tools, but the tools are different from those of traditional corporate bureaucrats. The new rewards are based

> *not on status but on contribution, and they consist not of regular promotion and automatic pay raises but of excitement about mission and a share of the glory and the gains of success. The new loyalty is not to the boss or to the company but to the projects that actualize a mission and offer challenge, growth, and credit for results.*

With schools discarding their own mind-numbing, shackling images of the past, and adopting the merits of individual growth, loyalty to a mission, and a drive for positive results, they can not only turn around years of educational decline but they can make the schools a challenging, even enjoyable place to work that will attract quality professionals.

School practitioners have complained for decades that the reason the schools were failing was because the individual schools had little power and were operated at the mercy of a political bureaucracy that did not have the best interests of the child as its priority. However, when the scores were low, the parents angry, and the students disgusted and dropping out, those in power pointed the accusing finger at the practitioners in the schools and the teachers' unions.

The board and superintendent must be held accountable. The future of Effective Schools is the restructuring of the district school systems. It is making the central office work for the schools, and not for the whims of the superintendent and board. It is also a matter of the schools, the individual campuses, insisting on a higher standard of performance and cooperation than practiced in the past.

Although the Effective Schools practitioners work hard on the imperatives of innovation and responsiveness within their systems, there seems to be unanimous agreement that there is one factor that is outside their control, but that is extremely important in their success: higher education.

Right now the training of teachers in many teaching institutions is derelict. The teachers are arriving at public and private schools without any knowledge of cooperative learning, mastery learning, or even fundamental instruction techniques for heterogeneous populations. These teachers are not taught how to teach to high expectations in a heterogeneous population; they are given little instruction in the proper management of classroom time; and they have no discernible training in the interpretation of testing and measurement, or in decision-making skills. Unfortunately, these teachers arriving at the classroom door are often replacing teachers who also did not have these skills. And they work alongside teachers whose education was just as deficient.

School systems are spending considerable time and money in retraining teachers. The task is made more difficult by the depth of the cultural bias against high expectations for all children held by many teaching graduates—a bias that was learned by observation in elementary and secondary school, and reinforced in college. Today, colleges are often no better than the public schools at establishing a climate of high expectations for success.

For all the voice and fist raising in the direction of elementary and secondary schools, it is unfortunate that a similar call to reform and accountabilty is not aimed at higher education. Critics point out that in the United States only 27 percent of undergraduates complete the requirements for a four-year baccalaureate degree in five years or less. If you turn that around, that is a stopout/dropout rate of 73 percent. The average for secondary schools is between 20 and 25 percent.

Higher education may be suffering from the same ills that plague the public schools: low expectations and a lack of leadership. Many students and tenured professors do not feel any pressure to be held accountable. And, like the schools, higher education seems to be suffering from poor management and organization. There are reports that even some graduate business schools are encountering trouble balancing their budgets.

Higher education maintains that one of their problems is that they must deal with the graduates of the public schools. Public school practitioners insist that one of their problems is that they must deal with the graduates of higher education. No one wins in this chicken and egg argument. In fact, both entities are guaranteed to lose. The losses begin taking on human faces in the first grade.

There are three forces at work in the United States that make change in education essential and inevitable, if not imminent: the cutback in public education funds at all levels; the increase in funds needed for social services (in 1989, the federal government spent $21.5 billion on welfare programs for families started by teenagers); and the increasing numbers of poor and minority citizens. These forces are working to create a demand for accountability as the only means we know to pull this country out of its quagmire of dismal mediocrity in education.

Effective Schools has come forward with a process for change that reinstates accountability by demanding justifiable outcomes. It requires a professional attitude and professional behaviors, and, at a time when society seems to have more excuses than reasons, Effective Schools allows *no* excuses.

It is often enlightening to watch students' reactions to the implementation of the correlates. The students are not threatened by them; the correlates provide a stability, a guiding force, that helps them know how much "wiggle room" they have. But they also see something more in the correlates. They say the correlates can be applied personally, to life, to how we should live responsibly: mission, safe environment, opportunity to learn, high expectations, leadership, frequent monitoring, and positive home-school relations.

This lesson—the personal application of the correlates—may come in handy as the responsibilities of the public schools continue to expand. If we can keep the moral imperative intact—the belief that all children can learn and that by teaching all children we enhance and enlighten our democratic society—we will be on a course that preserves the best in us while challenging our untapped potential.

Despite the best intentions of our forebears, the United States has always been a very class-conscious, class-oriented society. We have even supported our biases by faulty intelligence test interpretation and the misuse of methodological research. Our history is an unfortunate accumulation of beliefs and policies that have, in large measure, served to track only the chosen onto journeys of prosperity. Now we have reached that point where our dogma has caught up with us and we must either change or lose all that we have tried so diligently to preserve.

The President and Congress are calling for a reform plan to save the public schools (the New American Schools initiative). They are even establishing experimental schools to determine what is the best way to go about this reform. The practitioners in Effective Schools can only shake their heads as more money is wasted.

A startling and depressing example of how ludicrous and ill-directed school reform can be is happening in Houston. With great expense of time and talent—and with extravagant fanfare—the University of Houston has involved its business school faculty in an extensive program to investigate the implementation possibilities and problems of school-based management in the Houston Public Schools. Right next door is one of the nation's front-running, successful, school-based management systems: Spring Branch did it with the Effective Schools Process and their own people.

Unfortunately, there is a plethora of examples such as this. The Education Secretary, Lamar Alexander, and David Kearns, former chairman of the Xerox Corporation, are calling for businesses to become involved in the nation's schools. Leaders of Effective Schools just smile as they point to their own schools' partnerships—with as many as 20 and 30 businesses, agencies, and nonprofit organizations involved—going back a decade.

There are other proposed reform elements: increased teacher training and in-service programs; revised curriculum; programs that address past generations as well as future; stiffer graduation requirements; more frequent and comprehensive testing; alignment of social services within the schools; creation of specific management guidelines; solicitation of outside resources.

All of these proposals have been in operation in Effective Schools for over the last decade. They may come under different headings and various groups may claim credit. Indeed, reform programs are many and varied in name and nature. It is the Effective Schools Process that has committed itself to the teaching for learning for *all*, that has provided the means and skills to accomplish that, and that has proven it is the belief in the teaching and learning for *all* that transforms declining school systems—no matter where they are or what their population—into improving school systems. Effective Schools is the road to school reform and school renewal, and is inconclusive in its action.

So, yes, we know how to change our schools, how to restructure them. We know how to build accountability. We know how to inspire and enlighten. We don't need more studies or experimental schools. We know the way. Some

25 years ago, Ron Edmonds and other researchers started gathering research data that produced the progressive findings that now demonstrate, very specifically, how to create Effective Schools. Now, thousands of such schools exist. It hasn't taken the infusion of millions of dollars. It has taken some tough, thoughtful leadership and people with courage and high expectations of themselves and others.

But it's not enough. Children are still being denied the knowledge and confidence to fulfill their dreams. It was one thing when we failed because we didn't know the best way to teach all children, or the best way to lead and restructure. But now we do know, and not doing so now is indefensible. There is no possible excuse for *our* failure. And it is ours, not theirs.

America's children have entrusted us with their dreams. They come to us able, brave, and willing. We are stewards of their future, as they are of ours.

For the Record

After an agonizing personal/professional knock-down-drag-out fight with herself, Suzanne Still decided in the summer of 1991 to leave the Hollibrook School for a teaching and research position at Texas A&M. "There has to be more than one Hollibrook. This change is a chance for me to impact higher education," she says. "What good does it do for us to continue to put out the same Beaver Cleaver teachers who don't understand what is needed in our schools today?"

Still and the faculty assisted in choosing Still's successor, Roy Ford. The teachers admit to some initial angst at her departure, but say they knew that in time her unique talents would take her elsewhere. They are working closely with Ford, who believes (as Still had forecast in this book) that he must have done something incredibly good in this life to now have the principalship of Hollibrook. The school continues to grow and improve.

"I got sick and tired of hearing that Hollibrook worked because of Suzanne Still," says Still. "It works because of the teachers and now it's a chance for them to prove to all the know-it-alls that they are the real decision makers, that they are professional educators."

She insists, "My heart is there everyday," but says her work now is "my real calling." In September, a Hollibrook student wrote a book, *Miss Still Is Missing*. "It broke my heart," Still says. "It was about how they came back this fall and I wasn't there and they felt cheated. But on the last page, it said, 'But Hollibrook is OK, so I guess college and other schools need her more than we do.'"

In South Carolina, there is a new superintendent of education, Barbara Nielsen, who is inspiring change and optimism. According to Jean Norman, Nielsen is working on process, attitude, and philosophy. "There's still so much to be done, but I think we're moving a little more quickly in the right direction." Norman also reports some increased pockets of help from higher education. "It's difficult with the economy the way it is, but there are some exciting, stimulating things going on. We're progressing."

And Jamie Summers, principal of the O. P. Earle School in Landrum, South Carolina tried to retire, but the parents in the school wouldn't let her.

In Spencerport, New York, both Bob Sudlow and Joe Clement have retired. The district's program, More Effective Schools/Teaching Project, was approved by the National Diffusion Network of the United States Department of Education in April 1992. This project was envisioned, planned, and implemented using the Effective Schools Process in its most comprehensive form.

Bibliography

Achilles, C. M. 1987. "A Vision of Better Schools," in William Greenfield, ed., *Instructional Leadership,* pp. 17–37. Boston: Allyn and Bacon.

Anderson, Carolyn S. 1985. "The Investigation of School Climate," in Gilbert R. Austin and Herbert Garber, eds., *Research on Exemplary Schools,* pp. 97–126. Orlando: Academic Press.

______. 1987. "How Effective Are School Effectiveness Instruments?" Paper prepared for the Illinois Association for Research and Evaluation.

Argyris, Chris. 1980. "Making the Undiscussable and Its Undiscussability Discussable," *Public Administration Review,* 40(3): 205–213.

Arnn, John W. Jr. and Mangieri, John. 1988. "Effective Leadership for Effective Schools: A Survey of Principals' Attitudes," *NASSP Bulletin,* 72(505): 1–7.

Austin, Gilbert R. 1978. *Process Evaluation: A Comprehensive Study of Outliers.* Baltimore: Maryland State Department of Education.

______. 1979. "Exemplary Schools and the Search for Effectiveness," *Educational Leadership* 37: 10–14.

Austin, Gilbert R., and Holowenzak, Stephen P. (1985). "An Examination of 10 years of Research on Exemplary Schools," in Gilbert R. Austin and Herbert Garber, eds., *Research on Exemplary Schools,* pp. 65–82. Orlando: Academic Press.

Azumi, Jann E. 1989. "Effective Schools Characteristics, School Improvement and School Outcomes: What are the Relationships?" Paper delivered at the annual meeting of the American Educational Research Association, Washington, DC, April.

Bamburg, Jerry and Andrews, Richard L. 1987. "Goal Consensus in Schools and Student Academic Achievement Gains." Paper delivered at the annual meeting of the American Educational Research Association, Washington, DC, April.

Bennis, Warren and Nanus, Burt. 1985. *Leaders: The Strategies for Taking Charge.* New York: Harper Collins.

Berliner, David. 1986. "In Pursuit of the Expert Pedagogue," *Educational Researcher,* 15(7): 5–13.

Block, James H., Efthim, Helen, E., and Burns, Robert B. 1988. *Building Effective Mastery Learning Schools.* New York: Longman.

Bloom, B. S. 1974. "Time and Learning," *American Psychologist,* 29: 682–688.

______. 1976. *Human Characteristics and School Learning.* New York: McGraw-Hill.

Blum, Robert E. 1984. *Onward to Excellence: Making Schools More Effective.* Portland, OR: Northwest Regional Educational Laboratory.

Brookover, Wilbur B. 1985. "Can We Make Schools Effective for Minority Students?" *The Journal of Negro Education,* 54(3): 257–268.

Brookover, Wilbur B. and Lezotte, Lawrence W. 1979. "Changes in School Characteristics Coincident with Changes in School Achievement." East Lansing, MI: Michigan State University Institute for Research on Teaching Occasional Paper No. 17. Ed 181005.

Brookover, Wilbur B. and Schneider, Jeffrey M. 1975. "Academic Environments and Elementary School Achievement," *Journal of Research and Development in Education,* 9(1): 82–91.

Brookover, Wilbur B., et al. 1979. *School Social Systems and Student Achievement. Schools Can Make a Difference.* New York: Praeger.

———. 1982. *Creating Effective Schools.* Holmes Beach, FL: Learning Publications.

Brousseau, Bruce A. 1988. *A Test of Five Correlates from Effective Schools Research Using Hierarchical Linear Modeling.* Unpublished Ph.D. Dissertation, Michigan State University, Lansing.

Bryk, Anthony S. and Thum, Yeow Meng. 1989. *The Effects of High School Organization on Dropping Out: An Exploratory Investigation.* New Brunswick, NJ: Center for Policy Research in Education, Rutgers University.

Canady, Robert Lynn. 1988. "A Cure for Fragmented Block Schedules in Elementary Schools," *Educational Leadership,* 46(2): 65–67.

———. 1989. "Design Scheduling Structures to Increase Student Learning," *Focus in Change,* 1(2). Nat'l Ctr. for Effective Schools Research & Development.

Canady, Robert Lynn and Hotchkiss, Phyllis R. 1985. "Scheduling Practices and Polices Associated With Increased Achievement for Low Achieving Students," *Journal of Negro Education,* 54(3): 344–355.

Carroll, John B. 1963. "A Model of School Learning, *Teachers College Record,* 64: 722–733.

———. 1977. "A Revisionist Model of School Learning," *Review of Education,* 3: 155–167.

Clark, David L., Lotto, Linda S., and Astuto, Terry A. 1984. "Effective Schools and School Improvement: Comparative Analysis of Two Lines of Inquiry," *Educational Administration Quarterly,* 20(3): 41–68.

Cohen, David K. 1988. "Teaching Practice, Plus Que Ca Change . . . ," in Phillip W. Jackson, ed., *Contributing to Educational Change,* pp. 27–84. Berkeley, CA: McCutchan.

Coleman, J. S., Campbell, E. O., Hobson, C. J., McPartland, J., Mood, A. M., Weinfeld, F. D., and York, R. L. 1966. *Equality of Educational Opportunity.* Washington, DC: U.S. Office of Education, National Center for Educational Statistics.

Comer, James P. 1987. "New Haven's School-Community Connection," *Educational Leadership,* 44(6): 13–16.

———. 1988. "Educating Poor Minority Children," *Scientific American,* 259(5): 42–48.

Conley, Sharon, C. 1989. "'Who's on First?': School Reform, Teacher Participation, and the Decision-making Process." Paper delivered at the annual meeting of the American Educational Research Association, San Francisco, March.

Cooper, Eric J. 1989. "Toward a New Mainstream of Instruction for American Schools," *The Journal of Negro Education,* 58(1): 102–116.

Cooper, Eric J. and Levine, Daniel U. 1988. "An Effective Schooling Network with a Legislative Emphasis," *Educational Horizons,* Fall/Winter: 40–41.

Corbett, H. Dickson, Firetone, William A., and Rossman, Gretchen, B. 1987. "Resistance to Planned Change and the Sacred in School Cultures," *Educational Administration Quarterly,* 23(4): 36–59.

Corbett, H. Dickson and Rossman, Gretchen B. 1989. "Three Paths to Implementing Change: A Research Note," *Curriculum Inquiry,* 19(2): 164–190.

Covey, Stephen R. 1989. *The Seven Habits of Highly Effective People.* New York: Simon & Schuster.

David, Jane L. 1989. "Synthesis of Research on School-Based Management," *Educational Leadership,* 46(8): 45–53.

Davis, Gary A. and Thomas, Margaret A. 1989. *Effective Schools and Effective Teachers.* Boston: Allyn and Bacon.

Deal, Terrence E. 1985. "The Symbolism of Effective Schools," *The Elementary School Journal,* 85(5): 601-620.

Deal, Terrence E. and Kennedy, Allen. 1982. *Corporate Cultures.* Reading, MA: Addison-Wesley.

Deal, Terrence E. and Peterson, Kent D. 1990. *The Principal's Role in Shaping School Cultures.* U.S. Department of Education.

Edmonds, Ronald R. 1978. "Alternate Patterns for the Distribution of Social Services," in Walter Feinberg, ed., *Equality and Social Policy.* University of Illinois Press.

Edmonds, Ronald. 1978. "A Discussion of the Literature and Issues Related to Effective Schooling." Paper prepared for the National Conference on Urban Education. Cemrel, St. Louis.

Edmonds, Ronald. 1979. "Effective Schools for the Urban Poor," *Educational Leadership,* October, pp. 15-24.

Edmonds, Ronald R. and Frederickson, John R. 1979. *Search for Effective Schools. The Identification and Analysis of City Schools That Are Instructionally Effective For Poor Children.* Ed 170 396.

Edmonds, Ronald et al. 1973. "A Black Response to Christopher Jencks' Inequality and Certain Other Issues," *Harvard Educational Review,* 43(1): 76-91.

Elmore, Richard F. 1987. "The Culture of Authority in Schools," *Educational Administration Quarterly,* 23(4): 60-78.

Eubanks, Eugene E. and Levine, Daniel U. 1983. "A First Look at Effective Schools Projects in New York City and Milwaukee," *Phi Delta Kappan,* 64(10): 697-702.

Firestone, William A. and Corbett, H. D. 1988. "Planned Organizational Change," in Norman J. Bogan, ed., *Handbook of Research on Educational Administration,* pp. 321-338. New York: Longman.

Firestone, William A. and Wilson, Bruce L. 1989. "Using Bureaucratic and Cultural Linkages to Improve Instruction: The Principal's Contribution," in Joel L. Burdin, ed., *School Leadership,* pp. 275-296. Beverly Hills, CA: Sage.

Fiske, Edward B. 1991. *Smart Schools, Smart Kids.* New York: Simon & Schuster.

Frederick, Judith M. and Clauset, Karl H. 1985. "A Comparison of the Major Algorithms for Measuring School Effectiveness." Paper delivered at the annual meeting of the American Educational Research Association, Chicago, April.

Fullan, Michael. 1982. *The Meaning of Educational Change.* New York: Teachers College Press.

Gauthier, William J. Jr., Pecheone, Raymond L., and Shoemaker, Joan. 1985. "Schools Can Become More Effective," *Journal of Negro Education,* 54(3): 388-408.

Glass, G. V. and Smith, M. L. 1978. *Meta-analysis of Research on the Relationship of Class Size and Achievement.* San Francisco: Far West Laboratory for Educational Research and Development.

Good, Thomas L. and Brophy, Jere E. 1986. "School Effects," in Merlin C. Wittcock, ed., *Handbook of Research on Teaching,* pp. 570-602. New York: Macmillan.

Guthrie, Hal, Mathews, Gary, and Wells, Bob. "Campus Improvement Planning," *Instructional Leader,* 2(3).

Hall, Gene E. and Hord, Shirley M. 1987. *Change in Schools.* Albany: State University of New York Press.

Hallinger, Philip and Murphy, Joseph. 1985. "Instructional Leadership and School Socioeconomic Status: A Preliminary Investigation," *Administrator's Notebook,* 31(5).

______. 1987. "Instructional Leadership in the School Context," in William Greenfield, ed., *Instructional Leadership,* pp. 179-202. Boston: Allyn and Bacon.

Henderson, Anne and Lezotte, Larry. 1988. "SBI and Effective Schools: A Perfect Match," *NETWORK for Public Schools,* 13(5): 1, 3-5. National Committee for Citizens in Education, Washington, D.C.

Henderson, Anne T., Marburger, Carl L., and Ooms, Theodora. 1985. *Beyond the Bake Sale.* Columbia, MD: National Committee for Citizens in Education.

Huberman, A. Michael and Miles, Matthew B. 1982. *Innovation Up Close: A Field Study in 12 School Settings.* Andover, MA: The Network.

Huff, Sheila, Lake, Dale, and Schaalman, Mary Lou. 1982. *Principal Differences: Excellence in School Leadership and Management.* Boston: McBer.

Jencks, Christopher, et al. 1972. *Inequality: A Reassessment of the Effect of Family and Schooling in America.* New York: Basic Books.

Joyce, B. and Showers, B. 1980. "Improving Inservice Training: The Messages of Research," *Educational Leadership,* 379–385.

Kanter, Rosabeth Moss. 1989. *When Giants Learn to Dance.* New York: Simon & Schuster—Touchstone.

———. 1989. "New Managerial Work," *Harvard Business Review* (Nov.–Dec.)

Kelly, Thomas F. 1989. "What's New in Effective Schools Research." Paper prepared for the BOCES III-Suffolk, New York Effective Schools Consortium.

———. Updated. "Clear Data: The Lever for Change in Schools." Unpublished paper.

Keppel, Francis. 1966. *The Necessary Revolution in American Education.* New York: Harper & Row.

Kijai, Jimmy. 1988. "Discriminating Ability of the School Effectiveness Correlates." Paper delivered at the annual meeting of the American Educational Research Association, New Orleans, April.

Klitgaard, R. E. and Hall, G. R. 1973. *A Statistical Search for Unusually Effective Schools.* Santa Monica, CA: Rand Corporation.

Kouzes, James M. and Posner, Barry Z. 1987. *The Leadership Challenge.* San Francisco: Jossey-Bass.

Kozol, Jonathon. 1991. *Savage Inequalities.* New York: Crown Publishers.

Leiberman, Ann. 1988. "Teachers and Principals: Turf, Tension, and New Tasks," *Phi Delta Kappan,* 69(9): 648–653.

Leithwood, K. A. and Montogomery, D. J. 1982. "The Role of the Elementary School Principal in Program Improvement," *Review of Educational Research,* 52(3): 309–339.

———. 1985b. "School Improvement Based on Effective Schools Research: A Promising Approach for Economically Disadvantaged and Minority Students," *The Journal of Negro Education,* 54(3): 301–312.

Levin, Henry M. 1987. "New Schools for the Disadvantaged." Paper prepared for the Mid-continent Regional Educational Laboratory, Denver, June.

———. 1988. *Accelerated Schools for Students at Risk.* New Brunswick, NJ: Center for Policy Research in Education, Rutgers University.

Levine, Daniel U. 1975. "Educating Alienated Inner-City Youth: Lessons for the Street Academies," *The Journal of Negro Education,* 44(2): 138–148.

———. 1985. "A Mini-Description of Initially-Unsuccessful Attempts to Introduce Outcomes-Based Instruction," *Outcomes,* 4(2): 15–19.

———. 1988. "Teaching Thinking to At-Risk Students: Generalizations and Speculation," in Barbara Z. Preisseisen, ed., *At-Risk Students and Thinking: Perspectives from Research,* pp. 117–137. Washington, D.C.: NEA.

Levine, Daniel U., ed. 1985. *Improving Student Achievement Through Mastery Learning Programs.* San Francisco: Jossey-Bass.

Levine, Daniel U. and Eubanks, Eugene E. 1983. "Instructional and Organizational Arrangements at an Unusually Effective Inner City Elementary School in Chicago." Paper delivered at the annual meeting of the American Educational Research Association, Montreal, April.

———. 1989. "Organizational Arrangements at Effective Secondary Schools," in Herbert

J. Walberg and John J. Lane, eds., *Organizing for Learning,* pp. 41–49. Reston, VA: National Association of Secondary School Principals.

Levine, Daniel U. and Havighurst, Robert J. 1989. *Society and Education.* 7th ed. Boston: Allyn and Bacon.

Levine, Daniel U. and Jones, Beau F. 1988. "Mastery Learning," in Richard A. Gorton, Gail T. Schneider, and James C. Fisher, eds., *Encyclopedia of School Administration and Supervision,* pp. 166–167. Phoenix: Oryx.

Levine, Daniel U. and Leibert, Robert E. 1987. "Improving School Improvement Plans," *Elementary School Journal,* 87(4): 397–412.

Levine, Daniel U. and Lezotte, Lawrence W. 1990. *Unusually Effective Schools, A Review and Analysis of Research and Practice.* National Center for Effective Schools Research & Development. University of Wisconsin–Madison.

Levine, Daniel U. and Ornstein, Allen C. 1990. "Research on Classroom and School Effectiveness and Its Implications for Improving Big City Schools," *The Urban Review* (in press).

Levine, Daniel U., and Sherk, John K. 1990. *Effective Implementation of a Comprehension Development Approach in Secondary Schools.* Kansas City: University of Missouri-Kansas City (title tentative, in press).

Lezotte, L. W. 1986. "School Effectiveness: Reflections and Future Directions." Paper delivered at the annual meeting of the American Educational Research Association, San Francisco, April.

Lezotte, L. W., and Bancroft, B. A. 1985. "School Improvement Based on Effective Schools Research: A Promising Approach for Economically Disadvantaged and Minority Students," *The Journal of Negro Education,* 54(3): 301–312.

Lezotte, Lawrence, Edmonds, Ronald, and Ratner, Gershon. 1974. *Remedy for School Failure to Equitably Deliver Basic School Skills.* Cambridge, MA: Center for Urban Studies, Harvard University.

Lezotte, Lawrence W., et al. 1980. *School Learning Climate and Academic Achievement.* Tallahassee: Florida State University Teacher Education Projects.

Little, Judith W. 1982. "Norms of Collegiality and Experimentation: Workplace Conditions of Success," *American Educational Research Journal,* 19(3): 325–40.

Little, Judith Warren and Bird, Tom. 1987. "Instructional Leadership 'Close to the Classroom' in Secondary Schools," in William Greenfield, ed., *Instructional Leadership* pp. 118–138. Boston: Allyn and Bacon.

Loucks-Horsley, Susan. undated. "Managing Change: An Integral Part of Staff Development." Paper prepared for the Regional Laboratory for Educational Improvement of the Northeast and Islands.

Louis, Karen S. and Miles, Matthew B. 1990. *Improving Urban High Schools: What Works and Why.* New York: Teachers College Press.

Mace-Matluck, Betty J. undated. *The Effective Schools Movement: Its History and Context.* Austin, TX: Southwest Educational Developmental Laboratory.

McCormack-Larkin, Maureen and Kritek, William J. 1982. "Milwaukee's Project RISE," *Educational Leadership,* 40(3): 16–21.

Madden, Nancy A., Slavin, Robert E., Karweit, Nancy L., and Livermon, Barbara J. 1989. "Restructuring the Urban Elementary School," *Educational Leadership,* 46(5): 14–18.

Maeroff, Gene I. 1988. *The Empowerment of Teachers.* New York: Teachers College Press.

Manasse, A. Lori. 1984. *How Can We Recognize Effective Principals?* Alexandria, VA: National Association of State Boards of Education.

Marburger, Carl L. 1985. *One School at a Time.* Columbia, MD: National Committee for Citizens in Education.

Maryland State Department of Education. 1978. *Process Evaluation: A Comprehensive Review of Outliers.* Baltimore: Maryland State Department of Education.

Miller, Stephen K., Efthim, Helen, Koppel, Sheree, and Sayre, Kathleen. 1985. "Measuring School Improvement Implementation: A School Effectiveness Structural Components Inventory (Executive Summary)." Paper delivered at the annual meeting of the American Educational Research Association, Chicago, April.

Morgan, Gareth. 1986. *Images of Organization.* Newbury Park, CA: Sage.

Mortimore, Peter, et al. 1988. *School Matters.* Berkeley: University of California Press.

Murphy, John A. and Waynant, Louise F. 1989. "Reaching for Excellence and Equity in Prince George's County Public Schools," in Barbara O. Taylor ed., *Case Studies in Effective Schools Research.* Madison, WI: National Center for Effective Schools Research and Development.

Murphy, Joseph. 1989. "Principal Instructional Leadership," in P.W. Thurston and L.S. Lotto, eds., *Advances in Educational Leadership.* Greenwich, CT: JAI Press.

Murphy, Joseph. 1991. *Restructuring Schools: Capturing and Assessing the Phenomena.* New York: Teachers College Press.

Murphy, Joseph and Hallinger, Philip. 1985. "Effective High Schools—What Are the Common Characteristics?" *NASSP Bulletin,* 69(477): 18–22.

Murphy, Joseph and Hallinger, Philip, eds. (forthcoming) *Restructuring Schooling: Learning from Ongoing Experiences.* Beverly Hills: Corwin-Sage.

Murphy, Joseph, Weil, Marsha, Hallinger, Phillip, and Mitman, Alexis. 1982. "Academic Press: Translating Expectations Into School Level Policies and Classroom Practices," *Educational Leadership,* 40(3): 22–26.

New York State Office of Education Performance Review. 1974. *School Factors Influencing Reading Achievement: A Case Study of Two Inner-City Schools.* Albany, NY: Department of Education.

Olson, Lynn. 1986. "Effective Schools," *Education Week.* January 15: 11–22.

Pecheone, Raymond and Shoemaker, Joan. 1984. *An Evaluation of School Effectiveness Program in Connecticut.* Hartford: Connecticut State Department of Education.

Peters, Tom J. 1988. *Thriving on Chaos.* New York: Knopf.

Peters, Tom J. and Austin, Nancy K. 1985. *A Passion for Excellence.* New York: Random House.

Peters, Tom J. and Waterman, Robert. 1982. *In Search of Excellence.* New York: Harper and Row.

Peterson, Kent D. 1989. "Secondary Principals and Instructional Leadership: Complexities in a Diverse Role," National Center for Effective Secondary Schools.

Pink, William T. 1987. "In Search of Exemplary Junior High Schools: A Case Study," in George W. Noblit and William T. Pink, eds., *Schooling in Context: Qualitative Studies,* pp. 218–249. Norwood, NJ: Ablex.

Pollack, Sally, Watson, Dan, and Chrispeels, Janet. 1987. "A Description of Factors and Implementation Strategies Used by Schools in Becoming Effective for All Students." Paper delivered at the annual meeting of the American Educational Research Association. Washington, DC, April.

Pollack, Sally, et al. 1988. "A Description of District Factors that Assist in the Development of Equity Schools." Paper delivered at the annual meeting of the American Educational Research Association, New Orleans, April.

Porter, Andrew. 1989. "A Curriculum Out of Balance," *Educational Researcher,* 18(5): 9–15.

Purkey, Stewart C. and Smith, Marshall W. 1983. "Effective Schools-A Review," *Elementary School Journal,* 83: 427–52.

Ravitch, Diane. 1983. *The Troubled Crusade.* New York: Basic Books.

Rosenholtz, Susan J. 1985. "Effective Schools: Interpreting the Evidence," *American Journal of Education,* 93(3): 352–388.

Rossman, Gretchen B., Corbett, H. Dickson, and Firestone, William A. 1988. *Change and Effectiveness in Schools.* Philadelphia: Research for Better Schools.

Rowan, Brian, Bossert, Steven L., and Dwyer, David C. 1983. "Research on Effective Schools: A Cautionary Note," *Educational Researcher,* 12(4): 24–31.

Rutter, Michael, et al. 1979. *Fifteen Thousand Hours.* Cambridge, MA: Harvard University Press.

Sarason, Seymour B. 1990. *The Predictable Failure of Educational Reform.* San Francisco: Jossey-Bass.

Saxl, Ellen R., Kaplan, Meryle, Robinson, Jennifr J. and Springer, Carolyn M. 1989. *Project BASICS in the Schools: There for the Long Haul.* New York: Center for Policy Research.

Schein, Edgar H. 1985. *Organizational Culture and Leadership: A Dynamic View.* San Francisco: Jossey-Bass.

Schön, Donald. 1983. *The Reflective Practitioner.* New York: Basic Books.

School Effectiveness Unit. 1989. "The School Effectiveness Report: History, Current Status, Future Directions." Paper prepared for the Connecticut State Board of Education, Middletown, February.

Shoemaker, Joan. 1982. "Effective Schools: Putting the Research to the Ultimate Test," *Pre-Post Press,* 7(2): 1.

______. 1984. *Research-Based School Improvement Practices.* Hartford: Connecticut State Department of Education.

Sizemore, Barbara A. 1985. "Pitfalls and Promises of Effective Schools Research," *Journal of Negro Education,* 54(3): 269–288.

______. 1987. "The Effective African American Elementary School," in George W. Noblit and William T. Pink, eds. *Schooling in Social Context: Qualitative Studies,* pp. 175–202. Norwood, NJ: Ablex.

Slavin, Robert E. and Madden, Nancy A. 1989. "What Works for Students at Risk: A Research Synthesis," *Educational Leadership,* 46(5): 4–13.

Slavin, Robert E., et al. 1989. "Can Every Child Learn? An Evaluation of 'Success for All' in an Urban Elementary School," *The Journal of Negro Education,* 58(3): 357–366.

Stringfield, Sam and Teddlie, Charles. 1987. "A Time to Summarize: Six Years and Three Phases of the Louisiana School Effectiveness Study." Paper delivered at the annual meeting of the American Educational Research Association, Washington, DC, April.

Stringfield, Sam, Teddlie, Charles, and Suarez, Sandra. 1986. "Classroom Interaction in Effective and Ineffective Schools: Preliminary Results From Phase III of the Louisiana School Effectiveness Study," *Journal of Classroom Interaction,* 20(2): 31–37.

Taylor, Barbara A. O. 1984. *Implementing What Works: Elementary Principals and School Improvement Programs.* Ph.D. Dissertation, Northwestern University, Evanston, IL. #8502445 University Microfilms International, Ann Arbor.

Taylor, Barbara O., ed., *Case Studies in Effective Schools Research.* National Center for Effective Schools Research & Development. University of Wisconsin–Madison.

Teddlie, Charles, Kirby, Peggy C., and Stringfield, Sam. 1989. "Effective Versus Ineffective Schools: Observable Differences in the Classroom," *American Journal of Education,* 97(3): 221–236.

Teddlie, Charles and Stringfield, Sam. 1985. "A Differential Analysis of Effectiveness in Middle and Low Socioeconomic Status Schools," *Journal of Classroom Interaction,* 20(2): 38–44.

______. 1989. "The Ethics of Behavior for Teachers in Four Types of Schools," *Ethics in Education.*

Terman, Lewis. 1923. "Intelligence Tests and School Reorganization." New York: World Book Co., p. 28.

Tichy, Noel and DeVanna, Mary Anne. 1986. *Transformational Leader.* New York: John Wiley.

U.S. Department of Education. 1987. *Schools That Work Educating Disadvantaged Children.* Washington, DC: U.S. Government Printing Office.

Venezky, Richard L. and Winfield, Linda F. 1979. *Schools That Succeed Beyond Expectations in Teaching Reading.* Newark, DE: University of Delaware. Ed 177 484.

Villanova, Robert. M. 1984. "A Comparison of Interview and Questionnaire Techniques Used in the Connecticut School Effectiveness Project." Paper delivered at the annual meeting of the American Educational Research Association, New Orleans, April.

Weber, George. 1971. *Inner-City Children Can Be Taught to Read: Four Successful Schools.* Washington, DC: Council for Basic Education.

Wehlage, Gary G. 1983. *Effective Programs for the Marginal High School Student.* Bloomington, IN: Phi Delta Kappa.

Wehlage, Gary G. Rutter, Robert A., and Turnbaugh, Anne. 1987. "A Program Model for At-Risk High School Students," *Educational Leadership,* 44(6): 70–73.

Weiss, Albert S. 1984. *The Effectiveness of Project RISE in Raising Achievement Levels of Pupils in Milwaukee Public School Inner-City Schools.* Unpublished Ph.D. Dissertation, Marquette University, Milwaukee.

White, Paula. 1988. *Resource Materials on School-Based Management.* New Brunswick, NJ: Center for Policy Research in Education, Rutgers University.

Wick, John W. and Turnbaugh, Roy C. 1983. "A Successful Program to Improve Student Performance." Paper published by the Northwestern University School of Education Division of Field Studies, Evanston.

Wimpelberg, Robert. 1987a. "Managerial Images and School Effectiveness," *Administrator's Notebook,* 32(4): 1–4.

Wimpelberg, Robert, Teddlie, Charles, and Stringfield, Samuel. 1989. "Sensitivity to Context: The Past and Future of Effective Schools Research," *Educational Administration Quarterly,* 25(1) (in press)

APPENDIX A

Definition of the Effective Schools Model or Process

The Effective Schools Model or Process is a framework for school reform that is based on evolving research from both empirical investigations and case studies of schools across the country that have been successful in teaching the intended curriculum of basic skills to *all* their students. (Basic skills may include comprehensive reading skills, oral and written communication skills, computing skills, problem solving, higher-order thinking skills, and social skills.)

In this model the individual school is viewed as the targeted unit of improvement. Each school, through a faculty-administrator team-planning approach, utilizes the concepts and elements of the Effective Schools Process to develop and implement a long-range improvement plan. In addition, the model promotes districtwide restructuring for improvement. To become effective requires that the district be committed to the program for at least three to five years.

Two criteria for measuring effectiveness have evolved: quality and equity. Having a quality standard assures that the level of achievement in a school is high. Having an equity standard assures that the high achievement does not vary significantly across the subsets of the school's student population. Not only are these standards critical to the definition of Effective Schools but they are fundamental when planning and implementing the Effective Schools Process for school improvement.

Two elements are key to the success of the model. First, the schools and district must develop and state school and district missions. Second, the schools and district must be willing to accept the Effective Schools Program as a *comprehensive* plan. Developing a school improvement plan on a piecemeal basis and focusing on only two or three of the characteristics (correlates) that define an Effective School destroys the cohesiveness of the program and decreases the chance for significant results and lasting improvement of the school.

Many schools achieve most of the characteristics, or correlates, of Effective Schools, and have thus improved the instructional climate or culture of the school. But unless the comprehensive model is carried out in its entirety, few new and substantially different behaviors will occur in the classroom, including a marked increase in the performances of all students.

The seven characteristics of Effective Schools that define the educational programs at these schools tend to work together to foster the organizational dynamics and the context of shared values that promote a school climate or culture conducive to teaching for learning for *all.* The model is guided by shared decision making at the school site, which is based largely on data collected by schoolwide and districtwide monitoring systems.

The decision-making and planning process itself is an heuristic procedure, wherein the principal and the school council or improvement team (made up of the principal, teachers, support staff and community members, including parents) carry out data-gathering and strategic planning on a regular basis. The planning helps to coordinate and integrate curricular development with organizational development at the school-site level, and gives information to the district office and board of education for their own planning and policy-making functions. In this way the two levels of the school organization are aligned for more efficient as well as more effective operations.

The National Center for Effective Schools Research and Development uses the capitalized phrases *Effective Schools Research* and *Effective Schools Model or Process* to denote the comprehensive model espoused by the National Center and founded upon the research literature. "Effective Schools" is a service mark (SM) of the National Center for Effective Schools Research and Development.

The National Center for Effective Schools Research and Development
Wisconsin Center for Education Research, Suite 685
University of Wisconsin-Madison
1025 West Johnson Street
Madison, Wisconsin 53706
(608) 263-4730

Richard A. Rossmiller, Director
Edie L. Holcomb, Associate Director for Training and Technical Assistance
Anne Turnbaugh Lockwood, Assistant Director for Communications
Barbara O. Taylor, Associate for Planning and Institutional Relations

APPENDIX B

A Short History of the Effective Schools Movement in the United States

The Sixties: A Watershed Period for American Educational Philosophy

The 1966 Coleman study, *Equality of Educational Opportunity*, and the 1972 Jencks study, *Inequality: A Reassessment of the Effect of Family and Schooling in America*, found that the large variance in acquisition of basic skills and in academic outcomes of students in U.S. schools could largely be explained by the "attitude of the student" and with the general social context of his or her family and social background. The public inference from these findings was that "Schools don't make a difference." In other words, student and family characteristics rather than school characteristics accounted for student attitude about schooling and therefore his or her achievement in school. What happened in public schools could not change the destiny of students from low-income and working-class families, no matter what school inputs and outputs were measured, studied, and applied.

At the same time, researchers were studying the fundamental relationships of classroom variables such as time-on-task, opportunity to learn, student aptitude, and quality of instruction. Benjamin Bloom and his colleagues built upon John Carroll's (1974) earlier model of "school learning," and produced a new teaching process called *Mastery Learning*.

The key concept of Mastery Learning is that all students can achieve mastery in basic skills if given the proper amount of time (not too much or too little), individualized teaching techniques, and prompt feedback on achievement so he or she doesn't fall behind the rest of the class. Bloom also included the finding that, given proper pedagogical processes and student monitoring, *all* children can learn.

The primary research question emanating from these two studies was: If we can, in theory, teach all children and enable them to master basic skills, then what kind of schools do we need to assure this mastery? Certainly the schools Coleman, Jencks, and their associates studied were not teaching all children. Were there schools that actually existed where children from low-income families were learning, beating the statistical odds stacked against them, and mastering basic skills and knowledge? If there were schools where all children were learning, what were the characteristics of these exceptional schools?

The Early Effective Schools Research (1971–1980)

Beginning in the late sixties and early seventies, researchers challenged and reinterpreted Coleman's and Jenck's findings and began their investigations into what turned out to be important studies on school effectiveness. George Weber (1971), Klitgaard and Hall (1973), and a number of other researchers went about identifying and describing schools that were unusually effective at teaching for learning for all students. Especially interesting were "outlier" studies that looked at schools whose student scores on standardized achievement tests were at the highest end and at the lowest end of a given sample group of schools. These schools were then compared on certain attributes. The New York State Department of Education (1974, 1976), the Maryland State Department of Education (1978), and a study in Detroit by Lezotte, Edmonds, and Ratner (1974) produced consistent results, although some of the research designs were slightly flawed.

In the early seventies, a group of researchers at Michigan State University set out to *find* schools, that, contrary to Coleman's and Jenck's findings, were successful in teaching children from low-income families. Wilbur Brookover, a sociologist at Michigan State, and his early colleagues had an exceptionally good research idea: They studied schools in inner-city Detroit that were all-black, with students from families with low incomes. When they found schools where students were achieving significantly higher than the average of their sample of schools, they would call these schools "effective," and study their characteristics and ways of operating. Brookover and his colleagues found eight such schools.

This study was originally reported in 1973, and entitled "Elementary School Social Environments and Achievement." The original school characteristics identified in all of these investigations came to be known as "correlates of effective schools," and were described as follows in these early days:

1. The staff is pulled together by the principal (or other leader) to form a consensus and shared values about the *mission* of the school.

2. The staff and administration establishes a climate of *high expectations* for students and their ability to achieve.
3. The classroom shows a "purposeful atmosphere" that results from high expectations, and is business-like, but not oppressive.
4. Student progress is monitored frequently (the Mastery Learning process) and teaching is adjusted to keep the class moving and all children learning.
5. There is an emphasis on the teacher as the locus of responsibility for student *learning*, not merely for producing good lesson plans, "coverage" of material, or special lesson and teaching procedures.

An effective school, as defined by early researchers, was one in which essentially all of the students acquire basic skills and knowledge, and other desired behavior within the school. To measure whether all students were acquiring basic skills, teachers and administrators had to take *aggregated* data from several sources (standardized norm-referenced tests, criterion-referenced tests, teacher-made tests, student attendance and tardiness records, for example) and disaggregate these data. The process of disaggregation meant taking the data set and breaking it down to form subsets of students based on socioeconomic status (middle income, low income), gender (boy, girl), or race/ethnicity. These subsets of data in an *effective school* would show all subgroups distributed similarly across the statistical curve used (J curve, normal curve). In an "ineffective school" there would be gaps in the reported average scores of low-income students when compared to middle-income students, and many more middle-income students (proportionately) would be in the top percentiles of the curve used.

The disaggregation of data became the tool used to demonstrate to school staff and administrators that they had work to do to teach all children. A typical school in the United States would teach only a small percentage of low-income students, and by using the disaggregation process, the discrepancy between middle- and low-income children became evident. If the staff truly believed that "all children can learn," then they would set about changing the learning climate of the school, and the way they taught.

Creating Effective Schools: The Move into the Field of Public Schools (1978–1985)

In 1978, Gilbert Austin and his associates studied elementary schools with "high residual effects" and "low residual effects" on students' achievement in basic skills test scores, and found what Brookover had found in the earlier study: Certain characteristics were commonly found in high-residual schools that were not present in low-residual schools.

At the same time, completely independently of the work done in the United States, Michael Rutter and his colleagues in England studied the characteristics of effective high schools in the classic study *Fifteen Thousand Hours: Secondary Schools and Their Effects on Children* (1979). Remarkably, Rutter's findings agreed with those in the United States, although the configuration of characteristics and emphasis differed because high schools are organized quite differently from elementary schools.

Also, a researcher named Ron Edmonds of Michigan State University collaborated with colleagues at Michigan State and John R. Frederickson to complete an extensive study of several inner-city schools of Detroit that were found to be instructionally effective for poor children. While working on this project, Edmonds had joined the faculty of Harvard University School of Education (where he had been pursuing independent study) as director of the Center for Urban Studies (1973). From this vantage point, he planned the first demonstration project for creating effective schools. In 1978, he took the position of Senior Assistant for Instruction, New York Public School System, to carry out the first demonstration project on Effective Schools, as he and Larry Lezotte began consulting in Milwaukee public schools on the RISE project (Rising to Individual Scholastic Excellence), the second demonstration project on Effective Schools to be carried out in the United States.

Edmonds, a black scholar with a fiesty temperament, the hardy stamina of conviction, and a brilliant mind, had pulled together a number of strands from a variety of academic disciplines. In a paper titled *A Black Response to Christopher Jenck's Inequality and Certain Other Issues* (1973), he and other black scholars explained the relationship between desegregation policies, concerns about equity in the schools, and true integration in the public schools. Edmonds had worked with Brookover and Lezotte at Michigan State, and had become aware of the seemingly innocuous but harmful practices that tended to follow minority children into schools where they were bused: inequitable discipline and suspension procedures, tracking throughout the grades into "fast" and "slow" groups, discriminatory diagnosis for special education and learning-disabled children, and discriminatory teaching procedures and practices in the classroom.

Edmonds's interest in creating effective schools became an overwhelming political call to action for him and his followers, as he went about restructuring public schools so that the classroom teacher would be supported in her or his attempts to teach *all* children. To Edmonds, equity defined quality education as much as excellence did.

Effective Schools Programs began to sprout all over the United States in the late seventies and early eighties. Some, such as the SHAL project in St. Louis, RISE in Milwaukee, and statewide efforts in Michigan and Connecticut were well planned and well executed, given the narrow "craft knowledge" on school improvement that existed in that period.

Many other schools and some districts and most state departments began to apply Effective Schools literature during this period. It remained for others, however, to complete the Effective Schools Process for school improvement after the untimely death of Edmonds in July 1983. While the Effective Schools Movement was well launched at this time, research findings were slow to materialize because of two competing factors: the excellence movement and research university criticisms of the early findings of research on effective schools.

The Effective Schools Movement Slows: Research on Effective Schools Matures and Becomes Multidisciplinary (1985–present)

In 1985, the U.S. Office of Education funded two Research and Development Centers on Effective Schools: the Center for Effective Elementary and Middle Schools at Johns Hopkins University and the National Center for Effective Secondary Schools at the University of Wisconsin–Madison. These two centers were founded amidst a turbulent era in public education.

Since its inception, the Reagan administration had encouraged criticism of the public schools. Studies such as *A Nation at Risk* (1983), followed by *Action for Excellence* and *Education and Economic Progress*, sounded the clarion call to school reform.

But most of the early attempts to "reform" schools tended to talk about better programs for the gifted and talented, merit pay for teachers, and higher high school graduation standards. There was little state or national policy that addressed the discriminatory activities and behaviors of the classroom that continued to exist. The political fight in 1985 was plainly educational *excellence* versus *equity*.

The Reagan administration encouraged the excellence movement, seemingly unaware of the building demographic data that predicted heavy increases in poor, minority students over the next 20 years. In 1985, it was difficult for those working within the Effective Schools Movement to continue to come out strongly for equity. In 1987, the Johns Hopkins research and development center dropped "effective" from the name of their center, even though individual researchers there were still convinced the equity component inherent in Effective Schools was crucial to successful school improvement. This event of renaming was indicative of the discomfort many felt with concerns for equity during the heyday of the "excellence movement."

However, some consultant-researchers and practitioners in the field in the mid-eighties interpreted the original Effective Schools as inherently harboring equity (all students learning) *as well as* excellence (a high level of achievement). Researchers such as Levine and Eubanks (1986), Levine and Leibert

(1987), Purkey and Smith (1983), Purkey, Rutter, and Newmann (1987), Shoemaker (1986), and Bamburg and Andrews (1990) began to expand the concepts of the early Effective Schools research findings even as they criticized some of the research methodologies of these findings. State departments of education shepherded the school effectiveness/teacher effectiveness development. Where state departments encouraged and supported training to bring about the restructuring of schools so the teachers could teach all children, much was learned about the interaction of organizational dynamics of schools within the tried and true tenets of organizational theory. In short, the field began to learn why Effective Schools work. (The field learned especially what not to do in school reform during 1983–87.) The literature of Effective Schools research was being applied on a wide scale.

By 1987, enough was known about the need to change district and state department of education structures, as well as individual school structures, to expand the development and consulting base of the Effective Schools Movement. There was a need for more consistency in implementation of the Effective Schools Process Model, and a group of the early workers in the Effective Schools field came together to found the National Center for Effective Schools Research and Development (NCESRD). Originally housed at Michigan State, and subsequently moved to the University of Wisconsin–Madison, the center was a resource to "assure more Effective Schools today and tomorrow" (its mission).

Organized to be responsive to development efforts by individual school districts, the NCESRD held summer and fall conferences and kept extensive files on school improvement and Effective Schools research. NCESRD also formed a Cadre of Fellows (see Appendix D) made up of educators who held full-time jobs in universities, state departments of education, and in the field, but also consulted with state departments of education, districts, and schools on implementing the Effective Schools Process. The NCESRD's focus was on field development and documentation of results from successful Effective Schools efforts nationwide.

Research continued to be done on defining Effective Schools, and investigating their creation, largely outside the NCESRD. An extensive synthesis of research on Effective Schools, incorporating research on the implementation of school improvement programs, was written in 1988 by Daniel Levine and Lawrence W. Lezotte (*Unusually Effective Schools, A Review and Analysis of Research and Practice,* 1990). This synthesis (the reference section of which comprises 13 pages of relevant studies from 1971 to 1988) plus the NCESRD publication of a set of case studies from 11 districts and one educational resource center (*Case Studies in Effective Schools Research,* 1990) allowed the field to understand what was known about creating Effective Schools and districts and what they actually looked like.

At the present time, 1992, after a decade of development, enough is known about the Effective Schools Process to mount a national training program for practitioners. The training materials (titled "School-Based Instructional Leadership"), which are partnership modules for professional development, were worked out and written over a period of three years by many practitioners, the Cadre of Fellows of the NCESRD, and the present staff of the NCESRD. Beginning in 1992, the training program will exist for those practitioners and professional trainers who wish to learn the ropes to create and sustain Effective Schools, where all children learn well.

APPENDIX C

A Selected List of School Districts That Have Implemented Effective Schools Successfully

Listed here are names of districts that have been implementing the *comprehensive* Effective Schools Process for school improvement for at least three years, some of them for as long as nine years. These districts have continued to meet the criteria listed on page 433 to the satisfaction of staff and the Cadre of Fellows of the National Center for Effective Schools Research and Development, University of Wisconsin–Madison.

Although the list is selective because it meets most of these criteria to a high standard, it is not inclusive. Enumerating all the districts in the United States that have successful and ongoing Effective Schools Programs would be a monumental task. Over the last decade, educators from the Regional Educational Laboratories, from many other universities, from intermediate districts in the various states, from state departments of education, proprietary consultants, as well as personnel connected with the National Center for Effective Schools, have all done training, facilitating, and consulting both at state and local levels to bring about Effective Schools.

The Effective Schools movement continues to grow. The General Accounting Office (GAO) estimates over 41 percent of school districts have implemented some sort of Effective Schools Process (*Effective Schools Programs: Their Extent and Characteristics,* 1988, GAO/HRD-89-132BR, General Accounting Office, Washington, DC 20548.) This list includes some of the most successful examples of district and school reform using the Effective Schools Process.

Adams County School District #14, Commerce City, Colorado 80022
Adlai E. Stevenson High School District 125, Prairie View, Illinois 60069
Ann Arbor Public Schools, Ann Arbor, Michigan 48104
Austin Independent School District, Austin, Texas 78703
Beaverton School District, Beaverton, Oregon, 97075

Camp Lejune School District, Camp Lejune, North Carolina 28452
Carroll County Public Schools, Westminster, Maryland 21157
Cumberland County Schools, Fayetteville, North Carolina 28302
Danville Public Schools, Danville, Virginia 24543
Deer Valley Unified School District #97, Phoenix, Arizona 85027
Dodge City Unified School District #443, Dodge City, Kansas 67801
Edgecombe County Schools, Tarboro, North Carolina 27886
Ferris Independent School District, Ferris, Texas 75125
Frederick County Public Schools, Frederick, Maryland 21701
Geary County Unified Schools (District #475), Junction City, Kansas 66441
Glendale Union High School District, Glendale, Arizona 85301
Guilford County School System, Greensboro, North Carolina 27401
Halton Board of Education, Burlington, Ontario L7R 3Z2
Jackson Public School District, Jackson, Mississippi 39225
Laurel County Board of Education, London, Kentucky 40741
Littleton Public Schools, Littleton, Colorado 80120
Lonoke School District, Lonoke, Arkansas 72086
Manchester School District, Manchester, Connecticut 06040
Milwaukee Public Schools: RISE Project, Milwaukee, Wisconsin 53211
Nampa School District (District #13), Nampa, Idaho 83651
Natrona County School District #1, Casper, Wyoming 82601
New Hanover County Schools, Wilmington, North Carolina 28401
Newport News Public Schools, Newport News, Virginia 23606
Newton-Conover City Schools, Newton, North Carolina 28658
Niagara Falls City School District, Niagara Falls, New York 14301
New York City, Spanish Harlem (District #6), New York 10030
Norfolk Public Schools, Norfolk, Virginia 23501
North York Board of Education, Willowdale, Ontario M2R 2V4
Pasadena Public Schools, Pasadena, Texas 77502
Pearl River Union Free School District, Pearl River, New York 10965
Phoenix Union High School District, Phoenix, Arizona 85012
Portland Public Schools, Portland, Maine 04103-5599
Portsmouth Public Schools, Portsmouth, Virginia 23705
Prince George's County Public Schools, Upper Marlboro, Maryland 20770
Red Bank Public Schools, Red Bank, New Jersey 07701
Rutland City School District, Rutland, Vermont 05701
Sacramento County Office of Education, Sacramento, California 95827
San Diego Office of Education, Sacramento, California 92111
San Marcos Unified School District, San Marcos, California 92069
School City of Mishawaka, Mishawaka, Indiana 46544
School District #73-1/2, Skokie, Illinois 60076

Seattle Public Schools, Seattle, Washington 98109
Sheboygan Area School District, Sheboygan, Wisconsin 53081
South Redford School District, South Redford, Michigan 48239
Southwest Vermont Supervisory Union, Bennington, Vermont 05201
Spencerport Central Schools, Spencerport, New York 14559
Spirit Lake Community School District, Spirit Lake, Iowa 51360
Spring Branch Independent School District, Houston, Texas 77224
Stanley County School District, Albemarle, North Carolina 28002-1399
The School Board of Seminole County, Sanford, Florida 32771
Victoria Independent School District, Victoria, Texas 77901
Wetzel County Board of Education, New Martinsville, West Virginia 26155

Criteria Important in Deciding Progress of Districts and Schools Using the Effective Schools Process

The National Center for Effective Schools Research and Development suggests the inclusion of the following criteria for assessing progress of districts and schools using the Effective Schools Process for school improvement:

1. The board of education has endorsed the Effective Schools Process and supports the effort in its annual budget.
2. The board of education has stated a district mission; the schools have stated their school missions.
3. The district has decentralized its day-to-day decision making in the form of school-based management (site-based improvement) (e.g., the schools have active, functioning building leadership teams and improvement strategies that vary from school to school).
4. The district is committed to continuing staff development by budgeting funds for this purpose and sponsoring an integrated professional training program that is sensitive to the specific needs of various schools and teachers.
5. There is an ongoing monitoring system that is used by the district and by classroom teachers to keep all students up to date and learning.
6. The district has disaggregated student performance data, and principals and teachers use these data and other outcome data as a basis for decision making.
7. The district has shown progress in student achievement, indicated by various student performance data and other indicators, across all subsets of students, for at least three years.
8. The community, citizens, and especially parents are aware of improved student achievement and the faculty's teaching for learning success with all children.
9. Each school's improvement plan is reviewed annually and updated accordingly.

APPENDIX D

The Cadre of Fellows of the National Center for Effective Schools Research and Development Foundation

While the nation ponders the New American Schools program, an agile group of distinguished educators is already working hard to disseminate hands-on skills and knowledge and to build Effective Schools and districts all over the country. These educators, the Cadre of Fellows of the National Center for Effective Schools Research and Development Foundation (NCESRDF), are probably unique in the history of dissemination of new program initiatives in the field of education. The fellows are all professional educators of high standing, but rather than work full time for NCESRDF, they work full time as superintendents, associates in regional educational laboratories, members of university faculties, school principals, and in central office staffs in school districts. In addition to these regular commitments, they devote from one to three days a month to service to the field by giving Effective Schools awareness speeches and consulting, facilitating and training in partnerships with practitioners in districts and schools nationwide. The Cadre of Fellows of the NCESRDF are truly ambassadors of Effective Schools Research.

The Cadre has been instrumental in the development of the "school-based instructional leadership modules" for professional development, which are now being tested at the National Center. When completed, which is expected in mid-1992, these models will be refined and then used by the Cadre of Fellows and other professional trainers and facilitators in the field to help school personnel, districts, and schools become proficient in implementing correctly and consistently the comprehensive Effective Schools Process for school improvement.

Dr. Henriette L. Allen
Administrative Assistant for Planning & Evaluation
Jackson Public Schools
Jackson, MS 39225-2338

Dr. John W. Amos
Director, Elementary Education
Pittsylvania County Schools
Chatham, VA 24531

Dr. Patricia L. Anderson
Director of Secondary Education
Geary County USD #475
Junction City, KS 66441

Dr. Richard L. Andrews
Dean, College of Education
University of Wyoming
Laramie, WY 82071

Dr. George W. Bailey
Consultant
Cheyenne, WY 83007

Dr. Beverly A. Bancroft
Consultant/Researcher
Michigan State University
Okemos, MI 48805

Dr. C. M. Bernd
Superintendent
San Marcos Unified Schools
San Marcos, CA 92069

Mr. Ben A. Birdsell
Director
Association for Effective Schools, Inc.
Stuyvesant, NY 12173

Ms. Nancy R. Bishop
Director of Staff Development
Prince George's County Public Schools
Landover, MD 20785

Dr. Robert E. Blum
Director, School Improvement Program
Northwest Regional Educational Laboratory
Portland, OR 97204-3213

Mr. Edgar A. Burnett
Administrators Association
St. Louis Public Schools
St. Louis, MO 63108

Dr. R. Lynn Canady
Associate Professor, School of Education
University of Virginia
Charlottesville, VA 22903

Dr. Robert V. Carlson
Director of Educational Development Program
University of Vermont
Burlington, VT 05404

Dr. Aurora Chase
Director of Instruction
Elementary School District #20
Hanover Park, IL 60103

Dr. Janet A. Chrispeels
Coordinator
San Diego County Office of Education
San Diego, CA 92111

Mr. Joseph Clement, Jr.
Superintendent
Spencerport Central Schools
Spencerport, NY 14559

Dr. Richard P. DuFour
Superintendent
Adlai E. Stevenson High School
Prairie View, IL 60069-2815

Mrs. Susan Schaefer Durns
Instructional Coordinator
Busch Magnet School
St. Louis, MO 63109

Dr. Robert Eaker
Dean, College of Education
Middle Tennessee State University
Murfreesboro, TN 37132

Dr. Laile E. Fairbairn
Assistant Superintendent for Educational Services
South Country Central School District
East Patchogue, NY 11722

Dr. David Flowers
Assistant Superintendent for Instruction
Geary Country USD #475
Junction City, KS 66441

Dr. Robert N. Fortenberry
Executive Director
Public Education Forum of Mississippi
Jackson, MS 39201

Dr. Willis J. Furtwengler
Professor
Wichita State University
Wichita, KS 67208

Dr. William J. Gauthier, Jr.
Superintendent
Public Schools
Naugatuck, CT 02887

Dr. Gerald E. George
Superintendent
Glendale Union High School District
Glendale, AZ 85301

Ms. Gwendolyn Gholson
Principal
Ravenswood Middle School
East Palo Alto, CA 94303

Mr. Eddie D. Hall
Principal
Larchmont Elementary School
Norfolk, VA 23508

Dr. Philip Hallinger
Director, Center for Advanced Study of Educational Leadership
Vanderbilt University
George Peabody College of Education
Nashville, TN 37203

Mr. Wilbert E. Hawkins, Jr.
Director
Prince George's County Maryland's Tomorrow
Upper Marlboro, MD 20772

Dr. Max O. Heim
Superintendent
Geary County USD #475
Junction City, KS 66441

Dr. Swinton A. Hill
Administrative Assistant for Staff Development
Jackson Public Schools
Jackson, MS 39225-2338

Ms. Susie B. Hinton
Principal
Noah Webster School
Hartford, CT 06105

Dr. Shirley M. Hord
Senior Research Associate
Southwest Educational Development Laboratory
Austin, TX 78701

Dr. James Huffman
Professor, College of Education
Middle Tennessee State University
Murfreesboro, TN 37132

Dr. Barbara C. Jacoby
Effective Schools Consultant
Naples, FL 33963-8073

Mr. Henry R. Kelly
Director
Federal/State Programs
Bridgeport Board of Education
Bridgeport, CT 06606

Dr. Judith M. Lawrence
Bureau Manager
School Improvement
New Jersey Department of Education
Trenton, NJ 08625

Dr. Lawrence W. Lezotte
Senior Vice President
Effective Schools Products, Ltd.
Okemos, MI 48864

Ms. Ann B. Madison
Director of Human Relations and Staff Development and Student Affairs
Norfolk Public Schools
Norfolk, VA 23501

Dr. Gary S. Mathews
Associate Superintendent for Instructional Services
Spring Branch ISD
Houston, TX 77224-9432

Dr. Pamela Sue Mayer
Senior Program Associate
Center for Creative Leadership
Greensboro, NC 27438-6300
919 288-7210

Ms. Lydia L. McCue
Director of Adolescent Education
Putnam County Schools
Winfield, WV 25213

Dr. David P. Meaney
Sacramento County Superintendent of Schools
Sacramento, CA 95827

Dr. H. W. "Bud" Meyers
Associate Professor, College of Education and Social Services
University of Vermont
Burlington, VT 05405

Dr. Stephen K. Miller
Associate Professor, Foundations of Education
University of Louisville
Louisville, KY 40292

Dr. Joseph F. Murphy
Professor & Chair, Department of Educational Leadership
Vanderbilt University–Peabody College of Education
Nashville, TN 37203

Dr. Jean M. Norman
Director, School Council Assistance Project, College of Education
University of South Carolina
Columbia, SC 29208

Dr. M. John O'Connell
Coordinator of School-Based Instructional Decision Making
Prince George's County Schools
Upper Marlboro, MD 20772

Dr. Marie A. Parker
Associate Director for Planning and Development
Arkansas Department of Education
Little Rock, AR 72201

Dr. David W. Pearsall
School/District Improvement Specialist
New Jersey Department of Education
Manasquan, NJ 08736

Mr. Michael F. Pockl
Executive Assistant for School Improvement
Akron Public Schools
Akron, OH 44308

Dr. Sally Pollack
Coordinator
San Diego County Office of Education
San Diego, CA 92111-3799

Dr. Gerrita L. Postlewait
Superintendent
Wetzel County Schools
New Martinsville, WV 26155

Dr. Patrick Proctor
Superintendent of Schools
Windham Public Schools
Williamantic, CT 06226

Dr. Russell J. Quaglia
Assistant Professor, College of Education
University of Maine at Orono
Orono, ME 04469

Dr. William Rauhauser
Consultant
Lewisville, TX 75067

Ms. Claudia L. Risnes
School Improvement Coordinator
Anoka-Hennepin School District #11
Coon Rapids,MN 55433

Dr. Beatrice E. Rock
Director of School Improvement Programs
Wayne-Finger Lakes BOCES
Stanley, NY 14561

Dr. Joan Shoemaker
Educational Consultant
Connecticut State Department of Education
Middletown, CT 06457

Dr. Samuel C. Stringfield
Principal Research Scientist
John Hopkins University
Center for Social Organization of Schools
Baltimore, MD 21218

Dr. Robert E. Sudlow
Effective Schools Consultant
Spencerport, NY 14559

Dr. Charles B. Teddlie
Associate Professor and Assistant Chair
College of Education
Louisiana State University
Baton Rouge, LA 70803-4721

Mr. Gerald D. Vance
Executive Director
Compact for Educational Opportunity
Milwaukee, WI 53212

Dr. John Van Schoonhoven
Principal
Greenbelt Center School
Greenbelt, MD 20770

Dr. Albert S. Weiss
Principal
Maryland Avenue School
Milwaukee, WI 53211

Mrs. Sheila Grimes Williams
St. Louis Public Schools
Staff Development Supervisor
Curriculum Division
St. Louis, MO 63112

Ms. Mary Jackson Willis
Executive Assistant for Education
Office of the Governor
Columbia, SC 29211

Mrs. Delester B. Young
Supervisor of Curriculum and
Staff Development
St. Louis Public Schools
St. Louis, MO 63113

Dr. Rufus Young, Jr.
Consultant
University City, MO 63132

Dr. Savannah Miller Young
Principal
Shepard Elementary School
St. Louis, MO 63118

Index

J

K

L

M

N

O

P

R

S

T

U

V

W